The Penguin Guide to the
1000 Finest Classical Recordings

Re

The Penguin Guide to the

1000 Finest Classical Recordings

The Must-Have CDs and DVDs

Revised Edition

**Ivan March, Edward Greenfield,
Robert Layton** *and* **Paul Czajkowski**

*Edited by Ivan March and Paul Czajkowski
Assistant Editor Alan Livesey*

PENGUIN BOOKS

PENGUIN BOOKS

Published by the Penguin Group
Penguin Books Ltd, 80 Strand, London WC2R ORL, England
Penguin Group (USA) Inc., 375 Hudson Street, New York, New York 10014, USA
Penguin Group (Canada), 90 Eglinton Avenue East, Suite 700, Toronto, Ontario,
Canada M4P 2Y3 (a division of Pearson Penguin Canada Inc.)
Penguin Ireland, 25 St Stephen's Green, Dublin 2, Ireland (a division of Penguin Books Ltd)
Penguin Group (Australia), 707 Collins Street, Melbourne,
Victoria 3008, Australia (a division of Pearson Australia Group Pty Ltd)
Penguin Books India Pvt Ltd, 11 Community Centre, Panchsheel Park,
New Delhi – 110 017, India
Penguin Group (NZ), 67 Apollo Drive, Rosedale, Auckland 0632, New Zealand
(a division of Pearson New Zealand Ltd)
Penguin Books (South Africa) (Pty) Ltd, Block D, Rosebank Office Park,
181 Jan Smuts Avenue, Parktown North, Gauteng 2193, South Africa

Penguin Books Ltd, Registered Offices: 80 Strand, London WC2R ORL, England

www.penguin.com

First published 2011
This edition published 2012
001

Copyright © Ivan March Publications, 2011

Typeset in 8.1/10.5 Fresco
Typeset by Jouve (UK), Milton Keynes
Printed in Great Britain

ISBN: 978-0-141-3997

www.greenpenguin.co.uk

MIX
Paper from
responsible sources
FSC
www.fsc.org   FSC™ C018179

ALWAYS LEARNI

Coventry City Council	
EAR*	
3 8002 01777 657 8	
Askews & Holts	Oct-2012
781.680266	£14.99

Contents

Introduction

With our 2010 edition the *Penguin Guide to Recorded Classical Music* reached its maximum capacity, and we realized that a new approach was needed to advise readers as to the most desirable recordings available. Our chosen answer is to plan a more compact survey centring on 1,000 of the very finest issues. But, apart from operas, very few CDs or DVDs include just a single work, which means that our coverage is much greater than the book's title would suggest. In addition, the important collections grouped under a single artist often include a great variety of music, which again considerably expands the repertoire being discussed. Ballet music is given a separate survey at the beginning of the book. Otherwise there are no better examples than Simon Preston's collection of Bach's organ music, the six volumes of music by Frank Bridge conducted by Richard Hickox on Chandos, Decca's coverage of Pavarotti's recitals or the EMI anthology devoted to Maria Callas which includes all her key recitals and complete opera sets, running overall to a box of 70 CDs.

Even more ambitious is the distinguished survey – not yet complete – of Bach's 200-plus magnificent cantatas on BIS, performed by the Japan Bach Collegium, directed by Masaaki Suzuki. This is one of the crowning achievements of the present-day record catalogues; moreover, their SACD recordings offer remarkable realism. Although we have treated them as a set, for the moment they must be explored individually. Each has its own documentation, and all will give great pleasure and refreshment. BIS promise that one day (probably in two or three years' time) the complete set will be ready to be published in an album, and then arrangements will be made so that the balance of the series can be added to those already acquired.

In the field of opera, where there are desirable DVD and CD versions of a given work, both will be included side by side. This applies notably to operas in which there are two generations of key recordings of comparable desirability, one on CD and one on DVD. Sometimes in other fields there is also a second outstanding version of a work that cannot be ignored, and this may also be mentioned in the text.

Our experience of the early-vintage LP catalogue, much of which is now reappearing on CD, means that we are able to expand our coverage in this area – often grouped under the name of the performer(s). These compilations include many valuable recordings of British music and are perhaps headed by the extensive anthologies of Ansermet's recordings which Australian Decca are now making available, impressively remastered.

Although our coverage is wide, this survey is in no way intended to be a balanced one. But all the recordings listed and recommended are indispensable to one or to all of us, and we hope our readers will find our comments to be a guide to their discovery and acquisition. Some recordings may require perseverance to obtain, but all are worth seeking out. The important Australian Eloquence series of recordings is now available in the UK and they can also be obtained by American readers.

Catalogue Numbers

Great care has gone into the checking of CD and DVD catalogue numbers and contents to ensure that all details are correct, but the major companies are at present totally reorganizing their catalogues to make them more attractive and more competitive. EMI have brought out a huge number of reissues (usually at lower prices). There are many reissues, too, from Universal (Decca, DG and Philips), while the new catalogues (from the UK and USA) of the combined labels of Sony and RCA have caused us insoluble problems in determining which CDs are currently available and which catalogue numbers are now correct on each side of the Atlantic. The editors and publisher therefore cannot be held responsible for any mistakes which may have crept in despite all our zealous checking. When ordering recordings, readers are urged to provide their source with full details of the music and performers, as well as the catalogue number.

Deletions

Compact discs regularly succumb to the deletions axe, and many highly praised CDs are likely to disappear during the lifetime of this book. But most really important and desirable recordings are eventually reissued, usually costing less!

As for the others, we can only suggest to readers that if a recording we have enthused about appears to be deleted, keep your eyes on the lists of reissues, as it will surely reappear before too long, unless it has repertoire which has little public support.

Acknowledgements

Our thanks to Roger Wells, who copy-edited the raw material for this edition; and to Kathleen March, who frequently discovers musical errors, and to Alan Livesey, who as Assistant Editor proof-reads the copy meticulously throughout at great speed, and manages to uncover still existing mistakes that occurred earlier in the assembly of the book's text! Grateful thanks also go to all those readers who write to us to point out factual errors and to remind us of important recordings that have escaped our notice.

IVAN MARCH,
ROBERT LAYTON,
PAUL CZAJKOWSKI
and EDWARD GREENFIELD

Downloads

For some classical CD collectors, the word 'download' may provoke a blank stare or even a feeling of queasiness which new technology often generates. Both these responses are understandable, but two things are certain about downloads: (i) they are here to stay, and (ii) there is nothing to fear from them.

First of all, what is a 'download'? It is simply a way of 'downloading' music directly from the Internet on to your computer, where it can then either be transferred to a blank CD, played on an iPod (or various other MP3 players), or simply played on your computer. And you don't have to download the entire contents of a CD, only the music you want. But more of this below.

Will downloads take over from CDs? While there has been an explosion of growth in this new way of acquiring music (especially in the pop-music world), it seems not to have resulted in a comparable reduction of CD sales. Collectors regard the CD (as they did the LP) as more than just a medium to play music. The artwork, sleevenotes, presentation, etc., are all part of the CD 'experience'.

Whether or not the teenagers of today, who download music as a matter of course, will regard these matters as being of the same importance remains to be seen, but the basic urge to buy something which you can physically hold, touch and feel is unlikely to go away. On a practical level, opera libretti, texts and translations etc. are a key area where CDs score over downloads: the idea of following texts on a computer is impractical and undesirable. And, just like book-lovers, record collectors like to have their recorded music on shelves around them.

The sound quality is another area in which hi-fi enthusiasts are suspicious of downloads. While it is true that the sound quality of most downloads is not quite that of the equivalent CD, the difference is relatively small and, when played through computers, MP3 players, iPods, headphones or car stereos, this is perhaps not of the greatest importance.

On top-quality hi-fi equipment, sound is very important, and this is being addressed by the record industry. High-quality downloads are becoming available with full CD sound-quality. For the technically minded, CDs are coded to play back at 16bit/96 kHz and this will be the standard of these new downloads.

Even more impressive will be the availability of an 'ultra'-hi-fi audio-quality download – in theory better than CD sound – which may well be available from some companies during the lifetime of this book. These downloads will be using impressive 24-bit technology, which is the level at which many new recordings are made. This will be the format to convert and excite hi-fi enthusiasts to this new medium.

One of the great advantages downloads offer is the sheer quantity of music which is being made available. Never again will the dreaded word 'deleted' strike the horror it once did. Not only that, but the ability to pick and choose which track you want to buy is a clear advantage over a CD; the occasions when one wants to buy only the rare fill-up or coupling on a CD provokes frequent annoyance to collectors.

The relative cheapness of downloads may encourage one to explore new repertoire, as well as duplicating favourite repertoire without adding to your storage problems. Most sites offer a free one-minute sample of each track – a real encouragement to experiment and expand one's repertoire knowledge. Also, downloads offer the chance to experiment with new music without having to face the sometimes intimidating atmosphere of a classical record department.

Computers often (and justifiably so) rate as one of the top causes of frustration in modern life. But they are growing more reliable and easier to use. As long as you have a broadband connection, downloading is a relatively easy procedure since the on-screen instructions are pretty obvious. The download may be a bit time-consuming but this is becoming a faster procedure as time goes by, with broadband connections getting better all the time. Indeed, within a comparatively short space of time it will take a matter of seconds to download a complete opera – through we are not there yet.

Many of the recordings discussed in this book will be available to download (a quick check on the relevant company's website will tell you if this is so). A dedicated download site, such as iTunes, is an obvious place to start, but many record companies offer their own download facility. TheClassicalShop.net offers many high-quality downloads and a host of independent labels to choose from and is well worth exploring.

The performances heard via downloads remain the same, whatever format they are presented on (taking note of the above remarks on sound quality).

An International Mail-order Source for Recordings in the UK

Readers are urged to support a local dealer if he is prepared and able to give a proper service, and to remember that obtaining many CDs involves expertise and perseverance. However, in recent years many specialist sources have disappeared; for that reason, if any difficulty is experienced in obtaining the CDs you want, we suggest the following mail-order alternative, which offers competitive discounts in the UK but also operates world-wide. Through this service, advice on choice of recordings from the Editor of the *The Penguin Guide to the 1000 Finest Classical Recordings* is always readily available to mail-order customers:

Squires Gate Music Centre Ltd (PG Dept)
615 Lytham Road
Squires Gate, Blackpool
Lancashire FY4 1RG
UK
Tel./Fax: (+44) (0) 1253 405599
Website Address: www.lprl.demon.co.uk
Email Address: sales@lprl.demon.co.uk

This organization can supply any recording available in Britain and patiently extends CD and DVD orders until they finally come to hand. A full guarantee of safe delivery is made on any order undertaken. Please write or fax for further details, or make a trial credit-card order, by fax, email or telephone.

Squires Gate also offers a try-before-you-buy weekly loan service (within the UK only) so that customers can try out recordings at home for a small charge, without any obligation to purchase. If a recording is subsequently purchased, it will be discounted and the trial charge waived. Full details sent on request.

Squires Gate Music Centre also offers a simple two- or three-monthly mailing, listing a hand-picked selection of current new and reissued CDs, chosen by the Editor of the *Penguin Guide*, Ivan March. Customers of Squires Gate Music Centre Ltd, both domestic and overseas, can receive the bulletin as available, and it is sent automatically with their purchases.

Foreword

As a Foreword to this edition, we offer below a brief but comprehensive history of recorded sound, from Thomas Alva Edison's first cylinder of 1877 and Emile Berliner's disc system of the early 1890s, to the arrival of electric recording, which transformed the sound fundamentally, while the debut of the LP in 1950 at last brought continuity to major works. Stereo enormously enhanced realism a decade later, and the compact disc virtually removed both background noise and wear and tear on the disc itself; with the coming of DVD, listeners are able to watch as well as hear distinguished artists making music.

The earliest years of recording: Edison's cylinder phonograph
When in 1877 Edison first demonstrated the cylinder phonograph in his factory to an assembled staff, and the words 'Mary had a little lamb' came clearly out of its tin horn, he could hardly have envisaged the full potential of his invention. Indeed, its first commercial use, as exploited by the inventor's Columbia Phonograph Company, was as an office machine, to record dictation. Understandably, this was not welcomed by office staff and its career was short-lived. Instead, in the 1880s, coin-in-the-slot novelty phonographs were devised, equipped with ten sets of ear tubes through which the reproduced sound travelled simultaneously. These were rented out to showmen at fairs, who charged five cents from each listener to experience the primitive sound, and soon these reproducing machines spread to shops and saloons.

The arrival of the recording industry's first key artistic figure: Fred Gaisberg
This innovative change to the world of entertainment brought with it the recording industry's first A&R (artists and repertoire) man, Fred Gaisberg, a remarkably gifted man of Bavarian extraction, whose family had emigrated to New York in 1854. Young Fred, with the encouragement of his highly musical mother, soon developed into a first-rate musician and a fine pianist. He also received much early support as a boy from the famous bandmaster/composer John Philip Sousa, who encouraged him to stand beside the maestro at open-air concerts on windy days and turn over and hold down the music. Such continued exposure to the popular hits of the time must have been invaluable to young Fred, and he soon became a very highly accomplished and much sought-after accompanist.

It was not surprising that, while he was still at school, the Columbia Phonograph Company heard of Gaisberg's talents and in 1889 they offered him the post of producer/pianist (who could play loudly and clearly!) for their expansion into a wider range of repertoire. The first star of this innovative repertoire was John York Artee who, unaccompanied, could clearly enunciate prose as diverse as Mark Antony's famous speech from *Julius Caesar* and the Lord's Prayer. But he was primarily employed as a whistler and as such he was celebrated in duet with the sixteen-year-old 'Professor' Gaisberg (piano) for such virtuoso items as 'The Whistling Coon' and 'The Mocking Bird', which Artee himself announced in stentorian tones.

The simple early cylinder recording technology

Gaisberg's early recordings were made straight into the recording horn, itself attached to a stylus which travelled laterally across a hollow wax cylinder. Simultaneously this was rotated by a hand crank – allowing the sound track to cut across the wax surface turning underneath it, with the vertical motion of the vibrating stylus mirroring the sound signal. It played for up to two minutes. By a resourceful additional expansion it was possible to place up to three horns close together and thus make three recordings at once. However, when Sousa's band came to record, such was the volume that as many as ten recordings could be made simultaneously! Yet every purchaser of such a recording could justly claim that they had a master copy.

Emile Berliner and his flat disc recording system

By the beginning of the 1890s the cylinder technology had been considerably improved, and in 1891 Gaisberg spent several months expanding his own knowledge of the acoustic recording technology at his company's factory at Bridgeport, Connecticut. He was thus equipped to meet and work with the most brilliant inventor of all, the man who devised an innovative new recording system which was destined to replace the cylinder altogether. It was conceived by Emile Berliner, whose family had emigrated from Germany to America in 1870. With little in the way of financial resources and working first in a small laboratory in New York, Berliner had devised a zinc disc on which a recording could be etched as it turned, giving a virtually immediate playback facility. Because the recording stylus vibrated and etched laterally on a flat surface, not rising and falling as in the phonograph's 'hill and dale' recording process, it made a steady progress which produced an improvement in the smoothness of the reproduced sound.

Most important of all, the use of a flat disc as the source of the recording meant that having cut his master into the disc, Berliner could then create a negative image and from that reverse master, in which the groove stayed at a consistent depth, he could press copies. This created a mass-production manufacturing process which provided almost unlimited quantities of listenable discs, pressed from that reverse master and, with the first single-sided discs, 5 and 7 inches in diameter, the gramophone record was created.

Gaisberg joins Berliner

In 1893 Fred Gaisberg was invited by Berliner to his house, where a demonstration showed unequivocally how his new gramophone method was superior to the cylinder-playing phonograph, even though the playback mechanism was still hand-cranked. Gaisberg immediately sought a promise from Berliner that when his 'gramophone', as it was called, was at the marketing/development stage he could join the working team. A year later he did so, moving to 1410 Pennysylvania Avenue, the address of Berliner's modest new laboratory in Washington, DC. There Gaisberg was to record a demonstration programme of songs and music to be used to raise capital to market the new company's products.

The technical success of the gramophone was thus assured, but not its financial backing. Numerous demonstrations were given but, despite their artistic success, potential investors were sceptical and resistant when asked for money. However, this delay was not entirely disadvantageous for, during this waiting period, Berliner found a new material with which to press his records. Developed by the Durinoid Company of Newark, New Jersey (who were button manufacturers), it was a mixture of powdered shellac and byritis, bound by cotton flock and coloured with lamp-black. It was rolled out into 'biscuits' which, when heated, were easily moulded under pressure and which, when cooled, admirably retained the impression of the recording grooves pressed into them. Thus was born what was eventually to become the 78-r.p.m. 'shellac' record familiar for half a century until it was eclipsed by the vinyl LP and, later, the CD.

Gramophone companies appear in the USA and Europe

It was the discovery of this new plastic material which finally convinced investors of the potential of Berliner's invention, and in October 1895 the United States Gramophone Company was incorporated in Philadelphia to control the patents. This, as it happened, was opportune; in his machine shop, just across the Delaware river in Camden, New Jersey, a young mechanic called Eldrige Johnson had perfected a practical gramophone motor that was simple and cheap to make. Thus the last hurdle was crossed, and Berliner no longer had to rely on hand-cranking.

Soon a promotional office was organized in New York, and in 1897 Gaisberg was to mastermind the first recording studio in 12th Street in Philadelphia, and he was given carte blanche as to the choice of artists and repertoire.

So great was the success of the venture in the USA, it soon became obvious that a European equivalent should be set up without delay, and in 1898 the new British-based Gramophone Company was incorporated in Maiden Lane in London, initially to import records and record-playing machines from America. But the choice of location for the factory where the new records were to be made was not England but Hanover, where German technology reigned supreme. Moreover the chairman of the new company, Trevor Williams (a brilliant addition to the board), realized immediately that the success of the (initially UK) venture depended on being able to record European performers in repertoire of European interest. Someone with recording experience and wide musical knowledge had to mastermind this expansion, and the choice was obvious.

Gaisberg as the first outstanding recording producer

Thus it was that Fred Gaisberg would cross the Atlantic to set up a new base in London; the artistic success of the new catalogue would be ensured as it was to include the most famous operatic stars of the time. Above all, Gaisberg had the skill to determine whether a singer would record well. The most famous example of his instant recognition of a great voice comes in the often-told story about his discovery of Caruso. In 1902, the young tenor was singing at La Scala opera house in Milan in an opera that was very popular at the time, Francetti's *Germania*. He held the audience spellbound and Gaisberg realized that this was a very special voice indeed. Caruso was approached through an intermediary and was asked whether he would be willing to record ten arias. He agreed, but insisted they all be recorded in one session, and he asked for a fee of £100. Gaisberg cabled London for permission and received the stark reply: 'Fee exorbitant. Forbid you to record.'

But Gaisberg was so sure of his own judgement that he went ahead anyway, hiring a private drawing-room on the third floor of the Grand Hotel. A bell-shaped metal horn was suspended five feet from the floor to pick up both the singer's voice and the accompanying piano. The selection was to include '*Questa O quella*' from *Rigoletto*, '*Celeste Aida*' and the 'Dream song' from *Manon*, and Caruso went through the whole programme as fast as the wax discs could be put on to the recording machine. But Gaisberg was right: Caruso's voice recorded perfectly and the result was an artistic and technical triumph; the subsequent success of the ten records not only produced an immediate profit of £15,000 but also encouraged other – previously reluctant – singers to come into the recording studio. For the acoustic recording system was above all suitable for recording the human voice, which in Gaisberg's hands it often did with uncanny realism. The 'orchestral' accompaniments were much less successful and had to be rescored to concentrate on wind and brass sonorities rather than strings, although the piano sometimes reproduced reasonably well.

Gaisberg remained the key international recording manager for the Gramophone Company until 1925, when the coming of electric recording required new skills and produced many new problems outside his previous experience, but also, at last, the ability to record a symphony orchestra with adequate realism. In 1931 the Gramophone Company (affected by the Depression) merged with their main competitor, Columbia, to become Electric and Musical Industries Ltd (EMI) and it was Gaisberg who was appointed to manage the new combined HMV International Department, which now had access to a galaxy of new names. They included Beecham, Gieseking, Szigeti, Bruno Walter and Weingartner, to say nothing of the Victor American catalogue, which featured Horowitz, Rubinstein, Heifetz and Toscanini, among many others – in essence a roster of the greatest artists in the world.

What remained to be done was to perfect the technique of recording and reproducing sound and to keep under contract artists who had an affinity with the music they recorded. Thus the editing of various 'takes' could ensure that the performance was musically and stylistically accurate. But it soon became obvious that if recordings of real distinction were to be achieved, then a combined team of producer and recording engineer was necessary, with the producer dominant and soon to achieve a reputation and influence of real significance, especially at EMI, where Walter Legge's name soon became as famous as those of the artists he recorded.

The LP arrives

When the long-playing record made its appearance in 1950 most listeners thought that the final stage in the development of sound reproduction was at hand. Yet, astonishingly, EMI held back, concentrating instead on smaller, 7-inch vinyl discs mainly used for singles, which hardly proved suitable for classical repertoire. This left a glaring gap in the marketplace, which was eagerly taken up by the burgeoning new Decca Record Company (London Records in the USA). Decca had the advantage, in Arthur Haddy, of the most brilliant technical director the record industry has ever known and, in John Culshaw, an equally able and imaginative producer. They made a perfect team.

At the end of the 78-r.p.m. era, Haddy had developed a new extended-range recording system which soon became famous under its logo, ffrr (full frequency range recording). This was incorporated into the Decca/London LP technology to produce recordings of remarkable range and definition. Culshaw took full advantage of the technical improvement which ffrr provided, and soon Decca LPs took the market lead both technically and musically, a lead which they never really lost, although EMI caught up in the 1960s with their remarkable artists' roster, and both Deutsche Grammophon in Germany and Philips in Holland also brought comparable competition of high quality.

The coming of stereo in the UK

It was A. D. Blumlein of the British Columbia Gramophone Company who, in 1931, conceived and patented the idea of stereo recording on disc. He noted at the time that the coarse shellac composition with which records were then made was unsuitable for the process. But in 1952 Arthur Haddy at Decca realized that the vinyl material used for LPs would indeed be suitable and he devised a 45/45 stereo recording system, based on Blumlein's ideas, in which the two channels could be cut in the two walls of the record groove at 45 degrees to the surface plane. By 1954 the Decca British and German engineers had combined to produce a recording machine and reproducing pick-ups using this technology, and from that time onwards all major works were recorded at Decca for later issue as both stereo and mono LPs. Although this research was kept secret, other companies were pursuing similar goals, so in March 1958 Haddy arranged a demonstration in New York to show the feasibility of the Decca 45/45 system, and this was adopted universally. Very soon Decca stereo LPs were on the market using the logo ffss (full frequency stereophonic sound) and, with the enhancement obvious to virtually all ears, the future of the stereo disc was assured.

Stereo arrives in the USA

In the USA, the new RCA Victor Company had formed an existence independent of its old affiliation with what had now become EMI, although retaining the famous HMV 'dog and trumpet' logo (to which they had equal rights) for their classical catalogue. They too had been secretly experimenting with stereo from 1953 onwards, and in February 1954 the RCA producers John Pfeiffer and Richard Mohr took their new equipment to Boston's Symphony Hall, which had the finest acoustics for recording in the whole of the USA. They recorded experimentally Munch and his Boston vocal and orchestral team in Berlioz's *Damnation of Faust,* using a pair of microphones and two-track tapes. It was subsequently discovered that Chicago's Symphony Hall also had an acoustic ambience ideal for stereo, and so from 1958 until the early 1960s a series of 'Living Stereo' recordings was made in either venue, featuring artists of the calibre of Arthur Fiedler (ideal for ballet music), Munch, Fritz Reiner, Stokowski, Heifetz, Rubinstein and others. The simplest microphone techniques were used: the sound was recorded on either two or three tracks, and the result was remarkably successful.

In 2006 John Newton and his technical team at Sound Mirror Inc. in Boston returned to these master tapes and re-transferred them to Super Audio CDs (SACDs), using either two or three channels as available; however, the result proved fully compatible using a normal CD player. The reproduction is astonishingly realistic. The performances are all outstandingly fine, the balance is superb, with the hall acoustics truthfully caught, and these remain among the finest stereo recordings ever made. Many of them will be found in our pages.

At this point we need to remind readers of another, much smaller American record company which produced early stereo recordings ahead of its time. The production team of Mercury combined a first-class producer in Wilma Cozart and a brilliant engineer in Bob Fine. Wilma, who was a trained musician, favoured a natural sound-balance and Bob (who was eventually to become her husband) pioneered the use of just two or three microphones for his stereo recordings (some say that RCA borrowed the idea from Mercury!). The catalogue was imaginatively chosen, including much contemporary American music, and the brilliant sound gave the best Mercury issues a lead over many of their competitors.

The CD takes over, SACD adds realism, and the DVD offers a further new dimension

One problem remained: background noise. Even well-cared-for LPs gathered extraneous noise as they were played, with sudden clicks and pops (often caused by dust particles) particularly irritating. Even when digital recording sharpened the clarity of the sound image, these disturbances persisted. Finally, with the arrival of the compact disc in the early 1980s this problem was overcome and the newer digital recordings could be heard against a background of absolute silence. Even digitally remastered analogue CDs could be enjoyed with just a minimum of hiss from the master-tape. Moreover, modern technology has managed to reduce background noise considerably even from cleverly transferred recordings with a shellac, 78-r.p.m. source.

One further refinement was to come. In the 1960s several of the major companies experimented with quadraphonic surround sound, but the system failed to catch on, and some say this was because the fair sex refused to accept the presence of four large speakers in the living-room. However, the coming of compatible SACDs revived the project. The back speakers can be very small, even hidden, for their purpose is only to add a subtle background ambience to the recording. With small groups of artists this can bring a subtle but tangible feeling of presence; with large-scale works, especially choral music, the result can be a very thrilling fourth dimension, and one really has the sense of sitting in the concert hall itself.

The appeal of the DVD is so obvious that it hardly needs any advocacy from us. We are discovering that the major international opera houses have been recording (in stereo) and filming their key productions for several decades now, and there is much treasure to be discovered in their archives. The quality of both picture and sound is generally remarkably good, often really excellent. Those music lovers seeking to watch instrumental and vocal soloists, choirs, and famous orchestras playing under key conductors will not be disappointed either. No better examples exist than the superb DVD of Bach's *Brandenburg Concertos* recorded at Castle Cöthen by the wonderfully alive and stylish Freiburg Baroque Orchestra, or the series of recordings Bernstein made in New York and Boston not long before he died, full of musical joy and brimming over with an exuberant life force.

A Timeline for Key Composers Included in Our Choices

11th–12th centuries: Hildegard of Bingen (1098–1179); Perotinus (c. 1160–1225); Léonin (c. 1153–1201)

The earliest music of our culture has not survived, as it was not possible until the twelfth century to write it down in such a way as to determine the pitch of the notes and their relationship to one another. Then, for the first time, the austere but haunting two-part plainchant of Léonin, the resident composer at the cathedral of Notre Dame in Paris, was written on a 'stave' (a series of horizontal lines), and this was extended by his colleague Magister Perotinus to three and four parts, which characterized a style of writing called organum.

But, astonishingly, it was a woman who was to compose the first music to survive into regular present-day performance. Besides her remarkable gifts as a composer, Hildegard of Bingen had mystic visions throughout her life and believed that God was communicating directly to her. The church (and indeed the pope) accepted that her experiences were genuine, and this gave her far-reaching philosophical power as a confidante of the church authorities, including the pope. She believed that the world should be experienced and enjoyed jointly by man and woman, yet be balanced by resistance to sin. 'Only thus is the world fruitful,' she suggested. Her music is a simple, soaring monody with immediate appeal.

15th–17th centuries: Josquin Desprez (c. 1440–1521); Thomas Tallis (c. 1505–85); William Byrd (1543–1623); Carlo Gesualdo (1561–1613); Claudio Monteverdi (1567–1643); Orlando Gibbons (1583–1625); Henry Purcell (1659–95)

By the time Josquin Desprez arrived, medieval polyphony had matured into vocal writing of great feeling and intensity, whether in Mass settings of great eloquence in four or five parts or in simpler motets, which are still very telling. Carlo Gesualdo's motets bring astonishing dissonances and chromaticisms, often flagrantly pungent, which surely reflect his own personal life. Byrd and Tallis were the two great composers in Elizabethan England.

Monteverdi, whose life spanned half of both the 16th and 17th centuries, is however surely the key figure in Italian vocal music of this period. The expressive range of his eight books of madrigals is remarkable, and Book 8 includes the unique pair of dramatically inspired mini-operas, *Il ballo delle ingrate* and *Il combattimento di Tancredi e Clorinda*.Their intensity and originality are however capped by his 1610 *Vespers* and the three major operas, *L'Incoronazione di Poppea*, *L'Orfeo* and *Il Ritorno d'Ulisse in patria*.

Turning to England, we encounter some of the greatest instrumental music to have appeared so far: the sublime *Fantasias* for viol consort by Orlando Gibbons lead on naturally to the *Fantasias* of Purcell. So little is known of this great composer, except his music and the fact that he was honoured enough in his time to be buried in Westminster Abbey.

17th–18th centuries: Antonio Vivaldi (1678–1741); Georg Telemann (1681–1767); Johann Sebastian Bach (1685–1750); George Frideric Handel (1685–1759)

Two key baroque composers dominate the first half of the eighteenth century: Johann Sebastian Bach and George Frideric Handel. Bach's influence was initially in German music, while Handel (born within a short distance of Bach) left his native Saxony and made his career in England. Both were musical geniuses of the highest order, yet fascinatingly they never met. They also chose to explore quite different musical genres.

The peak of Bach's achievement in vocal music lay in 300 church cantatas (of which about 200 survive) and included the great Passion oratorios, and a uniquely original and expansive Mass. He was a famous organist and composed much commanding organ music. He also wrote relatively lightweight, Vivaldi-style concertos and a great deal of extraordinarily original harpsichord music (now often heard on the piano). Equally memorable is his solo instrumental music, suites and partitas for cello and violin.

Handel developed the Corelli-influenced *concerto grosso*, and wrote keyboard suites that were quite different from Bach's. But he is most celebrated for his Italian operas, the English oratorios of comparable calibre (not least *Messiah*, the most performed of all choral works), and the *Fireworks* and *Water Music*, written for the king, which were to become some of the first suites of popular orchestral music, vividly scored.

Antonio Vivaldi was justly famous in Italy in his own time as priest/musician and writer of countless concertos for diverse instruments. A wag once said that 'he wrote the same concerto five hundred times,' but that is patently not true; his invention is inexhaustible in its diversity, in both his instrumental and (more recently revived) vocal music (secular and sacred). It seems remarkable that after he died, in 1741, his output was all but forgotten until Louis Kaufman and the Concert Hall Chamber Orchestra directed by Henry Swoboda revived and recorded *The Four Seasons* in Carnegie Hall in December 1947. The work has now become the most popular classical work in the whole repertoire.

The entertaining German composer Georg Telemann was almost equally prolific and his music is certainly comparably attractive, specializing (besides concertos) in colourful baroque orchestral suites, often engagingly pictorial and featuring local scenes in Hamburg, where he lived.

18th–19th centuries: Thomas Arne (1710–78); Joseph Haydn (1732–1809); Wolfgang Amadeus Mozart (1756–91); Ludwig van Beethoven (1770–1827); Franz Schubert (1797–1828)

Thomas Arne in England, following in Handel's footsteps, had success with both instrumental music and opera (at Covent Garden) and his *Artaxerxes* was the first *opera seria* with words in English. The score has had to be reconstructed, but is well worth investigating, full of attractive numbers colourfully orchestrated.

The period between 1732 and 1827/8 is without doubt the richest section of our musical timeline and one cannot consider any of these four great linked composers without remembering the other three. Haydn, living for much of his life at Esterháza, commented that, isolated as he was, he *had* to be original. But he was not just original, his originality was extraordinarily prolific. His most precious contribution was the virtual invention of the string quartet, and he left us nearly 80 of them, including six very agreeable works for a long time attributed to him as Opus 3 but actually written by Romanus Hoffstetter, which he acknowledged as authentic in his complete works, perhaps one of his light-hearted jokes. But they are not unworthy, and the rest are magnificent, desert-island fare (for I.M.).

Haydn also gave us 104 hardly less stimulating symphonies, of which undoubtedly the last twelve, written for London, are among the finest. It now seems difficult to believe that before the Second World War most of Haydn's earlier symphonies had not even been printed, and their availability owes much to the research of a brilliant musicologist, H. C. Robbins Landon, whose *Symphonies of Joseph Haydn* was first published in 1955. The sad thing is that many of these early and middle-period works, which are of the highest quality, are still very seldom heard in the concert hall. But of course they are all available on CD. Haydn was not a concerto specialist, but he wrote a single trumpet concerto for the new keyed instrument when it arrived, and it has never been equalled since, let alone surpassed. However, he wrote some excellent works for cello, and his keyboard concertos, for piano or harpsichord, are by no means to be dismissed. His *Creation* and *Seasons* are among the first great English choral works.

There are many who consider Mozart to be a greater composer than Haydn, and in the case of certain very special works they may be right. The operas, *Così fan tutte*, *Don Giovanni*, *Le nozze di Figaro* (especially) and *Die Zauberflöte* are indispensable, as are the *Clarinet Concerto* and *Clarinet Quintet*, many of the piano concertos, but especially No. 23 in A, K.488, and the *Double Piano Concerto*, K.365. The five violin concertos are also memorable, capped by the masterly *Sinfonia concertante for violin and viola*. The last four symphonies will be among many readers' special favourites, as will the six quartets dedicated to Haydn, and the *String Trio in E flat* and the *G minor String Quintet*. But Haydn's contribution overall remains colossal and so, with proper respect, we place the achievements of these two masters side by side.

Beethoven stands alone and supreme at the centre of the pantheon of great composers. He began writing music of his own time, then expanded every musical form - symphonies, concertos, chamber, instrumental, piano and choral music - and took them forward into the future. None more so than the string quartets, of which the first six are supremely classical and the late works have a sublimely subtle inner essence to which the listener raptly responds without seeking or needing analysis.

Schubert is the great musical lyricist, both in his countless songs and in the glorious chamber and piano music. The symphonies have a powerful simplicity, the *Unfinished* marks the true beginning of Romantic music. His last instrumental works, including the *String Quintet* and the final *B flat major Piano Sonata*, take us into an Elysian musical world unsurpassed even by Beethoven.

18th and 19th centuries (in the opera house): Gioachino Rossini (1792–1868); Gaetano Donizetti (1797–1848); Vincenzo Bellini (1801–35)

Rossini and Donizetti showed us that great art, besides being musically satisfying, could also make us smile with pleasure. Beethoven greatly admired *The Barber of Seville*, an opera which matches stylish melody with sparkling humour. Donizetti's *Don Pasquale*, *L'Elisir d'amore* and *La Fille du régiment* are all great fun, often made at the expense of a pompous central character – the epitome of *opera buffa*. But Donizetti could also write serious opera, of which *Lucia di Lammermoor* is justly the most famous, and Bellini followed in his wake.

19th century (first part): Hector Berlioz (1803–69); Felix Mendelssohn (1809–47); Frédéric Chopin (1810–49); Franz Liszt (1811–86); Richard Wagner (1813–83); Giuseppe Verdi (1813–1901); Charles Gounod (1818–93); Jacques Offenbach (1819–80); Anton Bruckner (1824–96); Johannes Brahms (1833–97); Georges Bizet (1838–75); Peter Tchaikovsky (1840–93); Antonín Dvořák (1841–1904); Edvard Grieg (1843–1907)

Hector Berlioz burst into the nineteenth century with the *Symphonie fantastique*, the first epic Romantic programme symphony, written only a few years after Beethoven's death, yet conceived in spectacle and hyperbole, and orchestrated with a brilliance none of the composer's predecessors could have dreamed of. The comparably masterly concert overture *Le Carnaval romain*, less than ten minutes long, is in some ways even more breathtaking, as is his *Requiem*.

Mendelssohn is credited with bringing the fairies into the orchestra in his exquisite *Midsummer Night's Dream Overture and Incidental Music*, and he also travelled to Scotland to create an unsurpassed musical seascape in the *Hebrides Overture*.

Chopin and Liszt then stepped on to the concert platform with their romantic piano music, matching delicate poetry with sparkling virtuosity. At the same time Verdi and Gounod romanticized the operatic stage, and Wagner imbued his characters and the large accompanying orchestra with an overwhelming chromatic sensuality, although they usually took a long time to sing what they had to say.

French composers can usually be relied on to write racily exuberant music, and Offenbach was perhaps the wittiest of them all, providing a perfect counterpart to Wagner's melodramatic hyperbole. In Germany, Bruckner added weight and expansive length to his nine symphonies while Brahms in his four symphonies, *Violin Concerto*, and two great *Piano Concertos* sensed that he was regarded by his compatriots as a natural successor to Beethoven. When quizzed about the obvious similarity between the great, expansive melody in the finale of his *First Symphony* and the main theme of the finale of Beethoven's *Ninth*, his scornful reply was, 'Any fool can see that.'

Bizet wrote just one symphony, in C major, but it is sheer delight, especially in the hands of Beecham. He also gave us one of the most popular of all operas, *Carmen*, which Oscar Hammerstein greatly praised for the sheer number of 'hits' that he acknowledged the score contains.

The music of both Dvořák and Tchaikovsky is permeated with the rich folklore of their respective homelands. Indeed Stravinsky stated, 'Tchaikovsky was the greatest Russian of us all.' Yet Dvořák wrote his finest symphony, the '*New World*', while he was in America, and the folk influence in the beautiful main theme of its justly famous slow movement has as much of an American influence as Czech.

Tchaikovsky, alongside Schubert, was the greatest melodist of all time, and every one of his works overflows with memorable tunes. He told us that he would often wake up in the middle of the night with a new theme running through his consciousness, complete with harmony and orchestration. He had to get up immediately and write it down, for he would have forgotten it by morning. Tchaikovsky befriended Grieg when the two composers came together to England to receive honorary doctorates at Cambridge University. They liked each other immediately and Tchaikovsky greatly admired the haunting simplicity of Grieg's music with its strong, Norwegian folk flavour.

19th century (second part): Gabriel Fauré (1845–1924); Leoš Janáček (1854–1928); Edward Elgar (1857–1934); Giacomo Puccini (1858–1924); Gustav Mahler (1860–1911); Richard Strauss (1864–1949)

If it is the refined delicacy of the lyricism of Gabriel Fauré which captivates the listener, it is the sharp, pungent originality of Janáček's writing that catches the ear with its often abrasive orchestration. Elgar was truly English, very proud of his patriotism and conscious of his heritage. He did not seek dissonant textures in the orchestra but scored traditionally, with sonorously expansive string and brass and a reliance on rich melodic lines and strong rhythms and, in outer movements, a thrusting, vigorous impetus, finding its zenith in the *Pomp and Circumstance Marches* which are famous. His greatest work was *The Dream of Gerontius*.

Puccini and Richard Strauss were also both both supreme melodists and scored richly and romantically for the orchestra. Puccini's masterpiece, *La*

Bohème, has a continuous inspired melodic flow from the first note to the last and Strauss's *Rosenkavalier* brings an utterly magical 'Presentation of the Silver Rose' scene and an unforgettable final Trio. Their principal works between them have helped to keep opera alive and popular since the era of Verdi.

Gustav Mahler is a very different musician from Bruckner, while springing from the same roots. Like Bruckner, he left us nine very expansive symphonies, but with greater orchestral and vocal variety between them. No. 2 is subtitled the 'Resurrection' because of its spectacular Judgement Day choral finale, and No. 8 is called the 'Symphony of 1000' because of the huge musical forces required for performances. But Nos. 1 and 4 have an endearing lyrical warmth, No. 5 has a glorious slow movement and No. 4 has a simple song for its finale.

Claude Debussy (1862–1918); Frederick Delius (1862–1934); Maurice Ravel (1875–1937)

Debussy was in many ways the most original orchestral composer of the twentieth century. None of his music is predictable, especially in its harmonic and melodic language; virtually all of it is impressionistic, and its vivid use of colour and drama is uniquely compelling. Ravel's muse is more subtle, the lusciously sensuous *Daphnis et Chloé* and the delicate *Ma Mère l'Oye* are among the most beautiful scores of the whole century, with an almost Mozartian refinement of texture; yet much of his music glitters with colour and sparkles with rhythmic intensity. The English composer Frederick Delius also creates glowing luxuriance and gentle suggestion in his orchestral writing, with its very English pastoral evocation, although there is passion too. He needs a special sensitivity from his performers and that is something Beecham above all other conductors brought to his music.

Jean Sibelius (1865–1957); Ralph Vaughan Williams (1872–1958); Sergei Rachmaninov (1873–1943); Alexander von Zemlinsky (1871–1942); Gustav Holst (1874–1934)

Sibelius, Vaughan Williams and Rachmaninov were key symphonists of this era, spanning the period between the 19th and 20th centuries. All three composers wrote naturally symphonically, thrillingly using themes of real memorability. Rachmaninov was the most romantic of his time and wrote four memorable piano concertos and the *Rhapsody on a Theme of Paganini*, a set of brilliant variations for piano and orchestra on a familiar theme which calls for great pianistic imagination and virtuosity from the soloist. Zemlinsky's music is even more ripely sensuous and full of inventive sonorities and luscious invention. His most celebrated work is the passionately poetic *Lyric Symphony*, which includes two vocal soloists. Holst is most famous for his vividly characterized orchestral suite, *The Planets*. In many ways this is a unique programme symphony in seven diverse movements, ranging from the ferocious 'Mars the bringer of war,' to 'Saturn' with its closing mystic diminuendo of female voices. 'Jupiter' is the jolliest, with its famous, very English central tune.

Arnold Schoenberg (1874–1951); Charles Ives (1874–1954); Béla Bartók (1881–1945)

Arnold Schoenberg's early music (notably the symphonic poem *Pelleas und Melisande* and *Verklaerte Nacht*) has a sensuous richness of texture which appeals to listeners in a way that much of his later, more 'modern' music fails to communicate. But the American composer Charles Ives, while flouting convention in every way in his use of enigmatic dissonance, has no communicative problems, rather bringing astonishment in the daring originality and sheer personality of his music.

Béla Bartók, once a seemingly daunting modernist writer, breaking new ground, has found his way into the popular repertoire by vividly coloured orchestration, drawing on earthy Hungarian and Romanian folk music. Indeed the *Concerto for Orchestra* has now become a favourite demonstration of orchestral virtuosity.

Igor Stravinsky (1882–1971); Nikolai Miaskovsky (1881–1950); Bohuslav Martinů (1890–1959); Serge Prokofiev (1891–1953); Francis Poulenc (1899–1963)

Stravinsky was discovered and nurtured by the impresario Serge Diaghilev and, after beginning with his ballets, *The Firebird* (with echoes of Rimsky-Korsakov) and *Petrushka*, went on to write one of the great masterpieces of the twentieth century, the *Rite of Spring*, then moving on to write music of great originality in almost every other sphere. He was not a natural melodist, but borrowed from Russian folksongs instead. His compatriot, Serge Prokofiev's, peak achievements include the richly melodic ballet score for *Romeo and Juliet* and the equally inspired monumental opera based on Tolstoy's novel, *War and Peace*. But he wrote masterpieces in every form, including memorable concertos for cello, piano and violin, superb ballet music, and seven highly stimulating symphonies, plus chamber music. Miaskovsky's mellow, seemingly old-fashioned Russian style, full of nostalgia and poignant lyricism, may seem backward-looking, yet it is easy to come under the spell of the elegiac mood which is his speciality.

The Czech composer Bohuslav Martinů's *Concerto for Double String Orchestra, Piano and Timpani* is one of the most powerful works of the twentieth century. He too was prolific, writing six symphonies that show real vision, concertos and much chamber music of great appeal for a variety of instruments.

Poulenc's *Les Biches* (another Diaghilev ballet) is a favourite score of ours. It is skittish, high spirited and fresh, and delectably melodic as only French music can be. The original choreography takes place near the beach with the corps de ballet in skimpy swimming costumes, and later having a vigorous tussle around a sofa. But there is an underlying feeling of naughtiness in the choreography which suggests that all is not what it seems.

20th century: Aaron Copland (1900–1990); Samuel Barber (1910–81)

Of all the USA's twentieth-century composers it is Aaron Copland whose music hauntingly captures the vast open spaces of the American continent best and, like Stravinsky, it was the ballet which inspired his greatest music. Leonard Kerstein of the New York City Ballet tried to commission a score from him without success until one day he left behind on the composer's piano a book of cowboy songs, including one of the most famous, 'Old Paint'. The result was the masterly *Rodeo*, and *Billy the Kid*. But Copland's masterpiece, *Appalachian Spring*, was written for Martha Graham's ballet company and is a truly unforgettable score, climaxing with variations on the delightful Quaker melody, 'The gift to be simple'.

Samuel Barber's *Adagio for Strings* is for Americans what 'Nimrod' from the *Enigma Variations* is for the British public; it is actually a version for full strings of the slow movement of his *String Quartet*. But all Barber's music is rewarding, and his glorious *Violin Concerto* now holds its place among the greatest international works in this form.

William Walton (1902–83); Benjamin Britten (1913–76); Malcolm Arnold (1921–2006)

The distinguished (Manchester-born) music critic Neville Cardus declared William Walton's *First Symphony* the finest since Sibelius, and it is good to see that after a period of eclipse it has now returned to the concert hall. Walton's output was comparatively small but includes outstanding concertos for all the major stringed instruments, some outstanding film music, two splendid coronation marches with *nobilmente* tunes worthy of Elgar, and in *Belshazzar's Feast* one of the very finest choral works written in English. And we must not forget *Façade*, a series of delicious orchestral vignettes designed as a backcloth to all but inconsequential poems by Edith Sitwell, but which stand up equally well in their ballet form, without the words.

Benjamin Britten was infinitely more prolific than his predecessor; because he wrote so much vocal music, of which the delightful *Ceremony of Carols* remains one of the most inspired examples, his music is now better known than Walton's. He wrote a remarkable number of songs, which he performed with his musical and personal partner, Peter Pears, and it was Pears who took the lead role in *Peter Grimes*, an operatic masterpiece if ever there was one. Among Britten's orchestral works are the engaging *Simple Symphony for Strings*, the superbly inventive *Variations on a Theme of Frank Bridge* and, of course, the *Young Person's Guide to the Orchestra*, in which he writes variations on a comparatively little-known theme of Purcell.

We have a special place in our hearts for Malcolm Arnold, an orchestral trumpeter-turned-composer who wrote tuneful, stimulating and friendly music (including nine splendid symphonies) and many shorter works, vividly coloured and never short of good tunes. Alas, he lived and composed at a time when writing tunes and music which communicated readily to the public was unfashionable, and the adverse reception from his critics all but broke his spirit.

Dmitri Shostakovich (1906–75)

Many would regard the Russian genius, Dmitri Shostakovich, as the greatest and most highly original composer of the twentieth century. He lived in Soviet Russia under Stalin and endured constant vitriolic criticism from inferior musicians in the Soviet hierarchy who were unfit to pass any musical judgements at all. But the Russian people did not desert him, and for them he wrote an enormous range of music in all forms, including 14 symphonies, many of which recorded recent Russian history, or made disguised comments on the repressive communist lifestyle. His dance and ballet music is spontaneously tuneful (his arrangement of 'Tea for two' a particular delight) and his powerful opera, *Lady Macbeth of Mtsensk*, is among the most memorable of the twentieth century. He wrote some fine piano music too, but he reserved his inner feelings for his chamber music. The string quartets are the most personal and deeply expressive of all his works.

Olivier Messiaen (1908–92); Einojuhani Rautavaara (born 1928)

Olivier Messiaen is the true mystic of French music. His *Turangalîla Symphony* (the title comes from Sanskrit) is on an epic scale to embrace 'almost the totality of human experience'; his single, masterly chamber work, the visionary *Quatuor pour la fin du temps*, composed during his days in a Silesian prison camp, is unforgettably haunting. But much of his other music (especially the works for organ) is concerned with religious experience and his sense of the eternal, while his *Catalogue d'oiseaux* for piano is immersed in bird-song which he loved so much.

Rautavaara's is another wholly original voice of our time, though by no means a formidable one. His symphonies are readily approachable, full of colour and atmosphere, and he has written a series of concertos for different instruments, which are all hauntingly accessible and richly evocative. The most famous is the *Cantus arctcus*, using tape recordings of Arctic bird calls against an orchestral backcloth.

John Adams (born 1947); Thomas Adès (born 1971)

Here, finally, are two relatively new names, one English, the other American. Thomas Adès writes brilliantly for the orchestra, combining intricate rhythms with dazzling use of colour. But it is his opera, *The Tempest*, which has placed him firmly on the musical map. He writes very imaginatively for voices and his vocal lines are both melodic and singable. This is a work that could well make it into Covent Garden on a regular basis.

The American, John Adams, however, has already written a superb opera which is bound to join the international operatic repertoire. If *Nixon in China* seems an unlikely subject, it has all the drama one could ask for, particularly in the choral and ensemble writing and the vividly rhythmic orchestral accompaniment. Moreover Adams has the rare twentieth-century gift of writing lyrical lines for the soloists that are grateful to sing and moving to listen to. Adams's other orchestral music with its extended minimalist style is original, ear-catching and inventive, and there is a great deal of it, nearly all of high quality.

Ballet Music

Some classic ballet recordings

The idea of dancing to music is of course not a new one. Both ritual and popular dancing took place in ancient Egypt and Greece, but the idea of it being a theatrical entertainment is more recent. It was during the Renaissance that the dancing art-form really began to develop, though mainly as court entertainment. Its development was speeded up through the increasing popularity of opera and oratorio. Early ballets comprised music, poetry and dance, melding into a single entertainment, but this soon morphed into a melodramatic form of ballet, in spirit a sort of miniature opera.

Lully was the first great master of this form; he revolutionized the way ballets were written. He made them a complete artistic whole and his collaboration with Molière from 1671 raised the standard to new heights. A two-CD set with Minkowski and the Musiciens du Louvre from Warner (*Les Comédies Ballets*) captures the often brilliant style of his writing in which the combination of melody and often outrageous burlesque represents an unparalleled comic partnership between composer and playwright (Warner Apex 2564 62184 (2)). Rameau consolidated Lully's achievements and wrote much striking ballet music, and the catalogue is now rich with fine examples of his art .

However, it was with Gluck's *Don Juan* (1761) that the real turning point in ballet music occurred. It was the first ballet written by a truly important composer and it also provided music for the dance, with no singing or speaking of any kind. It was also one of the first works in which the choreography made serious attempts to represent the drama. The music is a delight: distinctive, tuneful and very danceable. Marriner's classic pioneering ASMF Decca/Argo account is available on Australian Decca Eloquence (476 2440) alongside Gardiner's period performance on Warner (8573 89233-2). Both are excellent.

Neither Haydn nor Mozart (*pace Les Petits Riens*) made great contributions to the genre, but Beethoven did with his ballet, *The Creatures of Prometheus*. Mackerras, with the Scottish Chamber Orchestra, gives a fresh, vigorous version of this score on Hyperion, now on their bargain Helios label (CDH 55196).

After the death of Gluck, ballet remained an integral part of French opera, with most composers writing a fair amount of ballet music for their operas – Gossec, Grétry, Auber, Boïeldieu and others. In fact, it was an iron-clad rule of the Paris Opéra that all operas performed there must have their own ballet sequence (even Wagner's). This was at the insistence of the all-powerful Parisian Jockey Club, whose members ogled the corps de ballet to select their mistresses. The ballet had to take place during the second half of the opera, as over-indulgence at dining precluded attendance before then. The results of this tradition produced a good deal of very attractive 'light' music of the best kind, of which perhaps the most famous was Gounod's famous ballet from *Faust*, which the composer ingeniously fitted into the plot. But Donizetti, Rossini and Verdi also composed some equally tuneful and vivacious music, combining melody, wit and vivacity.

Minkus was the first composer to establish ballet music as an entertainment in its own right. Between 1871 and 1903 he established a partnership with the famous Russian choreographer, Marius Petipa, for whom he wrote a great deal of engagingly colourful and tuneful music, beginning in 1869 with *Don Quixote*. However, in Rudolf Nureyev's revised version of the ballet, the eponymous character does not feature strongly in the action, which concentrates on a triangular love story between Kiri, Basilio and the rich, elderly Gamache. In 1857 Minkus had also composed music for Petipa's '*Grand pas classique*', the only part of the ballet *Paquita* to survive. But the key collaboration between Minkus and Petipa was the exotic *La Bayadère* (1877), set in India, which has survived as a complete work.

The Italian, Riccardo Drigo, is also remembered for an attractive *pas de deux* which was originally interpolated into Adam's *Le Corsaire* in 1899. But before that, in the 1840s and 1850s, the Royal Danish Ballet flourished under the choreographer Bournonville, and the Danish composers Edward Helsted, Holger Paulli and Niels Gade provided tuneful music for three ballets: *Napoli*, *The Kermesse in Bruges* and *Flower Festival at Genzano*. Those interested in the development of ballet music will find a well-played and -recorded EMI two-CD set – with the Minkus scores arranged and conducted by John Lanchbery and the others by Terence Kern and Ole Schmidt. It is well worth seeking out (6 48640-2).

But the first major ballet in the repertoire that is independent of opera and which is performed regularly to this day is Adolphe Adam's *Giselle*. This ballet, along with Delibes's *Coppélia* and *Sylvia* and Tchaikovsky's *Swan Lake*, *Sleeping Beauty* and (for Christmas) *The Nutcracker*, are the great ballets of the romantic era. They have survived partly because of the excellence of the narrative, but far more importantly because of the quality of the music. These ballets are discussed under their respective composers, but there is plenty more music which, while not reaching the artistic heights of those masterpieces, is entertainingly melodic and memorable.

Richard Bonynge

No conductor has done more for this area of the repertoire on record than Richard Bonynge, who has resurrected many rare ballets during his recording career, and Decca have put a collection of them into a 10-CD bargain box called *Fête du Ballet* (468 57-2). In it you will find Auber's tuneful score for *Marco Spada* (Auber had the knack of writing memorable tunes), and the set also includes a delightful confection of this composer's music, arranged by Constant Lambert for the ballet *Les Rendez-vous*, plus Auber's short but catchy *Pas Classique*. Lecocq's effervescent score for the ballet *Mam'zelle Angot* (arranged by Gordon Jacob) is very successfully presented here too – an enticing bouquet of tunes, very brightly and wittily orchestrated.

The composers who wrote for the Imperial Theatres in Russia are again represented here, with more music by Minkus and Drigo, including the latter's complete *La Flûte magique*, well crafted and orchestrated and of better quality than its reputation implies. Bonynge's classic ballet sets, 'Homage to Pavlova' and 'The Art of the Prima Ballerina', comprise very attractive, short ballet excerpts, ranging from the well-known to the completely obscure, as well as including the only complete recording of Luigini's *Ballet Egyptien* – and enjoyably tuneful it is too. Among the more modern ballets represented are the Rossini/Britten *Soirées musicales* and *Matinées musicales* and Désormière's arrangement of the Strauss family's music, to form the ballet *Le Beau Danube*. Other highlights include Burgmüller's *La Péri*, written in the wake of the success of *Giselle* for the reigning prima ballerina at the Paris Opéra, Carlotta Grisi.

Offenbach's delightful *Le Papillon* is featured only as a suite, but readers are urged to investigate the complete version of the ballet (see under Offenbach), which is one of the finest of all Bonynge's ballet discoveries. The classic coupling of suites from Massenet's *Le Cid* and Meyerbeer's *Les Patineurs* is also included and, though it is not ballet music, Massenet's *Scènes alsaciennes* and *Scènes dramatiques* sit very well on an all-Massenet CD, which also includes the *Waltz* from *Le Roi de Lahore* and the sparkling *Marche des princesses* from *Cendrillon*. The sound throughout these recordings is of Decca's best quality.

Serge Diaghilev

The early-twentieth-century ballet scene was dominated by the figure of Serge Diaghilev, the mastermind of a small group of famous designers of scenery and costumes, musicians and writers in St Petersburg. In 1908 he created a sensation in Paris with a season of Russian operas, and the following year he gave his first ballet season with his Ballets Russes, now regarded as the greatest ballet company in the history of the medium, creating a sensation across Europe (and especially in England). Through his genius of collaboration, Diaghilev inspired composers, dancers, designers and choreographers, including Balanchine, to create some of the greatest ballets of the twentieth century, commissioning masterly scores from Stravinsky, Debussy, Ravel, de Falla and Prokofiev, as well as music from Les Six, notably Poulenc (*Les Biches* a supreme example) and Milhaud, as well as eliciting contributions from such unlikely sources as the English composer, Constant Lambert.

Diaghilev's other main achievement lay in getting composers to arrange music already written for other purposes in creating new ballets. Among his greater successes were Schumann's *Carnaval* (piano music orchestrated by several Russian composers, available on Australian Decca Eloquence 480 038) conducted by Ansermet, coupled with that conductor's classic account of *The Seasons*. Weber's *Le Spectre de la rose* appears in Berlioz's orchestrated version, and Respighi's arrangement of music by Rossini, *La Boutique fantasque*, has been preserved in Ansermet's magical mono version of that score, available on Somm CD027 (coupled with his equally famous mono *Petrushka*).

In their excellent historical two-disc ballet music series, EMI also offer Offenbach's *Gaîté Parisienne* played by the Monte Carlo Philharmonic Orchestra directed by its arranger, Manuel Rosenthal, which also usefully offers a complete listing of the sources of all twenty numbers. This is combined with Prêtre's complete Philharmonia recording of Poulenc's *Les Biches* with chorus, John Lanchbery's vivid account with the Bournemouth Symphony Orchestra of the only available full version of Messager's *Two Pigeons* and Mackerras's Philharmonia account of *Les Patineurs* (both ballets choreographed by Sir Frederick Ashton) (6 48656-2).

In similarly tuneful style, Hérold's *La Fille mal gardée* should not be overlooked and John Lanchbery's *Tales of Beatrix Potter* is another delightful confection of tunes, mainly from the Victorian era, but so skilfully arranged one would think it an original ballet score (EMI 9498392).

During this fertile period, splendid ballet scores were also written by Britten (*The Prince of the Pagodas*), Florent Schmitt (the exotic *La Tragédie de Salomé* (available on CD on Hyperion CDA 67599, coupled with the composer's spectacular *Psalm* XLVII), and Albert Roussel (see under the composer), as well as Arnold (*Homage to the Queen* – available on a new Chandos CD of Arnold's ballet scores, including much that is rare (Chan. 10550), *Miracle in the Gorbals* by Bliss (Naxos 8.553698), and of course Bartók.

Herbert von Karajan was a naturally sympathetic conductor of ballet music, and DG have gathered together some of his best recordings on a bargain two-CD set (459 445-2). In it you will find an unsurpassed performance of Chopin's *Les Sylphides* (in Roy Douglas's uniquely masterful arrangement), with very stylish accounts of Ponchielli's *Dance of the Hours*, Gounod's *Faust* ballet music, Delibes's *Coppélia Suite* and Offenbach's *Gaîté Parisienne* – as well as a splendidly played *Sleeping Beauty Suite* of Tchaikovsky.

Other colourful ballet scores well worth hunting out are Glazunov's *Raymonda* (there is a lovely DVD of the Bolshoi performing it on Arthaus DVD 100 719), and particularly that masterpiece of colour and melody, *The Seasons* (see under Glazunov). The Armenian composer Aram Khachaturian must be mentioned; his ballets *Gayaneh* and *Spartacus*, especially the former, are among the most vivid Russian scores in the repertoire (see under Khachaturian). Massenet wrote three ballets, two of which have been recorded by Richard Bonynge: *Le Carillon* and *Le Cigale*. Both have a unique French charm and sophistication, and are richly scored; *Le Carillon* is coupled with Delibes's *Coppélia* (Decca 444 836-2) but *Cigale* is at present out of the catalogue, although available as a download (from iTunes). For perhaps the ultimate Massenet ballet though, one must turn to Leighton Lucas's masterful arrangement of Massenet excerpts which form the ballet *Manon* – with the famous *Elégie* returning throughout the score as an *idée fixe*. It is a gorgeous score, full of melody, colour and imagination, sumptuously recorded by Decca and most understandingly conducted by Bonynge, with the Covent Garden Orchestra (Decca 470 525-2 (2)).

Balanchine

Unquestionably the greatest choreorapher of the twentieth century was George Balanchine (1904–83). Born in St Petersburg, he became a member of the Russian Imperial Ballet, where he worked as both dancer and choreographer. He went to Paris in the 1920s and joined the Ballets Russes as one of Diaghilev's key choreographers, achieving a close personal relationship with Stravinsky as well as many other composers. He stayed until Diaghilev's death in 1929, then worked with a number of ballet companies in Europe, until in 1933 he was invited to move to New York by Lincoln Kirstein; here he worked with the resident American Ballet Company of the Metropolitan Opera until 1938. He then worked with various companies until he was able to create the New York City Ballet in 1948, with which he stayed until his death. It was here that he established an American style of ballet movements which was as original as it was imaginative. His choreography is as individual as it is unpredictable, full of surprises and wonderfully entertaining to watch. He drew on orchestral music already written in other forms, using many works of Tchaikovsky, creating new and unconventional dance movements that are unsurpassed and unsurpassable.

Fortunately the excellent EMI two-CD ballet music series includes some of the finest music he chose, and EMI have provided excellent recordings. The first of two sets (6 48625-2) includes one of his earliest works, the 1934 *Serenade,* using the work by Tchaikovsky for strings, yet placing the slow movement, *Elégie,* as the finale and combining individual dances for each performer but climaxing with a dazzling ensemble. Hickox's performance of the music with the City of London Sinfonia is fully worthy. Bizet's *Symphony in C,* another favourite, was adapted for the Paris Opéra Ballet in 1947 but was also used for the inauguration of the New York City Ballet a year later. The choreography is based on the individual style of each of the four movements, with a different group of dancers for each. In the dazzling finale all four groups join together in a spectacularly thrilling apotheosis. The performance on CD is the finest on record, directed by Sir Thomas Beecham. *Allegro brillante* (in fact Tchaikovsky's *Third Piano Concerto*) came a decade later, in 1956, excellently played by Peter Donohoe and the Bournemouth Symphony Orchestra, conducted by Rudolf Barshai. The other major work included here is *Jewels,* which dates from 1967. It is in three parts, with the dancers' costumes simulating the title. The first, *Emeralds,* is set to gently lyrical pieces by Fauré, taken from his incidental music to *Pelléas et Mélisande* and *Shylock,* sensitively played by the Toulouse Capitole Orchestra conducted by Michel Plasson. The second, *Rubies,* turns to Stravinsky's *Capriccio for Piano and Orchestra* (brilliantly played by Michel Béroff and the Orchestre de Paris under Ozawa) and the dancing evokes the New York style of jazz and Broadway musicals. For *Diamonds,* the closing part, Balanchine moved to Tchaikovsky's (*Polish*) *Third Symphony*, omitting the first movement ('Always Tchaikovsky for dancing,' he commented), and indeed this work, as played by the Philharmonia Orchestra under Muti, has a distinct ballet flavour.

The second EMI Balanchine collection (6 48620-2) also includes Muti's recording of *Diamonds* from *Jewels* and two other Tchaikovsky works, *Ballet Imperial* (1941), set to the uncut version of the *Second Piano Concerto*, which here uses another superb recording by Peter Donohoe and the Bournemouth orchestra with Barshai. Most valuable of all is the *Theme and Variations* (1947) taken from the *Orchestral Suite No. 3 in G*, splendidly played by the La Scala, Milan, Orchestra, directed by Lovro von Matačić. As a bonus, the disc offers more Tchaikovsky, *Onegin*, produced by the Stuttgart Ballet in 1965. This features the same Pushkin story as is used in the opera *Eugene Onegin*, but not the music. Instead, the choreographer, John Cranko, chose orchestrations of piano pieces, including *The Seasons*, by Kurt-Heinz Stolze, but for his finale he used the thrilling closing section of *Francesca da Rimini*, beginning with the seductive clarinet solo which accompanies Francesca's entry.

Another key Balanchine ballet score is *Night Shadow*, with a dazzling selection of tunes taken from the operas of Bellini, arranged and scored by Vittorio Rieti. The story follows that of *La Sonnambula* and the piece was premiered by the Ballet Russe de Monte Carlo in New York in 1946, then revived by the New York City Ballet in 1965 when Balanchine became director. This is coupled with Sir Frederick Ashton's *The Dream*, using excerpts from Mendelssohn's incidental music for *A Midsummer Night's Dream*, played by Previn and the LSO with wonderful freshness, employing soloists and the Finchley Children's Music Group, and truly bringing the fairies into the orchestra. Then comes *The Lady and the Fool*, created for Sadler's Wells by John Cranko and Sir Charles Mackerras, and brilliantly played by the LPO conducted by Mackerras.

The second of the two CDs contains four Chopin *Nocturnes* chosen in 1970 by Jerome Robbins for *In the Night*, beautifully played by Garrick Ohlsson. Then come orchestral versions of Erik Satie's three *Gymnopédies* for his sensuous *Monotones*, choreographed by Sir Frederick Ashton for Covent Garden. This is followed by *The Dying Swan*, Michel Fokine's ballet for Pavlova, with music by Saint-Saëns, played by the CBSO under Louis Frémaux, and finally Weber's *La Spectre de la Rose* ('Invitation to the Dance', orchestrated by Berlioz), again with Fokine's choreography, gloriously played by the Philharmonia Orchestra under Karajan (EMI 9 49849-2).

Those wanting to find out more about Balanchine and the New York City Ballet should look on line under the choreographer's name, and this entry also includes a performance of the finale of Bizet's *Symphony in C*.

Opera: A Historical Timeline

According to the *Oxford English Dictionary*, the origin of the word 'opera' (derived initially from Latin and then from Italian) meant 'labour' or 'work', an entirely appropriate description, for opera was to become the most complicated and demanding of all musical art forms. It brought solo singing of the most spectacular virtuosity, balanced by a rich depth of feeling and capable of firmly establishing the character of the role of the singer, plus an equally impressive choral contribution. Dancing, too, soon became an important feature, while the orchestral accompaniment, as the years passed, grew in importance and size. A successful opera also had to have both a good plot and a good libretto, both poetic and humanly dramatic, even humorous, which the vocal music could illustrate. Costumes could be exotic, and spectacle itself was soon prized by early opera lovers, and elaborate stage machinery made this possible.

The key composer at the birth of opera was indisputably Claudio Monteverdi, whose Italian setting of the famous classical story of *Orfeo* created the début of this new art form in 1607 – the very beginning of the seventeenth century. Within a decade Monteverdi had moved to Venice, and the first opera-house for paying audiences opened, so that this new dramatic experience now had the widest popular following. Venetian audiences were first able to see and hear *Il ritorno d'Ulisse in patria* staged in 1640, and then, three years later, what is perhaps the composer's most successful opera, *L'Incoronazione di Poppea*. This was based on characters from ancient Rome, including the Emperor Nero, and created opera's first female opera star (or 'diva' as such creative singers came to be called) in Anna Renzi in the role of Ottavia. With its basic story combining lust, sex and infidelity and with a memorable closing duet the work could not fail.

There were also a pair of memorable shorter works which might be described as the first chamber operas, the extraordinarily vivid narrative piece, *Il combattimento di Tancredi e Clorinda* and the more lyrical opera-ballet, *Il ballo delle ingrate*, featuring Pluto, Amor and Venus and a small female chorus of ungrateful souls. The work was given its début at a wedding, and was designed to warn the ladies in the audience (including the bride) not to scorn their lovers' advances and consequently be punished by Pluto with banishment to the underworld!

Francesco Cavalli followed Monteverdi in the direction of Venetian operas in 1668, but he also composed a dozen himself in a musical style which is sensuously very appealing. His most famous work is *La Calisto*, staged in 1651, returning to a mythological subject. It is full of erotic seductions, primarily between the heroine (the determinedly chaste Calisto) and Jove who, to ensure her compliant response, takes the form of the goddess Diana, whose kisses she will not resist. But the real Diana loves the shepherd Endimione and they also embrace with passion. There are the inevitable complications, but each couple is reunited at the end of the opera.

Jean-Baptiste Lully was the composer who dominated French opera in the seventeenth century and he established the French tradition of introducing dances and divertissements as an essential part of the entertainment, and from then on no opera could be staged in Paris without a ballet. The librettos were derived from mythology, and the term '*comédie-ballet*' came into use. Lully's domination meant that his successor, Marc-Antoine Charpentier, had to delay the production of his masterpiece, *Medée*, until 1693, and even then Lully's admirers prevented its immediate acceptance. But in this setting of the Greek story of the sorceress, Medea, who in her anger slays her own children, Charpentier created one of the most memorable of seventeenth-century French operas.

Jean-Philippe Rameau, too, at first suffered from Lully's dominance, yet he soon established his individuality and excellence. But his music really belongs to the eighteenth century and he truly established the opera-ballet in 1735 with *Les Indes Galantes*, an ingenious collection of four *entrées*, each with a different geographical location, Turkey, Peru, Persia and North America, with ballet music to match.

Meanwhile in England music for the stage was in the hands of one of our greatest composers, Henry Purcell. He left us a whole series of plays with musical interludes and masques, often described as semi-operas, including *The Fairy Queen*, which interpolates the action of Shakespeare's *A Midsummer Night's Dream*. Even so, he only wrote one work which can truly enter the operatic firmament. Yet *Dido and Aeneas* ends with Dido's Lament, 'When I am laid in earth', one of the greatest, most touchingly expressive arias ever written. It is an excerpt that, in spite of many later fine recordings, Dame Janet Baker has made her own.

Vivaldi is of course best known for his countless concertos and in particular for *The Four Seasons*. Yet he also wrote many operas, of which over a dozen survive. Arias from some of these are celebrated in various collections listed below. Singers love to perform these excerpts for they are immensely demanding vocally, and equally rewarding if sung with panache. However, the best known of the complete works, *Orlando Furioso* (which includes one of opera's first mad scenes), has been excellently recorded and is well worth having on record. Its attractive melodic invention is matched by exciting vocal virtuosity and imaginatively vivid orchestration.

Apart from a huge output of other music, orchestral, instrumental, choral and solo vocal (to say nothing of the oratorios, which were often opera substitutes with biblical characters), it was Handel who introduced *opera seria* to English audiences, sung in Italian, which he wrote himself. The first, *Rinaldo*, dates from 1711. Handel had played the violin in the orchestra in Hamburg, but he moved to London with George I (the former Elector of Hanover) in the early 1700s. *Opera seria* consisted of arias, choruses and recitative, the arias expressing the music's feeling and the response of the characters to their situation within the plot, while the recitative – sung dialogue, accompanied simply by keyboard and other continuo instruments – is concerned with advancing the interplay of the characters within the action of the story. Among his operas *Giulio Cesare*, one of the longest, stands out, while we have a very soft spot for the shortest, *Acis and Galatea*, in Boult's starrily cast version from Chandos, with Owen Brannigan an unforgettable Polyphemus. Among the oratorios, apart from the supreme Handelian masterpiece, *Messiah*, *Judas Maccabaeus* and *Solomon* are both unforgettable. But it was Christoph Gluck who decided in 1714 to reset the famous story of *Orfeo ed Eurydice* a century after Monteverdi's version. Many would say, with reason, that he surpassed the latter, and because of its success he wrote three versions, with the final Paris setting of Orfeo's role thrillingly allotted to a high tenor.

Arne's *Artaxerxes* (1762) followed the Handel style of *opera seria*, but chose the English language, and was in fact the first of such operas to be sung in English, which immediately increased its appeal to English opera-lovers, and it enjoyed a great success.

Haydn himself acknowledged that his operas were musically no match for those of Mozart, although undoubtedly entertaining. Besides offering normal staged performances, Esterháza's speciality was a series of marionette operas which were elaborately and expensively produced, and also included human characters. The only work to have survived is *Philemon und Baucis*, probably the first Haydn wrote, and it was performed in honour of Empress Maria Theresia on her visit on 1 September 1773.

With Mozart we come to the high peak of operatic composition, never surpassed. He began with *opera seria*, *Mitridate, Re di Ponto*, written when he was only 14. *Lucio Silla* came two years later; *Il re pastore* followed in 1775, *Idomeneo, Re di Creta*, acknowledged as the finest of the series, dates from 1780–81 and *La clemenza di Tito*, Mozart's penultimate *opera seria*, is certainly enjoyable if perhaps not one of his greatest inspirations. The first of his masterpieces is *Die Entführung aus dem Serail*, written for Vienna, in the form of a German *Singspiel*, with spoken interludes of dialogue. It is delightful, wonderfully fresh and tuneful, but perhaps not quite as unforgettable as the three totally inspired works with libretti by Lorenzo da Ponte – *Le nozze di Figaro, Don Giovanni* and the delicious *Così fan tutte*. To these we must add the captivating *Die Zauberflöte*, a charming folk tale with symbols of freemasonry (of which the composer was a member). Its winning libretto, written appropriately by a freemason colleague, Emanuel Schikaneder, introduces the irresistible Papageno (an appropriately costumed bird-catcher) and Papagena, who is to become his beloved partner. This is surely the ideal work to introduce children to the opera house.

Italian opera

With the opening of the nineteenth century, opera found its home in Italy, where it stayed for more than a hundred years. Gioachino Rossini, its first exponent, happily wrote both *opera seria* and the humorous *opera buffa*, but it was in the latter that he especially shone. His masterpiece, *Il barbiere di Siviglia* (1816), in which the heroine, Rosina (a mezzo role), is happily united with her lover, Count Almaviva, through the machinations of the barber Figaro, was admired by Beethoven. Other entertaining works followed, including *L'Italiana in Algeri*, *La Cenerentola* (loosely based on the story of Cinderella), *Le Comte Ory* and *La gazza ladra*, which has a serious underplot as the heroine, Ninetta, is threatened with execution as a thief, when the culprit is really a magpie.

Il viaggio a Reims was the first opera Rossini wrote in France. It is on a large scale, designed for simply the greatest singers of the day, with lavish costumes, elaborate sets and a ballet of 40 dancers to complete the sumptuousness of this work, first performed in 1825. Conceived as part of the festivities to honour the coronation of Charles X, its plot involves a group of travellers waiting to be taken to Rheims, with one would-be traveller after another doing his or her party piece, and with a whole range of nationalities involved. One of the most spectacular numbers in the operas, the *Gran Pezzo Concertanto a 14 Voci* ('*Ah! A tal colpo inaspettato*'), begins slowly and unaccompanied (on the news that no horses are available) and builds up, in true Rossini fashion, to a spectacular cabaletta with all 14 soloists singing about their changed circumstances, to electrifying effect. The finale gives a great opportunity for Rossini to employ 'local' colour – Russian, Spanish, French, etc. – in various national toasts in the celebratory finale.

All these operas are framed by more serious works, Rossini's first *opera seria*, *Tancredi*, and the dramatic *Guillaume Tell*, whose overture is more famous than the opera itself! Indeed Rossini's overtures are a delectable art form in their own right, famous for their ingeniously contrived crescendos, which Schubert tried unsuccessfully to imitate.

Vincenzo Bellini's operas explore a style called *bel canto* (beautiful song) and their world is very different from Rossini's *opera buffa*. The *Oxford English Dictionary* defines the term as 'a lyrical style of singing using a full, rich, broad tone and smooth phrasings'. Bellini's operas *Beatrice di Tenda*, *I Puritani* and *La Sonnambula* (with its famous sleepwalking scene) have proved splendid vehicles for Joan Sutherland, and Maria Callas joins her in the most famous work, *Norma*.

Gaetano Donizetti, who mastered both *bel canto* and *opera buffa*, was for a time almost submerged beneath Bellini's vocal opulence, yet he had an engaging melodic gift and sparkle which ensured that, in the field of *opera buffa*, *L'Elisir d'amore*, *Don Pasquale* and *La Fille du régiment* are a match for Rossini. Among his more serious works are *Anna Bolena* and *Maria Stuarda* (both based on English history of dubious authenticity). But *Lucia di Lammermoor* (with another mad scene) is the finest and proved another joint vehicle for Callas and Sutherland.

But it is Giuseppe Verdi whom we must turn to as the greatest, most prolific composer of the nineteenth century. His first success was in 1842 with *Nabucco* (with its celebrated Chorus of Hebrew Slaves, '*Va pensiero*'). The

Shakespearean *Macbeth* (with the evil Lady Macbeth strongly characterized) followed in 1846/7. Then came the triology of great operas of the 1850s, which immediately captured a permanent world-wide public. *Rigoletto* came first in 1851 with its extraordinarily powerful casting of a baritone in the name role, and its three unforgettable hits, '*Questa o quella*', '*La donna è mobile*' and the heroine, Gilda's, '*Caro nome*', to say nothing of a celebrated Quartet. *Il trovatore* was next (1853). Caruso later declared that all that this opera needed was the four greatest singers in the world; and certainly its melodrama is well imbued with superbly powerful music. Its most memorable character is the gypsy, Azucena, who in an electrifying scene in Act II tells the hero, Manrico, that by mistake she murdered her own baby in a fire. (This opera is a favourite opera of I.M.) But *La traviata* (1853/4) is the public's favourite with its story of an impossible but passionate liaison between the courtesan, Violetta, and the respectable Alfredo, which is tragically ended by Alfredo's father in a famous scene in Act II.

The very romantic *Un ballo in maschera* followed, then *La forza del destino* (written for performance in St Petersburg in 1861). It introduces an unforgettable tune in the overture which Callas made famous in the aria itself. *Don Carlos* with its remarkable inquisition scene came next, then *Simon Boccanegra* (1881), which had a particularly celebrated closing scene. But this was all-but dwarfed by the spectacular *Aida* (1871) with its triumphal march sequence, the opera appropriately given its début in Cairo. The masterly *Otello* (1887), Verdi's finest Shakespearean adaptation, brings a very convincing villain in Iago, and Desdemona is given a very beautiful scene before she is murdered. Finally in 1893 came Verdi's last work, *Falstaff*, a remarkable comic opera, set to Boito's adaptation of *The Merry Wives of Windsor*, which showed the composer was not content to sit on his laurels, for it is written as a continuous *parlando* conversational interplay.

Umberto Giordano's *Andrea Chénier* (1896), Leoncavallo's *Pagliacci*, and justifiably the most popular *Cavalleria rusticana* (also 1896) of Mascagni are the three prime examples of what is described as *verismo* opera, as they are based on the lives of ordinary people, and the latter pair of works are usually successfully presented as a double bill.

Giordano's *Fedora* followed in 1898 in the wake of the overwhelming success of *Cavalleria rusticana* and it has become almost equally popular. Again, the composer chose a story with revolution hovering in the background, but this time it takes place in St Petersburg. Princess Fedora's fiancé, Count Vladimiro, is mortally wounded by Count Loris Ipanov. Fedora seeks revenge but allies herself with Loris when she learns that it was over a matter of honour (Vladimiro was caught dallying with Ipanov's wife). Loris and Fedora end up living together in Switzerland and, when news arrives that Loris's brother drowned in his cell when the Neva overflowed, his mother dies of grief and Loris suspects that Fedora has been persecuting his family. Fedora takes poison, then begs Loris's forgiveness and, while she is dying, Loris does so, with a final kiss. The opera's most celebrated aria is *'Amor ti vieta'* ('Love forbids you'), sung by Loris (a tenor) but there is much attractive music in the score, not least in the sequence where a pianist entertains guests at a *soirée* with a rather beautiful Chopinesque piece, while Fedora and Loris engage in conversation.

If Delibes' *Lakmé* is famous for its 'Bell Song', *La Gioconda* (1876) by Ponchielli is famous for its ballet, the *Dance of the Hours*, immortalized (not very respectfully) in Walt Disney's film, *Fantasia*. All the characters have plenty of opportunity to express themselves in passionate exchanges, with some striking arias, while the chorus, with its mob scenes, festive crowds, sailors and a masked ball, provide plenty of spectacle. The story is about La Gioconda, a local singer who is desired by Barnaba, a spy of Badoero, the chief of the Venetian inquisition. Gioconda is repelled by him and, in revenge, Barnaba whips up the crowd against her blind mother, who is saved only by the inter- vention of Laura, Badoero's wife, to whom her mother gives a rosary in thanks. Barnaba contrives a plan to hurt La Gioconda by reuniting Laura with her for- mer lover, Enzo – now in love with La Gioconda – in order that Badoero can catch them together. La Gioconda overhears this plot, goes to confront Laura and is about to stab her when she sees the rosary her mother once gave to her. As Badoero approaches, she helps Laura to escape. Later, an outraged Badoero orders Laura to take poison, but La Gioconda gives her a sleeping draught to make her appear dead, then has her summoned to meet Enzo. To ensure Enzo's freedom, La Gioconda offers Barnaba her body and when he comes to claim it, she stabs herself.

If Verdi dominated Italian opera in the nineteenth century, Puccini took over at the turn of the twentieth. *La Bohème*, his finest work, dates from 1896 and has become the most popular opera of all time. Quite apart from its wonderful melodies, which flood the work from the first bar to the last, its con- struction itself is perfect. As Edward Greenfield has pointed out in his book on the composer, the opera might be compared to a symphony, with a finely balanced first movement, set in a garret high above Paris. Here the four male principals indulge in horse-play, ending with the most rapturous duet in all opera when Mimì enters and meets Rodolfo. She loses her key and, in search- ing for it, their hands touch, to produce one of the most familiar lines in all opera: Rodolfo's 'Your tiny hand is frozen' (*'Che gelida manina'*). Then follows the spectacular Café Momus scene, dominated by Musetta, who loves Marcello – a scherzo in all but name. During the slow movement, set outside an inn near the gate of Paris, which takes place two months later, all four lovers, Rodolfo and Mimì, Marcello and Musetta, meet to try to settle their differences, result- ing in a magnificent quartet. The finale recapitulates the opening music from Act I, until the sudden arrival of Musetta with the dying Mimì, and the poign- ant end of the opera is almost unbearably touching. Puccini himself wept when composing the final scene.

But Puccini's first operatic success in 1893 had been *Manon Lescaut*, following much the same story as had been previously used by Massenet, about a profligate heroine who chooses the riches of the high life to her real lover, Des Grieux. She is deported, and the only drawback of a lyrically inspired work is that the final Act in the Louisiana desert, where she dies in her lover's arms, is unconvincing.

The ultra-passionate *Tosca* came next (1900) and is full of thrilling music. Tosca, herself an opera singer, has the famous autobiographical *'Vissi d'arte'*, Tosca's lover, Cavaradossi, sings one of Puccini's most potent arias, *'E lucevan le stelle'* and Puccini interpolates a superb choral *'Te Deum'* for Scarpia, the Roman police chief. In the opera's key scene, when he tries to seduce Tosca, she stabs him instead.

Puccini also had a great regard for *Madama Butterfly* (1902/3), another top favourite with the public, and he incorporated some pseudo-Japanese themes into the highly lyrical score. 'One fine day' is another of the composer's most memorable arias, and the haunting 'Humming Chorus' when Butterfly antici-pates her lover Pinkerton's return, is equally moving.

La Fanciulla del West, set among American gold miners (1910), is under-rated, as is *Il Trittico* (combining *Il tabarro* with the affectingly sentimental *Suor Angelica* and the engagingly humorous *Gianni Schicchi*). But the last is often heard on its own (and has one very famous aria for Schicchi's daughter, Lauretta, *'O mio babbino caro'*). Puccini's least-known opera – undeservedly so, for it is a real charmer – is *La Rondine*, originally intended for a Viennese debut, but because of World War I eventually first performed in Monte Carlo in 1917. Set in Paris, it has something of the lighthearted flavour of Viennese operetta, and Puccini's melodic gift is unabated, with the heroine, Magda's, lovely *'Che il bel sogno di Doretta'* totally memorable. The plot has something in common with *La Traviata*, although the poet, Prunier, is an important subsidiary char-acter. But Magda is a sophisticated and self-contained heroine and when, at the close, Ruggero, her lover, cannot marry her because his respectable family will not accept a courtesan wife, the lovers part sadly but not tragically.

Turandot, Puccini's last opera, which he left unfinished, was effectively completed by Franco Alfano. It is a tale of a formidable princess who will only accept the hand of a suitor if he can answer three seemingly impossible rid-dles. Prince Calaf, the hero, is successful and so avoids the death sentence. The opera is most famous for *'Nessun dorma'*, a splendid aria which Pavarotti has proved he can sing perfectly ten times out of ten. The heroine also has the memorable, soaring *'In questa reggia'*, while the subsidiary character, the slave girl Liù, sings the enchanting *'Signore ascolta'*. There is light relief from the emperor's ministers, Ping, Pang and Pong, but the great success of the opera rests on the great choral scenes.

German opera

In the German repertoire Beethoven's *Fidelio* (1805) stands high among other nineteenth-century operas, a work in which he celebrates the loyalty and dedication of a woman. Florestan, falsely imprisoned by the governor, Don Pizarro, is saved and freed by his devoted wife, Leonora, who adopts the breeches role of Fidelio to gain access to the prison. The music is magnificent (especially the Prisoners' Chorus), and Beethoven wrote four different overtures for the work, *Leonora Nos. 1, 2* and *3*, and the simpler *Fidelio*, which he finally chose to use.

Weber had one great operatic success in *Der Freischütz* (1821). The characterization of the lovers is not strong, but their music is engagingly, tunefully romantic. Agathe's two arias are unforgettable. Max has to win his beloved, Agathe, in a shooting contest. To ensure his success, in an electrifying scene in Wolf's Glen, he bargains with the demon, Samiel, for magic bullets. But the opera ends happily with Max's weakness forgiven and his bride restored to him.

Three immensely successful light operas must not be overlooked. Humperdinck's *Hänsel und Gretel*, faithfully based on the fairy tale and with most engaging music (not least in the Overture), was premièred with Richard Strauss conducting in 1893, and it became an enduring popular success, famous for the children's Dance Duet, the Sandman's lovely music and the 'Witches' Ride'.

Lehár's 'Merry Widow' (*Die lustige Witwe*) arrived in 1905, a lighthearted Viennese-style frolic about the wooing of wealthy Hanna Glawari by her previous lover, Count Danilo, for purely financial reasons that are connected with the finances of Pontevedro, where they live. The operetta fizzes with vivacious numbers, but its most famous hit is the lovely waltz duet, *'Lippen schweigen'*, which comes at the very end of the piece and is surprisingly short.

With the *Land of Smiles* (1929), both Tauber's fame and Lehár's commercial success were at their height. The story of Lisa, an aristocratic Viennese girl, falling in love with a Chinese prince gave the opportunity for Lehár to embrace the opulent sound-worlds of both Puccini and Richard Strauss, though of course translated into Lehár's brand of melancholy lyricism. Unlike most operettas, this one has a more downbeat ending: Lisa is unable to accept the conventions of the Chinese in which all passions have to remain concealed behind disciplined smiles, and the lovers renounce their love. One of the work's most celebrated numbers, *'Dein ist mein ganzes Herz'*, is particularly gorgeous. Much of this score demands a high standard of singing, not least in the fine duets.

Of course we cannot miss out Johann Strauss the younger, whose *Die Fledermaus* (1874) is the finest of all Viennese operettas, with a marvellously sparkling score. The title comes from Dr Falke's bat (*Fledermaus*) costume in which he is forced to find his way home from an earlier party, and he wants to avenge himself by playing a joke on Eisenstein, the man who left him in this predicament. But the operetta centres on Prince Orlofsky's masked party, which everyone attends, including Eisenstein's wife, Rosalinde, and her maid Adele. Eisenstein, who is due to serve a prison sentence at 6 a.m., flirts with a supposed Hungarian Countess (in fact his wife in disguise) who pockets her husband's watch in order to embarrass him, while Rosalinde in turn flirts with

Alfred (a singing teacher). All is sorted out at the prison before the end of the piece and the cast finally toast the effect of champagne to one of the composer's finest tunes. *Der Zigeunerbaron* followed, made famous by a tune which we know as 'One day when we were young' but, enjoyable as it is, it has never had the success of *Die Fledermaus*.

Wagner

For most listeners, Wagner's music represents the zenith of German romantic opera, and his huge musical influence, not least its passionate chromaticism, extended to every other musical format. In order to have complete control over his works, he wrote the librettos himself and even built a Festspielhaus at Bayreuth dedicated to their performances, in particular the four *Ring* operas. He wanted the productions to be as realistic as possible, and in this respect alone his influence failed to survive, for there are few other areas of opera in which modern producers mount performances which are so at odds with the music and the composer's intentions. We recall a Covent Garden production of *Siegfried* which opened up with a child's pram in front and a German aircraft dominating the back of the stage. Many of his other works have endured similarly crass interference from producers seeking to overlay performances with their own interpretative ideas which have little to do with the music. Patrice Chéreau's 1976 *Ring* costumed the gods in modern business clothes, yet audiences accept such anachronisms and so do the critics.

Wagner's first three important operas, *Der fliegende Holländer* (1843), *Tannhäuser* (1845 and 1861) and *Lohengrin* (1850), steadily moved away from the relatively conventional format of opera, although the *Dutchman* still had romantic arias and lively choruses. In *Tannhäuser* the layout, while still featuring arias and choruses, also uses a more narrative style, and *Lohengrin* moves nearer still to the continuous writing of the four *Ring* operas.

In *The Flying Dutchman* the central character is cursed to sail the sea forever, but once in every seven years he may move ashore to seek a lover who will prove faithful to him. At last he meets Senta, the daughter of the captain of another ship, and at the opera's close the pair are swallowed up by the sea together.

Tannhäuser, with its famous 'Pilgrims' Chorus', exists in two versions, the first mounted in Dresden, the second in Paris sixteen years later. But the story remains virtually the same, concerning a song contest which will determine whom the heroine marries. Tannhäuser himself has been seduced by Venus (to strikingly sensuous music) but he breaks free and is reunited with his beloved Elisabeth, only to disgrace himself by extolling the virtues of sensual love. He journeys to seeks forgiveness in Rome but is rejected. The pilgrims return without him, and Elisabeth dies in distress. But in heaven she redeems her lover, who then joins her.

The heroine of *Lohengrin*, Elsa, is accused of murdering her brother, but she states that a knight will appear and be an advocate of her innocence. When

Lohengrin arrives anonymously on a swan, she happily agrees to marry him, but is told she must not ask his identity. But the villainess, Ortrud, interferes and persuades Elsa not to trust the knight, so Elsa asks him to reveal his name, which means he must leave and return to the place of the Holy Grail from which he came. When he departs, Elsa dies of grief.

Tristan und Isolde (which followed in 1865) is about a human love so powerful that it transcends everything in its rapture, and can find a solution only in death for the lovers. Tristan brings Isolde (who earlier had saved his life) on his ship to Cornwall, where she is to marry his uncle, King Marke. When Tristan is forced to ignore her because of his relationship with his uncle, Isolde asks her attendant, Brangäne, to bring poison, and she and Tristan both drink it together. But Brangäne has substituted a love potion, and they are soon passionately in each other's arms. That night in the Cornish castle, Tristan and Isolde are temporarily united, while King Marke is off on a hunting expedition with Tristan's friend, Melot. Brangäne warns the lovers of their danger as dawn approaches. But Marke returns and, discovering them together, blames Melot for the liaison. Tristan fights Melot in a duel and is mortally wounded. He is taken back to his home in Brittany and Isolde follows to nurse him, but he dies in her embrace. The other characters follow, with Marke determined that Tristan and Isolde shall after all be allowed marry. But he is too late, for the pair die a 'love-death' in each other's arms.

After all this passion and mayhem, it is good to welcome at last a cheerful Wagnerian comic opera, *Die Meistersinger von Nürnberg* (1868), with richly mellow music to match. The overture alone is both resplendent and optimistic, and there are plenty of fine arias, with the 'Prize Song' particularly memorable. Walther, a knight, wants to marry Eva, a goldsmith's daughter, but he discovers that he must win a song contest in order to secure her hand. He consults the wise and lovable Hans Sachs and his apprentice, David, for advice on the necessary style of the song. At the song school in the church Walther meets other mastersingers, whom he fails fully to impress. His principal adversary is Beckmesser, who intends to serenade Eva that night. But Eva's nurse, Magdalene, takes the place of Eva, and a fracas ensues, as David is in love with Magdalene himself. The day of the competition arrives, and Beckmesser has high hopes of winning, using poetry written by Sachs. But he fails, and Walther's fine singing secures him his beloved bride and membership of the mastersingers.

Wagner's greatest operatic work, *Der Ring des Nibelungen*, spans four linked operas, lasting together nearly 16 hours: *Das Rheingold*, *Die Walküre*, *Siegfried* and *Götterdämmerung*. Understandably, they are usually performed separately! Wagner spent not far short of three decades writing them and they were premièred at the Festspielhaus in 1876. Their narrative is based on mythology and folklore and the music includes some 200 leitmotifs, brief musical themes which Wagner used and re-used to give underlying illustration to the music and the events of the narrative. The key characters include Wotan (lord of the gods, and later to be described as the Wanderer), Alberich (lord of the Nibelungs), Loge (the god of fire), the incestuous twins Siegmund and Sieglinde, Brünnhilde (Wotan's favourite daughter), Mime (a Nibelung blacksmith), Siegfried (a *helden-tenor* (high tenor), Wotan's grandson and the opera's hero), Gunther (king of the Gibichungs), Gutrune (his sister) and Hagen (their half-brother). Of course there are many other subsidiary characters too.

Das Rheingold opens with three beautiful nymphs pleasurably swimming in the Rhine. Full of lust, Alberich emerges from his subterranean world and is told that whoever fashions a ring made from the gold in the river will also have complete power and unlimited wealth; but he must also reject love. Alberich willingly does this and escapes with the gold. In their fortress the gods hear of the theft and Wotan and Loge determine to get it back. Meanwhile Alberich tries out the *Tarnhelm*, a helmet fashioned from the Rhine gold by his brother, Mime, which makes him invisible, and he also has an all-powerful ring made from the gold. Alberich then makes the Nibelungs pile up a stack of gold in order to rule the universe. But Loge cunningly makes Alberich turn himself into a toad, and Wotan and he make Alberich their prisoner. The gold and the ring are then given to Wotan in return for Alberich's release, but before parting with the ring he casts a spell of death upon it and it ends up in the hands of the giant, Fafner. A storm then provides a rainbow bridge which the gods cross into their new home, Valhalla.

Die Walküre introduces Sieglinde and Siegmund (children of Wotan) who fall in love, in spite of Sieglinde's being already married to Hunding, who says that Siegmund and he must fight until one of them is dead. However, Sieglinde tells her brother of a hidden sword which he finds and calls 'Nothung'. Meanwhile Wotan has ordered Brünnhilde to ensure that Hunding's sword will kill Siegmund, but after he and Sieglinde have slept in each other's arms, Brünnhilde unsuccessfully tries to protect him. Wotan intervenes and Siegmund dies. Then Wotan kills Hunding. In the mountains, to the music of the famous 'Ride of the Valkyries', slain battle heroes are collected by Brünnhilde and her followers, to be taken to Valhalla. Brünnhilde, however, saves the now pregnant Sieglinde by sending her east, out of Wotan's reach, and gives her part of *Nothung* for her son when he is born. In a very telling scene, Wotan banishes his daughter to a sleep that will last until a man claims her. Brünnhilde asks that she shall be surrounded by a ring of fire so that only a hero can do so. In one of the most moving scenes in the opera, Wotan sadly bids her farewell and Loge provides the ring of fire.

Siegfried takes us to a cave where Sieglinde's son, Siegfried, has been brought up by Mime, who plans to use the pieces of the sword *Nothung* (if it can be repaired) to get the ring from Fafner, now turned into a dragon. Wotan, disguised as the Wanderer, tells Mime that it can be forged only by a fearless man. And Mime tells Siegfried that he might discover fear in an encounter with Fafner. Siegfried jubilantly forges the sword and then cuts the anvil in two. That night both Wotan and Alberich wait outside Fafner's cave, and as day breaks Siegfried joins them and blows his horn. Fafner awakes and Siegfried kills him. A bird tells him to fetch both the ring and the *Tarnhelm* from the cave and, forewarned by Mime of his danger, Siegfried kills him too. The bird then leads him to where Brünnhilde lies, where, encountering Wotan, he destroys his spear. He walks through the fire without fear and kisses her and she falls instantly in love with him.

At the opening of *Götterdämmerung* the three Norns anticipate the end of the reign of the gods. Brünnhilde and Siegfried share a cave together and before he departs heroically they exchange gifts. He gives her the ring, and she gives him her horse, Grane. Meanwhile at their Rhine palace, Hagen suggests to King Gunther (both new characters in the story) that he marry Brünnhilde and that a love potion could ensure that Siegfried will marry Gunther's sister, Gutrune. The result of swallowing the potion is that Siegfried forgets Brünnhilde and falls in love with Gutrune. Siegfried is now also willing to obtain Brünnhilde for Gunther. He arrives back at the cave at nightfall and, using the magic helmet to change to an image of Gunther, he snatches the ring from Brünnhilde. Then they sleep together innocently. The next day Siegfried returns to Gutrune, and Gunther brings Brünnhilde, whom Siegfried does not acknowledge, and she accuses him of betrayal. The Rhinemaidens appear to warn Siegfried of his danger but, after Hagen's further potion recalls Brünnhilde to him once more, Hagen kills him. But Brünnhilde gets the ring back, and, at the opera's finale, she rides into Siegfried's flaming funeral pyre. The Rhinemaidens find the ring and drown Hagen, and the gods and Valhalla are also destroyed in the conflagration.

Parsifal (1882) was Wagner's last opera, and its curious mixture of religious feeling, compassion (which Wagner thought important), sexuality and ceremonial philosophy perplexes some music lovers. Based on a thirteenth-century legend, it is set in Monsalvat, the Spanish name for the stronghold of the Holy Grail, which reputedly carried the blood of the crucified Christ. The opera has a mixture of characters, centring on Amfortas (son of Titurel), who is guardian of the Holy Grail, whose side has been pierced by the magician, Klingsor, using the holy spear that also pierced the body of Christ. The wound will not heal. The innocent Parsifal (described as 'a guileless fool made wise by pity') arrives with a swan (which he has shot) and is introduced to Gurnemanz, a senior figure among the knights, and also to Kundry. She is a sorceress who has been ordered by Klingsor (an evil, disgraced knight) to be a seductress in a garden full of beautiful women, similarly alluring. She knows Parsifal's background, calling him by name, and tries unsuccessfully to seduce him. Then she passes him over to Klingsor, who throws the holy spear at him. It hovers over him and Parsifal uses it to create the sign of the cross. The castle sinks into the earth.

Some years pass and Parsifal returns on Good Friday (to Wagner's most ravishing music), again to meet Gurnemanz. He is dressed in black armour which he removes on request, and is recognized and welcomed by all. He is hailed as the king of the knights. He places the spear on Amfortas's wound and it is miraculously healed; after a great procession, including the funeral procession of Titurel, Kundry and the others kneel in tribute to him. Kundry dies and Holy Grail is seen to glow.

Richard Strauss

Richard Strauss's 15 operas provided a *fin de siècle* for the tradition of German romantic opera, but in 1905 *Salome* first daringly took his music firmly into the twentieth century with writing full of tension and dissonance and a thrilling orchestral setting of the famous 'Dance of the Seven Veils'. The biblical tale, with Herod's lust for the repulsive heroine, and her demanding, receiving, and kissing John the Baptist's head (an extraordinary sequence in the Decca recording) makes a gripping if hardly tasteful operatic experience.

Elektra (1909) continued the interplay of repulsive characters, with murder and vengeance within the family, and Elektra herself also has another weird dance to climax the story. This opera began the partnership between Strauss and the legendary librettist, Hugo von Hofmannsthal, which reached its zenith in the composer's greatest opera, *Der Rosenkavalier* (1911).

With its almost Mozartian elegance, *Rosenkavalier* overflows with glorious music, including a ravishing duet between the lovers, Octavian and Sophie, a delectable waltz sequence, an unsurpassed closing trio for three female voices (which Strauss loved to juxtapose), followed by a charming closing duet as the young lovers go off happily together.

Ariadne auf Naxos (1916) combines two stories, the first a production of a double opera (*seria* and *buffa*) in the hands of the composer and major-domo, and the second the supposed mythological opera itself, with its love between Ariadne and the young Bacchus, which brings ravishing music.

Sir Georg Solti wanted to record the little-known *Die Frau ohne Schatten* (1919) before he died, and legend has it that the Decca recording cost £1 million. It centres on the empress who has no shadow but who finally achieves one after first trying to find one among the humans, Barak and his wife, and then deciding that she cannot ruin their marital happiness.

Arabella followed in 1933, another engaging love story in which the heroine seeks 'Mr Right' (Mandryka); and her sister (Zdenka), disguised in a breeches role, after causing complications of identity, is also happily betrothed to her lover (Matteo).

French opera

La Dame Blanche (1825) is the most successful and enduring of François-Adrien Boieldieu's operas. Its appeal lies not only in its melodic invention, but in the subtle colour of the orchestration and harmony which gives delicious piquancy to the often very charming melodies. One only has to listen to the work's overture – a masterpiece of the genre – to be captivated by the writing. Inspired by a story of Sir Walter Scott, its Scottish setting, a castle allegedly haunted by a ghost (the white lady), gave the composer plenty of opportunity for 'local colour' and some wonderfully atmospheric, richly romantic writing which ensured the work's popularity throughout the nineteenth century. Today one admires it for both the wit and sophistication of the writing, all of it given a deliciously Gallic flavour.

Giacomo Meyerbeer was above all famed for operatic spectacle. *Les Hugue-nots* (1836) was his most famous and finest opera, but it is seldom staged because of the huge cost. However, there is a fine recording and it is detailed fully under its entry under the composer. For similar reasons Berlioz's *Les Troyens*, written between 1856 and 1860, has resisted performances, and it was never produced during the composer's lifetime. But its glories have now been fully revealed under the auspices of both James Levine (on DVD at the Met. in 1983) and Sir Colin Davis (on CD in London).

Gounod's masterpiece was *Faust* (1859), which had enormous success both in France and in the rest of the world. The story is of Faust's pact with the devil to restore his youth, and his seduction of Marguerite, while her final redemption is set to one of the most thrilling tunes in the whole of opera. The work is made irresistible by the vividness of the narrative and the profusion of attractive tunes throughout. Having its début in France, it also had to include a ballet, and the ballet suite is now, rightly, just as famous as the opera.

Delibes's *Lakmé*, with its colourful, exotic setting, has survived in the repertoire primarily as an excellent vehicle for a soprano to show how her prowess in the work's most famous aria, the 'Bell Song', as well as many other equally appealing delights on the way (not least a celebrated duet exploited by a certain airline advert on British television). Its story, concerning the hatred of the Brahmin priests in nineteenth-century India for the English invaders, provided the composer with a chance to show off his gift for exotic harmonies and colourful orchestration. While the story is typical of nineteenth-century opera, it is far from unsophisticated. The key aria is not only a display piece for the soprano, it provides a significant part of the plot, when Lakmé is forced to sing it in public to bring out her lover, Gerald (a dreaded Englishman), in order that Nilakantha, the Brahmin priest (Lakmé's father), kill him for daring to love his daughter. But the opera is not all death and horror, for much of it is touchingly lyrical; there is humour too, especially in the scenes with the English governess, Mistress Bentson.There is also a delightful 'market scene' with some very attractive ballet music.

Bizet had an enormous success with *Carmen* (1875), another masterpiece which is called an *opéra-comique*, because it includes spoken dialogue. Set against the background of a Spanish bull-ring, its gypsy heroine is the seductress par excellence who is first is attracted to Don José but who then deserts him for the bullfighter Escamillo (called a toreador, which description does not exist in Spanish!). Oscar Hammerstein once commented that the opera could not fail as it had so many hit numbers.

Jules Massenet's most successful opera was *Manon* (1884), set to the same story as Puccini's *Manon Lescaut*. Although its music is not overall superior to

Puccini's, it is of consistently high quality and has one totally memorable aria in Act II when Manon sings a farewell to her *'petite table'*. Generally the development of the story is very attractively detailed and the end of the opera avoids the scene in the Louisiana desert. Massenet was successful with two other operas: *Thaïs*, most famous for its celebrated *Méditation* (now best known as a violin solo), and *Werther*, probably his finest work, but which was first rejected by the Paris Opéra for its pervading tragic atmosphere, ending with Werther's suicide. It was therefore first performed in Vienna (in 1892).

'There is good music, bad music, and the music of Ambroise Thomas,' so the acerbic Chabrier rudely said of the composer of *Mignon* (1866). Yet by any standards, *Mignon* is a fine score. It has never entirely faded from the repertoire because of its charming story, based on a Goethe novel, which mixes elements of the romantic and Gothic with great atmosphere and charm and, above all, it offers a string of gorgeous tunes and arias, both lively and sentimental. The story of Mignon, rescued from gypsies by Wilhelm, her love for him and her involvement with a group of travelling actors, including her love-rival Philine, provided plenty of scope for the usual operatic shenanigans, the end of which finds Mignon reunited with her marquis father, and all ends with general rejoicing. The two most famous and stand-out arias, Philine's dazzling show-piece, *'Je suis Titania'*, and Mignon's wonderfully sentimental *'Connais-tu le pays'*, both feature in the work's superbly constructed overture. The Minuet is a peach of a piece and was once very popular in collections of music of 'light music' (as indeed was the splendid overture, *Raymond*). Those who respond to this work should also explore Thomas's *Hamlet* (1868) which includes, among other things, a heady drinking song, a celebrated mad scene (followed by a very eerily beautiful death scene, with a humming chorus as Ophelia slips beneath the water) and some of the most delightful ballet music you'll ever hear.

In its day, the idea for setting the biblical subject of Samson and Delilah to an opera was controversial, and Saint-Saëns's opera had to wait some years before it was first performed (1877). However, its eventual success was resounding and prolonged, for a very good reason: the score is tuneful, colourful, theatrical and very well constructed. The story of *Samson et Dalila* provided the composer with plenty of scope for spectacle, but he imbued it with much subtlety too, with, for example, each of Dalila's three arias adding another dimension to her character. Her most famous aria, in which she tries to seduce Samson, is *'Mon cœur s'ouvre à ta voix'*, one of the most popular in the repertoire. The ballet sequence, the *Bacchanale*, is a popular orchestral show-piece.

Lalo's melodramatic overture to *Le Roi d'Ys* is comparatively well known, but not the opera (1888) from which it derives. Its lively Breton story, set in the city of Ys, opens with the people celebrating peace, brought about by the betrothal of Margared (the king's daughter) and Karnac, who were once enemies. However, nothing is straightforward: Margared loves someone else, and Karnac swears revenge on the city of Ys. It all goes from bad to worse and the opera ends in a spectacular flood scene, caused by Margared, furious that her real love, Mylio, has married her sister, Rozenn. Karnac then opens the floodgates which protect the city, and Margared in a fit of remorse hurls herself into a watery grave. While Lalo uses genuine Breton folksongs, the score is also influenced by Wagner, not least in drawing from legendary Celtic stories, and while in the main it is through-composed, there are many stand-out arias and some rather good choruses too. The opera is unfailingly entertaining.

Yet it was Offenbach who secured a special affection with the public with his mastery of French operetta – *opéra bouffon* with a special sparkle. *Orphée aux enfers* (1858) with its famous story altered, the heroine being reluctant to return to Orpheus, and *La belle Hélène* (1864) with the action audaciously centring on Helen in her double-bed, were both great successes, each parodying famous Greek mythology. But *La Vie Parisienne* (1866), set nearer home, was equally effervescent. Sadly, Offenbach did not live to see his masterpiece, *Les contes d'Hoffmann*, performed. It has a linking prologue and epiloque and in between come three of Hoffmann's tales, with the soprano role in each usually given to single singer. Productions which try to include all the available music are only partly successful, but Bonynge's superb (1971) recording solved the textual problems to perfection, including all the best numbers.

Gustave Charpentier was a one-work opera composer, but *Louise* (1900) has held the stage in Paris and, although its music is eclectic, its Montmartre atmosphere is appealing and it is certainly worthy of a recording. The story of Louise who loves a poet, Julien, against her parents' wishes has a happy ending with the lovers together, which perhaps accounts for its success.

But French opera was to be transformed and taken firmly into the twentieth century by another single-opera composer, Claude Debussy, who, while certainly coming under the influence of Wagner in his *Pelléas et Mélisande* (1902), created an entirely individual style, changing the presentation of his narrative to a unique flowing of words and music. Sensuous in atmosphere, simmering with underlying passion, and with the often restrained orchestration every bit as important as the voices, it created an entirely new amalgam of vocal and instrumental writing.

Ravel's two contributions to the opera genre, *L'Enfant et les sortilèges* and *L'Heure espagnole*, are highlights of twentieth-century opera. *L'Heure espagnole* is something of a French farce, with Concepción facing the problem of how to get her lover, unnoticed, into her bedroom. Set in a clockmaker's shop, the obvious answer is to smuggle him up in a grandfather clock with the assistance of the unknowing but obliging muscular muleteer, Ramiro. Naturally things get more complicated when a second rival arrives and is similarly hidden in another clock, which is also taken up by the ever-obliging Ramiro (who eventually ends up with Concepción himself) and then down the stairs, several times – with all the characters getting very frustrated. The ingenious plot is really an excuse for Ravel to display his orchestral prowess, along with a chance to mock human weakness in a most engaging way; his depiction of all sorts of clocks for the clockmaker's house is sublime.

L'Enfant et les sortilèges casts the same sort of magic as Tchaikovsky's *The Nutcracker*, with Colette's novel embracing an *Alice in Wonderland*-type fantasy. A child, fed up with his homework, decides to sabotage his books, pets, the furniture and even the wallpaper, all of which come to life and are full of animosity towards him. The melancholy humour is irresistible, particularly from the clock that can't stop itself from chiming as its pendulum has been taken away; it can no longer tell the time, and has a terrible tummy-ache with a draught right through its middle. Then there is the teapot saying (in English, of course) to the cup, 'How's your mug?' 'Rotten,' comes the reply. Most touching of all is the princess who doesn't know her fate, as the child tore up the book she came from. Feeling miserable about his situation, the child retreats to the garden, but his creatures, which have long been subjected to his cruelty, are eager to take their revenge. However, a little squirrel is wounded in an incident and the child binds its paw. Realizing that the child is injured too, and reflecting on the child's act of kindness, the animals take him home, shouting out, 'Mama!' As the child holds out his arms to her, the opera is suddenly over. The score is an absolute delight, full of vivid scenes and, with Ravel's miraculous ear for orchestral detail, the composer brings Colette's curiously touching story to vivid life.

Russian opera

There is a famous (true) story that when the St Petersburg Conservatoire was first opened Tchaikovsky rushed inside and played the familiar overture to Glinka's *Ruslan and Ludmilla* through on the piano. He (rightly) considered that Glinka's influence on Russian music was fundamental and that therefore he should be the first to be heard in the new building. Certainly the opera itself is rich in very Russian arias and dance music. But it was Mussorgsky who wrote the two great nationalistic operas, *Boris Godunov* (1874) and *Khovanshchina* (1886), although the latter had to be completed by Rimsky-Korsakov and Shostakovich. Both have complicated plots.

Boris Godunov opens with the spectacular scene of his coronation. But Boris is haunted by the suggestion that he was responsible for the murder of the young Dmitri, his brother's son, who would have been his true successor to the throne, and this obsession with his possible guilt dominates the story. There is also a false Dmitri, pretender to the throne; the heroine, Marina, is willing to marry him in order to become tsarina. The opera ends with Boris's death and introduces the extraordinary character of the Simpleton repeating the accusation of the murder.

Khovanshchina has a magical orchestral prelude, picturing dawn rising above the Kremlin. Even more than *Boris Godunov* it contains much wonderful folk-inspired music, especially in the choruses. Its basis is the conflict between the ruling tsars and the Old Believers, led by Prince Ivan Khovansky. They are a political/religious group who oppose any kind of political or religious reform and the adoption of Western ideas. There are various love entanglements, but essentially the opera is about the defeat of the Old Believers, who are dramatically consumed in a final conflagration in a moving choral finale.

But it was Tchaikovsky who wrote Russia's most popular opera, *Eugene Onegin* (1879), and the one which Russians consider gives a true picture of Russian country life in the nineteenth century. Tatyana, a young, inexperienced girl, falls instantly in love when she meets Yevgeny Onegin, a friend of Lensky (her sister Olga's fiancé). That evening in one of the greatest arias in all opera, she writes him a letter expressing her love and on the morrow he returns to dismiss her proposal quite brusquely. Later, at a party for Tatyana, Onegin flirts with Olga and is challenged to a duel by the jealous Lensky, who is shot dead. Three years later, at a ball in St Petersburg, Prince Gremin arrives with his wife, none other than Tatyana, whom he loves very much. But Onegin is also a guest, and the pair now both confess their renewed love for each other to music which Tchaikovsky had already used in the famous letter scene. Tatyana, however, while admitting her feelings, stays faithful to her husband, and Onegin is left with his new passion unrequited. Tchaikovsky's music for the whole opera is inspired and he writes a famous waltz and an equally celebrated polonaise for the two dancing scenes.

Tchaikovsky's second operatic success was *Queen of Spades (Pique Dame)*, a macabre tale in which the composer is much more sympathetic to its principal character, Herman, than was Pushkin, who wrote the short story on which the opera is based. Tchaikovsky, surprisingly, identified with a man who came to be obsessed by gambling, which he considered more important than his love for Liza. She is the daughter of the Countess, who has the secret of three winning cards. Herman demands to be told this secret from her at pistol point, and she dies of shock. Liza then drowns herself, and Herman returns to the gaming table. But when he calls the third card, the Queen of Spades appears in his hand instead, and the Countess's ghost also appears. Terrified, he commts suicide.

The composer's final opera, *Iolanta*, which dates from 1892, the year before he died, is written in a very different, fairy-tale mood. It has a delightful score, not unlike his finest ballet music, and concerns a princess, blind from birth, who does not know of her affliction. Her father is told that she can be cured, but only if she is told about her blindness (which he has resisted doing) and is determined to be cured. A visiting knight, Vaudémont, unwittingly reveals her affliction, but then the way is open for her to achieve her sight, and the opera has a happy ending and charms the listener from the first note to the last.

Prokofiev's *War and Peace*, based on Tolstoy, which the composer worked on from 1941 to 1952, is another opera, not only of great length (at over four hours), but one that makes great production demands. It is now accepted in the repertoire, and there have been several recordings. The opera is cleverly dominated by the sympathetic character, Pierre, who stands in the background of the action. Part I is a simple triangular love story between Natasha and the widowed Prince Andrey. But his father does not approve of the match and sends him away. Meanwhile Natasha meets the renegade Prince Anatole and is tempted to elope with him. But Pierre tells her that Anatole is already married, and she asks him to persuade Andrey to forgive her for her unfaithful behaviour. At that moment Napoleon begins his invasion of Russia and in Part II the fierce Russian resistance is shown when the Muscovites set fire to Moscow. Prince Andrey joins the army and is mortally wounded. The Russian Field Marshal Prince Kutuzov (given a magnificent aria) now becomes the hero of the hour, but he decides to abandon Moscow, and Napoleon's army is forced to retreat, defeated by the severe Russian winter. Andrey does not survive the battle, but Natasha is able to ask him to forgive her before he dies. Pierre is rescued by Russian partisans and reflects that Natasha is a woman he too could love.

Prokofiev's *The Fiery Angel* had a very long gestation period (1919–23; 1926–7), was revised several times and was not staged during the composer's lifetime. The story, taken from one of Russia's greatest symbolist poets (Bryussov), is a study of neurotic female sexuality, full of demonic visions and horrific images. Although we may question whether they are real or imagined, they clearly are very real for the lead character, Renata, who is obsessed with the idea of her protective angel, Madiel. Her obsession causes havoc with the men in her life, especially with Ruprecht, who loves her, and who is enlisted to track down her erstwhile lover, Count Heinrich, whom she regards as 'Madiel', but who has deserted her. This leads Ruprecht dangerously into the world of the occult and the black arts, although it is Renata who ends her life condemned to torture and death, but not before corrupting the nuns in the convent she enters to punish her own sinfulness. Though religion is mixed up with black magic and the occult, the opera packs a considerable emotional punch, while Prokofiev's chromatic writing is particularly striking. Some of the music found its way into the composer's *Third Symphony*.

Czech opera

Smetana's comic opera, *The Bartered Bride* (1866), understandably made him famous, not least for its sparkling overture. It is full of spirited music, including lively Czech dances, and tells of the love between Mařenka and Jeník. However, her father is indebted to Micha and wants her to marry Micha's son, Vašek, a stammering simpleton. There is a memorable part for the marriage broker, Kecal, whom Jeník manages to fool so that he is given Mařenka's hand and at the same time clears his father's debts. In the middle of all this the travelling circus arrives. Vašek is persuaded to take the part in the costume of a dancing bear, which means that Micha can no longer take him seriously as a suitor, and the lovers can be married.

Dvořák's one success in the field of opera was *Rusalka* (1900), a romantic tale about a water nymph who falls in love with a prince, but Rusalka is mute and cannot speak to him, although she can sing; and her lovely 'Song to the Moon' is the opera's most famous aria. The story does not end well, for the prince is unfaithful to her, and in the end when she kisses him he dies, and Rusalka disappears back into the lake.

With the arrival of the twentieth century the old conventions of *opera seria*, *opera buffa* and *bel canto* disappeared, glowing lyricism lost its domination and harmonic writing was often far from mellow. This certainly applies to the operas of Janáček, which have achieved a wide public following. The work that put him on the operatic map was a Czech adaptation of the *verismo* style. *Jenůfa* (1904) has a grim story, taking place in an isolated Czech village. Jenůfa conceives a baby whose father is Steva, the local mill-owner. However, the baby is murdered by Kostelnička, Jenůfa's stepmother, when Steva refuses to marry her. Jenůfa forgives Kostelnička and is now willing to marry Laca, Steva's half-brother.

In *Osud*, written immediately after *Jenůfa*, the core of the story is about the composer, Zivný, and Míla, the married woman he loves; it finds the composer's inspiration at its brightest, from the exhilarating opening waltz ensemble onwards, a passage that vividly sets the scene in a German spa at the turn of the century.

Káta Kabanová (1921) is regarded as Janáček's masterpiece, and when writing it the composer himself had an affair with a married woman. Its heroine, Káta, does not love her husband, Tichon, and arranges a moonlight tryst with her lover, Boris. But she later confesses her sinful unfaithfulness to her husband and commits suicide in the Volga river.

Janáček's next opera, *The Cunning Little Vixen* (1924), is a complete contrast in which animals and humans mix, singing and dancing in a fairy-tale world, and the music has an original charm deriving from both animal sounds (female voices) and human responses (male voices).

The Makropulos Affair (1926) has a weird story about Elina Makropulos, born in 1575, who is now 337 years old, achieved by using an elixir of life. She arrives in Prague in 1912 as an opera singer. The plot centres on an estate owned by Jaroslav Prus but which a document proves was left to her son. She obtains it by spending the night with Jaroslav and then dies, claiming she has found that a long life is unrewarding.

Janáček's last opera, *From the House of the Dead* (1930), is a dismal story about life in a labour camp and features various prisoners and their tedious lives. Gorjančikov, a politician, is the central character; he teaches a young boy, Aljeja, to read and write. An eagle becomes a symbol of the freedom which Gorjančikov achieves at the end.

Other 20th- and 21st-century operas

Composed in 1904-6, the exhilarating score of *Maskarade* was composed by Carl Nielsen in the wake of his giving up playing after 16 years in the Danish Royal Theatre Orchestra, and this freedom no doubt accounts for the exuberance of his writing and the light-hearted nature of the piece. The work has understandably become something like the Danish national opera. Set in

Copenhagen in 1723, the story of an arranged marriage between Jeronimus's son, Leander, and Leonora, the daughter of his friend Leonard, is, of course, bound to run far from smoothly; both have fallen in love with other people. Unbeknown to them (for they met each other at a masked ball) the marriage has been arranged for *them*, which they discover only at the end of a masquerade when they take off their masks, so all can end very happily. The ball scenes gave Nielsen a chance to write some of the most sparkling music he ever composed, though both Leander and Leonora are given music – in particular a duet – of surprising emotional power and depth.

Rutland Boughton's once immensely successful opera, *The Immortal Hour* (1910–12), is famous for two things: the *Faery song* ('How beautiful they are'), which is first heard hauntingly at the end of Act I from a chorus in the distance; and secondly the equally immortal line, 'They laugh and are glad and are *terrible.*' This gently lyrical evocation of Celtic twilight took London by storm in the 1920s and 1930s with its simple tunefulness and fine atmosphere, compensating for any shortcomings of the verse. Its romantic escapism was right for the times, and its neglect following the Second World War is rather unfair.

Bartók's only opera, *Duke Bluebeard's Castle* (1918), is a sinister retelling in operatic form of Perrault's *La Barbe Bleue*. A spoken narrator introduces a dialogue between Bluebeard and his latest wife, Judith, who insists on opening the seven bolted doors of his castle. Judith is convinced he has murdered all his previous wives, but she still loves him. He tries to dissuade her from opening the seventh door, but finally gives her the key and she passes through into the darkness of night.

At the age of 23 Korngold had his operatic masterpiece, *Die tote Stadt* (1920), presented in simultaneous world premières in Hamburg and Cologne! The score includes many echoes of Puccini and Richard Strauss, but its youthful exuberance carries the day. The opera, about Paul who is obsessed with the memory of his dead wife Marie, sets Act II entirely in Paul's imagination, which features an amazing sequence of scenes, including one where his new love, Marietta, is seen rising from her coffin. By the time Paul wakes up at the end of Act III, he has come to the realization that his period of mourning is now over. It is an opera obsessed with ideas of death and rebirth and was an ideal story for a composer who enjoyed one of the most successful of all careers in Hollywood as a film composer.

Doktor Faust is Busoni's masterpiece. Alas, he died before it was finished, but Philipp Jarnach, his student, completed the score. However, in 1974, further missing sketches were found and Antony Beaumont managed to complete the work in an even more satisfactory manner. In Busoni's version of the well-known Faust narrative, all the dark-romantic elements of this endlessly fascinating story are richly conveyed, with a comparable tapestry of colour to match the imagination of the narrative, from the introspective broodings of Faust to much brighter, extrovert episodes. The score is given a unified, taut structure, with the composer's gift for striking sonorities particularly apparent.

The opera, while markedly different in almost every way from Gounod's version, has been revived many times in recent years and seems unlikely to disappear from the repertoire.

Kurt Weill collaborated with Bertholt Brecht in 1928 to write his down-to-earth *Threepenny Opera* (a new kind of lower-class, cynical *verismo*). It mixes ballads with spectacular ensemble scenes. Its most famous number is the ballad, 'Mac the Knife', and its principal characters are Mr and Mrs Peachum, petty criminals who unsuccessfully try to prevent their daughter, Polly, from marrying Macheath. However, Macheath later renews a relationship with Jenny, a prostitute. The Peachums take him to court, but finally forgive him, and he is made a peer of the realm instead!

George Gershwin's *Porgy and Bess* (1935) is the one truely American opera, although mention must also be made of the Jerome Kern musical, *Show Boat*, for its serious story involving the theme of miscegenation makes it every bit worthy to be considered a semi-opera. Its musical score, too, is of the highest quality, including one of the most famous of all American songs, 'Ol' man river'. *Porgy and Bess* also incorporates the style of traditional African-American music of all kinds. Its story concerns the love between the two principal characters, but Bess has another boyfriend in Crown, whom the jealous Porgy stabs. At the opera's close, the unfaithful Bess runs off with another lover, Sportin Life; and Porgy, coming out of prison, sets off to follow her to New York. Famous songs include 'A Woman is a sometime thing', 'It ain't necessarily so' and 'Bess, you is my woman now'.

Stravinsky's *The Rake's Progress* (1951) is one of the surprises that this unpredictable composer was always giving us, equally surprisingly given its première in Venice. Using the Hogarth prints as his inspiration, he persuaded W. H. Auden and his associate, Chester Kallman, to provide a libretto for him, to which he wrote a pastiche opera, unashamedly lyrical, spiced with ironic, even grotesque humour, yet which ends tragically with the hero, Tom Rakewell, consigned to a mental asylum. In the Epilogue he uses the words 'For idle hands and hearts and minds the Devil finds a work to do.'

Oedipus Rex is described by Stravinsky as an 'opera-oratorio after Sophocles', scored for orchestra, speaker, soloists and male chorus. Stravinsky's libretto was written by Jean Cocteau in French and then translated by Abbé Jean Daniélou into Latin (the narration, however, is performed in the language of the audience). It was written at the beginning of the composer's so-called neo-classical period. He set it in Latin, stating it was a language 'not dead but turned to stone'. The characters remain immobile on the stage, being able to gesture only with their hands and heads; thus the heroic tragedy is told within an antique convention, though employing many charactertistics of the musical style of nineteenth-century opera.

The narrator greets the audience, explaining the nature of the drama they are about to see, and setting the scene: Thebes is in the grip of a plague, and the Thebans implore King Oedipus, the conqueror of the Sphinx, to rescue them, which he promises to do. Creon (Oedipus's brother-in-law) reports from the oracle that Thebes is harbouring the murderer of the previous king, Laius, who has brought plague on the city. Oedipus questions the soothsayer Tiresias, who refuses to speak. In a fit of anger, Oedipus accuses Tiresias of being the murderer; the latter then states that the murderer is a king. Oedipus promptly accuses Tiresias of plotting with Creon, whom he believes covets the throne. At that moment, Oedipus's wife, Queen Jocasta, appears.

Act II finds Jocasta calming things down by telling them that the oracles always lie, and gives an example: an oracle had once predicted that Laius would die at his son's hand, when in fact he was murdered by bandits at the crossing of three roads. However, this only has the effect of upsetting Oedipus even further, as he recollects killing an old man at a crossroads before coming to Thebes. A messenger arrives with the news that King Polybus of Corinth (whom Oedipus believes to be his father) has died, though he then also discovers that Polybus was only the foster-father of Oedipus, and Oedipus is in fact a foundling. A shepherd arrives and says it was he who had found the child Oedipus in the mountains. Jocasta, suspecting the horrible truth, flees. A shattering revelation is now announced: Oedipus is the child of Laius and Jocasta, and therefore Oedipus killed his father, and married his mother. The truth now out, Jocasta hangs herself, and Oedipus breaks into her room and puts out his own eyes with her pin. He departs Thebes for ever, as the chorus at first vent their anger, and then mourn the loss of the king they loved. A background knowledge of the story is helpful to understand the work fully, such as the fact that Oedipus merely suspects that he is the murderer of King Laius, that he does not realize he was also his son. While the structure of the opera is highly original, the music not only embraces Italian operatic influences, Verdi, Bellini and Puccini, but also that of Handelian opera, and the characterization of the roles is remarkable: Oedipus, for example, at first has brilliantly virtuosic writing, which diminishes with his self-confidence, until his last utterances are completely unadorned.

Amahl and the Night Visitors has become an annual television event in the USA since its first broadcast in 1951, and it is easy to see why. The sentimental story concerns Amahl, a cripple whose mother steals part of the treasure offered by the three kings for the Holy Child; Amahl offers his crutch as a gift instead and is miraculously healed; and then he joins the kings in search of the Christ Child. For this simple tale, Menotti provided some absolutely charming music and the composer insists that a boy should always sing the part of Amahl, not a soprano.

Although Walton's *Troilus and Cressida* (1954) has not received universal praise, few operas since Puccini have such a rich store of memorable tunes, often paralleling the early Walton of *Belshazzar's Feast* and the *Symphony No. 1* in style. Set with the backdrop of the Trojan War, Cressida, daughter of the High Priest of Troy, is in love with Troilus but through events agrees to marry Diomede, and in the end stabs herself. There is humour in the work too, especially in the role of Pandarus, Cressida's manipulative uncle, and if the work's libretto can be partly blamed for the opera's relative failure, the often beautiful and compelling music is more than compensation.

Tippett's *Midsummer Marriage* (1955) is loosely based on the story of Mozart's *The Magic Flute*, with two couples, one 'royal' and one 'common', tracing the path to marriage: Jenifer and Mark (Pamina and Tamino), the earthy Jack and Bella (Papageno and Papagena), with King Fisher (Queen of the Night), and so on. It is a work that we believe should be in the standard repertoire, alongside Britten's *Peter Grimes*, for the music consistently has that inspired melodic flow which distinguishes all great operas. There are few operas of any period which use the chorus to such glorious effect, often in haunting offstage passages; but as a work as a whole it is hard to resist, even for those not normally fond of modern opera. The so-called 'difficulties' of the libretto, with its mystical philosophical references, fade when the sounds are so honeyed in texture, and so consistently lyrical, while the story – for all its complications – preserves a clear sense of emotional involvement throughout. The impressive orchestral *Ritual Dances* heard in the opera have a concert life outside that of the opera.

Leonard Bernstein's comic operetta *Candide* (1956) (of which we have not been able to include a recording) is a kind of ironic send-up of Voltaire. After the appalling things that happen to its heroine, Cunegonde, whose hit number (quoted in the superb overture) is 'Glitter and be gay', unlike Voltaire's original novel it has an optimistic ending, a characteristic Bernstein ballad, 'Make our garden grow'. But this splendid and very entertaining piece has not achieved the success of *West Side Story* (1957), Bernstein's masterpiece with its Romeo and Juliet story set in New York, and including some of his finest tunes, especially 'Maria', 'One hand, one heart' and the soaring 'Tonight'.

Samuel Barber composed *Vanessa* in 1956–7. The rather melodramatic story in the manner of a Gothic romance, concerning the return of a lover (who turns out to be the son of the hero) to Vanessa's household and the ensuing emotional havoc caused, suits the essentially romantic idiom of Barber's harmonic language. Maria Callas refused to sing it (on the grounds that she thought it lacked melody, though the more likely reason was that her rival in the opera gets all the best numbers). To ears accustomed to contemporary opera, the work is richly romantic and readily appealing (Barber said, 'There's no reason music should be difficult for an audience to understand, is there?'). Its instant success at its first performance can be understood on listening to the first-class RCA recording of 1958.

Poulenc's *Dialogue des Carmélites* (1957) is so unlike his usual piquant, witty style that it is difficult at times to believe he wrote this powerful, unrelenting score for a story about a group of nuns who finally take a vow of martyrdom under the guillotine. Blanche, the key figure in the story, returns at the last minute to join her sisters as they wait for death, which is achieved musically with a *'Salve regina'* with voices departing, one at a time, to the sound of the guillotine. It is a denouement to a narrative that listeners either embrace or reject as unacceptably grim.

Assassinio nella cattedrale (1958) is the only Pizzetti opera to have been professionally staged in England. It is based on Alberto Castelli's translation of T. S. Eliot's play, which portrays the assassination of Archbishop Thomas Becket in Canterbury Cathedral in 1170. However, Pizzetti shortened and adapted the narrative: he omits the knights' justification of the murder of the archbishop in Eliot's epilogue. The opera is compact, but it is totally compelling, both musically and dramatically. The musical flow is dignified and stately, as befits the subject matter, and the orchestral palette is subtle in its colouring. There are moments when its melodic lines suggest that the lessons of Mussorgsky and Debussy's *Pelléas* have been observed, as well as late Verdi, and the choral writing has an almost symphonic sweep. *Assassinio nella cattedrale* has been absurdly neglected on the stage (as indeed has Pizzetti generally) but a DVD recording of this work brings home the beauty and nobility of this score.

Benjamin Britten's operas dominated the English stage for three decades, beginning with his semi-comic *Albert Herring* of 1943 (which we have also seen successfully performed in Hamburg with the comedy coming over well to a German audience). His last, much more serious *Death in Venice* was staged in Aldeburgh in 1973. Throughout, his partnership with the tenor, Peter Pears (personal as well as musical), was part and parcel of each production. But his supreme masterpiece is *Peter Grimes*, which achieved worldwide success. It is about a relationship between a fisherman and his boy apprentice, and caused a sensation at its first production in 1945, its music instantly appealing and its tragic story of the death of the boy and the antagonism of the villagers of the Borough totally arresting. The orchestral music depicting the sea includes four unforgettable descriptive interludes, and also a marvellous effect when the door to the inn opens and the storm outside floods in orchestrally.

Billy Budd (1951) is considered by some to be Britten's greatest opera. It is set on a naval vessel, the warship *Indomitable*, commanded by Captain Vere. Claggart, Master-at-Arms (an Iago-like villain), accuses the newest member of the crew, Billy, of fomenting mutiny, and in return Billy strikes him and he falls dead. The penalty is execution by hanging, but Billy accepts his fate with dignity.

The Turn of the Screw (1954) is Britten's other undoubted masterpiece, adopting a weird Henry James story about two children, Miles and Flora, under the care of a governess, but who appear to be under the influence of the previous governess, Miss Jessel, and Peter Quint, both now dead,. The latter is finally responsible for the death of Miles. Britten's music is stark and hauntingly atmospheric, especially the orchestral interludes.

A Midsummer Night's Dream (1960) follows Shakespeare pretty closely, and Britten's music does too, with ear-tickling tuned percussion used to create the fairy music, comparatively straightforward vocal lines for the lovers, but excelling in the ensemble music for the rustics, who all but steal the show.

Death in Venice, Britten's last opera (1973), is based (not always closely) on the novella by Thomas Mann. Its hero is Aschenbach, a celebrated writer and philosopher who, staying in Venice, meets and falls in love with a young boy, Tadzio. Yet he also is haunted by the influence of Apollo and Dionysus, symbolizing life and death, the latter of which takes over at the end of the opera. Britten himself was dying at the time of the opera's completion.

Nixon in China (1987) provides an extraordinary narrative for an opera, but it was an immediate, remarkable success and is John Adams's masterpiece so far. The opera, an embroidery of a historical event, has a remarkable cast-list of characters: President Nixon himself and his wife Pat, Henry Kissinger, Chou En-Lai, plus Mao Tse-tung and his wife, Chiang Ch'ing, who has an unforgettable aria at the end of Act II. The meeting of Nixon and Chou brings a mutual expression of goodwill, but the evening performance of a revolutionary ballet is not well received by the visitors, and the opera ends with Chou's philosophical acceptance that events always seem to move beyond their control. The opera is notable for its splendid choral scenes, and it grips from beginning to end.

The Minotaur, Harrison Birtwistle's eighth opera, like his earlier commission from Covent Garden, *Gawain*, has a libretto by David Harsent, using a language nicely balanced between poetry and the vernacular, while Birtwistle's idiom, always abrasive, has developed here a more lyrical strain. As in previous operas Birtwistle is not only preoccupied with Greek myth but with central characters who are anti-heroes. In *The Minotaur* the opera rises to a superb final climax, when Theseus has killed the minotaur (in this incarnation possessing a bull's head and a human body), and the monster is finally allowed to speak. This means that the concluding monologue, as he is dying, echoes directly the Death of Boris in Mussorgsky's *Boris Godunov*, a likeness that Birtwistle intends. With typical ingenuity Birtwistle has created a lyrical thread passed from instrument to instrument, symbolizing the thread that Ariadne gives to Theseus to lead him back through the minotaur's maze. The role of the minotaur as a sort of Jekyll and Hyde figure was expressly designed for John Tomlinson, the famed Wotan from Bayreuth, and centrally cast too in Birtwistle's earlier *Gawain*.

Thomas Adès's setting of Shakespeare's *The Tempest* was another unexpected triumph at Covent Garden in 2004. Its libretto by Meredith Oakes took considerable liberties with Shakespeare's text, but the result, with Ian Bostridge as Caliban and Simon Keenlyside as Prospero, was totally convincing at the opera's début. Yet it was Ariel, sung by the spectacular American coloratura Cyndia Sieden, who stole the show with her shimmering stratospheric roulades, and it is she who ends the work hauntingly.

The Penguin Guide to the
1000 **Finest Classical Recordings**

ADAM, Adolphe (1803-56)

Giselle (ballet: complete, DVD version) (Choreography: Jean Coralli and Jules Perrot, revised Marius Petipa and Peter Wright)
Opus Arte DVD OA0993D. Cojocaru, Kobborg, Soloists & Corps of the Royal Ballet, ROHCG O, Gruzin (Producer: Peter Wright)

Giselle (ballet: complete, CD version)
Ⓜ Decca 4783625-2 (2). ROHCG O, Bonynge

Adam's *Giselle* is the first of the great classical ballets. The story has a simple romantic opening Act, with plenty of chances for the principal dancers to shine, but the drama rises to a peak in the second, where the female corps de ballet take the form of Willis, deserted maidens who have each died of a broken heart. Urged on by their imperious queen, Myrtha, they are able to return from the grave to entice any unfaithful male lover into a dance leading to death from sheer exhaustion. However, the heroine Giselle forgives her lover and success-fully pleads for his life from the queen and her companions, before returning to the underworld. The choreography is richly traditional but includes an extraordinary hopping step for the corps de ballet in Act II, which is uniquely memorable.

The ballet has been extraordinarily successful on DVD with fine versions from Kirov (Warner) and Paris (TDK). But the most recent recording comes from a BBC transmission in January 2006. It is marvellously danced, with the Romanian ballerina, Alina Cojocaru, in the title role and the Danish virtuoso, Johan Kobborg, as Albrecht. They are a touching pair and the remaining roles are no less brilliant and as strongly characterized. The Royal corps de ballet is superb. A compelling performance, with finely supportive playing from the Covent Garden orchestra under Boris Gruzin and expert video direction throughout.

Bonynge's CD performance offers the complete original score, exactly as Adam wrote it, with all repeats. Also included are the *Peasant pas de deux* in Act I with music by Frédéric Burgmüller, and two other insertions, possibly by Minkus. The playing is polished and warmly sympathetic. Bonynge's tempi are very much of the ballet theatre, but the overall tension is well maintained and detail is affectionately vivid. Recorded in London's Henry Wood Hall, with its glowing acoustics, the sound is richly coloured and sumptuous, the bass resonance almost too expansive, and this is one of the most successful and satisfying of Bonynge's many ballet recordings made for Decca over the years.

ADAMS, John (born 1947)

John Adams is undoubtedly now the most important contemporary composer in the United States and is already making a worldwide reputation for music which is listener-friendly, highly imaginative and original. He tells us that the first major piece of classical music he experienced in his youth, heard within the glorious acoustic of Boston's Symphony Hall, was Vaughan Williams's *Fantasia on a Theme by Thomas Tallis* conducted by Koussevitzky, which made an overwhelming impression on him.

Having then encountered Webern (which he described as 'the strangest musical experience in my whole life'), Adams believes that 'in the distant future musicians will look back on a period in the twentieth century – the era of Schoenberg, Stockhausen and Boulez – when composers aggressively destroyed the pulse and tonal syntax of music', and this is a view with which we have considerable sympathy.

After a year's sabbatical in 1974 he was exposed to the music of Steve Reich, notably *Drumming*. But he later moved on from the 'Minimalism' for which Reich is famous, finding it provided only a limited musical experience. 'Its emotional bandwidth was very small,' he said, 'so I tried to stretch it.' He did just that, and the result has been most illuminating.

(i) *The Chairman Dances*; (ii) *Grand Pianola Music*; (iii) *Shaker Loops*; (i) *Short Ride in a Fast Machine*

Ⓑ EMI 2 06627-2. (i) CBSO Rattle; (ii) Random Wilson, NY Soloists; (iii) NY Soloists, Warren-Green

Under Rattle the foxtrot *The Chairman Dances* has unabated energy. It is an extraordinary adjunct to Adams's opera *Nixon in China*, but not part of it, for Madame Chou outrageously dances a foxtrot in front of the assembled dignitaries at a banquet. Rhythmically unpredictable in its minimalist patterns, its kaleidoscopic scoring is ear-catching. The whizzing *Short Ride in a Fast Machine* and the exhilarating concertante (and tuneful) *Grand Pianola Music* both have immediate hit potential; the latter has a thrilling climax. *Shaker Loops* was the work that first alerted us to the originality and intensity of Adams's earlier music and Christopher Warren-Green here directs its recording début.

Harmonielehre; *Short Ride in a Fast Machine*

SFS 0053. San Francisco SO, Michael Tilson Thomas

This superb disc is as fine a place as any to start exploring the music of America's greatest contemporary composer, and the performances, splendidly recorded live at the Davies Symphony Hall, are unsurpassed. Adams was influenced by Schoenberg but rejected his atonal compositional style. His *Harmonielehre* throbbingly moves in arch form from white-hot, energy-absorbing minimalism to poignantly expressive yearning, before returning to the energetic thrust of the opening. 'The Anfortas Wound', pictured in the second movement, can never be healed and is evoked with plangent yearning; then the finale – inspired by the composer's young daughter – at first is glitteringly light-hearted, then becomes a tender *berceuse*, before gathering pace and culminating in a tidal wave of minimalist brass and percussion. The brief, succinct *Short Ride in a Fast Machine* is, in the composer's words, 'a cranked up, high velocity, orchestral juggernaut insistently urged on by the unyielding pulse of the wood block'.

Nixon in China (opera: complete)
Ⓑ Naxos 8.669022/24 (3). Orth, Kanyova, Hammons, Heller, Dahl, Opera Colorado Ch., Colorado SO, Alsop

Nixon in China is Adams's masterpiece, an inspired and wholly original opera, worthy to stand alongside the great operas of the past based on historical subjects and matching Britten's *Peter Grimes* in its immediacy and melodic flow. If it seems an extraordinary conception to base a stage work on President Nixon's visit to communist China in 1972, it projects grippingly in the theatre, and it stands up just as compellingly musically on record. Adams's special brand of minimalism works magnetically in the rich orchestral accompaniment, and the music has a lyrical flow absent from most modern operas. Adams really can write for the voice and the choral music too is especially telling, but many of the solo arias are magnetic. Marin Alsop has this music in her very being, and her version is cast from strength. Robert Orth is a strong Nixon and his wife Pat is intensely and sympathetically characterized by Maria Kanyova. But Tracy Dahl steals the show in her sympatheic portrayal of Madame Mao, particularly in the coloratura of the closing Act. An unforgettable set, which won the 2010 *Gramophone* Opera Award.

In some respects the earlier, St Luke's recording, conducted by Edo de Waart (Ⓑ None. 79177-2 (3), Sylvan, Craney, Maddalena, St Luke's Ch. & O), is more sophisticated, particularly the chorus, and Madame Mao (Trudy Ellen Craney) sings splendidly at the climax of the opera's third Act.

ADÈS, Thomas (born 1971)

(i-ii) *Asyla, Op. 17*; (i; iii) *. . . But All Shall be Well, Op. 10*; (iii-iv) *Chamber Symphony for 15 Players, Op. 2*; (iii-v) *Concerto conciso for Piano & Chamber Orchestra, Op. 18*; (i; iii) *These Premises are Alarmed, Op. 18*
EMI 5 03403-2. (i) CBSO; (ii) cond. Rattle; (iii) cond. composer; (iv) Birmingham Contemporary Music Group; (v) with composer (piano)

Thomas Adès's brilliant orchestral piece, *Asyla*, with its exotic use of a vast range of percussion instruments, was Simon Rattle's choice of work to complete his inaugural programme as the new music director of the Berlin

Philharmonic in November 2002. The *Chamber Symphony* is extraordinarily intricate in its rhythmic ideas, developing ear-tickling colouristic patterns. The *Concerto conciso* has the solo piano well integrated into the instrumental group, where rhythms are free and jazzy, but it brings a calm central chaconne before the closing 'Brawl'. *These Premises are Alarmed* is a brief, witty apoplexy, designed as a brilliant orchestral show-piece for the Hallé Orchestra. Balance is restored in . . . *But All Shall be Well*, the title coming from 'Little Gidding', the last of T. S. Eliot's *Four Quartets*. Remarkable music, splendidly played and most vividly and atmospherically recorded.

The Tempest (opera: complete)

EMI 6 95234 2 (2). Keenlyside, Sieden, Bostridge, Royal, Spence, Langridge, ROHCG
    Ch. & O, composer

Many composers have attempted to turn Shakespeare's last masterpiece, *The Tempest*, into an opera, but few have succeeded as strikingly as Thomas Adès, who wrote his 2004 version for Covent Garden. With Meredith Oakes adapting the text in rhymed couplets, the elaborate plot was neatly simplified, with Adès composing each of the principal roles specifically for particular singers, rather in the way Britten did. The result is well constructed and dramatically effective in its clever timing and contrasted textures. The climax at the end of Act III brings a beautiful love duet for Miranda and Ferdinand (the mezzo, Kate Royal, and the high baritone, Toby Spence, a handsome couple). An impressive passaclaglia ensemble follows, before the opera ends with a poignant duet for Caliban (Ian Bostridge, a high tenor role) and Ariel, with its stratospheric chir-rupings expressly designed for the dazzling American coloratura, Cyndia Sieden. Also notable is the powerful tonal aria in Act II for Caliban, a character here inspiring more sympathy than usual. The late Philip Langridge in one of his last performances at Covent Garden also makes a memorable King of Naples, while Adès's evocative orchestration with its percussion effects vividly conjures up the atmosphere of the magic island of Prospero, a role written for the clear, fresh-voiced baritone of Simon Keenlyside, noble if youthful-sounding. 'O brave new world,' sings Miranda near the end, inspiring Prospero's comment, 'Oh simple girl.' The whole opera fades into the distance at the end to Ariel's increasingly faint flutings. A strong and memorable opera, which makes a splendid add-ition to the repertory, here recorded live in transparent yet atmospheric sound in the 2007 revival, conducted powerfully by the composer.

ALBÉNIZ, Isaac (1860–1909)

Iberia (complete); *Navarra*

Ⓜ Double Decca (ADD) 448 191–2 (2). Alicia de Larrocha (with **GRANADOS**:
    Goyescas)

Alicia de Larrocha has recorded *Iberia* three times with almost equal success, but her 1972 analogue version is rather special. She has a unique feeling for this repertoire, and plays with great character, losing little by comparison with the later digital version (also for Decca). The piano recording is most realistic and the Double Decca reissue is highly desirable for being coupled with an equally recommendable set of Granados's *Goyescas*.

ALBINONI, Tomaso (1671–1751)

Oboe and Double-Oboe Concertos: *12 Concerti a cinque, Op. 7*; *12 Concerti a cinque, Op. 9*; *Sinfonia*
Chan. 0602; 0579; 0610. Robson, Latham, Col. Mus. 90, Standage

Like Vivaldi's, Albinoni's concertos offer a seemingly infinite variety of invention and imagination within his musical language. His music is more than merely melodically appealing, his occasional quirks of harmony and rhythm keep the listener on his toes and offer a great source of pleasure. Simon Standage's survey of oboe and double-oboe concertos on Chandos is top choice in this repertoire. Anthony Robson plays all eight solo concertos from Opp. 7 and 9 using a period oboe. His tone is most appealing and his phrasing and musicianship are second to none. Simon Standage provides alert accompaniments, also using original instruments, and creates bright, athletic string timbres. Catherine Latham joins him to complete the Collegium Musicum 90 sets of Opp. 7 and 9, including the works for strings. The artistic results are very lively and refreshing, although the balance is rather close.

Simon Standage has also recorded the composer's equally appealing Op. 5 concertos (CHAN 0663) – full of lovely melodic invention – and very recently, Albinoni's rarely recorded Op. 10 set, which includes much delightful music, not least the vivid evocation of flamenco style in the *Eleventh Concerto* (CHAN 0769).

ALFVÉN, Hugo (1872–1960)

Midsummer Watch, Op. 16 (Swedish Rhapsody); *Adagio*; *Andante religioso*; *King Gustav II Adolf*; *Legend of the Skerries*; *The Mountain King Suite*; *The Prodigal Son: Suite*; *Symphonies 1–5*
Ⓜ BIS CD1478/80(5). Royal Swedish O, Neeme Järvi (with soloists)

Alfvén was one of the leading nationalist composers working in Scandinavia at the turn of the nineteenth and twentieth centuries. For three decades he was conductor of the celebrated Uppsala male choir, Orfei drängar (Sons of Orpheus). His *Midsummer Watch* brings the magic of the Swedish midsummer vividly to life and has a wholly individual character, and intoxicating atmosphere. So too has the affecting *Elegy* from the incidental music to the play *Gustav II Adolf*. The symphonies are less perfect but are well worth investigating all the same, especially when the five discs are economically priced for the cost of only three. Neeme Järvi conducts his Swedish forces with enthusiasm and authority, and this is altogether most rewarding and not music one meets readily.

ALKAN, Charles-Valentin (1813–88)

Concerto for Solo Piano, Op. 39/8–10; *Troisième Recueil de chants, Op. 65*
Hyp. CDA 67569. Marc-André Hamelin

12 Etudes in the Minor Keys: Symphony for Piano, Op. 39/4–7; *Alleluia, Op. 25*; *Salut, cendre du pauvre!, Op. 45*; *Super flumina Babylonis, Op. 52*; *Souvenirs: 3 Morceaux dans le genre pathétique, Op. 15*
Hyp. CDA 67218. Marc-André Hamelin

Grande sonate (Les Quatre Ages); *Barcarolle*; *Le Festin d'Esope*; *Sonatine, Op. 61*
Hyp. CDA 66794. Marc-André Hamelin

All lovers of the piano repertoire must surely come across the remarkable piano music of Charles-Valentin Alkan some day. His music has a reputation for being fiendishly difficult, but his great range and variety of pieces ensured that he was admired by Liszt, Busoni and many others. Marc-André Hamelin continues his remarkable traversal of Alkan's work with the *Concerto for Solo Piano*, a gigantic score, the first movement of which alone takes just under half an hour. The *Symphony for Piano* comprises four movements (Nos. 4–7) from the *Douze études*. The *Symphony* and the other pieces on Hyperion must sound effortless, just as a great dancer must seem weightless, and Hamelin makes light of their many difficulties. Superb playing and very good recording – and noteworthy not only for its virtuosity but for its refined music-making. Alkan's *Grande sonate* over its four massive movements represents the hero at various ages, with the second, *Quasi-Faust*, the key one. The *Sonatine*, the most approachable of Alkan's major works, is done just as dazzlingly, with the hauntingly poetic *Barcarolle* and the swaggering *Festin d'Esope* as valuable makeweights.

ALWYN, William (1905–85)

William Alwyn composed vigorously over the whole span of his musical life. His music is recognizably English and has an enticing amalgam of romantic as well as neoclassical character. In spite of a wide coverage of excellent recordings, he has never made it into the mainstream concert hall, although there is evidence that his music is coming back into fashion. It is certainly rewarding enough to do so.

(i) **Autumn Legend** (for cor anglais); (ii) **Lyra Angelica** (concerto for harp); (iii) **Pastoral Fantasia** (for viola); **Tragic Interlude**
Chan. 9065. (i) Daniel; (ii) Masters; (iii) Tees; City of L. Sinfonia, Hickox

Autumn Legend (1954) is a highly atmospheric tone-poem, very Sibelian in feeling. So too is the *Pastoral Fantasia*, yet the piece has its own developing individuality. The *Tragic Interlude* is a powerful lament for the dead of wars past. But the highlight of this disc is the *Lyra Angelica*, a radiantly beautiful, extended piece (just over half an hour in length) inspired by the metaphysical poet Giles Fletcher's *'Christ's victorie and triumph'*. The performance here is very moving, and the recording has great richness of string tone and a delicately balanced harp texture. Rachel Masters's contribution is distinguished. The classic Lyrita recording of *Autumn Legend* and *Lyra Angelica*, under the direction of the composer, is still also available on SRCD 230.

ANSERMET, Ernest (conducting various orchestras)

BACH: *Cantata 31: Sonata.* **HAYDN**: *Symphony 22.*
BEETHOVEN: *Symphony 4.* **WEBER**: *Der Beherrscher der Geister: Overture; Preciosa: Overture.* **MENDELSSOHN**: *Ruy Blas; Overture.* **BORODIN**: *Polovtsian Dances.* **LIADOV**: *Kikimora.* **STRAVINSKY**: *Scherzo à la Russe; Pulcinella: Suite.* **SIBELIUS**: *Symphony 4.* **DELIBES**: *Coppélia:* excerpts; *Sylvia:* excerpts. **FRANCK**: *Le Chasseur maudit.* **CHABRIER**: *Joyeuse Marche*; **Danse Slave.** **FAURÉ**: *Masques et Bergamasques*; *Pénélope: Prélude.* **SCHUMANN**: *Carnaval.* **RAVEL**: *Le Tombeau de Couperin.* **DEBUSSY**: *6 Epigraphes Antiques*; *Petite Suite.* **RESPIGHI**: *Fountains of Rome; Rossiniana.* **HONEGGER**: *Pacific 231; Le Roi David.* **DUKAS**: *La Péri.* **RIMSKY-KORSAKOV**: *Dubinushka.* **MARTIN**: *Concerto for 7 Wind Instruments, Timpani, Percussion & String Orchestra*
Ⓑ Decca (ADD) 475 8140 (6)

It was the advent of Decca's Full Frequency Range Recording recordings (ffrr) in the late 1940s that put both Ansermet and Decca at the forefront of hi-fi classical recordings. Ansermet's mono accounts of *La boutique fantasque* and *Petrushka* are landmarks in recording history. During the 1950s and '60s,

Ansermet made an extraordinary number of LPs, mainly with his Suisse Romande Orchestra. He became especially famous for his interpretations of twentieth-century repertoire (though not the exponents of the twelve-tone row) and French music. If many of Ansermet's performances can be criticized for their lack of polish and sheer virtuoso brilliance, they (usually) make up for it in terms of character and musical substance. Ansermet sparkles in the lighter French repertoire: Chabrier's *Joyeuse marche* and *Danse slave* are among the best performances of these works on disc. Just listen to the sense of exhilaration in the music-making, not achieved by mere speed: it is the rhythmic pulse which makes them so striking, along with the 1964 recording. Decca provide similar brilliance in the *Tarantella* from *Rossiniana*, the most entertaining movement from the Rossini/Respighi suite.

The Delibes items show Ansermet's gift for ballet music (both his complete *Coppélia* and *Nutcracker* are classics). The *Mazurka* from *Coppélia* positively dances out of the speakers, while *Les Chasseresses* from *Sylvia* is rich in pageant and classical drama. We are strikingly summoned to attention with Dukas's *Fanfare* from *La Péri*, and the ensuing ballet music is both lively and sharply characterized. A rarity on this disc is an orchestrated version (by Glazunov, among others) of Schumann's *Carnaval* and it works surprisingly well in its nineteenth-century orchestral dress. César Franck's ominous hunting calls in *Le Chasseur maudit* sound splendid in Ansermet's 1961 performance, building up a fine sense of drama (what a wonderfully entertaining work this is!). Ansermet's classic version of Fauré's *Masques et Bergamasques*, dating from 1961, finds the conductor on top form, with light and sensitive playing making the most of this delightful music.

Ravel and Debussy are composers with whom Ansermet often excelled. Ansermet fans will recognize the oboe almost like an old, if not always completely stable, friend. Still, the finely etched colours of Ravel's *Le Tombeau de Couperin* are well brought out and there is a cool beauty in the charming *Petite Suite*. Ansermet's extensive and innate understanding of orchestral texture is well displayed in his orchestration of Debussy's *Six Epigraphes Antiques*. This was originally written as a piano duet but Ansermet's orchestration fits the music perfectly. The mono sound is very good but it is a pity he didn't re-record it in stereo.

It is hard to imagine a more powerful performance of Honegger's masterpiece, *Pacific 231*, than Ansermet's 1963 account: the opening tingles with excitement, with Honegger's steam-engine brought to startling life. The same composer's 'Dramatic psalm', *Le Roi David*, is a distinctive pageant offering very agreeable musical ideas in the composer's distinctive sound-world. The performance is strong in character and, with its distinguished French cast (Suzanne Danco is especially impressive), it is completely idiomatic.

Frank Martin is represented by his *Concerto for Seven Wind Instruments, Timpani, Percussion and String Orchestra*. The shifting emotions of the music, with its unusual colours and the angular quality of the melodic lines, make for a highly rewarding and distinctive piece. Again, the woodwind playing is not the last word in brilliance (that oboe again!), but the performance is concentrated and full of conviction.

With his ear for colour, it is not surprising that Ansermet made some impressive LPs of Russian music. His *Polovtsian Dances* may not be in the Solti league of exhilaration, but the orchestra is lively enough, even if the chorus is a bit limp. Liadov's *Kikimora* and Rimsky-Korsakov's *Dubinushka* receive excellent performances.

Stravinsky's *Scherzo à la Russe*, a relaxed reading, allows the textures to shine out, deliciously so in the quiet, chamber-like section of the work. *Pulcinella* was one of Ansermet's most successful stereo Stravinsky recordings, not least because of the vividness of the 1956 recording. True, it sounds a little dry by today's standards, but it has an intimate quality which is most attractive. Listen to the double basses in the *vivo* section and the rasp of the brass – crisp and vibrant. The gentleness of the following *Minuetto* is quite melting and one even forgives the oboe player's lack of polish.

Ansermet was a mathematician and there is a sense that his mathematical mind sometimes worked too hard in the romantic repertoire. His Beethoven cycle is unfailingly interesting though, and his poised, direct approach works well (the *Ninth Symphony*, with Joan Sutherland, won universal praise). The *Fourth Symphony* with its subdued opening is almost chilling in its beauty here, and he warms up nicely in the main *allegro*. Ansermet's always reliable sense of phrasing makes the string playing especially enjoyable, with the articulation in the finale particularly memorable.

The Weber overtures, *The Ruler of the Spirits* and *Preciosa*, are highly enjoyable, the latter with its sparkling Turkish music section. Ansermet's account of Mendelssohn's *Ruy Blas Overture* is among the very best versions with its vivid sound and sense of drama.

Most unlikely repertoire for Ansermet is Bach, but actually he was rather warm-hearted when playing this composer: listen to the vitality of the opening of *Cantata 31*. Ansermet's Haydn is memorable too, mainly for its elegant phrasing of the strings. The finale of *Symphony No. 22* is especially enjoyable, with its hunting rhythms, all very lively but not at all forced.

Sibelius's *Fourth Symphony* is the least successful item here. Those who know this symphony well will get something out of this performance, because Ansermet always has a way of illuminating strands of a score in an interesting way. However, the tension notably sags in the slow movement and the performance as a whole lacks enough concentration to hold the work compellingly together.

Ansermet was the opposite of the flashy showman conductor: the excitement of listening to Ansermet performances is more in the detail than overt brilliance. But they are always enjoyable for their spontaneity.

ANSERMET, Ernest, with the Suisse Romande Orchestra

'Ouvertures Françaises': LALO: *Le Roi d'Ys*. AUBER:
Le Domino Noir; Fra Diavolo. HÉROLD: *Zampa*. THOMAS:
Mignon; Raymond. BOIELDIEU: *La Dame Blanche*.
OFFENBACH: *La Belle Hélène; Orphée aux enfers*
Ⓜ Australian Decca Eloquence (ADD) 4800023

This recording of once popular French overtures was always one of Ansermet's most successful records. Lalo's *Le Roi d'Ys* is full of melodrama and builds up to a particularly exciting finale, while *La Dame Blanche* receives a suitably more reserved, though delicately stylish, reading. Auber's infectious overture, *Le Domino noir*, with its string of colourful, formal dances, goes splendidly, with Ansermet's strikingly articulated strings (at 5 minutes 40 seconds) in the crescendo á la Rossini particularly effective. The opening section of the *Fra Diavolo Overture* is also effectively pointed – what a fine overture that is! Both the Offenbach overtures come off very well, with *La Belle Hélène* (in Haensch's ingenious arrangement) sounding most enticing with its many wittily memorable tunes. If the final *Can-can* in the *Orphée aux enfers* overture is taken at a slower speed than one might expect, it is invested with such rhythmic vigour that music sounds freshly minted. *Zampa* also receives one of its best performances on disc, with the dramatic tremolo strings near the beginning sounding especially vibrant. With both of Thomas's most famous and delightful overtures (*Mignon* is an inspired piece, beautifully scored), this makes a most welcome reissue, with any slight imperfections of ensemble easily forgivable in the fresh, lively music-making.

ARENSKY, Anton (1861–1906)

(i) *Piano Concerto in F min., Op. 2; Fantasia on Russian Folksongs.
To the Memory of Suvorov; Symphonic Scherzo*
ⒷⒷ Naxos 8.570526. (i) Scherbakov; Russian PO, Yablonsky

Arensky occupies a small but not insignificant place in the history of Russian music. While not possessing the distinction of, say, Rimsky, his music has genuine merit and often has considerable melodic appeal. This inexpensive Naxos CD is an ideal way to explore his orchestral music. Not surprisingly, these performances are very Russian in feeling, and after a bold opening both orchestra and the excellent soloist make the very most of the concerto's memorable secondary theme. The *Fantasia on Russian Folksongs* is hardly less idiomatic, and again shows the pianist, Konstantin Scherbakov, in brilliant form. There are attractive couplings too; the commemorative march celebrates *General Suvorov* with plenty of fanfare, yet has a contrasting, folksy centrepiece, and the lively *Symphonic Scherzo* shows the composer's orchestral palette vividly. A most enjoyable collection.

Violin Concerto in A min., Op. 54

Hyp. CDA 67642. Gringolts, BBC Scottish SO, Volkov – **TANEYEV**:
Suite de concert, Op. 28

The concerto's second theme is an adorable idea that is both touching and difficult to dislodge from one's memory. Ilya Gringolts plays it with disarming elegance and warmth, yet elsewhere he offers effortless brilliance and is expertly and sensitively partnered by Ilan Volkov and the BBC Scottish Orchestra. The balance between soloist and orchestra is truthful and most musically judged. If you fancy the attractive Taneyev coupling, this can be strongly recommended.

ARGENTA, Ataulfo (with various orchestras)

CHABRIER: *España*. **RIMSKY-KORSAKOV**: *Capriccio espagnol*. **GRANADOS**: *Andaluza*. **MOSZKOVSKY**: *Spanish Dances, Book 1* (with LSO). **DEBUSSY**: *Images* (with SRO). **LISZT**: *Piano Concertos 1 & 2* (with Katchen, LPO); *Faust Symphony* (with Paris Conservatoire O); *Les Préludes* (with SRO). **ALBÉNIZ**: *Iberia Suite*. **BERLIOZ**: *Symphonie fantastique*. **TURINA**: *Danzas fantásticas* (with Paris Conservatoire O). **TCHAIKOVSKY**: *Violin Concerto* (with Campoli, LSO); *Symphony 4* (with SRO)
Ⓑ Decca mono/stereo 475 7747 (5)

Argenta's early death came before he realized his full potential. His recording career was cut short, but before then he made a series of colourful records for Decca which have been gathered here complete for the first time. The first CD in the box is a vintage, early stereo collection, *España*, mainly from the pens of non-Spaniards, but readily displaying the conductor's flair, not least in the sparkling account of Chabrier's title-piece. The slight but endearingly dated Moszkowski dances are stylishly played, and the last three are especially successful. The highlight of the disc is Rimsky's *Capriccio espagnol* which (alongside Maazel's DG Berlin version from the same period) has seldom been matched for its brilliance and Mediterranean colour, with real virtuosity from the LSO. The 1957 Kingsway Hall recording with its glittering percussion is dazzling in this CD transfer, and only a slight tightness in the upper range of the strings gives a hint that this is not a new recording. The Debussy *Images*, recorded in Geneva the same year, shows the conductor's fine ear for intricate detail, so well etched by the recording; but the response from the SRO has less body of tone than that produced by the LSO. The more familiar Liszt *Piano*

Concertos with Katchen are brilliantly extrovert readings, vividly recorded. The Berlioz *Symphonie fantastique* (stereo) is an individual account, with the balance between reflection and neurosis remarkably well judged. The orchestral playing is impressive and the French brass is full of character. Argenta observes the repeat in the *March to the Scaffold* (for the first time on LP) and the finale is strong on atmosphere as well as drive. What both *Les Préludes* and the *Faust Symphony* lack in the polish of the orchestral playing they more than make up for in character and personality. The mono sound is again excellent. Argenta is again on top form in Albéniz's *Iberia* and Turina's *Danzas fantásticas*, though he characteristically brings out the colour rather than the sensuousness of the music. The 1953 mono sound is sharp and vivid. It is good to have a reminder of the art of Campoli; his account of the Tchaikovsky *Violin Concerto* has always been praised for its combination of technical brilliance and a natural sense of style. The soloist's judicious editing of his part does not interfere with the music's impulse and line and, although this is a personal reading, its natural warmth and spontaneity are appealing. The stereo sound is exceptionally warm and vivid for its date (1956). The *Fourth Symphony*, however, is not on the same adrenalin level, though it is a decent, lusty account, with characterful rather than brilliant playing from the orchestra, and good early stereo sound from 1955.

ARNE, Thomas (1710–78)

8 Overtures (1751); *Overtures*: *Alfred*; *Thomas and Sally*
Chan. 0722. Col. Mus. 90, Standage

Thomas Arne, the composer of *Rule Britannia*, was a highly active composer for the theatre, owing in part to his Catholic religion which precluded him from posts in the church. He had a flair for writing simple, attractive melody, and his set of *Eight Overtures*, published in 1751, was an attempt to broaden his appeal through a series of separate publications. The invention is tuneful and elegant, cosmopolitan in style; they also have a certain eighteenth-century English pastoral spirit which is very refreshing. The two theatre overtures make for equally enjoyable listening, with the Scottish Gavotte of *Thomas and Sally* adding a dash of 'local' colour. Very stylish and alert playing from Simon Standage and Collegium Musicum 90, and the sound is vivid and full. An unexpectedly distinctive and enjoyable collection, easy to live with.

Artaxerxes (English opera: complete)
Ⓜ Hyp. CDD 22073 (2). Robson, Bott, Partridge, Spence, Edgar-Wilson, Hyde, Parley of Instruments, Goodman

Artaxerxes was the first *opera seria* with words in English, and this sparkling, lively performance impressively explains why Arne's opera was such a success when it was first performed at Covent Garden in February 1762, three years after Handel died. One reason for its success was that it provides a splendid challenge to the singers, most of all to the soprano who takes the role of Mandane, sister of Artaxerxes, whose love for Arbaces, her brother's friend, provides a central theme of the libretto, translated from Metastasio. The one number that has latterly become popular – largely thanks to Joan Sutherland's brilliant recording – is 'The soldier tir'd', but that dazzling climactic number is only one of Mandane's formidable solos, whether expressive or vehement. Catherine Bott gives a masterly performance, with the counter-tenor Christopher Robson also impressive in the castrato title-role, and with Ian Partridge pure-toned and incisive in the role of the villain, Artabanes, even if his sweet tenor hardly conveys evil. With the mezzo-soprano Patricia Spence taking the role of Arbaces, the others are first rate too. On two well-filled CDs, the set owes much of its success to the inspired direction of Roy Goodman who, from the overture onwards, electrifies the players and singers, pointing rhythms and aerating textures to bring out the charm as well as the vigour of the writing. The reconstruction of the score – involving the recitatives which were separated from the original – has been capably achieved by Peter Holman, who contributes an effective note. Full texts are included.

ARNOLD, Malcolm (1921–2006)

Anniversary Overture, Op. 99; Beckus the Dandipratt (Comedy Overture), Op. 5; The Fair Field, Op. 110; A Flourish for Orchestra, Op. 112; A Grand Grand Festival Overture, Op. 57; Peterloo Overture, Op. 97; Robert Kett Overture, Op. 141; The Smoke, Op. 21; A Sussex Overture, Op. 31; Tam O'Shanter Overture, Op. 51
Chan. 10293. BBC PO, Rumon Gamba

Arnold was master of the short orchestral form, his *English Dances* being a supreme example. However, he wrote a series of strikingly attractive overtures, which have been gathered together on this mightily impressive Chandos recording. *Beckus the Dandipratt* came first in 1943, possibly something of an uninhibited self-portrait. *Tam O'Shanter* is another flamboyant portrayal, with a spectacular realization of bagpipes at its witty climax. *A Grand Grand Festival Overture* came a year later. The scoring included four vacuum cleaners and a floor polisher. (On the night of its première, they were dispatched by the rifles of a firing squad!) But this is far more than an occasional piece, not least because it has a really good tune. The noisily dramatic *Peterloo* also has one – but then, so have all the other works here. They are marvellously played, with a truly Arnoldian infectious exhilaration, and the Chandos recording is in the demonstration bracket.

(i; ii) *Double Piano Concerto* (three hands); (iii) *English Dances 3 & 5*;
(iv) *Beckus the Dandipratt: Overture*; (i) *Peterloo: Overture*; (v)
Solitaire; *Symphonies*: *1*; (iv) *2*; (i) *5*; (iii) *Tam O'Shanter*
Ⓑ EMI mono/stereo 3 82146-2 (2). (i) CBSO; (ii) Cyril Smith, Phyllis Sellick (piano duo, 3
   hands); (iii) Philh. *o*; (iv) RPO; (v) Bournemouth SO; all cond. composer

Sir Malcolm Arnold was the finest of the twentieth-century English composers
who suffered from the destructive era of atonalism, the weird experimentation
of Stockhausen, and the music of Boulez and his followers, which failed to
communicate with the ordinary music-lover. Melody became unfashionable
and traditional writing, however original, fell completely by the wayside.
Arnold was a natural melodist and musical communicator and, while he survived by writing film scores, his serious works gradually became unfashionable
and absent from the concert hall. But fortunately much of his music has
survived on record (including the remarkable symphonies).

   He was a brilliant advocate of his own works, revealing their emotional
depth but also their passages of electrifying exuberance. *Symphonies 1, 2* and *5*
are just three of the treasures in this superb compilation, which brings together
all the recordings Arnold made for EMI. *Beckus the Dandipratt* is a deliciously
light-hearted characterization hailed as a cross between Strauss's *Till* and
Walton's *Scapino*. *Tam O'Shanter* is another flamboyant portrayal. The *Concerto
for Two Pianos* ends with a delightfully infectious rumba, full of cross-rhythms.
No Arnold collection captures his special magic quite as compellingly as this.

4 Cornish Dances; *8 English Dances, Sets 1 & 2*; *4 Irish Dances*;
4 Scottish Dances; *4 Welsh Dances*
ⒷⒷ Naxos 8.553526. Queensland SO, Penny

This disc was an early Naxos success and enjoys the inclusion of all six sets of
the dances which are among Arnold's most spontaneous and attractive shorter
works. The cheerful, tuneful ebullience of the masterly *English Dances* came
first in 1950–51 and the others followed on, with wide changes of mood to continually capture the ear. The performances have the composer's imprimatur
(he was present at the recording sessions) and can be recommended as an ideal
representation of Arnold's spontaneous orchestral writing.

AUBER, Daniel (1782–1871)

Overtures: *Le Domino noir*; *Le Cheval de bronze*; *Crown Diamonds*;
Fra Diavolo; *Masaniello*
Ⓜ Australian Decca Eloquence (ADD) 480 2385 (2). Paris Conservatoire *o*, Wolff (see also
   under the conductor: **WOLFF, Albert**)

Auber had the knack of writing catchy tunes and he stuffed the best of them into his superbly crafted overtures. Take *The Crown Diamonds*, for example – after a long string cantilena, Auber gives the first section of the Allegro over to brass and woodwind, and a delicious effect his scoring makes. *Fra Diavolo*, with its side-drum introduction followed by a dainty tune on the violins before moving on to the vivacious militaristic aspects of the score, is as enjoyable as any of the overtures by Rossini. Each of these works is hugely enjoyable.

BACH, Carl Philipp Emanuel (1714–88)

Cello Concertos: in A min., Wq.170; in B flat, Wq.171; in A, Wq.172
BIS CD 807. Hidemi Suzuki, Bach Col., Japan

These works show their fine composer at his most inventive. Hidemi Suzuki, who is soloist/director here, is another fine artist from this remarkably talented family, and he creates a dashing flow of energy in the orchestral ritornellos of outer movements; and the Bach Collegium play with great zest and commitment. In slow movements Suzuki's eloquent phrasing, warmth of feeling and breadth of tone are totally compelling, producing a cello line of heart-stopping intensity. The recording is splendid.

(i) Flute Concertos: in D min., Wq.22; in A min., Wq.16; in B flat, Wq.167; in A, Wq. 168; in G, Wq.169. Sonata for solo flute, Wq.132
ⓑⓑ Naxos 8.555715/16. Patrick Gallois, (i) Toronto Camerata, Mallon

Patrick Gallois is a masterly flautist, and he gives a set of superb performances of these fine concertos, written for the court of Frederick the Great and arranged by the composer from works originally featuring the harpsichord as soloist. There is much sparkling vivacity in the Allegros, and the expressive range of the solo instruments, sometimes quite dark in feeling, is fully captured by both Gallois and the Toronto Camerata under Kevin Mallon.

6 Hamburg Sinfonias, Wq. 182/1–6
ⓑⓑ Naxos 8.553285. Capella Istropolitana, Benda

The *Six Hamburg String Sinfonias* are particularly striking in their unexpected twists of imagination, and they contain some of Bach's most inspired and original ideas. Using modern instruments at higher, modern pitch, Benda directs light, well-sprung accounts with extra light and shade. The excellent sound is full and open as well as immediate, and these winning works are well worth exploring.

Keyboard sonatas Wq. 52/4; 59/1; 61/2; 65/17 & 31; 65/32: Andante only Rondos in A. Wq 58/1; in C min, Wq59/4; in D min Wq 61/4.
Ⓜ DG 469 0356 Mikhail Pletnev (piano) (with BEETHOVEN: *Piano Sonata 26 (Les Folieux)*)

Altogether remarkable playing even by Pletnev's exalted standards. He finds both the wit and depth of this music and his resource of keyboard colour and refinement of articulation are pretty awesome. The Beethoven Sonata comes as a digital bonus online.

BACH, Johann Christian (1735-82)

Harpsichord or Clavier Concertos, Opp. 1, 7, 13 & 14 (complete)
Ⓑ CPO 999930-2 (6). Halstead, Hanover Band

Bach's early Berlin concertos (from the 1750s) undoubtedly influenced the young Mozart. These splendid performances from Anthony Halstead directing the Hanover Band from a Broadwood piano are appealingly fluent, full of flair and vitality. Slow movements are deeply expressive and outer movements bustle vigorously. Halstead has recorded Op. 7 in chamber form with just an accompanying string trio. His solo playing is very persuasive and the result is delightfully intimate. Bach's Op. 13 appeared in 1777 and shows him still developing in ideas and orchestration. Op. 14 is more ambitious, although it may have been written earlier. Halstead accompanies himself brightly and gracefully.

6 Sinfonias, Op. 3; 6 Sinfonias, Op. 6; 3 Sinfonias, Op. 8; Sinfonias in C (Venier 46 – 2 versions); *in F* (manuscript); *Sinfonias, Op. 9/1–2* (standard and original versions), *Op.9/3; Sinfonia in E flat with Clarinets; 6 Sinfonias, Op. 18*
Ⓜ CPO 999896-2 (5). Hanover Band, Halstead

Anthony Halstead continues his exploration of J. C. Bach with his *Sinfonias*, which share the same three-part format as the Italian overture, and at the time the descriptive titles were interchangeable. Indeed, as we discover in Opp. 9 and 18, Bach borrowed overtures from his own operas to include in his published sets. The works were initially intended for his London concerts and this is the first complete coverage on period instruments – and very impressive it is.

BACH, Johann Sebastian (1685-1750)

Brandenburg Concertos 1–6, BWV 1046–51; (i) *Harpsichord Concertos 1–7, BWV 1052–8;* (i-ii) *Double Harpsichord Concertos 1–3, BWV 1060–62;* (i-iii) *Triple Harpsichord Concertos 1–2, BWV*

1063–4; (i–iv) *Quadruple Harpsichord Concerto, BWV 1065*; (i; v; vi) *Triple Concerto for Flute, Violin & Harpsichord, BWV 1044*; (vi; vii) *Double Concerto for Oboe & Violin, BWV 1060*; (vii) *Oboe d'amore Concerto, BWV 1055*; (vi) *Violin Concertos 1–2*; (vii–viii) *Double Violin Concerto, BWV 1041–3*; *Orchestral Suites 1–4, BWV 1066–9*

Ⓑ DG 477 9510 (8). English Concert, Trevor Pinnock; with (i) Pinnock; (ii) Kenneth Gilbert; (iii) Lars Ulrik Mortensen; (iv) Nicholas Kraemer; (v) Lisa Beznosiuk; (vi) Simon Standage; (vii) David Reichenberg; (viii) Elizabeth Wilcock

This admirable box collects together, on eight CDs, the English Concert's recordings of Bach, directed by Trevor Pinnock and made in the 1970s and early 1980s, which have dominated the catalogue ever since. Pinnock's *Brandenburg Concertos* represent the peak of his achievement as an advocate of authentic performances, with sounds that are clean and refreshing but not too abrasive. Interpretatively, he adopts faster speeds in outer movements, but is relatively slow in *Andantes*, a style that others have followed since, yet from first to last there is no routine. The soloists are outstanding.

In the solo concertos he plays with real panache, his scholarship tempered by excellent musicianship. Pacing is again brisk but, to today's ears that are used to period performances, the effect is always convincing when the playing is so spontaneous and the sound so bright and clear. The transcribed *Concertos for flute, violin and harpsichord, for oboe and violin* and *for oboe d'amore* are equally persuasive, both vigorous and warm, with consistently resilient rhythms, while the *Violin Concertos* are equally welcome. Rhythms are again crisp and lifted at nicely chosen speeds – not too fast for slow movements – and the solo playing here, led by Simon Standage, is very stylish.

In the *Orchestral Suites* Pinnock improves on his readings of many years earlier, with sound that is rather warmer and string-tone sweeter. In the dance movements of the *Suite No. 2* Lisa Beznosiuk takes her flute solos faster and more brilliantly than her predecessor, Simon Preston, but otherwise speeds are a fraction broader in all four *Suites*, with *Allegros* more jauntily sprung and phrasing a degree more *espressivo*. Above all, the great *Air* of *Suite No. 3* sounds far warmer, persuasively played on multiple violins instead of on a single, acid-toned instrument.

Those hankering after first-class modern-instrument performances of the *Violin Concertos* might add Grumiaux's fine mid-priced analogue disc (Decca 420 700-2) in which he is satisfyingly joined in the *Double Concerto* by Hermann Krebbers and in the *Concerto for Violin and Oboe* by the equally distinguished Heinz Holliger. This is in every way satisfying.

Brandenburg Concertos 1–6, BWV 1046–51

Ⓜ EuroArts Invitation DVD 2050316. Freiburg Bar. O, Von der Gölz

The beautifully handwritten score for Bach's *Brandenburg Concertos* was presented to Christian Ludwig, Margrave of Brandenburg, in 1721, to whom they were dedicated in French. We are not told whether he liked them or not, but they have since become the composer's most familiar and cherished orchestral works. Their design (with stimulating contrasts between the full ensemble and the *concertino* of soloists) shows strong Italian influences, notably that of Vivaldi, and their performance requires considerable virtuosity, notable from the pair of horns in No. 1, the solo trumpet in No. 2, the obbligato harpsichord in No. 5 and the violas and cellos in No. 6.

The very finest of all DVDs of these highly rewarding works is by the Freiburg Baroque Orchestra directed by Gottfried von der Gölz. Visually entrancing, it is appropriately photographed against the magnificently restored Spiegelsaal of the Castle Cöthen, which has an ideally spacious acoustic. The performance itself, on period instruments, is freshly spontaneous in the most appealing way and the imaginative video direction often takes us among the players to create the complete illusion of being present. Tempi are ideally chosen and the performance has great finesse and easy virtuosity. The recording is in the demonstration bracket.

Orchestral Suites Nos. 1–4, BWV 1066/9 (with *alternativements* dances)
Harmonia Mundi HMC 90 2113/14. Freiburg Bar. O, Gottfried von der Goltz

As we have discovered in their outstanding DVD of the *Brandenburgs*, the Freiburg Baroque Orchestra are unsurpassed in this repertoire, their performances consistently stimulating and splendidly recorded. But they also include the *alternativements* dances in all four suites, which gives them a competitive edge over all other versions. This is a key recording, although the sound is a little dry.

Clavier Concertos 1–7, BWV 1052–8; (i) Double Clavier Concertos 1–3, BWV 1060–62; (i-ii) Triple Clavier Concertos 1–2, BWV 1063–4; (iii) Triple Concerto for Flute, Violin & Harpsichord, BWV 1044. Italian Concerto in F, BWV 971
Ⓑ Decca 478 2363 (4). András Schiff (piano), with (i) Peter Serkin (piano); (ii) Canino (piano); (iii) Nicolet (flute), Shiokawa (violin), CO of Europe or Camerata Bern

As is instanced by the performance of the *Italian Concerto*, splendidly articulated and alive, and by his other Bach solo records, Schiff's control of colour and articulation never seeks to present merely a harpsichord imitation, and in the concertos his shaping of Bach's lovely slow movements brings finely sustained lines and a subtle variety of touch. In the composite concertos, joined by Bruno Canino, Aurèle Nicolet and Yuuko Shiokawa – equally fine artists – he and they are just as satisfying. He directs both the Chamber Orchestra of Europe (in the solo concertos) and the Camerata Bern from the keyboard and chooses spirited, uncontroversial tempi for Allegros, at the same time providing decoration that always adds to the joy and sparkle of the music-making. This makes a clear first choice for those who, like us, enjoy Bach on the piano, and the composite concertos are particularly successful, notably BWV 1044.

(Unaccompanied) Cello Suites 1–6, BWV 1007–12
EMI DVD DVA 5 99159-9 (2). Rostropovich

Whether on DVD (filmed against the comparatively severe backcloth of the Basilique Sainte-Madeleine, Vézelay, in France) or on the companion CD version, both of which are included here, Rostropovich's performances are masterly and all-involving, drawing distinctions between each work in his spoken introductions, although one can choose to hear the music without the commentaries. Unsurpassed and unsurpassable. There is also a CD-only set, offered less expensively on EMI 5 18158-2, which is just as welcome.

Unaccompanied Violin Sonatas 1–3, BWV 1001, 1003 & 1005; Violin Partitas 1–3, BWV 1002, 1004 & 1006
Hyp. CDA 67691/2. Alina Ibragimova

The young Russian virtuoso Alina Ibragimova has been making waves for some time, but in these accounts of the Bach solo sonatas and partitas her mastery is very striking indeed. Hers are traditional readings and they pay no homage to the authentic-instrument lobby. She brings a refined, quiet sensitivity to the slow sarabandes of the *First* and *Second Partitas* as well as to the slow openings of the three *Sonatas*, and finds great spirit and incisiveness in the more vigorous movements. There is elegance and character in every single piece. We have a special affection for Grumiaux (Philips 438 736-2) and Milstein (DG 457 702-2) in these works, but this modern version from Hyperion is outstanding in every way.

Goldberg Variations, BWV 988
Sony 696998924322. Perahia (piano)

We are agreed that Murray Perahia's set of the *Goldberg Variations* is uniquely revealing, essentially thoughtful and intimate, often introvert, and with his involvement and dedication present in every bar. The piano recording, too, is wonderfully natural. An obvious first choice. Even so, Rosalyn Tureck's VAI account is very special indeed, with insights all its own. For I.M. it is enormously compelling and would be a desert island choice (VAI VAIA 1029); but Perahia's account is hardly less inspired.

15 2-Part Inventions, BWV 772–86; 15 3-Part Inventions (Sinfonias), BWV 787–801; 6 Little Preludes, BWV 933–8; 6 Little Preludes, BWV 939–43 & 999; 6 Little Preludes from the Clavierbüchlein for Wilhelm Friedemann Bach, BWV 924–31; 3 Fughettas, BWV 952, 953 & 961; Prelude and Fugue, BWV 895; Preludes and Fughettas, BWV 899, 900, & 902a; French Suite 6, BWV 817; Partita 2, BWV 826
Dynamic CDS 629/1-2 (2). Andrea Bacchetti (piano)

Bach's Klaviermusic (including the 2-Part Inventions and the rather more complex 3-Part Sinfonias) was mainly written in Köthen from 1717 to 1723 for Bach's eldest son, Wilhelm Friedmann, and the Sixth French Suite and Second Partita also seem to come from the end of this period. So for Andrea Bacchetti to include them in his survey seems very appropriate, and they are wholly welcome musically. The monothematic Inventions are simply structured and usually brief, but their very simplicity adds to their immediacy of appeal, with changes of style from dance to fugue, from expressive writing to canon. Bacchetti, who has already given us a first-rate DVD of the Goldberg Variations (Arthaus 101447), plays them with spontaneous freshness and plenty of expressive life, and these two discs make very appealing listening. The Inventions are also available, admirably played on the harpsichord, by Masaaki Suzuki (BIS CD 1009), but he does not include the other items, and in any case this simple music makes its mark more readily on the piano.

Partitas 1–6, BWV 825–30
Sony BMG 88697443612 (1, 5 & 6); 88697226952 (2, 3 & 4). Perahia (piano)

Bach's six Partitas appeared one at a time at approximately yearly intervals between 1725 and 1730. He obviously valued them highly for they were the first works he published at his own expense. With the character of French dance movements underlying the writing, they show true mastery of the style français and are as diverting to listen to as they are demanding to play. Murray Peahia is again in his element here. Bach keyboard playing does not come any finer than this. A set of true distinction, most truthfully recorded.

Allabreve in D, BWV 589; Aria in F, BWV 587; Canzona in D min., BWV 588; Canonic Variations on 'Vom Himmel hoch', BWV 769; Chorale Partitas, BWV 766-8, 7; Clavier-Übung (Prelude & Fugue in E flat, BWV 552/1-2 & Chorale settings, BWV 669-89; 4 Duets, BWV 802-5); Concertos for organ solo, BWV 592; (after Vivaldi), BWV 593, 594 & 596; (after Ernst, Prince of Sachen-Weimar), BWV 592. Fantasia, BWV 562; BWV 563 (con imitazione); BWV 570; BWV 572; Fantasia and Fugue, BWV 537 & BWV 542; Fugue on a theme by Giovanni Legrenzi, BWV 574; Fugues, BWV 575, 577-8; Fugue on a theme of Corelli, BWV 579; Orgelbüchlein: Chorales BWV 599-644; Kirnberger Chorales, BWV 691-713 & Chorale settings, BWV 714-41 & BWV 753; 764, BWV AnH. ll/55 & without BWV number. 18 Leipzig Chorales, BWV 651-68; 6 Schübler Chorales, BWV 645-50; 18 Chorales of diverse kinds, BWV 659-67; Passacaglia & Fugue in C minor, BWV 582; Pastorale, BWV 590; Pedal-Exercitium, BWV 598; Preludes, BWV 568; 569 (con organo pleno); Preludes & Fugues, BWV 531-46; 543; 551; 535a; Toccatas and Fugues (Dorian), BWV 538; 540; in D min., BWV 565; BWV 566; Toccata, Adagio & Fugue,

BWV 564; Trio Sonatas 1–6 BWV 525–30; Trios, BWV 583 & BWV 586

ⓑ DG 477 8628 (14). Simon Preston (various organs)

Simon Preston's survey was recorded digitally over more than a decade, from 1987 onwards, beginning with the solo *Concertos*. The performances which set the standard for the whole series are first class in every way and the recording of the various organs (from Lübeck Cathedral, Tonbridge School, Kent, St Peter's Waltrop, Saint John's, Smith Square, Klosterkirke, Sora, Trinity College, Cambridge, Nidaros Domkirke, Trondheim, among others) is admirably clear, yet with an attractive ambient resonance. Preston revels in the extrovert brilliance of the early Weimar *Preludes and Fugues* (and indeed also the flamboyant *Toccatas*) with their virtuoso use of pedals; but he also relishes the more tightly structured works, which he plays with genuine panache. Another highlight of the series is the (1993) set of *Trio Sonatas* on the first disc, recorded on the Klais organ at St Katharina, Blankenburg (near Bonn). Some of the repertoire has been recorded on separate discs, including a few works omitted here, such as the *8 Little Preludes and Fugues* which are wrongly attributed to Bach. But apart from these few omissions the whole set now reappears in a DG bargain box, with the various genres sensibly grouped together. The performances are consistently alive and distinguished and the choice of organs ear-tinglingly perceptive. The reissued box includes a new analysis of the music by Dorotheas Schröder.

A generous and well chosen 146-minute collection of major Bach organ works taken from Peter Hurford's alternative cornerstone Decca survey on 17 discs (444 410-2) makes a recommendable alternative choice. This selection, devised for the general collector, brings two separate recitals, each framed by major concert pieces, with beautifully played chorales used in between the large-scale works to add contrast. The analogue recordings are splendidly remastered.

Complete Cantatas: ongoing BIS Masaaki Suzuki Series with Japan Bach Collegium (also Concerto Palatino), Masaaki Suzuki; Volumes 1–47 (Soloists include: Kurisu, Tachikawa, Kantano, Kooy, M. Suzuki, Yanagisawa, Mera, Türk, Sakurada, Schmithüsen, Frimmer, Blaze, Urano, Persson, Wessel, Nonoshita, Sollek-Avella, Kupfer, MacLeod, Hatano, Gilchrist, Kobow, Hida, Taylor, Kenworthy-Brown, Rydén, Bertin, Mields, Sampson, Weller, Kobow, Wörner, Blažíková, Nicholls).

Vol. 1: *Cantatas BWV 4*; *150*; *196* (BIS CD 751); Vol. 2: *BWV 71*; *106*; *131* (BIS CD 781); Vol. 3: *BWV 12*; *54*; *162*; *182* (BIS CD 791); Vol. 4: *BWV 163*; *165*; *185*; *199* (BIS CD 801); Vol. 5: *BWV 18*; *143*; *152*; *155*; *161* (BIS CD 841); Vol. 6: *BWV 21* (with alternative movements); *31* (BIS CD 851); Vol. 7: *BWV 61*; *63*; *132*; *172* (BIS CD 881); Vol. 8: *BWV 22*; *23*; *75* (BIS CD 901); Vol. 9: *BWV 24*; *76*; *167* (BIS CD 931); Vol. 10: *BWV 105*; *179*;

186 (BIS CD 951); Vol. 11: *BWV 46*; *95*; *136*; *138* (BIS CD 991); Vol. 12: *BWV 21*; *147* (BIS CD 1031); Vol. 13: *BWV 25*; *50*; *64*; *69a*; *77* (BIS CD 1041); Vol. 14: *BWV 48*; *89*; *109*; *148* (BIS CD 1081); Vol. 15: *BWV 40*; *60*; *70*; *90* (BIS CD 1111); Vol. 16: *BWV 119*; *194* (BIS CD 1131); Vol. 17: *BWV 73*; *144*; *153*; *154*; *181* (BIS CD 1221); Vol. 18: *BWV 66*; *67*; *134* (BIS CD 1251); Vol. 19: *BWV 37*; *86*; *104*; *166* (BIS CD 1261); Vol. 20: *BWV 44*; *59*; *173*; *184* (BIS CD 1271); Vol. 21: *BWV 65*; *81*; *83*; *190* (BIS CD 1311); Vol. 22: *BWV 7*; *20*; *94* (BIS CD 1321); Vol. 23: *BWV 10*; *93*; *107*; *178* (BIS CD 1331); Vol. 24: *BWV 8*; *33*; *113* (BIS CD 1351); Vol. 25: *BWV 78*; *99*; *114* (BIS CD 1361); Vol. 26: *BWV 96*; *122*; *180* (BIS CD 1401); Vol. 27: *BWV 5*; *80*; *115* (BIS CD 1421); Vol. 28: *BWV 26*; *62*; *116*; *139* (BIS SACD 1451); Vol. 29: *BWV 2*; *3*; *38*; *135* (BIS SACD 1461); Vol. 30: *BWV 51*; *1127* (BIS SACD 1471); Vol. 31: *Cantatas BWV 91*; *101*; *121*; *133* (BIS SACD 1481); Vol. 32: *BWV 111*; *123*; *124*; *125* (BIS SACD 1501); Vol. 33: *BWV 41*; *92*; *130* (BIS SACD 1541); Vol. 34: *BWV 1*; *126*; *127* (BIS SACD 1551); Vol. 35: *BWV 74*; *87*; *128*; *176* (BIS SACD 1571); Vol. 36: *BWV 6*; *42*; *103*; *108* (BIS SACD 1611); Vol. 37: *BWV 35*; *169*; *170*; *200* (BIS SACD 1621); Vol. 38: *BWV 52*; *55*; *58*; *82* (BIS SACD 1631); Vol. 39: *BWV 28*; *68*; *85*; *175*; *183* (BIS SACD 1641); Vol. 40: *BWV 79*; *137*; *164*; *168* (BIS SACD 1671); Vol. 41: *BWV 56*; *82*; *84*; *158* (BIS SACD 1691); Vol. 42: *BWV 13*; *16*; *32*; *72* (BIS SACD 1711); Vol. 43: *BWV 57*; *110*; *151* (BIS SACD 1761); Vol. 44: *BWV 43*; *88*; *146* (BIS SACD 1791); Vol. 45: *BWV 39*; *129*; *187*; *Sinfonia in D, BWV 1045* (BIS SACD 1801); Vol. 46: *BWV 17*; *19*; *45*; *102* (BIS SACD 1851); Vol. 47: *BWV 27* (with appendix); *36*; *47* (BIS SACD 1861); Vol. 48: *BWV 34*; *98*; *117*; *120* (BIS SACD 1881); Vol. 49: *BWV 156*; *159*; *171*; *188* (BIS SACD 1891); Vol. 50: *BWV 49*; *145*; *149*; *174* (BIS SACD 1941); *Secular Cantatas, BWV 210 (Wedding)*; *211 (Coffee)* (BIS CD 1411); *Christmas Oratorio, BWV 248* (BIS 941/2)

Ⓑ BIS CD 9030/32 Volumes 21–30 (Limited Edition)

Bach's more than two hundred cantatas were among his most amazing achievements, especially when one remembers that he actually composed about 300 in all, and the remainder are lost. Although some of Bach's earliest cantatas date from before he became court organist at Weimar in 1708, most of the surviving cantatas were composed during two inspired periods, between 1713 and 1716 in Weimar (where he was expected to provide a new work every month), and between 1723 and 1729 in Leipzig. At Cöthen, between 1717–23, cantatas were not required but, once established at Leipzig, he wrote five annual cycles (for use during all the Sundays and Festivals of the liturgical year) at the almost incredible rate of one a week. The first two *Jahrgang* (volumes) of 1724 and 1725 have come down to us nearly complete, but many works from the remaining three are, alas, no longer preserved.

All these cantatas are of the highest musical quality and many show Bach at

his most inspired. Their formal design is simple, usually framed by two choruses, with solo movements at the centre plus a central chorale. The Weimar
cantatas are more adventurous in style, often including recitative and arias,
with a *da capo* return to the opening section. The imaginative reader might picture his many sons gathered round the composer during the week, helping to
copy out the solo vocal, choral, instrumental and continuo parts ready for
the forthcoming weekend's rehearsal and performance.

There are about five recorded surveys of this richly rewarding repertoire,
three of them still in progress; but, to our minds, Suzuki's BIS series with the
Japan Collegium stands as a clear first choice and one of the gramophone's
greatest achievements, offering performances of total conviction and consummate artistry. They are certainly among the finest ever, radiating freshness, and
their vitality is matched by a wonderfully rich and present recording, which in
the later volumes, with the addition of the surround sound of SACD, is very
realistic indeed; one has the feeling of sitting in the auditorium where the
performances are taking place. Played back through ordinary CD equipment,
the effect is hardly less impressive. With Carolyn Sampson, Robin Blaze and
Yukari Nonoshita, among others, joining the soloists once the series got well
under way, the quality of the solo singing, and indeed of the instrumental
obbligati, seems unsurpassable.

Suzuki is proceeding chronologically, using a higher pitch (A = 465), with its
concomitant brighter sound, which is especially effective against the warmly
expansive background acoustic. The strings are clean yet have bloom, and the
sense of inhibition – of excessive awareness of the constraints of period performance – is refreshingly absent here. The set which comes, CD by CD, with
texts and translations included, is fully documented, and the BIS recordings
are altogether exemplary. The CDs, all available separately, are in the premium
price range. It will probably be two more years before the set is complete, so we
suggest collectors interested in collecting this wonderful music should simply
explore the individual issues, any one of which is worthy for inclusion in our
1,000 finest recordings. The celebrated *Christmas Oratorio* (also available separately) is in essence a special collection of six linked cantatas, in which Bach drew
on earlier music. It was written for Christmas in Leipzig in 1734-5, performed
over six feast days from Christmas Day to Epiphany (6th January). Suzuki's
performance is a joyfully alive reading, with good soloists and a first-class choral
contribution.

Cantatas (i) *82*; (i–iii) *159*; (ii) *170*
Ⓜ Decca Australian Eloquence (ADD) 476 2684. ASMF, Marriner, with (i) Shirley-Quirk;
   (ii) Baker; (iii) Tear

Classic accounts of three cantatas, including *Sehet, wir gehn hinauf gen Jerusalem* (BWV 159) – one of Bach's most inspired works. Particularly glorious is the
meditation, *Es ist vollbracht* ('It is finished'), with its poignant oboe obbligato

(played by Roger Lord). Both Dame Janet Baker and John Shirley-Quirk are in marvellous voice, as they are in Nos. 82 and 170 – hardly less inspired works and performances. Indeed, this group of cantatas ought to be in every collection, and the recordings (mid-1960s) are of Decca's best vintage quality.

Mass in B min., BWV 232 (DVD version)

Virgin DVD 0094637063699. Ziesak, DiDonato, Taylor, Agnew, Henschel, Maîtrise
Notre-Dame de Paris, O Ens. de Paris, Nelson

Mass in B min., BWV 232 (CD version)

DG 415 514-2 (2). Argenta, Dawson, Fairfield, Knibbs, Kwella, Hall, Nichols, Chance,
Collin, Stafford, Evans, Milner, Murgatroyd, Lloyd Morgan, Varcoe, Monteverdi Ch., E.
Bar. Sol., Gardiner

John Nelson gives Bach's great Mass a highly distinguished DVD début, with a deeply expressive performance, full of life. His soloists, including Daniel Taylor and Joyce DiDonato, are all first rate. Ruth Ziesak sings radiantly and her duet with DiDonato in the *Kyrie* is an early highlight. The choral group is dominated by the female voices, but the singing in the *Gloria, Sanctus*, and notably the *Osanna* is thrilling. Nelson's tempi cannot be faulted, and the performance moves forward spontaneously to its richly satisfying closing *Dona nobis pacem*. The authentic-sized orchestra achieves a compromise, playing modern French instruments, and Olivier Simonnet's video coverage is fully worthy of the performance.

On CD, John Eliot Gardiner gives a magnificent account of the *B minor Mass*, one which attempts to keep within an authentic scale, but which also triumphantly encompasses the work's grandeur. Gardiner masterfully conveys the majesty (with bells and censer-swinging evoked) simultaneously with a crisply resilient rhythmic pulse. The choral tone is luminous and powerfully projected. The regular solo numbers are taken by choir members, making a cohesive whole. The recording is warmly atmospheric, but not cloudy.

Motets: Singet dem Herrn ein neues Lied, BWV 225; Der Geist hilft unser Schwachheit auf, BWV 226; Jesu, meine Freude, BWV 227; Fürchte dich nicht, ich bin bei dir, BWV 228; Komm, Jesu, Komm!, BWV 229; Lobet den Herrn, alle Heiden, BWV 230; O Jesu Christ, mein Lebens Licht, BWV 118; Ich lasse dich nicht, du segnest mich den, BWV Anh. 159

BIS SACD 1841. Nonoshita, Matsui, Guillon, Mizukoshi, Bach Col. Japan, Masaaki Suzuki

Bach's *Motets*, which include some of the greatest music he ever wrote for chorus, have previously been recommended by us in a fine performance by the Stockholm Bach Choir under Harnoncourt. This is one of his best CDs and, beautifully recorded, it is still worth exploring at mid-price (Teldec 0630 17430-2). But the newest collection from Japan is finer still, and it includes also

Ich lasse dich nicht, du segnest mich den, BWV Anh. 159 (which was only partly written by Bach, but includes richly complex polyphony which is most appealing) and the sonorous *O Jesu Christ, mein Lebens Licht*, lavishly scored, alternatively for strings and brass, so making a resonantly sonorous close to the collection. The familiar motets are memorable too, the opening *Singet dem Herrn* particularly fresh, and *Jesu, meine Freude* strikingly beautiful. So is the recording, particularly fine using surround sound in the Kobe Shoin Women's University Chapel in Japan.

St John Passion, BWV 245

TDK DVD DV-BAJPN. Türk, Midori Suzuki, Blaze, Urano, MacLeod, Bach Col. Japan, Masaaki Suzuki

Recorded in Suntory Hall, Tokyo, on 28 July 2000 – the day marking the 250th anniversary of Bach's death – this is an outstanding version on DVD of the *St John Passion*, another tribute to the work of Masaaki Suzuki in Japan. In a brief interview which comes as a supplement, he comments on the intensive training in period performance he undertook in Holland, and this performance consistently demonstrates the vigour and sensitivity of his approach to Bach. The interpretation remains very similar to Suzuki's earlier CD account on BIS, with fresh, light textures and generally brisk speeds, which yet allow for depth of feeling; and the sense of occasion is irresistible. Only Gerd Türk as the Evangelist is presented as a soloist in front of the choir, giving an achingly beautiful performance, with his profound involvement all the more evident when seen as well as heard. Türk also sings the tenor roles, and the other soloists, all first rate, also have double roles, singing in the sixteen-strong choir (4-4-4-4) before stepping forward when needed as soloists, Stephen MacLeod singing Christus as well as the bass arias, Chiyuki Urano singing Pilate and other incidental solos, Robin Blaze a superb soloist, and the ravishing Midori Suzuki in the two soprano arias.

St Matthew Passion, BWV 244 (CD version)

Ⓜ Decca 478 2194 (2). Johannes Chum, Hanno Müller-Brachmann, Christina Landshamer, Marie-Claude Chappuis, Maximilian Schmitt, Thomas Quasthof, Klaus Häger, Leipzig Thomanerchor, Tölz Boys' Ch., Leipzig GO, Chailly

Riccardo Chailly's glorious new live account of the *St Matthew Passion*, recorded in the ideal acoustic of the Leipzig Gewandhaus in 2009, is very recommendable indeed. The balance is excellent, as is immediately shown in the opening double chorus, which has striking but not exaggerated antiphonal separation, and there is an ideally wide range of dynamic between soloists and chorus, so the effect is very real, with a fine bloom on the solo voices. Indeed the soloists sing very beautifully, with Johannes Chum's dedicated Evangelist standing out. The two great arias in Part II, Marie-Claude Chappuis's *Erbarme dich* and Christina Landshamer's *Aus Liebe will mein Heiland sterben* (with its

delicately played obbligato acompaniment for flute and two oboes da caccia)
are movingly beautiful, as indeed are the chorales. Chailly's pacing is freshly
resilient and the refined orchestral playing often has the lightest touch.

Chorale Preludes: *Ein' feste Burg ist unser Gott; Komm, süsser Tod;*
Mein Jesu, was vor Seelenweh. Christmas Oratorio: Sinfonia.
English Suite 2 in A min., BWV 807: Bourrée. Fugue in G min.,
BWV 578 (Little Fugue); Orchestral Suite 3 in D, BWV 1068:
Air on the G String. Passacaglia and Fugue in C min., BWV 582;
Toccata and Fugue in D min., BWV 565; Violin Partitas: 1 in B
min., BWV 1002: Sarabande; 3 in E, BWV 1006: Preludio
(with Bonus DVD: **DEBUSSY**: *Prélude à l'après-midi d'un faune*)
Ⓜ EMI Legend (ADD) 557758. Symphony O, Stokowski

Stokowski was a conducting phenomenon. Perhaps his very showmanship has
in the past overshadowed his reputation as a 'great' conductor, but great he
certainly was. He moulded his orchestras into the sound he wanted and created great warmth and tension in the strings. The results were often electrifying.
In these times, when so-called 'authenticity' is paramount, his arrangements
of Bach are the antithesis of modern orchestral practice but, taken on their
own terms, they remain just as valid and enjoyable as ever, with one marvelling
anew at the sheer richness of sound Stokowski created. The American (Capitol)
late-1950s recordings of Bach arrangements have tended to be overshadowed
by his later, more flamboyant, Decca Phase Four recordings (now, alas, deleted).
The earliest versions here were made in 1957, and if the sound, understandably, displays a degree of thinness, it is still remarkably warm and well balanced,
and certainly impressive for its time. Stokowski's brand of lyricism is apparent
throughout, with the conductor clearly wallowing in the sheer richness of
sound he creates in the quiet numbers (which predominate). They may be
inauthentic but are often very moving. The *Chorale Preludes* are played with
great intensity, while in the obvious show-pieces, such as the *D minor Toccata*
and Fugue and the *Passacaglia*, with their splashes of romantic colour, plenty
of electricity is generated. As a DVD bonus we are offered the 1972 film of
Debussy's *Prélude à l'après-midi d'un faune*, recorded at the Royal Festival Hall,
in which Stokowski is a joy to watch – marvellously intense and magical.

'Johann, I'm only Dancing': *Brandenburg Concerto 3, BWV*
1048; Harpsichord Concerto in F min., BWV 1056: Arioso. Double
Violin Concerto in D min., BWV 1043: Largo. (Orchestral) Suite 2
in B min., BWV 1067: Minuet & Badinerie. Cello Suite 6, BWV
1012: Prelude in D. English Suite 3 in A min., BWV 807: Bourrée.
Sarabande. Flute Sonatas: in A, BWV 1032: Largo e Dolce; in C,
BWV 1033: Allegro; in E min., BWV 1034: Andante. Harpsichord
Prelude in G min., BWV 885. Oboe Sonata in G min. BWV 1020;

Prelude & Fugue in C min., BWV 847. Toccata in D, BWV 1012.
Toccata and Fugue in D min., BWV 565; Violin Partita in E, BWV
1006: Prelude
Red Priest Recordings RP 007. Red Priest (Piers Adams (recorders); Julia Bishop (violin);
Angela East (cello); Howard Beach (harpsichord))

A brilliantly and affectingly different collection of transcriptions of favourite
Bach movements, at times uniquely exhilarating, at others showing Bach at his
most expressively touching, as in the lovely *Arioso* from BWV 1056, the slow
movement of the transcribed *Double Violin Concerto* and Howard Beach's
delicate solo harpsichord contributions. Piers Adams's recorder playing is
musically dazzling (the *Badinerie* from the *Second Orchestral Suite* is uniquely
virtuosic) but the other players complete an ensemble which is delightfully
fresh and alive, and most effectively balanced. The sleeve-picture might suggest that the group are jazzing up Bach, but they certainly don't do that; instead
they make his music come to life and communicate with wonderful freshness.
The recording is admirably vivid and present.

BAKER, Janet (mezzo)

'The Beloved Mezzo': **BRAHMS**: *Alto Rhapsody* (with John
Alldis Choir). **WAGNER**: *Wesendonck-Lieder*. **R. STRAUSS**:
Liebeshymnus; *Das Rosenband*; *Ruhe, meine Seele*; *Muttertändelei*
(with LPO, Boult). **ELGAR**: *Sea Pictures* (with LSO). *Dream of*
Gerontius: Angel's Farewell (with Choirs, Hallé O). **BERLIOZ**: *Nuits*
d'été. **RAVEL**: *Shéhérazade* (with New Philh. O; all cond. Barbirolli).
CHAUSSON: *Poème de l'amour et de la mer* (with LSO, Previn).
MAHLER: *Kindertotenlieder*; *5 Rückert-Lieder*; *Lieder eines*
fahrenden Gesellen (with Hallé O or New Philh. O, Barbirolli); *Symphony*
2: Urlicht (with CBSO, Rattle). **HANDEL**: *Messiah: He was despised*
(with ECO, Mackerras). *Ah! Crudel nel pianto mio, HWV 478*; *Armida*
abbandonata, HWV 105 (with ECO, Leppard). **BACH**: *Cantata 82,*
Ich habe genug: Schlummert ein (with Bath Festival O, Y. Menuhin);
Christmas Oratorio: Bereite dich, Zion. St John Passion: Es ist
vollbracht. Bist du bei mir (with ASMF, Marriner). Early English Songs:
DOWLAND: *Come again, sweet love*. **CAMPION**: *Never love*
again unless you can; *Oft have I sighed*; *If thou longst so much to*
learn; *Fain would I wed* (with Robert Spencer, lute). **PURCELL**:
Sleep, Adam, sleep; *Lord what is man*. **BOYCE**: *Tell me, lovely*
shepherd. **MONRO**: *My lovely Celia*. **ARNE**: *Where the bee sucks*
(with Martin Isepp (harpsichord), Ambrose Gauntlett (viola da gamba)). Lieder:
SCHUBERT: *Gretchen am Spinnrade* (with Gerald Moore (piano));

*Heidenröslein; An die Musik; Die Forelle; Auf dem Wasser
zu singen; Du bist die Ruh; Nacht und Träume; An Sylvia.*
MENDELSSOHN: *Neue Liebe; Auf Flügeln des Gesanges;
Nachtlied.* **LISZT**: *Lorelei; Über allen Gipfeln ist Ruh* (with
Geoffrey Parsons (piano)). **SCHUMANN**: *Frauenliebe und -Leben,
Op. 42* (with Daniel Barenboim (piano))
ⓑ EMI (ADD) 2 08087-2 (5)

Indeed Janet Baker was one of the most loved English singers of our time and
this admirable anthology covers her key recordings between 1965 and 1980,
with the voice staying ever fresh. She had a remarkable communicative ability.
As John Steane comments in the booklet which accompanies this set: 'For
those who heard her "in the flesh" the voice commanded immediate attention.
If you happened to be looking down at your programme, with the first sung
notes you looked up. She had a way of so directing the voice that everybody felt
she was singing for them. And she was lucky in being one of those whose
recordings preserve a true reflection.'

Whether in English, French or German song, she felt the idiom naturally
but there was also a special feeling for Mahler, encouraged by her association
with Barbirolli. But others formed serendipitous musical partnerships with
her, not least Sir Adrian Boult, whose account of Brahms's *Alto Rhapsody* opens
this programme arrestingly. She closes with Lieder, the intimacy of which
found a special place in her heart, especially when singing with her favourite
accompanist, Geoffrey Parsons. Indeed this is a treasurable set, and one can
only feel a little disappointed by EMI's decision not to include translations.

BAKER, Janet, with the Melos Ensemble of London

'French Songs': **RAVEL**: *Trois poèmes de Stéphane Mallarmé;
Chansons Medécasses.* **CHAUSSON**: *Chanson perpétuelle,
Op. 37.* **DELAGE**: *Quatre poèmes hindous*
Ⓜ Australian Decca Eloquence (ADD) 480 3670

A classic disc if ever there was one. This beautiful recital was made in 1966 and
sounds as fresh today as the day it was made. Chausson's cycle of a deserted
lover has a direct communication, which Janet Baker contrasts with the subtler
beauties of the Ravel songs. She shows great depth of feeling for the poetry
here, and an equally evocative sensitivity to the songs about India written by
Ravel's pupil, Maurice Delage, in 1912. The superb playing from the Melos
group adds much to the pleasure of this recording, with the exquisite instrumental writing which is such a part of this repertoire brought out with both
vividness and delicacy, helped by vintage Decca sound. This may be placed
among Janet Baker's most outstanding recordings.

BANTOCK, Granville (1868-1946)

Caristiona; *A Celtic Symphony*; *Cuchullan's Lament*; *The Cyprian Goddess (Symphony 3)*; *Dante and Beatrice*; *Fifine at the Fair*; *Hebridean Symphony*; *Helena Variations*; *Kishmul's Galley*; *Omar Khayyám: Prelude & Camel Caravan*; *Overture to a Greek Tragedy*; *Pagan Symphony*; *Pierrot of the Minute*; *Processional*; *Sapphic Poem for Cello & Orchestra*; *Sappho*; *The Sea Reivers*; *Song of Songs (Prelude & extracts)*; *Thalaba the Destroyer*; *The Wilderness and the Solitary Place*; *The Witch of Atlas*
Hyp. CDS 44281/6 (6). Lloyd Webber; Bickley; Connell; Begley; RPO (with Ch.), Handley

Between 1990 and 2003 Vernon Handley recorded all the principal orchestral works of Bantock (although the complete *Omar Khayyám* had to wait until 2006/7 and now appears on Chandos CHSA 5051 (3)). It was a considerable achievement, revealing Bantock as a major figure in English music in the late nineteenth and early twentieth century. Handley is a dedicated advocate and the standard of performances and recordings in this box is very high indeed. If you have not already invested in this rewarding composer, Hyperion's box (with the sirens visually enticing on the front cover) offers a chance to respond to their allure, with a promise of many rewards from this often sumptuously scored and consistently inventive music.

BARBER, Samuel (1910-81)

Complete Orchestral Works (as below)
⓫ Naxos 8.506021 (6). Soloists, RSNO, Marin Alsop

Adagio for Strings; (i) *Cello Concerto, Op. 22*. *Medea* (ballet suite), *Op. 23*
⓫ Naxos 8.559088. RSNO, Alsop; (i) with Wendy Warner

(i) *Canzonetta for Oboe & Strings*; (i-ii) *Capricorn Concerto*. *Fadograph of a Yestern Scene*; *Mutations from Bach*; (iii) *A Hand of Bridge* (opera). *Vanessa* (opera): *Intermezzo*
⓫ Naxos 8.559135. RSNO, Alsop; with (i) Stéphane Rancourt; (ii) John Gracie, Karen Jones; (iii) Lesley Craigie, Louise Winter, Simon Wall, Roderick Williams

(i) *Piano Concerto*. *Commando March*; *Die Natali, Op. 37*; *Medea's Meditation and Dance of Vengeance*
⓫ Naxos 8.559133. RSNO, Alsop; (i) with Steven Prutsman

(i) *Violin Concerto*. *Music for a Scene from Shelley, Op. 7*; *Serenade for Strings, Op. 1*; *Souvenirs* (ballet suite), *Op. 28*
⓫ Naxos 8.559044. RSNO, Alsop; (i) with James Buswell

First Essay for Orchestra, Op. 12; **The School for Scandal Overture,**
Op. 5; *Symphonies 1, Op. 9*; *2, Op. 19*
ⓑ Naxos 8.559024. RSNO, Alsop

Second Essay for Orchestra, Op. 17; **Third Essay for Orchestra,**
Op. 47; (i) *Toccata Festiva for Organ & Orchestra, Op. 36*;
(ii) **Knoxville: Summer of 1915, Op. 24**
ⓑ Naxos 8.559134. RSNO, Alsop; with (i) Thomas Trotter; (ii) Karina Gauvin

This is among Marin Alsop's finest achievements to date, among her many
other impressive recordings, and this box can hardly be recommended too
highly. Barber's *Cello Concerto* of 1945 is more elusive than his *Violin Concerto*
but Wendy Warner concentrates on its sometimes wry lyricism, and she articulates with brilliant point in the gentle scherzando passage of the finale. Alsop
is a persuasive partner, relishing the often plangent orchestral backcloth and
securing a splendidly committed response from the Scottish players, both here
and in the often astringent score for *Medea*. The selection is generous, with the
atmospheric central portrait of Medea herself and her dance of vengeance
made the final point of the score. The famous *Adagio for Strings* then becomes
essentially an elegy, but reaches a passionate climax.

The neoclassical *Capricorn Concerto*, which takes its name from the house
that Barber and Menotti shared, is a relative rarity, but this Scottish account is
in every way appealing. The *Canzonetta* was left in short score on Barber's
death, but this arrangement with strings is expertly done, and the piece is as
moving as the very best of Barber. The *Fadograph of a Yestern Scene* is another
rarity, a ruminative and reflective score with a strong vein of melancholy to
sustain it. The witty ten-minute opera, *A Hand of Bridge*, which Barber wrote
for Menotti's festival at Spoleto, also comes off well. In short, this is a most
pleasurable disc and repays repeated listening.

Stephen Prutsman gives a powerful reading of Barber's formidable *Piano
Concerto*, fully in command of the bravura writing of the outer movements and
tenderly expressive in the central *Canzonetta*. Again with Marin Alsop a most
sympathetic Barber interpreter, the *Concerto* is effectively supplemented by the
well-known concert work drawn from the *Medea* ballet, the genial and colourful fantasia on Christmas carols, *Die Natali*, written at the same period as the
Concerto in memory of Serge and Natalie Koussevitzky, and the wartime *Commando March*.

Marin Alsop then backs up the masterly *Violin Concerto* with the witty and
delightfully parodic ballet, *Souvenirs*, and two early works, the evocative *Scene
from Shelley* and a long-neglected three-movement *Serenade*, which is based on
a string quartet written when Barber was nineteen and which anticipates the
Adagio for Strings. James Buswell is a refined, sensitive soloist in the *Concerto*,
warm without being soupy, if not quite as individual as Ehnes in his vintage
version with Tovey.

In the fifth Naxos collection, the two *Symphonies* are played by the Scottish orchestra with passionate commitment and deep lyrical feeling. The account of the complete *Second Symphony* will surely confirm the reputation of a wartime work which the composer partly withdrew in despondency after its neglect. The *First Essay for Orchestra* also generates a powerful atmosphere when played with such depth of expression, helped by the spectacular recording.

Marin Alsop's final outstanding collection gathers together a most attractive group of works, including one of the most popular of all, the evocative setting of a prose poem by James Agee, *Knoxville: Summer of 1915*, with the Canadian soprano Karina Gauvin as the opulent soloist. The voice is so rich that the diction is not as clear as it might be, but happily the booklet provides the full text. Alsop's reading brings out the contrasts between the different sections more sharply than usual; similarly, in both of the *Essays* (No. 3 a late work, written in 1976) she highlights contrasts to bring out the feeling in each of these compressed symphonic structures. The *Toccata Festiva* for organ and orchestra, written for the unveiling of a new organ for the Philadelphia Orchestra, is an exuberant piece that brings the widest expressive range in the organ part and, with the orchestral contribution colourful too, the work (surprisingly) is a great rarity on disc. But, like the whole six-disc collection, it is superbly played and recorded.

Adagio for Strings, Op. 11

Ⓜ Decca (ADD) 475 8237. ASMF, Marriner (with **COWELL**: *Hymn and Fuguing Tune;* **CRESTON**: *Rumour;* **COPLAND**: *Quiet City;* **IVES**: *Symphony 3*)

Americans have now adopted Barber's *Adagio* (a transcription of the slow movement of a string quartet) as their equivalent to Elgar's *Nimrod* favoured by listeners on this side of the Atlantic. Marriner's nobly restrained performance with the ASMF, which dates back to 1976, is still unsurpassed. Its climax is absolutely gripping and the remastered Argo recording shows just how good Decca string-sound was in the mid-1970s. The couplings are as attractive as they are imaginative, and this splendid anthology shows five twentieth-century American composers all on top form.

Violin Concerto, Op. 14

Onyx 4016. Ehnes, Vancouver SO, Tovey – **KORNGOLD**; **WALTON**: *Violin Concertos*

Barber's *Violin Concerto* grows in stature with every hearing, and the young Canadian violinist James Ehnes proves an ardent and committed advocate, mirrored by Bramwell Tovey's glowing partnership, particularly in the lyrical, beautiful slow movement, which has exquisite delicacy of feeling. It is an inspired coupling, as well as a generous one, having the Barber alongside two other high-romantic concertos together. Ehnes gives superb performances of all three, bringing out their full emotional thrust without vulgarity or exaggeration. An altogether indispensable CD.

Vanessa (complete)

Ⓜ RCA (ADD) 88697446172 (2). Eleanor Steber, Nicolai Gedda, Rosalind Elias, Regina Resnik, Giorgio Tozzi, Met. Op. O, Mitropoulos

Vanessa inhabits much the same civilized world as Strauss or Henry James. Although it has not held the stage, its melodic freshness and warmth will ensure a reversal of its fortunes some day. This recording was made at the time of its first performance in 1958, but no apologies are needed for its quality; it stands the test of time as well as does the opera itself, and this reissue is well worth seeking out.

BARBIROLLI, Sir John, with various orchestras

IRELAND: *A London Overture* (with LSO). **VAUGHAN WILLIAMS**: *Fantasia on 'Greensleeves'*; *Fantasia on a Theme by Thomas Tallis* (with Sinfonia of London); *Symphonies: 2 (London)* (with Hallé O); *5 in D* (with Philh. O). **BAX**: *The Garden of Fand* (with Hallé O); *Tintagel*. **DELIUS**: *The Walk to Paradise Garden* (with LSO); *In a Summer Garden*. **BUTTERWORTH**: *A Shropshire Lad*. **SIBELIUS**: *Finlandia*; *Karelia Suite*; *Pohjola's Daughter*; *The Swan of Tuonela*; *Valse triste* (with Hallé O). **ELGAR**: *Cello Concerto* (with Navarra, Hallé O); *Enigma Variations* (with Philh. O); *Introduction and Allegro* (with Allegri String Qt, Sinfonia of London); *Sea Pictures* (with Baker, LSO); *Serenade in E min., Op. 20* (with Sinfonia of London); *Elegy*; *Sospiri* (with New Philh. O); *Symphony 1* (with Philh. O). **MAHLER**: *5 Rückert-Lieder* (with Baker, New Philh. O); *Symphony 5* (with New Philh. O). **DEBUSSY**: *La Mer*. **RAVEL**: *Daphnis et Chloé: Suite 2*; *Ma Mère l'Oye: Suite*; *La Valse* (with Hallé O). **TCHAIKOVSKY**: *Serenade in C for strings* (with LSO); *Symphony 4 in F min.* (with Hallé O). **BRAHMS**: *Tragic Overture*; *Symphony 3* (with VPO). **PUCCINI**: *Madama Butterfly* (excerpts, with Scotto, Stasio, Palma, Panerai, Morresi, Opera Theatre O, Rome). **BERLIOZ**: *Les Nuits d'été* (with Baker, New Philh. O)

EMI (ADD) 457767-2 (10)

Sir John Barbirolli, born in London of Italian and French parents, was one of the finest and most successful British conductors of the last century. He was especially associated with the Hallé Orchestra, which he took over in 1943 when it was reduced to only 23 players. Over the next few years he built it up to stand alongside London's finest orchestras. Barbirolli was an outstanding interpreter of the late-romantic classics, particularly Mahler, Sibelius and Brahms, but perhaps his greatest sympathy was with British music, of which he was a supreme champion.

CD 1 opens with Ireland's *London Overture* with its pithy main theme – and very successful it is too. This is followed by his very special (1957) recording of Vaughan Williams's *London Symphony* – an inspirational reading that gathers power as it proceeds. The slow movement has great intensity and eloquence, with the Hallé strings surpassing themselves. Bax's *Garden of Fand* follows, recorded at the same time – another performance full of character and atmosphere.

CD 2 opens with Barbirolli's almost Italianate Delius – richly romantic accounts of *The Walk to the Paradise Garden* and *In a Summer Garden*, with different orchestras, but both with passionate and characteristically arching string phrasing. Next (and new to CD) is a 1957 performance of Butterworth's *A Shropshire Lad*, with its opening as rapt and as haunting as can be imagined. Vaughan Williams's *Symphony No. 5* which follows is one of Barbirolli's greatest recordings, opening magically and unsurpassed in lyrical intensity, with many wonderfully glowing moments.

CD 3 reminds us what an excellent Sibelian Barbirolli was, especially with *Pohjola's Daughter*: it is an extremely impressive performance, spacious, yet no less exciting for its slower than usual tempi. Curiously, Barbirolli's 1957 recording of the *Cello Concerto* with Navarra has been chosen, rather than the iconic reading he made later with Du Pré. The performance culminates in a most moving account of the Epilogue. Only the Scherzo falls short – slower than usual and not completely assured.

Disc 4 begins with the 1969 reading of Mahler's *Fifth Symphony* – one of the most warmly affecting performances ever committed to disc, expansive, yet concentrated in feeling, especially the *Adagietto*. The recording sounds excellent, and this is undoubtedly one of the classic versions of this much recorded symphony.

CD No. 5 shows Barbirolli's feeling for the French repertoire too, with his 1959 Hallé version of *La Mer* fully encompassing the work's atmosphere and vivid impressionism. In Ravel's *Daphnis et Chloé Suite*, Barbirolli's characteristically languorous shaping of Ravel's yearning string phrase in *Daybreak* brings a real sense of ecstasy. He has the advantage of using a chorus, well balanced into the texture; the 1959 recording is full and luminous. The flute playing in the *Pantomime* is brilliant and sensitive; the *Danse générale* sparkles, with the chorus contributing very vividly to the climax. *La Valse* also has plenty of temperament and excitement, and *Ma Mère l'Oye* has delicacy and innocence, and the ear would hardly guess that this later recording derives from a 1957 mono master, so translucent the sound.

CD6 is devoted to Tchaikovsky and includes Barbirolli's exciting (1957) account of the *Fourth Symphony*, but is not one of his great recordings. After a lively first movement, the elegantly structured *Andantino* has many characteristic touches of individuality. The following *Serenade for Strings* (1964) is characteristically ripe and romantic, especially in the *Élégie*. In the first movement, Barbirolli is surprisingly metrical when the second subject arrives, but he is naturally expressive in the *Waltz* and prepares the bustling finale with subtle, loving anticipation.

CD 7 includes some of Barbirolli's finest Elgar recordings. His *Introduction and Allegro* and *Serenade in E minor* are certainly among them and the *Elegy* and *Sospiri* are hardly less fine, while the Vaughan Williams *Tallis Fantasia* which follows is a uniquely inspirational performance. The magically quiet playing of the second orchestra is unforgettable. The recording has magnificent definition and sonority, achieving dramatic contrasts between the main orchestra and the ethereally distanced solo group. The CD ends with Barbirolli's full-blooded (1967) account of Bax's *Tintagel*, another of his greatest recordings, with the sea vistas magnificently evoked by players and recording engineers alike, and Sir John sees that the memorable principal tune is given a fine romantic sweep.

CD 8 brings Janet Baker's unforgettable recording of the *Sea Pictures*. Like Du Pré, Baker is an artist who has the power to convey on record the vividness of a live performance. With the help of Barbirolli she makes the cycle far more convincing than it usually seems, with the words clothed in music that seems to transform them. The *First Symphony* which follows is very good, without possessing the surging exhilaration of his earlier, Pye account. Barbirolli is perhaps just a bit too affectionate here, though his identification with the music is not in doubt.

Again in Brahms's *Third Symphony* (CD 9), dating from 1967, with the Vienna Philharmonic Orchestra, one feels that Barbirolli is just that bit too indulgent with this score. To sustain a performance as slow as this demands the keenest concentration, and though the playing of the VPO is refined and beautiful, tension tends to fall. The *Tragic Overture* is similarly expansive, but full of vigour. This CD is completed by Barbirolli's superb (1962) account of Elgar's *Enigma Variations*. It was a work that Barbirolli, himself a cellist, made especially his own, with wonderfully expansive string-playing and much imaginative detail. The recording was made when he was at the very peak of his interpretative powers.

The final CD (No. 10) is devoted to Barbirolli's classic opera and vocal recordings. *Madama Butterfly* (1967) inspired the conductor to make a recording in which the singers perform with a dedication and intensity rare in opera recordings made in Italy, and the whole score glows more freshly than ever. (The complete opera is also available on EMI 5 67885-2.) There is hardly a weak link in the cast and the ardour and perception of Renata Scotto's portrayal of Butterfly more than make up for any shortcomings in the basic beauty of her tone colour. Following *Butterfly* comes the magical Berlioz cycle, *Les Nuits d'été*. The collaboration with Janet Baker produced some remarkable records. Even if the great singer is admittedly just slightly strained in the first song, *Villanelle*, the half-tones in the middle songs are exquisitely controlled and the elation of the final song, *L'Île inconnue*, with its vision of an idyllic island, has never been more rapturously captured on record. Finally, Dame

Janet's totally idiomatic recording of the 5 *Rückert-Lieder* completes this CD. Her range of tone and colour is matched by dedicated playing from the New Philharmonia, and this recording is first class.

BARTÓK, Béla (1881–1945)

Concerto for Orchestra; *Dance Suite*; *Divertimento*; *Hungarian Sketches*; *The Miraculous Mandarin: Suite*; *Music for Strings, Percussion & Celesta*; *Romanian Folk Dances*
(M) Double Decca 470 516-2 (2). Chicago SO, Solti

A self-recommending collection of Solti's digital Bartók recordings which has special individuality and distinction. Solti had a great and natural affinity with Bartók and, although his Chicago performances may not have the searing intensity of his vintage LSO accounts (alas, not currently available), the extra warmth of the music-making brings out the lyrical qualities of the music. The *Concerto for Orchestra* has great zest and bold colouring; the *Divertimento* is superbly done, incisive and full-blooded; and the *Hungarian* and *Romanian Dances* have all the atmosphere one could wish for. In short, this is excellent value in the Double Decca series and brings particularly fine Decca sound.

(i–ii) *Piano Concertos 1–3*. *Violin Concertos*: (iii–iv) *1*; (iii; ii) 2
Double Decca (ADD/DDD) 473 271-2 (2). (i) Ashkenazy; (ii) LPO; (iii) Chung; (iv) Chicago SO; all cond. Solti

If, in the *Violin Concertos*, Chung is rather forwardly balanced, the hushed intensity of the writing, as well as the biting Hungarian flavour, is caught superbly, thanks to Solti as well as to the soloist, and there is no sentimental lingering. In the *Piano Concertos*, the partnership between Ashkenazy and Solti works equally well. The *Second* and *Third Concertos* spark off the kind of energy one would expect from a live performance. The *First Concerto* (digital) is even tougher, urgent and biting, and the slow movements in all three works bring a hushed inner concentration, beautifully captured in warmly refined sound. Indeed, the recording throughout, whether analogue or digital, is of vintage Decca quality.

String Quartets 1–6
Decca 455 292-2 (2). Takács Qt

The Takács Quartet bring to these masterpieces the requisite virtuosity, tonal sophistication and command of the idiom, as well as passion. These are full-blooded accounts of enormous conviction, with that open-air quality which suggests the Hungarian countryside. The recording too is wholly natural. These works have been lucky on disc, but this Decca set remains unsurpassed.

(i–iii) *Sonata for Two Pianos & Percussion*; (i) *Out of Doors*; *Sonatina*
Ⓜ Decca (ADD) 478 2467. (i) Kovacevich; (ii) Argerich; (iii) Goudswaard, Roo (with: (i; ii)
   MOZART: *Andante with five Variations in G for Piano Duet, K.501.*
   DEBUSSY: *En blanc et noir*)

Recorded in 1977, this strongly atmospheric and finely characterized performance of the *Sonata for Two Pianos and Percussion* still remains a top choice. This
is most imaginative playing and the recording is exceptionally wide-ranging
and truthful. It is difficult to imagine a more eloquent or better-recorded
account of this powerful work. The rapport between the artists produces
undoubted electricity, and sparks fly in the brilliant finale and in the Allegro of
the first movement. Comparable rapport is also found in the delightful Mozart
Variations which follow. Although they are taken at quite a brisk tempo, the
playing is unfailingly sensitive and vital. Debussy's *En blanc et noir* is one of the
composer's most neglected works. It comes from the last years of his life and
is full of unexpected touches. This account, also from 1977, was then the finest
version to have appeared, with both artists at their imaginative and sensitive
best. The solo piano pieces were recorded in 1969 and emerge with immediacy
and tremendous freshness here. Indeed, the piano sound is outstanding by any
standards, and Stephen Bishop Kovacevich gives splendidly vivid readings
and plays with tremendous fire and intensity. The opening of *Out of Doors* is
thrillingly vibrant, as is the final 'Chase', and there is contrasting light delicacy
in the intervening movements (*Night's Music* is hauntingly atmospheric), as
there is in the closing section of the *Sonatina*.

Allegro barbaro; *14 Bagatelles*; *3 Burlesques*; *Dance Suite*;
4 Dirges; *10 Easy Pieces*; *2 Elegies*; *7 Esquisses*; *First Term at the
Piano*; *For Children, Books 1–4*; *3 Hungarian Folksongs from Csik*;
3 Hungarian Folk Tunes; *15 Hungarian Peasant Dances*; *Petite
Suite*; *Improvisations on Hungarian Peasant Songs*; *Kossuth*;
9 Little Piano Pieces; *Marche funèbre from Kossuth*; *Mikrokosmos*
(complete); *Out of Doors*; *4 Pieces*; *Rhapsody 1* (2 versions); *Romanian
Christmas Carols*; *2 Romanian Dances*; *6 Romanian Folk Tunes*;
3 Rondos on Folk Tunes; *Sonatina*; *Sonata*; *3 Studies*; *Suite*
Ⓑ Decca 478 2364 (8). Kocsis

Decca have restored Zoltán Kocsis's coverage of the complete piano music to
the catalogue, and it remains the classic set for the foreseeable future. Bartók
playing doesn't come any better than this – nor does piano recording. Kocsis
penetrates to the very centre and soul of this music more deeply than almost
any rival. Scrupulously attentive to the composer's wishes, Kocsis can produce
power and drama when required, but he also commands a wide-ranging palette
and a marvellously controlled vitality. His playing calls to mind Bartók's own
injunction that performances must be 'beautiful but true'.

Bluebeard's Castle (DVD version)
Decca DVD 074 3254. Sass, Kováts, LPO, Solti (V/D: Miklós Szinetár)

Solti made his electrifying video recording of *Bluebeard's Castle* in 1981. His two soloists could not have been better chosen, for both the dark-timbred Kolos Kováts and the rich-voiced Sylvia Sass are totally convincing in their roles as a grim, unmoving Bluebeard and an increasingly apprehensive but determinedly wilful Judith. The sets in Miklós Szinetár's production are extraordinarily imaginative, creating an uncannily gloomy atmosphere as Duke Bluebeard and his wife make their way slowly through the dank, ill-lit passages of his castle, and always bringing a vivid surprise to the viewer as well as to Judith as each door is opened. The tension steadily increases until the seventh door reveals Judith's own destiny. With the LPO responding with great concentration, Solti's orchestral commentary is superbly controlled: the taut grip for which his conducting is celebrated is felt at its most magnetic, and the powerful closing scene is haunting. The recording and camerawork are of the highest quality and, for good measure, Chris Hassall has provided the translation for the subtitles

Kertész also set new standards when he made his analogue recording in 1966 with Walter Berry and Christa Ludwig, not only in the playing of the LSO at its peak and the brilliance of the recording, but also in the firm sensitivity of the soloists, with the natural Hungarian inflexions inspired by the conductor (Decca 466 377-2).

BARTOLI, Cecilia (mezzo-soprano), with the Orchestra La Scintilla, directed by Ada Pesch

'Maria': DVD 1: *Arias from*: **GARCIA**: *La figlia dell'aria*.
PERSIANI: *Ines de Castro*. **MENDELSSOHN**: *Infelice*.
ROSSINI: *La Cenerentola*; *Otello*. **BALFE**: *The Maid of Artois*.
HUMMEL: *Air à la Tirolienne avec Variations*. **BELLINI**:
La Sonnambula. **MALIBRAN**: *Oh Dolce Incanto* (from *L'Elisir d'amore*); *Rataplan*. **GARCIA**: *El poeta calculista*. DVD 2:
'Malibran Rediscovered – The Romantic Revolution' (documentary)
Decca DVD 074 3252 (2)

This two-DVD set is Cecilia Bartoli's tribute to Maria Malibran, one of the great legends in operatic history, and it includes much interesting repertoire. The first DVD is from a concert in Barcelona's magnificent Palau de la Musica Catalana in November 2007, and includes some of the most sparklingly tuneful *bel canto* examples, not only with famous items of Rossini and Bellini, but with surprises such as Mendelssohn's vibrant *Infelice*, with its pleasing violin obbligato. The Balfe aria (sung in English) is especially enjoyable. Hummel's variations are brilliant and sparkling and are tremendous fun – Bartoli's person-ality comes through superbly here, as it does in the vivacious *Rataplan* number by Malibran herself. The items by Malibran's father, Manuel Garcia, are well worth having, particularly the colourful piece from *El poeta calculista,* with its guitars and castanets. The concert was clearly a success and the excitement of the occa-sion comes over well in this handsomely produced DVD. The documentary on DVD 2, 'Malibran Rediscovered', talks about Bartoli's relationship with her illus-trious predecessor and her journey of discovery, highlights of which include a scene with Decca's great opera producer, the late Christopher Raeburn.

BAX, Arnold (1883–1953)

The Garden of Fand; *Mediterranean*; *Northern Rhapsody No. 3*; *November Woods*; *Tintagel*
Lyrita (ADD) SRCD 231. LPO, Boult

Both *The Garden of Fand* and *Tintagel* precede Bax's symphonies, and are his most inspired pieces, tone-poems rich in melodic invention and opulence of orchestral colour. They are glorious and every bit as evocative and atmospheric as any of Delius's tone-pictures. Sir Adrian was a consistent champion of the composer and an eloquent interpreter of this appealing music.

Symphonies 1–7
Chan. 10122 (5). BBC PO, Handley

The seven symphonies of Arnold Bax (1922–39) bestride the inter-war years but are totally at variance with its turbulent ethos. Bax described himself as an 'unashamed romantic' and the symphonies are rich in invention and bold in colour, totally unlike any of his British or European contemporaries. Little known in Europe, the symphonies are now beginning to make their way, and the present box is no small measure the cause of this. Vernon Handley is in total sympathy with Bax's muse and his direction is authoritative as well as idiomatic. Superb sound from the Chandos and BBC engineers. We would not be without this set.

Tintagel
EMI (ADD) 3 79983-2. LSO, Barbirolli (with **DELIUS**: *La Calinda; In a Summer Garden; Irmelin Prelude; A Song of Summer; The Walk to the Paradise Garden.* **IRELAND**: *London Overture*)

For collectors wanting *Tintagel* alone, Barbirolli's LSO version is the finest ever recorded and is unlikely ever to be surpassed. The performance has a great romantic sweep and the full-bodied 1965 recording still sounds splendid. The couplings too are of a comparable vintage.

BEECHAM, Sir Thomas (with London Philharmonic Orchestra, Royal Philharmonic Orchestra or French National Radio Orchestra)

Although together representing a single overall anthology, the following five boxes are available separately. Each includes a booklet with first-class notes by the Beecham expert and aficionado, Lyndon Jenkins.

Sir Thomas Beecham, 'The Great Communicator' (a documentary by Jon Tolansky)
Ⓑ EMI (DDD/ADD) 9 09964-2 (4)

This documentary covers Sir Thomas's life and career as impresario and conductor – Monteux admiringly dubbed him 'Le Grand Bâton' – through the memories and accounts of 25 eyewitness communicators, including John Amis, Geoffrey Brand, David Cairns, Lyndon Jenkins, Felix Abrahamian, Jon Vickers and many other contributors, including orchestral musicians, writers, critics, broadcasters, audience members, and also one of Sir Thomas's sons. The voice of Sir Thomas himself is heard in previously unpublished rehearsal recordings from the EMI archives and in a spoken presentation to an invited audience. Musical illustrations are taken from EMI recordings made between 1916 and 1959, as well as a previously unpublished recording of a 1947 concert at the Royal Albert Hall.

Beecham was ever resourceful, and when Walter Legge at EMI wanted him to record Sibelius's *Fourth Symphony*, which was never as popular as Nos. 1, 2 or 5, the problem would be the cost of rehearsal time for such an unfamiliar work. 'Leave that to me,' Sir Thomas said, and he told Legge that he would take the work on a provincial tour. 'You will be at every rehearsal with the score,' he said; and every morning he rehearsed Sibelius's *Fourth* and in the evening substituted it for whatever popular symphony was in the programme. Before he began, he gave the audience one of his inimitable speeches. He told them that he had been given to understand that they were over-familiar with the main programmed work and congratulated them on their perspicacity in asking him 'to let them hear what is undoubtedly the greatest symphony written in the twentieth century'. The orchestra then played the Sibelius *Fourth*, and on return to the EMI studios the orchestra was fully prepared to make the recording.

I.M. recalls going to hear Beecham live on two occasions. The first was at the Royal Albert Hall during the war years, when Beecham had returned briefly to England. In his LPO programme was Chabrier's *España*, which scintillated so infectiously that he felt he was hearing an orchestra for the first time. The second occasion was at a rehearsal in post-war Birmingham. Beecham went through the familiar repertoire selectively, and in the main was concerned with the inner balance, especially of the woodwind. After about half the allotted time he was obviously satisfied, for he said to the players, 'We don't need any more of this, do we,' and, with a twinkle, 'Shall we go home?' 'Yes, Sir Thomas,' came the enthusiastic reply, and they did.

We are grateful, in re-surveying his many recordings, to draw on the notes provided by the Beecham expert and aficionado, Lyndon Jenkins, which are consistently illuminating and enjoyable to read.

'The Classical Tradition'

HAYDN: (i) *Symphonies 93; 94 (Surprise); 95; 96 (Miracle); 97; 98; 99; 100 (Military); 101 (Clock); 102; 103 (Drum Roll); 104 (London) (London Symphonies);* (i–ii) *The Seasons* (oratorio) **MOZART**: (i; iv) *Violin Concerto 3 in G, K.216;* (i) *Divertimenti 2 in D, K.131; 15 in B flat (Theme & Variations and Meneutto only); March in D (Haffner), K.249;* (iii) *Overtures: Don Giovanni; Le nozze di Figaro. Symphonies 29 in A, K.201; 31 in D (Paris), K.297; 34 in C, K.338; 35 in D (Haffner), K.385; 36 in C (Linz), K.425; 38 in D (Prague), K.504; 39 in E flat, K.543; 40 in G min., K.550; 41 in C (Jupiter), K.551. Thamos, King of Egypt, K.345: Entr'acte 2* (only)

Ⓑ EMI (stereo/mono) 9 09946-2 (10). (i) RPO; (ii) with Morison, Young, Langdon, Beecham Ch. Soc.; (iii) LPO; (iv) Gioconda de Vito

Mozart and Haydn were at the very heart of Beecham's repertoire and he made his stereo recordings of Haydn's *London Symphonies* in 1958/9. The recordings sound admirably full-blooded, with sound that is both full and vivid. The RPO performances are both sensitive and invigorating. The art of phrasing is one of the prime secrets of great music-making, and no detail in these performances goes unattended. They also have both drama and warmth and at times a unique geniality. The playing too has an inner life and vitality that put it in a class of its own.

In *The Seasons* Beecham, while not using a scholarly edition, makes the most of Haydn's expressive tone-painting, and his team of soloists is as good as could be desired. Elsie Morison's flexible voice and wide range are matched by Alexander Young's finely controlled and rock-steady technique, while the bass, Michael Langdon, has a fine reserve of power. The Beecham Choral Society provides a backbone of sound which brings Haydn's score vividly to life, and the recording is excellent.

The Mozart *Symphonies* have fine polish and a unique elegance which make them very different from today's period-instrument approach, with beauty of timbre and warmth, especially in the strings, pre-eminent. These are Beecham's pre-war recordings with the LPO (which he founded in 1932), made between 1937 and 1940 with Walter Legge as producer. The interpretations are both characteristically vital and relaxed, except for *No. 29 in A major*, which is perhaps too affectionate, even languorous. When this recording was issued on six 78-r.p.m. sides it competed with Koussevitzky's Boston version which fitted neatly on to four, as his tempo for the opening movement was almost twice as fast as Beecham's. Yet, heard independently, both readings worked effectively enough.

The *D major Divertimento* is a large-scale performance, but none the worse for that (with some superb horn-playing), but the highlight of the last disc is Gioconda de Vito's memorable (1949) account of the *G major Violin Concerto* with its exquisitely played *Adagio* and light-hearted finale.

'The Later Tradition'

BEETHOVEN: *Symphonies 2; 7*; (i-ii) *Mass in C*; (i) *The Ruins of Athens* (incidental music). **BRAHMS**: *Symphony 2; Academic Festival Overture*; (i) *Song of Destiny*. **LISZT**: (i; iii) *A Faust Symphony. Orpheus*; (i; iv) *Psalm XIII*. **MENDELSSOHN**: *Overtures: A Midsummer Night's Dream; Die schöne Melusine*. **SCHUBERT**: *Symphonies 3 in D; 5 in B flat; 6 in C*. **R. STRAUSS**: (v) *Don Quixote, Op. 35; Le Bourgeois gentilhomme, Op. 60* (excerpts); (vi) *Ein Heldenleben, Op. 40; Feuersnot, Op. 50, Love scene. Intermezzo, Op. 72: Entr'acte in A flat. Salome: Dance of the 7 Veils*. **SUPPÉ**: *Overture, Poet and Peasant*. **WAGNER**: *Die Meistersinger Overture*

Ⓑ EMI stereo/mono 9 18611-2 (8). RPO; with (i) Beecham Ch. Soc.; (ii) Vyvyan, Sinclair, Lewis, Nowakowski; (iii) Alexander Young; (iv) Midgley; (v) P. Tortelier; Lampe; (vi) Steven Staryk

After the Second World War Beecham returned permanently to England from America and, finding that he could not again take over artistic control of the LPO, in 1946 founded the Royal Philharmonic Orchestra. Among his last stereo recordings with this orchestra were Beethoven's *2nd* and *7th Symphonies*, highly personal readings but still among the finest performances on disc. The *Second* brought a brilliant first movement and a contrasting, warmly beautiful *Larghetto*; the *Seventh* was an even more brilliant account, with a thrilling finale, the horns singing out spectacularly in the climaxes of the outer movements. The *Mass in C* was recorded in 1958, and Beecham provided a magnificent performance. Both Richard Lewis and Jennifer Vyvyan were in excellent voice, with Monica Sinclair and Marian Nowakowski a little way behind in sheer quality, but not so far as to spoil the ensemble. The chorus was first rate and, combined with the orchestra, afforded a wide and exciting dynamic range. *The Ruins of Athens* incidental music is equally vibrant, and the transfer is vivid and lively, with clear choral sound.

Though the opening of the transfer of Brahms's *Second Symphony* brings some background noise, the sound is vivid enough and the Beecham magic makes this volatile reading consistently compelling. The accompanying booklet reveals that it was recorded at no fewer than six separate sessions, spread between November 1958 and November 1959. The quirkiness of the performance reflects that. The horns at the opening may be rather subdued, but the first movement is then urgently riveting at speeds faster than usual. Beecham is also on the fast side in the second-movement *Adagio*, but his fine detailing there and in the third movement is totally distinctive, and the finale brings an exhilarating close. The *Academic Festival Overture* and the rarer *Song of Destiny* are equally desirable, the latter sung in Vaughan's English translation.

Beecham's classic (1958) recording of Liszt's *Faust Symphony* for long dominated the catalogue, and it is well transferred to CD, although Richard Gooch's balance is rather forward, brightening the brass, notably so in the first movement's famous dominating theme. But the splendid performance shows its conductor, an instinctive Lisztian, at his most illuminatingly persuasive. His control of speed is masterly, spacious and eloquent in the first two movements without dragging, brilliant and urgent in the finale without any hint of breathlessness. It provides a uniquely warm and understanding reading of this equivocal piece, hard to interpret.

Orpheus was inspired by an Etruscan vase in the Louvre depicting Orpheus singing to his lyre, and Beecham's recording remains the most poetic and unaffected yet to be committed to disc. It sounds uncommonly fresh and spacious, and the performance is magical. The account of *Psalm 13* is hardly less impressive. It is sung in English, with the legendary Walter Midgley gloriously open-voiced; but the recording here is drier and more monochrome. All the same an indispensable reissue.

Mendelssohn's *A Midsummer Night's Dream Overture* opens gently and magically, with the first tutti contrasting in its bold drama, and the closing section Elysian in its beauty. *Die schöne Melusine* is perhaps less inspired, but was another of Beecham's favourites; and it is played with much affection, but it is the *Poet and Peasant Overture* that he transmutes from a pot-boiler into a work of dignity and lyrical memorability, to all but match the *Die Meistersinger Prelude*.

The triptych of Schubert *Symphonies* is another of his finest records, in which every phrase breathes. There is no substitute for imaginative phrasing and each line is shaped with distinction and spirit. The *Allegretto* of the *Third Symphony* is an absolute delight, matched by the delicacy of the opening of the *Fifth* and the simple lyrical beauty of its *Andante*, while few conductors have been as persuasive as Beecham in the *Sixth, C major, Symphony*. The sound is generally faithful and spacious.

Beecham with Tortelier recorded their mono version of *Don Quixote* in 1947 during Strauss's visit to London. The playing is pretty electrifying, with the then newly formed RPO on their best form. Tortelier had performed the work under the composer himself and here he plays for all the world as if his life depended on it. There is great delicacy in *Le Bourgeois gentilhomme* and some delicious playing from the RPO's then leader, Oscar Lampe. The account of *Ein Heldenleben*, made in the same year, also remains a model of its kind, authoritative, marvellously paced and beautifully transparent in its textures. A glorious performance which long held sway until Karajan's 1959 account came along. The other Strauss excerpts, hardly less seductive, were recorded in 1947, before the advent of the mono LP.

'English Music'
DELIUS: (i) *Brigg Fair*; (i; iii) *Violin Concerto*; (i) *Dance Rhapsodies 1 & 2*; *Fennimore and Gerda (Intermezzo)*; *Florida Suite* (rev. Beecham);

Irmelin Prelude; *Marche caprice*; *On Hearing the First Cuckoo in Spring*;
On the Mountains (Pas vidderne); *Over the Hills and Faraway*; *Sleigh Ride*;
A Song Before Sunrise; *Summer Evening*; *Summer Night on the River*;
(i; iv) *Sea Drift*; (i; v) *The Song of the High Hills*; (i; vi) *Songs of Sunset*;
(i; vii) *A Village Romeo and Juliet* (complete opera). (i) **BANTOCK**:
Fifine at the Fair. (i) **BAX**: *The Garden of Fand.* (ii) **BERNERS**:
The Triumph of Neptune (ballet: excerpts). (ii) **GERMAN**: *Gypsy Suite*

Ⓑ EMI stereo/mono 9 09915-2 (6). (i) RPO; (ii) LPO; with (iii) Jean Pougnet; (iv) Gordon
Clinton & Ch.; (v) John Cameron, Maureen Forrester, Beecham Ch. Soc.; (vi) Freda Hart,
Leslie Jones, Luton Ch. Soc.; (vii) Margaret Ritchie, René Soames, Denis Dowling,
Frederick Sharp, Lorely Dyer, Gordon Clinton, Dorothy Bond & Ch.

Few if any conductors have been associated more indelibly with a single composer than Beecham with Delius, with whom he formed a lifelong friendship;
and this series of recordings of the major orchestral works, recorded between
1956 and 1957 at Abbey Road, is one of the highlights of the EMI catalogue.
The remastering of the orchestral sound (mostly done in 2001) continues
to demonstrate a technological miracle. The result brings these unsurpassed
performances into our own time with great beauty and an uncanny sense of
realism and presence. The delicacy of the gentler wind and string textures is
something to marvel at, as is the orchestral playing itself. Beecham's fine-spun
magic, his ability to lift a phrase, is apparent from the very opening of *Brigg
Fair*, which shows Delius at his most inspired and the Royal Philharmonic
Orchestra at their most incandescent. It is good that the rarely heard *Florida
Suite*, Delius's first orchestral work (1888/90), is included, for it is brim full of
delightful melody and orchestral colour. The tune we know as *La Calinda* makes
its début in the first movement. This and the third movement both incorporate
African-American folk dances which reflect Delius's earlier stay on a plantation
in Florida. *La Calinda,* like the equally delectable *Sleigh Ride*, became two of
Beecham's celebrated 'lollipops', often used as concert encores. Jean Pougnet's
1946 mono recording of the *Violin Concerto* is also welcome: it was later upstaged
by Menuhin's version, but here sounds wonderfully fresh.

Of the choral works, Beecham's performance of *Sea Drift* conveys the surge
of inspiration that so readily matches the evocative colours of Walt Whitman's
poem about the seagull, a solitary guest from Alabama, and the *Song of the
High Hills* is permeated with a feeling of joy and exhilaration, whereas the
Songs of Sunset brings a more sensuous mood in this setting of poems of Ernest
Dowson.

The studio recording of *A Village Romeo and Juliet* was made in the days of
78s in 1948, and although the mono sound is limited in range it is well focused,
and Beecham's ability to mould Delius's melodic lines gives it extra warmth.
However, he also made a live radio recording with a similar cast for the BBC
Third Programme only a week before he went into the EMI studios! The wonder is how different it is interpretatively. The timing alone provides an indication

of the contrast, with the studio recording some 11 minutes shorter. Moreover the radio recording (available on Somm BEECHAM 12-2) is the one which sounds the more passionately spontaneous at almost every point. But in both versions René Soames as the hero, Sali, sings with fresh, cleanly focused tone, so the better-balanced studio version is worth hearing in its own right.

The four extra items by other composers on the last disc are treasurable. Beecham always had a soft spot for Bantock's atmospheric and colourfully scored *Fifine at the Fair*, and his advocacy is so persuasive that one could wish for the piece to be restored to the repertoire. The early (1949) mono sound emerges warmly and vividly, with the CD transfer making the most of the 78 master. In Bax's *Garden of Fand*, Beecham related its atmospheric feeling to the music of Delius, and it is played superbly here, especially by Jack Brymer in his spectacular clarinet cadenza, and by the strings in the lovely theme in the second part of the piece. The 1947 recording is a bit confined and two-dimensional, but it is again very well transferred to CD. German's slighter *Gypsy Suite*, too, benefits from Sir Thomas's affectionate treatment. But the highlight is undoubtedly Lord (Gerald) Berners' suite, *The Triumph of Neptune*, drawn from the ballet performed by Diaghilev's Ballets Russes in London in 1926. The composer was often called the English Satie, and Satie's love of circus music was echoed by Berners' taste for the music hall. Beecham responded readily to the music's mixture of wit and charm (it even, unexpectedly, includes a baritone voice singing an excerpt from 'The Last Rose of Summer'). The 78s were long cherished by us and it is good to have this rare work back in the catalogue.

'French Music'
BERLIOZ: (i) *Symphonie fantastique, Op. 14*; *Overtures*: (ii) *Le Carnaval romain, Op. 9*; (iii) *Le Corsaire, Op. 21*; *Le Roi Lear, Op. 4. La Damnation de Faust: Danse des sylphes*; *Menuet des follets. Les Troyens, Act I: Trojan March*; (iii; iv) *Act IV: Royal Hunt and Storm*. **BIZET**: (iii) *L'Arlésienne: Suites 1 & 2*; (i) *Carmen: Suite 1*; (iii) *Patrie, Op. 19*; *Roma: Carnaval*; (i) *Symphony in C*. **CHABRIER**: (ii) *España*; (iii) *Joyeuse marche*; (i) *Gwendoline Overture*. **DEBUSSY**: (iii) *Prélude à l'après-midi d'un faune*; *L'Enfant prodigue: Cortège et air de danse*. **DELIBES**: (iii) *Le Roi s'amuse (ballet music: suite)*. (i) **FAURÉ**: *Dolly suite, Op. 56* (orch. Rabaud); *Pavane, Op. 50*. **FRANCK**: *Symphony in D min.* (orch. Rabaud). (iii) **GOUNOD**: *Faust ballet music*; *Roméo et Juliette: Le Sommeil de Juliette*. **GRÉTRY**: *Zémir et Azor: Ballet music* (ed. Beecham). (i) **LALO**: *Symphony in G min.* (iii) **MASSENET**: *Cendrillon: Valse. La Vierge: Le Dernier sommeil de la Vierge*. **SAINT-SAËNS**: *Le Rouet d'Omphale*; *Samson et Dalila: Danse des prêtresses de Dagon*; *Bacchanale*. **VIDAL**: *Zino-Zina Gavotte*

Ⓑ EMI stereo/mono 9 09932-2 (6). (i) Fr. Nat. R. O; (ii) LPO; (iii) RPO; (iv) Beecham Ch. Soc.

Attempts have frequently been made to explain the consistently scintillating quality of Beecham's performances and his own explanation, 'I simply get the best players, and let them play,' undervalues the special genius of his music-making. Never more so than his 1959 account of Berlioz's *Symphonie fantastique*, still unsurpassed. It has a demonic intensity that is immediately compelling and holds the listener on the seat-edge until the work's electrifying close. In EMI's latest (2003) transfer, in which every detail is crystal clear, the strings have a rich sheen and the brass a sonority and depth more telling than in previous incarnations of the recording. Even the tolling bells of the finale deserve a credit for their remarkable tangibility, while the warm acoustic of the Salle Wagram, Paris, frames a concert-hall balance of remarkable realism. The tinglingly atmospheric accounts of the *Royal Hunt and Storm* (with chorus), the *Trojan March* and the *Overture, Le Corsaire* are no less memorable. The two mono recordings, *Le Carnaval romain*, played by the LPO and dating from 1936, and RPO's *Le Roi Lear*, made in the Kingsway Hall in 1947, are also full of excitement.

Among the other symphonies Beecham recorded, the Bizet *C major* work stands out. Beecham's magical touch is especially illuminating and the music sounds freshly minted. The oboe soloist in the slow movement distinguishes himself and the finale is full of zest. Bizet's *Roma Symphony* was written some years later but is more uneven in quality, so Beecham chose to play and record its best movement, its gay finale, *Carnaval*, with its pleasing secondary tune, not taking it too fast in order to respond to the composer's markings of *plus vite* and *più presto* towards the close.

Beecham is also masterful in the rhythmic bite he gives to the great syncopated melodies that swagger their way through the outer movements of the Franck *Symphony in D minor* – the second subject in the first movement, and the opening theme of the finale. But he has to work harder with the Lalo *G minor* work when the material is thinner and the argument in the first movement lacks tautness. However, the second-movement Scherzo, with its highly effective flute writing, partly compensates, inspiring Beecham to a delectably pointed performance.

He was undoubtedly at his finest in the two *L'Arlésienne Suites* of Bizet, still unsurpassed, and here the early (1956) stereo gives the woodwind striking luminosity, yet plenty of body. Beecham's own arrangement of a suite from Grétry's *Zémir et Azor* in his own words offered music which possessed 'a lightness, a grace and a melodic invention surpassed only by Mozart', and in his hands the *Pantomime* movement made an exquisite effect and audiences would sometimes not be able to resist giving spontaneous applause. This movement was often played separately as one of Beecham's celebrated 'lollipops', as were the airy waltz from Massenet's *Cendrillon*, Gounod's fragile picture of Juliet asleep, and Vidal's delectable *Gavotte* from his ballet, *Zino-Zina*.

No one conducts Bizet's *Carmen Prélude* with quite Beecham's flair, set off by an explosive cymbal crash, while in his hands the *Patrie Overture*, even though it is played by the English RPO, it is as ebulliently Gallic as *La Marseillaise*, with a degree of brashness for good measure. The *Gwendoline Overture* has contrasting charm. The seven numbers of Gounod's elegantly vivacious *Faust* ballet music, delightfully characterized, were recorded in Walthamstow, along with the delicately fragile *Last sleep of the Virgin* of Massenet (another 'lollipop'). But the incomparably effervescent performance of Chabrier's *España* used the Kingsway Hall and is one of the highlights of this collection, both for its unique exuberance and for the amazingly realistic mono recording of the LPO, with the percussion condiment glittering. It was produced by Walter Legge in 1939. Complete on two 78-r.p.m. sides, with each recorded separately nearly two weeks apart, the result, when they are joined together as here, is absolutely seamless as if the music was put on disc at a single session.

Fauré's *Dolly Suite* brings the consistently imaginative and poetic phrasing that distinguished Beecham's best performances, and the *Berceuse*, *Le Jardin de Dolly* and *Tendresse* (in Rabaud's orchestration) are exquisite, while *Le Pas espagnol* has the kind of dash one expects from Beecham's Chabrier. Fauré's enchanting *Pavane* was Beecham's last recording, yet it is as captivating as any music which had come earlier. Similarly, Beecham's unsurpassed account of Saint-Saëns's *Le Rouet d'Omphale* brings delicacy of string textures and wind playing (notably the flute) which is utterly beguiling, with its closing section particularly haunting. By contrast the *Bacchanale* from *Samson and Delilah*, like Chabrier's *Joyeuse Marche*, has wonderful dash and flair, and one can imagine the twinkle in Sir Thomas's eye.

Surprisingly, he recorded little Ravel or Debussy, but the *Prélude à l'après-midi d'un faune* brings a ravishingly diaphanous web of sound, and the *Cortège et Air de danse* is exquisitely done. Delibes' pastiche ballet score, *Le Roi s'amuse*, is given the special elegance that Sir Thomas reserved for music from the past, unashamedly re-scored to please the ear of later generations. After Delius this is all repertoire which showed him at his very finest. The remastering is marvellously managed, and all the recordings sound wonderfully vivid and fresh.

BEETHOVEN, Ludwig van (1770–1827)

Piano Concertos 1–5 (CD version)
Ph. 462 781-2 (3). Brendel, VPO, Rattle

This Philips set is Brendel's third and finest survey of the Beethoven concertos, made in Vienna with Rattle; each concerto was recorded immediately after live performances, producing extra spontaneity. The dynamic range is greater too with hushed *pianissimos* more intense. The ambience of the Musikverein casts a warm, natural glow over the sound and adds the necessary breadth to the *Emperor*. A fine set – Brendel admirers should be well satisfied.

(i–ii) *Piano Concertos 1–5*. (ii) *Creatures of Prometheus:* excerpts; (ii–iii) *Symphonies 1–9*; (ii) *Overtures: Coriolan; Egmont; King Stephen; Leonora III. String Quartet, 14, Op. 131* (arr. for string orchestra); (ii; iv) *Choral Fantasy;* (v) *Missa solemnis*

Ⓜ DG DVD 073 4500 (7). (i) Zimerman; (ii) VPO; (iii) with G. Jones, Schwarz, Kollo, Moll, Konzertvereinigung & V. State Op. Ch. in *No. 9*; (ii; iv) with Homero Francesch, V. Jeunesse Ch.; (v) Moser, Schwarz, Kollo, Moll, R. Hilversum Ch., Concg. O; all cond. Bernstein

Bernstein's outstanding Beethoven collection – including some of his finest Beethoven recordings – was recorded over the late 1970s and 1980s. The original intention was to include all five of the piano concertos, but the conductor's death in 1990 prevented that, and Zimerman directed the first two concertos from the keyboard with impressive grip and command and with playing that is technically immaculate. In the last three concertos there is close support and unity of purpose between conductor and pianist. In many ways they are differing musical personalities, Zimerman commanding, poised and aristocratic, Bernstein displaying a full-blooded brilliant temperament. But their collaboration is a triumphant success and these readings are in many ways the most stimulating available, both compelling and thoughtful. No. 3 is quite inspired. (They are also available in a separate 2-DVD box: 073 4269)

The symphony cycle, dramatic, perceptive, rich in emotion but never sentimental, has a natural spontaneous quality. With Bernstein's electricity matched against the traditional warmth of Viennese playing the results are consistently persuasive, and the cameras consistently show his pleasure and involvement in the music-making. First-movement exposition repeats are observed consistently and very effectively. The first two symphonies are presented as large-scale works with fast Allegros made sharply rhythmic. Yet there is an underpinning of classical elegance. The *Eroica* brings a strong, dramatic, though not over-forced approach, with a superb, dedicated account of the *Funeral March*. In No. 4 Bernstein's taut manner brings out the compactness and geniality of the argument, and there is warmth and resilience too, with the finale especially involving. Bernstein has rethought his reading of the *Fifth*, giving it resonance and spaciousness as well as drama, ending with a blazing account of the finale. Joy and serenity are combined in the *Pastoral*, while in the *Seventh* the extra spring and exhilaration of the lilting rhythms of the first movement are balanced by the reposeful *Allegretto*, and the last two movements have the adrenalin flowing freely. The set culminates in a superb triumphant account of the *Ninth* with a fast, tense first movement, a resilient Scherzo, a hushed, expansive reading of the *Adagio* and a dramatic account of the finale. With such consistently fine performances and excellent video direction from Humphrey Burton, this is a very enjoyable set indeed. The overtures are lively and sympathetic, the *Choral Fantasy* is most engagingly done, and Bernstein and Beethoven are at their most seductive in the *Creatures of*

Prometheus ballet music. But what caps the collection is the outstanding account of the *Missa solemnis* with a spiritual intensity matched by very few rivals. Edda Moser is not an ideal soprano soloist, but the others are outstanding, and the *Bendictus* is made angelically beautiful by the radiant playing of the Concertgebouw concertmaster, Herman Krebbers.

In performing the arrangement of the Op.131 *String Quartet* for full strings, Bernstein is following the practice of Toscanini and Mitropoulos, and there is no doubt as to the commitment and depth of the playing, nor the richness of its lyrical feeling. If such a transcription is to be made at all, it could not be done with more eloquent advocacy than it is here.

Violin Concerto in D, Op. 161
RCA (ADD) SACD 09026 61742-2. Heifetz, Boston SO, Munch - **BRAHMS**: *Violin Concerto*

His supreme mastery has Heifetz finding time for individuality and imagination in every phrase. For some, the comparative lack of serenity in the first movement (though not in the *Larghetto*, which is wonderfully poised) may be a drawback, but the drama of the reading is unforgettable. Heifetz's unique timbre is marvellously captured on SACD, as is Munch's conducting, with its distinctive character, notably its clarity and crispness. This recording is available either coupled to the Brahms *Violin Concerto* (with Reiner conducting in Chicago) or with the Mendelssohn *Violin Concerto* (with Munch - SACD 61391-2). However, the Brahms coupling is one of the outstanding SACD transfers made by John Newton for RCA, with Heifetz's unique timbre superbly captured.

Those seeking a modern recording which is both beautiful and stimulating should turn to Vadim Repin's ravishing DG account (477 6596) with the VPO under Muti, in which the exquisitely sensitive slow movement recalls Schneiderhan's vintage (1962) DG version. The coupling is a charismatic account of the *Kreutzer Violin Sonata* with Argerich. This is a favourite disc of I.M.'s.

Triple Concerto in C for Violin, Cello & Piano, Op. 56
Ⓑ EMI Masters (ADD) 6 31768-2. David Oistrakh, Rostropovich, Sviatoslav Richter, BPO, Karajan - **BRAHMS**: *Double Concerto*

Even in the days of star-studded recordings, the roster of artists on the EMI Masters reissue from 1969 is breathtaking. EMI plotted for a long time to capture the celebrated trio, and to have as spectacular a conductor as Karajan in addition is almost too good to be true. The results are aptly opulent, with Beethoven's priorities between the soloists well preserved in the extra dominance of Rostropovich over his colleagues. This warm, expansive music-making confirms even more clearly than before that the old view of this as one of

Beethoven's weaker works is quite wrong. The three Soviet soloists revel in the multiplicity of ideas, with Richter in the spare piano part providing a tautening influence. The recording is over-reverberant, which clouds some climaxes, but this is not too serious.

Symphonies 1–9
Sony DVD 88697195389 (1–4); 88697195399 (5–8); 88697195409 (9). BPO, Karajan

Recorded in the early to mid-1980s at the Philharmonie, with Karajan himself overseeing the video production, this cycle is very recommendable indeed and shows the conductor at his finest. The performances are marvellously polished yet free from any kind of glamour or glitz. They have the musical strengths of all Karajan's Beethoven cycles with the visual dimension that adds to the immediacy of effect. However, nowhere in the presentation material are the excellent soloists in the *Ninth* identified.

Symphonies 1 in C, Op. 21; 2 in D, Op. 36
Pentatone Surround Sound SACD PTC 5186 118. ASMF, Marriner

Although the atmosphere of the eighteenth century is still apparent in his first two symphonies, Beethoven made his immediate break away from tradition by opening the *First* with a discord. Not a very pungent discord, it is true, and it is immediately resolved. But it serves to establish the way forward.

Marriner presents both symphonies with a Mozart-sized orchestra. The result is lithe and fresh and with plenty of character. Dramatic contrasts are powerful, yet the music's proper scale is retained and the result is completely satisfying. The 1970 recordings were originally made in quadraphony, and the result on SACD is of remarkably realistic quality with a natural balance for the strings, to make a splendid introduction to this repertoire.

Symphonies 3 in E flat (Eroica), Op. 55; 6 in F (Pastoral), Op. 68; 8 in F, Op. 93; Overtures: Coriolan; Creatures of Prometheus; Egmont; Fidelio
⑱ EMI Gemini 3 71462-2 (2). LPO, Tennstedt

Tennstedt's outstanding and unerringly paced account of the *Eroica* derives from a 1991 performance in the Royal Festival Hall, and it has the true hallmark of a live occasion, natural spontaneity and gripping tension throughout. *Nos. 6* and *8* were recorded at Abbey Road between 1984 and 1986. The fresh, alert, yet imaginative performance of the *Pastoral* brings a radiant reading of the finale, with beautiful string playing from the LPO. The *Eighth* is an equally enjoyable reading, in which the second-movement *Allegretto* is made into a Scherzo and the Minuet is spaciously lyrical. The overtures are all vividly dramatic. Altogether an unmissable bargain set for Tennstedt admirers, and a splendid general recommendation.

Symphony 4 in B flat, Op. 60
Testament SBT 1430. BPO, Karajan – **R. STRAUSS**: *Ein Heldenleben*

Karajan's Beethoven *Fourth* was recorded when the Berlin Philharmonic came to London in 1985. Its excellence speaks for itself and the coupling is equally memorable.

Symphonies 5 in C min., Op. 67; 7 in A, Op. 92
Ⓜ DG (ADD) SACD 471 630-2 or 447 400-2. VPO, Carlos Kleiber

A justly famous coupling that stretches back to the LP era. In Carlos Kleiber's hands the first movement of the *Fifth* is electrifying, yet still has an underlying hushed intensity. The slow movement is tender and delicate; then, after a Scherzo in which the horns are superbly arresting, the finale emerges into pure daylight. In the *Seventh* the symphonic argument never yields to the charm of the dance. Incisively dramatic, his approach relies on sharp rhythmic contrasts and thrustful rhythms, with the finale racing to its conclusion with great impetus and the horns again dominating the texture.

Symphony 6 (Pastoral); Overtures: Coriolan; Creatures of Prometheus; (i) Egmont Overture and Incidental music: Die Trommel Gerühret; Freudvoll und leidvoll; Klärchens Tod, Op. 84
Ⓜ EMI (ADD) 5 67965-2. Philh. O, Klemperer; (i) with Nilsson

The *Pastoral* is I.M.'s favourite Beethoven symphony, and he first heard it in 1941 (in abbreviated form) in Walt Disney's *Fantasia*, gloriously played by Stokowski and the Philadelphia Orchestra. The swinging melody on which the finale is based is one of the richest that Beethoven (or anyone else for that matter) ever wrote, and in the film the climax accompanies the sun god, Apollo, driving his chariot across the heavens – a spectacularly appropriate visual conception.

This account of the *Pastoral* stands out among Klemperer's Philharmonia Beethoven recordings (alongside his live Testament version of the *Choral Symphony* – SBT 1177). It is famously controversial, with its legendary story of the Scherzo, taken by Klemperer at an unusually relaxed tempo. At the studio rehearsal the record's celebrated producer, Walter Legge, stopped the performance with the comment, 'Isn't that a little slow, Otto?' 'You will get used to it,' was the conductor's immediate reply, and he continued in measured fashion as before. And indeed, such is the magnetism of the Philharmonia playing that one does indeed get used to it, and the performance overall is memorable for its combination of warmth and drama. The couplings are memorable too, and Birgit Nilsson is in her prime in the *Egmont* music.

Symphony 9 in D min. (Choral), Op. 125 (CD version)
Ⓜ LPO Live 0026. Popp, Murray, Rolfe Johnson, Pape, LPO Ch., LPO, Tennstedt

Klaus Tennstedt's outstanding *Choral Symphony* was recorded live in October 1992 at the Royal Festival Hall. Terminally ill as he was, a fact widely known, this made each of his last concerts into an event, which added to tensions. The performance stands comparison with any rival version in the thrusting intensity of the playing, brisk in the first movement with timpani prominent, lilting in the Scherzo (though with no repeats observed), radiant in the slow movement, with the LPO strings at their most mellifluous, and violent at the start of the choral finale, leading to an exceptionally intense and well-coordinated account, with outstanding soloists and chorus. The sound, although on the dry side, is vividly clear.

Wellington's Victory (Battle Symphony), Op. 91

Ⓜ Decca (ADD) 475 8508. Cannon & musket fire directed by Gerard C. Stowe, LSO, Dorati (with separate descriptive commentary by Deems Taylor) – **TCHAIKOVSKY**: *1812* etc.

This most famous of all Mercury records (now released on Decca) was one of the most successful classical LPs of all time, selling some two million copies in the analogue era. Remastered for CD, it sounds even more spectacular than it ever did in its vinyl format, vividly catching Beethoven's musical picture of armies clashing. The presentation, with excellent documentation, now comes as one of Decca's 'Originals'.

Piano and Wind Quintet in E flat, Op. 16

EuroArts DVD 2072308. James Levine, Ens. Wien-Berlin (with bonus items by Ligeti, Berio, Mozart & Françaix) (V/D Jean-Pierre Ponnelle)

In this coupling of equally inspired works for piano and wind instruments, we used to judge that Mozart scored marginally over Beethoven in felicity in using his simple forces. Not so here. Fine as the Mozart performance is, the Beethoven is even more memorable because of the unforgettably beautiful playing of James Levine, especially in the slow movement, which is presented with Elysian delicacy. In all other respects this is a treasurable performance, splendidly played and recorded, and most realistically videoed.

Piano Trios: 4 in B flat, Op. 11; 5 in D (Ghost), Op. 70/1; 7 in B flat (Archduke), Op. 97

Ⓜ Ph. (ADD) 464 683-2. Beaux Arts Trio

The Beaux Arts Trio are on top form here and the recording has been given a pleasing bloom by the CD transfers. All three performances are first rate and there is plenty of drama and intensity in the *Ghost Trio* to ensure that it matches its companions.

Septet in E flat, Op. 20; Sextet for Wind in E flat, Op. 81b

Ⓑ Hyp. Helios CDH 55189. Gaudier Ens.

The *Septet* is one of the young Beethoven's most joyfully carefree inspirations and the Gaudier Ensemble play it with an infectious mixture of elegance and exuberance. The rarer *Sextet* for two horns and string quartet provides an equally winning coupling. Excellent sound makes this a highly desirable bargain.

String Quartets: Vol. 1: *1 in F; 3 in D; 4 in C min., Op. 18/1, 3 & 4; 10 in E flat (Harp), Op. 74; 13 in B flat, Op. 130; 14 in C sharp min., Op. 131* (EMI DVD 3 8567-9); Vol. 2: *2 in G, Op. 18/2; 7 in F (Rasumovsky 1), Op. 59/1; 11 in F min., Op. 95; 12 in E flat, Op. 127; 15 in A min., Op. 132* (EMI DVD 3 8580-9); Vol. 3: *5 in A; 6 in B flat, Op. 18/5 & 6; 8 in E min. (Rasumovsky 2), Op. 59/2; 9 in C (Rasumovsky 3), Op. 59/3; Grosse Fuge in B flat, Op. 133; 16 in F, Op. 135*
EMI DVD 3 8592-9. Alban Berg Qt
Ⓑ Decca CD 454 062-2 (10) Italian Qt

The Alban Berg cycle is the only complete DVD cycle to have appeared so far. It was recorded in Salzburg in 1989, a couple of years after the fine LP (and later CD) set which the Alban Berg Quartet made for EMI. In terms of sheer quartet-playing these players are difficult to fault: ensemble is flawless, intonation perfect, and their mastery unimpeachable. The video presentation is totally free from affectation; the vision is straightforward and never draws attention to itself. Some readers may find the dynamic contrasts a shade exaggerated, but most collectors will find much musical satisfaction here.

The fine complete Quartetto Italiano survey, first issued on Philips and superbly stylish, is again available, and is undoubtedly the CD choice of preference for these masterpieces. The latest Philips remastering is most impressive, the sound much smoother than before. Moreover the *Second* and *Third Rasumovsky Quartets*, originally recorded quadrophonically, have additionally been reissued on the Pentatone label in very natural surround sound. With tempi perfectly judged and every phrase sensitively shaped, this separate disc is very desirable indeed (Pentatone SACD PTC 5186 176).

The Borodin Quartet's survey is also deeply felt and their performances, recorded between 2003 and 2006, can also be recommended alongside the very finest of recent years, if not a first choice. Recorded in the Grand Hall of the Moscow Conservatoire, the sound is satisfyingly warm and present (Chan. Ⓜ 10553 (8)) and the presentation is economical.

String Trios: 1 in E flat, Op. 3; 3 in G; 4 in D; 5 in C min., Op. 9/1–3; Serenade in D, Op. 8
Ⓜ Hyp. Dyad CDD 22069 (2). Leopold String Trio

The young Beethoven, in preparation for writing string quartets, composed the three Op. 9 *String Trios* in 1798. They have a winning originality, each well contrasted with the others. The six-movement Opus 3 *Trio* was composed three years earlier and, with its pair of *Minuets* framing the central *Adagio*, appears to have been modelled on Mozart's *Divertimento* in the same key. It is most appealing, but the delightful seven-movement *Serenade*, published in

1797, is even more so. The performances by the Leopold Trio are particularly alive and fresh and the Hyperion recording is remarkably real and vivid.

Piano Sonatas 1–32

EMI DVD 3 68993-9. Daniel Barenboim (with masterclasses including Saleem Abboud Ashkar, Alessio Bax, Jonathan Biss, Shai Wosner, David Kadouch, Lang Lang)

Barenboim's Beethoven cycle drew full houses and critical accolades in London a few years ago, and this set, deriving from eight concerts in Berlin, is hardly less imposing. This is Beethoven playing of the most impressive artistry and highest accomplishment, displaying a total concentration and profound musical intelligence. In addition to the cycle there are six masterclasses of almost an hour each, in which Barenboim coaches some excellent younger players; Barenboim is extraordinarily illuminating and full of insight, and his generosity of spirit and intuitive understanding are always in evidence. All pianists and music-lovers, whether expert or less knowledgeable, will learn a lot from them – as we have.

Piano Sonatas 1–32; Bagatelles, Opp. 119, 126

Ⓑ EMI Classics 5 62700-2 (9). Stephen Kovacevich
ⒷⒷ Regis (mono) RRC 9016 (9)

Piano Sonatas 8 (Pathétique); 14 (Moonlight); 21 (Waldstein); 23 (Appassionata); 25 in G, Op. 79; 26 (Les Adieux); 29 (Hammerklavier)

Ⓑ EMI Masters 9 65922-2 (2) (from above). Kovacevich
Ⓜ RCA (ADD) SACD 88697 68882-2 (Sonatas 8,14, 23, 26 & 29 only). Rubinstein

The catalogue is rich in Beethoven *Piano Sonata* cycles – Schnabel, the very first, Ashkenazy (Decca), Kempff's, Paul Lewis, Gilels and Solomon's outstanding mono cycle (Regis/9010), RRC, all enjoy legendary status. Stephen Kovacevich recorded his set between 1991 and 2003, and among modern accounts it is difficult to equal, let alone surpass. In terms of artistry and musical wisdom, it ranks alongside Solomon and in authority matches Kempff. Its *Hammerklavier* and *C minor*, Op. 111, are both magisterial and eclipse most rivals, while throughout the series the piano sound is wonderfully vivid and fresh. Those wanting a shorter selection of the named sonatas including the *Hammerklavier* should be happy with the two-disc set in the Masters series.

The alternative group is Rubinstein's very first recording of Beethoven's *Moonlight Sonata* and, like the other works on the RCA disc, it dates from the early 1960s. It is an unforgettable account, with an improvisatory feel to the opening movement, which is also felt in *Les Adieux*. The *Pathétique* contrasts a youthful zest in the outer movements with an *Adagio cantabile* of melting simplicity, while the *Appassionata* has all the surging impetus one could wish for. The master recordings, made in the Manhattan Center, were originally registered in three-track stereo and they have been superbly remastered by John Newton to bring a sense of remarkable realism and presence. This is one of Rubinstein's very finest records and will give enormous satisfaction.

33 Variations on a Waltz by Diabelli, Op. 120
EuroArts DVD 3079238. Stephen Kovacevich (with **BACH**: *Partita 4 in D, BWV 828.*
   SCHUMANN: *Kinderszenen, Op. 15*)
Onyx CD ONYX 4035 (with **BACH**: *Partita 4*)

Stephen Kovacevich first recorded the *Diabelli Variations* in 1968. Forty years and much experience (including recording the 32 *Sonatas* and the *Concertos*) separate it from these newcomers. This extraordinary work explores the virtuosic possibilities of variation form – technical and intellectual – over the most ambitious span, yet always with a profound underlying emotional basis. It is custom built for Kovacevich. Nothing this artist does is less than compelling, and both these masterly new accounts enrich his discography with their sweep and control, and depth of feeling. Both are very well recorded, the EuroArts DVD live at the Verbier Festival, where Martial Barrault's camera angles achieve a nice balance to catch both an overall picture and a close-up of his hands. Both DVD and CD include equally fine accounts of the Bach *Partita*, but the DVD offers also a memorably poetic account of Schumann's *Kinderszenen*.

Fidelio (complete, DVD version)
DG DVD 073 4159. Janowitz, Popp, Kollo, Sotin, Jungwirth, Dallapozza, V. State Op. Ch. &
   O, Bernstein

Beethoven's *Fidelio* is a rare opera with a happy ending, celebrating a brave, faithful and loving wife, Leonora, who hopes to save her imprisoned husband (Florestan) from certain death by disguising herself as a young man and seeking employment as the gaoler's assistant at the prison in which he is held. Her task is made the more practical, since the gaoler's daughter, Marzelline, falls in love with 'her' and the gaoler welcomes the 'match'. Rescue comes just in time (heralded by the trumpet calls made famous in the *Leonora* Overture) and the villainous despot (Pizarro) ends up cast into the same cell in which his prisoner has previously languished. The music is powerfully lyrical and includes a moving Prisoners' Chorus in which the gaoler sympathetically allows the other prisoners briefly to come out of their dungeon cells into the daylight.

   Bernstein conducts a classic DVD account of Beethoven's inspired score with an outstanding cast. This live recording is first class in every way. Gundula Janowitz sings gloriously as Leonora, with Lucia Popp radiant as Marzelline. All the male soloists are firm and clear, each of them at his peak, not least René Kollo as Florestan and Hans Sotin as Pizarro, the villain. The great finale of Act II in particular conveys a rare dedication. The production and sets are impressively realistic.

BELLINI, Vincenzo (1801-35)

Beatrice di Tenda (CD version)

Ⓜ Decca (ADD) 433 706-2 (3). Sutherland, Veasey, Pavarotti, Ward, Opthof, Ambrosian
Op. Ch., LSO, Bonynge

Beatrice di Tenda was Bellini's last but one opera, coming after *Sonnambula* and *Norma* and before *I Puritani* (the latter written for Paris). It had an unfortunate birth, for the composer had to go to the law courts to wring the libretto from his collaborator, Romani, and it has been felt that the result is not dramatically compelling. The story involves a whole string of unrequited loves – X loves Y who loves Z who loves . . . and so on, and the culminating point comes when the heroine, Beatrice, wife of Filippo, Duke of Milan, is denounced falsely for alleged infidelity. Bellini always intended to revise the score, but failed to do so before his death. There is an impressive trial scene – closely based on the trial scene of Donizetti's *Anna Bolena* – and the unfortunate Beatrice is condemned to death and executed despite the recantation of false witnesses. As it is, the opera remains essentially a piece for an exceptional prima donna with a big enough voice and brilliant coloratura. Joan Sutherland naturally made it her own, and though in this (1966) recording she indulges in some of the mooning one hoped she had left behind, the many dazzling examples of her art on the three CDs are a real delight. The other star of this set is Sutherland's husband, Richard Bonynge, whose powers as a Bellini conductor are most impressive: just listen to the way he moulds the exhilarating Act I finale, with the beautifully sprung rhythms rushing headlong to a thrilling conclusion. The supporting cast could hardly be more impressive, with Pavarotti unusually responsive for a modern tenor. Outstanding recording too, vividly transferred to CD, with arias from *Norma*, *I Puritani* and *La Sonnambula* included as a bonus.

Norma (CD version)

Ⓜ Decca (ADD) 470 413-2 (3). Sutherland, Horne, Alexander, Richard Cross, LSO Ch.,
LSO, Bonynge

It was a measure of Joan Sutherland's (and Bonynge's) concern for musical values that she deliberately surrounded herself with singers who match her own quality and not (like some divas have done) with singers who stand no chance of distracting one from the star's glory. She is joined here by an Adalgisa in Marilyn Horne whose control of florid singing is just as remarkable as Sutherland's own, and who sometimes even outshines the heroine in musical imaginativeness. But fine as Horne's contribution is, Sutherland here marked a new level of achievement in her recording career. Accepting the need for a dramatic approach very much in the school of Callas, she then ensures at the same time that something as near as possible to musical perfection is achieved. Her old trouble of diction with the words masked is occasionally present, and on the whole Sutherland's old account of '*Casta Diva*' on her early recital disc,

The Art of the Prima Donna, is fresher than this. But basically this is a most compelling performance, musically and dramatically, and in this Sutherland is helped by the conducting of her husband, Richard Bonynge. On this showing, there have been few finer Bellini conductors in the recording studio, for in many of the conventional accompaniment figures he manages to keep the musical interest alive with sprung rhythms, and with the subtlest attention to the vocal line. The other soloists are all very good indeed, John Alexander and Richard Cross both young, clear-voiced singers.

One cannot mention this opera without reference to Callas, of course. Her two commercial EMI recordings, one mono (5 62638-2 (3)), one stereo (5 66428-2 (3)), both supremely conducted by Serafin, have much to commend them. The earlier set finds Callas in better voice, but the later recording boasts a finer cast, with Corelli and Christa Ludwig adding much to the electricity which a Callas recording usually generates.

I Puritani (CD version)

Decca (ADD) 417 588-2 (3). Pavarotti, Sutherland, Ghiaurov, Luccardi, Caminada,
  Cappuccilli, ROHCG Ch. & O, Bonynge

Ten years after her first recording of *I Puritani*, made in Florence, Joan Sutherland returned to this supremely enjoyable score of Bellini's, an opera which requires, not one star but four great singers, which this 1973 recording certainly has. 'Opera must make people weep, shudder, die through the singing,' Bellini wrote to his librettist, and this sharply committed performance – with all the cuts opened up – brings to thrilling life the potentially limp story about Cavaliers and Roundheads. Sutherland's singing here is brighter and fresher than in her earlier recording, with the lovely aria *'Qui la voce'* no longer a wordless melisma, and the great show-piece, *'Son vergin vezzosa'*, is taken at a dangerously fast pace: the extra bite and tautness are exhilarating. Pavarotti, then the possessor of the most radiantly beautiful of tenor voices, shows himself a remarkable Bellini stylist, rarely if ever coarsening a legato line, unlike so many of his Italian colleagues. Ghiaurov and Cappuccilli make up a uniformly impressive cast list. The recording is vivid and atmospheric and one marvels at Bellini's gorgeous melodies, some very exciting duets and one of the most thrilling of all operatic barn-storming finales, with Sutherland, Bonynge and all on electrifying form.

La Sonnambula (CD version)

Ⓜ Decca (ADD) 448 966-2 (2). Sutherland, Monti, Elkins, Stahlman, Corena, Ch. & O of
  Maggio Musicale Fiorentino, Bonynge

This recording was one of the early Sutherland/Bonynge triumphs. It is, in fact, Richard Bonynge's favourite opera, and although he recorded it again with an even starrier cast, this early version is perhaps marginally the finest. Sutherland is on top form. Her *'Ah non giunge'* is fabulous, and this recording, unlike the later digital re-make, includes Bellini's longer postlude, with the dramatic crashing chords which end the opera, but which were cut from the later recording. Bonynge's conducting is in fact one of the great assets of this set, as outstanding in its way as his wife's singing. If some commentators have taken a swipe at Bonynge's conducting ability, this set proves that even early on in his career there was no question whatsoever of his tagging along on her coat-tails, for the playing and singing here, from a group not normally remarkable for alertness, has a crispness of discipline which had not been heard in opera sets from Italy for a long time. The *Polonaise* in Act II before Amina's entry has a wonderful sparkle. The rest of the cast is no let-down. Nicola Monti has a charming voice, and though he does not always use it with imagination he gives continual enjoyment – which is more than you can often say about Bellini tenors. Both Sylvia Stahlman as Lisa and Margreta Elkins as Teresa sing most beautifully and with keen accuracy. Corena's *buffo*-style Rodolfo has attractive vitality – indeed, at the time of the original review, we thought him rather coarse, but we would be glad to have some of his stylish singing character in today's opera houses. The recording still sounds vividly dramatic and full, and this is a far better way of getting to know this curiously compelling opera than the new Decca DVD – spoilt by an unspeakably ghastly production.

BERG, Alban (1885–1935)

(i) *Violin Concerto*. *Passacaglia* (realized by Borries & Venzago); *Lulu: Symphonic Pieces*. *Piano Sonata, Op. 1* (orch. Verbey); *3 Pieces, Op. 6*; *Wozzeck: 3 Fragments*. *Der Wein* (sung in (ii) French (iii) German). Transcription of Johann **STRAUSS** Jr: *Wein, Weib und Gesang!*

Ⓜ Chan. SACD CHSA 5074 (2). Gothenburg SO, Venzago, with (i) Keulen; (ii) Murray; (iii) McGreevy

An outstanding new collection of the key works of Berg, spanning the creative career of the composer, with a few novelties thrown in too. These include Theo Verbey's superb orchestration of Berg's solo *Piano Sonata*, which transforms the piece into virtually a new work. In the *Passacaglia* fragment (1913), each variation builds on the former one rather than on the original theme, and the result is an intense piece of orchestral writing, put together from the composer's sketch by Christian von Borries. The concert aria, *Der Wein* ('The Wine') is heard here in two performances, one in the usual German by Geraldine McGreevy, and the other in French by the tenor, Robert Murray. The latter, in Baudelaire's original French, is markedly sweeter in tone. The main orchestral works come off extremely well here: both the soloist and the conductor bring out all the colours which make up the *Violin Concerto*, and the orchestral suites from *Wozzeck* and *Lulu* have both intensity and atmosphere. The *Three Pieces*, Op. 6, have more warmth here than usual, though the finale has a fine sense of impending doom. The disc ends with Berg's enjoyable arrangement of Strauss's *Wein, Weib und Gesang!* Throughout, these performances benefit from superb Chandos SACD sound and excellent playing from the Gothenburg orchestra. The two CDs are offered for the price of one.

Wozzeck (complete)

Ⓜ Decca 478 3408 (2). Waechter, Silja, Winkler, Laubenthal, Zednik, Jahn, Malta, Sramek, VPO, Dohnányi - **SCHOENBERG**: *Erwartung*

Dohnányi, with refined textures and superb playing from the Vienna Philharmonic, presents an account of *Wozzeck*, cast from strength, that is not only more accurate than any other on record but also more beautiful. At midprice, coupled with Schoenberg's *Erwartung*, this is an outstanding set in every way.

BERGANZA, Teresa (mezzo-soprano)

'A Portrait': Arias from: **ROSSINI**: *Il barbiere*; *La Cenerentola*; *L'italiana in Algeri* (with LSO, Gibson). **MOZART**: *Così fan tutte*; *Le nozze di Figaro* (with LSO, Prichard). **GLUCK**: *Alceste*. **CHERUBINI**: *Medea* (with ROHCG O, Gibson). **HANDEL**: *Alcina* (with LSO, Bonynge). **BIZET**: *Carmen* (with LSO, Abbado). Songs/Arias: **MOZART**: *Ch'io mi scordi di te? . . . Non temer, amato bene* (with LSO, Prichard). **CHERUBINI**: *Ahi! Che forse ai miei di*. **CESTI**: *Intorno all'idol mio*. **PERGOLESI** (attr.): *Confusa, smarrita*. **SCARLATTI**: *Chi vuol innamorarsi*; *Elitropio d'amor*; *Qual mia colpa, o sventura . . . Se delitto è l'adorarvi*; *La Rosaura*. **LAVILLA**: *Cuatro canciones vascas*. **TURINA**: *Farruca. Saeta en forma de Salve a la Vergen de la Esperanza*. **GRANADOS**: *La maja dolorosa*; *El majo timido*; *El tra-la-la y el punteado* (with Felix Lavilla, piano). **FALLA**: *7 Canciones populares españolas*. **GUERRERO**: *Sagrario's Romanza*. **MARQUES**: *Margarita's Romanza* (O, cond. Lauret). **ARÁMBARRI**: *Ocho canciones vascas* (O, cond. Gombau)

ⒷⒷ Decca (ADD) 475 518-2 (2)

A truly memorable Teresa Berganza compilation. Naturally, there is a good sprinkling of her classic early operatic recordings of Rossini and Mozart, which sparkle as brightly as ever and have rarely been out of the catalogue. All the other items on the first disc, from the Gluck and Handel items to the Bizet, also show her on top form, a real star mezzo of character and style. The second CD is packed full of her native Spanish repertoire, most of which has not been widely available on CD before, some being transferred for the first time. Her recordings with Felix Lavilla, made at the beginning of the 1960s, are especially enjoyable, and on their original release were compared with Victoria de los Angeles. Undoubtedly the arias by Cherubini and Scarlatti, and others, would have gained from more than a piano accompaniment, but the classical quality of the singing is most beautiful, and the recording has transferred well to CD. The *Ocho canciones vascas* ('Eight Basque Songs') and *Sagrario Romanza* and *Margarita's Romanza* derive from two EPs from the late 1950s, and these simple, naive songs are sung to perfection. The group of Basque songs is especially captivating: they were arranged in their present form by Jesús Arámbarri in 1931, and his discreet and delicate orchestral accompaniments subtly underline the mood of each item. The sound is a little dated and sometimes is not quite sharply focused, but they are warm and highly atmospheric. At bargain price, this is one of the most enterprising collections in Decca's 'Portrait' series.

BERKELEY, Lennox (1903–89)

Divertimento in B flat, Op. 18; *Partita for Chamber Orchestra, Op. 66*; *Serenade for Strings, Op. 12*; (i) *Sinfonia concertante for Oboe & Chamber Orchestra, Op. 84: Canzonetta* (only). *Symphony 3 in 1 Movement, Op. 74*; *Mont Juic* (with Britten), *Op. 9*
Lyrita (ADD) SRCD 226. LPO, composer; (i) with Winfield

Lennox Berkeley was typical of the English composers whom Lyrita championed in the 1970s, and this beautifully planned collection introduces some of the most elegant and enjoyable music that he ever wrote. Chandos took over the Berkeley cause in the 1990s (and that of his son, Michael) but this is a very good place to start the music of the father. The *Divertimento* is enchanting, with its four stylish and highly inventive movements, while the *String Serenade*, similarly in four sections, is hardly less attractive and brings a beautiful *Lento* closing movement. In its rather weightier tone of voice the *Partita* belies that it was written originally with a youth orchestra in mind, while the fourth movement from the *Sinfonia concertante* makes a splendid interlude before the closing *Symphony No. 3*. This is a concise, one-movement work, slightly more austere in its lyricism, but with a popular element entering the finale. Here at times one has the feeling that the composer would have created an even stronger effect had he held the performance more tautly, but it remains a distinctive account. The recording, from the early 1970s, is first class, and the CD transfers only improve the sense of presence and realism. The programme opens with the charmingly spontaneous *Mont Juic Suite* which Berkeley wrote in collaboration with Benjamin Britten, two movements each (Berkeley contributing the opening pair), and the work was later published jointly as Berkeley's Op. 9 and Britten's Op. 12.

BERLIOZ, Hector (1803–69)

Overtures: Béatrice et Bénédict; Benvenuto Cellini; Le Carnaval romain; Le Corsaire. Roméo et Juliette: Queen Mab Scherzo. The Trojans: Royal Hunt and Storm
RCA 9026 61400-2. Boston SO, Munch (with SAINT-SAËNS: *Le Rouet d'Omphale*)

Berlioz overtures encompass much of the extraordinary original writing which made their composer one of the outstanding geniuses of the early Romantic era. They are dazzlingly orchestrated, consistently melodic, and hugely enjoyable show-pieces for orchestra. This RCA collection ranks alongside Munch's classic account of *Daphnis and Chloé*, and is undoubtedly one of the great recordings of the last century. It comprises, among other delights, dazzlingly brilliant performances of four favourite overtures: the virtuosity of the Boston players, especially the violins in *Béatrice et Bénédict* and *Le Corsaire*, is breathtaking. But it is for the wonderfully poetic and thrilling account of the *Royal Hunt and Storm* from *Les Troyens* that this CD earns its accolade. The horn solo is ravishing and the brass produce a riveting climax as the storm reaches its peak. Then the sense of rain-drenched countryside is magically evoked as the horn steals back in the closing bars. The early stereo (1958/9) is remarkable: one really feels the hall ambience, and John Pfeiffer's remastering is expert. *Romeo and Juliet* was recorded in 1961, and again one marvels at the articulation of the Boston violins and horns. The Saint-Saëns bonus is the earliest recording of all (1957). It is beautifully played and, after a robust climax, has the most delicate *pianissimo* ending.

However, Sir Colin Davis also made an outstanding recording of Berlioz overtures, with the Dresden State Orchestra, and it includes such rarities as *Le Roi Lear*, *Waverley* and the masterful *Les Francs-juges Overture* with its memorable main theme and sonorous writing for brass. It too is a splendidly played and recorded CD, available on RCA (82876 65839-2), but the Munch recordings remain unique and indispensable classics.

(i) *Harold in Italy*. *Les Troyens: Ballet Music*
Ⓑ LSO Live LSO 0040. (i) Zimmermann; LSO, C. Davis

Sir Colin Davis again demonstrates here his supreme mastery as a Berlioz interpreter in a recording of *Harold in Italy*, recorded live with the magnificent soloist, Tabea Zimmermann, who is rightly balanced as part of the orchestra instead of being spotlit, for this is an inspired concertante symphonic poem and not a concerto. The *Ballet Music* from *Les Troyens* provides an attractive and warmly atmospheric bonus. The disc is made the more attractive by its bargain price.

Symphonie fantastique, Op. 14
Pentatone Surround Sound SACD PTC 5186-184. Concg. O, C. Davis

In 1974 Sir Colin Davis chose the *Symphonie fantastique* for his first (Philips) recording with the Amsterdam Concertgebouw Orchestra, and in so doing entirely superseded his earlier version with the LSO. Pentatone returned to the original quadraphonic master tape for this reissue, which is spectacularly realistic. Gounod wrote about this extraordinarily original symphony that 'with Berlioz all impressions, all sensations – whether joyful or sad – are expressed in extremes to the point of delirium'. The results place the disc as a primary recommendation, comparable with Beecham's EMI version.

L'Enfance du Christ, Op. 25

Ⓜ Hyp. Dyad CDD 22667 (2). Rigby, Miles, Finley, Aler, Howell, Corydon Singers & O, Best

The atmospheric oratorio for Christmas, so different from any other Berlioz work, is beautifully recorded in sound which is immediate but warm. Matthew Best's version offers a keenly dramatic view. So Alastair Miles conveys pure evil in Herod's monologue at the start, and with words exceptionally clear Joseph's pleas for shelter are movingly urgent. Jean Rigby is a fresh, young-sounding Mary, with Gerald Finley warm and expressive as Joseph. John Aler is a powerful reciter and Gwynne Howell a strong, benevolent-sounding father of the family. The famous Shepherds' Chorus is beautifully sung and this makes an ideal choice for those wanting an intimate view and a superb, modern recording.

Les Nuits d'été (song-cycle)

Ⓜ Decca 475 7712. Crespin, SRO, Ansermet – RAVEL: Shéhérazade. DEBUSSY; POULENC: Songs

Crespin's sheer richness of tone and a style which has an operatic basis do not prevent her from bringing out the subtlety of Berlioz's writing. Le Spectre de la rose (a wonderful song) for instance has a bigness of style and colouring and an immediate sense of drama that immediately conjures up the opera house. But this is not a criticism. With Ansermet brilliantly directing the accompaniment this glowing performance is a tour de force. The Ravel coupling is equally inspired, and the superb transfers enhance the listener's pleasure further. This supreme performance is truly legendary and fully worthy of a place among Universal's 'Originals'.

Requiem Mass, Op. 5

Pentatone Surround Sound SACD PTC 5186 -191 (2). Dowd, Wansworth School Boys' Ch., L. Symphony Ch., LSO, C. Davis

Sir Colin Davis's inspired Philips recording of the Berlioz Requiem was made in Westminster Cathedral. As in the companion issue of the Symphonie fantastique, quadraphonic sound was used and the set is reissued by Pentatone in four-channel surround sound. The result, especially in the Dies irae–Tuba mirum, outshines all other versions in amplitude and spectacle. The large-scale brass and drum climaxes are quite astonishing and the choral fortissimos glorious, helped by the fresh cutting edge of the Wandsworth School Boys' Choir and the LSO's incisive accompaniment. The result is a triumph.

Roméo et Juliette, Op. 17 (DVD version)

Arthaus DVD 102 017. Schwarz, Langridge, Meven, Bav. R. Ch. & SO, Colin Davis (V/D:
  Klaus Lindemann)

Sir Colin Davis is without peer as a Berlioz interpreter and it is good to have
this fine (and often inspired) account of the master's dramatic symphony on
DVD. Recorded fairly early in his days in Munich with the Bavarian Radio
Orchestra, it has great fire and dramatic intensity – as well as the sensibility
and poetic feeling we associate with him. Quite apart from the virtuosity of this
wonderful orchestra, listeners will be riveted by the singing of the three soloists: Hanna Schwarz, whom we associate mainly with Wagner, the impeccable
Philip Langridge and the splendid, dark-toned Peter Meven, who died in 2003.
The video direction of Klaus Lindemann could hardly be bettered. A thrilling
performance.

Les Troyens, Parts I & II (complete, DVD version)

DG DVD 073 4310 (2). Troyanos, Norman, Domingo, Monk, Plishka, NY Met. Op. Ch.,
  O & Ballet, Levine

Les Troyens, Parts I & II (complete, CD version)

Ⓑ LSO Live 0010CD (4). Heppner, DeYoung, Lang, Mingardo, Mattei, Milling, L. Symphony
  Ch., LSO, C. Davis

Recorded at the Met. in 1983, this very fine account of Berlioz's epic opera, *Les
Troyens*, features the most starry cast of soloists, all at their peak, and is
strongly directed by James Levine. Jessye Norman is magnetic in the Fall of
Troy, commanding in her prediction of doom. Plácido Domingo is at his most
heroic in both halves of the massive narrative, as Aeneas both in Troy and in
Carthage. As Dido, Tatiana Troyanos is tough and tender, more vulnerable by
far than as Cassandra in the first opera. The staging is nicely stylized with
grandly traditional costumes and unobtrusive hangings in the set. The recorded
sound is remarkably good, and Brian Large's video direction is characteristically well managed. This version is very rewarding on all counts and it makes
an obvious principal DVD recommendation for the foreseeable future.

For those seeking Berlioz's *Trojans* on CD, Sir Colin Davis's second live
recording, made in the Barbican in London, magnificently crowns his whole
career as a Berlioz interpreter on record, generally outshining even his pioneer
version of 30 years earlier. The first wonder is that the sound of the chorus and
orchestra is even fuller, more spacious, and certainly brighter and clearer than
on the earlier, Philips recording, or even the opulent digital recording given to
Charles Dutoit in his Montreal set for Decca. Davis is marginally faster in all
five Acts, a degree more thrustful, with the excitement of a live occasion consistently adding extra intensity. The casting too is margially even finer than
before. Petra Lang, a last-minute substitute as Cassandra, is superb, firm, rich
and intense, investing every phrase with emotional power, instantly establishing her dominance in the very first scene. Opposite her Peter Mattei makes a

powerful Choroebus. Both in *The Fall of Troy* and *The Trojans at Carthage* Ben Heppner excels himself, not just heroic with his unstrained Heldentenor, but finding a degree of refinement in the love duet of Act III that few rivals can match, let alone on disc. Michelle DeYoung may not be quite as rich and firm a Dido as Josephine Veasey on Davis's earlier set, but the vibrancy of her mezzo is warmly caught by the microphones, and her death monologue is the more moving for the vulnerability she conveys. The rest make an excellent team without any significant shortcomings. Though the set comes on four discs at bargain price, full libretto and notes are provided, printed in very small type.

BERNERS, Lord (1883–1950)

The Triumph of Neptune (ballet): *extended suite*; *Fantaisie espagnole*; *Fugue for Orchestra*; *3 Morceaux*; *Nicholas Nickleby* (film music)
Olympia OCD 662. RLPO, Wodsworth

It was Sir Thomas Beecham who discovered and introduced us to the music of Lord Berners with *The Triumph of Neptune* ballet and its interpolated 'Last rose of summer' in the days of 78s. Nothing we have since discovered quite matches this in quirky audacity, but it all gives pleasure in its tongue-in-cheek individuality. Berners was a colourful eccentric. He dyed the pigeons at his house all the colours of the rainbow, had a clavichord installed in the back of his Rolls-Royce, and had a folly built in his garden, saying, 'The great point of the tower is that it will be entirely useless,' and he put up a notice which read, 'Members of the public who commit suicide from the tower do so at their own risk.' His inclusion in this book reflects our affection for his comparatively small output, and he would no doubt have been very amused that any of it would make the 1,000 greatest recordings. But he is a unique character, endlessly fascinating and never less than entertaining. Barry Wordsworth captures the music remarkably well. The *Trois morceaux* and the *Fantaisie espagnole* are Gallic in inspiration and are attractively imaginative. The *Fugue for Orchestra*, described as a 'serious' work by the composer, turns out to be the most amusing of the lot. The recording is good, but not in the demonstration bracket, but never mind that. Berners gave himself a very appropriate epitaph which sums up his character:

> Here lies Lord Berners,
> One of the learners.
> His great love of learning
> May earn him a burning,
> But Praise to the Lord!
> He seldom was bored.

And neither are we.

BERNSTEIN, Leonard (1918-90)

Reflections (an autobiographical film produced, directed and photographed by Peter Rosen): *Introduction*; *Teaching*; *Mentors*; *Musical Ambassador*; *Composing*; *Tonality*; *American Music*
Medici Arts DVD 3078728 NTSC. Soloists, Israel PO, Indiana University School of
Music Op. Theatre, Rinat Ch., Jerusalem Academy Ch., Sharonit Ch.; cond.
Bernstein, Lukas Foss, John Mauceri, Mark James. Leonard Bernstein (speaker),
nar. Peter Thomas; Directed by Humphrey Burton & Yves-André Hubert
(with bonus: **MILHAUD**: *Le bœuf sur le toit* (complete ballet), O Nat.
de France, Bernstein)

Peter Rosen's fascinating autobiographical interview with Leonard Bernstein, with supporting performance excerpts, dates from 1977, with much riveting archive film included and interspersed with short but vivid excepts from the *Serenade*, *Symphonies 2 (Age of Anxiety)*, *3 (Kaddish)*, *Mass*, *On the Town*, *West Side Story*, *Wonderful Town*, etc., recorded in Israel. But the main content of the DVD is of Bernstein himself, cigarette in hand, charismatically reflecting on his life (beginning with his remarkable 1943 Carnegie Hall début as substitute for a sick Bruno Walter), the influence of Koussevitzky and others, his views on composition and his passionate adherence to tonalism as a creative basis and the importance of musical communication, at which he is peerless. An altogether unforgettable visual and aural experience, for no one communicates like Bernstein either vocally or in his music. If he had written only *West Side Story*, he would be a genius; as it is, he is uniquely gifted, America's greatest musician. The scintillating account of Milhaud's exhilarating *Le bœuf sur le toit* alone is worth the cost of the DVD – and what a joy he is to watch, enjoying himself hugely.

Symphonies: (i) *1 (Jeremiah)*; *2 (The Age of Anxiety)*; (ii) *Chichester Psalms*
Ⓜ DG (ADD) 457 757-2. Israel PO, composer; with (i) Ludwig; (ii) soloists from Vienna
Boys' Ch.

The *Jeremiah Symphony* dates from Bernstein's early twenties and ends with a moving passage from *Lamentations* for the mezzo soloist (Christa Ludwig). As its title suggests, the *Second Symphony* was inspired by the poem of W. H. Auden, though no words are set to music in this purely orchestral work. The *Chichester Psalms* is one of the most attractive choral works written in the twentieth century; its jazzy passages are immediately appealing, as is the intrinsic beauty of the reflective passages. These live performances with the Israel Phiharmonic may lack the last degree of polish, but the warmth of the writing is fully conveyed in these excellent recordings. With a playing time of just under 80 minutes, this DG 'Originals' CD is excellent value.

Mass (for the Death of President Kennedy)

Sony SM2K 63089 (2). Titus (celebrant), Scribner Ch., Berkshire Boy Ch., Rock Band & O, composer

It is typical of Bernstein that he conceived this remarkable setting – among his most extended works – not just basing it on the Catholic Mass but as a piece embracing all religions. He wrote it for the opening of the Kennedy Center for the Performing Arts in Washington, describing it as a 'Theater Piece for Singers, Players and Dancers'. It is a full-length entertainment, outrageously eclectic in its borrowings from a range between pop and the avant-garde. Its scenario boldly defies good taste, with the Celebrant finally smashing the holy vessel before the altar.

If the writing at times seems dangerously thin, the concentration of Bernstein holds the piece together, most strikingly of all in this first recording, conducted by the composer himself, intermittently available from Sony in different formats. Central to the performance's success is the clear, finely focused singing of Alan Titus as the Celebrant, bringing tenderness as well as power to the keynote *Simple Song*, with its '*Lauda, laude*' refrain. The echoes of *West Side Story* are many, with each section of the Catholic Mass amplified in Introits, Tropes and Meditations coming at suitable points. The work ends triumphantly with a section entitled *Pax: Communion* ('Secret Songs'). A flawed work but a memorable one, indispensable to all admirers of America's greatest musician/composer. The newest Naxos version under Marin Alsop (559622/23) also has many excellent qualities, but it is rather less intense and suffers from a Celebrant (Jubilant Sykes) who croons his part, not hitting the notes cleanly, under the note and sliding. The modern, digital recording is cleaner, but not always any clearer, and it is the composer's own recording which remains an obvious first choice.

West Side Story (complete)

DG 457 199-2. Te Kanawa, Carreras, Troyanos, Horne, Ollman, Ch. & O, composer

The composer's own recording of the masterly score to *West Side Story*, musically his greatest achievement, is now available on a single CD. There are those who suggest that the frankly operatic approach to its casting is less than ideal, but we find the result highly successful, for the great vocal melodies are worthy of voices of the highest calibre; Tatiana Troyanos, herself brought up on the West Side, spans the stylistic dichotomy to perfection in a superb portrayal of Anita. Moreover Bernstein's son and daughter speak the dialogue most affectingly. With the composer conducting a superb instrumental ensemble group of musicians 'from on and off Broadway' the power of the music is greatly enhanced by the spectacularly wide dynamic range of the recording.

Wonderful Town

Ⓜ EMI DVD 9 67136-2. Criswell, McDonald, Hampson, Barrett, Gilfry, L. Voices, Birmingham Contemporary Music Group, Rattle

Reissued in EMI's American Classics series, *Wonderful Town* was one of Bernstein's earliest successes and it still stands up well. Here in a fizzing account, starrily cast, Rattle gives a performance that is vigorously idiomatic and warmly refined in the many lyrical moments. The two characterful sisters finding their feet in the big city are brilliantly characterized by Kim Criswell and Audra McDonald, not just charismatic but singing superbly. Thomas Hampson as Robert just as commandingly bestrides the conflicting problems of Broadway and the classical tradition, and Brent Barrett in the secondary role of Wreck delightfully brings in the cabaret tradition. Such numbers as 'Ohio', 'A little bit in love', 'Conversation piece' and 'Wrong note rag', rounded off by the big tune of 'It's love', can be appreciated for their full musical quality, with Rattle and his talented Birmingham group relishing the jazzy idiom. Bright, forward sound to match. The only loss is the full text, included in the original booklet, and now replaced by a synopsis.

BERWALD, Franz (1796–1868)

Symphonies 1 (Sérieuse); 2 (Capricieuse); 3 (Singulière); 4 in E flat
BIS-CD 795/96. Malmö SO, Sixten Ehrling

The Berwald symphonies all come from the four years 1842–5, when he had returned to Sweden from Berlin where he had run an orthopaedic clinic. He spent much of the 1850s running a sawmill and sandworks in northern Sweden. The symphonies are highly individual and finely crafted; Sixten Ehrling's fresh approach is admirable and the playing of the Malmö orchestra lively and well disciplined. The *Sinfonie sérieuse* was recorded in 1970 and is arguably the finest account of the work ever recorded, and there is plenty of sparkle in the *E flat Symphony* too.

BIBER, Heinrich (1644–1704)

Battaglia à 10; (i) Requiem à 15
Alia Vox AV 9825. (i) Soloists, La Capella Reial de Catalunya; Le Concert des Nations, Savall

Biber's music is highly original and imaginative, using vocal and choral effects with equal resourcefulness. His *Battle* sequence has some bizarre instrumental effects, well realized by Jordi Savall and his group. They open with dance-like vigour and create plenty of light and shade. The closing *Lament* is gently touching. The *Requiem* is recorded, like the *Missa Bruxellensis* below, in Salzburg Cathedral, which Savall accommodates in a spacious performance that moves forward strongly – in every way a superbly eloquent account with splendid soloists. The overall balance is amazingly successful, the separation is natural but is all bathed in the richly resonant cathedral ambience. This is a magnificent disc in every way and almost certainly first choice for the *Requiem*.

Mystery (Rosenkranz) Violin Sonatas (complete)
Virgin 5 62062-2 (2). Holloway, Moroney, Tragicomedia

Biber's set of *Mystery* (or *Rosary*) *Sonatas* for violin and continuo tells the
Christian story in instrumental terms. There are 15 sonatas, divided into three
groups: *The Five Joyful Mysteries* (the Annunciation; Visitation; Nativity; Presentation of the Infant Jesus; and the Twelve-year-old Jesus in the Temple);
The Five Sorrowful Mysteries (Christ on the Mount of Olives; the Scourging at
the Pillar; Crowning with Thorns; Carrying of the Cross; and the Crucifixion)
and *The Five Glorious Mysteries* (the Resurrection; Ascension; Descent of the
Holy Ghost; Assumption of the Virgin; and Coronation of the Virgin). The work
ends with an expressively powerful extended slow *Passacaglia* which becomes
steadily more complex. John Holloway's strong instrumental personality is
very telling. Davitt Moroney (chamber organ or harpsichord) and Tragicomedia
provide an imaginative continuo, using viola da gamba, lute, harp and a regal
for the Crowning with Thorns. The recording gives a most vivid presence to the
soloist.

Missa Bruxellensis
Alia Vox AV 9808. Soloists, La Capella Reial de Catalunya, Le Concert des Nations, Savall

This gloriously festive *Missa Bruxellensis* – a late (perhaps final) work, dating
from 1700 – is scored for two eight-voice choirs, groups of wind, strings, and a
bass continuo of organs and bassoons. The disposition of the soloists, choristers and instruments in the stalls, around the transept, and in the cathedral
choir was designed to add to the sense of spectacle, and the music is fully
worthy of its ambitious layout. Its imaginative diversity, with continued contrasts
between *tutti* and *soli* of great expressive power, shows the composer working
at full stretch. The *Kyrie* opens in great splendour with the two antiphonal
choirs and festive trumpets (*cornets à bouquin*). The closing *Agnus Dei* has the
soloists singing radiantly, but with piercing dissonances from Biber's extraordinary sustained suspensions, with the full forces then entering for the closing
Amen. The performance here, superlatively recorded in the echoing – but never
blurring – acoustics of Salzburg Cathedral, re-creates the work's première and
is truly inspired. This marvellous disc cannot be recommended too highly.

BIRTWISTLE, Harrison (born 1934)

The Minotaur (DVD version)
Opus Arte DVD OA1000D. Tomlinson, Reuter, Rice, Watts, Langridge, Echalaz,
    ROHCG O & Ch., Pappano (Dir.: Stephen Langridge)

This, Birtwistle's eighth opera, like *Gawain,* his earlier commission from Covent Garden, has a libretto by David Harsent, using a language nicely balanced

between poetry and the vernacular, while Birtwistle's idiom, always abrasive, has developed here a more lyrical strain. As in previous operas Birtwistle is not only preoccupied with Greek myth but with central characters who are anti-heroes. In *The Minotaur* the piece rises to a superb final climax when, after Theseus has killed the Minotaur (in this incarnation with a bull's head and a human body), the monster is finally allowed to speak, so that the concluding monologue as he is dying echoes directly the Death of Boris in Mussorgsky's *Boris Godunov*, a likeness that Birtwistle intends. With typical ingenuity Birtwistle has created a lyrical thread passed from instrument to instrument symbolizing the thread that Ariadne gives to Theseus to lead him back through the Minotaur's maze.

The impact of the opera is greatly heightened not just by the casting but by the staging by Stephen Langridge at the Royal Opera House, Covent Garden, very well filmed on this DVD with simple yet vividly atmospheric designs by Alison Chitty. The role of The Minotaur as a sort of Jekyll and Hyde figure was expressly designed for Sir John Tomlinson, famed Wotan from Bayreuth and centrally cast too in Birtwistle's earlier *Gawain*. His voice may no longer be as steady as it was, but his singing could not be more moving. There are no reservations whatever about Christine Rice as Ariadne, superb in every way, and other fine contributions come from the bass-baritone, Johan Reuter, as Theseus and Philip Langridge as the Oracle, while Antonio Pappano, Music Director at Covent Garden, excels himself, conducting an electrifying performance with orchestra and chorus finely coordinated.

BIZET, Georges (1838–75)

L'Arlésienne (incidental music): *Suites 1–3* (*Suite 3* compiled Minkowski); *Carmen: Suite*
Naïve V 5130. Lyon Nat. Opéra Ch., Musiciens du Louvre, Minkowski

Minkowski's compilation from Bizet's *L'Arlésienne* offers the most generous available selection of music from this delightful score, fitting a third suite between the familiar *Suites 1* and 2, with the chorus adding much beauty to the *Pastorale*, the Second Act *Tableau* and extra vividness to the *Farandole*. The orchestral playing is first rate in every way, with an especially delicate contribution from the flutes, and the famous string *Adagietto* is tenderly played *Andante quasi Adagio*, as the composer indicated. The *Carmen Suite* is vivaciously colourful and, throughout, the recording is of demonstration quality. As if this were not enough, the handsome packaging, in a beautifully printed book form, is a pleasure in itself, interspersed with famous French paintings by Van Gogh, Gauguin and others.
Symphony in C – see under Beecham: 'French Music'.

Carmen (DVD version)

TDK DV-CLOPCAR. Obraztsova, Domingo, Buchanan, Mazurok, V. State Op., Ch. & O,
Carlos Kleiber (Stage and V/D: Franco Zeffirelli)

Carmen (complete, CD version)

Ⓜ EMI 5 67357-2 (3). De los Angeles, Gedda, Micheau, Blanc, Fr. R. Ch. & O, Beecham

Zeffirelli's 1978 live DVD recording will be hard to surpass. Eleana Obraztsova
and Domingo are ideally cast as Carmen and Don José. They act very convincingly and sing gloriously (the *Flower Song* is as memorable as Carmen's hit
numbers). Moreover, for once there is a totally convincing Micaëla in Isobel
Buchanan, who also sings ravishingly. Her Act III scene and aria is a highlight
of the opera. From the opening Prelude Carlos Kleiber directs with fizzing
vitality and drama, yet creates a warmly sympathetic backcloth for the voices
in the lyrical writing: the close of Act II is unforgettable, as, of course, is the
opera's final scene. Zeffirelli's production is predictably spectacular (especially
in the outer Acts) and traditional in the best possible way, and the camera follows the action admirably. The sound cannot be faulted. The set is additionally
offered in a reduced-price box with Giordano's *Fedora* and Verdi's *Il trovatore*,
both with Domingo, and *Il trovatore* conducted by Karajan (TDK Gold Edition:
DV-GOLDBOX2).

Victoria de los Angeles's portrayal of Carmen is absolutely bewitching, and
when in the Quintet scene she says '*Je suis amoureuse*' one believes her absolutely. Naturally the other singers are not nearly as dominant as this, but they
make admirable foils; Nicolai Gedda is pleasantly light-voiced as ever, Janine
Micheau is a sweet Micaëla, and Ernest Blanc makes an attractive Escamillo.
The hall acoustic makes the chorus sound very resonant but gives an attractive
theatrical atmosphere to the solo voices, caught naturally and without edginess, and well balanced in relation to the orchestra. At its mid-price, this
famous set reasserts its position near the top of the list of recommendations
and makes a worthy addition to EMI's 'Great Recordings of the Century'. Beecham adds his own special touch to the orchestral interludes. The documentation
cannot be faulted, including session photographs and a full translation.

BLISS, Arthur (1891–1975)

(i) ***Adam Zero*** (ballet): ***Suite***; ***Mêlée fantasque***; ***Hymn to Apollo***;
(i–ii) ***Rout for Soprano & Orchestra***; (iii) ***Serenade for Orchestra &
Baritone***; (iv) ***The World is charged with the grandeur of God***

Lyrita SRCD 225. LSO, (i) cond. composer; (ii) with Rae Woodland; (iii) Shirley-Quirk, cond.
Brian Priestman; (iv) Amb. S., cond. Ledger

This CD does not contain Bliss's most memorable piece of music (the *March*
from *Things to Come* – see below), but it does contain a varied and very attractive

collection of pieces which show the composer at his most entertaining. The *Dance of Spring* from *Adam Zero* is exhilarating in its rhythmic drive and pounding timpani, while the following *Bridal Ceremony* – and especially the lively *Dance of Summer* – are equally enjoyable. The *Mêlée fantasque* (well named) is even more striking, with strong Stravinskian influences but with a characteristic elegiac section at its centre. After the *Hymn to Apollo*, although the rest of the programme is primarily vocal, it is in fact the orchestral writing that one remembers most vividly, for the *Serenade* has two purely orchestral movements out of three. The second, *Idyll*, shows Bliss's lyrical impulse at its most eloquent. The orchestra is almost more important than the voice in *Rout*. The solo vocal performances throughout this CD are of high quality, and John Shirley-Quirk's swashbuckling account of the gay finale of the *Serenade* must have pleased the composer greatly. In *The World is charged with the grandeur of God*, the invention is less memorable, and it is again the orchestration that shows the composer's imagination at work, notably the atmospheric scoring for the flutes in the second section. The recordings date from the early 1970s and are of high quality.

Film Music: *Caesar and Cleopatra: Suite*; *The Royal Palaces: Suite*; *Things to Come: Concert Suite*; *War in the Air: Theme*. *Welcome the Queen*
Chan. 9896. BBC PO, Rumon Gamba

It seems extraordinary that Bliss's great pioneering film score for *Things to Come*, some 45 minutes of music, became lost in its original form. Now, thanks to Philip Lane, we can at last hear this inspired music, a wonderfully orchestrated score, as Bliss conceived it, with the closing *Epilogue* full of Elgarian *nobilmente* spirit. The *March* – perhaps the composer's finest inspiration – is played with tremendous verve here, and elsewhere the score's dramatic moments make a great impact. *Caesar and Cleopatra* exists in a faded working manuscript, and again it shows him in inspirational form. The three *Dance Interludes* are all very different, yet conjure up a warm, nostalgic glow. *War in the Air*, with its Waltonesque opening fanfare, was a splendid title- and closing-credits piece of considerable panache. The *Royal Palaces Suite* displays plenty of regality and also shows the composer at his most diverting and tuneful in the charming *Waltz* from *The Ballroom in Buckingham Palace*; and altogether this splendid CD confirms Bliss as a composer of resource who could write good tunes to order – at least in the early part of his career. Bliss's rollicking *Welcome the Queen* gets the CD off to a splendid start, and the Chandos recording is first class.

Checkmate (ballet): *Suite*
ⓑ Hyp. Helios CDH 55099. E. N. Philh. O, Lloyd-Jones – **LAMBERT**: *Horoscope*;
 WALTON: *Façade*

David Lloyd-Jones is a highly sympathetic advocate of Bliss's ballet suite, and he includes also the *Prologue*. The Hyperion recording, while warm enough to convey the score's lyricism, has plenty of bite in the *Red Knight's Mazurka*. This is most enjoyable, but it is the superb couplings that make this triptych both distinctive and even more desirable at Helios price.

(i) *Clarinet Quintet*. *String Quartet 2*

ⓑⓑ Naxos 8.557394. Maggini Qt; (i) with David Campbell

Bliss's masterly *Clarinet Quintet* is given a searching account by David Campbell with the Maggini group; the latter go on to offer an equally dedicated performance of the *Second Quartet*, full of intensity and imagination. An altogether memorable coupling, very well recorded.

BLOCH, Ernest (1880–1959)

Schelomo (Hebraic Rhapsody) for Cello & Orchestra

DG (ADD) 457 761-2. Fournier, BPO, Wallenstein – **BRUCH**: *Kol Nidrei;* **LALO**: *Cello Concerto*. **SAINT-SAËNS**: *Cello Concerto 1*

Bloch's most famous piece of music is undoubtedly *Schelomo* ('A Voice in the Wilderness') – a rhapsody for cello and orchestra. Its exotic, Semitic harmonies create a richly coloured atmosphere which is quite compelling and almost hypnotic. If Fournier is a bit too closely balanced in this fervent account from 1966, he is excellently supported by Wallenstein, and the sound, apart from the balance, is excellent.

BOCCHERINI, Luigi (1743–1805)

(i) *Cello Concerto 9 in B flat* (original version, revised Gendron); (ii–iii) *Flute Concerto in D, Op. 27* (attrib.; now thought to be by Franz Pokorny); (iv) *Symphonies 3 in C; 5 in B flat, Op. 12/3 & 5;* (v) *Guitar Quintets 4 in D (Fandango); 9 in C (La Ritirata de Madrid);* (vi) *String Quartet in D, Op. 6/1;* (iii) *String Quintet in E, Op. 13/5: Minuet* (only)

Decca 438 377-2 (2). (i) Gendron, LOP, Casals; (ii) Gazzelloni; (iii) I Musici; (iv) New Philh. O, Leppard; (v) Pepe Romero, ASMF Chamber Ens.; (vi) Italian Qt

Surely no one can hear Boccherini's 'Minuet' without thinking of *The Lady Killers* – it is a real charmer of a work and, of course, has to be included on any 'Best of Boccherini' collection, such as this. In fact, Boccherini wrote much music of equally melodic appeal and this inexpensive two-CD set is a good way to start to explore it. It includes Gendron's version of the *Cello Concerto*; it was he who pioneered the return of the original version (without Grützmacher's re-working), and what an enjoyable work it is too. Equally pleasing (and one can see why it was attributed to Boccherini) is the *Flute Concerto*, a splendidly sparkling *galant* work with a very catchy finale. Splashes of Spanish colour are found in the *Guitar Quintet No. 4* with its Fandango finale, and in the *Quintet No. 9* ('*La Ritirata di Madrid*'), both works reflecting his time spent in that country. Both receive excellent performances from Pepe Romero and the ASMF Chamber Ensemble. The *Symphonies* are full of vitality in these excellent performances under Raymond Leppard and are very well recorded. The Italian Quartet's performance of the *D major Quartet* is notable for its freshness and refinement – and its minor-keyed slow movement is as memorable as its charming finale. All these recordings encourage one to explore more of this composer's output, and with many fine recordings available from CPO, Naxos, Hyperion, Virgin, Chandos and others, there is plenty of exploring to do.

Cello Quintet (for cello & strings), Op. 37/7
Ⓜ Australian Decca Eloquence 421 637-2. ASMF, Marriner – **MENDELSSOHN**: *Octet, Op. 20*

Boccherini's *Quintet* is an inspired piece and makes this disc worth getting for its own sake, though the coupled performance of the Mendelssohn *Octet* is a particularly fine one. The opening movement is curiously haunting, and while the following *Menuett* is charmingly light in spirit, and its finale as jolly as can be, the slow movement has great eloquence, making this a more substantial work than might be expected from this composer. The 1968 recording remains rich and full.

BOÏELDIEU, François (1775–1834)

Harp Concerto in 3 Tempi in C
Ⓜ Decca (ADD) 425 723-2. Marisa Robles, ASMF, Brown – **DITTERSDORF**; **HANDEL**: *Harp Concertos*, etc.

Boïeldieu's *Harp Concerto* is a work which brings real delight. This (originally Argo) recording is still in the demonstration class and very sweet to the ear. The finale lingers in the imagination long after the music has ended: its mixture of melody, wit and a touch of melancholy is very seductive. To make this reissue even more attractive, three beguiling sets of variations have been added, including music by Beethoven and a *Theme, Variations and Rondo Pastorale* attributed to Mozart.

La Dame Blanche (opera: complete)
Ⓑ EMI 3 95118-2 (2). Rockwell Blake, Naouri, Fouchécourt, Deletré, Massis, Delunsch, Brunet, Dehont, Vajou, R. France Ch., Paris Ens. O, Minkowski

Boïeldieu's engaging overture to *La Dame Blanche* is one of the true miniature masterpieces of light music. (It is worth including here a true story of the experience of a first-class bassoon player (William Greenlees) who went straight from the Royal Manchester College of Music to a seasonal summer engagement with the Spa Orchestra at Scarborough. They gave concerts daily, playing everything from sight – something for which British musicians are famous. Bill was warned by his professor at the College to beware of *The White Lady Overture*, in which the bassoonist turns a page immediately before the second subject arrives, heralded by fast *solo* bassoon arpeggios (noticeably audible with a small orchestra). Having watched out carefully for the arrival of the piece on a daily basis, Bill realized that his moment had come only when he turned the page of *La Dame Blanche* and realized that he had been caught out! Instantly translating the title in his head, with great resource he looked quickly at the key signature and quickly filled in the gap by playing *a tempo* semiquaver scales in the correct key. Afterwards the conductor, Jan Hurst, congratulated him for being the first bassoonist in the history of the concerts not to break down altogether!)

The opera itself is a charmingly delicate score which uses the Scottish-based melodies (from the opera) which the composer infused with a typically Gallic flavour to piquant effect. The opera was hugely successful in its day, but this is its first complete modern recording, and it is a delightful set in every way. Completed in 1826, this light-hearted adaptation of Sir Walter Scott's novel sparkles from first to last, helped by the inspired direction of Marc Minkowski with an excellent team of soloists who all sing with a natural feeling for the idiom. This is a piece which, with its many lively ensembles, points directly forward to Donizetti's *Daughter of the Regiment* and even to Offenbach's two gendarmes from *Geneviève de Brabant*. Good teamwork in this opera is more important than great solo singing; but here the cast has no weak link, with the outstanding Rossinian tenor, Rockwell Blake, matched by the others, not least by Annik Massis as Anna and Mireille Delunsch as Jenny. For some non-French speakers there may be rather too much dialogue, but that can easily be excised on CD. Warm, well-balanced sound. It is now available at bargain price, though, alas, without texts or translations.

BONYNGE, Richard

'Overtures and Ballet Music of the Nineteenth Century'
(with (i) New Philh. O, or (ii) LSO): Disc 1: (i) Overtures: **AUBER**: *Marco Spada*; *Lestocq*. **ADAM**: *Giralda*; *La Poupée du Nuremberg*. **LECOCQ**: *La Fille de Madame Angot*. **THOMAS**: *Mignon*. **PLANQUETTE**: *Les Cloches de Corneville*. **BOIELDIEU**: *Le Calife de Bagdad*; *La Dame Blanche*. (ii) Ballet Music: **MEYERBEER**: *Le Prophète: Coronation March*. **MASSENET**:

La Navarraise: Nocturne. **GOUNOD**: *La Reine de Saba, Act II: Waltz*. **BIZET**: *Don Procopio*. Disc 2: (ii) Overtures: **DONIZETTI**: *Roberto Devereux*. **ROSSINI**: *Torvaldo e Dorliska*. **MAILLART**: *Les Dragons de Villars*. **OFFENBACH**: *La Fille du tambour-major*. **VERDI**: *Giovanna d'Arco*. **HÉROLD**: *Zampa*. **WALLACE**: *Maritana*. **AUBER**: *La Neige*. **MASSENET**: *Chérubin, Act III: Entr'acte*; *Don César de Bazan: Entr'acte Sevillana*; *Les Erinnyes: Invocation*. **GOUNOD**: *Le Tribut de Zamora, Act III: Danse grecque*. **SAINT-SAËNS**: *Henry VIII, Act II: Danse de la gypsy*. **DELIBES**: *Le Roi l'a dit, Act II: Entr'acte*

Ⓑ Double Decca (ADD) 466 431-2 (2)

This superb programme is based on three Richard Bonynge LPs, two with the LSO and one with the New Philharmonia Orchestra, again from the late 1960s-early 1970s. The repertoire of once-popular music is deliciously programmed, and although some of the repertoire is available elsewhere (the *Zampa* and *Mignon Overtures*, for example) much of it is still only heard on these recordings. Of the three Auber overtures – all of them rarities – *Marco Spada* has a most evocative opening, suggesting a sunrise, before bursting into one of the composer's typical galloping *Allegros*; *Lestocq* contains a memorably wistful theme on the oboe, before again launching into an irresistibly jaunty *Allegro*, while *La Neige*, more subtle than usual, shows the composer's gift for writing catchy tunes quite early in his career. Adam's *Giralda* and *La Poupée de Nuremberg* display all the delicacy and skill we know from his ballet scores; the former includes glittering castanets for a dash of local colour while the latter features an unexpected passage for string quartet. Boieldieu's charming *La Dame Blanche* is as light as thistledown and *The Caliph of Bagdad* has never sounded more resplendent. Lecocq's *La Fille de Madame Angot* is quite felicitous. Among the LSO performances, *Maritana* stands out. Bonynge presents this with great affection, the melodramatic opening arresting and the hit tune, 'Scenes that are Brightest', lusciously presented. Rossini's *Torvaldo e Dorliska* is interesting in including the second subject of the *Cenerentola Overture*, while Donizetti's *Roberto Devereux* even draws on 'God Save the Queen'. Offenbach's winning *La Fille du tambour-major* is piquantly scored, ending with an exuberant *Can-can* played with superb gusto. We also turn to the LSO for the ballet music. Besides a brilliant account of Meyerbeer's *Coronation March*, there is a series of *bon-bouches*, including Massenet's haunting *Invocation*, a cello solo from *Les Erinnyes*) and the *Nocturne* from *La Navarraise*. Gounod's *Grande valse* from *La Reine de Saba* sounds as though it has been left over from the *Faust* ballet music, while Saint Saëns's *Gypsy Dance* from *Henry VIII*, with its ominous timpani strokes, turns into a tuneful *valse macabre*. The programme ends with a charming pastiche *Minuet* from Delibes's *Le Roi l'a dit*. Bonynge is a complete master of this repertoire, which he clearly loves, and all this music is chic and poised in his hands and, of course, brilliantly played, so that enjoyment is assured.

BORODIN, Alexander (1833–87)

'The World of Borodin': (i) *In the Steppes of Central Asia. Prince Igor*: (ii) *Overture*; (ii–iii) *Polovtsian Dances*; (iv) *Symphony 2 in B min*. (v) *String Quartet 2: Nocturne*; (vi) (Piano) *Scherzo in A flat*; (vii–viii) Song: *Far from the shores of your native land*; (vii; ix) *Prince Igor: Galitzky's Aria*

ⓜ Decca 444 389-2. (i) SRO, Ansermet; (ii) LSO, Solti; (iii) with L. Symphony Ch.;
    (iv) LSO, Martinon; (v) Borodin Qt; (vi) Ashkenazy; (vii) N. Ghiaurov; (viii) Z. Ghiaurov;
    (ix) L. Symphony Ch., LSO, Downes

It is not often that a composer's output can be encapsulated on a single disc in 76 minutes. Solti's *Prince Igor Overture* shows him at his finest and the *Polovtsian Dances* follow on excitingly. Ansermet's contribution, *In the Steppes of Central Asia*, too is impressive, as are the *Nocturne* and the solo vocal items. But the highlight of the disc is Martinon's unsurpassed (1960) LSO account of the *Second Symphony*, ideally paced, where the sound has remarkable presence and sparkle. Indeed, the opening of this striking symphony grabs you by the throat in this recording and makes an unforgettable impression, though it is the colour of the score and its memorable tunes which give the most lasting impression.

BOUGHTON, Rutland (1878–1960)

The Immortal Hour (opera: complete)
ⓑ Hyp. Dyad CDD 22040 (2). Kennedy, Dawson, Wilson-Johnson, M. Davies,
    George Mitchell Ch., ECO, Melville

Enormously successful in its day, to modern ears much of *The Immortal Hour* may seem like Vaughan Williams and water. But with its famous hit, the *Faery Song*, its simple tunefulness is most appealing. This fine performance, conducted by a lifelong Boughton devotee, brings out the hypnotic quality which had 1920s music-lovers attending peformances many times over, entranced by the lyrical evocation of Celtic twilight. The excellent cast of young singers includes Anne Dawson as the heroine, Princess Etain, and Maldwyn Davies, headily beautiful in the main tenor rendering of the delightful *Faery Song*. Warm, reverberant recording, enhanced by its CD format, this engaging opera is not to be missed at its reissued Dyad price.

BOULANGER, Lili (1893–1918)

Faust et Hélène; Psaume 24; Psaume 130; Du fond de l'abîme; D'un matin de printemps; D'un soir triste
Chan. 9745. Dawson, Murray, Bottone, MacKenzie, Howard, CBSO Ch., BBC PO, Y.-P.
   Tortelier

There is a haunting and often poignant quality to the music of Lili Boulanger, in part because she died so young. *Faust et Hélène* has astonishing beauty and a natural eloquence. Like *Psaume 24, Du fond de l'abîme* and the other music on this disc, it offers testimony to an altogether remarkable talent. There is a distinguished team of soloists (Lynne Dawson and Bonaventura Bottone in the cantata and Ann Murray in one of the Psalms) and first-rate contributions from the Birmingham chorus and the BBC Philharmonic under Yan-Pascal Tortelier. An altogether magical collection.

BOWEN, York (1884–1961)

(i) *Piano Concerto 1, Op. 11*; (ii) *Violin Concerto, Op. 33*
Ⓜ Dutton CDLX 7169. BBC Concert O, Handley, with (i) Michael Dussek;
   (ii) Lorraine McAslan

The *Piano Concerto* is an early work, composed when Bowen was nineteen. There are some reminiscences of Saint-Saëns and Litolff, but the piece has refreshing fluency and charm. The *Violin Concerto* failed to find a persuasive champion and soon disappeared from the repertoire until this excellent recording restored it to circulation. As an eight-year-old boy, York Bowen made his début in a Dussek concerto, so it is appropriate that Michael Dussek, who is descended from the composer, should play it here.

(i) *Piano Concertos 2 (Concertstück), Op. 17; 3 (Fantasia), Op. 23. Symphonic Fantasia, Op. 16*
Ⓜ Dutton CDLX 7187. (i) Dussek; BBC Concert O, Handley

This couples the *Second Concerto* (subtitled *Concertstück*) with the *Third* (1907) and the *Symphonic Fantasia*, which no less a conductor than Hans Richter championed with the LSO. Bowen was still in his early twenties when they were written and these pieces all have a youthful freshness and generosity of feeling. Excellent notes from Lewis Foreman enhance the appeal of these most welcome and admirably performed issues.

Ballade 2; 3 Miniatures, Op. 44; 3 Pieces, Op. 20; from 3 Preludes: 2 & 3; 3 Serious Dances, Op. 51; 3 Songs without words, Op. 94
Chan. 10506. Celis

24 Preludes, Op. 102; *Sonata 6 in B flat min., Op. 160*; *Reverie, Op. 86*

Chan. 10277. Celis

The Dutch pianist Joop Celis proves an enthusiastic and highly virtuosic exponent of York Bowen and he offers a valuable anthology of his solo piano music.
Apart from the shorter pieces, he is very impressive in the magnificent *Sixth
Sonata*, and even more rewarding in the *24 Preludes*, eclectic but with something unmistakably English about them.

The *B flat minor Sonata*, Op. 160, was York Bowen's last composition, composed just before he died in 1961, and he never wrote anything finer. It is a
magnificent work. But it is the *24 Preludes*, in all the major and minor keys,
written just before the Second World War, which demonstrates the full range
of Bowen's piano writing. Stephen Hough has already recorded a selection, but
the Dutch pianist, Joop Celis, gives us the lot and shows us just how fascinating and rewarding they are. There are touches of Rachmaninov, Scriabin and
Debussy, and they stem from the spiritual world of Brahms – yet, like in the
Sonata, there is something unmistakably English about them. Fine, realistic
recording makes this a most desirable issue.

BRAHMS, Johannes (1833–97)

(i) *Piano Concertos 1 in D min., Op. 15*; *2 in B flat, Op. 83*. *Fantasias, Op. 116*

Ⓜ DG (ADD) 447 446-2 (2). Gilels; (i) BPO, Jochum

This set represents Gilels at his finest, and his partnership with Jochum is
similarly masterly. The opening of the *Second Concerto*, with its glorious
Brahmsian horn solo so beautifully matched by Gilels's reponse, is unforgettable; but all three performances are unsurpassed and the remastered recording
is outstanding.

Violin Concerto in D, Op. 77

RCA (ADD) SACD 09026 61742-2. Heifetz, Chicago SO, Reiner – **BEETHOVEN**:
   Violin Concerto

Like the Beethoven with which it is coupled, the SACD transfer of Heifetz's
dazzling performance makes vivid and fresh what on LP was originally rather
harsh Chicago recording, more aggressive than the Boston sound in the
Beethoven. However, with the new CD transfer the excellent qualities of RCA's
Chicago balance for Reiner come out in full, giving a fine, three-dimensional
focus. The EMI mono Milstein/Steinberg performance should also not be
forgotten. It is simply glorious: a performance of surpassing beauty, its virtuosity effortless, and with a tremendous breadth, warmth and eloquence (EMI
5 67583-2).

Double Concerto for Violin, Cello & Orchestra, Op. 102

EMI DVD 490449-9. D. Oistrakh, Rostropovich, Moscow PO, Kondrashin (with
   BACH: *Unaccompanied Cello Suite 1: Bourrées 1–2; Double Violin Concerto).*
   MOZART: *Sinfonia concertante for Violin, Viola & Orchestra, K.364*
   (both with I. Oistrakh, cond. Menuhin)
Ⓑ EMI CD (ADD) 6 31768-2. D. Oistrakh, Rostropovich, Cleveland O, Szell –
   BEETHOVEN: *Triple Concerto*

The DVD Brahms and Mozart recordings were made during the Moscow Philharmonic's visit to London in October 1965 and September 1963 respectively.
The *Double Concerto* is a highly charged account which shows both David Oistrakh and Rostropovich at their most emotionally intense yet profoundly
disciplined. Mozart's heavenly *Sinfonia concertante* with Oistrakh *père et fils* was
recorded in the Royal Albert Hall and with Menuhin rather than Kondrashin at
the helm. David Nice's notes speak of 'the elegance and focused tone David
Oistrakh draws from the viola', and this is a joy in itself. The Bach *Double Concerto in D minor* was recorded in Paris earlier, in October 1958, and affords an
admirable opportunity for contrasting the golden tone of the one with (on this
occasion) the seraphic playing of the other. Rostropovich's very intense accounts
of the two solo *Bourrées* make a welcome bonus. Of course the sound calls for
some tolerance, but this film is a rarity and it is to be treasured.

The Cleveland version was made in 1969 in Severance Hall. In most respects
this is even finer than the earlier London account, having claims to be considered the most desirable of versions, even though the recording is not ideally
smooth. With Szell at the helm this is perhaps the most powerful performance
since the days of Heifetz and Feuermann, or Thibaud and Casals, and it deserves
the strongest recommendation.

(i) Serenades 1 in D, Op. 11; (ii) 2 in A, Op. 16

ⒷⒷ Warner Apex 2564 61138-2. (i) Royal Stockholm PO, Andrew Davis;
   (ii) Ens. Orchestral de Paris, Jordan

It is a pity that Kertész's Decca coupling of both Brahms *Serenades* has been
withdrawn as a single disc, but Andrew Davis and the Stockholm Orchestra give
a spirited account of the D major work, and Davis's direction is as sympathetic
as the players' response. The recording is very good too, even if the texture
could be more transparent. For the budget reissue, it is joined by Armin Jordan's more mellow performance of the companion A major work, which has a
warmly played slow movement and an engaging closing Rondo. Again, the
sound is pleasingly full with a nice bloom on the woodwind. This is excellent
value at Apex price and fills an important gap in the catalogue.

Symphonies 1–4

Ⓑ DG Virtuoso (ADD) 4284218 (1&3); 4284219 (2&4)

Karajan's set dates from the late 1970s and is unsurpassed among modern
recordings, although the Furtwängler performances (see below under the

conductor) are not quite eclipsed. Karajan demonstrates that his readings of the Brahms symphonies, with lyrical and dramatic elements finely balanced, changed little over the years, though it is worth noting that his approach to No. 1, the work with which he most completely identified, is even bigger in scale than his earlier Berlin version of 1964. The commanding new version of No. 2 brings a finale which is now very fast, challenging even the Berlin players, while No. 3 has become stronger and more direct. In No. 4 Karajan refuses to overstate the first movement, starting with deceptive reticence (rather like Boehm). His easily lyrical style is fresh and unaffected, and highly persuasive. The Scherzo, fierce and strong, leads to a clean, weighty account of the finale. The playing of the Berlin Philharmonic remains uniquely cultivated, the ensemble is finely polished, and yet there is no lack of warmth or impetus throughout the set. Reissued on a pair of virtuoso separate virtuoso reissues, this is altogether most satisfying.

(i) *Clarinet Quintet, Op. 115*; (ii) *Clarinet Trio in A min.*
Hyp. CDA 66107. Thea King, with (i) Gabrieli Qt; (ii) Georgian (cello), Benson (piano)

Thea King and the Gabrieli Quartet give a radiantly beautiful performance of the *Clarinet Quintet*, as fine as any put on record, expressive and spontaneous-sounding, with natural ebb and flow of tension as in a live performance, and the *Trio* is hardly less persuasive. The recording of the strings is very vivid and real.

(i-iii) *Horn Trio in E flat*; (ii-iii) *Violin Sonata 1, Op. 78*; (iii) *7 Fantasias, Op. 116*
HM HMC 90 1981. (i) Van der Zwart; (ii) Faust; (iii) Melnikov

Brahms specifically wrote his warmly romantic *Horn Trio* for the natural Waldhorn, without valves, and here we have an inspired performance in which Teunis van der Zwart uses such a natural horn. This means that he has to 'stop' the notes which are not natural harmonics by putting his right hand firmly inside in the instrument's bell to make them sound in tune; it also alters their timbre. This is a unique performance and the result is a triumph, with 'stopped' notes adding to the range of colour, as the composer intended. Isabelle Faust and Alexander Melnikov make fine partners and the lovely *Violin Sonata* is also played with much warmth.

Piano Quintet in F min., Op. 34
Virgin 3 951413-2. Andsnes, Artemis Qt (with **SCHUMANN**: *Piano Quintet*)

The Brahms and Schumann *Piano Quintets* are both passionately romantic works in which the piano often leads the ensemble strongly. They make a perfect coupling. Andsnes, whose playing is full of personality, and the Artemis Quartet, who have a fine presence, give a magisterial account of the Brahms and are no less compelling in the Schumann. The recording is natural and vivid, and this pairing is unlikely to be surpassed.

String Quintets 1 in F, Op. 88; 2 in G, Op. 111
ⓑ Hyp. Helios CDH 55369. Raphael Ens.

These are fine, vital performances of both works from the Raphael Ensemble. The *First Quintet* opens seductively, and the playing in both works is on the same level of distinction as their accounts of the *String Sextets* and, like that companion Hyperion disc, the recording is very present indeed.

String Sextets 1 in B flat, Op. 18; 2 in G, Op. 36
Hyp CDA 66276. Raphael Ens.

The *Sextets* are among Brahms's most appealing chamber works, and the Raphael Ensemble are fully responsive to their vitality and warmth. In short these are superb performances, and the recording is very vivid and immediate.

Violin Sonatas 1, Op. 78; 2, Op. 100; 3, Op. 108
Sony 88697 623842. Liebeck, Apekisheva

Many discs offer the three Brahms *Violin Sonatas* as an ideal coupling, but few are as satisfying as this Sony issue, with the prize-winning British virtuoso, Jack Liebeck, joined in a remarkable partnership with the Russian pianist, Katya Apekisheva. Where other virtuoso violinists sometimes tend to regard their pianist merely as an accompanist, this young duo work as equals, each responding to the other in performances that consistently sound spontaneous.

They also bring out the subtle contrasts between the three works. In No. 1 the lyrical warmth of the first movement is set against the deeply meditative quality of the slow movement, leading on to the finale, which is played with almost Mendelssohnian lightness. The compact structure of No.2 suits them equally well, with the first movement bringing the subtlest contrasts of tone from Liebeck, down to a hushed *pianissimo*. The brief, wistfully lyrical slow movement leads to a warm, strong account of the finale with its main 'travelling' theme. The dramatic strength of No. 3 with its minor-key intensity brings another contrast, with Liebeck again finding the widest tonal range in lightness and agility set against power. The dedicated account of the slow movement leads to big, dramatic contrasts in the finale. It is remarkable that each of the players brings such expressive depth to their performances, with echo sequences never played mechanically. Excellent, well-balanced sound.

Piano Music (i) for four hands: *21 **Hungarian Dances*** (original version); (ii) *16 Waltzes, Op. 39*. Solo Piano: *4 Ballades, Op. 10*; *7 Fantasias, Op. 116*; *3 Intermezzi, Op. 117*; *6 Pieces, Op. 118*; *4 Pieces, Op. 119*; *2 Rhapsodies, Op. 79*; *Sonata 3 in F min., Op. 5*; *16 Waltzes, Op. 39*; *Variations and Fugue on a Theme by Handel, Op. 24*; *Variations on a theme by Schumann, Op. 9*
ⓑ Regis/Vox CD5X 3612-2 (5). Walter Klien; with (i) Brendel; (ii) Beatriz Klien

Walter Klien's recordings derive from the Vox catalogue in the early days of stereo LP. They are very distinguished and this collection makes an admirable way to explore Brahms's most familiar and rewarding piano repertoire. Klien's performance of the *F minor Sonata* is unsurpassed, with all the spontaneous buoyancy of youth. He is equally at home in the classicism of the *Handel Variations* and the romanticism of Brahms/Schumann, while his natural sensitivity in the shorter *Pieces* and *Intermezzi* is magical. Alfred Brendel, also early in his career when he was still a Vox recording artist, joins him very successfully for the piano-duo original version of the *Hungarian Dances* and the latter are infectiously jolly. Beatriz Klien is a hardly less successful partner in the *Waltzes*. Fortunately the Vox engineers were at their best, and the piano tone is fully convincing. However, this set may be difficult to get.

Variations and Fugue on a Theme by Handel, Op. 24; 6 Pieces, Op. 118; 4 Pieces, Op. 119; 2 Rhapsodies, Op. 79
Sony 8869 772725-2. Murray Perahia

Murray Perahia's 2010 Brahms collection, recorded in Berlin, is one of his finest CDs yet. The set of *Handel Variations* is both elegant and totally authoritative, and the pair of passionate *Rhapsodies* and two infinitely varied sets of *Pieces*, Opp. 118 and 119, are equally compelling. Published in the year of the composer's sixtieth birthday, they were the last of Brahms's solo piano music. Excellent, vivid recording makes this an indispensable example of Perahia's special identification with the composer.

Liebeslieder Waltzes, Op. 52; New Liebeslieder Waltzes Op. 65; 3 Quartets, Op. 64
Ⓜ DG 477 8619. Mathis, Fassbaender, Schreier, Fischer-Dieskau, with Wolfgang Sawallisch or Karl Engel (piano)

Brahms is reputed to have written on the score of Johann Strauss's *Blue Danube*, 'Unfortunately not written by me', but he was a dab hand at writing seductive waltz sequences for voices, as these *Liebeslieder Waltzes* show. They are surprisingly difficult for the singers, but one would never guess this from the beguiling performances here, with the voices of these four celebrated soloists blending enchantingly, and given admirably lilting backing by the two celebrated pianists in turn. The remastered CD (from 1983) has fine realism and presence.

German Requiem, Op. 45
DG DVD 073 4398. Janowitz, Van Dam, V. Singverein, VPO, Karajan

Karajan's DVD of the *German Requiem*, recorded live at the 1978 Salzburg Festival, is another of his unsurpassed recordings – of a work that he clearly loved greatly. He may keep his eyes closed, but his conducting is very physical and the cameras reveal him as deeply impassioned. His two soloists are first rate: Gundula Janowitz sings gloriously, matched by José van Dam's full tone and sense of drama. The arresting timpani in *Denn alles Fleisch, es ist wie Gras* shows that this is to be a performance of both fervour and fully revealed detail. The huge chorus visually creates a magnificent backcloth; their singing is increasingly rich and powerful and the closing section very moving.

EMI have also reissued Klemperer's measured and monumental Philharmonia recording (with Schwarzkopf and Fischer-Dieskau) in their bargain 'Masters' series. With dynamic contrasts underlined and superb singing from chorus and soloists alike, the result is uniquely powerful and can certainly be considered by Klemperer addicts (EMI 9 65925-2).

BRIDGE, Frank (1879-1941)

Orchestral Works (complete recording)
BBC Nat. O of Wales, Hickox:

Vol. 1: *Enter Spring*; *Isabella*; *Mid of the Night*; *2 Poems for Orchestra*
Chan. 9950

Vol. 2: *Dance Poem*; *Dance Rhapsody*; *5 Entr'actes*; *Norse Legend*; *The Sea*
Chan. 10012

Vol. 3: *Coronation March*; (i) *Phantasm*. *Sir Roger de Coverley (A Christmas Dance)*; *Summer*; *There is a Willow Grows aslant a Brook*; *Vignettes de danse*
Chan. 10112 ((i) with Shelley)

Vol. 4: *Allegro moderato*; *Lament for String Orchestra*; (i) *Oration (Concerto elegiaco)*. *Rebus – Overture for Orchestra*; (ii) *A Prayer* (for chorus & orchestra)
Chan. 10188 (with (i) Gerhardt; (ii) BBC Nat. Ch. of Wales)

Vol. 5: *2 Entr'actes*; *2 Intermezzi from 'Threads'*; *2 Old English Songs*; *Sir Roger de Coverley (A Christmas Dance)*; *Suite for Strings*; *Todessehnsucht*; *Valse Intermezzo à cordes* (arr. Hindmarsh); (i) *The Hag*; *2 Songs of Robert Bridges*
Chan. 10246 ((i) with Williams)

Vol. 6: *Berceuse*; *Chant d'espérance*; *The Pagent of London*; *A Royal Night of Variety*; *Serenade*; (i) *Adoration*; (ii) *Berceuse*; (i) *Blow Out, You Bugles*; (ii) *Day After Day*; (i) *Love Went A-Riding*; (ii) *Mantle of Blue*; *Speak To Me*; (i) *Thy Hand In Mine*; *Where She Lies Asleep*
Chan. 10310 (with (i) Langridge; (ii) Connolly)

Richard Hickox's comprehensive survey of Frank Bridge's orchestral music with the BBC National Orchestra of Wales is one of the highlights of the Chandos catalogue. Volume 1 begins with his fresh and bracing rhapsody, *Enter Spring*, dating from 1927, while his second tone-poem, *Isabella* (1907), brooding and haunting, fully captures Keats's gruesome story which inspired this Lisztian tone-poem. In the longest work on this volume, *Mid of the Night*, Liszt is recalled again, and one has the feeling of a young composer (24) spreading his wings and exploring orchestral colour. The *Two Poems for Orchestra* (1915), the first chromatically sinuous and the second a lively orchestral dance, are also vividly scored.

Volume 2 includes Bridge's most celebrated piece, the tone-poem, *The Sea*, and it here receives a superbly briny performance. The disc opens with an exceptionally lively *Dance Rhapsody* (1908), again brilliantly orchestrated. The light but very charming folk-tune-inspired 5 *Entr'actes* come from the music Bridge wrote for a play, *The Two Hunchbacks*, while the more experimental *Dance Poem*, premièred in 1914, is harmonically and melodically more diffuse. This is followed by the short but beautiful *Norse Legend*, an evocative miniature tone-poem, originally written for violin and piano in 1905, but later (1938) orchestrated.

Volume 3 begins with the stirring *Coronation March* of 1911, which just misses having a truly memorable big tune. *Summer* (1914) evokes a summer's day in the country while *Phantasm* finds Bridge at his most searching and exploratory. As Paul Hindmarsh writes in the sleevenotes, 'it inhabits a spectral world of dreams and ghostly apparitions'. Howard Shelley is the responsive soloist. *There is a Willow Grows aslant a Brook* is hauntingly dark and bleak, as befits its Shakespearean inspiration: Gertrude's Act IV speech in *Hamlet*, in which she describes the drowning of Ophelia. The *Vignettes de danse* are orchestrations of earlier piano pieces, as is the much more famous and hugely enjoyable *Sir Roger de Coverley*, which ends this disc in its full orchestral version.

Volume 4 contains perhaps Bridge's finest orchestral work, the *Oration* for cello and orchestra. Alban Gerhardt's performance can stand alongside the finest earlier accounts. Rarities on this disc include the *Rebus Overture*, the composer's last completed work (1940), and, although the textures are sparer than in his earlier music, the scoring is characteristically original. The *Allegro moderato* (or *Symphony*) *for String Orchestra*, completed by Anthony Pople, shows Bridge at his most deeply eloquent, as does the poignant *Lament* (1915), written for a young friend who died with her family when the *Lusitania* was sunk. *A Prayer*, an anti-war work completed in orchestrated form in 1918, is Bridge's only setting for chorus and orchestra. Deliberately written to be performed by amateur choral societies, its relatively simple style is direct and affecting. The performance and recording here – and throughout this CD – is excellent.

The highlight of Volume 5, the *Suite for Strings* (1909), is full of delightful pastoral writing and piquant colour. Of the *Two Intermezzi from 'Threads'*, the second movement, a pastiche of a Viennese dance, is sparklingly toe-tapping. Both the *Two Old English Songs*, 'Sally in Our Alley' and 'Cherry Ripe', are imaginatively scored, with the former in lush harmonies and the latter turned into a virtuoso string tour de force for strings, where the tune only emerges from the hustle and bustle towards the close. *Todessehnsucht* is an arrangement of Bach (the funeral chorale, *Komm, Süsser Tod*) which is Stokowskian in its sumptuous grandeur. The nostalgic pair of *Entr'actes* are orchestrated piano works and evoke much warm nostalgia. The *Valse Intermezzo à cordes* is a stylish early student work, beautifully crafted and surprisingly memorable. Roderick Williams is the superb baritone in the lively setting of Robert Herrick's poem, *The Hag*, and the *Two Songs of Robert Bridges* are no less colourfully evocative.

The final volume largely comprises Bridge's orchestral songs, beginning with the stirring *Blow Out, You Bugles*, based on Rupert Brooke's most famous war poem. The contrasting *Berceuse* is also memorable, with again Bridge's orchestral colour very telling. Sarah Connolly sings it most beautifully too, as she does in all her items. *Love Went A-Riding*, with its galloping accompaniment, is very enjoyable, with the late Philip Langridge lustily vigorous. The orchestral items here include the colourful suite, *The Pageant of London* for wind orchestra, written for a pageant performed at the Crystal Palace in 1911. These are lively music vignettes of 'Ye Olde England' and they receive their première recording here in their original version. The *Berceuse, Chant d'espérance* and *Serenade* are all orchestral miniatures of much pastoral charm. The CD ends with the brief *A Royal Night of Variety*, written for the BBC in 1934, which starts robustly and ends unexpectedly quietly.

Throughout these six collections the BBC National Orchestra of Wales are on top form; they obviously enjoy the music. Hickox is persuasively idiomatic and spontaneous, and the Chandos recording is first class.

Phantasm for Piano & Orchestra

Ⓜ Dutton CDLX 7223. Stott, RPO, Handley (with **IRELAND**: *Piano Concerto*);
   WALTON: *Sinfonia concertante*

Bridge's curiously titled *Phantasm* is a large-scale piano concerto, some 26 minutes long, in a single, massive movement. Kathryn Stott, most sympathetically accompanied by Vernon Handley and the RPO, proves a persuasive, committed interpreter, matching her achievement in the other two works on the disc, and especially the delightful Ireland *Piano Concerto*. Warm, generally well-balanced (originally Conifer) recording.

(i) Piano Quintet. 3 Idylls; String Quartet 4

Hyp. CDA 67726. (i) Lane; Goldner Qt

The *Piano Quintet* dates from 1905, but Bridge completely re-wrote it in 1912. The passionate energy of the original first movement remains, but it is the memorable secondary theme that all but dominates. The broodingly enticing *Adagio* frames a sparkling Scherzo, and the finale reintroduces the main ideas from the first movement at its climax. It is altogether most rewarding and, with Piers Lane leading the Goldner Quartet, the performance here has irresistible impetus and responds to the music's rich, lyrical feeling.

The *Three Idylls*, the second of which Britten used for his celebrated *Variations,* are sheer delight, the first ravishingly, delicately sensuous, and the third more animated but no less winning. They are most beautifully played here. The *Fourth Quartet* (1937), Bridge's last chamber work, is thematically and harmonically much more forward-looking, although it is not atonal. Its atmosphere has a haunted quality, with even the central *Quasi minuetto* far from conventional. The finale is pithily energetic, and once again Bridge closes with quotations from his first movement. But the work has moments of ethereal beauty that place it among the composer's most deeply felt music.

BRITTEN, Benjamin (1913-76)

The Hidden Heart – A Life of Benjamin Britten and Peter Pears
EMI DVD 50999 2 16571-9 (Editor: Jake Martin; Exec. Producers: Nicolas Kent, Vanessa Phillips; Producer/Director: Teresa Griffiths)

This fine documentary, originally produced for Channel 4, offers an intimate and sympathetic portrait of the composer and his friend and interpreter, Peter Pears. Those taking part include Pears's niece and, briefly, members of the Britten family, Donald Mitchell and John Evans. The programme is full of valuable documentary and archival material and concentrates on three periods of Britten's life: *Peter Grimes* from the war's end, with an engaging contribution from the original apprentice; the *War Requiem* from the 1960s; and his last opera, *Death in Venice*, imaginatively pictured and evoked, with Robert Tear in the role of Aschenbach, and an illuminating commentary by James Bowman and John Amis. It brings both the composer and Peter Pears vividly to life and affords many insights into their achievements.

(i) *Violin Concerto*; (ii) *Serenade for Tenor, Horn & Strings, Op. 31*
Ⓑ CfP 5 75978-2. (i) Rodney Friend; (ii) Ian Partridge, Nicholas Busch; LPO, Pritchard (with **TIPPETT**: *Concerto for Double String Orchestra*)

Rodney Friend proves a masterful soloist in the *Violin Concerto*, combining expressive feeling with incisiveness. Ian Partridge then gives a consistently stylish reading of the *Serenade*, often strikingly new in its illumination, more tenderly beautiful than Peter Pears's classic recording with the composer, culminating in a heavenly performance of the final Keats setting. Excellent recording in both works, and Vernon Handley's Tippett coupling is no less memorable. This disc is inexpensive but would be a top choice if it cost far more.

(i) *Simple Symphony*; *Variations on a Theme of Frank Bridge*; (ii) *The Young Person's Guide to the Orchestra*

Decca (ADD) 417 509. Composer, with (i) ECO; (ii) LSO

This early CD compilation has remained at full price in the catalogue since its release in 1986. Lasting an unremarkable 60 minutes, it undoubtedly represents quality over quantity. Britten's *Simple Symphony* is a delight from beginning to end, and the warmth and vitality of the playing has striking presence in this 1969 recording. The strings at the opening sweep one into the fun spirit of this work immediately, and with superbly virtuoso playing in the *Playful Pizzicato* movement and the *Frolicsome Finale* - separated by the beautiful and surprisingly touching *Sentimental Sarabande* - this remains one of the most immediately appealing of all Britten's works. In the *Variations on a Theme of Frank Bridge*, Britten goes more for half-tones and he achieves an almost circumspect coolness in the waltz-parody of the *Romance*, though the *Aria Italiana* which follows is exhilarating; in the *Viennese Waltz* section later, he is again subtly atmospheric; and the *Funeral March* is one of the composer's most searingly haunting and striking pieces. The 1968 recording is again splendid. *The Young Person's Guide to the Orchestra* receives a blistering performance from the composer, which knocks spots off most rival recordings in terms of sheer brilliance, not only in the playing, but in the vivid recorded sound (from 1964). The performance is undoubtedly very fast - so fast, in fact, that even the LSO don't always quite keep up with Britten - but the sheer adrenalin of the music-making is impossible to resist.

(i) *Les Illuminations*; (ii) *Nocturne for Tenor, Seven Obbligato Instruments & Strings, Op. 60*; (i; iii) *Serenade for Tenor, Horn & Strings, Op. 31*

Ⓜ Australian Decca Eloquence mono/stereo 476 8470. Pears; (i) New SO, Goossens; (ii) LSO (members), composer; (iii) with Brain

The Australian Decca CD contains the early release the 1953 recording of the *Serenade for Tenor, Horn and Strings* and *Les Illuminations*, conducted by Goossens. Dennis Brain's horn playing is magical, almost ethereal in its beautiful timbre, with Pears superb in both these works, fresher than in the famous stereo versions under the direction of the composer. Goossens's conducting cannot be faulted - it is highly sensitive and strikingly alert, and the Decca sound is exceptionally good for its period; the voices emerge with uncanny warmth and vividness. The strings may be a little thin in the upper register, but their intensity is fully conveyed: these performances are full of atmosphere. The (1960) stereo recording of the *Nocturne* completes the CD, and we reproduce the original review from the 1961 *Penguin Guide* as not only does it remain as valid as when it was written (by E.G.), it gives a nostalgic reminder of the amount of space we were able to give a major new recording in those days: 'In this wide-ranging cycle on the subject of night and sleep, Britten chooses from a diverse selection of poets – Coleridge, Tennyson, Wordsworth, Wilfred Owen and Keats, and he finishes with a Shakespeare sonnet. The sonnet setting is a miraculous example of Britten's technique. The poem on the face of it seems one of the more trivial of Shakespeare's sonnets with puns and conceits of the most artless kind, but Britten in his setting finds an entirely new depth of meaning, so that what at first seemed mere playing on words appears in the song as a moving commentary on the absence of the beloved. One of my colleagues complained after the first performance that the music is too profound for the words, but that surely is to miss the point, and repetition on the gramophone shows the piece's true stature. This is a work full – as so much of Britten's output – of memorable moments. One thinks of the "breathing" motif on the strings which link the different songs, the brilliant dialogue for flute and clarinet in the Keats setting and above all the towering climax of the Wordsworth excerpt. Each song has a different obbligato instrument (with ensemble unified for the final Shakespeare song), and for the Wordsworth – an excerpt from *The Prelude* describing the poet's visit to Paris after the French Revolution – Britten chooses timpani obbligato from the ominous slow march setting. This is a long crescendo as the writer describes his increasing horror until finally the climax bursts out on the words "Sleep no more!" Heavy chords thunder out, only to subside into gentle thrumming on pizzicato strings for the Wilfred Owen setting with its heavy cor anglais obbligato. Though the *Nocturne* may not have quite the same charisma as its obvious predecessor, the *Serenade for Tenor, Horn and Strings*, it surpasses it in depth of insight.

'The performance is as nearly definitive as anything could be. Pears is the ideal interpreter, and the composer a most efficient conductor. The fiendishly difficult obbligato parts are played superbly, and it would be invidious to single anyone out. The recording is brilliant and clear with just the right degree of atmosphere, in the best Decca manner.'

The Prince of the Pagodas (complete ballet) (choreography by Kenneth MacMillan)

Warner DVD 9031-738262. Darcey Bussell, Jonathan Cope, Artists of the Royal Ballet, ROHCG O, Ashley Lawrence (V/D: Derek Bailey). Includes *Out of Line* (feature on Kenneth MacMillan by Derek Bailey)

Decca's early but vibrant stereo recording of Britten's colourful score is sadly not available at the moment. However, this superb DVD is. *The Prince of the Pagodas* is a masterly score that repays much repetition, and both the outer Acts are wonderfully inventive. The performances of Darcey Bussell as Princess Rose and Jonathan Cope as the Prince are every bit as impressive as we remember them, and MacMillan's choreography is, as always, distinguished by imagination and great musicality. The DVD also includes a feature on MacMillan by Derek Bailey which is full of interest and includes some excerpts from other ballets. Seeing MacMillan's choreography greatly enhances the musical experience.

(i) *A Ceremony of Carols*; (ii) *Deus in adjutorium meum*; *Hymn of St Columba*; *Hymn to the Virgin*; *Jubilate Deo in E flat*; *Missa brevis, Op. 63*

Hyp. CDA 66220. Westminster Cathedral Ch., Hill; with (i) S. Williams (harp);
(ii) O'Donnell (organ)

No collection of outstanding recordings would be complete without Britten's *Ceremony of Carols*, his first great hit, which did more than anything to establish his ascendancy as a composer of English vocal music. The singing of the Westminster boys here is particularly impressive, with perfect ensemble, the solo work amazingly mature, and a superb contribution from the solo harpist. The other, rarer pieces make up an altogether outstanding collection, beautifully and atmospherically recorded in an ideal ambience.

Saint Nicolas; *Hymn to Saint Cecilia*

ⓑⓑ Hyp. Helios CDH 55378. Anthony Rolfe Johnson, Corydon Singers, Girls of Warwick University Ch., Choristers of St George's Chapel, Windsor, Catherine Edwards & John Alley (piano duet), John Scott (organ), ECO, Matthew Best

For the first time in a recording the congregational hymns are included in Matthew Best's fresh and atmospheric account of *Saint Nicolas*, adding greatly to the emotional impact of the whole cantata. Though the chorus is slightly distanced, the contrasts of timbre are well caught, with the waltz-setting of *The Birth of Nicolas* and its bath-tub sequence delightfully carolled by the boy-trebles alone. The *Hymn to St Cecilia* is also beautifully sung, with gentle pointing of the jazzy syncopations in crisp, agile ensemble and with sweet matching among the voices.

War Requiem, Op. 66

Ⓜ Decca (ADD) 475 7511 (2). Vishnevskaya, Pears, Fischer-Dieskau, Bach Ch., L. Symphony Ch., LSO, composer

Britten's own 1963 recording of the *War Requiem* comes near to ideal and it has been splendidly remastered for this first reissue at mid-price, to take an honoured place among Universal's impressive series of 'Originals'. Full documentation is included.

Hickox's later recording (Chandos SACD CHSA 5007) has the advantage of SACD, with spectacular multi-channel surround sound. Moreover the boys' chorus from St Paul's Cathedral is exceptionally fresh. Another advantage is the choice of the golden-toned Heather Harper (who sang in the very first Coventry performance) as the soprano soloist. The composer's choice was Vishnevskaya; while having a Russian soloist was emotionally right, her actual singing is less honeyed. Nevertheless there is something very special about the Decca performance, which must remain a clear primary choice.

Albert Herring (DVD version)

Warner DVD 5046 78790-2. Graham-Hall, Kerns, Johnson, Palmer, Hammond-Stroud, Van Allan, Gale, Oliver, Opie, Rigby, Glyndebourne Ch., LPO, Haitink (V/D: Peter Hall)

Albert Herring (CD version)

Nim. NI 5824/6 (3). Pears, Cross, Parr, Kraus, Ashton, Evans, Lawson, E. Opera Group, composer

Peter Hall's DVD of Britten's engaging *Albert Herring* is wonderfully entertaining. John Gunter's sets are imaginatively, charmingly real, and the casting could hardly be better. John Graham-Hall in the title-role is splendidly offset by Patricia Kerns's portrayal of his dominating mother. Patricia Johnson's pompous but believable Lady Billows is almost but not quite an amusing caricature, and Felicity Palmer is a whimsically idiosyncratic Florence Pike. The rest of the cast sing splendidly and take their roles as to the manner born, and the whole show is conducted marvellously by Bernard Haitink.

The incredibly lively CD performance of *Albert Herring* cuts through any sonic limitations of this 1949 broadcast, conducted by the composer at the Theatre Royal, Copenhagen, on 15 September 1949. Indeed, it surpasses the composer's studio Decca recording in sparkle and life, made in the 1960s, with this cast largely comprising members of the first performance of this work. Pears here seems ideally suited as the gormless Albert Herring, but the entire cast is pretty well flawless (Otakar Kraus as Mr Gedge, the vicar, is a delight), and the excellence of the performance is reflected in the (unobtrusive) laughter from the audience. The diction of the cast is superb, with vowels beautifully enunciated (notably by Joan Cross) in ways which, sadly, belong to another era. Britten's electrifying conducting keeps the story rattling along with an exhilarating deftness and lightness of touch, but all sharply characterized. The booklet gives a fascinating, personal history of the opera by Nigel Douglas and a complete libretto is included. At the end, the composer thanks the audience in a short but charming speech, quoting Albert's key line, 'Thank you very much,' and we thank Nimbus very much for making this performance available once again. No admirer of this opera should be without this set.

Billy Budd (original 4-Act production; DVD version)

Decca DVD 074 3256. Pears, Glossop, Langdon, Bowman, Tear, Kelley, Amb. Op. Ch., LSO, Mackerras (Producer: Cedric Messina)

This outstanding film version, conducted by Mackerras, dates from as early as 1966, and immediately when this black-and-white film opens there is a compelling intensity to the performance which is almost unsettling. Peter Pears was a definitive Edward Fairfax Vere, a role with which he is inextricably linked.

With a supreme cast including Peter Glossop (memorable in the title-role) and Michael Langdon as the sinister Claggart, the performance could hardly fail – and it doesn't. Indeed it crackles with intensity, with superb direction and an excellent production. Mackerras secures plenty of electricity from the orchestra, with all the interjections from the brass heard crisply on the soundtrack.

Death in Venice (CD version)

Decca (ADD) 425 669-2. Pears, Shirley-Quirk, Bowman, Bowen, Leeming, E. Op. Group
   Ch., ECO, Bedford

Thomas Mann's novella, which made an expansively atmospheric film far removed from the world of Mann, here makes a surprisingly successful opera. Pears's searching performance in the central role of Aschenbach is set against the darkly sardonic singing of John Shirley-Quirk in a sequence of roles as the Dionysian figure who draws Aschenbach to his destruction and, though Steuart Bedford's assured conducting lacks some of the punch that Britten would have brought, the whole presentation makes this a set to establish the work outside the opera house.

A Midsummer Night's Dream (CD version)

Decca (ADD) 425 663-2 (2). Deller, Harwood, Harper, Veasey, Watts, Shirley-Quirk,
   Brannigan, Downside and Emanuel School Ch., LSO, composer

The beauty of the instrumental writing comes out in this recording even more than in the opera house, for John Culshaw, the recording manager, put an extra halo round the fairy music to act as a substitute for visual atmosphere. Britten again proves himself an ideal interpreter of his own music and draws virtuoso playing from the LSO. Peter Pears has shifted to the straight role of Lysander. The mechanicals are admirably led by Owen Brannigan as Bottom; and among the lovers Josephine Veasey (Hermia) is outstanding. Deller, with his magical male alto singing, is the eerily effective Oberon. For a DVD version of this work, we recommend Glyndebourne's 1981 production in which the atmospheric sets of John Bury exploit the limited space of the Glyndebourne stage in the old theatre. With Peter Hall an inspired director, the superb cast is conducted by Haitink, and it is available on Warner DVD 0630 16911-2.

Peter Grimes (DVD version)

Decca DVD 074 3261. Pears, Harper, Drake, Robson, Brannigan, Bainbridge, Gomes, Tear,
   Amb. Op. Ch., LSO, composer (Producer: John Culshaw; V/D: Brian Large)

While the original Decca CD set (475 7713) of *Peter Grimes* remains indispensable, one of the great achievements of the early analogue stereo era, the BBC's later (1969) recording must take its place as a primary recommendation. Pears remains superb in the title-role, every bit as compelling as on CD, yet with the additional projection possible with video. But what makes this performance so compelling is the excellence of the cast in general: from the beauty of Helen

Harper's Ellen Orford to the superb characterization of Ann Robson's Mrs Sedley. All the roles here are splendidly done and everything about the production and direction brings top quality.

The Turn of the Screw (CD version)

Decca mono 425 672-2 (2). Pears, Vyvyan, Hemmings, Dyer, Cross, Mandikian, E. Op.
  Group O, composer

Though the recording is in mono only, the very dryness and sharpness of focus give an extra intensity to the composer's own incomparable reading of this most compressed opera. The creepily ambiguous story (by Henry James) is beautifully evoked by Britten, who presents the narrative in almost cinematic terms. Indeed, so atmospheric and powerful is this performance, visuals become almost irrelevant, so vividly are pictures painted in the mind. Britten's construction of the score is marvellous, with its prologue and sixteen scenes, each preceded by a variation on the twelve-note 'Screw' theme, its mixture of tonality and dissonance highly compelling. Peter Pears as Peter Quint is superbly matched by Jennifer Vyvyan as the governess and by Joan Cross as the housekeeper, Mrs Grose. It is also fascinating to hear David Hemmings as a boy treble, already a confident actor.

BRUCH, Max (1838–1920)

Violin Concerto 1 in G min., Op. 26; *Scottish Fantasy, Op. 46*

Ⓜ Decca (ADD) 460 976-2. Chung, RPO, Kempe – **MENDELSSOHN**: *Violin
  Concerto*

Kyung-Wha Chung goes straight to the heart of Bruch's *G minor Concerto* and couples it, not only with the composer's other hit concertante work, the delightful *Scottish Fantasy*, but also with an equally sympathetic performance of Mendelssohn's *E minor Concerto*. Always a spontaneously inspired artist, Chung finds mystery and fantasy as well as the more extrovert qualities of the music. In the *Scottish Fantasy* her concentration transcends the episodic nature of the work to give the music unexpected depth, above all in the lovely slow movement. Kempe and the RPO are ideal accompanists, ever sympathetic, and the glowing recording is one of Decca's best.

Kol Nidrei

DG (ADD) 457 761-2. Fournier, LOP, Martinon – **LALO**: *Cello Concerto*. **SAINT-
  SAËNS**: *Cello Concerto 1*. **BLOCH**: *Schelomo*

Like Bloch's *Schelomo*, Bruch's *Kol Nidrei* is a Jewish rhapsody, even though Bruch was not himself Jewish. Like that work, it is an intensely atmospheric piece, with a gorgeously flowing Hebrew melody, and it is beautifully performed by Pierre Fournier, who is well supported by Jean Martinon. The early 1960s sound is excellent.

BRUCKNER, Anton (1824–96)

Symphonies 1–9 (complete)
Ⓜ DG (ADD) 477 7580-5 (9). BPO, Karajan

Karajan's magnificent cycle of Bruckner symphonies, recorded between 1976 and 1978, brings a yardstick by which others have been measured and – at mid-price – must be a clear first choice. We have sung the praises of these recordings loud and long, and in their new format they make outstanding value. There are many fine individual recordings of these works: Karl Boehm's strength in the *Fourth* gives the impression that in every bar he knows where he is going (Decca 475 8403); and Sinopoli's live recording of the *Fifth* brings playing of incandescent beauty from the Dresden Staatskapelle. But Karajan's readings are not just poised but superbly structured on every level, and the playing of the Berlin Philharmonic throughout the cycle is unforgettably fine, one of his finest achievements on record.

Symphony 4 in E flat (*Romantic*) (DVD version)
TDK DVD DVWW-COWANDS. N. German RSO, Wand (with **BEETHOVEN**
   Overture: Leonora No. 3)

Symphony 4 in E flat (*Romantic*) (CD version)
Decca (ADD) 475 8403. VPO, Boehm

This DVD performance comes from the Schleswig-Holstein Festival and was recorded in Lübeck Cathedral on 24 June 1990. It is an altogether magnificent reading, free from any kind of artifice. This is *echt*-Bruckner, the real thing without any attempt to inflate Bruckner's vision or take attention away from this inspired score. The production by Klaus Reinke and direction by Hugo Käch are wonderfully natural and could hardly be improved both in the symphony and in Beethoven's *Leonora No. 3 Overture* which precedes it.

There are many who admire Boehm's Bruckner, and he certainly controls the lyrical flow of the *Fourth Symphony* convincingly, helped by first-rate playing from the VPO and vintage Decca sound from 1973, with the advantage of the spacious acoustics of the Sofiensaal. The balance provides splendid detail and a firm sonority. Boehm's sobriety was also his strength; in every bar he gives the impression that he knows exactly where he is going and, choosing the Nowak edition, he shapes the structure compellingly.

Symphony 5 in B flat
DG 469527-2. Dresden State O, Sinopoli

Sinopoli's reading is characterful and strong in a positive, even wilful way that is distinctively his. The Dresden Staatskapelle responds with playing of incandescent intensity, totally allied with the conductor in silencing any stylistic reservations. This is a live recording, and the inspiration of the moment comes over at full force. The energy of the Scherzo and the passion of the slow movement complete the picture of an exceptionally high-powered reading, recorded in glowing sound.

Symphony 7 in E
Teldec 3984 24488-2. VPO, Harnoncourt

For I.M. the Bruckner *Seventh Symphony* is very special. He first heard it live at the beginning of the 1950s, played by the Hallé Orchestra under 'Glorious John' in the Albert Hall, Manchester (before the new concert hall was built). For the extra brass in the slow movement, members of the Brighouse and Rastrick Band were employed. At that time steam trains over the Pennines from Yorkshire were notoriously late, and we had to wait for their arrival before the performance could begin. The result was magnificent. Moreover the great cymbal crash in the slow movement (apparently not authentic) was included to great effect. In Harnoncourt's splendid version from Vienna, he omits it but that does not spoil the performance. With the advantage of the acoustics of the Sofiensaal the sound is splendid, the Viennese strings have a radiant sheen, and the brass is gloriously sonorous. The work is dedicated to Wagner, and in the beautiful coda Harnoncourt draws out the resemblance to *Das Rheingold* in the valedictory overlapping brass parts. The result is very moving, and the finale caps the performance admirably. This (unexpectedly) is one of Harnoncourt's best records and not to be missed by his admirers.

Symphony 8 in C min.
DG 427611-2. VPO, Karajan

Karajan's last version of the *Eighth Symphony* is with the Vienna Philharmonic Orchestra and is the most impressive of them all. The sheer beauty of sound and opulence of texture is awe-inspiring but never draws attention to itself: this is a performance in which beauty and truth go hand in hand. The recording is superior to either of its predecessors in terms of naturalness of detail and depth of perspective.

Symphony 9 in D min. (CD version)
Sony stereo/mono 518812-2. Columbia SO, Walter (with *Te Deum*: Yeend, Lipton, Lloyd, Harrell, Westminster Ch., NYPO, Walter)

Bruno Walter's 1959 account of Bruckner's *Ninth Symphony* represents the peak of his achievement during his Indian summer in the CBS recording studios, just before he died. His mellow, persuasive reading leads one on through the leisurely paragraphs so that the logic and coherence seem obvious where other performances can sound aimless. Some may not find the Scherzo vigorous enough to provide the fullest contrast, but the final slow movement has a nobility which suggests that, after this, anything would have been an anticlimax.

For the reissue Sony have added Walter's fine (1959) Carnegie Hall mono recording of the *Te Deum*, a characteristically spacious account with a well-matched team of soloists and an excellent contribution from the Westminster Choir. The transfer of the very good mono recording is well managed.

BUSH, Geoffrey (1920–98)

Symphonies (i) *1*; (ii) *2 (Guildford)*. (iii) *Music for Orchestra*;
(iv) *Overture Yorick*
Lyrita (ADD/DDD) SRCD 252. (i) LSO, Braithwaite; (ii) RPO, Wordsworth; (iii) LPO;
(iv) Philh. O; (iii–iv) Handley

This very well-filled disc brings together fine Lyrita recordings made between 1972 and 1982, and adds a superb, completely new recording of the *Symphony No.* 2. The vigorous *Yorick Overture* (1949), written in memory of the comedian Tommy Handley, opens this concert most invitingly. It has all the exuberance of a Walton overture and is an immensely jolly piece, with wit and warm lyricism nicely balanced; in one brief, syncopated idea it offers a rhythmic reminder of Lambert's *Horoscope*. The first of the two symphonies dates from 1954 and is a positive, three-movement structure centring on an elegiac slow movement with blues overtones, written in memory of Constant Lambert. The slow movement, *Elegiac Blues*, actually quotes from *The Rio Grande*. The work exhibits the traditional values of fine craftsmanship and directness of utterance by which Bush set great store. He did not shrink from the notion that music should entertain, and the main body of the first movement, as well as the finale, is much lighter in character than those of many contemporary British symphonists.

The *Second Symphony* is outgoing, too. This is no formal exercise but a warm statement of personal feeling. Its four clearly defined sections are played without a break, the first and last suitably genial and festive. Both the central slow movement and the witty Scherzo, with two catchy trios, draw on earlier material, which is then recapitulated in reverse for the finale. *Music for Orchestra* (1967) is also designed to be played continuously. It is, in the composer's words, 'a miniature symphony, with the string parts carefully written to be playable by amateur performers, yet with plenty of opportunities for bravura offered to the wind and brass.' Ample percussion and a piano add to the vividness. It is a formidable and by no means lightweight piece, with a bleakly poignant *Lento* at its centre, with the threads of the structure drawn together in the finale, called an *Epilogue* but which becomes energetic towards the close. All the performances and recordings are outstandingly good, notably that of the *Symphony No.* 2, conducted by Barry Wordsworth.

BUSONI, Ferruccio (1866–1924)

Piano Concerto, Op. 39
Hyp. CDA 67143. Hamelin, CBSO Ch., CBSO, Elder

Busoni's *Piano Concerto* is arguably the most formidable in the repertory, but in such an inspired reading as Hamelin's it emerges as a genuine Everest of a work. Even before the piano enters, the opening tutti (four minutes long) establishes the rapt, glowing intensity of the performance, thanks to Mark Elder's dedicated conducting of the Birmingham orchestra, with radiant recording to match. Above all, Hamelin and Elder bring out the warmer, more colourful qualities behind the five massive movements, the dedication of the long *Pezzo serioso* beautifully sustained.

Doktor Faust
Arthaus DVD 101 283 (2). Hampson, Groissböck, Kunde, Macias, Trattnigg, Ch. and O of
   Zurich Op., Philippe Jordan. (Director: Klaus Michael Grüber, V/D: Felix Breisach)

Doktor Faust is Busoni's last opera and it occupied him for the last two decades of his life. Much of it was composed in Zurich, where both *Turandot* and *Arlecchino* were premièred in 1917. But given the demands on his time made by concert tours, the score was left incomplete on his death and this production uses the edition prepared by his pupil, Philipp Jarnach. (The more scholarly reconstruction by his biographer, Antony Beaumont, has been recorded by Erato.) Jarnach's ending, prepared for the first performance in 1925, does not follow the detailed musical instructions left by the composer. It amounts to about four minutes of Jarnach, while the Beaumont edition, making use of manuscript sketches as well as other original material from 1923 and 1924, is more or less authentic Busoni. The composer Joseph Horowitz thought Antony Beaumont's completion 'perhaps less good' than that of Philipp Jarnach, but the fact remains that it does give us more of Busoni's original than the Jarnach. All the same, the present version is very powerful, particularly in the hands of Philippe Jordan and his impressive array of soloists – and most notably Thomas Hampson's account of the eponymous role. For many years Faust was identified with Dietrich Fischer-Dieskau, who rightly acclaimed it one of the greatest operas of the twentieth century, along with Berg's *Wozzeck* and Pfitzner's *Palestrina* (to which one might add *Peter Grimes* and *The Turn of the Screw*). The work has an unique expressive power, even among Busoni's finest compositions, and makes an indelible impression in this powerful production. Not only is its musical flow so potent and its dramatic intensity so strong, but the individual performances are commanding.

Faust is profound and the distillation of Busoni's life work. A memorable musical experience well served by the Zurich Opera's production team and the TV/Video engineers.

BUTTERWORTH, George (1885–1916)

The Banks of Green Willow; 2 English Idylls; A Shropshire Lad
(rhapsody) (with: **WARLOCK**: *An Old Song for Small Orchestra*.
HADLEY: *One Morning in Spring*)
Lyrita (ADD) SRCD 245. LPO, Boult – **HOWELLS**: *Elegy; Merry-Eye*, etc.

Butterworth's *Shropshire Lad* represents the English folk-song school at its
most captivatingly atmospheric – its opening is hauntingly magical – and the
other items are in a similarly appealing vein. Whether Butterworth would have
gone on, had he lived through the First World War, to develop as his friend
Vaughan Williams did is an interesting point, but the delicate genius here is
displayed at its most rewarding. Sir Adrian Boult, a tireless exponent of neglected English music, gives noble and radiant performances of these lovely
pieces. His natural feeling for the pastoral inflexions and the refinement of texture are unmatched by others, and the 1970s recording is delicately atmospheric.
The opening *English Idyll No. 1* is exhilarating in its freshness, and its charms
are impossible to resist, as is the catchy folk tune which begins *The Banks of
Green Willow*. These classic performances sound superb in their new CD transfer, which brought them to the CD world for the first time. Both the Warlock
and Hadley items make a very welcome bonus, the former richly pastoral in
nature, and the latter featuring some particularly felicitous woodwind writing.
All are outstandingly played and recorded, and the Howells couplings are no
less impressive.

Songs from *A Shropshire Lad: Loveliest of trees; When I was young
and twenty; Look not in my eyes; Think no more, lad; The lads in
their hundreds; Is my team ploughing?; Bredon Hill; O fair enough
are sky and plain; When the lad for the longing sighs; On the idle
hill of summer; With rue my heart is laden; I will make you
brooches; I fear thy kisses; Requiescat*. Folk Songs from Sussex:
*Yonder stands a lovely creature; A blacksmith courted me; Sowing
the seeds of love; A lawyer he went out one day; Come my own
one; The cuckoo; A brisk young sailor courted me; Seventeen
come Sunday; Roving in the dew; The true lover's farewell; Tarry
trousers*
ⓑⓑ Naxos 8.572426. Roderick Williams, Iain Burnside (piano)

Here are Butterworth's beautiful, melancholy song settings, including the
ravishing cycle from A. E. Housman's *A Shropshire Lad*, plus further folk songs
from Sussex and settings of poems by R. L. Stephenson, Shelley and Wilde.
Their delicate atmosphere is perfectly caught by Roderick Williams with his
gently glowing light baritone voice, and Iain Burnside's accompaniments are
equally sensitive.

BUXHEIMER ORGELBUCH, DAS (*c.* 1460)

Preludes; *Liturgical Melodies* (based on Chorales); *Transcriptions of (sacred) Motets*

Oehms SACD OC 645. Joseph Kelemen (organs of St Andreaskirche, Soest-Ostönnen, and Holfkirche, Innsbruck

The Buxheimer Organ Book, of course, has nothing to do with Buxtehude but dates from two centuries before that famous composer was born and is a collection of fourteenth- and fifteenth-century repertoire. Indeed, it contains the most extensive collection of keyboard music to have survived before 1600. It uses a system of tablature notation in which the upper voice is written out and the remaining voices are written as letters below, not unlike today's guitar notation. The music itself shows the transition from two-voice to three-voice counterpoint, with the occasional use of an extra fourth part, and its strongest characteristic is the use of rhythm, offering a fast, ornamented cantus moving over a calmer accompaniment. Twelve of the works included here have instructions for the use of pedal. Composers such as Johannes Ciaconia, Dunstable, Binchois and Dufay contributed.

Kelemen uses two organs, the first (whose builder is unknown), in the church of South Ostönnen which dates back to 1425. It was originally in another church but was moved to its present location in 1721/2 and has recently been restored. The second, in the Innsbruck Hofkirche, dates from 1558 and was built by Jörg Ebert. The music makes diverting listening when so well presented and splendidly recorded in SACD surround sound. The disc opens with the sonorous bell of the Ostönnen church, which dates from 1306.

BUXTEHUDE, Dietrich (*c.* 1637–1707)

7 Sonatas for 2 Violins, Viola da gamba & Harpsichord, Op. 1
Chan. 0766. Purcell Qt

Opus 1 was Buxtehude's first surviving collection of instrumental ensemble music, published in 1694. No doubt Bach encountered it (or its companion, Opus 2 of 1696) on his famous walking visit to Lübeck, ostensibly to hear Buxtehude play the organ. The fact that he overstayed his planned visit tells us how much he admired Buxtehude's instrumental music as well as his organ works, which undoubtedly had an influence on his own writing. Certainly these sonatas are inventive and full of life, and the later ones seem to get steadily more attractive. They are played by the Purcell group with pleasing vitality and freshness, and the Chandos recording is natural and warmly flattering.

*Ciacona in E min., BuxWV 160; Chorale Preludes: BuxWV 196;
BuxWV 207; BuxWV 220–21. Magnificat primi toni, BuxWV 203;
Praeludium in G min., BuxWV 148; Praeludium in A min., BuxWV
153; Toccatas: in D min. & F, BuxWV 155–6*
BIS SACD 1809. Masaaki Suzuki (organs of St Nicolai Church, Altenbruch, & St Jacobi
   Church, Lüdingworth)

Masaaki Suzuki offers a single admirable recital of some of Buxtehude's most
impressive works, using organs at two churches near the mouth of the river
Elbe. They could not be better chosen. First, they sound magnificent (especially in surround sound), and secondly, they were built by two organ builders
whom Buxtehude especially admired.

Suzuki's programme readily shows the diversity of the composer's invention and how his chosen forms set a pattern for music written by his successors,
including Bach. Indeed, remarkably the *Toccata in D minor* curiously antici-
pates the writing in Bach's famous BWV 565. The *Chorale Preludes* setting the
same chorale in pairs are strongly contrasted, one simple and the second complex. But it was Bach's son, J. C. Bach, who was so impressed by the *Chaconne
in E minor*, a set of variations on a four-bar bass theme that is repeated and
varied 31 times.

BYRD, William (1543–1623)

Masses for 3, 4 & 5 Voices; Ave verum corpus; Diffusa est gratia; Great Service
(with anthems); *Infelix ego; Ne irascaris; Domine; Nunc dimittis; Prevent us O
Lord; Tristia et anxietas; Vigilate.*
Gimell DVD GIMDP 902 or CDGIM 218 (2). Tallis Scholars, Peter Phillips

Because Byrd was the greatest composer of Elizabethan England, he was toler-
ated by his Queen, even though he was a devout Catholic, deploring the
reformation of the English church. His three great *Masses* (written for recusant
celebration) have striking beauty and intensity, and are presented here by Peter
Phillips and the Tallis Scholars with great eloquence. With the collection
expanded to include the *Great Service* and other memorable items, this is an
indispensible representation of some of Byrd's finest music, recorded creating
a warm, fresh sonority, either at Merton College, Oxford, or in Tewkesbury
Abbey (on DVD, with some pieces beautifully filmed by candlelight).

CALLAS, Maria (soprano)

Rather like the Decca and EMI surveys of Pavarotti's recordings, EMI, for the
eightieth anniversary of Callas's birth (and the fortieth of her death) brought

out three celebratory collections of her recordings, including this 70-disc complete survey. Most of these recordings have been discussed by us over the years and virtually all the operas are reviewed in our pages, so a list of recordings and dates is all that is needed here, plus a few general comments.

The Complete Studio Recordings (1949–69): **BELLINI**: *I puritani* (1953), with Di Stefano, Panerai, Rossi-Lemeni, La Scala, Milan, Ch. & O, Serafin. **BELLINI**: *Norma* (1954), with Filippeschi, Stignani, Rossi-Lemeni, La Scala, Milan, Ch. & O, Serafin. **BELLINI**: *Norma* (1960), with Corelli, Ludwig, Zaccaria, De Palma, La Scala, Milan, Ch. & O, Serafin. **BELLINI**: *La Sonnambula* (1957), with Cossotto, Zaccaria, Monti, Ratti, La Scala, Milan, Ch. & O, Votto. **BIZET**: *Carmen* (1964), with Gedda, Massard, Guiot, Ch. René Duclos, Children's Ch., Paris Nat. Op. O, Prêtre. **CHERUBINI**: *Medea* (1957), with Scotto, Pirazini, Picci, Modesti, La Scala, Milan, Ch. & O, Serafin. **DONIZETTI**: *Lucia di Lammermoor* (1953), with Di Stefano, Gobbi, Maggio Musicale Fiorentino Ch. & O, Serafin. **DONIZETTI**: *Lucia di Lammermoor* (1959), with Tagliavini, Cappuccilli, Ladysz, Del Ferro, Philh. Ch. & O, Serafin. **LEONCAVALLO**: *Pagliacci* (1954), with Di Stefano, Gobbi, Monti, Panerai, La Scala, Milan, Ch. & O, Serafin. **MASCAGNI**: *Cavalleria rusticana* (1953), with Di Stefano, Panerai, Canali, La Scala, Milan, Ch. & O, Serafin. **PONCHIELLI**: *La Gioconda* (1952), with Barbieri, Poggi, Turin Ch. & O, Votto. **PONCHIELLI**: *La Gioconda* (1959), with Cossotto, Companeez, Vinco, Ferraro, Cappuccilli, La Scala, Milan, Ch. & O, Votto. **PUCCINI**: Arias from: *Manon Lescaut*; *Madama Butterfly*; *La Bohème*; *Suor Angelica*; *Gianni Schicchi*; *Turandot* (1954), with Philh. O, Serafin. **PUCCINI**: *La Bohème* (1956), with Moffo, Di Stefano, Panerai, Spatafora, Zaccaria, La Scala, Milan, Ch. & O, Votto. **PUCCINI**: *Madama Butterfly* (1955), with Gedda, Danieli, Boriello, La Scala, Milan, Ch. & O, Karajan. **PUCCINI**: *Manon Lescaut* (1957), with Di Stefano, Fioravanti, Calabrese, Formichini, La Scala, Milan, Ch. & O, Serafin. **PUCCINI**: *Tosca* (1953), with Di Stefano, Gobbi, La Scala, Milan, Ch. & O, Victor de Sabata. **PUCCINI**: *Tosca* (1964/5), with Bergonzi, Gobbi, Paris Nat. Op. Ch., Paris Conservatoire O, Prêtre. **PUCCINI**: *Turandot* (1957), with Fernandi, Schwarzkopf, Nessi, La Scala, Milan, Ch. & O, Serafin. **ROSSINI**: *Il barbiere di Siviglia* (1957), with Alva, Gobbi, Ollendorf, Zaccaria, Philh. Ch. & O, Gallieri. **ROSSINI**: *Il Turco in Italia* (1954), with Rossi-Lemeni, Gedda, Calabrese, La Scala, Milan, Ch. & O, Gavazzeni. **ROSSINI & DONIZETTI** Arias (1964) from: *La Cenerentola*; *Guglielmo Tell*; *Semiramide*; *La Figlia del reggimento*; *Lucrezia Borgia*; *L'elisir d'amore* (with Paris Conservatoire O, Recigno). **VERDI**: *Aida* (1955), with Tucker, Barbieri, Gobbi, Modesti, Zaccaria, La Scala, Milan, Ch. & O, Serafin. **VERDI**: *Un ballo in maschera* (1956), with Di Stefano, Gobbi, Barbieri, La Scala, Milan, Ch. & O, Votto. **VERDI**:

La forza del destino (1954), with Tucker, Tagliabue, Rossi-Lemeni, Nicolai, Capecchi, La Scala, Milan, Ch. & O, Serafin. **VERDI**: *Macbeth* (1958): Mono version of *Sleepwalking Scene* (with Philh. O, Rescigno). **VERDI**: *Rigoletto* (1955), with Gobbi, Di Stefano, La Scala, Milan, Ch. & O, Serafin. **VERDI**: *La traviata* (1953), with Francesco Albanese, Savarese, Turin R. Ch. & O, Santini. **VERDI**: *Il trovatore* (1956), with Di Stefano, Panerai, Barbieri, La Scala, Milan, Ch. & O, Karajan. **VERDI**: Arias I (1958) from: *Macbeth*; *Nabucco*; *Ernani*; *Don Carlo* with Philh. O, Rescigno. **VERDI**: Arias 2 (1964) from *Otello*; *Aroldo*; *Don Carlo* with Paris Conservatoire O, Rescigno. **VERDI**: The 1964/5 Prêtre sessions: Arias from: *Aida*; *I Lombardi*; *Il trovatore*. **VERDI**: The 1969 recording sessions: Arias from: *I vespri siciliani*; *Attila*; *I Lombardi* (with Paris Conservatoire O, Rescigno)

Recitals: The first Recital (1949): Arias from: **WAGNER**: *Tristan*; **BELLINI**: *Norma*; *I Puritani* (with Turin R. O, Basile). *'Callas à Paris* 1' (1961): Arias by: **GLUCK**; **BIZET**; **SAINT-SAËNS**; **GOUNOD**; **THOMAS**; **MASSENET**; Gustave **CHARPENTIER** (with Paris R. O, Prêtre). *'Callas à Paris* 2' (1963): Arias by: **GLUCK**; **BERLIOZ**; **BIZET**; **MASSENET**; **GOUNOD** (with Paris Conservatoire O, Prêtre). *'Callas at La Scala'*: Arias from: **CHERUBINI**: *Medea*; **SPONTINI**: *La vestale*; **BELLINI**: *La sonnambula* (1955) with La Scala O, Serafin. *Lyric and Coloratura* arias by **CILEA**; **GIORDANO**; **CATALANI**; **BOITO**; **ROSSINI**; **MEYERBEER**; **DELIBES**; **VERDI** (1954) with Philh. O, Serafin. Mad Scenes (1958) from: **DONIZETTI**: *Anna Bolena*; **THOMAS**: *Hamlet*; **BELLINI**: *Il pirata* with soloists, Philh. Ch. & O, Rescigno. Arias by: **MOZART**; **BEETHOVEN**; **WEBER** (1963) (with Paris Conservatoire O, Rescigno)
ⓑⓑ EMI 3 95918-2 (70) Complete Callas Edition

Callas undoubtedly made her finest recordings early in her recording career, in the mid-1950s. Where she re-recorded operas later in stereo, the voice usually shows less security, often with hardness, even harshness above the stave, and the mono version remains a better choice. This certainly applies to her often thrilling 1953 performance of *Lucia di Lammermoor* as compared with the 1959 recording; and she was similarly at her peak in the 1954 *Norma* and less impressive in the 1960 stereo set. Her early Puccini recordings are all a success; she is a vibrant Mimì in *La Bohème* and, with Karajan directing, her *Madama Butterfly* is also memorable, while the close of *Manon Lescaut* is riveting. Not surprisingly, she makes a formidable Turandot, while her *Tosca*, with Gobbi as Scarpia, is unforgettable. Among the Verdi sets, *Aida* proves one of her finest roles, and *Forza del destino* and *La traviata* both find her movingly dramatic, while Karajan's presence again ensures an electrifying *Trovatore*. Perhaps more remarkable is her touching portrayal of Gilda in *Rigoletto*, where once again Gobbi is a superb partner. Not to be forgotten is her Rosina in Rossini's *Il barbiere*, a set which is still unsurpassed for its humour and lightness of touch from a very distinguished cast. *Carmen*, which one would have expected to be a triumph, is strangely disappointing, but still offers plenty to enjoy. All these recordings have survived in the catalogue for half a century, which says much for the Callas charisma. Often listed at well under £100, this 70-CD set is hardly an indulgence, but remains an essential purchase for all lovers not only of Maria Callas but of opera in general.

CAMPRA, André (1660–1744)

L'Europe Galante
Ⓜ Australian Decca Eloquence (ADD) 480 2374. ECO, Leppard – **LULLY**: *Pièces de symphonie*

The sheer tunefulness of *L'Europe Galante* has ensured that it hasn't disappeared for too long out of the catalogues: just sample the *Ragaudon I & II* for sheer catchiness. Campra, who was a few years older than Couperin, possessed keen melodic instincts and a genuine freshness. His work, partly thanks to this pioneering recording from 1966, seems to be gaining a wider following now, and this suite is marked by characteristic lyrical grace. It is given a thoroughly idiomatic performance, with modern instruments used to good effect, for Leppard had a fine sense of texture. The Kingsway Hall recording still sounds well, with added definition on CD.

CANTELOUBE, Marie-Joseph (1879–1957)

Songs of the Auvergne, Series 1–5 (complete)
Erato 0927 44656-2 (2). Dawn Upshaw, Lyon Op. O, Nagano (with **EMMANUEL**: *Chansons bourguignonnes*)

Dawn Upshaw follows in the wake of famous names like Victoria de los Angeles, Kiri Te Kanawa, Véronique Gens and Jill Gomez, who have all made these delightful songs their own. But Upshaw sings with a special blend of tenderness and character, and in the famous *Baïlèro* she uses greater variety of dynamic, even including an echo effect. Her line in the lyrical numbers is often very beautiful, while in the quirkier items her style is nearer to Natania Davrath's more folksy approach. She is persuasively accompanied by Kent Nagano and the Lyon Opera Orchestra with their distinctively French colouring. What makes this Erato set particularly enticing is the inclusion of half a dozen rather similar and no less captivating arrangements of Burgundian songs by Maurice Emmanuel. Full translations are provided, but in minuscule print.

CAVALLI, Francesco (1602–76)

La Calisto (DVD version)
HM DVD HMD 9909 001/2. Bayo, Lippi, Kammerer, Pushee, Winter, Visse, Oliver, Concerto Vocale, Jacobs

Cavalli was a natural successor to Monteverdi, and Jacobs is pretty faithful to the text of his most celebrated opera, making the love of Giove (Jupiter) and the nymph (La Calisto) central to the action. So Giove, when he is wooing Calisto, appears in drag, singing falsetto; the other characters too appear comically in drag, the irrepressible Dominique Visse as Furia and Alexander Oliver as Linfea. Though the fun is extreme, it can be argued that it follows period practice, and the sets with their elaborate trapdoors and gods descending from the heavens have a seventeenth-century flavour. There are also echoes of the *commedia dell'arte*, with Mercury a clown and Endimione a Harlequin figure. The sets dotted with nymphs are pretty and atmospheric.

CHABRIER, Emmanuel (1841–94)

España; Joyeuse marche; Habanera; Le Roi malgré lui: Danse slave; Fête polonaise. Suite pastorale
Ⓜ Australian Decca Eloquence (ADD) 480 0049 (2). SRO, Ansermet – **LALO**: *Andantino*, etc.

Now that Paul Paray's splendid Mercury collection has been deleted, Ansermet provides the best alternative. Indeed, many may prefer the more relaxed view he takes in the charming *Suite pastorale*. However, it is for the character of the performance that Ansermet provides in the famous *España* that this recording is so famous and for its technical brilliance. The bass drum is captured here by Decca (in 1964) as no other company could – it has a wonderfully deep and impressive presence, but the glittering percussion is no less memorable. The rhythmic snap Ansermet brings to the *Joyeuse marche* is very enjoyable too (again with Decca producing some superb bass drum thwacks) and the two scenes from *Le Roi malgré lui* have seldom sounded so lively and vivid before – what exhilaratingly tuneful music this is, brimming with melody, wit and invention. Decca have added the charming *Habanera*, dating from 1956 and sounding amazingly modern for its date, though obviously not as dazzling as the 1964 recordings.

CHARPENTIER, Gustave (1860–1956)

Louise (opera) complete

Ⓜ Sony 88697526312 (3). Ileana Cotrubas, Jane Berbié, Plácido Domingo, Michel
   Sénéchal, Gabriel Bacquier, Amb. Op. Ch., New Philh. O, Prêtre

Even more than Mascagni and Leoncavallo, Gustave Charpentier is a one-work
composer, and one might be forgiven for thinking that that work, the opera
Louise, is a one-aria opera. No other melody in this piece may quite match the
soaring lyricism of the heroine's *'Depuis le jour',* but this fine, atmospheric
recording from the mid-1970s certainly explains why *Louise* has long been
a favourite opera in Paris. It cocoons the listener in the atmosphere of Montmartre in the 1890s, with Bohemians more obviously proletarian than Puccini's,
a whole factory of seamstresses and an assorted range of ragmen, junkmen,
pea-sellers and the like, making up a highly individual cast list. Only four characters actually matter in a plot that remains essentially simple, even though
the music (not counting intervals) lasts close on three hours.

Louise is torn between loyalty to her parents and her love for the Bohemian,
Julien. The opera starts with a love duet and from there meanders along happily,
enlivened mainly by the superb crowd scenes. One of them, normally omitted
but included here, proves as fine as any, with Louise's fellow seamstresses
in their workroom (cue for sewing-machines in the percussion department)
teasing her for being in love, much as Carmen is treated in Bizet's opera. The
love duets too are enchanting, and though the confrontations with the boring
parents are far less appealing, the atmosphere carries one over.

Ileana Cotrubas makes a delightful heroine, not always flawless technically,
but charmingly girlish. Plácido Domingo is a relatively heavyweight Julien, and
Jane Berbié and Gabriel Bacquier are excellent as the parents. Under Georges
Prêtre, far warmer than usual on record, the ensemble is rich and clear, with
refined recording every bit as atmospheric as one could want. A splendid
reissue that fills an obvious gap in the catalogue.

CHARPENTIER, Marc-Antoine (1643–1704)

Médée: Suite from the opera

Australian Decca Eloquence (ADD) 480 2373. ECO, Leppard - **RAMEAU:** *Le Temple
   de la Gloire.* **GRÉTRY:** *Suite of Ballet Music*

'Marc-Antoine Charpentier is an attractive and often inventive composer
and this suite arranged from his opera *Médée* by Raymond Leppard offers some
pleasant, undemanding listening. The playing is immensely alert and undoubtedly stylish and the recording extremely fine.' That review was written in
1966, when the recording came out and, in spite of the authentic-movement

revolution, there is no reason to change our opinion. Indeed, these performances have stood the test of time remarkably well and remain hugely enjoyable. Highlights include the inventive overture, a very beautiful and melancholy *Prélude pour Médée seule*, the flute writing in the *Prélude* to Act IV, the piquant *Air des phantomes*, a lively *Air des combattans* and the nicely pointed final *Passepieds I et II*.

Leçons de ténèbre for Maundy Thursday & Good Friday
ⓑⓑ Virgin 2x1 5 22021-2 (2). Piau, Mellon, Lesne, Seminario Musicale, Lesne

The *Leçons de ténèbre* for Maundy Thursday and Good Friday from *Il Seminario Musicale* offer music of great variety and beauty, featuring soloists naturally attuned to this repertoire. The accompaniments are provided by a varied instrumental group, and their use is consistently imaginative and refreshing to the ear. The Psalms are sung by a smaller choral group. The effect is warm yet refined, the lyrical melancholy of much of this music is quite haunting, and the acoustic of L'Abbaye Royale de Fontevraud is ideal for the music. The reissued CDs are inexpensive and any collector attracted to this remarkable and inspired composer should consider them.

Médée (complete)
ⓑ*** Erato 2564 66305-7 (3). Hunt, Padmore, Deletré, Zanetti, Salzmann, Les Arts
    Florissants, Christie

In his second recording of this rare opera, again with his group Les Arts Florissants, Christie was glad to be able to open out the small cuts that were made before so as to fit the LP format. The success of his new interpretation is readily borne out in the finished performance, which easily surpasses the previous one in its extra brightness and vigour, with consistently crisper and more alert ensembles, often at brisker speeds, with the drama more clearly established. The casting is first rate, with Lorraine Hunt outstanding in the tragic title-role. Her soprano has satisfying weight and richness, as well as the purity and precision needed in such classical opera, and Mark Padmore's clear, high tenor copes superbly with the role of Jason, with no strain and with cleanly enunciated diction and sharp concern for word-meaning. The others follow Christie's pattern of choosing cleanly focused voices, even if the tone is occasionally gritty. Altogether this is a most welcome reissue.

CHAUSSON, Ernest (1855–99)

(i) Concerto for Violin, Piano & String Quartet; Piano Quintet; Piano Trio. String Quartet, Op. 33
Talent DOM 381 006/007 (2). Sharon Quartet, (i) with Ouziel

The four major chamber works on this two-disc set neatly encompass the full span of Chausson's all-too-short composing career. The *Piano Trio* is a teenage work, written when Chausson was still a student, and the liner note suggests the influence of Massenet, Franck and Wagner, but just as important an influence is Mendelssohn, reflecting the attractive lightness of the writing, its fairy quality, which hardly points to those more obviously direct influences.

At the other end of Chausson's career, he failed to complete his *String Quartet*, and it was with the greatest difficulty that his heirs were persuaded to allow Vincent D'Indy to complete the few bars needed to round off the third of the four projected movements. The *Piano Quintet* receives a strong, warm and purposeful performance from the Sharons, with Dalia Ouziel the excellent, agile pianist. Best known of Chausson's chamber works is the so-called *Concerto* for the unusual combination of piano, violin and string quartet. This version is most persuasive, with hushed tension in the slow movement and winning agility in the finale. Dalia Ouziel at the piano plays with dazzling brilliance and clarity of articulation.

(i) *Poème for Violin & Orchestra*; (ii) *Poème de l'amour et de la mer*

Chan. 8952. (i) Y. P. Tortelier; (ii) Finnie; Ulster O, Tortelier (with **FAURÉ**: *Pavane*; *Pelléas*).

No quarrels with Yan Pascal Tortelier's playing in the *Poème*, which he directs from the bow. There is consistent beauty of timbre and, what is more important, refinement of feeling. In the *Poème de l'amour et de la mer* Linda Finnie can hold her own with the very best; her feeling for the idiom is completely natural and her voice is beautifully coloured; among newer recordings this has very strong claims. Indeed, in rapport between singer and orchestra none is better.

Symphony in B flat; *Soir de fête, Op. 32*; *La Tempête, Op. 18*; *Viviane, Op. 5*

Chan. 9650. BBC PO, Tortelier

Like Franck and Dukas, Chausson wrote but one symphony – and what a splendid work it is. Much influenced in form by Franck and in spirit and harmonic language by Wagner, it is a richly and romantically charged work, full of both atmosphere and drama. It has been well served by the record companies, with classic accounts by Munch and Paray, and while vintage versions retain a unique magic, this modern performance more than holds its own. Moreover, it comes with some excellent rare orchestral works – the early romantic tone-poem *Viviane*, and his last orchestral work, *Soir de fête*, full of variety of mood and temperament, plus two charming pieces from *La Tempête*, music written for a marionette theatre production of Shakespeare's *The Tempest*. Excellent performances and sound.

While the electrifying Munch and Paray accounts are not currently available on CD, Ansermet's superbly recorded account has been re-released on Australian Decca Eloquence (480 0041). It is a warmly sympathetic account, if less well played than the Chandos version under Tortelier. It is, however, coupled with an outstanding version of Dukas's *L'Apprenti sorcier* and Roussel's *Symphonies, et al.*

CHERUBINI, Luigi (1760–1842)

String Quartets 1–4
BIS-CD 1003/4 (available separately). David Qt

Listening to Cherubini's *String Quartets* makes one realize the justice of Beethoven's admiration for the composer, for Cherubini's melodic inspiration is distinguished and instinctive, there is always a fine musical intelligence at work, and polished craftsmanship is always in evidence. The first four works bring an exhilarating response from the excellent BIS group who are superb individual players yet perfectly integrated tonally. They are thoroughly at home in Cherubini's sound-world. In short these modern-instrument performances could hardly be bettered and the recording, as one expects from this label, is in every way first class.

6 Keyboard Sonatas (1783)
RCA 88697057742. Andrea Bacchetti (piano)

This set of six Cherubini *Sonatas* was published in 1783 but was probably written earlier (perhaps 1780). They are most engaging two-movement works with a strong flavour of Mozart, but with *galant* touches to add charm. Their invention is appealingly diverse, and in these captivating performances one is drawn to return to them often. They are beautifully recorded.The Italian pianist, Andrea Bacchetti, is a relatively new name to us. He is an enterprising artist, willing to explore the keyboard repertoire, and his playing is always distinctive, cultivated and full of life.

(i–ii) *Marche religieuse*; (i; iv–v) *Mass in F (Di Chimay)*; (i–iii) *Mass for the Coronation of Charles X*; (vi) *Medea*: aria: *Dei tuoi figli la madre tu vedi*; (i; iv; vii) *Missa solemnis in D min.*; (i; iv; viii) *Missa solemnis in E*; (i–iii) *Missa solemnis in G (for the Coronation of Louis XVIII)*; (i; ix) *Motets: Antifona sul canto fermo 8*; *Nemo gaudeat*. (i–ii; x) *Requiem in C min.*; *Requiem in D min.*; (xi) *Overtures: Les Abencérages*; *Anacréon*; *Les deux journées*; *Eliza*; *Faniska*; *L'Hôtellerie portugaise*; *Medea*. (xi–xii) *Sonata 2* (for horn and strings)
Ⓑ EMI (ADD) 6 29462-2 (7). (i) Muti; (ii) Philh. O; (iii) Philh. Ch.; (iv) Bav. R. Ch. & SO; (v) Ziesak, Lippert, Abdrazakov; (vi) Callas, La Scala, Milan, O, Serafin; (vii) Tilling, Fulgoni, Streit, Tómasson, Suzuki, Schulist; (viii) Ziesak, Pizzolato, Lippert, Abdrazakov; (ix) Fleckenstein, Müller, Schneider, Meyer, Hartkopf, Bav. R. Ch.; (x) Amb. S.; (xi) ASMF, Marriner; (xii) Tuckwell

Cherubini's religious works came generally later in his career after his prime success as an opera composer. They combine the melodic flow he learned from his youthful studies with Sarti and the dramatic elements he had learned from the theatre.

His *Mass in F* (*Di Chimay*), written in 1809, broke a creative block. In his enthusiasm, Cherubini wrote what was then his most ambitious work. It is a massive 75-minute structure which in its inventiveness brings out the drama of the liturgy just as Haydn's last Masses had achieved in the immediately preceding years. Muti delivers his characteristic energy to this music, recorded live in 2003; his performances are not always perfectly polished, but in thrust and concentration they are most compelling, with the hushed account of the *Crucifixus* bringing a rapt choral response. Characterful soloists too, with the soprano Ruth Ziesak singing radiantly.

The *Missa solemnis in D minor*, written in 1811, is even longer and approaches Beethoven's *Missa solemnis* in its lyrical gravitas and depth. Cherubini makes great demands on his soloists, both individually and in concert, and on this live recording (2001) they are consistently impressive. The woodwind playing which opens the *Et resurrexit* is very beautiful indeed and the regal trumpets show the composer at his theatrical best. The sound is excellent, though the chorus could be more sharply focused.

The *Missa solemnis in E* of 1818 begins rather hauntingly in E minor. In terms of drama, this work is very much from a composer who wrote for the theatre, with its flamboyant *Amen* fugue at the end of the *Credo*. The bright trumpet fanfare which open the following *Sanctus* continues that theatrical atmosphere, though that is not to imply that this is in any way a work without deeper feelings; it includes a setting of the prayer, *O salutaris hostia* (not a usual part of the Mass), which is beautifully reflective. The *Mass* is followed by two beautiful Motets (*Antifona sul canto fermo* and *Nemo gaudeat*), rich in harmony and melody, and performed with great beauty.

The *Missa solemnis in G* (*for the Coronation of Louis XVIII*) was finished in 1819, but meanwhile Louis XVIII had postponed his coronation a number of times, and in the end it never took place. So Cherubini's Mass remained unperformed and the full score was prepared for publication only recently. Again, as is so often the case with Cherubini, the musical inspiration is not merely dignified but noble – and on occasion inspired. Muti (recorded in 1988) seems persuaded of its distinction and performs it with the LPO Chorus and Orchestra.

The *Coronation Mass for Charles X* dates from 1825, and there are signs in the *Gloria* that Cherubini was influenced by both Beethoven's *Fidelio* and the *Ninth Symphony*, and in the *Gloria Incarnatus* and *Crucifixus* by the *Missa solemnis*. But Cherubini's church music has a character of its own, beautifully crafted, with moments of real inspiration, such as in the closing bars of the *Kyrie*. Muti presents this music with an intensity to hide any limitations, and the chorus and orchestra both respond superbly. He secures the widest

dynamic refinements, and the digital sound (1984) is bold and full, with ceremonial trumpets braying magnificently. There is a musical appendix following
this work in the form of a *Marche religieuse*, a very fine piece.

Cherubini's finest achievements in his religious music are his two settings
of the Requiem Mass. His *C minor Requiem* was an instant success and achieved
lasting fame. It was commissioned by the government for the 1816 anniversary
of the execution of Louis XVI, and was composed at a very happy and secure
time in the composer's life when his creative powers were burning brightly. Its
admirers were many: Beethoven said that if he should write a Requiem, Cherubini's would be his model; Schumann and Brahms were equally enthusiastic
about it, and so too was Berlioz (it may have influenced his own *Grande Messe
des morts*). Muti directs a tough and incisive reading of this most dramatic setting of the Requiem, which reminds one that Toscanini also recorded it some
decades ago. Muti in the religious music of his own country believes in under-
lining the drama, and he is superbly well served both by his orchestra and by
his relatively small professional choir, and the full clear recording (from 1982)
is most satisfying.

It was also, incidentally, played at the funeral of Boïeldieu and, when the
Archbishop of Paris objected to its use of women's voices, Cherubini wrote his
D minor Requiem, *sans* women, to be played at his own funeral! Variety is produced in his using three-part textures in the choral writing, first and second
tenors, and basses, although the first tenor part is conceived for a high tenor,
similar to a counter-tenor, a voice which was then common in France. The
darkness of tone in the use of the male voices goes with much solemn minor-
keyed music and some striking anticipations of Verdi.

Rather like Rossini in his religious music, Cherubini sometimes lurches
into what can only be described as jauntiness, such as the writing 75 seconds
in from the beginning of the dramatic *Dies irae*. In this fine, committed performance under Muti (dating from 1973), the listener forgets the scarcity of
really memorable melodies, and relishes the drama and the distinctive textures, particularly in this outstandingly fine recording.

Included throughout these discs are Marriner's 1991 performances of
Cherubini's overtures, and if his performance of *Anacréon* does not have the
sheer incandescent energy of Toscanini, it is still brilliantly done. All these
overtures, which are brimming with attractive invention, are played with characteristic warmth and finesse by the Academy of St Martin-in-the-Fields.
L'Hôtellerie portugaise has much dexterity and charm, and the combination of
drama, energy and elegance in *Les deux journées* and *Faniska* is most winning.
Here, and even more in the witty touches in *Les Abencérages*, there are hints of
Rossini, but Cherubini's style is a bit weightier and the very fine *Concert Overture*, with its grave opening, is both dramatic and full of grace. These superb
recordings remind us again why Beethoven admired Cherubini so much. The
Sonata No. 2 for Horn and Strings is very pleasing indeed (with a rather catchy

Allegro movement), and the Callas excerpt from *Médée* (one of her most famous roles) is a nice addition.

CHOPIN, Frédéric (1810–49)

(i) *Piano Concerto 1. Ballade 1 in G min., Op. 23*; *Nocturnes 4 & 5, Op. 15/1–2*; *7, Op. 27/1*; *Polonaise 6, Op. 53*
Ⓜ EMI (ADD) 6 31780-2. Pollini; (i) Philh. O, Kletzki

Pollini's classic early EMI LP recital still – after many years – offers not only an unsurpassed reading of the *E minor Concerto* but five other items of equal distinction to make a perfect whole. This is playing of such total spontaneity, poetic feeling and refined judgement that any criticism is silenced. The recording is admirably truthful. Those seeking a coupling of the two concertos can turn to Zacharias, who directs the Lausanne Chamber Orchestra from the keyboard on MDG. The accompaniments to both works have never been more commanding, each slow movement is magical and the finales sparkle. Fine recording too. Another CD to treasure (MDG 340 1267-2).

Cello Sonata, Op. 63. Études: Op. 10/3; *Op. 10/5* (trans. Glazunov), *Op. 23/7. Introduction & Polonaise brillante, Op. 3*; *Nocturnes: 16, Op. 35/2*; *19, Op. 72/1* (arr. Mørk/Stott); *20, Op. posth. Preludes: 4* (arr. Mørk/Stott); *6. Waltz 3, Op. 14/2*
Virgin Classics 385784-2. Mørk, Stott

This collection of cello music centres on the two original cello works that Chopin wrote, one from each end of his career, the very early *Introduction and Polonaise brillante*, written when he was still in his teens, and the *Cello Sonata*, which was one of his last works, much influenced in its dark intensity by the break-up of his deep relationship with the novelist, Georges Sand. It would be hard to imagine a more powerful account of the *Sonata* than this one from the superb Norwegian cellist, Truls Mørk, well matched by the pianist, Kathryn Stott. The recording helps, made in collaboration with Norwegian Radio in the warm acoustic of Ostre Fredikstad Church in Norway, which suggests a substantial scale in the cello sound. There is similar rhythmic resilience in Mørk's performance of the *Introduction and Polonaise brillante*, with a delicious spring in the main polonaise theme, and with a thrilling speeding-up in the final coda. The cello transcriptions that make up the rest of the programme are all effective, with Mørk and Stott themselves responsible for two of the transcriptions and many of the items needing no arranger when the melodic line is so clear that cello and piano can readily play independently. Most haunting is the *Valse mélancolique* which the *Waltz*, Op. 14, No. 2, becomes.

Andante spianato & Grande Polonaise brillante; Barcarolle in F sharp; Berceuse in D flat; Nocturnes 1–19; Scherzi 1–4; Waltz in A flat, Op. 34/1
Ⓜ EMI mono 5 09668-2 (2). Rubinstein

EMI have reissued a set of some of Rubinstein's earlier mono Chopin record-ings, made between 1928 and 1937, as, rightly, one of their 'Great Recordings of the Century'. Many of them have not been equalled since, especially the *Nocturnes*, and all of them have not been surpassed, even by Rubinstein in his later stereo series for RCA. The current remastering by Andrew Walter has removed almost all the background noise, and the mono piano recording is miraculously real and vivid.

Ballades 1–4; Barcarolle; Fantaisie in F min.
DG 423 090-2. Zimerman

Krystian Zimerman's impressive set of the *Ballades* and the other two works on this disc are touched by distinction throughout and have spontaneity as well as tremendous concentration, bringing a remarkable combination of poetry and romantic feeling. The modern digital recording is one of fine quality.

Études, Op. 10/1–12; Op. 25/1–12
Sony SK 61885. Perahia

Murray Perahia's expressive range, variety of keyboard colour and musical imagination are of exceptional quality. His virtuosity is totally self-effacing so that the listener's engagement with Chopin's world is complete. The value and appeal of this set are further enhanced by the outstanding quality of the recording.

Mazurkas 1–59 (complete)
Ⓑ Double Decca (DDD/ADD) 448 086-2 (2). Ashkenazy

Piano Sonatas: 1 in C min., Op. 4; 2 in B flat min. (Funeral March); 3 in B min., Op. 58
Ⓜ Decca (ADD) 448 123-2. Ashkenazy

Vladimir Ashkenazy's recordings come from his distinguished comprehensive Decca 13-disc Chopin Edition (Decca 443 738-2), which is well worth having if you want to collect this composer's piano music as comprehensively as pos-sible. The Double Decca offers the most complete coverage available of the *Mazurkas*. They are finely articulated, aristocratic accounts of great character which have afforded us much pleasure. The *Sonatas* too enjoy classic status and, like the *Mazurkas*, are very well recorded, with vivid sound.

Waltzes 1–20 (complete)
Ⓜ EMI 6 98351-2. Ingrid Fliter

With recommended recordings by Rubinstein and Lipatti available it may seem remarkable that our first choice for the *Waltzes* is with the young Argentinian pianist, Ingrid Fliter. She plays twenty of them, including the two posthumously published works (in E flat and F sharp minor) marked by the composer *Sostenuto* and *Mélancolique*, respectively, plus another novelty in A minor that Chopin didn't write. Moreover her playing combines dazzling virtuosity with tenderness, lyrical delicacy and moments of playfulness, with every nuance exquisitely shaped. The whole collection is a joy and the recording is excellent, truthful, if a little dry in the bass.

Waltzes 1–14; Barcarolle; Mazurka in C sharp min., Op. 50/3; Nocturne in D flat, Op. 27/2
Ⓑ EMI Masters mono 9 65930-2. Lipatti

Dinu Lipatti's classic mono performances of the *Waltzes* were recorded by Walter Legge in the rather dry acoustic of a Swiss Radio studio in Geneva towards the end of the pianist's short life. In spite of the relative lack of bloom on the sound, they are very special and seem to have grown in wisdom and subtlety over the years.

CHRISTOFF, Boris (bass)

'Russian Opera, Arias and Songs': excerpts from: **MUSSORGSKY**: *Boris Godunov; Khovanshchina.* **BORODIN**: *Prince Igor.* **RIMSKY-KORSAKOV**: *Sadko; The Legend of the Invisible City of Kitezh.* **TCHAIKOVSKY**: *Eugene Onegin.* **MUSSORGSKY**: *Songs. Russian Folksongs*
Ⓜ EMI mono 392054-2

The magnetic quality of Christoff's singing is never in doubt here, and the compulsion of the singer's artistry as well as the vivid individuality of his bass timbres makes this a real portrait, not just a collection of items. These were his first recordings of the *Boris Godunov* excerpts (in which he assumes three different characters), and in musical terms he probably never surpassed them. But his characterization here is just as impressive as the singing itself, full of variety. The EMI transfers, of recordings made between 1949 and 1952, are bold and brightly focused with the most vivid projection.

CILEA, Francesco (1866–1950)

Adriana Lecouvreur (CD version)
Ⓜ Decca 475 7906 (2). Sutherland, Bergonzi, Nucci, d'Artegna, Cicuca, Welsh Nat. Op. Ch. & O, Bonynge

This is a curious but attractive opera with one pervading grand tune that should alone ensure its survival. It is the story of a great opera singer caught up in international intrigue and, in the manner of the veristic school, we are given a chance to observe her for a moment or two in her roles before she deals with her own life drama. Sutherland's performance could not be warmer-hearted, she impresses with her richness and opulence in the biggest test, the aria '*Io son l'umile ancella*', an actress's credo, and her formidable performance is warmly backed up by the other principals and equally by Richard Bonynge's conducting, not just warmly expressive amid the warmth of rich tunes, but light and sparkling where needed, easily idiomatic.

CIMAROSA, Domenico (1749–1801)

Il Maestro di Cappella
Ⓜ Decca 475 8490 (2). Corena, ROHCG O, Quadri - **DONIZETTI**: *Don Pasquale*

This sparkling 'intermezzo', lasting under 20 minutes, is one of the gems of the operatic catalogue. Corena's classic assumption of the role of the incompetent Kapellmeister is a joy from beginning to end. Corena shows complete mastery of the *buffo* bass style, and he is so little troubled by the florid passages that he can relax in the good humour. The vintage (1960) recording is both vivid and atmospheric, with the directional effects naturally conveyed. This music shows Cimarosa at his very best.

CLARKE, Rebecca (1886–1979)

(i–ii) *Dumka*; (i) *Chinese Puzzle*; *I'll bid my heart be still*; *Lullaby*; *Lullaby on an Ancient Irish Tune*; *Morpheus*; *Passacaglia on an Old English Tune*; (iii) *Prelude, Allegro & Pastorale*; (i) *Viola Sonata*
Ⓑ Naxos 8.557934. Dukes, with (i) Rahman; (ii) Hope; (iii) Plane

Rebecca Clarke's *Viola Sonata* is arguably the greatest work in that genre written in the twentieth century. It was written for the competition organized by Elizabeth Sprague Coolidge in 1919, and was counted equal first against Bloch's *Viola Sonata*, being relegated to second place only by casting vote. It is a ripely romantic piece, with echoes of English pastoral but with a very strong, far more international flavour, not least in the final meditative *Adagio*. The *Sonata*, superbly performed by Philip Dukes with Sofia Rahman, is well complemented by Clarke's other works for viola and piano, plus *Dumka* with violin added, and the *Prelude, Allegro and Pastorale*, for viola and clarinet in duet. Most of these works were unpublished at the time of Clarke's death, a composer, born in England, who spent the last 40 years of her life in New York, writing few but inspired works, all of them fresh, intense and inventive.

CLEMENTI, Muzio (1752–1832)

Symphonies: 1 in C; 2 in D; 3 in G (Great National Symphony); 4 in D
🅱🅱 Warner Apex (ADD) 2564 62762-2 (2). Philh. O, Scimone

Six of Clementi's 20 symphonies survive. The four numbered works are all scored for much larger forces than the Op. 18 set (included on an excellent Chandos CD, CHAN 9234, with the LMP and Bamert). Their musical content explains Clementi's high reputation in his lifetime as a composer for the orchestra, not just the piano. If the *Great National Symphony* is the most immediately striking, with *God Save the King* ingeniously worked into the third movement, the other works are all boldly individual. Scimone's Philharmonia performances from 1978 are both lively and sympathetic, and the recorded sound is excellent – and all at bargain price.

Piano Sonatas: Op. 24/2; Op. 25/5; Op. 40/2–3
🅱 Hyp. Helios CDH 55227. Demidenko

The spirit of Beethoven undoubtedly hovers over the dramatic opening of the *D major Sonata*, Op. 40/3, with which Demidenko opens his recital, and his performances of both this and the closing Op. 40/2 (both published in 1802) are very arresting. The *Molto adagio sostenuto* which acts as a prelude to this *B minor Sonata* is played with moving serenity and both the central *Largo mesto e patetico* and the *Lento patetico* of the *F sharp minor*, Op. 25/5, are very beautiful in Demidenko's hands. The *Allegro confuoco* of Op. 40/2 brings dazzling virtuosity, while he provides his own cadenzas for the first movement of Op. 24/2. Recorded at the Snape Maltings, Aldeburgh, in 1994, this reissue is a fine bargain. Those wanting to explore this rewarding repertoire further can turn to Hyperion's ongoing series of comparable distinction, played by Howard Shelley (CDA 67632, 67717, 67729, 67738, 67814 and 67819). Each is a double album with two discs offered for the price of one.

COATES, Eric (1886–1957)

Cinderella (Phantasy); *Dambusters March; Joyous Youth (Suite);*
London Suite; Miniature Suite; The Selfish Giant (Phantasy); *The*
Three Bears (Phantasy)
Chan. 9869. BBC PO, Gamba

Eric Coates is undoubtedly the greatest of the many fine British 'light music' composers. He was aptly described as 'the man who writes tunes' and, touchingly, just when his style of music was going out of fashion, he had one resounding and lasting hit at the end of his life with the *Dambusters March* – equal in impact to patriotic examples by Elgar and Walton if with a less *nobilmente* central tune. No praise could be higher, although we believe the piece was based on an earlier march which the composer replaced. This Chandos CD is arguably the finest single-CD collection of Coates's music before the public. It is a joy to hear his imaginatively coloured orchestration on a full-size orchestra with an ample string group, splendidly served by these superb performances and Chandos's demonstration-worthy recordings. The finest of the three *Phantasies* is *The Three Bears*, with its opening rhythmic phrase, 'Who's been sleeping in my bed?', and its later, beguiling waltz theme. *Cinderella* boasts another richly romantic example, and two more, both deliciously lightweight, close the *Joyous Youth Suite* and the *Miniature Suite*, which shows the composer at his most delicately elegant and graceful. (I.M. remembers that the latter was one of the first pieces he played when he first took up the French horn as a teenager with the Woolwich Civil Defence Orchestra during the war!) More robust is the *London Suite*, with its vigorous, pacy evocation of the old Covent Garden market, followed by a romantic portrayal of Westminster, complete with Big Ben chimes. The *Knightsbridge March* finale was famous as a signature tune for the BBC's *In Town Tonight* – the first radio 'chat show', in which guests who were 'in town' came into the studio to be interviewed. All orchestral musicians love playing Coates's music (particularly so as it is both rewarding and technically demanding) and this is conveyed by the orchestra throughout this wonderfully enjoyable collection.

Also worth considering is a long-available bargain two-CD collection on an EMI Classics for Pleasure (3 52356-2 (2)), conducted by either Groves, Kilbey or Mackerras – all the famous pieces are included, along with rarer items such as the *Saxo-Rhapsody*, in warmly sympathetic performances and in decent sound. Highlights in that set include Reginald Kilbey's performance of *The Three Elizabeths*, the composer's most inspired triptych, which is done with real flair in catching the composer's leaping *allegro* figurations in the first movement, and also in his shaping of the central slow movement – 'Elizabeth of Glamis', one of the composer's loveliest melodies (with a true Scottish snap in the rhythm and an affectionate grace) dedicated to the late Queen Mother.

The Dambusters March. From Meadow to Mayfair: Suite. The Merrymakers: Overture. Summer Days: Suite. Three Bears (Phantasy); Three Elizabeths Suite: March

Lyrita (ADD) SRCD 246. New Philh. O or LPO, Boult (with **GRAINGER**: *Over the Hills and Far Away*. **DELIUS**: *Marche Caprice*. **WALTON**: *Hamlet: Funeral March*. **VAUGHAN WILLIAMS**: *The Wasps: March Past of the Kitchen Utensils*. **ROSSINI**, arr. **BRITTEN**: *Soirées musicales: March*. **HOLST**: *Suite in E flat, Op. 28/1: March*)

As ever, Coates's music has great craftsmanship as well as good tunes and, lightweight though it is, it lies firmly within the English tradition. Here Boult finds its affinities with Elgar in delicacy of scoring and hints of nostalgia. *Summer Days*, written in the summer of 1919, was the first work that Coates composed as a former orchestral player. It includes a justly famous waltz, *At the Dance*, graciously elegant and with hardly any Viennese influence. The lollipops added for this reissue are equally welcome, particularly *The March Past of the Kitchen Utensils*, the hit number from Vaughan Williams's incidental music for *The Wasps*. The late-1970s recording is splendid, matching Lyrita's predictable high standard.

COLERIDGE-TAYLOR, Samuel (1875–1912)

Violin Concerto in G min., Op. 80; *Legend, Op. 14*; *Romance in G, Op. 39*
Lyrita SRCD 317. McAslan, LPO, Braithwaite (with **HARRISON**: *Bredon Hill*)

Coleridge-Taylor's beautiful *Violin Concerto* was one of the great discoveries of the Lyrita catalogue; although recorded in 1994 it was not issued until after 2007 (after two other versions had appeared). Lorraine McAslan's warmly lyrical performance is fully worthy of it and Nicholas Braithwaite and the LPO give passionate support. McAslan provides poetic performances of the *Legend* and *Romance*, both with memorable main themes, the *Legend* especially captivating. Then, for a valuable bonus, we are given the richly atmospheric *Bredon Hill* rhapsody of Julius Harrison, a lovely piece, obviously influenced by Vaughan Williams's *Lark Ascending*, but also by Butterworth – another memorable performance and admirably recorded.

Ballade in C min., Op. 73; *Clarinet Quintet in F sharp min., Op. 10*; *Piano Quintet in G min., Op. 1*
Hyp. CDA 67590. Nash Ens.

The *Piano Quintet*, written at the age of 18, is an astonishingly precocious work. It brims with assurance in its melodic sweep, and it is remarkable that this is probably its first performance since its première in 1893. Both Schubert and, especially, Dvořák's influence can clearly be heard in this work. Curiously, the finale is the darkest movement of the four, though this mood is dispelled by a surprise *fugato* section instead of a development section, and the work ends triumphantly in the major key. The *Clarinet Quintet*, written shortly after, is perhaps the greater work: it was inspired by a remark of Stanford, who made comment to the effect that after Brahms produced his clarinet quintet, no one would be able to compose another which did not show Brahms's influence. It was taken up as a challenge, and when he showed Stanford the result, he remarked, 'You've done it, me boy!' Again, the influence of Dvořák is most apparent. Its freshly energetic first movement is followed by an exquisitely beautiful slow movement which has, as the sleeve-note writer says, 'the qualities of an idealized folk song'. The Scherzo is a rhythmic tour-de-force, and the finale, with dashes of local colour in the form of a Scotch snap, is delightful.

The *Ballade* is a later work, written for the violinist Michael Zacherewitsh; it was first performed in Leeds in 1907. It is a wonderfully romantic, brooding work, with the spirit of Tchaikovsky (whom Coleridge-Taylor admired) and even of Rachmaninov. It is all masterfully performed by the Nash Ensemble whose unforced yet vital performances are a constant source of joy. Immaculate recording.

(i–iii) *Hiawatha's Wedding Feast*. (ii; iv) *Petite Suite de Concert, Op. 77*; (v) *La Bamboula (Rhapsodic Dance)*
Ⓑ CfP (ADD) 587 0242. (i) Richard Lewis & Royal Choral Soc.; (ii) Philh. O; (iii) Sargent; (iv) Weldon; (v) Bournemouth SO, Alwyn

Coleridge-Taylor's choral trilogy based on Longfellow's epic poem had its first performance under the composer at the Royal Albert Hall in 1900. It took a while to catch on, but in every year from 1924 until the outbreak of war in 1939 it was given a staged presentation at the same venue. Often nearly a thousand costumed 'Red Indian' performers came to enjoy themselves hugely, singing under the baton of their tribal chief, Sir Malcolm Sargent. His splendid record of *Hiawatha's Wedding Feast* (EMI) – the most popular part of the trilogy – remains unsurpassed to this day. This vintage recording – one of the highlights in the Classics for Pleasure catalogue – includes Richard Lewis's stylish performance of *Onaway! Awake, Beloved!*, but there is much else to enjoy, of course. The 1961 sound is warmly atmospheric. The *Petite Suite de Concert*, a salon pastiche, is the composer's best-known work and is music of great charm, with George Weldon's polished Philharmonia performance wholly sympathetic and not in the least sentimental, and in first-class sound. *La Bamboula*, which the composer wrote for his third visit to the USA in 1910, is a 'series of evolutions' on a West Indian dance also used by Gottschalk, and makes an attractive encore.

COLLINS, Anthony (1893–1963)

Eire; *Festival Royal – Overture*; *The Lady with a Lamp*; *Louis XV Silhouettes*; *The Saga of Odette*; *Santa Cecilia*; *Symphony 1 for Strings*; *Vanity Fair*; *Victoria the Great*
Dutton CDLX 7162. BBC Concert O, Wilson

Anthony Collins was the ideal recording conductor, as he was able to bring music vividly to life in the studio, and his Decca Sibelius cycle was a classic of the post-war LP era. This is the first CD devoted to his own highly enjoyable music. It opens with the patriotic *Festival Royal – Overture* (first performed in 1956) and, while it uses such obvious quotations as *God Save the Queen* and the 'Big Ben' chimes, it builds its own themes into a most entertaining work. The same patriotic spirit pervades his music to the 1937 film *Victoria the Great*.

Ear-tickling colours run through the delightful pastiche, *Louis XV Silhouettes*. The three-movement suite, *Eire*, based on Irish folk-tunes, is equally attractive, especially the toe-tapping final Reel, *Fluter's Hooley*. *Valse Lente* is a short and nostalgic evocation, originally used in the 1950 film *Odette*; and from the 1951 film *The Lady with a Lamp* the composer extracted the title theme and the music from the ball scenes to produce the *Prelude and Variations* included here. In the *Symphony for Strings* (1940), Collins's penchant for pastiche is to the fore. His most famous piece of all is the disarmingly simple *Vanity Fair*. First performed in 1952, this is the composition he most wanted to be remembered for, and indeed it is an exquisite little miniature of the sort that cheers you up every time you hear it.

CONNESSON, Guillaume (born 1970)

Cosmic Trilogy: Part 1: *Aleph*; Part 2: *Une lueur dans l'âge sombre*; Part 3: *Supernova*. (i) *The Shining One* (for piano & orchestra)
Chan. SACD CHSA 5076. RSNO, Stéphane Denève; (i) with Eric Le Sage

Guillaume Connesson is very much of the new generation of composers who have left atonalism well behind in favour of music designed to have a direct and immediate communication with listeners. His *Cosmic Trilogy* is accessible to anyone familiar with Stravinsky and borrows from that composer's idiom readily. Its climaxes are thrilling, its palette of colour continually captures the imaginative ear and there is no lack of firm melodic lines. The work is not only inspired by Connesson's response to the immensity of cosmic space, but also by his familiarity with Stephen Hawking's treatise *A Short History of Time* and with Wassily Kandinsky's painting, 'Quelques cercles'. *Cosmic Trilogy* is in three sections, of which Parts 2 and 3 are sub-divided. In mathematics, *Aleph* is the symbol of the power of infinity and, as Connesson's opening piece, it is a symphonic dance of life and vitality, the theme swirling giddily, making way at last for a winningly optimistic lyrical tune. The coda is a long ostinato crescendo, given its lift by the spirited woodwind. The first section of Part 2, *Une lueur dans l'âge sombre* ('A Glimmer in the Age of Darkness'), evokes the birth of the universe in a delicate spread of incandescence; the second section is ruminative and serene, and the dawning brilliance of light leads to a gentle closing diminuendo of haunting radiance. Part 3, *Supernova*, the composer tells us, 'puts us at the heart of the wondrous and tragic death of a star'. The evocation opens in darkness, and a crescendo mounts sinuously and with increasing power to reach a vibrating explosion which leads to the 'pulsating star' second section. Stravinsky's influence is strongly felt in the wild rhythms then generated, and the work ends in a burst of exciting cacophony.

The *Piano Concerto*, *The Shining One*, is an engaging lightweight miniature, only nine minutes long. The outer movements are lightly scored in scherzando fashion, while the lyrical central section makes a haunting contrast, with a virtuosic coda to make an exhilarating conclusion in which all participate, especially the soloist. Performances here are of the highest order, with Eric Le Sage, who gave the concerto's première, on glittering form and the RSNO on their toes throughout. Chandos's SACD recording is vividly spectacular.

COPLAND, Aaron (1900–1990)

(i) *Appalachian Spring*; *Billy the Kid* (complete ballets); (ii) *Dance Symphony*; (iii) *Danzón Cubano*; *El salón México*; (ii) *Fanfare for the Common Man*; *The Red Pony (Suite)*; (i) *Rodeo* (complete ballet)

Ⓑ EMI Gemini 3 81498-2 (2). (i) St Louis SO, Slatkin; (ii) Mexico City PO, Bátiz; (iii) Dallas SO, Mata

Copland wrote some of the most attractive of all American music, and this excellent bargain CD shows his amazing diversity, from the striking *Fanfare for the Common Man* to the colourful ballets, orchestral and film music. Slatkin's was the first complete recording of *Billy the Kid*. The complete *Rodeo* consists essentially of the usual four colourful movements, though here a piano interlude is included. Both are given first-rate performances and the sound is superb. *Appalachian Spring* is also complete and full of atmosphere. Altogether a remarkable triptych. Bátiz's orchestra doesn't have the technical excellence of Slatkin's but he is a lively and persuasive interpreter of Copland. The *Dance Symphony* is well done, though the ensemble is not as precise as it could be. *The Red Pony*, a colourful and nostalgic score for Lewis Milestone's memorable film, is among the most endearing lighter scores that Copland wrote and is very enjoyable. Mata's Dallas performances of *Danzón Cubano* and *El salón México* are as good as any – brilliant playing in demonstration sound. In every sense this set is a terrific bargain.

(i) *Clarinet Concerto*. *Dance Panels*; *Music for the Theater*; *Quiet City*

Ⓜ EMI 2 34439-2. NY Chamber Symphony, Schwarz, (i) with David Shifrin

David Shifrin's account of the *Clarinet Concerto* is among the best, the opening radiant in timbre and showing a natural fluency of phrasing, the later jazzy elements also well caught. What makes this collection especially attractive, apart from the beautifully played and evocative account of *Quiet City*, is the inclusion of the rare *Dance Panels*. Those who enjoy *Appalachian Spring* will surely respond to this inspired and diverse score, which typically moves with great ease from lyric tonal painting to jazzy dance rhythms. The *Music for the Theater* has comparable contrasts, The performances are of a high standard and the recording is vivid and with a particularly attractive ambience. Now offered at mid-price.

CORELLI, Arcangelo (1653–1713)

Concerti grossi, Op. 6/1, 3, 8, 9, 10, 11 & 12; Sonata a Quattro for Trumpet & Strings in D; Violin Sonata (for violin and harpsichord) in D min. (La Follia), Op. 5/12
Medici Arts DVD 207 2288. Sol. Ven., Scimone

Corelli is credited with inventing the *concerto grosso* format, with its concertino solo group contrasting with the main ripieno string ensemble – made famous later by Handel. This is not entirely true, but it was Corelli who surely developed and refined the form and who influenced many composers of his generation. The present works from Opus 6, dating from 1711/12, are among his most inspired, consistently inventive, melodic and stimulating, often with very beautiful and refined writing for the solo group. They are played here with great warmth and finesse by Claudio Scimone and his Venetian group, beautifully recorded (in 1986), and the performances evocatively photographed in the Basilica of San Marco in Rome. As a bonus we are given a miniature *Sonata for Trumpet and Strings* (with Guy Touvron the excellent soloist) and a superb account of Corelli's *Violin Sonata*, based on the famous Portuguese melody, *La Follia*, quite the best of the many settings of this famous tune.

CORIGLIANO, John (born 1938)

(i) *The Red Violin Concerto*; (ii) *Violin Sonata*
Sony/BMG 82876 88060-2. Bell, with (i) Baltimore SO, Alsop; (ii) Jeremy Denk

John Corigliano wrote the film score for *The Red Violin* (about a violin travelling through three centuries) and he had Joshua Bell as the 'voice' of the violin. He decided to transform the *Chaconne* of the film score, first into a concert piece for violin and orchestra, then later to expand it into a full-length concerto by adding a wild *pianissimo* Scherzo, with the soloist playing 'high, ethereal and dance-like'. A lyrical *Andante flautando* follows, with the soloist joining in a duet with the orchestra flute. The finale is 'a rollicking race in which the opposed forces of soloist and orchestra vie with each other' against extraneous non-musical sounds. There is a melancholy lyrical counterpart, before the *Chaconne* returns to complete the work. It is an unpredictable but fascinating work, and it could surely not be presented more excitingly than by Joshua Bell, with Marin Alsop and the excellent Baltimore orchestra. The recording is extremely vivid. The *Violin Sonata*, written much earlier (in 1962/3), is even more unpredictable, rhythmic patterns constantly changing, with two central slow movements framed by outer *Allegros*. The performance here is again surely definitive.

CORRETTE, Michel (1707-95)

Laudate Dominum (Psalm 148)
ⓑ Warner Apex 2564 60155-2. Alliot-Lugaz, Oudot, Lyon Vocal & Instrumental Ens.,
    Cornut - MONDONVILLE: Dominus Regnavit, etc.

We have a little gem here: Corrette's *Laudate Dominum*, based on the *Spring*
movement of Vivaldi's *Four Seasons*, is an indication of how popular the *Four
Seasons* remained in the years after his death, before it disappeared into obscur-
ity. Corrette's work dates from 1768, and Vivaldi's music is treated to some
especially felicitous writing (the adagio is hauntingly beautiful). As the sleeve-
note writer says, the work is full of Italianate freshness, with plenty of virtuosic
passages for flute, violins and voice. It is quite captivating and for most collectors will be a real find. Excellent performances and good (1975) sound.

 While introducing the little-known music of Corrette, readers are also
pointed to his delightful *Organ Concertos*, Op. 26/1-6, performed by René
Saorgin and the Nice Baroque Ensemble directed by Gilbert Bezzina (HM HMA
195 5148), which is another favourite discovery of ours. These lively and amiable concertos are given admirably buoyant performances, splendidly recorded
using period instruments. The orchestral detail is well observed, and Saorgin
plays vividly on an attractive organ of the period. Michel Corrette's invention
has genuine spontaneity, and this makes an enjoyable collection to dip into.
Not 'great' music perhaps, but attractively spirited - one does not want to eat
caviar every day.

COUPERIN, François (1668-1733)

(i) Apothéose de Lully; (ii) Les Nations: Premier ordre: 'La Françoise'; Deuxième ordre: 'L'Espagnole'
Australian Decca Eloquence (ADD) 480 2372. (i) ECO, Leppard; (ii) Jacobean Ens., Dart

A splendid reissue, made at the very beginning of the awareness of authentic-
performance practice. *Apothéose de Lully* is a piece of pure programme
music - Couperin's homage to the great French composer - and it contains
some remarkably inventive writing. The scurrying strings which begin *No. 5*
(track 2) are especially memorable, but the quirky string writing which follows
is hardly less so. The orchestration is the work of Raymond Leppard, who
directs some alert and stylish playing from the keyboard: the English Chamber
Orchestra respond excellently and the 1966 recording is quite superlative in its
range and clarity of definition. Thurston Dart was another pioneer in the
'authentic'-movement practice, and his version of *Les Nations* dates from 1962.
If, from today's point of view, the style inevitably sounds a little dated, it is

endearingly so, for the music contains some of Couperin's most imaginative writing. The sound is forward but warm and vivid.

Harpsichord Suites, Books 1–4: excerpts

Hyp. CDA 67440; CDA 67480; CDA 67520. Angela Hewitt (piano)

Having had great success with Bach's keyboard music, Angela Hewitt now turns to Couperin and in these three discs she chooses music that she feels is best suited to the piano. Her ornamentation is both crisply decorative and flexible and always inherent in the music's forward flow. CDA 67520 includes excerpts from Books I and II but centres on Book 3 (*Ordres 13* and *14*), and it includes *Les Folies françoises*, a miniature theme and variations on the famous *La Follia*, with each variation depicting a different character arriving at a masked ball in an invisible cloak. CDA 67440 continues Books 2 (*Ordres 6* and *8*) & 3 (*Ordre 18*). CDA 67480 is even more enticing in offering *Ordres 21* and *24–27*, with all the pieces having intriguing titles, many of them enigmatic; but the music itself is most engaging. With excellent documentation, every one of these discs can be enjoyed for the freshness of the music and performances.

COWARD, Noël (1899–1973)

'I went to a marvellous party': 45 Songs (1928–56) from: *Parisian Pierrot*; *On with the Dance*; *This Year of Grace*; *Lorelei*; *World Weary*; *Bitter Sweet*; *Private Lives* (including 2 spoken love scenes with Gertrude Lawrence); *Cochran's 1931 Revue*; *The Third Little Show*; *Cavalcade*; *Words and Music*; *Conversation Piece*; *Don't Put Your Daughter on the Stage*; *Tonight at 8.30*; *We were Dancing*; *Operette*; *The Stately Homes of England*; *Where are the Songs we Sung?*; *Dearest Love*. Wartime Songs: *London Pride*; *Could you please oblige us with a Bren Gun*; *Don't let's be beastly to the Germans.* **JEROME KERN**: *The Last Time I saw Paris*; *I'm Old-fashioned.* **COLE PORTER**: *You'd be so nice to come home to.* From 1945 onwards: Songs from: *Sigh No More*; *Pacific 1860*; *Ace of Clubs*; *The Globe Revue.* Cabaret Songs: *Alice is at it again*; *Time and again*; *A bar on the Piccola Marina.* **COLE PORTER**: *Let's do it, Let's fall in love*

Nim. Retrospective (ADD) mono RTS 4168 (2). Noël Coward, with Carol Gibbons (piano and with his orchestra) and various other orchestras

This treasurable collection compiled by Ray Crick and splendidly remastered by Alan Bunting is a total joy, bringing the 'Master', as Noël was known in the theatre, totally to life, his unique vocal personality vividly projected by the superb transfers here. Indeed the recordings, made over three decades, are astonishing in their presence and the way they capture his whimsicality, clear enunciation and sonorous, yet well-focused baritone. Perhaps the most cele-brated excerpts are spoken – the two infinitely memorable dialogues with Gertrude Lawrence in the finest of all his plays, *Private Lives*, which also includes the enchantingly nostalgic 'Someday I'll find you'. But so many numbers here are sentimentally indispensable, including 'I'll follow my secret heart', the touchingly patriotic 'London Pride' and, of course, 'I'll see you again' from *Bitter Sweet* – a show that urgently needs a revival. The silly songs, 'Mad Dogs and Englishmen' and 'A bar on the Piccola Marina', and a unique version of Cole Porter's 'Let's fall in love', with new words, are no less endearing. Accom-paniments are wonderfully stylish and there is excellent documentation. A pair of discs not to be missed on any account.

CRUSELL, Bernhard (1775–1838)

Clarinet Concertos: in E flat, Op. 1; in F min., Op. 5; in B flat, Op. 11
BIS-SACD1723. Fröst, Gothenburg SO, Kamu

Here is another example of a largely unknown composer who has been revived through recordings of his music. The Swedish clarinettist Bernhard Crusell was considered a supreme virtuoso/composer of his time and he left us three highly appealing and very tuneful concertos for his instrument. They are most elegantly played by the young Swedish clarinettist, Martin Fröst, and the fine Gothenburg orchestra under Okko Kamu. There have previously been excel-lent versions by Emma Johnson (ASV), by Antony Pay on a period instrument (Virgin), and dazzling virtuoso accounts by Kari Kriikku (Ondine). All are highly enjoyable, but this new BIS SACD seems to trump the others (except perhaps for Emma Johnson). Strongly recommended.

CURZON, Clifford (piano)

Decca recordings, Volume 2: 1941–72: **SCHUBERT**: *4 Impromptus, D.899; Piano Sonata 21 in B flat, D.960*. **MOZART**: *Piano Concertos 23 in A, K.488; 24 in C min., K.491* (with LSO, Krips). **BRAHMS**: *Piano Concerto 1 in D min., Op. 15* (with Concg. O, Beinum). *Piano Sonata 3 in F min., Op. 5; Intermezzi: in E flat, Op. 117/1; in C, Op. 119/3*. **GRIEG**: *Piano Concerto in A min., Op. 16* (with LSO, Fistoulari). **DVOŘÁK**: *Piano Quintet in A, Op. 81*. **FRANCK**: *Piano Quintet, in F min.* (with VPO Qt)
Ⓜ Decca (ADD) mono/stereo 475 084-2 (4)

This treasurable second anthology, which won the *Gramophone* 'Historical Instrumental Award' in 2003, surveys some of the very finest Clifford Curzon recordings for Decca made over three decades, including the early Schubert *Impromptus* (1941) and the remarkably beautiful performances of the two Mozart piano concertos, K.488 and K.491 (1953), with Josef Krips. Curzon was to record them again later in stereo, but the *C minor* (*No. 24*) in particular, with its exquisite *Larghetto*, remains very special. It appears here in its first international CD release. Curzon was also to record the Brahms and Grieg concertos again in stereo, the Brahms famously with Szell in 1962, but the earlier account with Van Beinum, if different in character, less pungently arresting, more warmly relaxed, brings the music's nobility out, especially in the slow movement. With the Grieg, Fistoulari proved a volatile partner, and again the slow movement is memorable, although in this instance the later, stereo version with Fjelstad brought out a specially idiomatic character to the orchestral playing. Both these earlier performances (from 1951) are also appearing on CD for the first time. In chamber music, Curzon's playing was no less magnetic, and the stereo coupling of the seductive Dvořák and Franck *Piano Quintets* was another landmark: the stereo recordings, made in the Sofiensaal (in the early 1960s), still sound very impressive. But it is the Brahms and Schubert *Sonatas* that sum up perfectly all that is uniquely cherishable in Curzon's art. The playing has great humanity and freshness. Both interpretations are totally spontaneous-sounding; yet in the Brahms, despite the underlying intensity, nothing is over-stated. And in the Schubert (as with the *Impromptus*) detail is finely drawn but never emphasized at the expense of the architecture as a whole. The stereo recording too is first class and balanced most naturally. A set which is not to be missed.

DEBUSSY, Claude (1862–1918)

Volume 1: *Berceuse héroïque*; *Images*; *Jeux*; *Marche écossaise*; *La Mer*; *Musiques pour le Roi Lear*; *Nocturnes*; *Prélude à l'après-midi d'un faune*; *Printemps*. Volume 2: *La Boîte à joujoux*; *Children's Corner* (orch. Caplet); *Danse* (orch. Ravel); (i) *Danses sacrée et profane*. (ii) *Fantaisie for Piano & Orchestra*; *La plus que lente*; *Khamma*; *Petite Suite* (orch. Büsser); (iii) *Première rapsodie for Clarinet & Orchestra*; (iv) *Rapsodie for Saxophone*

EMI Gemini (ADD) Vol. 1: 3 65235-2 (2); Vol. 2: 3 65240-2 (2). Fr. R. & TV O, Martinon; with (i) Jamet; (ii) Ciccolini; (iii) Dangain; (iv) Londeix

There have been many exceptional recordings of Debussy's orchestral music over the years, but for sheer value for money it is hard to beat Martinon's excellent survey from the 1970s, both for its overall quality and its comprehensiveness. Martinon's is a very good *Images*, beautifully played, with the orchestral detail vivid and glowing. *Jeux* is also very fine, with the sound attractively spacious. *La Mer* enjoys the idiomatic advantage of fine French orchestral playing, even if it does not quite match Karajan or Haitink. The *Musiques pour le Roi Lear* is a real rarity; the colourful *Fanfare* remains impressive and *Le Sommeil de Lear* is highly evocative. The *Nocturnes* are beautifully played, as indeed is *Printemps*, with Martinon penetrating its charm. *Children's Corner* and *La Boîte à joujoux* contain much to enchant the ear, as does the tuneful *Petite Suite*. A great rarity here is *Khamma*. This and the two *Rapsodies* are underrated and, although there are alternative versions of all these pieces, none is more economically priced. The performances are sympathetic and authoritative, and the recordings have been remastered successfully. The sound is full and spacious, with an attractive ambient glow. A bargain.

Fantaisie for Piano & Orchestra

Chan. CHSA 5084. Bavouzet, BBC SO Y. P. Tortelier (with **MASSENET**: 2
   Impromptus; 2 Pièces pour piano; Toccata; Valse folle) - **RAVEL**:
   Piano Concertos

This is simply one of the finest records of French piano music in the catalogue. Jean-Efflam Bavouzet has already given us unsurpassed accounts of Debussy's solo piano music, and here he turns to the little-known *Fantaisie for Piano and Orchestra*. It is an early work, cyclic in inspiration, but it has many hints of his later music, and its poise and refinement are matched by orchestration which is both colourful and subtle. The central slow movement is delicately poetic, and the brilliant finale also has a beautiful slow interlude. Bavouzet and Tortelier have the work's full measure and play it to perfection, helped by Chandos's really first-class recording. The Massenet miniatures are equally rewarding and, as Bavouzet comments in his note, 'their tenderness, not to mention their eccentricities, possess an engaging, if slightly old-fashioned charm'. There is brilliant virtuosity too, not least in the *Toccata*.

Images; La Mer; Prélude à l'après-midi d'un faune

Unitel Classics DVD 701608. O dell'Accademia Nazionale di Santa Cecilia, Bernstein (V/D:
   Horant Hohfeld)

Recorded live at the Accademia Nazionale di Santa Cecilia, Rome, in 1989, this is a key DVD if ever there was one. Bernstein is not famed for conducting Debussy, but this compellingly vivid and involving collection can easily match the more familiar recordings of Munch, Karajan and Ormandy. Bernstein was gravely ill at the time (the year before his death), yet one would never suspect it from the sheer joy of his music-making and his total control of the orchestra, who play with great intensity and precision. With Horant Hohfeld's close-up camera angles one is drawn to each of the solo players (especially the solo oboe and cor anglais). In response to Bernstein's inspired direction, the Santa Cecilia orchestra play with great virtuosity and all the subtlety of detail Bernstein can command, to say nothing of the electrifying intensity. The final climax of *Dialogue du vent et de la mer* is thrilling, after a performance in which every eddy and curlicue of the waves is pictorially vivid. The *Prélude à l'après-midi d'un faune* is richly atmospheric with a ravishing flute solo and a delicately sensuous climax in the strings. But these two performances are capped by the superbly detailed set of *Images* with *Les parfums de la nuit* in *Ibéria* wonderfully delicate in its nuancing and *Le matin d'un jour de fête* glittering with colour and bursting with energy.

La Mer

RCA (ADD) SACD 82876 61387-2. Boston SO, Munch – **IBERT**: *Escales.*
  SAINT-SAËNS: *Symphony 3*

La Mer; Prélude à l'après-midi d'un faune

Sony DVD 88697202449. BPO, Karajan – **RAVEL**: *Daphnis et Chloé: Suite 2*

To choose a single first choice from the many outstanding recordings of *La Mer* is very difficult, especially with Bernstein's DVD (above) to be taken into consideration. Munch's early account dates from 1956, yet this new SACD transfer makes it sound better than ever, incredibly vivid for its period (or any period, for that matter). Even though the sound is close-miked, the Boston acoustic provided plenty of atmosphere to match the performance's undoubted excitement. Outstanding couplings too.

But Karajan was always at his most inspired in this repertoire. His 1964 Berlin Philharmonic *La Mer* has long been recommended by us, and these, his last accounts of this and *Daphnis*, recorded in 1985, are masterly. The video presentation is expert and the sound vivid and well balanced. So for a marginal top recommendation this DVD holds its own.

Cello Sonata in D min.

Decca (ADD) 475 8239. Rostropovich, Britten – **SCHUBERT**: *Arpeggione Sonata.*
  SCHUMANN: *5 Stücke im Volkston*

Like Debussy's other late chamber works, the *Cello Sonata* is a concentrated piece, quirkily original and often hauntingly beautiful. The classic version by Rostropovich and Britten has a clarity and point which suit the music perfectly. The recording is first class and, if the couplings are suitable, this holds its place as first choice.

String Quartet in G min., Op. 10

Hyp. CDA 67759. Dante Quartet – **RAVEL**: *String Quartet; Violin Sonata in G*

We suspect that this coupling of the Debussy and Ravel *Quartets* will be to the present decade what the Quartetto Italiano and Melos Quartet couplings were for the 1970s and 1980s. The Dante Quartet, with Krysia Osostowicz as leader, has an impeccable sense of style and these are in every way beautifully played and recorded performances.

Complete Solo Piano Music: *2 Arabesques*; *Berceuse héroïque*; *Children's Corner*; *Danse bohémienne*; *Elégie*; *Hommage à Haydn*; *Mazurka*; *Morceau de concours*; *Nocturne*; *Page d'album*; *Le Petit nègre*; *La plus que lente*; *Rêverie*; *Suite bergamasque*
Chan. 10467

Ballade; *D'un cahier d'esquisses*; *Estampes*; *Images oubliées*; *L'Isle joyeuse*; *Masques*; *Pour le piano*; *Tarantelle styrienne*; *Valse romantique*
Chan. 10443

La Boîte à joujoux; *Jeux*; *Khamma*
Chan. 10545

Études, Books I & II; *Images, Series I & II*
Chan. 10497

Préludes, Books I & II
Chan. 10421. Jean-Efflam Bavouzet

Although there have been many outstanding Debussy collections published over the years, starting with Gieseking and including Zoltán Kocsis, Pascal Rogé, Noriko Ogawa, Jean-Yves Thibaudet and Jean-Philippe Collard, Jean-Efflam Bavouzet's survey steadily lived up to its initial promise as his five discs were issued one after the other. Moreover, included here are one or two novelties not offered in other groupings. Debussy playing does not come any better than this, and anyone starting to collect this excellent Chandos series need not really look any further. The CDs are available separately, each in turn was given a '*Gramophone* Award' and Chandos assure us that later this year a box of all five discs may be available.

Préludes, Books I & II (complete)
(M) EMI Masters mono 9 65931-2. Gieseking

Walter Gieseking's classic set of both Books of the Debussy *Préludes* (now reissued in the bargain 'Masters' series) is unsurpassed and the current remastering again confirms the natural realism of the 1953–4 Abbey Road mono recording, with Book I produced by Geraint Jones and Book II by Walter Legge. A set that should be in every collection.

3 Chansons de Bilitis
(M) Decca 475 7712. Crespin, Wustman (with recital of French song) – **BERLIOZ**: *Les Nuits d'été*. **RAVEL**: *Shéhérazade*. **POULENC**: *Songs*

These three exquisite songs of Debussy make a fine bonus to Crespin's legendary recordings of Berlioz and Ravel. Her instinctive understanding for the nuances of her own language is fully demonstrated here as she conjures up the haunting atmosphere suggested by the texts and, combined with Debussy's magical setting, makes for an unforgettable experience. What a great artist Crespin was.

Pelléas et Mélisande (DVD version)
DG DVD 073 030-9. Hagley, Archer, Maxwell, Cox, Walker, Welsh Nat. Op. Ch. & O, Boulez (V/D: Peter Stein)

Pelléas et Mélisande (CD version)
DG 435 344-2 (2). Ewing, Le Roux, Van Dam, Courtis, Ludwig, Pace, Mazzola, V. State Op. Ch., VPO, Abbado

Boulez's account of *Pelléas* with the Welsh National Opera was much admired at the time and, judging from the 1992 DVD recording, rightly so; Boulez produces much greater atmosphere than he did on his CD version. The soloists are impressive; Alison Hagley's Mélisande, especially, is both good to look at and to listen to. Her vocal and stage characterization is excellent, and she conveys an appealing sense of innocence. Neill Archer's Pelléas is no less intelligently projected, and Kenneth Cox's Arkel is splendidly sung and finely acted. Peter Stein's production is effective, simple and beautifully lit.

Claudio Abbado's outstanding *Pelléas* is just about the most strongly recommendable version of this opera on CD. One does not forget sublime accounts by Désormière and Ernest Ansermet, and also Karajan and Dutoit, but Abbado has the advantage of superb modern sound and a host of other merits in his favour. He satisfyingly presents a performance which is both sharply focused and freely flexible, which makes for compellingly dramatic results. The casting is simply superb, with no weak links at all.

'THE DECCA CLASSIC SOUND'
FALLA: *The Three Cornered Hat*; *La Vida breve*; **DEBUSSY**: *Images* (SRO, Ansermet). **CHABRIER**: *España*; **RIMSKY-KORSAKOV**: *Capriccio espagnol*; **GRANADOS**: *Andaluza*; **MOSZKOWSKI**: *Spanish Dances* (LSO, Argenta). **TCHAIKOVSKY**: *Violin Concerto* (Campoli, LSO, Argenta). **RACHMANINOV**: *Piano Concerto No. 3* (Ashkenazy, LSO, Fistoulari); *Piano Sonata No. 2* (Ashkenazy). **SIBELIUS**: *Symphony No. 1*; **MUSSORGSKY**: *Pictures at an Exhibition* (Philharmonia O, Ashkenazy). **BEETHOVEN**: Songs: *Che fa il mio bene?*; *Dimmi, ben mio*; *Ecco quel fiero istante!*; *In questa tomba oscura*; *T'intendo, si, mio cor*; **MOZART**: *Ridente la calma*; **SCHUBERT**: *Da quel sembiante appresi*; *Guarda, che bianca luna*; *Io vuo' cantar di Cadmo*; *Mi batte 'l cor*; *Mio ben ricordati*; *Non t'accostar all'urna*; *La pastorella*; *Pensa, che questo istante*; *Se dall'Etra*; *Vedi quanto adoro*; **HAYDN**: *Arianna a Naxos* (Bartoli, Schiff). **BARBER**: *Violin Concerto*; **BLOCH**: *Baal Shem*; **WALTON**: *Violin Concerto* (Bell, Baltimore SO, Zinman). **R. STRAUSS**: *An Alpine*

Symphony; *Don Juan* (San Francisco SO, Blomstedt). **BRUCKNER**:
Symphony No. 4 (Romantic) (VPO, Böhm). **J. STRAUSS I**: *Loreley-Rhein-Klänge* – waltz; *Radetzky-Marsch*; **J. STRAUSS II**:
An der schönen blauen Donau; *Auf der Jugd* – polka; *Bitte schön* –
polka; *Bei uns z'Haus* – waltz; *Leichtes Blut* – polka; *Pizzicato Polka*;
Tik-Tak – polka; *Wien, Weib und Gesang* – waltz; Eduard
STRAUSS: *Ohne Bremse* – polka; Josef **STRAUSS**: *Die
Emancipierte* – polka; *Moulinet* – polka; *Rudolfsheimer* – polka;
ZIEHRER: *Hereinspaziert*; **SUPPÉ**: *Overture: Die schöne
Galathee* (VPO, Boskovsky). **BRITTEN**: *War Requiem*
(Vishnevskaya, Pears, Fischer-Dieskau, Melos Ens., LSO, Composer).
MESSIAEN: *Turangalîla-symphonie* (Thibaudet, Concg. O, Chailly).
MENDELSSOHN: *Violin Concerto* (Chung, Montréal SO, Dutoit).
BRUCH: *Violin Concerto No. 1*; *Scottish Fantasia* (Chung, RPO,
Kempe). **MOZART**: *Piano Concertos Nos. 20 & 27* (Curzon, ECO,
Britten). **SCHOENBERG**: *Erwartung* (Silja, VPO, Dohnányi); **BERG**:
Symphonic Pieces from 'Lulu' (VPO, Dohnányi). **WEBERN**:
Im Sommerwind (Cleveland O, Dohnányi). **STRAVINSKY**: *The
Firebird*; *The Rite of Spring* (Detroit SO, Dorati). **RAVEL**: *Boléro*;
Ma Mère l'Oye; *Pavane pour une infante défunte*; *Le Tombeau
de Couperin*; *Valses nobles et sentimentales* (Montréal SO, Dutoit).
BRAHMS: *Piano Concerto No. 1* (Freire, Leipzig GO, Chailly).
SCHUMANN: *Carnaval* (Freire). **SHOSTAKOVICH**:
Symphonies Nos. 5 (Concg. O, Haitink) *& 9* (LPO, Haitink). **PURCELL**:
Dido and Aeneas (Bott, Kirkby, AAM, Hogwood). **BEETHOVEN**:
Violin Concerto (Jansen, Deutsche Kammerphilharmonie, Bremen,
Paavo Järvi). **BRITTEN**: *Violin Concerto* (Jansen, LSO, Paavo Järvi).
HOLST: *The Planets* (VPO, Karajan); *Egdon Heath*; *The Perfect Fool*
(LPO, Boult). **BARTÓK**: *Piano Concerto No. 3*; **RAVEL**: *G major
Piano Concerto*; **PROKOFIEV**: *Piano Concerto No. 3* (Katchen,
LSO, Kertész). **DVOŘÁK**: *Symphony Nos. 8* (LSO, Kertész) *& 9
(New World)* (VPO, Kertész). **HAYDN**: *Nelson Mass* (Stahlman, Watts,
Brown, Krause, Preston, King's College, Cambridge Ch., LSO, Willcocks);
Missa in tempore belli (Cantelo, Watts, Tear, McDaniel, St John's College,
Cambridge, Ch., ASMF, Guest). **GRANADOS**: *Goyescas* (Larrocha).
FALLA: *Nights in the Gardens of Spain* (Larrocha, LPO, Frübeck
de Burgos). **BEETHOVEN**: *Piano Sonatas Nos. 8 (Pathétique)*,
14 (Moonlight), *21 (Waldstein)*; *32 Piano Variations in C minor*
(Radu Lupu). **MENDELSSOHN**: *Symphony No. 3 (Scottish)*;
A Midsummer Night's Dream: Overture and Incidental Music (LSO,
Maag). **RESPIGHI**: *Pines of Rome*; *Roman Festivals*. **RIMSKY-KORSAKOV**: *Le coq d'or: Suite* (Cleveland O, Maazel). **JANÁČEK**:
Sinfonietta; *Taras Bulba*; *The Cunning Little Vixen: Suite* (VPO,
Mackerras). **TCHAIKOVSKY**: *Serenade for Strings*; *Souvenir de*

Florence; **GRIEG**: *Holberg Suite* (ASMF, Marriner). **IBERT**:
Divertissement; **SAINT-SAËNS**: *Danse macabre*; *Le Rouet
d'Omphale*; **BIZET**: *Jeux d'enfants* (Paris Conservatoire O, Martinon).
BORODIN: *Symphony No. 2* (LSO, Martinon). **VARÈSE**: *Arcana*;
Intégrales; *Ionisation*; **IVES**: *Symphony No. 2* (LAPO, Mehta).
RAVEL: *Daphnis et Chloé*; **ELGAR**: *Enigma Variations* (LSO,
Monteux). **BACH**: *Magnificat in D, BWV 243* (with Ameling, Bork,
Watts, Krenn, Krause); *Cantata BWV 10* (with Ameling, Watts, Krenn,
Rintzler); *Cantata BWV 140* (with Fontana, Winbergh, Krause) (Stuttgart
CO, Münchinger). **WAGNER**: *Der Ring des Nibelungen*: Extracts
(Birgit Nilsson, George London, Kirsten Magstad, Eberhart Walchter, Vera
Schlosser, Birgit Fasshender, Helen Watts, Wolfgang Windgasse, Gottlob Frick,
VPO, Solti). **PUCCINI**: *Turandot* – highlights (Sutherland, Pavarotti,
Caballé, Ghiaurov, LPO, Mehta). **SUSATO**: *Dansereye 1551* (New London
Consort, Pickett). **SAINT-SAËNS**: *Piano Concertos 2*, (i) *4*, *5* (Rogé,
RPO or (i) Philh. O, Dutoit). **PERGOLESI**: *Stabat Mater*; *Salve
Reginas in F min.*; *A min.* (Bonney, Scholl, Les Talens Lyriques, Rousset).
BACH: *Goldberg Variations* (András Schiff). **GLINKA**: *Ruslan and
Lyudmila: Overture*; **MUSSORGSKY**: *Khovanshchina: Prelude*;
Night on a Bare Mountain; **BORODIN**: *Prince Igor: Overture &
Polovtsian Dances* (LSO, Solti). **SUPPÉ**: Overtures: *Light Cavalry*;
Morning, Noon and Night in Vienna; *Pique Dame*; *Poet and
Peasant* (VPO, Solti). **MAHLER**: *Symphony No. 8 (Symphony
of a Thousand)* (Harper, Popp, Augér, Minton, Watts, Kollo, Shirley-Quirk,
Talvela, Chicago SO, Solti). **BEETHOVEN**: *String Quartets Nos. 11 &
13* (Takács Qt.). **PUCCINI**: *La Fanciulla del West*: Highlights
(Tebaldi, del Monaco, MacNeil, Tozzi, Santa Cecilia Ch. & O, Capuana).
MENDELSSOHN: *Octet*; **BEETHOVEN**: *Septet* (Wiener
Oktett). **WALTON**: *Belshazzar's Feast* (Terfel, Bournemouth SO & Ch.,
Litton); *Coronation Te Deum*; **PARRY**: *Blest Pair of Sirens*; *I Was
Glad*; *Jerusalem* (Winchester Cathedral Ch., Bournemouth SO, Hill).
Renée Fleming, 'Great Opera Scenes': Arias from: **MOZART**: *Le
nozze di Figaro*. **TCHAIKOVSKY**: *Eugene Onegin*. **DVOŘÁK**:
Rusalka. **VERDI**: *Otello*. **BRITTEN**: *Peter Grimes*, R.
STRAUSS: *Daphne* (LSO, Solti). José Carreras, Plácido Domingo,
Luciano Pavarotti, 'Three Tenors Concert, 1990': Arias from: **CILÈA**:
L'Arlesiana; **MEYERBEER**: *L'Africaine*; **PUCCINI**: *Tosca*;
Turandot; **LEHÁR**: *Das Land des Lächelns*; **SOROZÁBAL**:
La Taberna del puerto; Songs: *Core 'ngrato*; *Granada*; *Il lament di
Federico*; *Mattinata*; *O sole mio*; *Rondine al nido*; *Torna a Surriento*.
SCHIFRIN (arr.): *Medley* (Carreras, Domingo, Pavarotti, Teatro
dell'Opera di Roma O, Maggio Musicale Fiorentino O, Mehta). **Ute Lemper,
'Berlin Cabaret Songs': *Alles Schwindel*; *Eine kleine Sehnsucht*; *Das
Gesellschaftslied*; *Gesetzt den Fall*; *Ich bin ein Vamp!*; *Ich weiss*

nicht, zu wem ich gehöre; *L'heure bleue*; *Das lila Lied*; *Maskulinum–Femininum*; *Mir ist heut so nach Tamerlan!*; *Münchhausen*; *Peter, Peter, Komm zu mir zurück!*; *Raus mit den Männern!*; *Sex-Appeal*; *Der Verflossene*; *Wenn die beste Freundin*; *Wir wollen alle wieder Kinder sein!!*; *Zieh dich aus, Petronella!* (Lemper, Matrix Ens., Ziegler).
Joan Sutherland, Luciano Pavarotti, Marilyn Horne, 'Live from the Lincoln Center': Arias from: **VERDI**: *Ernani*; *Otello*; *Il trovatore*; **BELLINI**: *Beatrice di Tenda*; *Norma*; **PONCHIELLI**: *La Gioconda* (New York City Op. O, Bonynge)
Ⓑ Decca (ADD/DDD) 478 2826 (50)

Decca's Classic Sound box set comprises many of their classic recordings of the stereo era. Selecting which recordings to include must have been an all but impossible task, and, while we will all have a particular favourite recording which we feel should have been included, it is best to enjoy what actually has been included. The CDs are discussed in the alphabetical (by artist) order they appear in the set. A handsome booklet is included with many pictures and an excellent note by Decca's own Raymond McGill. The CDs are housed in their original artwork. Ernest Ansermet was one of Decca's most important conductors in the 1950s and '60s and the best of his recordings – of which two are included here – impress today: his vibrantly colourful *Three-Cornered Hat* is coupled with his meticulous and finely etched Debussy *Images*, both recorded in 1961, though you would never guess it from the immediacy of the sound. Ataúlfo Argenta made a series of lively recordings for Decca before his untimely death, the most famous of which, *España*, is included. Moszkowski's endearingly old-fashioned and tuneful *Spanish Dances* remain favourites of ours, and, along with equally successful performances of *Capriccio espagnol* and *España*, sound as fresh as the day they were first released (1958). The inspired coupling on this CD is of Alfredo Campoli's surprisingly little-known recording of the Tchaikovsky *Violin Concerto*: a performance full of style and imagination, with Argenta building up the climaxes with masterly skill and providing a finale which dazzles in its brilliance. The 1956 sound amazes in its vividness and warmth. Vladimir Ashkenazy is represented by his earlier recording of Rachmaninov's *Piano Concerto No. 3*, accompanied by another stalwart of Decca's early stereo days, Anatole Fistoulari, always a superb conductor of concertos as well as ballets. This account is fresher than his later account with Previn. Ashkenazy shows his full rapport with Rachmaninov in a highly sympathetic account of the original version of the *Second Piano Sonata* as a coupling. Ashkenazy is also a fine Sibelian, and, while his account of the *First Symphony* is not among the very finest, it is very good by any standards, and the same applies to his *Pictures at an Exhibition*, which follows. Cecilia Bartoli is one of Decca's stars of the digital era and, while some of her more recent recordings are marred by vocal mannerisms (usually related to her coloratura), the disc selected here of Beethoven and Schubert songs, accompanied by András Schiff, is delightful. Joshua Bell is represented by superb recordings of the Walton and Barber *Violin Concertos*, while, also from the 1990s, Herbert Blomstedt's impressive recording of the *Alpine Symphony* – one of the best of his San Francisco series – has been selected. Karl Böhm's classic account of Bruckner's *Fourth Symphony* had to be included, recorded in 1973 and still glowing as a performance and in richness of sound. Decca's first digital recording, the Vienna New Year's Day Concert 1979, conducted by a master of that repertoire, Willi Boskovsky, is always a joy to hear, with the audience participation in the *Radetzky March* possessing almost uncanny presence. Benjamin Britten's legendary recording of his own *War Requiem* (now on a single CD, lasting over 80 minutes), remains a classic of the recording age, with the shattering *Libera me* overwhelming in impact. Riccardo Chailly made many successful recordings for Decca, and his powerful 1992 account of Messiaen's *Turangalîla-symphonie* remains one of the most impressive this work has received. The violinist Kyung Wha Chung was an artist who never put a foot wrong in the studio, and her excellent Mendelssohn *Violin Concerto* (with Charles Dutoit), coupled with recordings of Bruch's equally popular *G minor Concerto* and the rare but gorgeous *Scottish Fantasia* (conducted by Rudolf Kempe), are together most enjoyable, though perhaps not quite as impressive as her Prokofiev, Stravinsky and Sibelius concerto recordings. Clifford Curzon, one of the great pianists of the twentieth century, is represented by two classic recordings of Mozart piano concertos, *Nos. 20* and *27*, conducted by Benjamin Britten. Inspired performances, recorded in 1970 but not released until 1982. Christoph von Dohnányi is represented by a triptych of twentieth-century works: Schoenberg's *Erwartung* (searingly intense music and performance, dating from 1979), Berg's *Symphonic Pieces from 'Lulu'* (a brilliant recording, from six years earlier 1973) and Webern's *Im Sommerwind* (from 1991) completing the portrait. Antal Dorati, especially famous for his Mercury repertoire, made many impressive recordings for Decca, not least his complete Haydn symphony survey. His recordings of Stravinsky's *The Firebird* and *The Rite of Spring*, from the early 1980s, remain impressive both for the energy of the music-making and for the sonic impact of the early digital recording. Charles Dutoit was in some ways the digital equivalent of Ernest Ansermet and covered much of the same repertoire. Although, at times, his recordings could seem a little bland, his Ravel records were especially famed, and the selection included here shows the beauty of detail and warmth of sound for which his partnership with the Orchestre Symphonique de Montréal was famous. Renée Fleming's recording of 'Great Opera Scenes' confirms her status as one of the great opera stars of today, and she is accompanied by one of the most significant conductors in Decca's history, Sir George Solti. Nelson Freire's account of Brahms's *Piano Concerto No. 1*, while excellent, does not quite equal Decca's famous Curzon/Szell recording in searing intensity, but it is impressive enough, and the Schumann *Carnaval* which follows is most enjoyable. Bernard Haitink's Shostakovitch symphony cycle, though always brilliantly recorded, did not always possess the white-hot excitement this music ideally needs. But his accounts of the *Fifth* and *Ninth Symphonies* do convey the artistic excellence of his performances, and the recordings have always been maintained by Decca in their catalogue. Dame Janet Baker's classic account of Purcell's *Dido and Aeneas* is supreme, but Decca have chosen Catherine Bott's 1992 version, with the Academy of Ancient Music, directed by Christopher Hogwood. While it offers many excellent qualities, it does not quite have the magical intensity of the earlier recording, though, of course, it is more 'authentic' in approach. Janine Jansen, a rising Decca star, is represented by excellent versions of the Beethoven and Britten *Violin Concertos*. Undoubted classic issues next, all dating from 1961: Herbert von Karajan's account of Holst's *The Planets* (with the VPO), a superb reading in every way, full of atmosphere and drama, is coupled with recordings by Sir Adrian Boult (with the LPO) of Holst's delightful *Perfect Fool* ballet and the more mysterious *Egdon Heath*, both full of character. Julius Katchen made many superb records for Decca, all noted for the boldness and vibrancy of the music-making; the three concertos included here, by Bartók, Ravel and Prokofiev, all conducted by István Kertész with the LSO, display the tremendous vitality for which both artists were renowned. Kertész died very young, but not before leaving us, among other things, a superb Dvořák cycle: included here are the glorious *Eighth Symphony*, with the LSO, and the earlier recording of the *New World*, with the VPO, in both cases, exhilarating, fresh, music-making at its most inspired. The Choir of King's College, Cambridge, under Sir David Willcocks, is represented (with the LSO) in a famous performance of the *Nelson Mass* of Haydn, while the St John's College, Cambridge, Choir, under George Guest, is represented by the dramatic *Missa in tempore belli*, both performances surpassed in scholarship, but not musicianship. Alicia de Larrocha, one of the most delightful and enchanting pianists of the modern age, was famous for her recordings of Spanish music, of which some of her finest solo 1970s performances of Granados are included here, as well as her 1983 account of De Falla's *Nights in the Gardens of Spain* (with the LPO under Rafael Frühbeck de Burgos). Quite a contrast of style comes in the music-making of Ute Lemper, whose vibrant accounts of 'Berlin Cabaret Songs' won her many fans across the world. Radu Lupu has maintained admirable integrity throughout his long career, partly by making comparatively few recordings. However, when he does enter the studio, something special is assured, as can be heard in his 1970s accounts of Beethoven's *Moonlight*, *Pathétique* and *Waldstein Sonatas*, along with the *32 Piano Variations*. Peter Maag also made comparatively few recordings, but his accounts of Mendelssohn's *Scottish Symphony* and *A Midsummer Night's Dream* music are undoubted classics, famous for both the zest of the music-making and the delicacy of musical nuance, and the 1950s/60s sound remains superb by any standards. Lorin Maazel made the majority of his finest records during the 1960s and '70s, and his vivid accounts of Respighi's *Roman Festivals* and *Pines of Rome*, coupled with a recording of Rimsky-Korsakov's dazzling *Le coq d'or* suite, are impressive examples. Sir Charles Mackerras, who made many famous records for various companies, was at his finest in the music of Janáček: his accounts of the *Sinfonietta* and *Taras Bulba* (with the VPO), coupled here with a recording of a suite from *The Cunning Little Vixen*, in their time helped to make Janàcek as popular as he is today. Sir Neville Marriner made countless recordings for Argo/Decca – his records of Vivaldi being notable for their freshness and fine musicianship. He is represented here by glorious accounts of Tchaikovsky's *Serenade for Strings* and *Souvenir de Florence* (slightly cut), as well as a recording of Grieg's *Holberg Suite*, repertoire ideally suited to this artist and his orchestra. The performances, like the sound, glow with radiant warmth. Jean Martinon made some memorable records for Decca. Included here are his electrifying (both sonically and musically) account of Borodin's *Second Symphony* (with the LSO), and his account of Ibert's *Divertissement* (with the Paris Conservatoire Orchestra), which receives a performance of unique vividness. The Saint-Saëns and Bizet items which complete the disc are hardly less successful. Zubin Mehta's heyday (recording-wise) was the 1960s/70s, and his sumptuous recordings of the Varèse orchestral works and Ives's *Second Symphony* remain an impressive tribute to the engineering of the 1970s. Pierre Monteux made many fine records, but none finer than his 1958 account of Elgar's *Enigma Variations*, one of the great recordings of the stereo era. His *Daphnis et Chloé* of Ravel (along with Munch's RCA account) is also one of the finest of this work ever committed to disc. All this music-making, with the LSO in the late 1950s, remains as fresh as the day the discs were made. Karl Münchinger's style may seem rather old-fashioned by today's standards, but his performances are blessed with innate musicianship, and, in planning his choral works, he often included superb soloists. His 1968 accounts of Bach's *Magnificat* and *Cantata* BWV *10* are two of his most impressive ventures, and, if in the later, digital recording of *Cantata* BWV *140* (1984) a hint of pedantry is more apparent, it remains enjoyable. Birgit Nilsson and Sir George Solti are synonymous with Decca, and a CD of highlights from the seminal recording of *Der Ring des Nibelungen* is understandably included. Equally synonymous with Decca is Luciano Pavarotti, and he is included in the famous 1990 concert with José Carreras and Plácido Domingo, certainly a part of Decca history and a resounding commercial success. But perhaps he is better heard in the highlights from Puccini's *Turandot* (also conducted by Mehta), an undoubted classic of the opera catalogue, with one of Joan Sutherland's finest portrayals in the title role. Philip Pickett's recording of Tielman Susato's *Dansereye* is one of the few early music performances included here. Pascal Rogé, a master of the French repertoire, is represented by Saint-Saëns's delightfully tuneful piano concertos, while Christophe Rousset combines both drama and expressive intensity in Pergolesi's *Stabat Mater* and two *Salve Reginas*, with Andreas Scholl and Barbara Bonney. András Schiff's 1982 recording of the *Goldberg Variations* of Bach remains very impressive indeed. Although the piece is performed on a modern piano, and Schiff's style is undoubtedly scholarly, the playing is imbued with a sense of wonder at the music's continued inspiration, and Schiff readily conveys his joy in the music-making. Have the *Ruslan and Lyudmila Overture*, *Prince Igor Overture* and *Polovtsian Dances* ever sounded more exciting than in the recordings by Sir George Solti with the LSO? We doubt it. Nor have there been more electrically charged recordings of the four Suppé overtures, recorded with the VPO. True, Solti may not bring out all the charm of these works, but they have never sounded more exciting! Another Solti classic is included in the form of his Chicago SO recording of Mahler's *Eighth Symphony*, dating from 1971, an inspiring performance, still packing a sonic punch. A more impressive trio of singers than Joan Sutherland, Luciano Pavarotti and Marilyn Horne is hard to imagine, and they appear together on 'Live from Lincoln Center', dating from 1981, all in superb voice, largely performing the bel-canto repertoire in which they all excelled, well supported by Richard Bonynge. The Takács Quartet offer thoughtful, beautifully performed and recorded accounts of two Beethoven string quartets from their complete cycle, and their stylishness makes one think anew about repertoire we know so well. Renata Tebaldi dominated the Decca catalogue in the 1950s and 1960 – a lovely soprano whose many fine recordings have stood the test of time. She was especially renowned for her Puccini arias, and highlights from one of her most successful opera recordings, *La Fanciulla del West*, are included here; her 'usual' tenor, the full-blooded Mario del Monaco, is hardly less impressive. The Wiener Oktett made a series of remarkable recordings in the 1950s and '60s for Decca, and many of their sessions remain supreme achievements. Their accounts of the Mendelssohn *Octet* and Beethoven *Septet* radiate both warmth and colour, with a glorious Viennese glow which seems to come from another age. The final CD, listed under Winchester Cathedral Choir, comprises stirring accounts of Walton's *Coronation Te Deum*, Parry's *I Was Glad* and *Blest Pair of Sirens* and Elgar's masterful orchestration of *Jerusalem*, all conducted by David Hill. The bulk of the CD, however, consists of a superb performance of Walton's *Belshazzar's Feast*, conducted by Andrew Litton. All in all, a most impressive box set and certainly worth its bargain price tag.

DELIBES, Léo (1836–91)

(i) *Coppélia*; (ii) *Sylvia*; (iii) *La Source* (with Minkus) (complete ballets)
Ⓑ Decca (ADD/DDD) 460 418-2 (4). (i) Nat. PO; (ii) New Philh. O; (iii) ROHCG O; Bonynge

Coppélia; Sylvia: Suite
Ⓜ Australian Decca Eloquence (ADD) 480 0083. SRO, Ansermet (with **RAVEL**: *Daphnis et Chloé: Suite 2*)

Coppélia marked a turning point in the history of ballet music. It possessed a quality which ballet music in the mid-nineteenth century rarely aspired to, and its success was instant and lasting. There is never a dull bar, and the sparkling succession of tunes are orchestrated with consistent flair and imagination and provide superb musical entertainment away from the theatre. *Sylvia*, written a few years later, was considered almost symphonic in style in its day, but today it is the colourful orchestration and melodiousness of the score which appeal. This box set also includes the complete ballet, *La Source*, written half by Delibes and half by Minkus. If it does not possess the consistent inspiration of the two great ballets, it is still very enjoyable indeed, with the music by Minkus of surprisingly good quality. Bonynge recorded *Coppélia* twice, the first time with the Suisse Romande Orchestra, and, excellent though that performance is, his digital re-make is included here. With its expert British sessions musicians, the National Philharmonic Orchestra is able to produce a more polished and no less spirited ensemble, and the wind solos are a constant delight. In moments like the delicious *Scène et valse de la poupée*, which Bonynge points very stylishly, the effect is Mozartian in its grace. Occasionally, the digital sound brings an emphasis on brilliance which isn't wholly natural, but the recording in most respects is praiseworthy, not only for the vividness of colour, but for the balance within a concert-hall acoustic. In the many colourful and elegantly scored interchanges for woodwind and strings the tangibility of the players is very striking. *Sylvia* does not quite possess the non-stop stream of insouciance which characterizes *Coppélia*, but it contains a great deal of attractive music, with such excitingly dashing numbers as *Les Chasseresses*, the *Marche et cortège de Bacchus*, and piquant items such as the *Pas des Éthiopiens* and the delightful *Pizzicato*. Bonynge plays the score with wonderful affection and polish, and, with the aid of glowing Decca sound (from 1974), all the felicities of the orchestration are brought out vividly.

The composition of the music for the earlier ballet, *La Source*, was divided between two composers, the established Minkus and the younger Delibes, who had not yet tried his hand in the field of ballet and for whom the commission was a godsend. He begins the second Act in the elegantly lightweight style of his colleague, but soon his stronger musical personality asserts itself with a romantic horn tune and, later, an even more memorable melody in the strings. The felicitous use of the orchestral palette is readily discernible; but, even so, this is clearly the forerunner for *Coppélia* and *Sylvia*, from a composer whose style is not yet fully individual. Minkus sets the style and atmosphere of *La Source* very much inherited from Adam, though with less melodrama. The music is attractive, its melodic contours less positive than those characteristic of Delibes; but the writing has distinct charm and its picaresque evocation suits the slight narrative line. Bonynge makes the entire score sparkle throughout and the Decca sound is, once again, superb. The boxed set comes with decent notes and a good synopsis of each ballet.

Special mention must be made of the newly reissued version of *Coppélia*, conducted by Ernest Ansermet. This version, along with his reading of *The Nutcracker*, shows Ansermet at his most magical. This performance crackles with a vitality which no other version matches (though Bonynge, in a different way, is equally recommendable). Items such as the *Musique des automates* sparkles like glitter, and the rhythmic vitality of the playing paints vivid images in the mind almost as clearly as a DVD version. The sound is astonishingly vivid and full for 1957, and virtually no allowances have to be made for its date in this splendid transfer. The four items from *Sylvia* are similarly vivid and brightly recorded. The Ravel bonus is unexpected and very welcome, for Ansermet was never less than interesting with this composer, and here the 1960 Decca sound amazes.

Lakmé (opera; complete)

Ⓜ Decca (ADD) 425 485-2 (2). Sutherland, Berbié, Vanzo, Bacquier, Monte Carlo Op. Ch. & O, Bonynge

Lakmé contains one of the most famous of all operatic arias as well as one of the most famous of all operatic duets, thanks to a television advert. However, this opera offers a lot more. It is full of exotic colour and melody as well as dramatic spectacle. The famous 'Bell Song' is not only a coloratura show-piece for the soprano (supremely sung by Sutherland, here), it is central to the storyline. The ballet music is charming, the Market Scene is vibrant with energy, and there is some delightful comedy supplied by the English Governess, Miss Bentson, played with relish by Monica Sinclair. In fact, this performance on Decca seizes all its opportunities with both hands. True, Joan Sutherland swallows her consonants, but the beauty of her singing, with its ravishing ease and purity up to the highest register, is what matters; and she has opposite her one of the most pleasing and intelligent of French tenors, Alain Vanzo. Excellent contributions from the others too, spirited conducting and brilliant, atmospheric recording from 1967.

DELIUS, Frederick (1862–1934)

(i) *Cello Concerto*; (i; ii) *Double Concerto*; (ii) *Violin Concerto*

Chan CHSA SACD 5094. (i) Watkins; (ii) Little; BBC SO, Andrew Davis

An ideal programme of Delius's richly textured concertos, performed by artists steeped in the British music tradition. Tasmin Little has made previous recordings of both the *Double Concerto* and *Violin Concerto* but these later performances are even finer. Her tone remains beautiful and pure through the range and she surmounts the technical difficulties with tremendous fluency and flair. Paul Watkins has used the original and more difficult version of the solo part in the *Cello Concerto*, though he makes light of the difficulties. As with Tasmin Little, he is at one with this music and is full of expressive power and imagination.

Sir Andrew Davis brings great ardour to the music-making and this is undoubtedly now the top choice in this repertoire and an instant 'classic' recording. The sound is of demonstration quality, being, like the music, both vivid and sumptuous.

(i) *A Mass of Life* (sung in German); (ii) *Requiem*

Chan. 9515 (2). (i) Rodgers, Rigby, Robson; (ii) Evans; (i–ii) Coleman-Wright; Waynflete
   Singers, Bournemouth Ch. & SO, Hickox

Hickox gives a glowing account of this ambitious setting of a German text drawn from Nietzsche's *Also sprach Zarathustra*. He is helped by excellent singing and playing from his Bournemouth forces, and by fine solo singing, notably from the soprano, Joan Rodgers. The full and atmospheric Chandos recording confirms the primacy of this version even over the excellent earlier recordings. The *Requiem*, half an hour long, makes the ideal coupling, emerging as a fine example of Delius's later work, not as distinctive in its material as the *Mass*, but with an element of bleakness tempering the lushness of the choral writing. Here too – with Rebecca Evans this time as soprano soloist – Hickox conducts a most persuasive performance, ripely recorded.

(i) *Sea Drift. Songs of Farewell*; (i–ii) *Songs of Sunset*

Chan. 9214. (i) Terfel; (ii) Burgess; Bournemouth Symphony Ch., Waynflete Singers,
   Southern Voices, Bournemouth SO, Hickox

In this second recording of Delius's masterpiece Hickox finds even more magic, again taking a spacious view – which keeps the flow of the music going magnetically. Bryn Terfel adds to the glory of the performance, the finest since Beecham, as he does in the *Songs of Sunset*, with Sally Burgess the other characterful soloist. The *Songs of Farewell*, helped by incandescent choral singing, complete an ideal triptych, presented in full and rich Chandos sound.

DÉSORMIÈRE, Roger, with the Paris Conservatoire Orchestra

Concert: **IBERT**: *Divertissement*. **IPPOLITOV-IVANOV**: *Caucasian Sketches: Suite 1*. **TCHAIKOVSKY**: *The Sleeping Beauty: Suite, Op. 66*. **SCARLATTI**: *The Good-Humoured Ladies: ballet* (arr. **TOMMASINI**)

Testament mono SBT 1309

Désormière was a stylist, and it shows in every bar. The 1951 recording of *Divertissement*, produced by John Culshaw (with the exception of Martinon's effervescent stereo version, with the same orchestra), remains unsurpassed in terms of sheer character and style, though there have been performances since that have been played with greater polish and been better recorded. Lovers of the sound of an authentic French-sounding orchestra (now long since gone) should consider this CD. The rest of the items are similarly individual: the *Procession of the Sardar* from the *Caucasian Sketches*, with its bright percussion effects, is particularly jaunty and catchy in Désormière's hands, and what *The Sleeping Beauty* lacks in rich sound it more than makes up for in theatricality. *The Good-Humoured Ladies* is deliciously pointed, the effect emphasized by the dry, up-front recording. Testament have also released another Désormière CD, which couples similarly characterful performances of Delibes's *Coppélia* and *Sylvia* ballet suites with Poulenc's *Les Biches*, the latter receiving one of its finest performances from the early LP era (SBT 1294).

DITTERSDORF, Carl Ditters von (1739–99)

Harp Concerto in A (arr. Pilley)
Ⓜ Decca (ADD) 425 723-2. Robles, ASMF, Brown – **BOÏELDIEU**; **HANDEL**: *Harp Concertos*, etc.

Dittersdorf's *Harp Concerto* is a transcription of an unfinished keyboard concerto with additional wind parts. It is an elegant piece, thematically not quite as memorable as the Boïeldieu coupling, but captivating when played with such style.

DONIZETTI, Gaetano (1797–1848)

Don Pasquale (DVD version)
Arthaus DVD 101303. Desderi, Giordano, Gatell, Cassi, Teatro Municipale di Piacenza Ch., Luigi Cherubini O, Muti (Director: Andrea De Rosa; V/D: Gabriele Cazzola)

Don Pasquale (CD version)
Ⓜ Decca (ADD) 475 8490 (2). Corena, Sciutti, Oncina, Krause, V. State Op. Ch. & O, Kertész – **CIMAROSA**: *Il maestro di cappella*

This live Arthaus recording from the 2006 Ravenna Festival is rather special. First it includes an unforgettable characterization of Don Pasquale himself from the veteran *buffo*, Claudio Desderi. Now in his sixties, he is still in fine voice, warm-toned in lyrical passages and with wonderful articulation in the famous patter-duet with the excellent Dottore Malatesta, Mario Cassi, at the end of Act III. Norina (Lauro Giordano), who studied with Maria Chiara, enters the action as a pretty, demure young thing, but becomes increasingly formidable as the opera progresses. But she is fully equal to the vocal bravura demanded of her, particularly in the closing scene. Francisco Gatell is her very convincing lover: he has a pleasingly light tenor voice which is at its finest in the nocturnal serenade at the end of the last Act. But the opera is dominated by Desderi's dignified portrayal of Pasquale, and it is given greater pathos than usual by his touching dismay at his increasingly untenable position, especially after Norina has slapped him. The Ravenna production is handsome, traditional in the best sense, and Muti keeps the action alive through every moment of Donizetti's miraculous score, which seems to get better and better as the opera proceeds. The recording and camerawork cannot be faulted.

Fernando Corena was an outstanding performer, and even if – on CD – he can't quite produce the semiquavers accurately, his sheer musical personality carries him through exuberantly. Graziella Sciutti is charming from beginning to end, bright-toned and vivacious, and remarkably agile in the most difficult passages. Juan Oncina (as often on record) sounds a bit strained, but the tenor part is very small; Krause makes an incisive and characterful Malatesta. Kertész directs proceedings with plenty of energy and the 1964 recording is excellent, with plenty of atmosphere and sparkle. The Cimarosa bonus makes this set especially attractive.

L'elisir d'amore (CD version)

Decca 475 7514 (2). Sutherland, Pavarotti, Cossa, Malas, Amb. S., ECO, Bonynge

Joan Sutherland makes Adina a more substantial figure than usual, full-throatedly serious at times, at others jolly, like the rumbustious Marie with her comic talents which came out delicately in her recording and stage performances of La Fille du régiment, fully on display here. In the key role of Nemorino, Luciano Pavarotti proves ideal, vividly portraying the wounded innocent. Spiro Malas is a superb Dulcamara, while Dominic Cossa is a younger-sounding Belcore, more of a genuine lover than usual. Bonynge points the skipping rhythms delectably, and the recording is sparkling to match. What helps to makes this recording so special, apart from the superb ensemble work – often very exciting – is the inclusion of the addition written for Malibran, the first interpreter of the role of Adina. Malibran was furious her part was not bigger, and she got her husband to write an extra aria. Richard Bonynge found it and had it orchestrated, and this show-stopper of an aria, 'Nel Dolce incanto', is gloriously performed by Sutherland.

La Fille du régiment (DVD version)

Virgin DVD 5099951900298. Natalie Dessay, Juan Diego Flórez, Alessandro Corbelli, Felicity Palmer, Donald Maxwell, ROHCG Ch. & O, Campanella (Director: Laurent Pelly; V/D: Robin Lough)

La Fille du régiment (CD version)

Decca (ADD) 414 520-2 (2). Sutherland, Pavarotti, Sinclair, Malas, Coates, ROHCG Ch. & O, Bonynge

Natalie Dessay establishes her star quality from her very first entry and vivaciously dominates Donizetti's delightful opera throughout. She is deliciously funny and often audacious in her variety of comic business, and she sings both brilliantly and movingly. In short, she is an unforgettably enchanting Marie, unlikely to be surpassed. Juan Diego Flórez as the opera's hero, Tonio, also sings and acts superbly, throwing off his famous repeated high Cs in '*Pour mon âme*' effortlessly. He creates an appealing lover figure for Marie. Moreover Laurent Pelly's production and staging are full of imaginative detail without making the comedy too broad. Coupled with unexpectedly original sets, excellent costumes and splendidly alive musical direction from Bruno Campanella, this version is for DVD what the famous Sutherland/Pavarotti version is for CD.

On Decca CD too, a fizzing performance of a delightful Donizetti romp that has achieved classic status, for both its comedy and fine singing. It was with this cast that the piece was revived at Covent Garden, and Sutherland immediately showed how naturally she took to the role of a tom-boy. Marie is a *vivandière*, in the army of Napoleon, and the jolly, almost Gilbertian, plot involves her translation back to a noble background from which as an infant she was lost. The original French version favoured by Richard Bonynge is fuller than the Italian revision and, with a cast that at the time of the recording sessions was also appearing in the theatre, the performances could hardly achieve higher spirits with keener assurance. Sutherland is in turn brilliantly comic and pathetically affecting, and no better sampler of the whole set need be suggested than near the end of the opera when Marie is reunited with her army friends (including the hero). Pavarotti is an engaging hero and his sequence of high Cs at the end of his aria, '*Pour mon âme*', must count as among the most dashing ever recorded. Monica Sinclair makes a formidable Countess, and even if the French accents are often suspect it is a small price to pay for such a brilliant, happy opera set.

Lucia di Lammermoor (CD version)

Decca (ADD) 410 1932 (3). Sutherland, Pavarotti, Milnes, Ghiaurov, Davies, Tourangeau, ROHCG Ch. & O, Bonynge

Lucia di Lammermoor is the role which catapulted Joan Sutherland to international fame and it was hardly surprising that ten years after her first recording of the role (with Pritchard conducting) Decca wanted to re-record the role with which she is inseparably associated. Though some of the girlish freshness of voice which marked the 1961 recording has disappeared, the detailed understanding has been intensified, and the mooning manner which in 1961 was just emerging had been counteracted. There has been no one in recent years to outshine Sutherland in this role and, rightly, for this recording she insisted in doing the whole of the Mad Scene in a single session, making sure it was consistent from beginning to end. Power is here as well as delicacy, and the rest of the cast is first rate. Pavarotti, not as sensitive as he can be through much of the opera (though still sounding superb), proves magnificent in his final scene. The text is absolutely complete and the recording first class in the vivid, Decca manner. It is now available in a beautifully packed hard-back book version to celebrate the fiftieth anniversary of Sutherland's 1959 Covent Garden performance, complete with all the pictures included in the original box set, as well as a bonus CD featuring excerpts from *Lucia* from earlier recordings, from Paris (1959) with Nello Santi, as well as from her complete 1961 recording with Pritchard.

In addition Regis have now reissued at budget price an excellent transfer of this 1959 collection (RRC 1364). As we said in our original review, no rave notice could really exaggerate the quality of this singing, which includes the exquisite first recording made by Sutherland of the *Lucia* Mad Scene which has not been surpassed by either of her complete recordings of the opera (1961, as above, and 1971). In fact this disc (which includes also *Ancor non giunse . . . Regnava nel silenzio* from *Lucia* and the delectable *Ah! tardai troppo . . . O luce di quest'anima* from *Linda di Chamounix*, plus two additional Verdi arias which show a comparable level of memorability) must be set on a pedestal as one of the finest and most dramatically thrilling displays of coloratura ever recorded. The youthful freshness of the voice is extremely appealing, and the tonal beauy is often quite magical. With an excellent stereo recording and fine accompaniments from the Paris Conservatoire Orchestra, conducted by Nello Santi, this remains one of the gramophone's great recital discs. As if this were not enough, Regis have added two arias from Handel's *Alcina*, recorded by Sutherland later.

Lucrezia Borgia (CD version)

Decca (ADD) 421 497-2 (2). Sutherland, Aragall, Horne, Wixell, London Op. Voices, Nat.
PO, Bonynge

Sutherland is in her element here – and what a wonderful score it is too, full of touches which make Donizetti's best operas so enjoyable. The last Act in particular is especially impressive, from its lusty opening chorus, the brilliant and jolly *Brindisi* (theatrically interrupted by death-tolling bells), a very touching duet between mother and son, and a breathtaking coloratura, show-stopping final aria. Sutherland is impressive throughout, achieving real pathos in the, let's face it, generally unsympathetic role of Lucrezia Borgia. Marilyn Horne has the odd moment of unsteadiness in the early parts of the opera, but she is impressive in the brilliant *Brindisi* of the last Act (a popular number since the days of 78-r.p.m.). Aragall sings stylishly too, and although Wixell's timbre is hardly Italianate, his is a commanding Alfonso. The recording is characteristically full and brilliant in the best Decca tradition.

Maria Stuarda (CD version)

Decca (ADD) 425 410-2 (2). Sutherland, Tourangeau, Pavarotti, Ch. & O of Teatro
Comunale, Bologna, Bonynge

In this Decca recording of Donizetti's tellingly dramatic opera on the conflict of Elizabeth I and Mary Queen of Scots, the contrast between the full soprano

Maria and the dark mezzo Elisabetta is underlined by some transpositions, with Tourangeau emerging as a powerful villainess in this slanted version of the story. Pavarotti turns Leicester into a passionate Italian lover, not at all an Elizabethan gentleman. As for Sutherland, she is at her most fully dramatic too, and the great moment when she flings out the insult *'Vil bastarda!'* at her cousin brings a superb snarl. (Sutherland, who had often been criticized for her diction, cannot be faulted here – she positively spits out her words!) Richard Bonynge directs an urgent account of an unfailingly enjoyable opera – full of superb tunes and exciting show-stopping arias. Unusually for Decca, the score is slightly cut, but this remains the most generally recommendable version of this marvellously dramatic work.

Fans of opera in English should investigate Janet Baker's fine performance, now on Chandos's 'Opera in English' label (CHAN 3017). It was a role she chose for her farewell performance to the London stage in 1982, and the role of the tragic queen was one of her most powerful creations. The rest of the cast, which includes John Tomlinson and Rosalind Plowright, is superb as well. The performance is also available on a Warner DVD (50467 0828), in John Copley's excellent production.

DOVE, Jonathan (born 1959)

Sacred Choral Music: *Bless the Lord, O my soul*; *Ecce beatam lucem*; *I am the day*; *In beauty may I walk*; *Into thy hands*; *Missa brevis*; *Wellcome, all wonders in one sight*; (i) *Run, shepherds, run!*. *Seek him that maketh the seven stars*; *The Star Song*; *The Three Kings*
Hyp. CDA 67768. Wells Cathedral Ch., Matthew Owens; Jonathan Vaughn (organ); (i) with
   Wells Cathedral School Chapel Ch.

The richness of Jonathan Dove's choral writing and his vividly colourful (yet sometimes sparing) use of the organ is heard again and again throughout this collection, so stirringly and beautifully sung by Wells Cathedral Choir, and recorded in the spectacular resonance of the Cathedral Church of St Andrew in Wells. The opening 'paean of praise', *Bless the Lord*, and the highly individual *Missa brevis* both demonstrate the composer at his most compelling, and the 'Agnus Dei' of the latter is profoundly moving. *I am the day* has a minimal-ist structure but after a mysterious opening is 'dancing and playful' and then quotes from the hymn, 'O come, O come Emmanuel'. The *a cappella Wellcome, all wonders in one sight* reflects the singing of the shepherds at Christ's birth., and the lightly rhythmic *Star Song* with its 'twinkling' organ part is another Christmas setting – of a poem by Robert Herrick. *The Three Kings* radiantly features two solo sopranos with the choir. But perhaps the most unusual set-ting is *Run, shepherds, run*, which introduces 'audience' participation, here a vigorous refrain from the second choir. *Ecce beatam lucem* is movingly serene, while *Seek him that maketh the seven stars* again features the organ, creating 'a musical image of the night sky'. The closing *Into thy hands* ends the programme in quiet dedication and calm. The composer suggests that 'it does not reach an ending, but simply, in trust, surrenders itself'.

The Adventures of Pinocchio (DVD version)

Opus Arte DVD OA 101 D2 (2). Simmonds, Summers, Plazas, Bottone, Broadbent,
    Clayton, Ch. & O of Opera North, Parry (Director: Martin Duncan; Sets & Costumes:
    Francis O'Connor)

In this operatic version in two substantial Acts, Jonathan Dove with his librettist, Alasdair Middleton, gives a much fuller idea of the story of Pinocchio, as told by Carlo Collodi, starting with the moment when Geppetto the woodman finds a talking log in the forest. He is about to chop it up when it speaks to him, demanding that he preserve it, later demanding that he bring out the secret it contains – nothing less than the puppet, Pinocchio, who kicks him as his legs appear.

Generally the scenes follow the development of Pinocchio from rebellious puppet to kind and considerate boy. One important detail in the story (much exploited by Disney) that the opera ignores completely is the varying length of Pinocchio's nose, depending on the number of lies he is telling: in the opera, no doubt for the convenience of the costume department, Pinocchio's nose remains long from beginning to end.

Dove's writing is characteristically colourful and vigorous, with inventive instrumentation; and the sharp, jazzy syncopations add to the attractiveness of the invention which is generally easily lyrical. The performance, filmed live, is conducted very ably by David Parry. Victoria Simmonds is excellent in the title-role, wearing a very convincing costume, with Jonathan Summers a pleasing Geppetto. A very welcome issue of a most attractive new opera.

DOWLAND, John (1563–1626)

Complete Solo Lute Music (collection)

Ⓑ BIS-SACD 1724 not compatible. Jakob Lindberg (8-course or 10-course lute or
    8-course orpharion)

Jakob Lindberg, a superb lutenist, provides us here with the complete solo lute and orpharion music of John Dowland, including two closing *Pavans* from J. D. Mylius's *Thesaurus gratiarum*, which has only recently been discovered. The orpharium, a flat-backed, wire-strung instrument, is used to atmospheric effect in the eleven works for which it was intended. This music can be dipped into at pleasure, for it is offered on a single SACD with an incredible playing time of four and a quarter hours (apparently achieved by using DVD technology for an audio-only SACD). Lindberg's playing is peerless and the result is totally realistic. One can pick out any one of the 92 items virtually instantaneously. A remarkable achievement, very well documented, and the ease of access gives Lindberg a lead over his competitors.

14 Ayres and 4 Lute Lessons, including: *Awake sweet love*; *Can she excuse my wrongs?*; *Come again! Sweet love*; *Fine knacks for ladies*; *Go crystal tears*; *Semper Dowland, semper dolens*; *Sorrow stay*; *Tell me true love*; *Captain Candish's Galliard Lady Laiton's Almain*; and more

ⓑⓑ Alto ALC 1048. James Bowman (countertenor), Robert Spencer (lute) (with 4 songs by Thomas Campion; 3 by John Danyel; 2 by Philip Rosseter)

This is another splendid super-bargain collection, originally issued as an LP on SAGA and much praised at the time (late 1970s). It plays for 71 minutes and contains songs from all three Bookes, and more besides, as well as some lute solos, played in exemplary fashion by Robert Spencer. In most respects this makes an ideal introduction to Dowland's art since it includes many of his most popular songs. Moreover they are sung with wonderful artistry by James Bowman, whose countertenor timbre is ravishing, and who brings sensitivity and intelligence to each song, and characterizes them far more tellingly than many of his colleagues in other collections. There is no lack of contrast and each phrase is floated with imagination. Amazingly for a record over 30 years old, the recording has outstanding realism and a natural presence. A true bargain.

DUKAS, Paul (1865–1935)

(i) *L'Apprenti sorcier*; *La Péri* (with Fanfare); (ii) *Polyeucte Overture*; *Symphony in C*; (iii) *Piano Sonata*; *La Plainte, au loin, du faune*; *Prélude élégiaque*

Ⓜ Chan. 2-for-1 241-32. (i) Ulster O; (ii) BBC PO; Y. P. Tortelier; (iii) Fingerhut

Dukas is primarily known for one of the most popular works in the repertoire, *L'Apprenti sorcier*. It is a brilliant orchestral show-piece which brilliantly conjures up the image of a hapless sorcerer's apprentice as his spell gets out of control. It is a tone-poem par excellence and fully deserves its fame. However, one must not overlook the composer's other works, including the splendid *Symphony* which, like the Chausson *Symphony*, is influenced in form by Franck and in spirit by Wagner – but in a language which is totally French. It is an impressive piece with some especially imaginative writing for brass. Tortelier's account is a clear primary recommendation (especially as Walter Weller's Decca account and Martinon's EMI version are no longer available), as is his *Polyeucte Overture*, an early piece with Wagnerian echoes.

Dukas's *La Péri* was written for Diaghilev in 1912, and again Yan Pascal Tortelier gives a very good performance of this colourfully imaginative score (including the introductory *Fanfare*, which precedes the tinglingly magical opening), with plenty of atmosphere and feeling. *L'Apprenti sorcier* is equally successful, though there is much competition for this work. Excellent Chandos recording in all four orchestral works ensures their success. Margaret Fingerhut's collection of the piano music is recommendable too, a distinguished survey, with the large-scale *Sonata* particularly authoritative. The Scherzo is quite dazzling and the Lisztian finale very commanding indeed. The *Prélude élégiaque*, written in 1910 to commemorate Haydn's death, and *La Plainte, au loin, du faune* are both more into the world of Debussian impressionism. Indeed, the latter piece was written a decade later as a *Tombeau de Claude Debussy* for Debussy, and it even includes quotations from *L'Après-midi*. They are both played very evocatively. An inexpensive and excellent survey of this fastidious composer's output.

Australian Decca Eloquence have issued Ansermet's outstanding version of *L'Apprenti sorcier*. The performance is relaxed yet has a cumulative effect: one has a feeling of real calamity before the magician hurriedly returns at the end to put right the mischief his apprentice has wrought. It is coupled with a brightly vivid account of *La Péri* – full of character and personality, and exceptionally vivid stereo sound from the late 1950s, plus recommendable versions of the Chausson *Symphony* and Roussel *Symphonies 3 & 4* (480 0041).

DURUFLÉ, Maurice (1902–86)

(i; ii; v) *Requiem, Op. 9*; (iii; iv; v) *Messe Cum jubilo, Op. 11*; (ii) *4 Motets on Gregorian Themes, Op. 10*; (v) (Organ) *Prélude et fugue sur le nom d'Alain, Op. 7*

ⓑⓑ Warner Apex 2564 61139-2. (i) Bouvier, Depraz, Philippe Caillard Ch., LOP; (ii) Stéphane Caillat Ch.; (iii) Soyer; (iv) O Nat. de l'ORTF; all cond. composer; (v) Duruflé-Chevalier (organ)

Duruflé wrote his *Requiem* in 1947, overtly basing its layout and even the cut of its themes on the Fauré masterpiece. A clear first choice is almost impossible to make; however, the Apex budget reissue is particularly valuable as it offers a spontaneously dedicated performance under the direction of the composer that blossoms into great ardour at emotional peaks. The less familiar but no less beautiful *Messe Cum jubilo* receives a comparably inspirational account, its gentler passages sustained with rapt concentration, with beautiful playing from the French Radio Orchestra. The soloists in both works rise to the occasion, and the choral singing combines passionate feeling with subtle colouring. The composer proves a splendid exponent of his own works, as does his daughter playing the *Prélude et Fugue* on the organ of Soissons Cathedral. The spaciously atmospheric recordings were made between 1959 (the *Requiem*) and 1971. Not to be missed.

DUTILLEUX, Henri (born 1916)

(i) Cello Concerto (Toute un monde lointain). Trois strophes sur le nom de Sacher

BIS SACD 1777. Christian Poltéra; (i) ORF V. RSO, Jac van Steen (with
  LUTOSŁAWSKI: *Cello Concerto*)

Rostropovich's classic coupling of these concertos under the composer has long reigned supreme and still remains beyond criticism. But this fine studio version from Vienna under Jac van Steen with the Swiss-born Christian Poltéra, a soloist of consummate artistry, will more than satisfy the discerning listener. The BIS recording has characteristic presence and definition, as usual, enhanced by SACD.

Symphonies 1–2

Chan. 9194. BBC PO, Y. P. Tortelier

Marvellously resourceful and inventive scores, which are given vivid and persuasive performances by Yan Pascal Tortelier and the BBC Philharmonic Orchestra. The engineers give us a splendidly detailed and refined portrayal of these complex textures – the sound is really state of the art. A most rewarding pairing.

DVOŘÁK, Antonín (1841–1904)

(i) Cello Concerto in B minor, Op. 104 (no. 2). In Nature's Realm; The Water Goblin

Telarc TEL 32927-02. (i) Bailey; Indianapolis SO, Märkl

Very few music lovers are aware that Dvořák wrote an earlier cello concerto before his masterpiece in B minor, which he was inspired to compose after hearing Victor Herbert's second concerto for that instrument. The early work is not without considerable merit, but the later work is almost certainly the greatest of all concertos for the instrument, alongside the quite different, nostalgic work by Elgar. Until now we have strongly recommended the DG recording by Rostropovich and Karajan, and that remains very fine. But this new version by Zuill Bailey and Jun Märkl, with the excellent Indianapolis Symphony Orchestra, has all the additional electricity and conveyed communicative warmth of live performance, and grips the listener from the very opening bars. The great tune, first heard on the horn, is gloriously played by Robert Danforth and later again taken up rapturously by the soloist, and the horns distinguish themelves in their chorale in the second movement. The woodwind, too, are exquisite at the opening of the slow movement, and Bailey plays the gently romantic closing section of the finale very touchingly indeed.

Altogether this is superb, and the two symphonic poems, the lyrical *In Nature's Realm*, and the sinister picture of *The Water Goblin*, are vividly realized.

Slavonic Dances 1–16, Op. 46/1–8; Op. 72/1–8
Ⓑ Sony (ADD) SBK 89845. Cleveland O, Szell

In Szell's exuberant and marvellously played set of the complete *Slavonic Dances* the balance is close (which means that *pianissimos* fail to register), but the character of the playing is unforgettable and, for all the racy exuberance, one senses a predominant feeling of affection and elegance. The warm acoustics of Severance Hall, Cleveland, ensure the consistency of the orchestral sound.

(i) Slavonic Dances, Op. 46/1, 3 & 8; Op. 72/9 & 10; (ii) Symphonic Variations, Op. 78
Ⓜ Decca (ADD) 475 7730. Kertész, with (i) Israel PO; (ii) LSO - **SMETANA**: *Bartered Bride Overture*, etc.

Kertész made this very successful Dvořák/Smetana coupling in the early 1960s and, alongside the symphonies, it remains a superb reminder of what a fine conductor he was. The Israel Philharmonic Orchestra was not at the time one of the world's most polished, but here the playing is irresistible in its high spirits and vivacious colouring. The furiants go with the wind, but Kertész maintains the underlying lyricism of the music. The fine performance of the splendid *Symphonic Variations* was recorded later, in 1970, and the sound quality is even finer. With the outstanding Smetana coupling, this makes an excellent pairing.

Symphonic Poems: *The Golden Spinning Wheel*; *The Noon Witch*; *The Water Goblin*; *The Wild Dove*
Sup. SU 4012. Czech PO, Mackerras

Dvořák's four symphonic poems are all based on gruesome folk tales, but so richly colourful is the composer's use of the orchestral palette, especially the woodwind, the ear is constantly diverted, and the music is overflowing with Czech melodies. As the evocative opening of *The Water Goblin* immediately shows, Sir Charles Mackerras gives marvellously atmospheric performances, and there is plenty of contrasting melodrama at the close, when the Goblin murders the baby of the kidnapped heroine. The Czech Philharmonic Orchestra is on top form throughout, and there is plenty of warm, tender playing, especially from the strings, with the orchestra given a lovely bloom from the acoustic of Prague's Rudolfinum. *The Golden Spinning Wheel* (a favourite of Sir Thomas Beecham's) opens with appropriately golden horn fanfares. This narrative brings the mutilation of the heroine, Dornicka, but she is magically restored at the close to provide, for once, a happy ending to the story. *The Noon Witch*, sinisterly characterized by a solo bass clarinet, again involves the murder of a child, but *The Wild Dove* involves a widow/poisoner, and the Dove represents the soul of the poisoned husband, and causes the conscience-stricken widow to commit suicide. Mackerras creates a vivid narrative flow throughout all four works and his pacing is wonderfully sympathetic and flexible, and this CD won the *Gramophone*'s Orchestral Award in 2010.

Symphonies 1–9; Overtures: Carnival; In Nature's Realm; My Home; Scherzo capriccioso

Ⓑ Decca (ADD) 430 046-2 (6). LSO, Kertész

Anyone collecting LPs in the 1960s would know these famous recordings with the striking Breugel pictures on the covers. It is still pretty difficult not to think of either Kertész or Dvořák today without thinking of the other, and these recordings have stood the test of time. All are characterized by a crisp, direct approach, with an equal measure of both drama and sensitivity given to scores to which the conductor was so naturally attuned.

This was the first complete recording of the *First Symphony* (*The Bells of Zlonice*), and although the fluency of this 54-minute work (written in early 1865) is not always matched by memorability of the material, it has much attractive writing in it which can be fully enjoyed. Zlonice was the place where Dvořák served his musical (as well as butcher's) apprenticeship, but the music is not intended to convey a programme.

The *Second Symphony*, written within months of the first, again is hardly vintage Dvořák. His publisher, Simrock, refused to take it when he submitted his *Symphonies 3 & 4*, even after it had been fully revised. Admittedly the ideas are not as strongly Dvořákian as they might be, and some movements outstay their welcome, but anyone who has been charmed by Dvořák's wide-open genius will find much to enjoy, notably in the highly engaging ideas in the first movement. One oddity – and weakness – is that each movement has a slow introduction, a case of the composer 'clearing his throat' before launching out.

The *Third Symphony* was the first of the composer's to show the full exuberance of his genius. When he wrote it in 1873, he was very much under the influence of Wagner, but nowhere do the Wagnerian ideas really conceal the essential Dvořák. Even the unashamed crib from *Lohengrin* in the middle section (D flat major) of the slow movement has a Dvořákian freshness, particularly when, as here, Kertész adopts a fastish speed – faster than the score would strictly allow – and deliberately lightens the texture. This very long slow movement is in any case the weakest of the three, but the outer movements are both delightful and need no apology whatever. The very opening of the symphony with its 6/8 rhythm and rising scale motifs can hardly miss, and the dotted rhythms of the second subject are equally engaging.

Compared to the exuberant music which flanks the *Fourth Symphony*, it is something of a disappointment. The opening theme – a fanfare-like motif – is not as characterful as one expects, but the second subject soars aloft in triple time. The slow movement begins with so close a crib from the *Pilgrims' Music* in *Tannhäuser* one wonders how Dvořák had the face to write it, but the variations which follow are attractive, and the Scherzo has a delightful lolloping theme, which unfortunately gives way to a horribly blatant march trio with far too many cymbal crashes in it. The finale, despite its rhythmic monotony, has at least one characteristic and attractive episode, and whatever the shortcomings of the work, there is much that is memorable.

The *Fifth Symphony* is a work of total genius. It is music to make one share, if only for a moment, the happy emotions of a saint – and what could be more welcome in a modern, nerve-racked life? The feeling of joy is here expressed so intensely that it provokes tears rather than laughter, and it is hard to understand why this work was neglected for so long. It used to be called the 'Pastoral', but although it shares Beethoven's key and uses the flute a great deal (a Dvořákian characteristic), the nickname is not especially apt. What initially strikes one are the echoes of Wagner – forest murmurs (Bohemian ones) in the opening pages, a direct lift from *Siegfried's Rhine Journey* in the second theme, and so on – but by the time he wrote the work, in 1875, Dvořák's individuality as a musician was well established, and the composer's signature was written on every bar. The slow movement is as beautiful as any in the symphonies, the Scherzo is a gloriously bouncing piece, with themes squandered generously, and the finale, though long, is intensely original in structure and argument.

If the previous symphonies reflect the influence of Wagner, the *Sixth* just as clearly reflects the influence of Brahms, and particularly Brahms's *Second Symphony*. Not only the shape of the themes but the actual layout in the first movement has strong affinities with the Brahmsian model; but Kertész's performance effectively underlines the individuality of the writing as well. This is a marvellous work that with the *Fifth* and *Seventh* forms the backbone of the Dvořák cycle – and that is hardly an idea we should have been likely to give before Kertész gave us fresh insight into these vividly inspired works. Kertész's reading is fresh, literal and dramatic in his characteristic Dvořák manner, and his tempi are eminently well chosen.

The *Seventh* is one of Dvořák's richest inspirations and Kertész offers a relaxed reading, beautifully recorded. In fact, on LP, we thought it slightly (and surprisingly) a bit under-characterized, but in its CD incarnation it emerged just as gripping as other performances in the cycle. This performance, with its many hauntingly yearning themes vibrantly conveyed, is perhaps most successful in the finale, which is magnificently done.

The *Eighth Symphony* – a popular favourite with many people – simply drips with gorgeous themes. It's a stunner of a symphony and Kertész's performance has always been a top choice: the reading is fresh, spontaneous and exciting. The slow movement is affectionate and captures the pastoral quality of the writing, and the tempo for the *Allegretto grazioso* is particularly well judged. The soaring theme in the strings which opens the third movement sweeps the listener along, and the finale is a blaze of colour and excitement.

The *Ninth Symphony* (*New World*) is understandably one of the most popular works in the concert hall and on CD – so popular, in fact, that it is possible to forget what an inspired work of genius it is. Although there have been plenty of superb recordings made since this one, it still deserves its place in the catalogue. Kertész recorded the work with the VPO before this recording, but over the years he had matured enormously, so that this version with the LSO was and remains one of the finest committed to disc. This time, Kertész included the exposition repeat, thus giving the first movement – otherwise very short – its proper stature. But it is in the slow movement that Kertész's sensitivity emerges most vividly. In essence his approach is as simple and straightforward as could be, yet the hushed intensity of the playing conveys a depth of feeling that makes one hear the music with new ears. Tempi in the last two movements are also perfectly judged – not too fast in the finale – and the recording quality is outstanding. Indeed, the recording quality is superb throughout this cycle. The box set includes some vivacious performances of the *Carnival Overture*, the *Scherzo capriccioso* and an exceptionally vivid performance of the tone-poem, *My Home*. In fact, Kertész made stunning recordings of Dvořák's tone-poems which were once available on a Double Decca CD, now deleted but which are worth looking out for.

Symphony 7 in D min., Op. 70
Ⓜ Decca Eloquence 480 5019. LSO, Monteux – **ELGAR**: *Enigma Variations*

Pierre Monteux's account of the *Seventh* has always been a strong contender at medium price. His performance, if perhaps originally not a first choice, is very much a favourite: it is exciting, idiomatic and pleasingly tinged with geniality. The orchestral playing is first class, and the Decca recording has stood the test of time. The beautiful opening and closing pages of the Poco adagio and the brilliant finale are highlights of a reading which, if it has a slightly mannered effect here and there, is very satisfying overall.

However this reissue is even more celebrated for its coupling, Elgar's *Enigma Variations* with its unforgettable performance of *Nimrod*.

Piano Quartets 1 in D, Op. 23; 2 in E flat, Op. 87
Hyp. CDA 66287. Domus

The Dvořák *Piano Quartets* are glorious pieces, and the playing of Domus is little short of inspired. This is real chamber-music playing: intimate, unforced and distinguished by both vitality and sensitivity. They are recorded in an ideal acoustic and in perfect perspective; they sound wonderfully alive and warm.

(i) Piano Quintet in A, Op. 81; String Quintet 2 in G, Op. 77
Hyp. CDA 66796. Gaudier Ens., (i) with Susan Tomes

With Susan Tomes the inspired pianist, the Gaudier Ensemble give a sparkling performance of the glorious *Piano Quintet* (one of I.M.'s favourite chamber works), full of mercurial contrasts that seem entirely apt and with rhythms superbly sprung. The account of the *G major String Quintet* has its warmth and humanity well caught, even if the performance is lighter than most rival versions, with speeds on the brisk side. Very well recorded, this is a highly recommendable coupling, although in neither work are the exposition repeats observed.

String Quartets 1–14; Cypresses, B.152; Fragments in A min. & F, B.120; 2 Waltzes, Op. 54, B.105
Ⓑ DG 463 165-2 (9). Prague Qt

Dvořák's *Quartets* span the whole of his creative life. The glories of the mature *Quartets* are well known, though it is only the so-called *American* (No. 12) which has achieved real popularity. The beauty of the present set, made in 1973–7, is that it offers more *Quartets* (not otherwise available), plus two *Quartet Movements*, in A minor (1873) and F major (1881), plus two *Waltzes* and the enchanting *Cypresses* (which Dvořák transcribed from the eponymous song-cycle) for good measure, all in excellent performances and decent recordings. The DG transfers are managed with a nice balance between warmth and presence. At bargain price, neatly packaged and with good documentation, this is self-recommending.

(i) Requiem, Op. 89; (ii) 6 Biblical Songs from Op. 99
DG 453 073-2 (2). (i) Stader, Wagner, Haefliger, Borg, Czech PO & Ch., Ančerl; (ii) Fischer-Dieskau, Demus

This superb DG set from 1959 brings an inspired performance of Dvořák's *Requiem*, which here emerges with fiery intensity, helped by a recording made in an appropriately spacious acoustic that gives an illusion of an electrifying live performance, without flaw. The passionate singing of the chorus is unforgettable and the German soloists not only make fine individual contributions but blend together superbly in ensembles. DG have added Fischer-Dieskau's 1960 recordings of six excerpts from Op. 99. He is at his superb best in these lovely songs. Jörg Demus accompanies sensitively, and the recording-balance is most convincing.

Rusalka (CD version)
Decca 460 568-2 (3). Fleming, Heppner, Hawlata, Zajick, Urbanová, Kusnjer, Kloubová, Kühn, Mixed Ch., Czech PO, Mackerras

This Decca recording of *Rusalka* is in every way a satisfying musical experience. This offers not only ripely atmospheric sound but what in almost every way is the ideal cast, with the Czech Philharmonic incandescent under Sir Charles Mackerras. Renée Fleming gives a heartfelt, sharply detailed performance, with the voice consistently beautiful over the widest range. Ben Heppner too, with his powerful tenor at once lyrical and heroic, is ideally cast as the prince. Franz Hawlata as the Watergnome, Rusalka's father, and Dolora Zajick as the witch, Ježibaba, are both outstanding too, with even the smaller roles cast from strength, using leading singers from the Prague Opera. In his inspired conducting Mackerras does not resist the obvious Wagnerian overtones, yet Czech flavours are never underplayed in the many colourful dance rhythms.

DYSON, George (1883–1964)

(i) *Violin Concerto*. *Children's Suite* (after Walter De La Mare)
Chan. 9369. (i) Mordkovitch; City of L. Sinfonia, Hickox

Dyson's *Violin Concerto* is a richly inspired, warmly lyrical work, and the third-movement *Andante* for violin and muted strings, divided into variations, brings a rare hushed beauty, superbly achieved in this dedicated performance. Lydia Mordkovitch gives a reading that is both passionate and deeply expressive. The *Children's Suite* reflects qualities similar to those in the *Concerto*, not least a tendency to switch into waltz-time and a masterly ability to create rich and transparent orchestral textures, beautifully caught in the opulent Chandos recording. Two rarities to treasure.

Symphony in G; *Overture: At the Tabard Inn*; *Concerto da chiesa for Strings*
(BB) Naxos 8.557720. Bournemouth SO, Lloyd-Jones

First heard in 1937, Dyson's *Symphony in G* is the most ambitious of his orchestral works, using ideas from *The Canterbury Pilgrims*, with majestic scoring for the brass. Helped by clear, well-balanced recording, David Lloyd-Jones conducts a brilliant performance which clarifies often heavy textures. In the *Concerto da chiesa for Strings* of 1949, each of the three movements develops a medieval hymn melody, with *Veni Emmanuel* inspiring a darkly dedicated slow first movement, among Dyson's finest inspirations. That melody returns, transformed, at the end of the finale, which is based on the vigorous psalm-tune, *Laetatus sum*. With solo strings atmospherically set against the full string band, this is a neglected masterpiece. *At the Tabard Inn* was originally designed as an overture for his choral work, *The Canterbury Pilgrims*, and completes a first-rate disc, superbly played.

(i–ii) *The Canterbury Pilgrims*. *Overture*: *At the Tabard Inn*; (ii) *In Honour of the City*
Chan. 9531 (2). (i) Kenny, Tear, Roberts; (ii) L. Symphony Ch.; LSO, Hickox

Dyson's best-known work is preceded by the *Overture* based on its themes. Here the soloists all have major contributions to make, for Dyson's characterization of the individual pilgrims is strong; but the glory of the piece is the choruses, which are splendidly sung here. *In Honour of the City*, Dyson's setting of William Dunbar, appeared in 1928, nine years before Walton's version of the same text; Dyson, however, unlike Walton, uses a modern version of the text, as he does in *The Canterbury Pilgrims*, and to fine, direct effect. The splendid Chandos recording is fully worthy of the vibrant music-making here.

ELGAR, Edward (1857–1934)

(i) *Cockaigne Overture*; (ii–iii) *Cello Concerto*; (iv; iii) *Sea Pictures*

Ⓑ EMI Masters 9 65932-2. (i) Philharmonia O; (ii) Jacqueline du Pré; (iii) LSO; (iv) Janet Baker; all cond. Barbirolli

A famous EMI coupling of the *Cello Concerto* and *Sea Pictures* has been expanded to include *Cockaigne* – one of the finest of all Barbirolli's Elgar records, his ripe yet wonderfully vital portrait of Edwardian London. Jacqueline du Pré's unsurpassed recording of the *Concerto* hardly needs any further recommendation from us, spontaneous in its freely rhapsodic style but with a very special kind of meditative feeling. In the very beautiful slow movement, brief and concentrated, her inner intensity conveys a depth of *espressivo* rarely achieved by any cellist on record. Brilliant virtuoso playing too in the Scherzo and finale.

Like Du Pré, Janet Baker is an artist who has the power to convey on record the vividness of a live performance. With the help of Barbirolli she makes the *Sea Pictures* far more convincing than it usually seems, with often trite words (by Lady Elgar) clothed in music that seems to transform them. The remastered recording in its entirety is very successful indeed. A concerto that should be in every collection.

(i) *Violin Concerto. Serenade for Strings*

Onyx 4025. (i) Ehnes; Philh. O, A. Davis

James Ehnes is the soloist in this exceptionally subtle and understanding account of the Elgar *Violin Concerto*. His half-tones are ravishing, and though he uses a wide vibrato the result is anything but sentimental. The second subject in the first movement is deeply expressive but not rhythmically distorted, and the whole performance benefits from Ehnes's flawless intonation. The final epilogue of the unaccompanied cadenza is deeply meditative, crowning a performance that stands out among recent recordings. Andrew Davis's lilting account of the *Serenade for Strings* makes an excellent fill-up. In addition, room must be found here to mention the Hallé recording by Thomas Zehetmair and Mark Elder, much praised by the *Gramophone* and in receipt of the magazine's 2010 Concerto Award (Hallé CDHLL 7521).

Enigma Variations (Variations on an original theme), Op. 36
Ⓜ Decca Eloquence 480 5019. LSO, Monteux – **DVOŘÁK**: Symphony 7

Pierre Monteux's Enigma remains among the freshest versions ever put on disc, and the music is obviously deeply felt. The reading is famous for the real pianissimo which Monteux secures at the beginning of Nimrod, the tension electric, and the superb climax is more effective in consequence. Differences from traditional tempi elsewhere are marginal and add to one's enjoyment. The vintage Kingsway Hall stereo recording was outstanding in its day, and it is almost impossible to believe that this dates from 1958.

The Dvořák coupling also shows Monteux on top form.

Enigma Variations; Pomp and Circumstance Marches 1–5, Op. 39
Ⓜ DG (ADD) 429 713-2. RPO, Del Mar

These supremely and rightly popular works of Elgar have been recorded many times but in the Enigma Variations Del Mar comes closer than any other conductor to the responsive rubato style of Elgar himself, using fluctuations to point the emotional message of the work with wonderful power and spontaneity. The RPO plays superbly, both here and in the Pomp and Circumstance Marches, which are given Proms-style flair and urgency – although some might feel that the fast speeds miss some of the nobilmente. The reverberant sound here adds something of an aggressive edge to the music-making. Monteux's equally glowing account of the Enigma Variations (Decca) has just been reissued – (see above).

(i–ii) Introduction and Allegro for Strings; (i) Serenade for Strings; (iii) Elegy, Op. 58; Sospiri, Op. 70
Ⓑ EMI 6 31788-2. (i) Sinfonia of London; (ii) Allegri Qt; (iii) New Philh. O, Barbirolli –
   VAUGHAN WILLIAMS: Greensleeves; Tallis Fantasia (with **DELIUS**: Brigg Fair (Hallé O))

This is almost certainly the very finest recording of English string music, combining four outstanding Elgar string works, including the superb Introduction and Allegro, with Vaughan Williams's supreme masterpiece, the great Tallis Fantasia. Moreover it might also be considered one of Barbirolli's very finest records, especially as his luxuriant performance of Delius's Brigg Fair has been added for this bargain reissue. The current remastering of an originally magnificent master loses nothing, combining bite and excellent inner definition with the fullest sonority.

Symphonies 1–2; Cockaigne; In the South
Double Decca (ADD) 443 856-2 (2). LPO, Solti

Before Solti recorded the First he made a searching study of Elgar's own 78-r.p.m. recording, and Solti seems freed from emotional inhibitions, with every climax superbly thrust home and the hushed intensity of the glorious slow movement captured magnificently on CD. The *Second* receives an equally incandescent reading, once again closely modelled on Elgar's own surprisingly clipped and urgent performance, but benefiting from virtuoso playing and, as with the *First*, vintage Decca sound. Fast tempi bring searing concentration and an account of the finale that for once presents a true climax. The original LPO couplings of the *Cockaigne* and *In the South* overtures were logical, even if *In the South*, recorded in 1979, is over-tense. However, this is an outstanding bargain and one of the glories of the Decca catalogue.

Symphony 2 in E flat, Op. 63; (i) Sea Pictures
Ⓑ CfP (DDD/ADD) 575 3062. LPO, Handley, (i) with Greevy

Vernon Handley's is the most satisfying modern version of a work which has been much recorded over the years. What Handley conveys superbly is the sense of Elgarian ebb and flow, building climaxes like a master and drawing excellent, spontaneous-sounding playing from an orchestra which, more than any other, has specialized in performing this symphony. The sound is warmly atmospheric and, at the peak of the finale, conveys the added organ part (which Elgar himself suggested 'if available'), a tummy-wobbling effect. As a generous coupling, Bernadette Greevy – in glorious voice – gives the performance of her recording career in *Sea Pictures*. Handley's sympathetic accompaniments are no less memorable, with the LPO players finding a wonderful rapport with the voice. In the last song Handley again uses an ad lib. organ part to underline the climaxes of each stanza.

Symphony 3; Pomp and Circumstance March 6; (i) Queen Alexandra's Memorial Ode (all realized by Anthony Payne)
Chan. CHSA 5057. BBC Nat. O of Wales, Hickox; (i) with Adrian Partington Singers

Richard Hickox's version of Andrew Paynes's realization of the *Third Symphony* is special, which is very compelling indeed. His reading is not only marginally stronger and more dramatic than the others, but it has the advantage of superb SACD surround sound and exceptionally attractive couplings. The *Memorial Ode for Queen Alexandra* as orchestrated by Payne, with the Adrian Partington Singers, is a tenderly moving piece, with Elgar in his role as Master of the King's Music setting a text by John Masefield. The *Pomp and Circumstance March No. 6*, like the symphony, was reconstructed and orchestrated by Payne, and in some ways is the most complex of all the *Pomp and Circumstance Marches*, a fine and valuable addition to an outstanding disc.

The Wand of Youth Suites 1 & 2; Organ Sonata in G
(orch. Gordon Jacob)
CfP 575 9792. RLPO, Handley

Handley's *Wand of Youth Suites* dates from 1988. He is a true Elgarian and catches all the impetuous energy of the *Sun Dance*, the intimate magic of the

Fairy Pipers and *Moths and Butterflies*, the warm serenity of the *Slumber Scene* and the contrasts of *Fairies and Giants* and the *Tame* and roisterous *Wild Bears*. The Liverpool orchestra plays with delicacy and vigour, warmth and finesse. It is welcome to have as an unexpected fill-up Handley's splendid account of the magnificent *Organ Sonata*, vividly orchestrated by Gordon Jacob, to create what might almost be counted Elgar's 'Symphony No. o'. The recording, from the partnership of Andrew Keener and Mike Hatch, is in every way first class.

(i) *Piano Quintet in A min., Op. 84. String Quartet in E min., Op. 83*
Chan. 9894. Sorrel Qt, (i) with Brown

The Sorrel Quartet, perfectly matched by Ian Brown in the *Piano Quintet*, give exceptionally searching readings of these two late chamber works of Elgar. These are dedicated performances which understandingly bring out the contrast between the expansive *Quintet*, bold in its rhetoric, and the more intimate *Quartet*, with its terse, economical structure. The breadth of expression, using the widest dynamic range down to the most delicate *pianissimos*, intensifies the impact of each performance, magnetic and concentrated as if recorded live.

Violin Sonata; *Canto popolare*; *La Capricieuse, Op. 17*; *Chanson de matin, Op. 15/2*; *Chanson de nuit, Op. 15/1*; *Mot d'amour, Op. 13/1*; *Offertoire, Op. 11* (arr. Schneider); *Salut d'amour, Op. 12*; *Sospiri, Op. 70*; *Sursum corda, Op. 11*
Chan. 9624. Mordkovitch, Milford

Along with the *Cello Concerto*, the *Piano Quintet* and the *String Quartet*, the *Sonata* belongs to Elgar's last creative period; all were composed at Brinkwells during 1918–19. Considering its quality, it is surprising how rarely it is given in the concert hall, though it has fared better on record. It is a work of striking power and eloquence and is not the least of these four great pieces. Lydia Mordkovitch here transforms the elusive Elgar *Violin Sonata*. In rapt and concentrated playing she gives it new mystery, with the subtlest pointing and shading down to whispered *pianissimos*. The shorter works include not only popular pieces like *Salut d'amour*, *Chanson de matin* and *Sospiri*, but rarities like a version of *Sursum corda* never previously recorded and a little salon piece of 1893 which Elgar inexplicably published under the pseudonym, Gustav Francke.

The Black Knight, Op. 3; *Scenes from the Bavarian Highlands, Op. 27*
Chan. 9436. L. Symphony Ch., LSO, Hickox

Richard Hickox recorded all the major choral works for Chandos with great success, and this coupling of two lesser-known works is especially valuable. The cantata *The Black Knight* is based on a similar story to that of Mahler's early cantata, *Das klagende Lied*. Hickox, helped by an exceptionally rich and full recording, with vivid presence, consistently brings out the dramatic tensions of the piece as well as the refinement and beauty of the poetic sequences, to make the previous recording under Sir Charles Groves sound too easy-going, enjoyable though it is. The part-songs inspired by the composer's visit to Bavaria then add even more exhilaration, with the vigour and joy of the outer movements – better known in Elgar's orchestral version – brought out winningly, and with the London Symphony Chorus at its freshest and most incisive. Anyone who doesn't melt on hearing the opening 'Dance' must surely have a heart of stone. A disc to win new admirers for two seriously neglected works.

(i) *Coronation Ode, Op. 44. The Spirit of England, Op. 80*

Chan. 6574. Cahill, SNO Ch. and O, Gibson; (i) with Collins, Rolfe Johnson, Howell

Gibson's performances combine fire and panache, and the recorded sound has an ideal Elgarian expansiveness, the choral tone rich and well focused, the orchestral brass given plenty of weight, and the overall perspective highly convincing. He is helped by excellent soloists, with Anne Collins movingly eloquent in her dignified restraint when she introduces the famous words of *Land of Hope and Glory* in the finale; and the choral entry which follows is truly glorious in its power and amplitude. *The Spirit of England*, a wartime cantata to words of Laurence Binyon, is in some ways even finer, with the final setting of '*For the Fallen*' rising well above the level of his occasional music.

The Dream of Gerontius (DVD and CD versions)

Warner DVD 3984 22351-2. Langridge, Wyn-Rogers, Miles, BBC Ch. & SO, A. Davis

Hallé CD CDHLD 7520 (2). Groves, Coote, Terfel, Hallé Ch. & Youth Ch., Hallé O, Elder

Andrew Davis and Mark Elder are among the most recent conductors in a distinguished line (including Sargent, Boult, Barbirolli and Britten) who made recordings of the work about which Elgar truthfully stated, 'This is the best of me.' At the time of writing his great oratorio (the turn of the nineteenth into the twentieth century) the composer still believed in Cardinal Newman's poem describing the journey of a Christian soul into heaven to meet his maker. With Elgar's inspired music added, it is so compelling that a Jewish friend of ours confessed to us that when he listened through *Gerontius* he became a Catholic for an hour and a half!

It was as well that Elgar wrote it when he did, for (although he was apparently buried within the Catholic rite) in the last years of his life his faith seemed less secure. But the music is wonderfully moving, especially the immediacy of the scene by the bed of the dying Gerontius, with the Priest's blessing and the overwhelmingly great 'Go forth' chorus. Then later the infinitely touching meeting with his guardian angel and their hesitant dialogue, the frantic 'Demons' chorus' in Purgatory, and at last a meeting with God himself, portrayed by an orchestral climax of tremendous splendour. Finally comes the most radiantly beautiful 'Angel's Farewell', first made famous by Janet Baker (in her recording with Barbirolli).

But Alice Coote sings radiantly for Mark Elder and Catherine Wyn-Rogers is hardly less touching for Andrew Davis. Philip Langridge, too, is at his very finest as Gerontius for Andrew Davis, and Alastair Miles admirably combines the roles of Priest and Angel of Agony. Similarly, Paul Groves is a most affecting Gerontius for Mark Elder and Bryn Terfel is predictably commanding in both his roles. Indeed, both these new versions are superb in their different ways, with the *Praise to the Holiest* chorus wonderfully powerful in both, the BBC Chorus especially telling in first accelerating and then pulling back for its climax, while the Hallé Chorus is richly expressive over the widest possible dynamic range. Both recordings are superb, as is the orchestral playing. On the DVD, Bob Coles's imaginative camera placing brings the usual added dimension to the communication of the performers, and it has the added optional advantage of subtitles offering Cardinal Newman's text to follow if you wish. It is impossible to declare which is the finer set; you must decide whether your priority lies with DVD or CD.

3 Partsongs, Op. 18; 4 Partsongs, Op. 53; 2 Partsongs, Op. 71; 2 Partsongs, Op. 73; 5 Partsongs from Greek Anthology, Op. 45; Death on the Hills; Evening scene; Go, song of mine; How calmly the evening; The Prince of Sleep; Weary wind of the West

Chan. 9269. Finzi Singers, Spicer

Elgar's part-songs span virtually the whole of his creative career and the 22 examples on this recording range from one of the most famous, *My love dwelt in a northern land*, of 1889 to settings of Russian poems (in English translation) written during the First World War. Even among Paul Spicer's many recordings with the Finzi Singers, this recording stands out as a highlight. Elgar's part-songs are richly lyrical, highly varied and astonishingly inventive. One is swept into the intimate nature of the writing in the opening number, *O Happy Eyes* (what a gorgeous tune it has), while *Owls* is intensely haunting and eerie in its vivid aural scene-painting and magical vocal effects. Paul Spicer delivers finely tuned, crisp and intense readings of all these pieces, and the Chandos sound is both vivid and warmly atmospheric.

The Spirit of England

Ⓜ Dutton CDLX 7172. Gritton, Kennedy, BBC Ch. & SO, Lloyd-Jones (with **KELLY**: *Elegy 'In Memoriam Rupert Brooke'*. **ELKINGTON**: *Out of the Mist*) – **GURNEY**: *War Elegy*. **PARRY**: *The Chivalry of the Sea*

It may come as a surprise even to Elgarians to find this new version of the cantata, *The Spirit of England*, labelled – like the other war-inspired items here – as a first recording. The explanation is that Elgar's original intention was to have two soloists, giving the outer movements ('The Fourth of August' and 'For the Fallen') to a soprano and the middle movement ('To Women') to a tenor. In practice, even by the time of the first performance Elgar suggested that a single soloist could readily sing all three settings of Laurence Binyon poems, and so it has been in the subsequent recordings. Here for the first time a tenor, the talented Andrew Kennedy, takes over for the central setting, and certainly the result is a degree more effective than with a single soloist. David Lloyd-Jones conducts a powerful performance, bitingly dramatic in 'The Fourth of August', with the chorus in superb form, and with the setting of 'For the Fallen' - its words much the best known - aptly elegiac, the more powerful for being taken at a flowing speed. Susan Gritton sings brightly and with clarity.

FALLA, Manuel de (1876-1946)

(i-ii) *Harpsichord Concerto*; (iii-v) *El amor brujo*; (iv; vi-vii) *Nights in the Gardens of Spain*; (viii) *The Three-Cornered Hat*; (ix) *La vida breve: Interlude and Dance*; (x) *Homenaje 'Le tombeau de Claude Debussy'*; (vii) *4 Spanish Pieces*; (xi) *7 Canciones populares españolas*; (ii; xii) *Psyché*

Double Decca (ADD/DDD) 466 128-2 (2). (i) Constable; (ii) L. Sinfonia, Rattle; (iii) New Philh. O; (iv) Frühbeck de Burgos; (v) Mistral; (vi) LPO; (vii) De Larrocha; (viii) Montreal SO, Dutoit; (ix) SRO, Ansermet; (x) Fernández; (xi) Horne, Katz; (xii) with Jennifer Smith

A myriad of performances have been perceptively gathered together for this 'Essential Falla' compilation, which is surely rightly named. Dutoit's 1984 complete version of *The Three-Cornered Hat* is wonderfully atmospheric as well as brilliantly played. Recorded in 1966, Frühbeck de Burgos's *El amor brujo* also enjoys exceptionally vivid sound, yet with plenty of light and shade, and the control of atmosphere in the quieter passages is masterful, while Nati Mistral has the vibrant, open-throated production of a real flamenco singer. Alicia de Larrocha's later, digital version of *Nights in the Gardens of Spain* is unsurpassed among modern recordings; her playing of the *Four Spanish Pieces* glitters. The other shorter works are especially worthwhile. Ansermet's *Interlude and Dance* from *La vida breve*, with its melodramatic opening and lively dance section, is always enjoyable, and Marilyn Horne's *Spanish Folksongs* are vibrantly idiomatic. John Constable's crisply vivid account of the delightful *Harpsichord Concerto* (with Rattle) and the haunting rarity, *Psyché*, for voice (Jennifer Smith a fine soloist) and orchestra complete an extraordinary survey. Readers may also want to sample Ansermet's Decca complete recordings of *The Three Cornered Hat* and *El amor brujo*, which are uniquely characterful and vibrantly recorded (466 991-2).

Siete canciones populares españolas (7 Spanish Popular Songs)

Testament mono SBT 1311. Souzay, Bonneau - **FAURÉ**: *Mélodies*. **RAVEL**: *Histoires naturelles*

Manuel de Falla's seven *Canciones populares españolas* could not be sung with greater feeling. The late Gérard Souzay is wonderfully captured here in this 1951 set, made only six years after his Paris début and finding the youthful bloom of his voice at its peak. Highly characterized performances, and expertly accompanied by Jacqueline Bonneau. No need to make any allowances for the age of the Decca recording in Paul Baily's scrupulous remastering.

FAURÉ, Gabriel (1845-1924)

(i) *Ballade for Piano & Orchestra, Op. 19*; (ii) *Berceuse for Violin & Orchestra, Op. 16*. *Caligula, Op. 52*; *Les Djinns* (orchestral version), *Op. 12*; (iii) *Elégie for Cello & Orchestra, Op. 24*; (i) *Fantaisie for Piano & Orchestra, Op. 111*. *Masques et bergamasques, Op. 112*; *Pelléas et Mélisande, Op. 80*; *Pénélope: Prélude*; *Shylock, Op. 57*

Ⓑ EMI 5 86564-2 (2). (i) Collard; (ii) Y. P. Tortelier; (iii) Paul Tortelier; Von Stade, Gedda, Bourbon Vocal Ens.; Toulouse Capitole O, Plasson

Although Fauré's most deeply characteristic thoughts are intimate rather than public, and his most natural outlets are the mélodie, chamber music and the piano, this set of the orchestral music contains much that is highly rewarding. It includes the delightful *Masques et bergamasques* and the *Pelléas et Mélisande* and *Shylock* music, as well as rarities such as *Les Djinns* and *Caligula*. Plasson gets an alert and spirited response from the orchestra and he shows a genuine feeling for the Fauréan sensibility, and the fine-spun lyricism of the *Nocturne* from *Shylock* is well-conveyed. The two works for piano and orchestra are particularly valuable; Jean-Philippe Collard gives a really distinguished account of the early *Ballade* and the seldom heard *Fantasie*, Op. 111. The recordings are generally very good indeed, though the piano tone (not the playing) is a trifle hard. Although the vocal items no longer have texts and translations, as on the original issues, the set is now offered at bargain price. Altogether, this is a lovely collection in every way, offering many delights, and cannot be too warmly recommended.

Piano Quartets: 1 in C min., Op. 15; 2 in G min., Op. 45; Piano Quintets: 1 in D min., Op. 89; 2 in C min., Op. 115

Hyp. CDA 66166 (*Quartets*); CDA 66766 (*Quintets*). Domus (available separately)

It goes without saying that the playing of all concerned here is uniformly excellent, alive and subtle, with expert and sensitive contributions from the distinguished pianist, who can hold her own in the most exalted company. Domus have the requisite lightness of touch and just the right sense of scale and grasp of tempi. Fauré's chamber music is masterly and this is an ideal way of acquiring a lot of the best of it. These performances make one fall for the music all over again. The *Second Quintet* is among the masterpieces of Fauré's Indian summer as he approached his eighties. The recording is excellent too.

Nocturnes 1–13 (complete)

Avie AV 2133. Charles Owen

The *Nocturnes* span Fauré's whole composing career, and while the earlier works inherit a moonlight romanticism from Chopin (although the *Second Nocturne* includes a turbulent centrepiece) the *Fourth in E flat is* deliciously sensuous, with a specially Fauréan delicacy. The *Ninth in B minor* is modally haunting, and the later works are rather more harmonically adventurous and develop an added internal intensity. All, however, are among his most rewarding piano miniatures and could not have been written by any other composer. Charles Owen is obviously completely at home in these sometimes elusive works and he plays them beautifully, with subtle feeling for their colour. He is very well recorded.

Mélodies: (i) *Après un rêve*; *Arpège*; *Automne*; *Au bord de l'eau*; (ii) *C'est l'extase langoureuse*; *Clair de lune*; *En sourdine*; *Green*; *L'Horizon chimérique* (cycle); *Mandoline*; *Prison*; *Spleen*
Testament mono SBT 1311. Souzay, (i) Bonneau or (ii) Baldwin - **FALLA**: *Canciónes populares*. **RAVEL**: *Histoires naturelles*

Writing in 1955, the authors of *The Record Guide* spoke of Souzay surpassing his earlier achievements, and they hailed these Fauré songs on Decca LXT 2543 (from which this Testament issue in part derives) as 'one of the most satisfactory LP song recitals yet issued'. Half a century later it has lost none of its ability to enchant and remains one of the most eloquent of all Souzay's song records.

Requiem (1893 version); *Ave Maria, Op. 67/2*; *Ave verum corpus, Op. 61*; *Cantique de Jean Racine, Op. 11*; *Maria, Mater gratiae, Op. 42*; *Messe basse*; *Tantum ergo, Op. 65/2*
Coll. (ADD) COLCD 520. Ashton, Varcoe, Cambridge Singers, L. Sinfonia (members), Rutter

Fauré's *Requiem* has received many fine recordings, but John Rutter's inspired reconstruction of the original 1893 score, using only lower strings and no woodwind, opened our ears to the extra freshness of the composer's first thoughts. Rutter's fine, bright recording includes the *Messe basse* and four motets, of which the *Ave Maria* setting and the *Ave verum corpus* are particularly memorable. The recording is first rate, though the choir and instruments are placed relatively close.

FERGUSON, Howard (1908–1999)

Piano Sonata in F min., Op. 8; *5 Bagatelles, Op. 9*; (i) *Partita for 2 Pianos, Op. 5b*; (ii) *Discovery* (song-cycle), *Op. 13*
⑱ Naxos 8.572289. Raphael Terroni; with (i) Vadim Peaceman; (ii) Phillida Bannister

Born in Belfast (in 1908), educated at Westminster School and the Royal College of Music, the young Howard Ferguson was encouraged to further his musical career by the pianist Harold Samuel at the Royal College of Music, and he subsequently studied composition with Vaughan Williams and formed a deep friendship with Gerald Finzi. But it was Samuel who was his mentor, and when the latter died suddenly in 1937 Ferguson was inspired to write his arresting *F minor Piano Sonata*. It was first performed by Myra Hess at the famous National Gallery wartime concerts, which Ferguson helped to organize. The work opens with a stormy introduction, intensively developed, but this soon leads into movingly dedicated secondary lyrical material and thence naturally into the delicate *Poco adagio*, full of reflected melancholy (and very beautifully played here by Raphael Terroni). The angular vitality with which the *Sonata* began returns in the finale, but there remains an underlying gentleness and an appealing romantic feeling until the final section springs to life with a return of the rhythmic intensity of the opening. The five quirky *Bagatelles* (1944) make an entertaining interlude, each distinctively characterized, with an endearingly whimsical closing *Allegretto*.

The song-cycle, *Discovery*, is a late work (1951), combining five brief, sensitive settings of verse by Denton Welch, with the central *Babylon* ravishingly lyrical, and the penultimate '*Jane Allen*' (just 36 seconds long) full of life. Phillida Bannister, the responsive soloist, responds ardently, with rich tone and no exaggerated vibrato. The cycle ends soaringly, with ringing bells from the piano, and it is not surprising to learn (from Richard Whitehouse's excellent notes) that the cycle was a favourite of Kathleen Ferrier's.

The pseudo-baroque *Partita for 2 Pianos* (1935/6), also available in an orchestral version, makes the most of the double-piano sonority. It opens *Grave*, but establishes its classical antecedents with a double-dotted *Allegro pesante*, then including a gracefully memorable Sarabande and closing with a perky Reel. All in all this is a most rewarding and attractive programme, splendidly played (and sung), and one's only regret is the absence of the song texts. The recording is absolutely truthful.

FERRIER, Kathleen (contralto)

'A Tribute': Arias from: **BACH**: *St Matthew Passion* (with Nat. SO, Sargent); *Mass in B min.*; *St John Passion*; **HANDEL**: *Judas Maccabaeus*; *Messiah* (with LPO, Boult). *Rodelinda*; *Serse*. **GLUCK**: *Orfeo ed Euridice* (2 excerpts, with LSO, Sargent & Southern PO, Stiedry). **MENDELSSOHN**: *Elijah* (with Boyd Neel O, Neel). **MAHLER**: *3 Rückert-Lieder* (with VPO, Walter). Songs & Lieder: **TRAD**.: *Down by the Salley Gardens*; *Drink to me only*; *Hark! The echoing air*; *I have a bonnet trimmed with blue*; *The Keel Row*; *Ma bonny lad*; *The Stuttering lovers*; *Ye banks and braes*. **BRAHMS**: *Botschaft*; *Geistliches Wiegenlied*; *Sapphische Ode*. **HANDEL**: *Atalanta*.

PURCELL: *Hark! The Echoing Air (from The Fairy Queen).*
SCHUBERT: *An die Musik; Gretchen am Spinnrade; Die junge Nonne; Der Musensohn* (with Spurr, piano). *Du bist die Ruh; Romance* (from *Rosamunde*) (with Walter, piano). **SCHUMANN**: *Er, der Herrlichste von allen* (with Newmark, piano). **STANFORD**: *A soft day.* **BRIDGE**: *Go not happy day.* **TRAD**.: *Come you not from Newcastle; Kitty my love* (with Stone, piano). *Blow the wind southerly*
Ⓑ Decca mono 475 078-2 (2)

This is the best Kathleen Ferrier collection available and it includes many of her famous recordings, from the delightfully fresh folksongs (the haunting, unaccompanied version of *Blow the wind southerly* has uncanny presence) to her celebrated recordings of Bach and Mahler. The noble account of *Oh rest in the Lord* from *Elijah* is another highlight, along with the Schubert lieder (*Die junge Nonne* and *An die Musik* are especially moving). Even better, Decca have remastered and improved the sound for this bargain two-CD set, and the booklet includes many fascinating pictures of the great contralto.

FIELD, John (1782–1837)

(i) *Piano Concertos 1–7; Divertissements 1–2; Nocturne 16 in F; Rondeau in A flat;* (ii) *Quintetto*
Ⓜ Chan. 10468 (4). O'Rourke; (i) LMP, Bamert; (ii) Juritz, Godson, Bradley, Desbruslais

The music of these concertos is uneven, but they are all easy to enjoy and most have their fair share of winning themes, with scintillating passagework, persuasively nocturnal slow movements, and often a catchy closing rondo. The soloist, Míceál O'Rourke, is very persuasive and he receives admirable support from Bamert and the London Mozart Players and first-class recording. The extra items which complete the CD containing the *Seventh Concerto* – the two *Divertissements*, a *Rondeau* and *Nocturne* – all include really good tunes, while the serene single-movement *Piano Quintet* is also delicately charming.

Nocturnes 1–9; Piano Sonatas 1 in E flat; 2 in A, Op. 1/1–2
Ⓑ Naxos 8.550761. Frith

Nocturnes 10–17; 18 (Midi); Piano Sonata 3 in C min., Op. 1/3
Ⓑ Naxos 8.550762. Frith

Benjamin Frith's playing is delectably coaxing, and he makes these *Nocturnes* so often seem exquisitely like Chopin, yet he still catches their naive innocence, especially in the *A flat major* work. He hops, skips and jumps delightfully in the *Irish Rondo* finale of the *First Sonata* and is hardly less beguiling in the rather more imposing opening movement of the *Second*.

The second CD includes the famous *Nocturne 18* whose original title was *Midi* (or 'Twelve o'clock Rondo'). The *Third Sonata* occupies the midway point in the recital. Its first movement is just a little hectoring (Beethovenian *con fuoco* was not Field's natural element) but the closing *Rondo* simulates another popular air for its basis. As before, the recording is very natural. What a charming composer Field was – it is easy to see why Chopin was influenced by him.

FINZI, Gerald (1901–56)

(i) *Cello Concerto*; (ii) *Clarinet Concerto*
Lyrita SRCD 236. (i) Ma, New Philh. O; (ii) Denman, RPO; Handley

In the *Cello Concerto*, Yo-Yo Ma, in his début recording, responds with the utmost sensitivity, sometimes playing on a mere thread of tone in his magical account of the *Andante quieto*. His is not a big performance but a greatly inspired one, and many will like his lightness of touch in the finale. The *Clarinet Concerto* is a comparable masterpiece. If it lacks the contemplative qualities of the *Cello Concerto*, its more extrovert character and consistent charm are no less compelling. John Denman's performance is entirely seductive. And in both works Vernon Handley's sensitive accompaniment brings first-rate playing, while the recording is of Lyrita's usual excellence.

Intimations of Immortality
Lyrita (ADD) SRCD 238. Partridge, Guildford PO Ch. & O, Handley – **HADLEY**: *The Trees so High*

This is an astonishingly compelling recording which should be in every English music lover's collection. Finzi's music, which is in the richest English choral tradition, is here performed with a passionate sense of commitment. In this the beauty and intensity of Ian Partridge's singing are a key factor, and equally the choral singing is richly committed, while the Guildford Philharmonic Orchestra is challenged to playing that would not disgrace a much more famous orchestra. The recording is also excellent and, with a most enterprising coupling, it cannot be too highly recommended.

FISCHER-DIESKAU, Dietrich (baritone)

'The Mastersinger', Arias from: **MOZART**: *Così fan tutte* (with BPO, Jochum); *Don Giovanni* (with Prague Nat. Theatre O, Boehm); *Le nozze di Figaro* (with German Op. Ch. & O, Boehm); *Die Zauberflöte*.
MAHLER: *Ich bin der Welt abhanden gekommen* (with BPO, Boehm). **ORFF**: *Carmina Burana*. **WAGNER**: *Die Meistersinger*

von Nürnberg (with German Op. Ch. & O, Jochum). *Das Rheingold* (with BPO, Karajan). **GLUCK**: *Orfeo ed Euridice*. **HANDEL**: *Giulio Cesare* (with Munich Bach O, Richter); *Serse* (with Munich CO, Stadlmair). **VERDI**: *Don Carlo* (with ROHCG O, Solti); *Macbeth* (with LPO, Gardelli); *Rigoletto* (with La Scala, Milan, O, Kubelik); *La traviata* (with Berlin RSO, Fricsay). **PUCCINI**: *Tosca* (with Santa Cecilia O, Maazel). **HAYDN**: *The Creation* (with BPO, Karajan). **R. STRAUSS**: *Arabella*; *Die Frau ohne Schatten* (with Bav. State O, Keilberth); *Elektra* (with Dresden State Op. O, Boehm); *Salome* (with Hamburg State Op. O, Boehm). Lieder: **SCHUBERT**: *Im Frühling* (with Richter, piano); *An Silvia*; *Erlkönig*; *Die Forelle*; *Heidenröslein*; *Ständchen* (with Moore, piano); *Der Musensohn* (with Demus, piano)
ⓑⓑ DG (ADD) 476 7111 (2)

A self-recommending set, originally released to coincide with Fischer-Dieskau's *Gramophone* Lifetime Achievement award in 1993. It must have been an impossibly difficult task to know what to include here (the DG Fischer-Dieskau Lieder Edition alone runs to 44 CDs!) and everything here is vintage stuff. Most of the items are operatic, drawn from both Decca's and DG's catalogues, and he is as impressive in the Verdi items (he is superb in *Don Carlos*, where as Rodrigo he rivals Gobbi in the Death scene) as he is in the Strauss items – his Orestes in *Elektra* is incomparable. He is always a delight in Mozart, particularly so as Papageno in *Die Zauberflöte* (a role he never assumed on stage) and he is no less stylish in the enjoyable baroque items included here. The lieder are, of course, wonderfully done and his subtle yet pointful shaping of the words is equally revealing in large operatic repertoire, where his highly individual portrayal of Sachs in *Die Meistersinger* is a highlight. The recital ends with a glowingly warm excerpt from Mahler's *Rückert-Lieder* which receives equally loving care from the conductor. The recordings – all good – date from the 1960s and '70s and, although the booklet notes are minimal (restricted to a short biography), this makes an excellent bargain sampler of Fischer-Dieskau's art.

FISTOULARI, Anatole, conductor (see also under: ROSSINI: *William Tell: ballet music*)

Ballet music: **STRAUSS/DORATI**: *Graduation Ball*. **MINKUS**: *Don Quixote: Pas de deux* (with New SO). **WEBER/BERLIOZ**: *Invitation to the Dance*. **LECOCQ**: *La Fille de Mam'zelle Angot*. **WALTON**: *Façade: Suites* (ROHCG O). **VERDI**: *Aida: ballet music*. **ROSSINI**: *William Tell: ballet music*. **SAINT-SAËNS**: *Bacchanale*. **MUSSORGSKY**: *Dance of the Persian Slaves* (with Paris Conservatoire O)
ⓑ Australian Double Decca mono/stereo 480 2391 (2)

Fistoulari made some superb recordings of concertos for Decca in the 1950s and '60s (many still top choices today, with Ashkenazy, Katchen, Ricci and others as soloists) and some equally remarkable recordings of ballet music. Many of these performances haven't been seen since the 1960s and '70s and this reissue makes one realize just how good they were. In the *Graduation Ball*, he manages to make this collection of miscellaneous Straussiana sound all of a piece, but also brings touches of affection and panache to the playing. One feels that he has the ballet in mind rather than the individual pieces of music of which it is composed. The mono sound is excellent. However, the star performances here are the Lecocq and Walton ballets. *La Fille de Mam'zelle Angot* was a highly successful operetta of the 1870s. The ballet dates from 1943, following the story of the operetta, but including music from other sources, all by Lecocq. The score is wittily arranged by Gordon Jacob in the manner of Constant Lambert's *Les Patineurs* (Meyerbeer). A strong flavour of Adam's style pervades some of the pieces (the adagio, for instance), and the spirit of Offenbach peeps in too, particularly in the final carnival scene. One could hardly imagine a better recipe for pure enjoyment, and Fistoulari's vivacious performance is well supported by the Decca (stereo) recording. His account of the *Façade Suites* is similarly brilliant and witty, and highlights include the delightfully delicate *Country Dance* and a superb *Old Sir Faulk* in which the foxtrot style of the 1920s is perfectly parodied. Again, the stereo sound is excellent. The mono version of the *Don Quixote Pas de deux* is a charming trifle, and the *Invitation to the Dance* displays a light touch for the waltz itself and finds much beauty and poise in the opening and closing pages. The *Dance of the Persian Slaves*, like the other stereo items with the Paris Conservatoire Orchestra, displays lively theatrical feeling, with the distinct sound of the Paris orchestra adding piquancy. Verdi's delightfully tuneful and vivacious ballet music from *Aida* is given a marvellously alive account; and, with such stylish pointing of strings, Rossini's ballet music to *William Tell* sounds freshly minted. The pseudo-exotic elements of the *Bacchanale* from *Samson and Delilah* are invariably enjoyable, but rarely do they achieve the adrenalin level of this performance: Fistoulari whips up the end of the piece in a frenzy of excitement. These recordings were last released on Eclipse LPs in the early 1970s and their reappearance on CD finds them sounding as fresh as paint. A highly enjoyable and varied collection of ballet music, performed by a master of the genre.

FOERSTER, Josef Bohuslav (1859–1951)

String Quartets: 1 in E, Op. 15; 2 in D, Op. 39; 3 in C, Op. 61 (rev.113); 4 in F, Op. 182; 5 in G sine Op.; Prayer for String Quartet, sine Op.; (i) Erinnerung for String Quartet & Harp sine Op. String Quintet, Op. 3; Allegro giocoso for String Quartet, sine Op.

Sup. 4050-2. Stamic Qt; (i) with Jana Bousková (harp)

Josef Foerster was naturally at home in the world of chamber music, and the nine works here span his composing career. The single-movement *String Quintet* came first, in 1886; the *First Quartet*, dedicated to and influenced by Tchaikovsky, followed two years later; and his *Fifth Quartet* was dedicated to his second wife, Olga. It closes with a touching slow movement which the composer left unfinished; as he commented, this was 'to symbolize one's path in life, which does not close with the physical departure from this earth'. The *Prayer* also has something of its dedicated feeling, while the *Erinnerung for String Quartet and Harp* shows a gentle, Mahlerian influence. Throughout, the music is influenced by Dvořák and Smetana, but it has a rich, flowing melodic lyricism which is all Foerster's own contribution. When played so expertly and with such sympathtic warmth, Foerster is revealed as a composer to return to and to give the listener much pleasure.

FOULDS, John (1880–1939)

A World Requiem

Chan. CHSA 5058 (2). Charbonnet, Wyn-Rogers, Skelton, Finley, Trinity Boys' Ch., Crouch End Festival Ch., Philh. Ch., BBC Symphony Ch. & O, Botstein

Foulds wrote his *A World Requiem* for the 1923 Festival of Remembrance, using over a thousand performers. The music is eclectic, with many derivations, and is essentially a cry for world peace. The work subdivides and opens darkly, but the call for deliverance in the second half is exuberant in its message that Christ's promise to mankind is the world's salvation. With these huge forces and four soloists, the vocal spectacle obviously recalls Mahler's *Third*, *Resurrection* and *Eighth Symphonies*, and certainly this performance exerts a gripping hold on the listener. The recording is very much in the demonstration bracket.

FRANÇAIX, Jean (1912–97)

(i–ii) *L'Horloge de Flore* (for oboe & orchestra); (i; iii) *Cor anglais Quartet*; (iii) *String Quartet*; (iv) *Trio for Oboe, Bassoon & Piano*
CPO 999 779-2. (i) Lencsés; (ii) Stuttgart RSO, Segal; (iii) Parisii Qt; (iv) Françaix Trio

L'Horloge de Flore is captivating. Inspired by the Linnaeus Flower Clock (which ingeniously conveys the time by its formation from different floral species, each of which blossoms at a different hour of the day or night), the music forms a suite of seven miniature movements, mainly gentle. It is beautifully played by Lajos Lencsés, and the accompaniment is admirably tasteful. In short, this is a miniature treasure, and it is supported by other inconsequential chamber works, all playful and presented with much finesse, and each as personable as it is slight. The closing *String Quartet* is full of whimsy and ends very gently with a *molto sostenuo*.

Ouverture anacréonique; Pavane pour un génie vivant; Scuola de ballo; Sérénade; Symphony 3 in G
Hyp. CDA 67323. Ulster O, Fischer

Françaix did not number his symphonies, but this amiable G major work is his *Third* (1953), composed light-heartedly in memory of Papa Haydn. What a happy work this is! The *Sérénade*, written 20 years earlier, is even more jocular, opening with fake-rhythmic abrasiveness before a melancholy bassoon introduces the *Andantino*. But high spirits return in the chirping *Poco Allegretto* and dashingly ribald finale. A touching calm then dominates the rather lovely opening of the *Ouverture anacréonique* (1978). But the music soon livens up vivaciously and reaches a confident, jazzy climax. The exquisite *Pavane pour un génie vivant*, a homage to Ravel, evokes that composer's world idyllically. The programme then ends winningly with a pastiche *Scuola de ballo*, based on the music of Boccherini. The whole programme is played with warmth, polish and vitality; the recording is first class and this is very highly recommended.

(i) Huit danses exotiques (for 2 pianos); (ii) Napoléon (suite for 4 hands); 15 Portraits d'enfants d'Auguste Renoir (for 4 hands); (i) Scuola di Ballo, sur des thèmes de Boccherini (for 2 pianos). Cinq 'Bis'; Cinq portraits de jeunes filles; Danse des Trois Arlequins; 'De la Musique avant tout chose'; Éloge de la danse (6 épigraphes de Paul Valéry); Huit Variations sur le nom de Johannes Gutenberg; Nocturne; La Promenade d'un Musicologue Éclectique; Pour Jacqueline; Scherzo; Si Versailles m'était conté...; Sonate pour piano; Trois esquisses sur les touches blanches (posth.)
Nimbus NI 5880 (3). Jones; with (i) McMahon; (ii) Farmer

Françaix's gifts, both as a creative artist and performing musician, were obvious from his early youth. He was praised by Ravel, and studied, like so many other twentieth-century musicians, with Nadia Boulanger. Then he won a 'premier prix' as a pianist at the Paris Conservatoire, and went on to give outstanding performances of his own works. He was a prolific composer and, although he wrote during a period dominated by atonalism, his writing resolutely avoids such excesses. His piano music is infectiously tuneful, graceful and full of charm and elegance.

This collection of all his works for solo piano, duo and duet is a delight from first to last. One might start on the first disc with its sparkling *Scherzo* and continue with the five *Portraits de jeunes filles*, each delectably characterized, notably 'La Capriceuse', the touching, neo-baroque 'La Tendre', the extravagantly ironic

'La Prétentieuse' and the closing, vivacious 'La Moderne'. The *Danse des Trois Arlequins*, a work that follows later on the disc, is also infectiously full of rhythmic uplift, and the *Éloge de la danse* offers six engaging vignettes in triple time, each describing the same woman.

Cinq 'Bis' (encores) increasingly demand real bravura. The first is invitingly named 'To entice the audiences', while the second, 'Pour les dames sentimentales', is romantically winsome, and the finale 'En cas de délire' unleashes a virtuoso moto perpetuo. The *Sonate pour piano*, however, is traditional in form, yet has a memorably personal central *Elégie*, while the *Gutenberg Variations* are predictably diverse. The first disc then ends with a delectable *Nocturne*.

The two remaining collections are no less appealing. *Huit danses exotiques* derive from Latin American dance music, although the finale is unexpectedly (and untruthfully) entitled 'Rock 'n' Roll'. The *15 Portraits d'enfants d'Auguste Renoir*, for 4 younger hands, are each hardly a minute long: every one is as simple as it is delectable. *Trois esquisses sur les touches blanches* is a gossamer triptych creating the ambience of a child's music lesson, with the finale bringing an irrepressible rejection from the pupil. The composer's last piano work, *La Promenade d'un Musicologue Éclectique*, is a tribute to six different composers, of which the miniature portrait of Scarlatti and a poignant evocation of Ravel are especially rewarding. The 'Petit Hommage à la Musique Contemporaine' defiantly 'cocks a snook' at the excesses of modernity.

'De la Musique avant tout chose' offers ten beautifully crafted 'pièces enfantines' picturing young children as they slowly mature, and the comparatively extended portrait *Pour Jacqueline*, dedicated to the composer's cousin (a very early composition), catches the young lady's unpredictable but exquisite femininity to perfection.

The third disc is devoted to highly effective piano transcriptions of Françaix's film and ballet scores. The score for the epic film *Napoléon* incorporates pastiches of national music, notably marches of all kinds, plus a mazurka and a polonaise, and many other tuneful snippets, all woven into a kaleidoscopic whole.

The suite from *Si Versailles m'était conté...* derives from the film of the same name covering the history of the famous palace. Its varied associations with hunting, past wars, courtly dancing, pastorale evocation and romance, are crowned with *La Marseillaise*. The *Scuola di Ballo* offers winning excerpts from a ballet score based on neatly varied and ever-catchy themes from Boccherini, taken mainly from his various string quintets.

We have devoted considerable space to describing this splendid anthology of piano music by this outstanding twentieth-century composer, music so little known, and we hope many readers will be tempted to acquire this rewarding box, with highly sympathetic and spontaneous performances throughout from Martin Jones, successfully partnered in the piano duos and duets by Adrian Farmer and Richard McMahon. The recordings are most natural and there are excellent notes.

FRANCK, César (1822–90)

(i) *Le Chasseur maudit*; (ii) *Les Éolides*; (i) *Psyché*; *Rédemption*; (i; iii) *Nocturne*
Ⓜ Australian DG Eloquence (ADD) 4762800. (i) O de Paris, Barenboim; (ii) SRO, Ansermet; (iii) Ludwig

What a good idea to gather together Barenboim's 1976 Franck recordings – and also that DG Australia did not include the obvious *Symphony*, which in any case was not one of Barenboim's successes instead of the rarer works here. *Rédemption* is given a splendidly convincing performance, with brass antiphonies gloriously brought out, making one wonder at the work's relative neglect. *Le Chasseur maudit* opens with a most evocative Sunday morning ambience; the devilish chase which follows is vividly exciting, with Franck's portrayal of the accursed huntsman superbly energetic with its arresting horn calls (an excellent version, though not eclipsing Munch's classic RCA account). The orchestral items from *Psyché* show real *tendresse*, and the relatively simple and brief *Nocturne*, beautifully done by Christa Ludwig, is equally beguiling. The 1967 sound for Ansermet's *Les Éolides* is even more vivid, with the conductor finding much feeling in the ebb and flow of the string writing of this haunting piece.

Symphony in D min.
ⒷⒷ RCA (ADD) SACD 82876 67897-2. Chicago SO, Monteux – **STRAVINSKY**: *Petrushka*

Pierre Monteux exerts a unique grip on this highly charged Romantic symphony, and his control of the continuous ebb and flow of tempo and tension is masterly, so that any weaknesses of structure in the outer movements are disguised. As soon as one begins this performance, one is hooked by the electricity of the music-making. The splendid playing of the Chicago orchestra is ever responsive to the changes of mood, and the most recent remastering for SACD brings further improvement to the 1961 recording; indeed, now the quality reflects the acoustics of Chicago's Orchestra Hall in the same way as Reiner's recordings, with textures full-bodied and glowing, without loss of detail. The newest coupling is Monteux's uniquely authoritative (1959) Boston recording of *Petrushka*.

String Quartet in D; (i) Piano Quintet in F min.
ⒷⒷ Naxos 8 572009. Fine Arts Qt; (i) with Ortiz

Cristina Ortiz and the Fine Arts Quartet couple Franck's two major chamber works and give very fine accounts of both masterpieces. They have ardour and finesse in equal measure. Of course, Curzon and the Amadeus have a special resonance in the *Quintet* but this bargain-label version has a very strong claim on the collector, and the pianist has both sensitivity and imagination.

(i) *Violin Sonata in A*; (ii) *String Quartet in D*

Ⓜ Australian Decca Eloquence (ADD/DDD) 476 8463. (i) Amoyal, Rogé; (ii) Fitzwilliam Qt

Franck's *D major Quartet* is highly ambitious in its scale; its almost orchestral texture and its complex use of cyclic form always seem on the verge of bursting the seams of such an intimate piece of chamber music. Yet as a very late inspiration it contains some of the composer's most profound, most compelling thought, and this magnificent performance by the Fitzwilliam Quartet, superbly triumphing over the technical demands with totally dedicated, passionately convinced playing, completely silences any reservations. In every sense this is a work which seeks to take up the challenges presented by the late Beethoven quartets in a way that few nineteenth-century composers attempted, not even Brahms. Richly recorded, with the thick textures nicely balanced, this was one of the finest chamber records of the late 1970s. It received a rosette on its original release, which it fully deserved. Amoyal and Rogé, richly recorded in 1995, also provide a superb account of the *Violin Sonata*, a performance full of fantasy and giving the impression of music emerging spontaneously on the moment.

FRESCOBALDI, Girolamo (1583–1643)

Keyboard Music, Volume 1: *Ancidetemi pur d'Arcadelt's passaggiatto*; *Capriccio 'Or che noi rimena'*; *Canzona Quarta; Cento Partite sopra Passacagli; 7 Toccatas*; Keyboard Music, Volume 2: *Balletto e Ciaccona*; *Corrente & Ciaccona; 5 Gagliardes; Partite sopra l'Aria di Monicha*; *Partite sopra l'Aria di Ruggiero; Partite sopra Ciaccona; Partite sopra Passacaglia; 7 Toccatas*; Keyboard Music, Volume 3: *Aria detta Balleto*; *Aria detta la Frescobalda; Balletto Primo – Corrente del Balletto*; *Balletto Seconda – Corrente del Balletto; Balletto Terzo – Corrente del Balletto – Passacagli; Canzona Prima; Canzona Quinta; Capriccio di Durezze; Capriccio fatto sopra La Cucchù; Capriccio Fra Jacopino sopra l'Aria du Ruggiero; Correntes 1–4; Capric sopra l'aria di Ruggiero*; *Ricercar 3; 4 Toccatas*

Nim. NI 5850 (Vol. 1); NI 5861 (Vol. 2) ; NI 5870 (Vol. 3). Richard Lester (harpsichord by Giovanni Battista Boni (*c*.1619), Italian harpsichord (*c*.1590), Siculus virginals (*c*.1540) or Vicentius Pratensis virginals (*c*.1600))

Girolamo Frescobaldi was born in Ferrara, but moved first to Brussels, then to Rome, before climaxing his career in the service of the Medici family in Venice. His music was as highly regarded as it was influential – and understandably so, as it was both highly inventive and spontaneous. The very first item on the first of these two discs, the *Capriccio 'Or che noi rimena'* (based on a Dutch student song) immediately demonstrates the quality and appeal of his variants, and the dance movements in Volume 2 are full of life, the opening gagliardas very jolly. The *Toccatas* make for an expressive contrast and perhaps include the finest music of all. Performance of Frescobaldi demands a free, improvisatory style of performance, of which Richard Lester is obviously a master. He plays a perfectly chosen harpsichord with a particularly attractive, warm sonority, not in the least 'clattery', with the sound perfectly focused in an ideal acoustic.

FURTWÄNGLER, Wilhelm

'The Great EMI Recordings': BARTÓK: *Violin Concerto 2* (with Y. Menuhin & Philh. O). BEETHOVEN: *Piano Concerto 5 (Emperor)* (with Edwin Fischer & Philh. O); *Violin Concerto* (with Y. Menuhin & Lucerne Festival O); *Overture Leonora 2* (with BPO); *Overture Coriolan*; *Symphonies 1–7* (with VPO); *8* (with Stockholm PO); *9 (Choral)* (with Schwarzkopf, Höngen, Hopf, Edelmann, Ch. & O of 1951 Bayreuth Festival); *Fidelio* (complete; includes *Leonora Overture 3*) (with Mödl, Windgassen, Edelmann, Frick, Jurinac, Schock, Poel, V. State Op. Ch., VPO). BRAHMS: *Violin Concerto* (with Y. Menuhin & Lucerne Festival O); *Double Concerto for Violin & Cello* (with Willi Boskovsky & Emanuel Brabec); *Hungarian Dances 1, 3 & 10*; *Variations on a Theme of Haydn (St Antoni Chorale)*; *Symphonies 1–4*. CHERUBINI: *Overture Anacréon* (all with VPO). FURTWÄNGLER: *Symphonic Concerto: Adagio* (with Edwin Fischer & BPO). HAYDN: *Symphony 94 in G (Surprise)*. LISZT: *Les Préludes* (with VPO). MENDELSSOHN: *Violin Concerto in E min., Op. 64* (with Y. Menuhin & BPO). MOZART: *Symphony 40 in G min., K.550* (with VPO). SCHUBERT: *Symphony 8 (Unfinished)*. R. STRAUSS: *Don Juan*; *Till Eulenspiegel*; *Death and Transfiguration* (all with VPO). TCHAIKOVSKY: *Symphony 6 (Pathétique)* (with BPO). WAGNER: *Tristan und Isolde* (complete) (with Suthaus, Flagstad, Thebom, Greindl, Fischer-Dieskau, Schock, ROHCG Ch. & Philh. O)
Ⓑ EMI (ADD) 9 07878-2 (21)

These analogue recordings, made between 1939 and 1954, have been excellently remastered, and they demonstrate how well balanced was the EMI sound afforded to Furtwängler in the 78 era. No apologies need be made: sonically they are most enjoyable to listen to, while they continually demonstrate the conductor's genius as an interpreter of the major classics, even as far forward as Bartók (with Yehudi Menuhin). This concerto is mandatory listening for anyone who admires the composer, and it sounds splendid in the new transfer, while Menuhin's noble (1947) Lucerne recording of the Beethoven *Violin Concerto* also has an authority and intensity that are almost unique in this repertoire. Edwin Fischer's 1951 recording of the *Emperor* with the

Philharmonia Orchestra is another of the great classics of the gramophone, both imperious and imperial.

By unearthing a live recording of No. 2, made in the Royal Albert Hall in 1948, and borrowing a radio recording of No. 8, made in Stockholm, EMI has put together a complete cycle of the Beethoven *Symphonies*. The sound of these two ad hoc recordings may be below the standard of the rest, but the performances are electrifying. No. 9 comes in the dedicated performance given at Bayreuth in 1951, but the others are EMI studio versions, not always as inspired as the conductor's live performances, but still magnetic, with well-balanced mono sound.

The 1953 recording of *Fidelio*, made in the Musikverein, omits the spoken dialogue, but the voices are very impressive, notably Martha Mödl, then new to the role of Leonora but already commanding. Sena Jurinac was a creamy-toned Marzeline, Otto Edelmann a sinister Pizarro, singing with wonderful clarity, and Wolfgang Windgassen as Florestan was heroic and totally unstrained. Gottlob Frick makes a magnificent Rocco, and Furtwängler is at his most inspired.

Furtwängler's 1949 account of the Brahms *Violin Concerto* with Menuhin, and the *Double Concerto* with (unexpectedly) Willi Boskovsky partnered by Emanuel Brabec, have been submerged under later versions, but in their way they are classic accounts. But the performances of the four Brahms *Symphonies* with the Vienna Philharmonic are in a class of their own. The live recording of the *First Symphony*, made in 1952, is partnered with live recordings of the remaining three symphonies, made in 1948–9 and 1952 and presumably taken from radio sources. The performance of the *First* is particularly fine, with a real feeling of apotheosis in the finale, from the horn call and the great string melody which follows, to the close. The electricity of Furtwängler in Brahms is vividly captured throughout. The music-making is obviously live, particularly at the thrilling close to each of the four *Symphonies*, except of course No. 3, which ends gently. The first movement of No. 4 is unexpectedly swiftly paced, although the *Adagio* makes a complete contrast, and the closing passacaglia is splendidly managed. The sound in all four works has been greatly improved in the present remastering, more full-bodied than in their last incarnation. The *Variations on a Theme of Haydn* are agreeably mellow and perceptively characterized.

It is good that the conductor's own rare but engagingly romantic *Adagio* from his *Symphonic Concerto*, beautifully played by Edwin Fischer, has survived. The performance of Haydn's *Surprise Symphony* is splendidly alive and elegant, with a very positive 'surprise', and the account of Mozart's *G minor* is one of the highlights of the set, the first movement taken briskly, making room for an exposition repeat, and the whole performance is full of character, as indeed is Liszt's *Les Préludes*, if of a very different kind, adding dignity to flamboyance and vigour.

Menuhin's unique gift for lyrical sweetness has never been presented on record more seductively than in his classic (1952) version of the Mendelssohn *Violin Concerto* with Furtwängler; the recording, made in the celebrated Berlin Jesus-Christus-Kirche, certainly does not sound its age. Nor does the balance of Schubert's *Unfinished Symphony*, played with warm lyricism, but with no lack of drama.

Don Juan and *Till Eulenspiegel* come from 1954, some months before the onset of deafness brought Furtwängler's career to an end, while *Death and Transfiguration* was recorded in Vienna in 1950. They are performances of commanding stature and have the glowing naturalness of utterance and mastery of pace that characterized the conductor at his best. *Don Juan* has real exuberance, *Till* is deliciously detailed and comes to a very dramatic end with rasping trombones, while *Death and Transfiguration* has real nobility at its climax. The recordings still sound glorious.

Tchaikovsky's *Pathétique Symphony* too is masterly, a truly great performance, with the tender second subject of the first movement matched by the work's poignant close in its feeling. And the Scherzo is transformed into its march apotheosis with splendid rhythmic power. The 1938 recording is astonishingly vivid and does not sound in the least dated.

This set of treasurable records is capped by the 1952 set of *Tristan und Isolde*, produced in the Kingsway Hall by Walter Legge. Furtwängler's concept is spacious from the opening *Prelude* onwards, but equally the bite and colour of the drama are vividly conveyed, matching the nobility of Flagstad's portrait of Isolde. The richly commanding power of her singing and her always distinctive timbre make it a uniquely compelling performance. Suthaus is not of the same calibre as a Heldentenor, but he avoids ugliness and strain. Among the others the only remarkable performance comes from the young Fischer-Dieskau as Kurwenal, not ideally cast but keenly imaginative. One endearing oddity is that – on Flagstad's insistence – the top Cs at the opening of the love duet were sung by Elisabeth Schwarzkopf. The Kingsway Hall recording was admirably balanced, catching the beauty of the Philharmonia Orchestra at its peak. It stands among Furtwängler's finest memorials, still unsurpassed by later versions in its spacious concentration and intensity.

'Remembering Furtwängler', written and narrated by Jon Tolansky: musicians who performed with Wilhelm Furtwängler, and others who saw him, recall how and why he excercised a magnetic and hypnotic effect over them and his audiences, illustrated by recordings made at rehearsals and performances. Our favourite story comes from the timpanist of the Berlin Philharmonic Orchestra. He tells us that at rehearsals he often followed a score during sections of the music in which he was not taking part. On one occasion the orchestra was rehearsing under another conductor and was playing well enough but with no particular distinction. Suddenly the sound changed and instantaneously possessed an extra radiance. He looked up from the score and saw that Furtwängler had just walked in at the door in full view of the orchestra.

Overall, this set is an essential purchase, and it is well documented.

GARDNER, John (born 1917)

(i) Piano Concerto 1, Op. 34. Overture: Midsummer Ale, Op. 73; Symphony 1, Op. 2
ⓑⓑ Naxos 8.570406. RSNO, Lloyd-Jones; (i) with Donohoe

This coupling of two of John Gardner's major works, plus a sparkling comedy overture, could not be more welcome, brilliantly played and recorded. Here is one of the most unjustly neglected composers of his generation. Born in 1917, he has always been astonishingly prolific, maybe one reason for his neglect when there is so much to choose from. At the last count in 2004 Gardner had clocked up no fewer than 249 opuses, most of them on commission, yet there have been disgracefully few recordings of his music. The *Symphony No. 1*, the most extended of the works on the new disc, is in four movements, spanning over 40 minutes. Though it was written in 1947, it was not performed until 1951, one of the pieces that Sir John Barbirolli introduced at the Cheltenham Festival. The idiom is more abrasive than in Gardner's later works, with a grinding slow introduction leading to an *Allegro* with echoes of Walton in its jazzy syncopations, though with sharper harmonies. As always in Gardner's music the orchestration is brilliantly clear, and after an interlude of stillness the work ends with a ripe and optimistic D major chord.

The *Piano Concerto No. 1* of 1957 offers a contrasted idiom in its percussive echoes of the Bartók *Piano Concertos*, suiting Peter Donohoe's strong style admirably in another performance brilliantly backed by David Lloyd-Jones and the Royal Scottish National Orchestra. The clangorous opening movement leads to a still, slow movement with more echoes of Bartók but also of John Ireland. The disc is dazzlingly rounded off with a rumbustious comedy overture, *Midsummer Ale*, written for the orchestra of Morley College, of which Gardner was music director. By rights this disc will bring renewed attention to the music of a most attractive composer.

GAY, John (1685–1732)

The Beggar's Opera (arr. Pepusch and Austin)
ⓑ CfP 575 9722 (2). Morison, Cameron, Sinclair, Wallace, Brannigan, Pro Arte Ch. & O,
Sargent – **GERMAN**: *Tom Jones*

The Beggar's Opera was the eighteenth-century equivalent of the modern American musical. It was first produced in 1728 and caused a sensation, burlesquing the sort of operas – stylized Italian opera favoured by Handel – the audiences were used to. This performance under Sargent is in every way first class, and the soloists could hardly be bettered, with Elsie Morison as Polly,

John Cameron as MacHeath and Owen Brannigan a splendid Peachum. The linking dialogue is spoken by actors to make the result more effective, with every word crystal clear. The chorus is no less effective and the 1955 recording has a most appealing atmosphere. It was one of EMI's first stereo successes and the chorus 'Let us take the road' (during which the singers recede into the distance) was understandably included on their stereo demonstration disc. It is now coupled with a delightful selection from Edward German's *Tom Jones*, which is hardly less vivid. Recordings of Britten's version of this score have been made, most recently by Chandos which is recommendable. His version is also available on a Decca DVD (074 3329) with a superbly vivid and memorable cast, recorded in 1963. Bonynge's souped-up version with a star cast, including Joan Sutherland and Angela Lansbury, is available on Australian Decca Eloquence, but this EMI is undoubtedly closest to the spirit of the work.

GERMAN, Edward (1862–1936)

Tom Jones (operetta: highlights)
ⓑ CfP 575 9722 (2). Harvey, Minty, Glover, Riley, Nigel Brooks Ch. & O, Gilbert Vinter –
   GAY: *The Beggar's Opera*

Listening to this sparkling selection, one's first impression is how like Sullivan is the basic idiom. The opening chorus might have come straight out of *Patience*, and there are many ensembles and solos that have a distinct reminder of one or other of the Savoy Operas, The librettist here even uses one of Gilbert's rhythms, *'Festina lente'*, as part of a song-title. But there is also music that could have only come from German's own pen, the really charming *Here's a paradox for lovers* and of course the delicate *Dream o'day* and the famous *Waltz Song*. They are all extremely well sung here by a solo group who, like the conductor, Gilbert Vinter, convey real enthusiasm for this tuneful score. The 1966 recording is excellent and has transferred vividly to CD. Splendidly coupled, this inexpensive set is not to be missed.

GERSHWIN, George (1898–1937)

(i) ***An American in Paris***; (ii) ***Piano Concerto in F***; (iii) ***Rhapsody in Blue***
Ⓜ Sony (ADD) 82876 78768-2. (i) NYPO, Bernstein; (ii) Previn, O, Kostelanetz; (iii)
   Bernstein (piano) with Columbia SO

An American in Paris; ***Rhapsody in Blue***
DG DVD 073 4513. NYPO, Bernstein (with **IVES**: *The Unanswered Question*;
   Symphony 2: Bav. RSO)

Bernstein's outstanding 1960 CD coupling of *An American in Paris* and *Rhapsody in Blue* has stood the test of time. Bernstein's approach in the *Rhapsody*, which he directs from the keyboard, is exceptionally flexible but completely spontaneous. It is a masterly account in every way, quixotic in mood, rhythmically subtle and creating a great surge of human warmth at the entry of the big central tune. The performance of *An American in Paris* is vividly characterized, brash and episodic, an unashamed American view, with the great blues tune marvellously phrased as only an American orchestra can do it. Both recordings still sound very good indeed. For this reissue Previn's account of the *Concerto in F* (made at the same time) with Kostelanetz, not surprisingly, has more pizzazz and is more telling stylistically than his later, HMV version with the LSO. Kostelanetz and his orchestra play a major part in the interpretation, especially in the brilliant finale. Once again the remastered sound is remarkably vivid. Altogether these classic versions remain unsurpassed.

Those wanting a DVD will find that again there is an authentically spontaneous command of idiom here; Bernstein is both a superb soloist and conductor in the *Rhapsody* and the New Yorkers respond in a proprietorial way. They also play with great concentration in *The Unanswered Question*. It is good also to see the Bavarian orchestra in the Ives *Symphony*, which they play to the manner born. The Gershwin was recorded at the Royal Albert Hall in 1976 and the Ives in 1987.

GESUALDO, Carlo de Venosa (c. 1561–1613)

Carlo Gesualdo was a great deal more than a musician/composer of distinction. He was also the powerful Prince of Venosa, and because of his rank he was not brought to book for the bloody double murder of his beautiful wife, Maria d'Avalos, and her lover, caught *in flagrante delicto* in his marriage bed. He was a writer of passionately expressive secular music, but he also wrote intensely felt and equally unpredictable liturgical settings for the church.

Leçons de ténèbres; *Responsories for Maundy Thursday*
Signum SIGCD 048. King's Singers

Gesualdo's responsories for Maundy Thursday of 1611, with their surprising chromatic dissonances, are among the most remarkable and original of all *Ténèbre* settings. Immediately *In Monte Oliveti* opens, the King's Singers demonstrate a very flexible approach to tempo and dynamic that is to characterize the whole performance. The impeccable intonation and tonal matching also give a special richness to the chordal writing and its moments of dissonance. The performance closes simply with the chant, *Christus factus est*, and this is treated as a brief recessional. In short this is a superbly sung performance, expressively poignant, but dramatic too, which brings a new dimension to this remarkable music, and the recording is outstanding.

Madrigals, Book 1 (1594)

ⓑⓑ Naxos 570548. Delitiæ Musicæ, Marco Longhini

It is against the background of the high point of his extraordinary life that Gesualdo wrote his madrigals. Obviously the 1590s were an extremely creative period for him, and these five-part madrigal settings clearly reflected the emotional turmoil of his own life. Their remarkable unpredictability of feeling, with pain, passion and joy side by side, was exhibited by their chromatic intensity and the spread of dissonances, the desperation in love of many of their texts, requited and unrequited.

The very first two madrigals in Book 1 are paired: *Baci soavi e cari . . . Quanto ha di dolce amore* ('Sweet and tender kisses . . . There is sweet love enough') brings a sophisticated mirror of erotic love-making with its sighs and physical responses with the very last word of part two, *morir!,* being a euphemism for orgasm. But others among these settings are of the joys of coupling, and the meaning of *Mentre madonna il lasso fianco posa* is even plainer: 'While my lady rested her weary limbs after erring happily and willingly'. The music itself is often serene or touchingly melancholy (*Tirsi morir volea*), although some settings move joyously and quickly. There is great variety here and the performances by this fine Italian vocal ensemble are rich in timbre and colour and beautifully blended and ever flexible in tempo. The clear recording in a warm acoustic is admirable and there are excellent notes and full text and translations.

GIBBONS, Orlando (1583–1625)

Consorts for Viols: *Fantasies a 3, 1–4*; *Fantasies a 6: 1–6*; *In Nomines 1–2*; *Keyboard Pieces arr. for Viols*; *Vocal Works arr. for Viols*
Avie AV 0032. Phantasm

The *Fantasies* for viol consort by Orlando Gibbons are among the most sublime works in the string repertory, leading on to the *Fantasias* of Purcell, even breathing the same air as the Beethoven late *Quartets*. Happily the group Phantasm is at once authoritative and beautifully matched. The complexities of the *Fantasies in six parts*, presented here as a cohesive group, are astonishing, both in rhythm and in counterpoint, and the two six-part *In Nomines*, more austere, have a similar intensity. Phantasm supplement the music written specifically for viols with transcriptions of keyboard and vocal works. The sound is admirably balanced and this is a highly satisfying collection.

Anthems and Verse Anthems

Gaudeamus CDGAU 123. King's College Ch., London Early Music Group, Ledger; Butt

This valuable anthology was the first serious survey of Gibbons's music to appear on CD. It contains many of his greatest pieces. Not only are the performances touched with distinction, the recording too is in the highest flight and the analogue sound has been transferred to CD with complete naturalness. Strongly recommended.

GIBSON, Alexander (conductor), with (i) New Symphony Orchestra or (ii) Orchestra of the Royal Opera House, Covent Garden

'Witches' Brew': (i) ARNOLD: *Tam O'Shanter Overture*.
MUSSORGSKY: *A Night on the Bare Mountain; Gnomus*.
SAINT-SAËNS: *Danse Macabre*. HUMPERDINCK: *Witch's Ride*. LISZT: *Mephisto Waltz 1*. (ii) GOUNOD: *Faust Ballet Music; Funeral March of a Marionette*
Australian Decca Eloquence (ADD) 442 9985

The bulk of this CD comprises a collection called 'Witches' Brew', originally issued on RCA in 1959, but recorded in 1957 by the Decca recording team. It was a collection that delighted us at the time, and it showed Gibson at his most spontaneous. The LP, long deleted, became something of a collector's item, and also a great favourite of the hi-fi enthusiasts. The sound still astonishes in its immediacy and rich detail. The performances are all excellent, but the *Tam O'Shanter Overture* is outstanding. It is one of Arnold's most brilliantly entertaining and evocative pieces, full of Scottish devilry, with the macabre humour delectably brought out – and especially so at the climax, when there is the most realistic portrayal of Tam's bagpipes, all achieved with orchestral instruments. Humperdinck's *The Witch's Ride* goes vividly too, and *A Night on the Bare Mountain* is spectacular – helped by the brilliance of the sound. For this reissue, Decca have added a very stylish account of the *Faust* ballet music, as well as the delectable *Funeral March of a Marionette* (Alfred Hitchcock's own familiar signature tune), both in vintage Decca sound from 1959. A disc well worth seeking out.

GIBSON, Alexander (conductor), with the Royal Scottish National Orchestra

'British Tone Poems': SMYTH: *The Wreckers: Overture*.
GERMAN: *Welsh Rhapsody*. HARTY: *With the Wild Geese*.
MacCUNN: *Land of the Mountain and the Flood*
Ⓑ CfP (ADD) 3 52405-2

Recorded in the Usher Hall in Edinburgh in April 1968, and almost never out of the catalogue since, this enterprising collection of British tone-poems remains one of Sir Alexander Gibson's finest records. Dame Ethel Smyth's opera, *The Wreckers*, was first performed in England in 1909. The story concerns the wrecking of ships by false signal-lights on the Cornish coast. Its overture is a strong, meaty piece which shows the calibre of this remarkable woman's personality – the first emancipated English feminist. While the material itself is not especially memorable, it is put together most compellingly and orchestrated with real flair.

With the Wild Geese was written a year later for the Cardiff Festival. It is another melodramatic piece, this time about soldiers fighting on the French side in the Battle of Fontenoy. The ingredients – a jolly Irish theme and a call to arms among them – are effectively deployed and though the music does not reveal a strong individuality in Harty as a composer, it is carried along by a romantic sweep which is well exploited here.

Edward German's *Welsh Rhapsody* was also written for the Cardiff Festival (in 1904) and makes a colourful and exciting finale for this well-chosen programme. German is content not to interfere with the traditional melodies he uses, relying on his orchestral skills to retain the listener's interest, in which he is very successful. The closing pages, based on 'Men of Harlech', are prepared in a Tchaikovskian manner to build to a rousing conclusion.

But undoubtedly Hamish MacCunn's descriptive Scottish overture *The Land of Mountain and Flood*, is the highlight of the disc. It is well crafted, has a really memorable tune and is attractively atmospheric. Gibson's performances are outstanding throughout in their combination of warmth, colour and atmosphere, and the recording still sounds very well indeed.

GINASTERA, Alberto (1916–83)

Glosses sobre temes de Pau Casals (2 versions): (i) *for String Quintet & String Orchestra, Op. 46*; *for Orchestra, Op. 48*. (ii) *Variaciones concertantes for Chamber Orchestra, Op. 23*
Naxos 8.572249. (i) LSO; (ii) Israel CO; Gisèle Ben-Dor

Naxos have already issued four collections of music by the rewarding Argentinian composer, Alberto Ginastera – the complete Ballets (8.557582), the Piano and Organ music (8.557911/12), the music for Cello and Piano (8.570569) and the complete String Quartets (8.570780). But if you want to explore the full range of the composer's melodic invention and vivid orchestral palette, you could hardly better this superbly played and recorded coupling of the *Glosses sobre temes de Pau Casals* in two different versions, and the almost kaleidoscopic *Variaciones concentantes*.

The *Glosses on Themes of Pablo Casals* (dedicated to the famous cellist, a great personal friend of the composer) began life as a work conceived for string quintet and string orchestra, celebrating the centenary of Casals's birth. The string quintet is placed separately from the main string group and acts rather like a concertino in a concerto grosso. The work is in five colourfully diverse movements, its *Introducció* drawing on a melancholy, folk-like theme, making an allusion to a Caribbean legend which alternates with a frenzied buzzing, very like a galaxy of insects. The following *Romaç* is an idyllic evocation recalling 'Three verses of love' composed by Casals in 1958 for his wife. *Sardanes*, which comes next, is a distanced hectic suggestion of the vibrant national dance of Catalonia, normally executed in a circle. The magical fourth movement, *Cant*, is nocturnal and Casals's familiar folk-song setting, 'The Song of the Birds', is heard as a gentle cello solo against a background of simulated birdsong. The aptly named finale, *Conclusió delirant*, is appropriately wild and frenzied.

Ginastera tells us that while composing *Glosses* for strings he felt the need to expand the scoring for full orchestra and, while the string version is by no means eclipsed, the generous expansion of the orchestration adds much to the music, for the instrumental additions were significant, including two flutes and piccolo, three each of oboes and clarinets and bassoons, three trumpets and trombones, four horns (the brass sonorities particularly telling), tuba, harp, piano, celesta and a full range of percussion.

The *Variaciones concertantes* for chamber orchestra includes double woodwind and horns, trumpet, trombone, timpani, harp and strings. The work is in twelve sections, with the theme introduced beguilingly on cello and harp. A string interlude acts as a bridge to the variations which follow, each variation in turn dominated by a solo instrument: flute, clarinet, viola, oboe and bassoon in canon, a rhythmic variation for trumpet and trombone, a *moto perpetuo* for violin, a lovely pastoral variation for horn. A further interlude for wind leads to a reprise of the main theme on a solo double bass and the spectacular finale, based on a virtuosic jousting dance, the *Malambo*, closes the work on full orchestra. These variations are as colourful and diverting as one could wish, and the solo playing from members of the Israel Chamber Orchestra is very winning indeed. First rate recording too.

GIORDANO, Umberto (1867–1948)

Andrea Chénier (DVD version)
TDK DVD DVWW OPACH. Guleghina, Cura, Guelfi, Teatro comunale di Bologna Ch. & O, Rizzi (Director: Giancarlo di Monaco; V/D: Paula Langobardo)

Recorded in Bologna in 2006, the DVD from TDK offers a traditional production with handsome stage pictures, strongly conducted by Carlo Rizzi. Act II even includes a statue of Marat murdered in his bath. José Cura in the title-role of the poet is not always as refined as he can be, though his singing in the big numbers is powerful, and for *Come un bel dì di Maggio* in Act IV he does find a gentle half-tone. Maria Guleghina as Maddalena sings with tender beauty, though she grows unsteady under pressure, as does the powerful Carlo Guelfi in the key role of Gérard, the proud servant in Act I who after the French Revolution becomes a leader. Very impressive among the lesser characters is Carlo Cigni as Roucher.

Fedora (DVD version)

TDK DVD DVWW OPFED. Freni, Domingo, Scarabelli, Corbelli, La Scala, Milan, Ch. & O, Gavazzeni (Director & V/D: Lamberto Puggelli)

Recorded at La Scala in 1993, the TDK version of Giordano's *Fedora* is valuable for capturing not only the moving characterization of the heroine, Fedora, by Mirella Freni, but for the glorious singing of Plácido Domingo as the hero, Loris. It is he who has the one sure-fire hit item, the brief aria, *Amor ti vieta*, and one longs to have a melody of similar quality in the rest of the piece, with its melodramatic story of Russia in 1881, based on a play by Sardou. The two other principals, Olga and De Siriex, are strongly taken by Adelina Scarabelli and Alessandro Corbelli, if with limited beauty of tone. The production is grandly traditional, with the darkness of the first two Acts giving way to lightness and beauty in the Alpine scene of Act III. Freni gives herself totally to the culminating scene, when she poisons herself rather than reveal that it is she who has betrayed Loris as a revolutionary to the police. The veteran conductor, Gianandrea Gavazzeni, is brilliant at bringing out the colour and drama of the piece.

GLAZUNOV, Alexander (1865–1936)

Violin Concerto in A min., Op. 82

Pentatone Surround Sound SACD PTC 5186 059. Julia Fischer, Russian Nat. O, Kreizberg – **KHACHATURIAN**: *Violin Concerto.* **PROKOFIEV**: *Violin Concerto 1*

Julia Fischer's coupling of three Russian violin concertos on Pentatone could hardly be more recommendable, with warmly compelling performances from the brilliant young German virtuoso, superbly recorded in full, bright, clear sound, given added sonority in SACD. In the Glazunov *Concerto* it is the clarity and subtlety of Fischer's playing that marks her reading out, in rivalry with even the finest. She finds yearning tenderness in the slow middle section of this one-movement work and gives an easy swing to the bouncy rhythms of the final section.

Raymonda – *'Dancer's Dream'* (Documentary)

Arthaus DVD 107 015. Principal Dancers & Corps de Ballet, with Paris Nat. Op. O, Anissimov (Director: François Roussillon)

A fascinating documentary (from 1999) about Glazunov's colourful ballet *Raymonda*, and its comparatively recent success with Rudolf Nureyev. The documentary is dedicated to the great ballet productions by Rudolf Nureyev performed at the Opéra National de Paris, of which Nureyev was artistic director from 1983. The documentary focuses on both the history of the ballet and Nureyev's work on it, and offers a fascinating series of interviews, interspersed with scenes from the ballet. Some of the material is archival, but the majority is of very beautiful recent productions, where both the colour of the music and the beauty of the dancing are well conveyed. The picture and sound quality are both first class. A thoroughly rewarding and civilized documentary – and a must for balletomanes.

Symphonies 1–8; Ballade in F, Op. 78; From Darkness to Light; Mazurka in G, Op. 38
BIS CD 1663/4 (5). BBC Nat. O of Wales, Otaka

A valuable set, offering all eight symphonies on five CDs for the price of two. They span just over two decades, the *First* being composed when Glazunov was a boy of sixteen and the *Eighth* completed when he was just forty. The symphonies are very consistent, both in substance and in character: if you have heard and liked one, its companions will offer few surprises and much satisfaction. The ideas are appealing and the craftsmanship and orchestration show an impressive mastery. Arnold Bax used to play them in duet form – understandably, for they are musically rewarding and are unlikely to be encountered in concert programmes. But they are decently represented on CD and have been out on individual discs for some time. The present issue represents a true bargain and the performances and recordings can hold their own against the Polyansky cycle on Chandos and other rivals.

GLINKA, Mikhail (1804–57)

Capriccio brillante on the Jota aragonesa (Spanish Overture 1); Kamarinskaya; Overture in D; Ruslan and Ludmilla: Overture and Suite. Souvenir of a Summer Night in Madrid (Spanish Overture 2); Symphony on Two Russian Themes; Valse-Fantaisie
Chan. 9861. BBC PO, Sinaisky

Kamarinskaya is a kaleidoscopic fantasy on two Russian folksongs. Tchaikovsky said it contained 'the whole of Russian music, just as the acorn holds within itself the oak tree'. The two *Spanish Overtures* created another genre, the orchestral 'picture postcard' which Russian composers brought home from their travels abroad. Glinka's two pieces have glitter and atmospheric appeal all of their own, especially the *Capriccio brillante*, featuring the 'jota aragonesa' also used by Liszt. But the seductive scoring of *Summer Night in Madrid* was in some ways even more influential. The *Valse-Fantaisie* is a real charmer, and the famous *Overture, March* and *Dances* from *Ruslan and Ludmilla* are fizzingly brilliant show-pieces for the orchestra. The playing of the BBC Philharmonic is both warmly responsive and sparkling, and the state-of-the-art Chandos recording is superb.

'GLORIOUS MAJESTY Music for English Kings and Queens'

HANDEL: *Music for the Royal Fireworks* (London Classical Players, Sir Roger Norrington). Coronation anthems: *Zadok the Priest*; *Let thy hand be strengthened*; *The King shall rejoice*; *My heart is inditing*. *Eternal source of light divine* (Soloists, King's College, Cambridge, Ch., AAM, Stephen Cleobury). **BYRD**: *O Lord make thy servant Elizabeth our Queen* (King's College, Cambridge, Ch., Stephen Cleobury). **PURCELL**: *Come ye sons of art away* (Soloists, Early Music Cons. of London, David Munrow); *Funeral Music for Queen Mary* (1695) (Soloists, King's College, Cambridge, Ch., AAM, (Stephen Cleobury). **ELGAR**: *Coronation Ode, Op. 44*. Arr. **ELGAR**: *National Anthem*. **PARRY**: *I was glad* (Soloists, King's College, Cambridge, Ch., New Philh. O, Band of Royal Military School of Music, Sir Philip Ledger). **ELGAR**: *Imperial March, Op.* 32 (LPO, Sir Adrian Boult); *O hearken thou (Offertory), Op.* 64 (LSO Ch., N. Sinf., Richard Hickox); *Coronation March, Op. 65*; *Nursery Suite: The Sad Doll* (RLPO, Sir Charles Groves). **WALTON**: *Crown Imperial*; *Orb and Sceptre (Coronation Marches)* (1937 & 1953) (LPO, Sir Adrian Boult). *Coronation Te Deum* (Worcester Cathedral Ch., CBSO & Ch., Louis Frémaux). **VAUGHAN WILLIAMS**: *O taste and see* (Chichester Cathedral Ch., Sir Philip Ledger); arr. *All people that on earth do dwell* (King's College, Cambridge, Ch., Stephen Cleobury). **BRITTEN**: *Jubilate Deo* (King's, College, Cambridge, Ch., Sir Phillip Ledger); *Gloriana: The Tournament*; *Courtly Dances* (Bournemouth SO, Uri Segal).
Ⓜ EMI 3 27285-2 (3)

It is appropriate in the year of the Queen's Diamond Jubilee that EMI should issue this magnificent anthology of music composed over the centuries and inspired by the British monarchy. The standard of these works is gloriously high and so is the consistent quality of the performances, and the EMI recordings. How lucky we were to have both Handel and Purcell to contribute; and later on Elgar and Walton kept up the standard. Walton's two *Coronation Marches* are among his most appealing music and the big tune at the centre of *Crown Imperial* rivals Elgar. To our delight, EMI have chosen the much admired

1937 mono recording of the latter, and it sounds as good now as it did when it was first issued on a 78. Britten's contribution is smaller but his pastiche dances for *Gloriana* are most engaging. A set not to be forgotten.

GLUCK, Christoph (1714–87)

Orphée et Eurydice (complete CD version of 1774 score)
Decca 478 2197 (2). Flórez, Garmendia, Marianelli, Madrid Ch. & SO, López-Cobos

Gluck wrote his most famous opera first in Italian in 1762, when the role of Orpheus was assigned to an alto castrato. Then, in 1769, he transposed this key part for a soprano castrato. Finally, in 1774 he made his third version for Paris, and as Parisians scorned the very idea of castrati he adapted the leading role for a *haute-contre* (a high tenor voice favoured as an alternative). The result is indeed challengingly high but here Juan Diego Flórez demonstates that the music sounds thrillingly effective in this stirring upwards transposition. He sings with power, lyrical élan and a wide range of dynamic. The lovely duets with the sweet-timbred Ainhoa Garmendia in the outer Acts are particularly successful and the most famous aria of all is most beautifully sung. Jesús López-Cobos conducts throughout with sensitivity and spirit, pacing admirably, and the choral and orchestral playing, especially in the ballet music, which comes at the close, is first class. Excellent recording too.

GOLDMARK, Karl (1830–1915)

Violin Concerto in A min., Op. 28
Delos DE 3156. Hu, Seattle SO, Schwarz (with **BRUCH**: *Violin Concerto 2*)

The Taiwanese soloist Nai-Yuan Hu (pronounced Nigh-Yen Who) makes an outstanding début on CD with a coupling of two underrated concertos which on his responsively lyrical bow are made to sound like undiscovered masterpieces. The Goldmark is a tuneful and warm-hearted concerto that needs just this kind of songful, inspirational approach: Hu shapes the melodies so that they ravishingly take wing and soar. Moreover, Schwarz and the Seattle orchestra share a real partnership with their soloist and provide a full, detailed backcloth in a natural concert-hall framework.

Rustic Wedding Symphony, Op. 26
Australian Decca Eloquence 476 8743. LAPO, López-Cobos – **GRIEG**: *Symphony*

López-Cobos directs a refreshing and attractively spirited reading of this engaging work (which Beecham premièred on record) with its particularly attractive first movement. His generally fast tempi may detract slightly from the charm of the piece, but the wide-ranging sound, which presents the Los Angeles orchestra untypically at a distance, means that this is an excellent way of sampling the by-ways of the classical repertoire. A bargain, when coupled to the rare Grieg *Symphony*.

GÓRECKI, Henryk (1933–2010)

Symphony 3 (Symphony of Sorrowful Songs), Op. 36
None. 7559 79282-2. Upshaw, L. Sinf., Zinman

When the *Third Symphony* first appeared, it immediately caught the attention of the wider musical public and was frequently played and broadcast. But more recently its fame has waned, undeservedly so. Scored for strings and piano, with soprano solos in each of the three movements, all predominantly slow, it sets three laments taking the theme of motherhood and is expressively most appealing. There are several available recordings of it, but the London Sinfonietta's fine performance, beautifully recorded, is a first choice, crowned by the radiant singing of Dawn Upshaw.

GOTTSCHALK, Louis (1829–69)

(i-ii) *Grand Tarantelle for Piano & Orchestra* (arr. Hershy Kay); (ii) *A Night in the Tropics (Symphony 1)*; (iii-iv) *The Union: Concert Paraphrase on National Airs, for 2 pianos, Op. 48* (arr. List); Music for Piano, 4 Hands: *L'Étincelle*; *La Gallina*; *La Jota aragonesa*; *Marche de Nuit*; *Orfa*; *Printemps d'amour*; *Radieuse*; *Résponds-moi*; *Ses yeux*; *Souvenirs d'Andalousie*; *Tremolo* (arr. Werner/List); (iii) Solo Piano: *The Banjo, Op. 15*; *Bamboula: Danse des nègres, Op. 2*; *Le Bananier, Op. 5*; *The Dying Poet*; *The Last Hope, Op. 16*; *The Maiden's Blush*; *Ojos Criollos (Danse Cubaine)*; *Pasquinade, Op. 59*; *La Savane*; *Souvenir de Porto Rico (Marche des Gibaros)*; *Suis-moi*; *Tournament Galop*
Van. (ADD) stereo/mono 1181 (2). (i) Nibley; (ii) Utah SO, Abravanel; (iii) List;
   (iv) Lewis, Werner

The Vanguard two-CD set includes a solo collection recorded as early as 1956; although the recording is mono, it is truthful and does not sound one-dimensional. Eugene List was just the man to choose for these solo items: he is marvellously deadpan. Whether tongue-in-cheek or not, he manages to sound stylish throughout. In the music for piano, four hands, he is joined by excellent partners; the performances have flair and scintillating upper tessitura.

The opening arrangement of the *Jota aragonesa* heads an ear-tickling pro-gramme with a neat touch of wit in the piece called *Tremolo*. When the participants move to two pianos for the outrageous *Union Paraphrase* the effect is properly flamboyant. In the quotation from 'Hail Columbia', the second pianist enterprisingly slipped a piece of paper into the piano across the lower strings to simulate a side-drum effect with great success. The orchestral items include a so-called symphony, *A Night in the Tropics*, which sounds suitably atmospheric in Utah, and Reid Nibley brings plenty of bravura to the concer-tante *Grand Tarantelle*.

GOUNOD, Charles (1818-93)

Faust (complete, DVD version)

EMI (DVD) 6 31611-9. Alagna, Gheorghiu, Terfel, Keenlyside, Koch, Royal Opera Ch.,
 ROHCG O, Pappano (DVD Producer: Ross MacGibbon)

Faust (complete, CD version)

Teldec 4509 90872 (3). Hadley, Gasdia, Ramey, Mentzer, Agache, Fassbaender, Welsh
 Nat. Op. Ch. & O, Rizzi

The EMI video recording of Gounod's *Faust* from Covent Garden is surely one of the finest achievements of DVD so far. It is magnificently photographed so that one might be sitting in an ideal seat in the stalls. The opera overflows with memorable tunes, presented virtually continuously, plus a ready supply of nineteenth-century melodrama, centring on Bryn Terfel's powerful, vividly evil personification of the Devil and ending with a truly thrilling climactic trio that precedes Marguerite's final redemption.

At the opening, Alagna dominates vocally in the name-role with a powerful heady lyricism (his rejuvenation scene in Act I is superbly managaged). Gheo-rghiu sings gloriously as a delightful Marguerite, but the action is underlined by the splendidly bold panache of Bryn Terfel's Méphistophélès, acting and singing to create a real sense of dominating evil. There is no weak link in the rest of the cast, Simon Keenlyside is a boldly resonant Valentin and Sophie Koch an engaging and touching Siébel. The Royal Opera Chorus rises to the occasion at all points of the narrative, and especially in the 'Soldiers' Chorus', and the diabolic ballet of Act V is no less memorable. Pappano conducts with delicacy, warmth and passion and also shows an obvious affinity with Gounod's colourful orchestration, holding the listener throughout - often through relaxed tempi, as in the seduction scene of Act III. To cap the excel-lence of this DVD, it also has a booklet with a vivid description by Patrick O'Connor of the background to the Paris of Charles Garnier's Opéra, 'where Faust was to hold sway for more than half a century as the most popular opera in the world'.

On CD, Rizzi, with an outstanding cast and vividly clear recording, makes the whole score seem totally fresh and new. Jerry Hadley as Faust has lyrical freshness rather than heroic power, brought out in his headily beautiful performance of '*Salut! demeure*' and, like Rizzi's conducting, his singing has more light and shade than that of rivals. The tenderness as well as the light agility of Cecilia Gasdia's singing as Marguerite brings comparable variety of expression, with the '*Roi de Thulé*' song deliberately drained of colour to contrast with the brilliance of the Jewel Song which follows. Her performance culminates in an angelic contribution to the final duet, with Rizzi's slow speed encouraging refinement, leading up to a shattering moment of judgement and final apotheosis. Alexander Agache as Valentin may be less characterful than some of his rivals, but his voice is caught richly; and it is the commanding demonic performance of Samuel Ramey as Méphistophélès that sets the seal on the whole set, far more sinister than many of his rivals in the past. This CD set includes a valuable appendix, not just in the full ballet music but numbers cut from the definitive score – a drinking song for Faust and a charming aria for Siébel.

Faust: ballet music

Ⓜ Australian Decca Eloquence (ADD) 476 2724. ROHCG O, Solti - **OFFENBACH**: *Gaîté Parisienne*. **RESPIGHI**: *Rossiniana*

Solti's 1959 account of the *Faust* ballet music is undoubtedly one of the liveliest (and most vividly recorded) versions committed to disc. While Beecham has offered more elegance in this repertoire (see above), no one beats Solti for sheer energy: Solti has a style of his own, and the final *Entrée de Phryné* almost goes off the rails with its hard-driven but exciting brilliance.

GRAINGER, Percy (1882–1961)

The Grainger Edition
Orchestral works: CD 1: *Blithe Bells*; *Colonial Song*; '*The Duke of Marlborough' Fanfare*; *English Dance*; *Fisher's Boarding House*; *Harvest Hymn*; *Green Bushes*; *In a Nutshell*; *Shepherd's Hey*; *There Were Three Friends*; *Walking Tune*; *We Were Dreamers*. CD 2: *Country Gardens*; *Dreamery*; *Early One Morning*; *Handel in the Strand*; *Irish Tune from County Derry*; *Mock Morris*; *Molly on the Shore*; *Shepherd's Hey!*; *The Warriors*; *Youthful Suite*. CD 3: *Colonial Song*; *English Dance 1*; *Green Bushes*; *Eastern Intermezzo*; *Hill Song 2*; *The Immovable Do*; *Irish Tune from County Derry*; *Lord Maxwell's Goodnight*; *The Merry King*; *The Power of Rome and the Christian Heart*; *Spoon River Ye Banks and Braes o' Bonnie Doon* (with BBC PO, Hickox).
Works for Chorus and Orchestra: CD 4: *Anchor Song*; *After-word*; *Brigg Fair*; *County Derry Air*; *Early One Morning*; *Handel in the Strand*; *I'm*

Seventeen Come Sunday; *The Lonely Desert-man Sees the Tents of the Happy Tribes*; *Marching Tune*; *Molly on the Shore*; *Shallow Brown*; *Six Dukes Went Afishin'*; *There Was a Pig Went Out to Dig*; *Thou Gracious Power*; *Two Sea Chanties*; *Ye Banks and Braes o' Bonnie Doon* (with Padmore, Varcoe, Thwaites, Joyful Company of Singers, City of L. Sinfonia, Hickox). CD 5: *Colleen Dhas*; *Colonial Song*; *Country Gardens*; *Dreamery*; *Handel in the Strand*; *Harvest Hymn*; *The Immovable Do*; *Lord Maxwell's Goodnight*; *The Lost Lady Found*; *The Love Song of Har Dyal*; *Mock Morris*; *My Robin Is to the Greenwood Gone*; *The Running of Shindand*; *Scotch Strathspey and Reel*; *The Sea-wife*; *Tiger-Tiger*; *We Have Fed Our Sea for A Thousand Years*; *The Widow's Party* (with Helen Stephen, Padmore, Varcoe, Tozer, Joyful Company of Singers, City of L. Sinfonia, Hickox). CD 6: *Danny Deever*; *Died for Love*; *Dollar and a Half a Day*; *Early One Morning*; *Irish Tune from County Derry*; *Love Verses from 'The Song of Solomon'*; *Molly on the Shore*; *The Merry King*; *Mock Morris*; *O Gin I Were Where Gadie Rins*; *The Power of Love*; *Random Round*; *Scherzo*; *Shepherd's Hey!*; *Skye Boat Song*; *The Three Ravens*; *Youthful Rapture* (with Gritton, Helen Stephen, Tucker, Varcoe, Hugh, Joyful Company of Singers, City of L. Sinfonia, Hickox). CD 7: *The Crew of the Long Serpent*; *Dalvisa*; *Danish Folk-song Suite*; *Fadir og Dóttir*; *Kleine Variationen-Form*; *The Merry Wedding*; *The Rival Brothers*; *A Song of Värmeland*; *Stalt Vesselil*; *To a Nordic Princess*; *Under en Bro* (Helen Stephen, Reuter, Danish Nat. R. Ch. & SO, Hickox)

Works for Unaccompanied Chorus: CD 8: *Agincourt Song*; *At Twilight*; *Australian Up-country Song*; *Early One Morning*; *The Gypsy's Wedding Day*; *Irish Tune from County Derry*; *Jungle-Book Verses*; *Love at First Sight*; *Mary Thomson*; *Mo Nighean Dubh*; *My Love's in Germanie*; *Near Woodstock Town*; *O Mistress Mine*; *Recessional*; *Six Dukes Went Afishin'*; *Soldier, Soldier*; *Ye Banks and Braes o' Bonnie Doon* (ASMF Ch., Hickox)

Works for Wind Orchestra: CD 9: *Colonial Song*; *Country Gardens*; *Faeroe Island Dance*; *The 'Gum-Suckers' March*; *Hill Song*; *Irish Tune from County Derry*; *The Lads of Wamphray March*; *Lincolnshire Posy*; *The Merry King*; *Molly on the Shore*; *Shepherd's Hey!*; *Ye Banks and Braes o' Bonnie Doon*. CD 10: *Bell Piece*; *Blithe Bells*; *Children's March*; *Hill Songs I & II*; *The Immovable Do*; *Irish Tune from County Derry*; *Marching Song of Democracy*; *The Power of Rome and the Christian Heart* (Royal N. College of Music Wind O, Reynish or Rundell)

Works for Chamber Ensemble: CD 11: *Arrival Platform Humlet*; *Colonial Song*; *Handel in the Strand*; *Harvest Hymn*; *The Maiden and the Frog*; *Mock Morris*; *Molly on the Shore*; *My Robin Is to the Greenwood Gone*; *The Nightingale and the Two Sisters*; *La Scandinavie*; *Shepherd's Hey!*; *The Shoemaker from Jerusalem*; *The Sussex Mummers' Christmas Carol*; *Theme and Variations*; *Youthful Rapture* (ASMF Chamber Ens., Sillito). CD 12: *Bold William Taylor*; *The Bridegroom Grat*; *Colonial Song*; *Died for*

Love; *Free Music*; *Harvest Hymn*; *Hubby and Wify*; *The Land o' the Leal*; *Lisbon*; *Lord Peter's Stable-boy*; *Lord Maxwell's Goodnight*; *Molly on the Shore*; *The Nightingale*; *The Old Woman at the Christening*; *The Only Son*; *The Power of Love*; *Sea Song*; *The Shoemaker from Jerusalem*; *The Twa Corbies*; *The Two Sisters*; *Walking Tune*; *Willow, Willow*; *Ye Banks and Braes o' Bonnie Doon* (with Della Jones, Hill, Varcoe, ASMF Chamber Ens., Sillito)

Songs for Mezzo-soprano: CD 13: *After-word*; *The Bridegroom Grat*; *Colonial Song*; *Dafydd Y Gareg Wen*; *Died for Love*; *Early One Morning*; *5 Settings of Ella Grainger*; *4 Settings from 'Songs of the North'*; *Harvest Hymn*; *Hubby and Wifey*; *In Bristol Town*; *The Land o' the Leal*; *Little Ole with His Umbrella*; *The Lonely Desert-man Sees the Tents of the Happy Tribes*; *The Love Song of Har Dyal*; *O Glorious, Golden Era*; *Near Woodstock Town*; *The Only Son*; *Proud Vesselil*; *A Song of Autumn*; *The Sprig of Thyme*; *Under a Bridge*; *Variations on Handel's 'The Harmonious Blacksmith'*; *Willow, Willow* (with Della Jones, Padmore, Varcoe, Thwaites, Lavender)

Songs for Tenor: CD 14: *Lord Maxwell's Goodnight*; *The Power of Love*; *3 Settings of Robert Burns*; *4 Settings from 'Songs of the North'*; *9 Settings of Rudyard Kipling*; *A Reiver's Neck-verse*; *The Twa Corbies* (with Hill, Thwaites)

Songs for Baritone: CD 15: *Bold William Taylor*; *British Waterside*; *Creepin' Jane*; *Hard Hearted Barb'ra (H)Ellen*; *The Lost Lady Found*; *The Pretty Maid Milkin' Her Cow*; *Sailor's Chanty*; *The Secret of the Sea*; *4 Settings from 'Songs of the North'*; *6 Settings of Rudyard Kipling*; *Shallow Brown*; *Six Dukes Went Afishin'*; *Willow, Willow* (with Varcoe, Thwaites)

Works for Pianos: CD 16: *In Bristol Town*; *Country Gardens*; *English Dance*; *Green Bushes*; *Harvest Hymn*; *Jutish Medley*; *The Keel-row*; *Let's Dance in Green Meadow*; *Random Round*; *The Warriors*; *'The Widow's Party' March*; *Ye Banks and Braes o' Bonnie Doon*; *Zanzibar Boat Song* (with Thwaites, Marshall, Lavender, Gillespie, Gray)

Solo Piano Works: CD 17: *Andante con moto*; *At Twilight*; *Eastern Intermezzo*; *English Waltz*; *Gigue*; *In Dahomey*; *Irish Tune from County Derry*; *Klavierstück in E*; *in D*; *in A min.*; *in B flat*; *Near Woodstock Town*; *Paraphrase on Tchaikovsky's Flower Waltz*; *Peace*; *Preludes in C & G*; *Sailor's Song*; *Saxon Twi-play*; *Scotch Strathspey and Reel*; *3 Scotch Folksongs*; *Seven men from all the world*; *Train Music*; *Walking Tune*. CD 18: *Arrival Platform Humlet*; *Australian Up-country Song*; *The Brisk Young Sailor (who returned to wed his true love)*; *Bristol Town*; *Colonial Song*; *Country Gardens*; *Died for Love*; *Gay but Wistful*; *The 'Gum-Suckers' March*; *Hard Hearted Barb'ra (H)Ellen*; *Handel in the Strand*; *Harvest Hymn*; *Horkstow Grange*; *The Hunter in His Career*; *Lisbon*; *The Merry King*; *Pastoral*; *Mock Morris*; *Molly on the Shore*; *My Robin Is to the Greenwood Gone*; *The Rival Brothers*; *Shepherd's Hey!*; *The Sussex Mummers' Christmas Carol*; *Sea-song Sketch*; *The Tents of the Happy*

Tribes; *Tiger-Tiger*; *The Widow's Party*. CD 19: *Beautiful Fresh Flower*; *Blithe Bells*; *A Bridal Lullaby*; *Bridal Lullaby Ramble*; *Children's March 'Over the Hills and Far Away'*; *Country Gardens*; *Danish Folk-song Suite*; *The Immovable Do*; *Irish Tune from County Derry*; *Lullaby from 'Tribute to Foster'* (2 versions); *Knight and Shepherd's Daughter*; *Now, Oh Now I Needs Must Part*; *One More Day, My John*; *Proud Vesselil*; *Ramble on the Last Love-Duet from Strauss's 'Der Rosenkavalier'*; *Rimmer and Goldcastle*; *To a Nordic Princess*; *Walking Tune* (with Thwaites)
ⓑⓑ Chan. 10638 (19)

Released by Chandos to mark the fiftieth anniversary of the composer's death, the Grainger Edition is the most comprehensive collection of his music available. The 19-CD set comprises almost – but not quite – all of the composer's output. This monumental project, which includes over 120 première recordings, was supervised by Barry Peter Ould of the Percy Grainger Society, as well as by other Grainger experts, notably Penelope Thwaites. You will find no concertos or symphonies here. The longest work, *The Warriors* (one of the composer's most inventive scores), lasts under 19 minutes. The bulk of Grainger's output are miniatures (a genre in which he excelled) and of which he famously wrote (or 'dished up', as the composer said) many versions of the same piece. That would be tiresome in less gifted hands, but Grainger was a master orchestrator and unfailingly conjured up an array of ear-tickling sonorities. His orchestrations are undoubtedly distinctive; but his ability, by rearranging works using different textures and harmonies to create, in effect, new works, is nothing short of miraculous. John Steane wrote in *Gramophone*, 'Grainger is the Jupiter of composers: the unfeigned, unforced, Bringer of Jollity,' and we heartily concur with his view. This set is available at the astonishing price of nineteen CDs for the cost of four, and it includes a superbly produced booklet with extensive notes on each piece and full texts. One of the great bargains of all time! Hickox is masterly in the orchestral items, with rhythms always resilient, both in bringing out the freshness of the well-known numbers like *Shepherd's Hey!*, *Handel in the Strand*, *Mock Morris* and various versions of the *Irish Tune from County Derry* (all of them quite different) as well as presenting the originality and charm of such little-known numbers as *Walking Tune*. The Suite, *In a Nutshell*, which includes pieces like the *Arrival Platform Humlet*, well known on their own, has at its core a powerful and elaborate piece, *Pastoral*, which with its disturbing undertow belies its title. But there are many such surprises and in the pastoral charm of such numbers as *English Dance No. 1*, one is constantly surprised by the twists and turns of Grainger's inventiveness, in melodic invention, orchestral colour and harmonic complexity. The items for chorus and orchestra provide wonderful sonorities. In the darkly intense *Shallow Brown* Hickox has a clear advantage in an excellent baritone soloist (Stephen Varcoe), with an equally fine vocal ensemble. Hickox's recording of the *Irish Tune from County Derry* (the 'Londonderry air') has an extended, elaborate setting. *Ye Banks and Braes* is another item given in a version previously unrecorded, with a whistled descant. Among the pieces completely new to disc are the *Marching Tune* and *Early One Morning*. Also most striking is the brief, keenly original choral piece, *The Lonely Desert-man Sees the Tents of the Happy Tribes*, here given a dedicated performance, with the tenor intoning a theme from Grainger's orchestral piece, *The Warriors*, and the distant chorus chattering a chant borrowed from his *Tribute to Foster*. Lusty items such as *The Widow's Party* raise a smile, while (in contrast to the other choral items) *The Running of Shindand* and *Tiger-Tiger* are both short, poignant works for cello quintet; the collection of works for chorus and orchestra is interspersed with other orchestral items, such as a particularly perky version of *Handel in the Strand*, and a première recording of a gorgeous work called *Dreamery*. The seven-minute *Scotch Strathspey and Reel* for chorus and orchestra is an exhilarating tour de force of invention and excitement. A third volume of works for chorus and orchestra contains many highlights, including his extraordinary *Random Round*: originally conceived as a piece to be improvised, the composer eventually wrote it out in a more conventional manner, but the result is not at all conventional and it builds up to a white-hot level of inspired excitement, its haunting harmonies lingering long in the mind after the music has ended.

From his earliest years Grainger was drawn to Scandinavian and Icelandic literature, and it is apt that a recording was made with the Danish National Radio Choir and Symphony Orchestra. This stimulating and rewarding collection centres on music directly influenced by his immersion in Scandinavian cultures and the repertoire is all little known, except perhaps the *Danish Folk-song Suite*, with its highly exotic orchestration, winningly presented here. Among the other orchestral items, the rollicking *Crew of the Long Serpent*, the colourful *Variations*, and the much more extended and lusciously scored *Tribute to a Nordic Princess* stand out. In the complex opening choral piece, *Father and Daughter*, a traditional Danish folk dance is mixed up with a theme of Grainger's own. The jolly, concerted *Merry Wedding* is sung in English: it draws on a folk poem for its text, but is musically original. *Dalvisa* is a delightful vocalise, using the same melody Alfvén featured as the centrepiece in his *Midsummer Rhapsody*. Splendid performances.

The St Martin's Academy Chorus sings beautifully in the favourite folk-songs, such as *Mo Nighean Dubh* (*My Dark-haired Maiden*), *Ye Banks and Braes*, *Early One Morning* and the *Londonderry Air*, all of which resound in the memory. There are many attractive novelties, too, such as Grainger's version of the *Agincourt Song*, the four diverse *Jungle Book* verses and *Love at First Sight* receiving their first recording. The latter was written by Grainger's wife, Ella, though harmonized and arranged for soprano solo and mixed chorus by her husband; she questions in a moment of happiness whether such love can really last after the seductive initial impulse. The result is charming.

The two wind-band collections are especially fun discs. The splendid players of the Royal Northern College of Music Wind Orchestra clearly enjoy

Grainger's rhythmic buoyancy, while relishing his feeling for wind colour. A good example is in the engaging *Hill Songs*, as well as the rich sonorities found in the powerful and remarkable *The Power of Rome and the Christian Heart*, and equally so in this characteristically imaginative arrangement of the *Londonderry Air* for band and pipe organ. *Bell Piece* (a 'ramble' on Dowland's melancholy air, *Now, O Now I Needs Must Part*) begins with a tenor solo with piano, before the wind players gently steal in. In the *Children's March* members of the band are invited twice to sing a vocalise when they are not playing. Many of the pieces are well known in Grainger's alternative arrangements, but this version of Grainger's most popular piece, *Country Gardens*, is not just an arrangement of the piano version, but, as he explained himself, 'a new piece in every way'. The *Faeroe Island Dance* in this late band version of 1954 has a pivoting ostinato for horns that echoes the opening of Vaughan Williams's *Fifth Symphony*, before launching into the dance proper, with echoes of *The Rite of Spring*. Altogether fascinating and greatly enjoyable programmes, strikingly well directed by Timothy Reynish and Clark Rundell.

The two volumes of chamber-music works show no lack of invention from the composer's colour palette. Indeed, Grainger's scoring is as ever vividly captivating, and never more so than in his arrangements of *Lisbon* and *Walking Tune* (both for wind quintet), or in the accompaniment to the delightful melody of *The Shoemaker from Jerusalem* (with flute, trumpet, strings and piano (four hands)). All the well-known numbers, such as *Handel in the Strand*, emerge as freshly enjoyable as in their bigger-clothed versions. Pieces like *La Scandinavie* show Grainger's mastery of the folk-music idiom, infusing his distinctive style into folk tunes to produces a totally convincing and utterly charming work. One relishes the lusty writing (and performance) of *Lord Peter's Stable-boy*, as well as the comic numbers such as *Hubby and Wifey*, as much as the reflective numbers such as *The Nightingale* (scored for cello and harmonium) and the poignant *Died for Love*. The performances, with the Academy of St Martin-in-the-Fields Chamber Ensemble and the assortment of vocal soloists, are quite superb.

The three volumes of songs are all characterfully done by Stephen Varcoe, Della Jones and Martyn Hill. Stephen Varcoe is obviously at home in his recordings of the folksongs. Most of them are set fairly simply, as in the lovely opening of *Willow, Willow*, or the bold, jiggy narrative of *The Lost Lady Found*, while the pretty maid milking her cow is very touching. Varcoe's vernacular account of Kipling's *Soldier, soldier come from the wars* is especially successful, searing in its intensity and one of the finest anti-war songs ever penned. *Hard Hearted Barb'ra* is delightfully done too, as is Grainger's own setting of Longfellow's *The Secret of the Sea*. *Shallow Brown*, which ends his programme, is very dramatic indeed. All the songs are helped by Penelope Thwaites's strong accompaniment; indeed, she makes an admirable contribution throughout both this and the other two CDs in this set.

Della Jones clearly relishes this repertoire and she brings out beautifully all the various and varied emotions the songs are intended to convey. In *Hubby and Wifey* she is joined by Stephen Varcoe, and the comic effect is delicious; while the *Colonial Song* is wonderfully sentimental. *The Lonely Desert-man Sees the Tents* is typical of Grainger's ability to paint beautiful mind-pictures with evocative accompaniments and haunting melody, and it is beautifully sung by Mark Padmore, as well as by Della Jones and Stephen Varcoe.

Martyn Hill provides almost operatic drama in his *Nine Settings of Rudyard Kipling*, but no more than the music can bear. The folksy elements of the *Three Settings of Robert Burns* are beautifully done, as is the memorable *The Twa Corbies*, performed with much character and feeling. Surprises and novelty abound in Grainger songs, and there is not a dull one anywhere.

The three volumes of solo piano music are performed by the indefatigable champion of Grainger, Penelope Thwaites. Another CD features no fewer than five pianists to perform Grainger's multi-piano works. Penelope Thwaites notes that 'the balancing of textures to bring out key melodic strands can often be achieved more clearly in Grainger's multi-piano versions', a remark noticeably true in *The Warriors*. *Random Round* is strikingly effective here and so too is the gentle *Ye Banks and Braes o' Bonnie Doon*, clearly one of his favourite folk tunes, which turns up in various guises throughout this box set, while it is almost impossible not to tap one's toes at the beginning of the jaunty *Jutish Medley* which follows. Chandos admirably surmount the complication of recording three pianos at once.

As for the three volumes of solo piano music, Penelope Thwaites understands the idiom totally. From the *Prelude in G* which opens the first of her three CDs, one is captivated by the charm of the music – in this case a very early work – as well as by all the various 'character' pieces. Naturally, there are piano versions of all the famous pieces, as well as all sorts of delightful surprises, all beautifully played and recorded.

(i–iii; vii) ***Bold William Taylor***; (iii–v) ***Brigg Fair***; (vi) ***Country Gardens***; (ii; v) ***Danny Boy***; (ii; v; viii) ***Died for love***; (i; iv; v; ix) ***Dollar and a half a day***; (ii; vii) ***The 'Duke of Marlborough' fanfare***; (ii; v) ***Green Bushes***; (ii; v; ix) ***The Hunter in his career***; (ii; vii; x) ***I'm Seventeen come Sunday***; (vii; xi) ***Let's dance gay in green meadow***; (ii; vii) ***Lisbon***; (ii; iii; vii) ***Lord Maxwell's goodnight***; (ii; vii; x) ***The Lost lady found***; (ii; v) ***The Merry king***; *Molly on the shore*; (ii; vii) ***My Robin is to the green wood gone***; (ii; iii; v) ***The Power of Love***; (ii; vii; x) *Scotch Strathspey and Reel*; (i; ii; vii; x) ***Shallow Brown***; (i; iv; v; ix) ***Shenandoah***; (iii; xii) ***Six Dukes went a-fishin'***; (iii; vii) **2 *Songs: The pretty maid milkin' her cow***; *The sprig of thyme*. (ii; vii) ***Shepherd's Hey***; (i; iv; v; ix) ***Stormy***; (x) ***There was a pig went out to dig***; (ii–v); ***The Three Ravens***; (i; ii; v; viii) ***Under a bridge***; (xiii) ***The Warriors***; (ii; iii; vii) ***Willow Willow***

Ⓜ Australian Decca Eloquence (ADD/DDD) 480 2205 (2). (i) Shirley-Quirk; (ii) ECO;
(iii) Pears; (iv) Linden Singers; (v) Bedford; (vi) composer; (vii) Britten; (viii) Reynolds;
(ix) Wandsworth Boys' Ch.; (x) Amb. S.; (xi) Tunnard; (xii) Ellis; (xiii) Philh. O, Gardiner

Percy Grainger's talent was smaller than his more fervent advocates would have us believe, but his imagination for arranging folksongs was prodigious. This two-CD collection includes Britten's classic 1968 recording, which is one of the best of all Grainger recitals in itself. Highlights include the *Willow Song*, which is a touching and indeed haunting piece and shows the quality of Grainger's harmonic resource. The *'Duke of Marlborough' Fanfare* is also strikingly original, and so too is *Shallow Brown*. The lusty choral singing in *I'm seventeen come Sunday* is very enjoyable, as is the marvellous *There was a pig went out to dig* – which is both catchy and haunting. The *Scotch Strathspey and Reel* is delightfully appealing with its quirky colourings and twists and turns with which the popular traditional songs are treated; it builds up to quite a frenzy in its central section, and the toe-tapping reel at the end is exhilarating. Indeed, each of the items is obstinately memorable, and the recording is extremely fine. The Steuart Bedford items are no less appealing, with richly recorded (in 1972) items such as *Molly on the Shore*, very atmospheric accounts of *Shenandoah* and *Brigg Fair* (with superb choral contributions), a gloriously nostalgic version of the *Irish Tune from County Derry* (*Danny Boy*), and a very piquant account of *Green Bushes*. The composer himself plays his most famous number of all, *Country Gardens*, in a performance dating from 1927. Fast-forward to the digital age and we have Gardiner's 1994 recording of *The Warriors*, a colourful and vigorous work described as 'an imaginary ballet for orchestra and three pianos', a characteristically extrovert show-piece, Grainger's largest work. With richly scored echoes of *Rosenkavalier* and *Petrushka* brought improbably together at the start, the piece throbs with energy, at one point – in a gentler interlude – involving an offstage orchestra in Ivesian superimpositions. If much of the writing, with the piano prominent in the orchestra, sounds as though it is about to turn into Grainger's *Handel in the Strand*, plus an echo or two of Eric Coates, the result is hugely enjoyable in such a fine performance as this. Dazzling sound.

GRÉTRY, André (1741–1813)

Suite of Ballet Music from the Operas
Australian Decca Eloquence (ADD) 480 2373. ECO, Leppard - **CHARPENTIER**:
   Médée: Suite. **RAMEAU**: *Le Temple de la Gloire*

This suite of ballet music from Grétry's operas was presumably chosen and arranged by the conductor, Raymond Leppard. At the time of the recording (1966) this was Sir Thomas Beecham repertoire and, like that great maestro, Leppard has skill in picking lollipops, but he added to his performances a feeling for the style of the period about which Sir Thomas would not have been quite so scrupulous. Even though the authentic movement has revolutionized performance of music from this period, these recordings remain highly enjoyable – not just mere nostalgia. Indeed, these are by any standards stylish readings; with well-sprung rhythms and nicely pointed string-playing in the delightful overture, the suite also includes two irresistibly catchy *Tambourins*. The gentle *Ballet des Nymphes de Diane* and *Chaconne* have a lovely laid-back insouciance which is utterly French in spirit, while the central *Minuet* – again very nicely pointed but not overly so – offers piquant use of the harp for further textural delight. This is the first time this recording has been issued on CD and should be snapped up immediately.

GRIEG, Edvard (1843–1907)

Piano Concerto in A min., Op. 16
Ⓜ EMI 5 03419-2. Andsnes, BPO, Jansons – **SCHUMANN**: *Piano Concerto*

The coupling of the Grieg and Schumann *Piano Concertos* has long been dominated by the superb pairing by Kovacevich and Colin Davis (Philips 475 7773). That remains highly desirable, but Leif Ove Andsnes enjoys the support of the Berlin Philharmonic Orchestra and a more modern sound. His virtuosity is commanding but it is never at the expense of tenderness and poetic feeling. The performance, recorded live in Berlin, is ever spontaneous-sounding, with soaring flights of the imagination, while the Berlin Philharmonic is at its warmest under Mariss Jansons. The Schumann, too, brings glorious playing from both soloist and orchestra; in short this is a gramophone classic for the present decade.

2 Elegiac Melodies; Holberg Suite, Op. 40; 2 Lyric Pieces, Op. 68; 2 Melodies, Op. 53; 2 Nordic Melodies, Op. 63
BIS SACD 1491. Bergen PO, Ruud

This is simply the most beautiful record of Grieg's string music in the catalogue and one of the most beautiful and realistic recordings of strings we have yet heard. It was made, appropriately, in the Grieg Hall in Bergen. The wonderfully vital account of the *Holberg Suite* is unsurpassed, even by Karajan's famous account, and the gentler pieces are exquisite, especially the *Two Nordic Melodies*, which are Elysian, and the closing *At the Cradle* from the *Lyric Pieces*, Op. 68. Truly marvellous playing from the Bergen orchestra and inspired conducting from Ole Kristian Ruud. The surround sound is in a class of its own. Try to hear the disc on SACD equipment with four speakers, though it sounds pretty marvellous on just two.

Lyric Pieces: Op. 12/1; Op. 38/1; Op. 43/1–2; Op. 47/2–4; Op. 54/4–5; Op. 57/6; Op. 62/4 & 6; Op. 65/5; Op. 68/2, 3 & 5; Op. 71/1, 3 & 6–7
Ⓜ DG (ADD) 449 721-2. Gilels

An unmissable selection of Grieg's delightful *Lyric Pieces*, from the well-known *Papillon*, Op. 43/1, to excerpts from the less often heard and highly poetic set, Op. 71. With Gilels we are in the presence of a great keyboard master whose characterization and control of colour and articulation are wholly remarkable. An altogether outstanding record in every way. The recording has been admirably remastered and reissued in DG's 'Originals' series; it is a CD that should be in every collection.

Peer Gynt (incidental music): extended excerpts
Virgin 5 45722-2. Mattei, Tilling, Hellekant, Ellerhein Girls' Ch., Estonian Nat. SO and Male Ch., Paavo Järvi

Paavo Järvi conducts his Estonian forces in warmly expressive, full-blooded readings of 40 items from Grieg's complete *Peer Gynt* music, including the content of the two orchestral suites and omitting only those pieces where spoken words predominate. The extra warmth of the performance is helped by the full, forward sound, recorded in a rather reverberant acoustic. Though their roles are limited, the soloists are first rate, with the baritone, Peter Mattei, giving a virile portrait of Peer Gynt in his *Serenade*. Järvi's account of *In the Hall of the Mountain King* is very exciting, with a wild accelerando and vigorous vocal contributions.

(i) Peer Gynt: Suites 1–2. In Autumn (Overture); An Old Norwegian Romance with Variations; Symphonic Dance 2
Ⓑ EMI Masters 965 9342. (i) Hollweg, Beecham Choral Society; RPO, Beecham

Beecham showed a very special feeling for Grieg's *Peer Gynt* music, and to hear 'Morning', the gentle textures of 'Anitra's Dance' or the eloquent portrayal of the 'Death of Aase' under his baton is a uniquely rewarding experience. Ilse Hollweg makes an excellent soloist. The recording dates from 1956 and, like most earlier Beecham reissues, has been enhanced by the remastering process. The most delectable of the *Symphonic Dances*, very beautifully played, makes an ideal encore after 'Solveig's Song', affectingly sung by Hollweg. The *In Autumn Overture*, not one of Grieg's finest works, is most enjoyable when Sir Thomas is so persuasive, not shirking the melodramatic moments. Finally, for the present reissue, we are offered *An Old Norwegian Romance with Variations*. It is a piece of much colour and charm, which is fully realized here.

Symphony in C min.
Ⓜ Australian Decca Eloquence 476 8743. Bergen SO, Anderson – **GOLDMARK**: *Rustic Wedding Symphony*

The *Symphony* is a student work, written while Grieg was living in Denmark, but he forbade performances of the work after hearing Svendsen's *First Symphony* in 1867, and the score was bequeathed to Bergen Public Library on the understanding that it was never to be performed. The work takes just over 37 minutes, and those expecting characteristic Grieg will be disappointed. In some ways the finale is the most confident of the four movements, though its seams are clearly audible. The ideas are fresher than in the inner movements and, although it is no masterpiece, the work is uncommonly assured for a youth of 20. It is persuasively played in Bergen, and the Decca recording is truthfully balanced, with good perspective and colour. At this price, it makes a fine coupling for the rare and colourful *Rustic Wedding Symphony* of Goldmark.

GROFÉ, Ferde (1892–1972)

Grand Canyon Suite
Telarc CD 80086 (with additional cloudburst, including real thunder). Cincinnati Pops O, Kunzel (with **GERSHWIN**: *Catfish Row*)

The Cincinnati performance is played with great commitment and fine pictorial splendour. What gives the Telarc CD its special edge is the inclusion of a second performance of *Cloudburst* as an appendix, with a genuine thunderstorm laminated on to the orchestral recording. The result is overwhelmingly thrilling, except that in the final thunderclap God quite upstages the orchestra, who are left frenziedly trying to match its amplitude in their closing peroration.

GUERRERO, Francisco (1528–99)

Missa De la batalla escoutez; Conditor alme siderum; Duo Seraphim clamabant; In exitu Israel; Magnificat octavi toni; Pange lingua gloriosi; Regina caeli
ⓑⓑ Hyp. Helios CDH 55340. Westminster Cathedral Ch., His Majestys Sagbutts and Cornetts, O'Donnell

Born in 1528 and trained by his brother, Pedro, and later, briefly, by Cristóbal de Morales, Guerrero spent virtually his whole musical life serving in Seville Cathedral as singer and composer, and he was able to play many instruments expertly. He was essentially Master of the Music, yet nominally the ageing Pedro Fernández held the post and Guerrero was his assistant until 1574, when at last he took over in his own right.

The performances here (even in the Mass) use brass instruments as well as voices, following the alternation style, which was a particular feature of Guerrero's music, where plainchant regularly alternates with polyphony. The Trinity motet, *Duo Seraphim*, opening descriptively with two solo trebles, uses twelve voices in three choirs to create wide contrasts of dynamic and texture. The *Missa De la batalla* for five voices uses a chanson of Jannequin, *La Guerre*, as its basis, indicated by including the French word 'escoutez' in its title. *Pange lingua gloriosi* uses a popular melody, a gently swinging Iberian song ornamented with counterpoint and moving from voice to voice, in many ways like a primitive theme and variations. Throughout the disc the eloquent singing, very well balanced and never overwhelming the brass choir, makes this a varied and highly enjoyable introduction to a remarkable composer of whom we shall undoubtedly hear more.

GURNEY, Ivor (1890–1937)

War Elegy

Ⓜ Dutton CDLX 7172. BBC SO, Lloyd-Jones – **ELGAR**: *The Spirit of England*.
　PARRY: *The Chivalry of the Sea* (with **KELLY**: *Elegy 'In Memoriam Rupert Brooke'*. **ELKINGTON**: *Out of the Mist*)

His deeply moving orchestral piece offers us a totally new view of the tragic Ivor Gurney. It is quite different from the charming songs and poems he wrote, even after he had been incarcerated in a mental home for the last 20 years of his life. That mental illness had been caused by his terrible experiences in the trenches in the First World War, something which this piece directly reflects in a powerful funeral march. After a single rehearsal run-through in 1920, it was totally neglected and here receives its very first professional performance, superbly conducted. On a fascinating disc of war-inspired pieces it stands out as a heart-stopping work, chilling in its power.

HADLEY, Patrick (1899–1973)

The Trees so High

Lyrita (ADD) SRCD 238. Allen, Guildford Philharmonic Ch., New Philh. O Handley –
　FINZI: *Intimations of Immortality*

For most of his working career, Hadley was the archetypal Cambridge composer, seduced by the charms of life as a senior member of the university from writing the music he plainly had in him. *The Trees so High*, described as a symphonic ballad, is a wide-ranging choral work, taking the folksong of that name as a base. The idiom is broadly in the Vaughan Williams school, but spiced with invention eclectically drawn from later composers. Thomas Allen makes an outstanding soloist and Vernon Handley draws persuasive singing and playing from his large forces. The music is beautifully recorded and the outstanding coupling is wholly apt.

HANDEL, George Frideric (1685-1759)

Concerti grossi, Op. 3/1-6 (including 4b), HWV 312-17
🆑 Hyp. Helios CDH 55075. Brandenburg Consort, Goodman

Concerti grossi, Op. 6/1-12
Chan. 9004/6. I Musici di Montréal, Turovsky

Handel re-fashioned the *concerto grosso* format and style which had been developed and refined by Corelli, to create two masterly sets of works in his own style. The result represents the very peak of his orchestral output. The music is endlessly inventive and gives the listener enormous stimulation and pleasure. As both these groups demonstrate (and the Boyd Neel Strings and ASMF before them), these works must be as much of a joy to play as to listen to.

In Opus 3 Roy Goodman achieves the best of both worlds by including the spurious (but very engaging) No. 4b and uses an authentic version of No. 6, while featuring the concertante organ at the close as a bonus. The playing is rhythmically very spirited and enjoyably light and airy: this is period-instrument music-making at its most seductive, helped by some delightfully sensitive flute and oboe contributions from Rachel Brown and Katharina Arfken respectively. First-class recording, natural and transparent within a pleasing ambience.

I Musici di Montréal follow on with an equally refreshing and stimulating set of Opus 6. The group uses modern instruments and Yuli Turovsky's aim is to seek a compromise between modern and authentic practice by paring down vibrato in some of the expressive music. The concertino, Eleonora and Natalya Turovsky and Alain Aubut, play impressively, while the main group (6,3,1,1) produces full, well-balanced tone, and Handel's joyous fugues are particularly fresh and buoyant. Turovsky paces convincingly, not missing Handel's breadth of sonority and moments of expressive grandeur, and the Chandos recording is excellent.

Harp Concerto, Op. 4/6; Variations for Harp
Ⓜ Decca (ADD) 425 723-2. Robles, ASMF, Brown – **BOIELDIEU**;
    DITTERSDORF: *Harp Concertos*

Handel's Op. 4/6 is well known in both organ and harp versions. Marisa Robles and Iona Brown make an unforgettable case for the latter by creating the most delightful textures, while never letting the work sound insubstantial. The ASMF accompaniment, so stylish and beautifully balanced, is a treat in itself, and the recording is well-nigh perfect.

Organ Concertos, Op. 4/1-6; Op. 7/1-6
🆑 Warner Apex 2564 62760-2 (2). Koopman, Amsterdam Bar. O

Ton Koopman's paired sets of Opp. 4 and 7 are offered economically on the Apex super-bargain label. They take precedence over all the competition, both as performances and as recordings. The playing has wonderful life and warmth, tempi are always aptly judged, and although original instruments are used, this is authenticity with a kindly presence. The warm acoustic ambience of St Bartholomew's Church, Beek-Ubbergen, Holland, gives the orchestra a glowingly vivid coloration and the string timbre is particularly attractive. So is the organ itself, which is spendidly played by Koopman and is just right for the music.

Music for the Royal Fireworks; Water Music (complete)
Ⓜ DG 477 7562. E. Concert, Trevor Pinnock

We would have liked very much to recommend the Orpheus Chamber Orchestra (also on DG) for this coupling, for they play all this music (on modern instruments) with a real sense of baroque style, crisp and buoyant, and with much elegance too. In addition the *Fireworks Music* brings a riveting sense of spectacle. However, this disc is currently deleted, and it seldom seems to stay in the catalogue for very long.

Fortunately Pinnock and his English Concert provide an admirable alternative. They play on period instruments with great zest, especially so in the *Fireworks Music*. Speeds are consistently well chosen. One test is the famous 'Air', which here remains an engagingly gentle piece. The recording is beautifully balanced and clear, and this coupling is very delectable indeed.

(i) Coronation Anthems (complete); (ii) Ode for the Birthday of Queen Anne
Ⓜ Australian Decca Eloquence (ADD) 466 676-2. (i) King's College, Cambridge, Ch., ECO, Willcocks; (ii) Kirkby, Nelson, Minty, Bowman, Hill, Thomas, Christ Church Cathedral Ch., Oxford, AAM, Preston

Willcocks's famous (1960) recording of these four anthems sounds much better on CD than it ever did on LP and is greatly enjoyable, especially *Zadok the Priest*. They are coupled with a fine performance of the *Ode for the Birthday of Queen Anne*, recorded in the late 1970s and sounding very good indeed. An excellent CD from Australian Decca.

Judas Maccabaeus (complete, CD version)
Ⓜ DG (ADD) 447 692-2 (3). Palmer, Baker, Esswood, Davies, Shirley-Quirk, Keyte, Wandsworth School Ch., ECO, Mackerras

Charles Mackerras's sparkling 1976 performance of *Judas Maccabaeus*, with its sequence of Handelian gems, is irresistible. Though not everyone will approve of the use of boys' voices in the choir, it gives an extra bit of character. Hearing even so hackneyed a number as *See, the conqu'ring hero* in its true scale is a delightful surprise. Ryland Davies and John Shirley-Quirk are most stylish, while both Felicity Palmer and Janet Baker crown the whole set with glorious singing. The recording quality is outstanding, fresh, vivid and clear.

Messiah (complete, DVD version)

Warner DVD 063017834-2. Nelson, Kirkby, Watkinson, Elliott, Thomas, Westminster
  Abbey Ch., AAM, Hogwood; Simon Preston (organ) (V/D: Roy Tipping)

Messiah (complete, CD version)

DG 477 5904 (2). Augér, Von Otter, Chance, Crook, Tomlinson, E. Concert Ch. & O,
  Pinnock

There have been many fine recordings of *Messiah* deserving of Handel's great
masterpiece over the years, but we must not forget one of the first and most
memorable, made in Huddersfield Town Hall in 1946 and splendidly conducted by Sir Malcolm Sargent. It is not quite complete, but no matter, it has
the tension of a live performance and includes the glorious soprano contribution of Isobel Baillie, whose 'I know that my Redeemer liveth' has never been
surpassed. This was also famous in its day as a 'single' and Isobel once told
I.M. that she felt slightly uncomfortable about its huge commercial success,
that it didn't somehow seem quite right that her royalties reached such a huge
figure. The other soloists were just as distinguished, including Gladys Ripley
(whose 'He was despised' was equally celebrated), while the Huddersfield
Choral Society was still singing at its peak (Dutton mono 2-CDEA 5010).

However, most collectors will want a modern CD recording, and an obvious
first choice remains with Trevor Pinnock's DG set with the English Concert
Chorus and Orchestra, who feature authentically scaled forces which, without
inflation, rise to the work's grandeur and magnificence, qualities Handel himself would have relished, while the period orchestra has plenty of body to the
sound. The soloists too are excellent, Arleen Augér radiantly pure, Anne Sofie
von Otter rich and steady, and John Tomlinson, firm, dark and powerful.

Those remembering with affection the vintage Huddersfield Choral Society
Messiah under Sargent will be glad to welcome a fine, new, traditional version
on Signum (SIGCD 246 (2)) in which the choir is supported by bright, lively
playing from the Northern Sinfonia, stylishly conducted by Jane Glover.
The four excellent soloists include Elizabeth Watts (soprano), Catherine
Wyn-Rogers (contralto), James Oldfield (bass) and – especially impressive –
Mark Le Brocq (tenor).

For DVD one can turn to Hogwood's enjoyably fresh 'traditional-period'
1982 account with the Academy of Ancient Music, and the soprano contribution shared by Judith Nelson and a very young Emma Kirkby. David Thomas is
particularly strong in the bass arias. Most enjoyable both to listen to and to
watch.

La Resurrezione

Virgin 50999 694567 01 (2). Camilla Tilling, Kate Royal, Sonia Prina, Toby Spence, Luca
  Pisaroni, Le Concert d'Astrée, Emmanuelle Haïm

In 1708, halfway through his four-year stay in Italy, the young Handel wrote
this refreshingly dramatic oratorio. With opera as such prohibited in Rome, it

served as a kind of substitute and, though it does not have the great choral music which is so much the central element of later Handel oratorios, the choruses which close each part of the work are memorable – and even more so is the bright orchestration, with brilliant use of woodwind and trumpets. Indeed the very opening has a most attractive introductory *Sonata*. Altogether it is a fine and many-faceted piece and Emmanuelle Haïm does it full justice with her excellent team of soloists. One has only to sample the brilliant virtuosity of Mary Cleophas's aria in Part I (Sonia Prina) or Mary Magdalene's touching *Per me già di morire* in Part 2 (Kate Royal) to hear the calibre of this singing; and the playing of Le Concert d'Astrée is equally impressive, and the recording is most effectively balanced.

Solomon

Ⓜ Decca 475 7561 (2). Watkinson, Argenta, Hendricks, Rolfe Johnson, Monteverdi Ch.,
  E. Bar. Sol., Gardiner

Gardiner's *Solomon* is the very finest of all Handel oratorio recordings after *Messiah* and *Judas Maccabaeus*. With panache he shows how authentic-sized forces can convey Handelian glamour even with sharply focused textures and fast speeds. The choruses and even more magnificent double choruses stand as cornerstones of a structure which may have less of a story-line than some other Handel oratorios – the Judgement apart – but which Gardiner shows has consistent human warmth. The Act III scenes between Solomon and the Queen of Sheba are given extra warmth by having in the latter role a singer who is sensuous in tone, Barbara Hendricks. Carolyn Watkinson's pure mezzo is very apt for Solomon himself, while Nancy Argenta is clear and sweet as the Queen; but the overriding glory of the set is the radiant singing of the Monteverdi Choir. Its clean, crisp articulation matches the brilliant playing of the English Baroque Soloists, regularly challenged by Gardiner's fast speeds, as in the *Arrival of the Queen of Sheba*: the sound is superb, coping thrillingly with the interplay of the double chorus.

Acis and Galatea (complete, CD version)

Ⓜ Chan. (ADD) 3147. Sutherland, Pears, Galliver, Brannigan, St Anthony Singers, L.
  Philomusica, Boult

In 1959, originally from Decca (Oiseau-Lyre), Boult provided the début stereo recording of Handel's delightful masque. Joan Sutherland in fresh, youthful voice makes a splendid Galatea, sparkling in the florid passages, warmly sympathetic in the lyrical music. Peter Pears, too, is at his finest, and although David Galliver is less striking, his contribution is still a good one, while Owen Brannigan was surely born to play Polyphemus, and he comes over as a very genial one-eyed giant, the villany muted. His lusty account of *O ruddier than the cherry* (heard in the version with treble recorder), in which he makes a positive virtue of intrusive aspirates, is alone worth the cost of the disc. Anyone hearing it who can resist smiling must be stony-hearted indeed. Although tempi are more relaxed than we would expect today, Boult's sympathetic direction ensures that the music-making has a lift throughout. The documentation includes a full text.

Berenice, Regina d'Egitto (CD version)

Virgin 50999 6 28536-2 (3). Ek, Bohlin, Fagioli, Basso, Nesi, Priante, Giustiniani, Il
    Complesso Barocco, Alan Curtis

Handel's ill-fated 1736/7 London season was the most ambitious he had ever attempted single-handed, including eight different opera productions, five of which were new to London. The result was the end of his career as an independent impresario, not helped by his suffering from a stroke in 1737 which paralysed his right arm and temporarily prevented him from playing the harpsichord. But at the same time he was able to complete Berenice, Regina d'Egitto. Its narrative deals with the problem of the young Egyptian queen, Berenice, who has to choose for her consort the Roman Alessandro, rather than her lover, Demetrio (who unfortunately loves her sister, Selene). However, the result is one of Handel's finest operas, with the most famous of many splendid arias, Vedi l'ape, sung by the Roman envoy, Fabio, its famous melody introduced as a largetto in the overture. The duet, Se il mio amor, between Berenice and Demetrio is particularly beautiful, as is so much of the music in this opera. Surprisingly, it ran for only three (maybe four) performances, so this splendid recording is most welcome, especially as Alan Curtis has restored music which Handel originally cut. The performance is admirably sung, dominated by Klara Ek's rapturous portrayal of Berenice, admirably partnered by Franco Fagioli's Demetrio, and with Romina Basso excellent in the mezzo part of Selena, and Ingela Bohlin an appealingly voiced Alessandro – his cavatina, Mio bel sol, a highlight of Act II. The opera is lightly scored (omitting flutes, recorders and brass) but using the plaintive oboe instead. Alan Curtis secures consistently fine playing from Il Complesso Barocco and directs the opera itself with a perfect combination of sensitivity and vitality.

Giulio Cesare (complete, CD version)

Ⓑ HM HMX 2901 385–7. Larmore, Schlick, Fink, Rorholm, Ragin, Zanasi, Visse, Concerto
    Köln, Jacobs

The casting of the pure-toned Barbara Schlick as Cleopatra on Harmonia Mundi proves outstandingly successful. Jennifer Larmore too, a fine, firm mezzo with a touch of masculine toughness in the tone, makes a splendid Caesar. Together they crown the whole performance with the most seductive account of their final duet. Derek Lee Ragin is excellent in the sinister role of Tolomeo (Ptolemy); so are Bernarda Fink as Cornelia and Marianne Rorholm as Sesto, with the bass, Furio Zanasi, as Achilla. René Jacobs's expansive speeds mean that the whole opera will not fit on three CDs, but the fourth disc, at 18 minutes merely supplementary, comes free as part of the package and includes an extra aria for the servant, Nireno, delightfully sung by the French couner-tenor, Dominique Visse. Fine, well-balanced sound. This now comes at bargain price with texts and translations included.

Hercules (complete, CD version)
Ⓜ DG 477 9112 (2). Tomlinson, Walker, Rolfe Johnson, J. Smith, Denley, Savidge, Monetverdi Ch., E. Bar. Sol., Gardiner

Gardiner's vital performance of *Hercules*, using authentic forces, conveys superbly the vigour of the writing, its natural drama; and the fire of this performance is typified by the outstanding singing of Sarah Walker as Dejanira. John Tomlinson makes an excellent, dark-toned Hercules. Fresh voices consistently help in the clarity of attack: Jennifer Smith as Iole, Catherine Denley as Lichas, Anthony Rolfe Johnson as Hyllus, Peter Savidge as the Priest of Jupiter. Refined playing and outstanding recording quality make this extremely welcome at mid-price.

9 German Arias; *Gloria*; *Trio Sonata in F, HWV 392*
BIS CD 1615. Emma Kirkby, L. Baroque

The *Nine German Arias* (written between 1724 and 1726) are the nearest Handel came to writing an intimate song-cycle. All the lyrics derive from Heinrich Brockes' set of poems ('Earthly delight in God', designed to be set as cantatas, with recitatives, which Handel chose not to use). Many of the poems are poetic paraphrases of Bible texts and every one of these arias has a winning Handelian flavour. There have been several recordings, and that by Carolyn Sampson on Hyperion (CDA 67627) is as fresh as it is tonally beautiful. However, Emma Kirkby's voice seems perfect for this repertoire and her performance is naturally appealing and just as fresh. Moreover this BIS CD includes also the beautiful *Gloria*, recently discovered in the music library of the Royal Academy of Music in London. It is a ravishing work in six sections, and Emma Kirkby sings it with full-voiced beauty. The London Baroque, who accompany splendidly, also provide a fine account of the *F major Trio Sonata* as a welcome interlude between the vocal works.

'Furore': Opera arias from: *Admeto*; *Amadigi*; *Ariodante*; *Giulio Cesare*; *Hercules*; *Imeneo*; *Semele*; *Serse*; *Teseo*
Virgin 50999 5 519038 2. Joyce DiDonato, Les Talens Lyriques, Christophe Rousset

All today's singers seem to want to aspire to a collection of Handel arias, and there are many desirable collections now available. Joyce DiDonato is one of the key virtuosic mezzos to have joined the throng, and she has already received a *Gramophone* award. She has a voice which is beautiful in legato yet very dramatic when opening her recital with *Crude furie degl'orridi abissi* ('Fierce furies of the dead abyss') from *Serse*. But in the following *Dolce riposo* (from *Teseo*) as Medea she has fallen obsessively in love with the hero, Theseus, and sings of her feelings touchingly, against an oboe obbligato. Yet when she discovers he will not return her love she vents her fury, proclaiming she will either have his love or destroy him: '*O stringerò nel sen*'. As Ariodante she again despairs at her lost love ('*E vivo ancora?* ('Am I still living?')). So throughout this boldly and dramatically sung recital the music swings between demanding, passionate feeling and unattained loss. Joyce DiDonato holds the listener in her grip through every response, and her bravura in anger is matched by her moments of tenderness. Christophe Rousset provides fine supportive accompaniments with Les Talens Lyriques, and if you enjoy vocal fireworks this can be strongly recommended. Full texts and translations are provided.

Overtures and Arias (1704–1726) from: *Almira*; *Amadigi di Gaula*; *Giulio Cesare in Egitto*; *Rinaldo*; *Rodelinda*; *Rodrigo*; *Scipione*; *Silla*; *Tamerlano*
(Hyp. CDA 66860)

Overtures and Arias (1729–1741) from: *Alcina*; *Arianna in Creta*; *Atalanta*; *Berenice, Regina d'Egitto*; *Deidamia*; *Ezio*; *Lotario*; *Partenope*; *Sosarme, re di Media*
(Hyp. CDA 67128). Emma Kirkby, Brandenburg Cons., Goodman (available separately)

It might be thought that a collection interspersing Handel arias and overtures would not be particularly stimulating. But Emma Kirkby (in glorious voice) and Roy Goodman (directing invigorating playing by the Brandenburg Consort) prove just how enjoyable such a concert, or pair of concerts, can be. The first disc covers the first half of Handel's operatic career. Volume 2 deals with Handel's later operas and opens with the virtually unknown overture to *Lotario* (1729). Queen Adelaide's feisty aria which follows shows Emma Kirkby at her nimblest, although she is hardly less dazzling in *Dite pace* from *Sosarme*. Perhaps the most delightful item here is *Chi t'intende?* from *Berenice*, where Kirkby clearly enjoys her continuing duet with the solo oboe.

HANSON, Howard (1896–1981)

(i) *Symphonies 1 (Nordic), Op. 21*; *Lament for Beowulf*; (ii) *2 (Romantic), Op. 30*; *Lux aeterna*; *Mosaics*; (iii) *3 in A min., Op. 33*; *Merry Mount Suite, Op. 31*; (iv) *4 (Requiem), Op. 34*; *5 (Sinfonia sacra), Op. 43*; *Elegy in Memory of Serge Koussevitzky*; *Dies natalis*
ⓑⓑ Naxos (i) 8.559700, with Seattle symphony Chorale in *Lament for Beowulf*;
  (ii) 8.559701; (iii) 8.559702; (iv) 8.559703. Seattle Symphony, Schwarz

Howard Hanson was the first American to win a 'Prix de Rome', in 1921, study-ing orchestration and composition with Respighi. He can best be described as a neo-romantic with a strong lyrical vein to his make-up. His musical sympa-thies lay with Scandinavia and Sibelius in particular (he was of Swedish descent), though it is the extrovert Sibelius of the warmly appealing first two symphonies that left the strongest imprint on his musical language. Gerard Schwarz has proved himself a master of Hanson's Nordic idiom and a consist-ently convincing and highly idiomatic interpreter of his works, and in the symphonies he secures playing of the highest quality from the Seattle Sym-phony. *Symphonies 1* and *2* are both hauntingly melodic, especially no. 2 (the popular favourite. The musical terrain of the *Third Symphony* is very similar to that of its predecessors, the string melodies surge purposely onward, and there are similar rhythmic patterns, while the *Fourth* again has strong Nordic influ-ences. The single movement *Sinfonia sacra* – inspired by Christ's Passion – is tellingly succinct. Of the shorter works, the *Lament for Beowulf* is an eloquent, elegiac piece with chorus, the *Elegy for Koussevitzky* is pensively touching, while the colourful *Merry Mount Suite* is also splendidly done. *Mosaics* is an inventive set of variations written in 1957 for Szell and the Cleveland Orches-tra. Throughout, these Seattle performances have plenty of breadth and vigour, and we await the reissue of two remaining symphonies and the concertante works which were included in the original Delos coverage.

HARTY, Hamilton (1879–1941)

A Comedy Overture; (i) *Piano Concerto*; (ii) *Violin Concerto*; (iii) *In Ireland (Fantasy)*. *An Irish Symphony*; (ii) *Variations on a Dublin Air*. *With the Wild Geese*. (iv) *The Children of Lir*; *Ode to a Nightingale*. Arrangement: *Londonderry Air*

Ⓜ Chan. 10194 X (3). (i) Binns; (ii) Holmes; (iii) Fleming, Kelly; (iv) Harper; Ulster O,
Thomson

Like Parry and Stanford, Hamilton Harty's music is essential listening for anyone interested in British orchestral writing in general. For many years, his excellent arrangements of the Handel *Water/Fireworks* music were the norm and on which many people (of a certain age!) grew up. His own music essen-tially (though not always) veers to the lighter side of the repertoire and is imbued with much melodic appeal and colourful orchestrations.

Bryden Thomson's box gathers together Harty's major orchestral and con-certante works with great success. The *Piano Concerto*, written in 1922, has strong Rachmaninovian influences, but the melodic freshness remains indi-vidual in this highly sympathetic performance. The *Violin Concerto* has no strongly individual idiom; the invention is fresh and is often touched with genuine poetry. The finale is an unmitigated joy: a gorgeous lilting tune, utterly memorable and totally captivating in its unforced, folksy charm. Ralph Holmes gives a thoroughly committed account of the solo part and is well supported by an augmented Ulster Orchestra under Bryden Thomson.

The *Irish Symphony* has won great acclaim for its excellent scoring and good craftsmanship. Its four movements are titled *On the Shores of Lough Neagh*, *The Fair Day*, *In the Antrim Hills* and *The Twelfth of July*, and the music is very evocative. The Scherzo is particularly engaging, though the finale too has a deliciously piquant folk melody that sticks in the mind. It is extremely well played here and the work is unfailingly enjoyable. The *Comedy Overture* makes for a bright and varied fifteen minutes' listening, with engaging themes and orchestration. The *In Ireland Fantasy* is full of delightful, Irish melodic whimsy with a wonderfully atmospheric beginning. Colourful melodrama enters the scene in the symphonic poem, *With the Wild Geese*, but its Irishry asserts itself immediately in the opening theme.

Harty's setting of Keats's *Ode to a Nightingale* is richly convincing, a piece written for his future wife, the soprano, Agnes Nicholls. The other work, *The Children of Lir*, is directly Irish in inspiration, evocative in an almost Sibelian way; it uses the soprano in wordless melisma, here beautifully sung by Heather Harper. Both works are imaginatively and vividly orchestrated. The performances are excellent, and the very appealing *Variations on a Dublin Air* and Harty's arrangement of the haunting *Londonderry Air* have been added as a most enjoyable bonus on this CD.

HAYDN, Joseph (1732–1809)

Complete Concertos: (i) *for Cello 1–3*; (ii) *for Horn in D*; (iii) *for Keyboard (Organ 1–3)*; (iv) *for Piano 1–4*; (v) *for Harpsichord 1–2*. Double Concertos for 2 lire organizzate 1–5: (vi) *for 2 Recorders 1–2*; (vii) *for Flute & Oboe 1–2*; (viii) *for 2 Flutes*. (ix) *Trumpet Concerto in E flat*; (x) *Double Concerto for Violin & Fortepiano*; (xi) *3 Violin Concertos*
(ⒷⒷ) Naxos 8.506019 (6). (i) Maria Kliegel; (ii) Dmitri Babanov; (iii; x) Harald Hoeren; (iv) Sebastian Knauer; (v) Ketil Haugsand; (vi) Daniel Rothert, Philipp Spätling; (vii–viii) Benoît Fromnger; (vii) Christian Hommel; (viii) Ingo Nelken; (ix) Jürgen Schuster; (x) Ariadne Daskalakis; (xi) Augustin Hadelich; Cologne CO, Helmut Müller-Brühl

This Naxos box, containing just Haydn's authenticated concertos, stands alone. All are new recordings, underpinned by warmly stylish accompaniments by the excellent Cologne Chamber Orchestra, spiritedly and sensitively directed by Helmut Müller-Brühl. If the *Trumpet Concerto* (still the finest ever written for this instrument, and splendidly played here) stands out, the fine *D major Cello Concerto*, Hob XVIIb/2, is also admirably presented by Naxos's star cellist,

Maria Kliegel, who then goes on to give a ravishing account of the *Adagio* of the early *C major Concerto* (only discovered in 1961).

Of the *Piano Concertos* the justly popular *D major*, with its catchy opening theme, could readily be placed alongside those of Mozart, especially in this sensitive performance by Sebastian Knauer. But listen to his engaging fluency in the *F major*, and the stylishness of his account of the following *Largo cantabile*, which is then matched by the memorable *Adagios* of both the *G major* and *D major* works. Lovely playing indeed.

The organ (with no pedals required) and harpsichord concertos are virtually interchangeable, the baroque scoring brightened by horns or trumpets, framing simple, expressive slow movements. The *Horn Concerto* receives easy virtuosity, especially in the slow movement, which soars up demandingly high.

The three *Violin Concertos* are perhaps not top quality Haydn, although Augustin Hadelich plays them spontaneously and with much finesse, and he phrases the *Adagio* of the *C major* most pleasingly, so that this work stands out among its companions. The little *Double Concerto for Violin and Harpsichord* is also most winning. The dialogue between the two instruments is most engaging, especially in the slow movement.

Finally, and also unexpectedly, the transcribed works for a pair of lire organizzate are most sprightly and pleasing. They were commissioned by the King of Naples to be played in duet with his teacher on a curious hybrid combination of hurdy-gurdy and organ. It is obsolete now, but Haydn arranged alternative transcriptions for varying woodwind instruments in pairs which are most effective, and the music is by no means trivial. Altogether this is a most rewarding compilation, with performances and recording of the highest quality and, with a handsome accompanying booklet, the set is offered in a most presentable box. An inexpensive feast.

Cello Concertos 1–2; *Violin Concertos: in G, Hob VII a, 4*; *in C, Hob VII, 1: Adagio* (transcribed for cello) (DVD version)
DG DVD 073 4351. Maisky, VSO - **SCHUMANN**: *Cello Concerto*

What a joy, as Maisky's performance of Haydn's *C major Cello Concerto* opens in the beautiful concert room of the Schloss Hetzendorf in Vienna, to hear the rich-timbred soloist and the lovely sounds of the Vienna strings playing on modern instruments, which Maisky himself directs with a combination of bow and body movements. These are simply glorious performances, beautifully photographed, and if Maisky sounds a little indulgent in the *Adagio* he has transcribed from the *C major Violin Concerto*, this and the complete G major work add to the pleasure of this superb DVD, one of the finest in the catalogue.

(i) *Piano Concertos: in G, Hob XVIII/4*; *in F, Hob XVIII/7*; *in D, Hob XVIII/11*. *Piano Sonatas 33, Hob XVI/20*; *60, Hob XVI/50*; *62, Hob XVI/52*; *Andante & Variations in F min., Hob XVII/6*
Virgin 2×1 5 61881-2 (2). Pletnev, (i) with Deutsche Kammerphilharmonie

Pletnev's reading of the *Sonatas* is full of personality and character. The *C major* is given with great elegance and wit, and the great *E flat Sonata* is magisterial. This playing has a masterly authority, and Pletnev is very well recorded. Now coupled with his equally memorable accounts of Haydn's three finest piano concertos, this reissue is a splendid bargain and one not to be missed.

Complete Symphonies 1–104; Symphonies A; B. Alternative versions: **Symphony 22 (Philosopher)**, 2nd version. **Symphony 63 (La Roxelane)**, 1st version. **Symphony 53 (L'Impériale)**, 3 alternative finales: (a) **A (Capriccio)**; (b) **C** (Paris version, attrib. Haydn); (c) **D: Overture in D** (Milanese version); **Symphony 103: Finale** (alternative ending); (i) **Sinfonia Concertante in B flat for Oboe, Bassoon, Violin & Cello**

Decca (ADD) 448 531-2 (33). Philharmonia Hungarica, Dorati, (i) with Engl, Baranyai, Ozin, Rácz

Haydn's *Symphonies* (along with the great symphonies of Mozart) represent a high water-mark of this form in the classical era. There is not a dull work among them: they are full of melody, forged through classical elegance combined with symphonic drama – but often it is his bubbling wit which is so engaging. His music is imbued with a genuine warmth and often a touching poignancy, especially in some of the slow movements, which contain music of surprising depth. Dorati was ahead of his time as a Haydn interpreter when, in the early 1970s, he made this pioneering integral recording of the symphonies. Superbly transferred to CD in full, bright, immediate sound, the performances are a consistent delight, with brisk *allegros* and fast-flowing *andantes,* textures remarkably clean. The slow, rustic-sounding accounts of the Minuets are more controversial, but the rhythmic bounce makes them attractive too. The set not only includes the *Symphonies A* and *B* (Hoboken Nos. 106 and 108) but also the *Sinfonia Concertante in B flat*, a splendidly imaginative piece with wonderful unexpected touches. Dorati's account – not surprisingly – presents the work as a symphony with unexpected scoring, rather than as a concerto. H. C. Robbins Landon tells us in the accompanying notes that the *Symphonies A* and *B* were omitted from the list of 104 symphonies in error as the first was considered to be a quartet (wind parts discovered later) and the second a divertimento. Dorati also includes as an appendix completely different versions of *Symphony 22* (*Philosopher*), in which Haydn altered the orchestration (a pair of flutes substituted for the cor anglais), entirely removed the first movement and introduced a new *Andante grazioso*; plus an earlier version of No. 63, to some extent conjectural in its orchestration, for the original score is lost. Of the three alternative finales for *L'Impériale* (No. 53), the first (*A*) contains a melody which, Robbins Landon suggests: 'Sounds extraordinarily like Schubert'; the second (*C*) seems unlikely to be authentic; but the third (*D*) uses an overture which was first published in Vienna. 'In some respects', Robbins Landon suggests, 'this is the most successful of the three concluding movements.' He feels the same about the extended finale of the *Drum Roll Symphony*, which originally included 'a modulation to C flat, preceded by two whole bars of rests'. But Haydn thought that made the movement too long and crossed out the whole section. Robbins Landon continues: 'Perhaps Haydn was for once in his life too ruthless here.'

Piano Trios 1–46, Hob XV:1–41; Hob XIV:C1 in C; Hob XV:C1 in C; Hob XIV6/XVI6 in G; Hob XV:fl in F min.; Hob deest in D
(complete)
Decca 454 098-2 (9). Beaux Arts Trio

Piano Trios: in F, Hob XV:2; in G, Hob XV:5; in F, Hob XV:6; in G, Hob XV:7; in B flat, Hob XV:8; in A, Hob XV9; in E flat, Hob XV:10; in E flat, Hob XV:11; in E min., Hob XV.12
Pentatone SACD Surround Sound PTC 5186 179 (2). Beaux Arts Trio

It is not often possible to hail one set of records as a 'classic' in quite the way that Schnabel's Beethoven sonatas can be so described. Yet this (Decca, originally Philips) set can be described in those terms, for the playing of the Beaux Arts Trio is of the very highest musical distinction. The contribution of the pianist, Menahem Pressler, is inspired, and the recorded sound on CD is astonishingly lifelike. The CD transfer has enhanced detail without losing the warmth of ambience or sense of intimacy. Offered in a bargain box of nine CDs, this is a set no Haydn lover should miss: it is desert island music.

However, those wanting a shorter selection could be well satisfied with the nine works on the Pentatone two-disc set in surround sound, which has marginally greater presence and warmth.

Piano Trios, Hob XV:24; 25 (Gypsy); 26; 27; 28; 29; 30; 31 (Jacob's Dream)
Hyp. CDA 67719 (24–27); CDA 67757 (28–31). Florestan Trio (available separately)

With Susan Tomes in the lead, these latest Florestan performances are also wonderfully fresh and appealing, alive, full of subtle detail and indeed joy in the music. They are vividly yet truthfully recorded. The first disc includes the *Trio* with the famous *Gypsy Rondo*; the second offers a two-movement work in which the second, a jaunty *Allegro* in E flat, pictures 'Jacob's Dream' from the Book of Genesis, in which Jacob dreams of a ladder that reaches from earth to heaven, with angels ascending and descending on it. But here the highlight is the opening *E major* work, No. 29, one of Haydn's most captivating, with its opening *Allegro* introducing a memorable main theme almost with the flavour of a folksong. Haydn's invention is remarkably unpredictable in the central *Allegretto* with its continuous 'walking' bass line.

String Quartets 1–83 (including Op. 2/1–6: Cassations, Op. 3/1–6, attrib. Hoffstetter); The Seven Last Words of Jesus Christ, Op. 51
Ⓑ Naxos 8.502400 (25). Kodály Qt

Haydn virtually invented the string quartet, and his 83 works in this form are among his greatest achievements, not least because every one is so enjoyable in showing the elegance, wit and friendliness of his invention. The complete survey by the Kodály Quartet was one of the recordings which first drew our attention to the Naxos label in its earliest days, and it remains one of the jewels in the Naxos crown. The playing has both warmth and refinement of detail and the readings are full of character. They never leave the impression that they are too studied or lacking in spontaneity; indeed, one often has the feeling in these studio recordings that one is listening to live music-making. The performances are flattered by the natural ambience of the Budapest Unitarian Church, which suits the players' mellow, civilized approach, although occasionally the Naxos engineers slightly miscalculated in the microphone balance and captured a little too much resonance, bringing a degree of tonal inflation. But the sound is always natural, the performances do not miss Haydn's subtleties or his jokes, and the group always communicates readily. The reissued set is absolutely complete, including the early *Cassations*, the engaging works by Hoffstetter, for long wrongly attributed to Haydn, and the *Seven Last Words* in its string quartet transcription. The set comes in a handsome box with a first-class booklet of documentation covering most of the composer's major works. It is undoubtedly a splendid bargain.

The Seven Last Words of Christ (String Quartet Version)
MDG SACD Surround Sound 9071550-6. Leipzig String Qt

Haydn composed his Passion music in 1776 for a priest in Cádiz. Originally written for orchestra, it was to become very successful, and the string quartet version soon followed. Haydn himself saw the difficulty of writing a series of movements in slow tempo and at the same time ensuring that the music reflected the sense of the priest's words. But in the event he created musical variety in a way that reflected the meaning of the text. The themes of the seven sonatas are introduced in each case by the first violin, and Haydn himself arranged to have Christ's words printed below the opening bars of the first violin part. Each sonata conveys in solemn music of the highest quality the emotional feeling expressed in the following text, with the last sonata given a special character by having the strings muted. The closing dramatic *Il terremoto*, marked *Presto e con tutta la forza*, represents the earthquake that occurred at the moment of Christ's death. The performance by the Leipzig Quartet is outstanding in every way, catching the changes of character and mood in each section with much feeling, and the recording in surround sound is very real and present.

Piano Sonatas 1–62 (complete); Seven Last Words of our Saviour on the Cross. Miscellaneous solo works, including Fantasia in C; German Dances & Minuets; Variations
Ⓑ BIS CD 1731/3 (15). Ronald Brautigam (fortepiano)

Piano Sonatas 1–61; Adagios in F & G; 2 Allegrettos in G; Arietta with 12 Variations in A; Fantasia in C; Variations (Sonata un piccolo divertimento) in F min.
ⒷⒷ Naxos 8.501042 (10). Jenö Jandö (piano)

There are no autograph manuscripts of Haydn's earliest sonatas, which were all written before 1766. The authenticity of No. 1 is certain, and many others of these early three-movement works bear the same fingerprints and a characteristic simplicity of style. But the later works have a boundless inventiveness characteristic of the composer. Ronald Brautigam's survey has great vitality and spontaneity and he is most realistically recorded. It you want a complete set of the Haydn piano sonatas, R.L. feels this would probably be first choice, providing you take to the fortepiano rather than a modern instrument. The documentation is excellent, and the 15 discs come for the price of three.

Those preferring the piano can turn to Jenö Jandö (I.M.'s choice), who seems to be in his element throughout. His freshness of approach and stylistic confidence match Brautigam's and the recording also is excellent. Overall this Naxos series can be recommended alongside its competitor on BIS. It comes with a comprehensive booklet detailing the *Piano Sonatas, String Quartets, Concertos* and *Symphonies*.

Sonatas 31 in A flat, Hob XVI/46; 39 in D, Hob XVI/24; 47 in B min., Hob XVI/32; 49 in C sharp min., Hob XVI/36
Chan. 10578. Jean-Efflam Bavouzet

Fresh from his triumphs in the Debussy cycle that he has just recorded for Chandos, Jean-Efflam Bavouzet now turns to the Haydn *Sonatas*, to which he brings the same mastery of style and range of keyboard colour. If the remainder of the sonatas are as good as these, it will be a set to treasure.

The Creation (Die Schöpfung) (in German; DVD version)
TDK DVD DVWW-COCREA. Augér, Sima, Schreier, Berry, Herrmann, Arnold Schoenberg Ch., Col. Aur., Kuhn (with documentary)

It is difficult to imagine a finer filmed and recorded account of Haydn's *Creation* than this TDK version, made doubly moving by the date of the performance in March 1982, the 250th anniversary of Haydn's birth. Moreover, the event took place in the Great Hall of the Old Vienna University where, on 27 March 1808, Haydn had attended a gala performance of his already celebrated masterpiece under the direction of Antonio Salieri. All this and more is related in a splendid documentary about the history and composition of the work. As for the performance, it is quite electrifying, but in the right way. Gustav Kuhn, with his lively temperament, conducts with an ideal combination of zest and depth of feeling. He opens with a true *pianissimo* and at the word 'Light' produces an overwhelming *fortissimo*. (It is recorded that at that moment at the gala performance Haydn was seen to look up at the heavens.) The soloists are unsurpassed on record. Arleen Augér (Gabriel) is at her glorious best, Peter Schreier (Uriel) sings with honeyed ardour, and Walter Berry is a powerfully resonant Rafael, with some wonderfully telling low notes. In Part Three, Gabriele Sima and Roland Hermann (looking at his partner with a benevolent twinkle) are perfectly cast as Adam and Eve. Throughout, the singing of the Arnold Schoenberg Choir is superb, the playing of the Collegium Aureum, using original instruments, gives constant aural pleasure and the work ends in a spirit of radiant joy, which is just what Haydn intented. The unfussy video direction by Franz Kabelka concentrates on the performers, so it is very like sharing the occasion with them.

The Seasons
HM HMC 801829.30 (2). Petersen, Güra, Henschel, RIAS Chamber Ch.,
   Freiburg Bar. O, Jacobs

It is astonishing that Haydn, at the end of his career, could write with such youthful exuberance in his culminating masterpiece, *The Seasons*. More than any other version, the period performance under René Jacobs brings out the joy in this piece, based on James Thomson's poem, as he nudges the music persuasively when Haydn has fun in imitating the lowing of cattle, the cry of the quail and the chirping of the cricket. With recording of ideal clarity and immediacy, Jacobs also brings out the boldness of the writing for brass and timpani in the finales of each section, notably in the drinking chorus which rounds off *Autumn*. Marlis Petersen is the fresh, agile soprano, Werner Güra the light, heady tenor and Dietrich Henschel the fine baritone, singing with a lieder singer's concern for detail. Excellent contributions too from the RIAS Chamber Choir and the splendid Freiburg Baroque Orchestra.

Philemon und Baucis (marionette opera, ed. Beil and Huss)
BIS SACD 1813. Genz, Engelhardt, Petryka, Vocalforum Graz, Haydn Sinf. Wien,
   Manfred Huss

Performances of marionette operas were a frequent and familiar feature at the elaborate marionette theatre at Esterháza, and it is fascinating and rewarding to have an edited example recorded on SACD. *Philemon and Baucis* was probably the first such opera that Haydn composed, and it was used for the inauguration of the theatre. The work was performed in honour of Empress Maria Theresia on her visit to Esterháza on 1 September 1773.

Philemon and Baucis is the only one of Haydn's marionette operas to have survived, and it has been reconstructed and edited by Hermann Beil and the conductor, Manfred Huss, as a way of presenting Haydn's music in a convincing manner. The opera's libretto is based on a play by Gottlieb Konrad Pfeffel.

It concerns an impoverished, elderly, virtuous couple who extend hospitality to Jupiter and Mercury when they decide to visit Earth. Two extra human characters are added, Aret and Narcissa, and the opera consists of spoken dialogue, sung arias, duets and ensembles, and as a finale the triumphal departure of Jupiter and Mercury, whose praises are sung by the four principal human characters and the chorus. It cannot be said that Haydn's music matches Mozart's operatic writing (Haydn acknowledged this himself), but the work has its moments and gathers strength as it proceeds. Indeed, the closing scene is very impressive. The singing of principals and chorus is of a high standard, as is the playing of the Haydn Sinfonietta and the direction of Manfred Huss. Recommended to the curious.

HAYDN, Michael (1737–1806)

Symphonies 14, P52; 17, P44; 19, P11; 24, P15; 29, P20; 33, P24; 40, P32; 41, P33; in F, P deest; 3 Marches, P59, 62 & 64

Ⓑ CPO 777 137-2 (2). Deutsche Kammerakademie Neuss, Frank Beermann or Johannes Goritzki

A good sampler collection of Michael Haydn's symphonies. There have been previous collections on Chandos, and a six-disc set by the Slovak Chamber Orchestra on CPO (999 591-2). But the present survey offers a coverage of the period extending approximately from 1760 to 1789, during which Haydn composed 41 symphonies. They have three or four movements, with orchestration varying among oboes and horns, two trumpets and timpani, and occasionally a solo flute or posthorn. They are very well played by the Deutsche Kammerakademie and make agreeable listening, but only serve to confirm that Michael's symphonies, although pleasingly constructed, were hardly ever a match for those of Joseph.

HENZE, Hans Werner (born 1926)

(i) *Barcarola*; *Symphonies: 7*; (ii) *9*; (iii) *3 Auden Songs*

Ⓑ EMI 2-CD 2 37601-2 (2). (i) CBSO, Rattle; (ii) Berlin R. Ch., BPO, Metzmacher; (iii) Bostridge, Drake

This two-CD set is invaluable while the DG box of the first six symphonies conducted by the composer is deleted. The *Seventh Symphony*, written for Simon Rattle and the CBSO in 1983/4, is not only the longest Henze has written, it is also the weightiest and most traditionally symphonic, Beethoven-like, in four substantial movements. Rather belying its title, the *Barcarola* presents a similarly weighty and massive structure, an elegiac piece of over 20 minutes, written in memory of Paul Dessau, and inspired by the myth of the ferryman, Charon, crossing the Styx.

Henze refers to his *Ninth Symphony* as a *summa summorum* of his musical output. It is choral throughout, a setting of seven poems by Hans-Ulrich Treichel based on Anna Seghes's *The Seventh Cross*, and there is no doubting the intensity and depth of feeling that lie behind the symphony. The recording derives from the première at the Philharmonie in 1997, and the singing of the Berlin Radio Choir is superb in every way. Powerful and impressive.

When Henze heard Ian Bostridge singing his *Three Auden Songs* he was so impressed that he wrote further settings for him. Listening to these compelling performances one can understand why the composer was attracted to Bostridge's unique vocal qualities and timbre. The one serious drawback to this reissue is that its presentation is remiss in omitting the texts.

Ondine (ballet: complete, DVD version)

Opus Arte OA 1030. Yoshida, Watson, Rosato, Cervera, Artists of Royal Ballet, ROHCG O, Wordsworth

Ondine (complete, CD version)

Ⓜ 478 3631 (2). L. Sinf., Knussen

Henze's *Ondine* was commissioned by Sir Frederick Ashton for Margot Fonteyn and the Royal Ballet, and was first produced at Covent Garden in 1958. Ashton wanted the movement to be fluid, like the surge and swell of the sea, and he choreographed Fonteyn's role full of aqueous imagery. She flickered and darted around the stage like a minnow, in small, swift toe-steps and with rippling arm movements, as though shaking drops of water from her fingers. Henze's luminous score, with its original and resourceful writing for harp, also conjures up water. Certainly the sense of the sea is marvellously conveyed in Act II, where Ondine and Palemon embark on board a ship. The movements of the dancers emulate the rocking of the ship, and the backdrops of the sets are painted on gauzes so that the harbour dissolves, to be replaced by a seascape, behind painted waves that go up and down. In the theatre itself it even induces some queasiness! In the finale Palemon and Ondine celebrate their wedding with a typical divertissement, before the latter's kiss seals his fate. Masterly dancing and a totally atmospheric account of a score that is haunting. The performances were recorded in June 2009 and if you were there (we were, on both the evenings listed here), the camerawork is completely unobtrusive and faithful.

The DG version of the score is given with sensitivity and authority by Oliver Knussen, one of Henze's most eloquent interpreters. Recorded in 1996, it is the product of Knussen's enthusiasm for the music, and this shows throughout. It is superbly realized by these fine musicians, and the excellent DG team serve them well with sound of great clarity and presence.

HÉROLD, Ferdinand (1791–1833)

La Fille mal gardée (ballet: complete, DVD version; choreography: Frederick Ashton)

Warner NVC Arts DVD 0630 19395-2. Collier, Coleman, Shaw, L. Edwards, Grant, Royal Ballet, ROHCG O, Lanchbery (Design: Osbert Lancaster; V/D: John Vernon)

La Fille mal gardeé (ballet, arr. Lanchbery) (complete, CD version)

Ⓜ Australian Decca Eloquence 442 9048 (2). ROHCG O, Lanchbery – **LECOCQ**: *Mam'zelle Angot*

The ballet *La Fille mal gardée* has had a fascinatingly long and varied history, and its origins as a subject for dance pantomime go back over two centuries. The first version was created by the French choreographer, Jean Dauberval, with the familiar plot and farmyard setting, but initially with a different title; and it was taken to London in 1791. The music included popular French folk material and operatic airs of the time. But when it reached Paris in 1828, a new score was written for it by Hérold. Much of the music was his own, but he also borrowed from Rossini and later Donizetti. In 1864 yet another new score was commissioned, from Peter Ludwig Hertel, which still included a good deal of Hérold's music.

The Royal Ballet *La Fille mal gardée*, with costumes and scenery by Osbert Lancaster, is a visual delight from beginning to end. Frederick Ashton's ever-inventive choreography is both witty and charming, and Lesley Collier and Michael Coleman are a most engaging pair of lovers and they dance with nimble grace. Brian Shaw's Widow Simone is the perfect foil, with the famous *Clog Dance* a captivating highlight, and Garry Grant is by no means outshone as the goofy Alain: he remains in our affections when his inept wooing comes to nought. The orchestra is again conducted by John Lanchbery, who has arranged this complex score so that it naturally follows every move of the dancers, while his constant drawing on familiar passages by Rossini adds to the listener's pleasure. The recording too is excellent, and the slight touch of thinness on the violin timbre is not a problem when the overall sound is so rich and resonantly full.

Lanchbery himself concocted the score for this fizzingly comic and totally delightful ballet. On CD, with sound of spectacular Decca fidelity, Lanchbery conducts a highly seductive account of the complete ballet with an orchestra long familiar with playing it in the theatre. It is coupled with Gordon Jacob's equally delicious confection, based on the music of Lecocq. Also available is a classic single CD offering an extended excerpts selection on Decca – a vintage Kingsway Hall recording. One cannot believe that it dates from 1962, for the combination of ambient bloom and the most realistic detail still places it in the demonstration bracket. The performance is also wonderfully persuasive and brilliantly played, displaying both affection and sparkle in ample quantity (430 196-2).

HERRMANN, Bernard (1911–75)

(i) *Marnie*; *Psycho*; *North by Northwest*; *The Trouble with Harry (A Portrait of 'Hitch')*; *Vertigo* ((ii) with: **WALTON**: *Escape Me Never*; *Richard III: Prelude*. **LAMBERT**: *Anna Karenina*. **BAX**: *Oliver Twist*. **BENJAMIN**: *An Ideal Husband*. **VAUGHAN WILLIAMS**: *49th Parallel*. **BLISS**: *Things to Come*. **SHOSTAKOVICH**: *Hamlet*)

Ⓜ Australian Decca Eloquence (ADD) 480 3787 (2). Herrmann, with (i) LPO; (ii) Nat. PO

Music from: *Citizen Kane*; *The Devil and Daniel Webster*; *The Day the Earth Stood Still*; *Fahrenheit 451*; *Gulliver's Travels*; *Jane Eyre*; *Jason and the Argonauts*; *Journey to the Centre of the Earth*; *Mysterious Island*; *The Seventh Voyage of Sinbad*; *The Snows of Kilimanjaro*

Ⓜ Australian Decca Eloquence (ADD) 480 3784 (2). LPO or Nat. PO, composer

Bernard Herrmann regarded himself as a composer who wrote music for film, rather than as a film-music composer, and these two compilations gather together all the recordings he made of his own music for Decca in the 1960s and 1970s. He was without doubt a master of the medium, and his collaboration with Alfred Hitchcock produced some of the most memorable of all film scores. Herrmann understood the medium perfectly and (before their famous falling-out) Hitchcock greatly respected his opinions. When, for example, Hitchcock told Herrmann that in the famous shower scene in *Psycho* he didn't want any music, Herrmann insisted that he listen to what he had written for that scene. The music stayed and those shrieking violins have achieved iconic status. In fact, it is the Hitchcock items which are the most enjoyable here: those arresting strings which play through the credits of *Psycho* give way to some wonderfully creepy and atmospheric writing when you can just sense the impending horror of the unfolding story. The bright, exhilarating music Herrmann provided for *North by Northwest* is brilliantly presented, while the hauntingly romantic scores for both *Marnie* (a hugely underrated film) and *Vertigo* (a masterpiece) are fully communicated. *The Trouble with Harry* is light, tuneful and wittily done.

The other two-CD compilation largely comprises music written for a sequence of fantasy films, and shows the composer's considerable skill in matters of orchestration, with vivid depictions of *The Giant Bee* and *Giant Crab* from the *Mysterious Island* being just two quirky examples. The artificially balanced Decca Phase 4 recordings are engineered for maximum colouristic effect, with the *Duel with the Skeleton* (from *The Seventh Voyage of Sinbad*) striking with its tangible percussive effects – one of the highlights in this collection. *Gulliver's Travels* features some especially delightful pastiche writing, with its 'regal' overture, a Haydn-esque *Minuetto*, but it is the *Lilliputians* music which is the most piquant item here. *Fahrenheit 451* features some especially atmospheric writing, and the *Citizen Kane* excerpts (the composer's first film score) show just how lively his musical imagination was from the beginning of his career. The *Memory Waltz* from *The Snows of Kilimanjaro* is lovely and wistful. The Hitchcock CD comes with a slightly less successful collection of British film music, and here the performances are a little earth-bound, though the Phase 4 recordings certainly make an impact. Lambert's *Anna Karenina* music is both rare and colourful, and the *Waltz* from *An Ideal Husband* is charmingly elegant. The Walton items lack the adrenalin of more famous performances, as does the brilliant *March* from *Things to Come*, though the vivid Shostakovich *Hamlet* suite finds the conductor back on top form.

HILDEGARD of Bingen (1098–1179)

(i) *Ordo Virtutum*; (ii) *In Portrait* (DVD version)

BBC Opus Arte DVD OA 0874 D (2). (i) Boothroyd, Hancorn, Mayfield, Chamber Op. Ch., Vox Animae, Fields, Adams, Devine (Directors: Michael Fields & Evelyn Tubb)

Confidante of popes, Hildegard was a genius in almost every field – composer, playwright, author, poet, artist, theologian, philosopher, visionary and prophet; and she taught that the world should be enjoyed by man and woman together: 'Only thus is the earth fruitful.' Her views were so remarkable in their time that it is a wonder they could be expressed and she survive. Because her mystic visions (in which she believed that God was communicating directly to her) were accepted by the Church as genuine, her power was remarkable and far-reaching. Moreover, she could speak plainly to those in authority above her and her criticisms would be accepted.

Her extraordinary sung and spoken mystery play, *Ordo Virtutum* ('The Play of the Virtues') celebrates her philosophy, based on the love of God and the enjoyment of life, alongside resistance to sin. Even with the music alone (which has been imaginatively recorded by Sequentia) this is a remarkable achievement, but to see it played out in glowing colours, imaginatively performed and beautifully sung, partly outside and partly inside, in splendidly chosen natural settings, adds an extra dimension to the drama, particularly in the dramatic passages in Scenes I and IV, where the Devil enters. The music, simple but soaring monody but with sparingly used harp, recorder and percussion accompaniments, is very beautiful in itself; its flowing lines haunt the memory and it is radiantly sung, while the drama of the piece comes over splendidly.

The accompanying second DVD includes a compulsive BBC 'Omnibus' dramatization of Hildegard's early life, before she set up her own order; and no better choice for the role of Hildegard could have been found than Patricia Routledge, who conveys the warmth and spiritual essence of her character. The additional items include 'A Real Mystic' (an interview with and lecture by Professor Matthew Fox, author of *Illuminations*, supplemented with an illustrative art gallery tour), while Mary Grabowsky considers Hildegard's spiritual significance for the twenty-first century.

'A feather on the breath of God': Hymns and sequences: *Ave, generosa*; *Columba aspexit*; *O Ecclesia*; *O Euchari*; *O ignis spiritus*; *O Jerusalem*; *O presul vere civitatis*; *O viridissima virga*
Hyp. CDA 66039. Kirkby, Gothic Voices, Muskett, White, Page

This Hyperion CD by the Gothic Voices was the disc which put Hildegard firmly on the map. It draws widely on the Abbess of Bingen's collection of music and poetry, the *Symphonia armonie celestium revelationum* – 'the symphony of the harmony of celestial revelations'. These hymns and sequences, most expertly performed and recorded, have excited much acclaim – and rightly so. A lovely CD.

HINDEMITH, Paul (1895–1963)

(i) *Horn Concerto*. *Concert Music for Brass and Strings, Op. 50*; *Nobilissima visione: Suite*. *Symphony in B flat for Concert Band*
Ⓜ EMI 7 63373-2. Philh. O, composer, (i) with Brain

These performances carry the authenticity of the composer's direction and also offer the unique playing of Dennis Brain, for whom Hindemith composed the concerto. Superb playing from the Philharmonia, then at the peak of its form, and no less superb sound, recorded in the early days of stereo, the producer being Walter Legge himself. Great music-making by any standards.

Mathis der Maler: Symphony. *Nobilissima visione: Suite*. *Symphonic Metamorphosis of Themes by Carl Maria von Weber*
EMI 555230-2. Phd. O, Sawallisch

An ideal introduction to Hindemith's world. The *Mathis Symphony*, which draws on three interludes from the opera of the same name, is a wonderfully inventive and satisfying score which the Philadelphians championed in the days of Eugene Ormandy. *Nobilissima visione* is a ballet written for Balanchine and has highly expressive music that is moving and eloquent. The somewhat later *Symphonic Metamorphosis of Themes by Carl Maria von Weber* is almost his most popular score, full of humour and brimming over with imaginative detail. Wolfgang Sawallisch conducts highly persuasive performances which find the Philadelphia Orchestra at its incomparable best.

(i) *Concert Music for Brass and Strings, Op. 50*; *Nobilissima visione: Suite*; (ii) *Symphonia serena*; (i) *Symphonic Metamorphosis on Themes by Carl Maria von Weber*; *Der Schwanendreher*;

Symphonie Mathis der Maler; (ii) *Symphonie die Harmonie der Welt*; (i) *Trauermusik*.
Ⓜ Decca 475 264-2 (3). (i) San Francisco SO; (ii) Leipzig GO, Blomstedt

Nobilissima visione, inspired by the frescoes of Giotto in Florence, ends with a noble passacaglia, and Blomstedt brings out the music's warmth as well as its rugged power. The *Symphonia serena* is a brilliant and inventive score, full of humour and melody, and there is plenty of wit in the Scherzo, which paraphrases a Beethoven march from 1809. Blomstedt again responds to this work sympathetically, and his reading of the *Symphonic Metamorphoses on Themes by Weber* is also appropriately light in touch, while the recording is exemplary in the naturalness of its balance. He also shows a strong feeling for *Mathis der Maler* and presents a finely groomed and powerfully shaped performance with lucid and transparent textures.

Die Harmonie der Welt comes from five years after the *Symphonia serena*. Like *Mathis der Maler* its three movements draw on material from an opera on the life of the astronomer Johannes Kepler (1571–1630), including the historical events that helped or hindered him, and the search for the harmony that undoubtedly rules the universe. Alongside the *Symphonia serena* this work is among the most impressive and powerful that Hindemith has given us, and Herbert Blomstedt and the Leipzig Orchestra are eloquent advocates of these two masterpieces.

The *Concert Music* is characteristic of Hindemith's early works with its chunky contrasts and emphatic rhymes set against a brief lyrical episode. *Der Schwartendrecher* is a concerto for Viola based on German folk themes, ending with a jolly set of variations. *Trauermusik* has a genuine elegiac quality and is enjoyable for its simple restrained eloquence.

HOLBORNE, Antony (*c.* 1560–1602)

Pieces for bandora: *Almain: The Night Watch*; *Fantazia*; *A Ground*; for cittern: *A French Toy*; *A Horne Pype*; *The Miller*; *Praeludium*; *Sicke Sicke and Very Sicke*; (i) for cittern with a bass: *Galliard*; *Maister Earles Pavane*; *Queenes Galliard*; for lute: Almains: *Almaine*; *The Choyce. Fantasia*. Galliards: *As it fell on a holie yve*; *The Fairy-rownde*; *Holburns passion*; *Muy linda*; *Responce*; *The teares of the muses*. Pavans: *Heres paternus*; *Pavan*, and *Galliard to the same*; *Posthuma*; *Sedet sola. A Toy*. Variations: *Il Nodo di gordio*
Gaudeamus CDGAU 173. Heringman, (i) with Pell

An entirely delightful representation on CD of an Elizabethan lutenist, composer and poet, now totally overshadowed by Dowland. Indeed, his melancholy pavane, *Posthuma*, has as much 'dolens' as almost anything by Dowland. It is this meditative quality which Jacob Heringman catches to perfection and which makes this collection so appealing. He improvises his own divisions when needed, as was expected by the composer, and his playing is appealingly spontaneous. But there is lively writing too, like *The Miller* and *A French Toy*; and how well they sound on the cittern, a robust-timbred instrument favoured mainly by the lower classes, and which came to be much played in barber's shops. Heringman is beautifully recorded in a most suitable ambience, providing the ideal CD for a late-evening reverie.

HOLMBOE, Vagn (1909–96)

Symphonies 1–13; *Sinfonia in memoriam, Op. 65*
Ⓑ BIS CD 843/46 (6 CDs for the price of 4). Aarhus SO, Owain Arwel Hughes
  (with Jutland Op. Ch. in *Sinfonia sacra*)

Vagn Holmboe is the leading Danish symphonist after Nielsen. He taught at the Conservatoire in Copenhagen. The general outlook of the *First Symphony* (*Sinfonia da camera*) is neoclassical and its proportions are modest, but one recognizes the vital current, the lucidity of thinking and the luminous textures. The last movement has an infectious delight in life. The *Second Symphony*, with its imaginative middle movement and vital companions, is a splendid piece. The *Third* (*Sinfonia rustica*), the first of his three wartime symphonies, also has an exhilarating finale. The *Fourth* (*Sinfonia sacra*) is a six-movement choral piece. It again encompasses a bracing vigour and underlying optimism, alongside moments of sustained grief. The *Fifth* makes a particularly good entry point into Holmboe's world. The only word to describe its outer movements is again exhilarating. But the slow movement, with its modal character, brings an anguished outburst in the middle to serve as a reminder that this is a wartime work, composed during the dark days of the Nazi occupation. The *Sixth Symphony* is even darker. Its distinctly Nordic world is established by the brooding slow-moving fourths of the long introduction, yet there is again a great luminosity too. The one-movement *Seventh* is a highly concentrated score, individual in both form and content, which encompasses great variety of pace and mood. The conductor penetrates the score of the *Eighth* with a particular sensitivity, and the Aarhus orchestra is equally persuasive in the *Ninth*, a dark, powerful work, among the finest Holmboe has given us. The *Tenth* is hardly less impressive, again dark, powerful and imaginative – again one of the Danish composer's most subtle and sensitive works, and the *Eleventh* also finds Holmboe at his most visionary. The *Twelfth* is tautly structured and well argued, although less inspired than the *Eleventh Symphony*. The *Thirteenth Symphony* is an astonishing achievement for a composer in his mid-eighties. The *Sinfonia in memoriam*, written much earlier, is another dark work of striking power and imaginative breadth and is masterly in every way. Every credit is owed to Owain Arwel Hughes and the Aarhus Symphony Orchestra for their fervent advocacy of all this music and to the splendid BIS engineers for the vivid and superbly natural sound. If you enjoy Sibelius, this is an inexpensive set and well worth exploring.

HOLST, Gustav (1874-1934)

(i) *Beni Mora (Oriental Suite), Op. 29/1*; *A Fugal Overture, Op. 40/1*; *Hammersmith – A Prelude & Scherzo for Orchestra, Op. 52*; (ii) *Japanese Suite*; (i) *Scherzo (1933/4)*; *A Somerset Rhapsody, Op. 21*
Lyrita (ADD) SRCD 222. (i) LPO; (ii) LSO; Boult

There is more to Holst than just *The Planets* and, from the 1970s, Lyrita led the way in showing us his orchestral range. Of all the Holst CD collections, this is perhaps the most attractive (though they are all worth exploring). *Beni Mora* (written after a holiday in Algeria) is an attractive, exotic piece that shows Holst's flair for orchestration vividly. Boult clearly revels in its sinuosity. *The Japanese Suite*, though not very Japanese, is curiously haunting and possesses much charm, particularly the piquant *Marionette Dance* and the innocuous *Dance under the cherry tree*. The most ambitious work here is *Hammersmith*, far more than a conventional tone-picture, and it is intensely poetic. Although conceived for military band, it was orchestrated a year later (1931). The *Scherzo*, from a projected symphony that was never completed, is strong, confident music. The *Somerset Rhapsody* is unpretentious but very enjoyable, and the brief, spiky *Fugal Overture* is given plenty of lift and bite to open the concert invigoratingly. As with other records in this Lyrita series, the first-class analogue recording has been splendidly transferred to CD.

Brook Green Suite for Strings; *Capriccio for Orchestra*; (i) *Double Violin Concerto, Op. 49*; (ii) *Fugal Concerto for Flute, Oboe & Strings, Op. 40/2*. *The Golden Goose* (ballet music, arr. Imogen Holst), *Op. 45/1*; (iii) *Lyric Movement for Viola & Small Orchestra*. *A Moorside Suite: Nocturne* (arr. for strings); *2 Songs Without Words, Op. 22*
Lyrita SRCD 223. ECO, I. Holst, with (i) Hurwitz, Sillito; (ii) Bennett, Graeme; (iii) Aronowitz

This generous programme (75 minutes) contains many interesting rarities. The *Capriccio* proves an exuberant piece, with some passages not at all capricciolike. *The Golden Goose* was written as a choral work for St Paul's Girls' School; these orchestral snippets were put together by Imogen Holst and, if comparatively slight, reflect the sharpness of an imagination which was often inspired by the needs of an occasion. The *Double Concerto*, with its bitonality and cross-rhythms, is grittier and with much less obvious melodic appeal, but it remains an interesting example of the late Holst. The first two movements of the

Fugal Concerto are much more appealing with their cool interplay of wind colour, particularly when the soloists are so distinguished. The *Lyric Movement for Viola and Small Orchestra* is certainly persuasive in the hands of Cecil Aronowitz and is one of the most beautiful of Holst's later pieces. The slow movement from the *Moorside Suite* – originally written for brass band – is heard here in the composer's own arrangement for strings; and the concert is completed with the comparatively familiar *Brook Green Suite* and two *Songs Without Words*, early works that are tuneful and colourful. All the performances are sympathetically authentic and the recording is well up to Lyrita's usual high standard.

Cotswolds Symphony in F (Elegy: In memoriam William Morris), Op. 8; Indra (Symphonic Poem), Op. 13; (i) Invocation (for cello & orchestra), Op. 19/2; (iii) The Lure (ballet music); The Morning of the Year: Dances, Op. 45/2. Sita: Interlude from Act III, Op. 23; (ii) A Song of the Night (for violin & orchestra), Op. 19/1; A Winter Idyll
Lyrita (DDD/ADD) SRCD 209. (i) Baillie; (ii) McAslan; LPO or (iii) LSO; Atherton

The earliest work here, *A Winter Idyll*, was written in 1897, the year after his fellow-student Hurlstone's *Variations on an Original Theme* when Holst was in his early twenties. Lewis Foreman's informative note speaks of the influence of Stanford, but both in this work and in the *Elegy*, which is a slow movement originally forming part of a *Cotswolds Symphony*, one can detect little of the mature Holst. The familiar fingerprints do surface, however, in *Indra* (1903) and *A Song of the Night* (1905), which is among the scores Colin Matthews has edited. *The Lure* (1921) was written at short notice for Chicago and is characteristic, but the inspiration is not of the quality of *The Perfect Fool*. When they were first performed at a BBC concert, the *Dances* from *The Morning of the Year* (1926–7) shared the programme with Honegger's *King David*, and they enjoy the distinction of being the very first commission made by the BBC Music Department. Holstians will need no urging to acquire this interesting, well-played and well-recorded disc. None of the music is perhaps Holst at his best, but it usefully fills in our picture of him.

The Planets (see also under Ormandy)
Ⓜ Decca (ADD) 475 8225. V. State Op. Ch., VPO, Karajan - **STRAUSS**: *Don Juan*

With Karajan at his peak, his extraordinarily magnetic and powerful (1961) Decca recording of *The Planets* is still uniquely individual, bringing rare tension, an extra magnetism, projected by superb Decca recording, produced by John Culshaw in the Sofiensaal. *Mars* is remorselessly paced and, with its whining Wagnerian tubas, is unforgettable, while the ravishingly gentle portrayal of *Venus* brings ardent associations with the goddess of love (not what Holst intended, but voluptuously compelling). The gossamer textures of *Mercury* and the bold geniality of *Jupiter* contrast with the solemn, deep melancholy expressed by the VPO strings at the opening of *Saturn*, while *Uranus* brings powerful playing from the Vienna brass, given splendid bite. A worthy candidate for Decca's 'Originals', especially with its new if unexpected Richard Strauss coupling.

HONEGGER, Arthur (1892–1955)

Pacific 231; Symphonies 2; 3 (Symphonie liturgique); 4 (Deliciae Basiliensis); (i) *Cantata de Noel*; (ii) *Le Roi David*

Ⓜ Decca Eloquence (ADD) 480 2316 (2). SRO, Ansermet, with (i) Mollet, R. Lausanne Ch. & Children's Ch.; (ii) Audel (narr.), Danco, Montmollin, Pauline Martin, Hamel –
MARTIN: *In terra pax*

This double CD set is almost worth its cost for the performance of *Pacific 231* – one of the most vividly descriptive tone-poems of the twentieth century. Indeed, it evokes the sort of imagery that Dukas achieved with *The Sorcerer's Apprentice*, only this time it is a powerful steam locomotive that is conjured up. It is a difficult work to perform and record, but Ansermet's is perhaps the finest ever committed to disc: it has a powerful, cumulative effect which is compelling from bar one, and the Decca recording handles the complex textures superbly. Indeed, it is a magnificent recording of a magnificent performance of a magnificent piece. The performances of the symphonies are at a slightly lower voltage (the *Third* is no match for the Karajan version listed below) but is decent enough and textually very clear. The *Fourth Symphony*, written for Paul Sacher and the Basle Chamber Orchestra, is full of character and invention, and is probably the most relaxed and unpretentious of the cycle. The *Christmas Cantata* was written in 1953 when the composer was ill in hospital during a painful illness which led to his early death, a couple of years later. It is an effective and often moving work and this performance, despite the odd lapses of intonation, is certainly effective. *Le Roi David* is full of atmospheric pageantry and was for years Honegger's best-known work (apart from *Pacific 231*). Ansermet's performance comes from the 1950s but one would hardly guess it from the vivid sound, and the performance has a wonderfully idiomatic feeling which is utterly convincing.

Symphonies 2 for Strings with Trumpet Obbligato; 3 (Symphonie liturgique)

DG 447 435-2. BPO, Karajan (with STRAVINSKY: *Concerto in D*)

An altogether marvellous CD. The playing of the Berlin strings in the wartime *Second Symphony* is superb, sumptuous in tone and refined in texture. The performance is quite masterly and the recording is splendidly balanced and richly sonorous. This is a first recommendation for both works, irrespective of alternative couplings. Karajan's sensitive feeling for texture can be seen at its finest in the coda of the *Liturgique*, which is quite magical.

HORNE, Marilyn (mezzo-soprano)

'The Complete Decca Recitals': CD 1 & 2 (with SRO, Lewis) 'Souvenir of a Golden Era': Arias from: **ROSSINI**: *Il barbiere di Siviglia*; *L'italiana in Algeri*; *Otello*; *Semiramide*; *Tancredi*. **BELLINI**: *I Capuleti e I Montecchi*. **BEETHOVEN**: *Fidelio*. **GLUCK**: *Alceste*; *Orphée et Eurydice*. **GOUNOD**: *Sapho*. **MEYERBEER**: *Le Prophète*. **VERDI**: *Il trovatore*. CD 3 (with V. Cantata O, Lewis). 'Bach and Handel Arias': Arias from: **BACH**: *Magnificat*; *St Matthew Passion*; *Notenbüchlein für Anna Magdalena Bach*; *Weihnachtsoratorium*. **HANDEL**: *Messiah*; *Rodelinda*. CD 4 (with ROHCG O, Lewis) 'Opera Arias': Arias from: **ROSSINI**: *La Cenerentola*; *L'italiana in Algeri*; *Semiramide*. **MEYERBEER**: *Les Huguenots*; *Le Prophète*. **MOZART**: *La clemenza di Tito*. **DONIZETTI**: *La figlia del reggimento*. CD 5 (with RPO, Lewis): 'Rossini Arias': Arias from: *L'assedio di Corinto*; *La donna del lago*. CD 6 (with V. Op. O, Lewis) 'Arias from French Opera': Arias from: **MASSENET**: *Werther*. **THOMAS**: *Mignon*. **BIZET**: *Carmen*. **SAINT-SAËNS**: *Samson et Dalila*. CD 7 (with LAPO, Mehta): **MAHLER**: *Lieder eines fahrenden Gesellen*; *Rückert-Lieder*. CD 8 (with RPO, Lewis) 'Mahler & Wagner Lieder': **MAHLER**: *Kindertotenlieder*. **WAGNER**: *Wesendonck-Lieder*. CD 9 (with Katz, piano) 'German Lieder': **SCHUBERT**: *Fischerweise*; *Im Frühling*; *Die junge Nonne*; *Nacht und Träume*. **SCHUMANN**: *Abendlied*; *Aus den hebräischen Gesängen*; *Die Kartenlegerin*; *Die Lotosblume*. **WOLF**: *Auf einer Wanderung*; *Der Genesene an die Hoffnung*; *Kennst du das Land?*; *Mein Liebster hat zu Tische*. **R. STRAUSS**: *Befreit*; *Für fünfzehn Pfennige*; *Schön sind, doch kalt die Himmelssterne*. CD 10 'French & Spanish Song': **BIZET**: *Absence*; *Adieux de l'hôtesse arabe*; *Chanson d'avril*; *Vieille chanson*. **DEBUSSY**: *La Flûte de Pan*; *La Chevelure*; *Le Tombeau des Naiades*. **FALLA**: *Siete canciones populares españolas*. **NIN**: *Villancicos españoles* (excerpts). CD 11 (with ECO, Carl Davis) 'Great American Songbook': **FOSTER**: *Beautiful Dreamer*; *Camptown Races*; *If You've Only Got a Moustache*; *I've Just Come from the Fountain*; *Jeannie with the Light Brown Hair*; *Sometimes I Feel Like a Motherless Child*. **MALOTTE**: *The Lord's Prayer*. **TRAD**.: *Battle Hymn of the Republic*; *Billy Boy*; *Shenandoah*; *When Johnny Comes Marching Home*. **NILES**: *Go 'Way from My Window*. Arr. **COPLAND** (from *Old American Songs*): *At the River*; *Ching-a-ring-Chaw*; *I Bought Me a Cat*; *Long Time Ago*; *Simple Gifts*. **COHAN**: *You're a Grand Old Flag*. **BERLIN**: *God Bless America*. **BRYAN** & **PIANTADOSI**: *I Didn't Raise My Boy to Be a Soldier*.

Ⓑ Decca (ADD/DDD) 478 0165 (11)

Marilyn Horne is one of the great mezzo-sopranos of the recording era and this bargain-box set gathers together all of her classical Decca recitals – an amazing feast of superb singing. The earliest recital (1964), CD 4, 'Opera Arias', was one of the most spectacular coloratura début records to appear since the war. Horne was immediately shown as having a really big, firm mezzo voice, yet finding no difficulty whatever in coping with the most tricky, florid passages, her musicianship (guided by her husband, the conductor Henry Lewis) impeccable. It set the standard for the rest of her recitals. This was made some years before her famous DG *Carmen* set appeared, but after we had heard her collaboration with Joan Sutherland, more than holding her own. Here as principal soloist she continually delights and astonishes. The range is astounding, just as free and unrestrained above the stave as below. When every single item brings wonderment it is impossible to single out one above the rest, and the recording is outstandingly vivid. The French recital is also very satisfying. The Massenet is beautifully done, and the lighter mood of the charming *Mignon* scene is perfectly managed. The vibrancy of the *Carmen* excerpts make a perfect foil for the Delilah characterization. The famous *Mon cœur s'ouvre à ta voix* is taken in a long-breathed, spacious manner to bring out the music's richly sensuous potential. Rossini was something of a speciality for Horne, and her Rossini recital is one of the most cherishable among all Rossini aria records ever issued. The voice is in glorious condition, rich and firm throughout its spectacular range, and is consistently used with artistry and imagination, as well as brilliant virtuosity in coloratura. By any reckoning, this is thrilling singing. The Handel arias from the Bach/Handel recital require a more florid, extrovert style, and the result is far more successful than her Bach singing (which does not show her at her most imaginative) with excellent accompaniments by Henry Lewis. She uses a beautiful mezzo voice for the *da capo* of '*Dove sei*', and in all three of the *Rodelinda* arias she finds her most sympathetic expressive style. Less successful is her version of Mahler's *Kindertotenlieder*, where the singing has a statuesque quality that does not suit Mahler's intensely personal inspiration. There is much to admire, and the voice is always beautiful, but tenderness is completely missing. The same can be said of the Wagner *Wesendonck-Lieder*: beautiful singing but lacking in emotional warmth. In her later Mahler recital (1979) with Mehta, in the *Lieder eines fahrenden Gesellen* and the *Rückert-Lieder*, Horne and Mehta are disappointing too. The unevenness of Horne's vocal production is exaggerated by close recording, and that balance undermines any refinement in the orchestral accompaniment. Yet the sheer power of Horne's voice can be exciting, as in the climax of *Um Mitternacht*. The two piano-accompanied recitals (with Martin Katz, 1972) are very enjoyable, and if one may now think of Horne as not always a totally idiomatic singer of German lieder, the results are surprisingly good. She sings with a wonderfully hushed, controlled intensity in Schubert's *Nacht und Träume*, and if the Schumann items are a little operatic at times, *Die Kartenlegerin* is delightfully done. Horne brings out much colour in the French and Spanish songs, with items such as Bizet's *Adieux de l'hôtesse arabe* most enjoyable. The most recent recording here, 'The Great American Songbook', was recorded digitally in 1985 and is a success in every way. Marilyn Horne is tangibly characterful in this American repertory, which draws from her a glorious range of tone, and she bridges stylistic gaps between popular and concert repertory with supreme confidence. The Copland songs are particularly delightful, and the Decca recording here – and throughout this set – is outstandingly vivid. Each of the recordings is presented in a cardboard sleeve with the original artwork – a nice touch – and the box artwork itself is striking. 'Souvenir of a Golden Era', included in this set, is available separately (475 8493).

HOROVITZ, Joseph (born 1926)

(i) *Clarinet & String Concerto*; (ii) *Concerto for Euphonium & Small Orchestra*; (iii) *Concerto for Violin & Strings*; (iv) *Jazz Concerto for Piano, Strings & Percussion*

Ⓜ Dutton CDLX 7188. Royal Ballet Sinfonia, composer; with (i) Cross; (ii) Mead; (iii) Haveron; (iv) Norris, Skelton

Joseph Horovitz is a composer of light music of the highest quality, at once light and lyrical, and beautifully crafted. This Dutton disc of four delightful concertos could not be more welcome. Horovitz unerringly brings out the special qualities of each solo instrument, not least the euphonium, subject of all too few concertos. The *Jazz Concerto for Piano, Strings and Percussion* brings out another side of Horovitz's writing, with its reliance on catchy syncopations, developing a quality that runs through all his music. Ideal performances under the composer's lively direction.

HOVHANESS, Alan (1911–2000)

(i) *Guitar Concerto 2. Fanfare for the New Atlantis*; *Symphony 63 (Loon Lake)*

ⓑⓑ Naxos 8.559336. RSNO, Robertson; (i) with Calderón

The *Second Guitar Concerto* was commissioned by Narciso Yepes. The solo guitarist (here the excellent Javier Calderón) dominates a kaleidoscope of orchestral chorale sonorities, pizzicati and fugati in the most inventive way. The *Fanfare* moves from a solo trumpet to the climax of the rebirth of Atlantis in the full orchestra. The *Symphony 63 (Loon Lake)* is characteristically evocative, spectacular in its washes of orchestral colour from both the strings and woodwind alike. Hovhaness's music is strangely haunting, when the performers are as dedicated and responsive as they are here, and the recording is worthy of the complex scoring.

HOWELLS, Herbert (1892–1983)

The B's (Suite for Orchestra); (i) *3 Dances for Violin & Orchestra*; (ii) *Fantasia*; *Threnody* (both for cello & orchestra) *King's Herald*; *Paradise Rondel, Op. 40*; (iii) *In Green Ways* (song-cycle); *Pastoral Rhapsody; Procession, Op. 36*
ⓑⓑ Chan. 2-for-1 241-20 (2). LSO, Hickox, with (i) Mordkovitch; (ii) Welsh; (iii) Kenny

The inspired suite, *The Bs*, celebrates the composer's musician friends and colleagues at the Royal College of Music at the beginning of the 1914–18 war. As such it has something in common with Elgar's *Enigma Variations*, although Howells clearly identified each dedicatee. 'Blissy' (Arthur Bliss) inspires a dainty, chimerical Scherzo on the second disc, with the piano an orchestral soloist. The shorter evocations are framed by an exuberant *Overture* with a *nobilmente* lyrical expansiveness representing the composer himself ('Bublum') and the finale ('Benjee' – Arthur Benjamin), which begins light-heartedly but ends grandiloquently, recalls the composer's own themes from the overture. The *Three Dances for Violin and Orchestra*, another wartime work (1915), are in the best English folk/pastoral tradition, with Lydia Mordkovitch a brilliant violin soloist; the song-cycle, *In Green Ways*, also includes poignant elegies. The English countryside is strikingly evoked in this group of five songs, using lyrics by Shakespeare and Goethe. Yvonne Kenny sings the whole group most affectingly and Richard Hickox and the LSO are ardent and communicative advocates of all this fine music.

The most personal works on the first disc are the *Fantasia* and *Threnody*, both for cello and orchestra, together forming a sort of rhapsodic concerto. Howells was reflecting his anguish over the death of his nine-year-old son, with flashes of anger punctuating the elegiac lyricism. The other major piece is the *Pastoral Rhapsody*, written in 1923. Similarly pastoral but predominantly vigorous, the *Paradise Rondel* of 1925 is full of sharp contrasts, with one passage offering clear echoes of the *Russian Dance* from *Petrushka*. The collection opens with the boldly extrovert *King's Herald*, bright with Waltonian fanfares. *Procession* brings more echoes of *Petrushka*, again reflecting Howells's response to the Diaghilev Ballets Russes' appearances in London. Helped by rich, atmospheric sound, Richard Hickox draws performances that are both brilliant and warmly persuasive from the LSO, with Moray Welsh a movingly expressive soloist in the concertante works. A most attractive bargain reissue, joining together two equally desirable discs.

(i-ii) *Elegy for Viola, String Quartet & String Orchestra*; (i) *Merry-Eye*; *Music for a Prince: Corydon's Dance*; *Scherzo in Arden*; (iii) *Procession for Small Orchestra*

Lyrita (ADD) SRCD 245. Boult, with (i) New Philh. O; (ii) Herbert Downes; (iii) LPO (with **WARLOCK**: *An Old Song for Small Orchestra*. **HADLEY**: *One Morning in Spring*) - **BUTTERWORTH**: *The Banks of Green Willow*, etc.

Of these short pieces the *Elegy* is much the most searching, a thoughtful and expressive inspiration, playing on textual contrasts such as make VW's *Tallis Fantasia* so moving in its restrained way. Written in 1917, it represents the sort of response to the First World War that one also finds in Vaughan Williams's *Pastoral Symphony*. The other pieces are relatively slight, but they present a welcome sample of the work of a highly discriminating composer. *Merry-Eye* offers some lively and very attractive invention, and the *Music for a Prince*, commissioned to mark the birth of Prince Charles, is hardly less enjoyable. Added to the original Howells programme is the short but colourful and effective *Procession*, apparently inspired by a dream the composer had in which he witnessed a sinister procession approaching and dispersing. It was so well received at the Proms in 1922 that it had to be repeated! Supreme performances and recording, with an outstanding coupling of Butterworth's items plus two excellent works by Warlock and Hadley.

HUMMEL, Johann (1778–1837)

Piano Concertos: in A min., Op. 85; in B min., Op. 89

Chan. 8507. Hough, ECO, Thomson

The *A minor* is Hummel's most often-heard concerto, never better played, however, than by Stephen Hough on this prize-winning Chandos disc. The coda is quite stunning; it is not only his dazzling virtuosity that carries all before it but also the delicacy and refinement of colour he produces. The *B minor*, Op. 89, is more of a rarity, and is given with the same blend of virtuosity and poetic feeling which Hough brings to its companion. He is given expert support by Bryden Thomson and the ECO - and the recording is first class.

Piano Quintet in E flat, Op. 87; Piano Septet in D min., Op. 74

Ⓜ Australian Decca Eloquence (ADD) 476 2447. Melos Ens. - **WEBER**: *Clarinet Quintet*

These two highly engaging works show the composer at his most melodically fecund and his musical craftsmanship at its most apt. One can see how Hummel charmed nineteenth-century audiences into regarding him as being a greater composer than he was, although newer recordings have certainly raised his claims in recent years. His skill at shaping and balancing a movement can be impressive: it is the ideas themselves (as in all music) that can make or break a structure, and here they are entirely appropriate to music designed to entertain. That these works certainly do in such spontaneous and polished performances – just try the opening movement of the *Septet* to sample the composer's felicity. The 1965 sound is warm, full and rich, and this is a vintage recording in every way. The coupling's a charmer too.

HUMPERDINCK, Engelbert (1854–1921)

Hänsel und Gretel (complete, DVD version)
EuroArts DVD 2055888. Papoulkas, Gabler, Vermillion, Ketelsen, Vilsmaier, Teuscher,
    Female & Children's Ch. of Dresden State Opera, Saxon State O, Hostetter (Stage
    Director: Katharina Thalbach, V/D: Andreas Morell)

Hänsel und Gretel (complete, CD version)
(B) EMI mono 6 40716-2 (2). Schwarzkopf, Grümmer, Metternich, Ilosvay, Schürhoff,
    Felbermayer, Children's Ch., Philh. O, Karajan

The EuroArts DVD offers a wholly enchanting production of Humperdinck's wonderfully tuneful children's opera that cannot be recommended too highly. It was the Dresden Semperoper's Christmas presentation in 2006 and it would be an ideal Christmas gift for any musical youngster – and it is very entertaining for adults too. There are no voices here of the calibre of Schwarzkopf and Grümmer, but Hans-Joachim Ketelsen (as Peter, the children's Father) sings his 'Tra-la-la-las' with richly resonant amiability, and Irmgard Vilsmaier as their Mother is unusually convincing dramatically. Iris Vermillion is a gloriously camp Witch (she enters glamorously and then changes into a seedier costume). But vocally the children dominate. Their *Dance Duet* is a real highlight, and Anna Gabler is vocally and dramatically strong as Gretel, while Lydia Teuscher sings charmingly as the Sandman and Dew Fairy. Michael Hofstetter directs with flair, pacing the opera spontaneously, yet finding much glowing detail in Humperdinck's score, especially the strings and horns, helped by demonstration-worthy sound in the lively opera-house acoustic. But it is Katharina Thalbach's production that makes this such an enchanting entertainment, full of imaginative detail, from the angels who either swing in on wires or come down a chute, to the Witch's house, made of eatable biscuits, which conveniently turns into the oven. And one must not forget the hugely real giant tortoise who stays around to guard the children; and the happy ending is exhilaratingly staged, with glorious singing from the chorus of women and children.

Karajan's classic 1950s set of Humperdinck's children's opera, with Schwarzkopf and Grümmer peerless in the name-parts, is hardly less captivating – this was an instance where everything in the recording went right. The original mono LP set was already extremely atmospheric. In most respects the sound has as much clarity and warmth as rival recordings made in the 1970s. There is much to delight here; the smaller parts are beautifully done and Else Schürhoff's Witch is memorable. This is now reissued as one of EMI's 'Classics' series, with a bonus disc including libretto and synopsis. For those who require a modern stereo version, there is John Pritchard's beautifully cast version version on Sony, which was the first in genuine stereo (in 1978) to challenge the vintage Karajan set. Cotrubas – sometimes a little grainy as recorded – and Von Stade both give charming characterizations, and the supporting cast is exceptionally strong, with Söderström an unexpected but refreshing and illuminating choice as the Witch. Pritchard draws idiomatic playing from the Gürzenich orchestra, and the recording is pleasingly atmospheric. This is, however, another of those Masterwork reissues in which the libretto is available only via a CD-ROM and a personal computer (Sony S2K 96455).

IBERT, Jacques (1890–1962)

Divertissement
Chan. 9023. Ulster O, Y. P. Tortelier (with MILHAUD: *Le Bœuf; La Création*) –
  POULENC: *Les Biches*

Yan Pascal Tortelier provides a splendid, modern, digital version of Ibert's sparklingly witty *Divertissement*. Verve is combined with much delicacy of detail, and the coupled works, Poulenc's *Les Biches* (equally witty) and the no less delectably spirited music of Milhaud are also most enjoyable. Marvellous, top-drawer, Chandos sound.

Escales
Ⓜ RCA (ADD) SACD 82876 61387-2. Boston SO, Munch – DEBUSSY: *La Mer*.
  SAINT-SAËNS: *Symphony 3*

Munch's *Escales* brings some ravishing textures from the Boston violins, and the finale, *Valencia*, has sparkling dance rhythms. The 1956 recording, if balanced rather closely, has brilliance and transparency, and sounds even better in this new SACD transfer.

INDY, Vincent d' (1851–1931)

(i) **Choral varié** (for solo saxophone & orchestra). **Diptyque méditerranéen, Op. 87; Istar, Op. 42: Symphony 3 (Sinfonia brevis), Op. 70**
Chan. 10585. (i) Flosason; Iceland SO, Gamba

D'Indy's *Jour d'été à la montagne*, inspired by Debussy's *La Mer*, used to appear regularly in the catalogue, but the exotic *Istar* has been rather more elusive. Premièred in 1897, it follows the story of Orfeo and Eurydice – only with the action reversed and a good deal more seductive, when the Assyrian goddess seeks to achieve the release of her lover from the Underworld. This she does by removing one of her seven garments (or ornaments) at each of the Seven Doors of the Dark Abode, finally revealing herself invitingly naked as she passes through the last door. The work is a richly scored set of variations, presented in reverse order, ending rather than opening with the memorable basic theme itself.

The concertante *Choral varié* for saxophone, written in 1903, exploits the melodic potential of a work based on a grave yet beautiful passacaglia theme developed within an imaginatively varied orchestral texture.

The *Second Symphony* has already been recorded successfully, but the powerful *Third* is again unfamiliar. Composed at the climax of the First World War, it is both patriotic and compelling, and often spectacularly orchestrated. Opening with a rocking *Lent et calme* it becomes bolder, with a piquant march in 6/8 tempo leading to a soaring theme on the horns, taken up by the full orchestra with hammering timpani. The second movement is more rustic, with fanfares, the third contrasts woodwind, strings and percussion colourfully. The finale is urgently rhythmic, but has a Gregorian Hymn (horn and flute) for contrast which is to reach a climax in the triumphant coda.

The *Diptyque méditerranéen* (1926) was D'Indy's orchestral swansong and reflects the composer's happy second marriage, to a younger woman; in its glowing invocation to nature, it mirrors the early *Jour d'été à la montagne*, evoking dawn (*Soleil matinal*) and evening (*Soleil vespéral*). The Iceland Symphony Orchestra and Rumon Gamba are thoroughly at home in all this music, and Sigurdur Flosason is a splendid soloist, phrasing with a rich, expansive tone. All four performances have striking spontaneity and the Chandos recording is very much in the demonstration bracket. If you are unfamiliar with D'Indy's music, this CD will make an admirable introduction to a very rewarding composer.

IRELAND, John (1879–1962)

(i) *Piano Concerto in E flat* (1930); *Legend for Piano and Orchestra* (1933). *3 Dances* (1913); *First Rhapsody in F sharp min.* (1906); *Indian Summer* (1932); *Pastoral* (1896); *A Sea Idyll* (1900)
ⓑⓑ Naxos 8.572598. Lenehan; (i) with RLPO, Wilson

John Ireland has written the most attractive of all English piano concertos, a piece which has not deserved its neglect since it was frequently played at the Proms in the 1930s and '40s. Worthy to rank with the finest twentieth-century works in this form, its poetic lyricism and distinctive melodic inspiration are in the ageless tradition of the finest English music. After its lively first movement it offers one of the most lyrically beautiful slow movements of any piano concerto written in the last century, and its sparkling finale has an indelible main theme that you will not be able to get out of your head once the work concludes. John Lenehan, following after Kathryn Stott, is at his finest here. The concertante *Legend* (written only three years after the concerto) is almost equally memorable. In both works the RLPO is on excellent form under the understanding direction of John Wilson, who is renowned as an idiomatic advocate of English music (shown again in the excellent anthology 'Made in Britain') and the Naxos recording is in the demonstration class. In the solo items, written earlier, Lenehan proves equally responsive. The *First Rhapsody* is passionately virtuosic, and the evocative *Pastoral* makes an appealing contrast to it. *Indian Summer* brings a brief but typically expressive song without words. The early *Sea Idyll* is in three contrasted rhapsodic sections and the *Three Dances* are folksy, simple but engagingly contrasted, the closing 'Reapers' Dance' infectiously vigorous, and again the Naxos recording is also very real and present. Not to be missed.

(i) *Piano Concerto*; *Legend for Piano & Orchestra. Overture: Satyricon*; *2 Symphonic Studies*; (ii) *These Things Shall Be*

Lyrita (ADD) SRCD 241. LPO, Boult, with (i) Parkin; (ii) Carol Case, LPO Ch.

This CD is included here for *These Things Shall Be*, one of the composer's most striking works. Alas, EMI have deleted Barbirolli's electrifying 78-r.p.m. recording, but Boult's version is the most successful in the stereo era. The composer chose exactly the right moment to write *These Things Shall Be* (1936-7). The words, taken from John Addington Symonds, are optimistic in an almost unbelievably naive way, but during the war when things were not going well the direct, life-assertive faith in a possible Utopian state of human relationships suited the need of the public mood and morale exactly. One can remember Prom performances of great power and eloquence, and certainly the music, with its mixture of Elgar *nobilmente* and Waltonian declamation (without the dissonant bite of *Belshazzar's Feast*), is very effective and easy to enjoy. This recorded performance has less thrust and conviction than those far-off wartime accounts, but it is well sung and played and a good deal of the impact of the writing comes through. The music itself is melodic, spacious in phrase and readily enjoyable at its face value. The performance of the superb *Piano Concerto* is first class, both as a performance and as a recording, and if the rest of the disc shows the composer at less than first-rate quality, it is all worth hearing: the *Legend for Piano and Orchestra* is a bit rambling, though quite appealing, and the *Satyricon Overture* is enjoyable without being as memorable as the *London Overture*. The *Two Symphonic Studies* are arranged by Geoffrey Bush; the first begins in a rather broody manner but develops into quite a vigorous fugue, while the second, which begins quietly, turns into a lively *Toccata*. Both are colourfully orchestrated. The recordings throughout are of vintage Lyrita quality from the 1960s and '70s.

(i-ii) *Violin Sonatas 1 & 2*: (i; iii) *Cello Sonata*
ⓑⓑ Naxos 8.572497. (i) Benjamin Frith; (ii) Lucy Gould; (iii) Alice Neary

John Ireland's two *Violin Sonatas*, both early works, were what first alerted serious music-lovers to the arrival of a distinctive new voice among young British composers. In 1911 the *First Sonata* won first prize out of 134 entries in the third Cobbett Competition for chamber works, on this occasion not for the Phantasy form which Cobbett wanted to encourage, but simply for pieces for violin and piano. The powerful first movement leads on to an easily lyrical slow movement featuring a simple melody repeated an octave higher. The flowing music of the finale rounds the work off very effectively. The *Second Sonata* of 1915 had even greater success when it was first performed, receiving rave reviews and wide audience acclaim. It too is in three nicely balanced movements, ending with an energetic finale. Lucy Gould, one of the leading British violinists of her generation, is most sympathetically accompanied by Benjamin Frith, a pianist who should be far more widely acclaimed. Naxos generously offers as an extra the similarly striking *Cello Sonata* of 1923. This too receives an outstanding performance from Alice Neary with Frith again an ideal accompanist. With well-balanced sound, the disc makes a very welcome addition to Naxos's growing library of British chamber works.

IVES, Charles (1874-1954)

Symphonies 1-4; *Central Park in the Dark*; (i) *General William Booth enters into Heaven*
Hyp. SACDA or CDA 67540 (*Symphonies 1, 4 & Central Park*); SACDA or CDA 67525
 (*Symphonies 2 & 3, General Booth*). Dallas SO, Litton; (i) with Albert, Dallas
 Symphony Ch.

Recorded live in Dallas in 2004 and 2006, Andrew Litton's two discs cover the symphonies of Ives in the most logical way, with the four main works supplemented by two of his most striking shorter pieces, a coupling offering an advantage over rival versions. Litton is totally in sympathy with Ives's distinctive use of hymns and marches. The *First Symphony*, with its echoes of Dvořák's *New World*, already points forward to the composer's later radical development. The *Fourth Symphony* (with Litton supported in the extraordinarily complex writing by the assistant conductor, Daniel Rechev) emerges as a masterpiece. Amazing music to have been conceived as early as it was, with the contrapuntal element so important in Ives's writing clarified, and the hilarious introduction of 'Yankee Doodle' in the fourth movement given delightful point. The *Second Symphony*, while still retaining links with the nineteenth-century tradition, is distinctively Ivesian in many of its procedures, with hymns and marches superimposed on more conventional passages, often celebrating the American brass band. The hilarious finale, brilliantly caught in Litton's performance, is a quodlibet with one theme piled on another, erupting finally in a shattering *fortissimo* account of *Columbia, the Gem of the Ocean*. On the face of it, the *Third Symphony* is less radical than the others; it is entitled *The Camp Meeting*, with the three movements based on organ pieces Ives wrote early in his career. *Central Park in the Dark* emerges as the most vividly atmospheric piece, evoking the impressions of someone at night, sitting in the park and hearing a kaleidoscope of subtle sounds of the surrounding city. *General William Booth enters into Heaven* is an orchestral development of one of the most stirring of Ives's songs, a setting of a poem by Vichel Lindsay. With soloist and chorus joining the orchestra, it develops to a massive climax, vividly caught in Litton's performance with Donnie Ray Albert as soloist. The sound, though not the most immediate, is vivid too, and is particularly spacious on SACD, with textures commendably clear, as in Ives's use of the piano as part of the orchestra in No. 4.

(i) *Symphony 2*; (ii) *The Unanswered Question*

DG DVD 073 4513. (i) Bav. RSO; (ii) NYPO; Bernstein (with **GERSHWIN**: *An American in Paris; Rhapsody in Blue*; Bernstein, piano, & NYPO)

An indispensable DVD. To watch Bernstein conduct these supreme masterpieces of American music is a joy and a privilege in itself, his face expressing almost every emotion and his communication with the orchestral players absolute. The richly resonant acoustic of the Royal Albert Hall casts a glow on the glittering rhythmic detail of *An American in Paris* from every member of the NYPO (especially the solo brass), which is as unforgettable as the arrival of the great blues centrepiece. Taking the solo role in the *Rhapsody*, Bernstein dominates completely, playing with a spontaneous freedom of tempo and nuance (his virtuosity is tangible), while in the Ives *Symphony* he produces radiantly expressive string textures from the Bavarian strings and captivates the ear with the composer's kaleidoscopic quotations of popular tunes. The symphony's close is all but overwhelming, to be followed by the epilogue of *The Unanswered Question* with its insistent, haunting trumpet solo. At a Harvard University lecture Bernstein said, 'I'm no longer sure what the question is, but I do know the answer is "Yes".' After the music drifts into silence he leaves the podium to delay any applause. (The DVD includes a talk about the symphony by Bernstein himself.)

JANÁČEK, Leoš (1854–1928)

(i) *Sinfonietta*; *Taras Bulba*; (ii) *Lachian Dances*; (iii; iv) *Capriccio 'Vzdor'* (for piano & chamber ens.); *Concertino*; (iii; v) *Dumka* (for violin & piano); (vi) *Mládí*; (iii; vii) *Pohádka*; *Presto* (for cello & piano); (iii; v) *Romance* (for violin & piano); (viii) *String Quartets 1*; *2 (Listy Důvěrné)*;

(ix) *Suite for String Orchestra*; (iii; v) *Violin Sonata*; (iii) *In the Mists*;
On an overgrown path; *Reminiscence*; *Teme con variazioni
(Variations for Zdenka)*; (x) *Glagolitic Mass*; (iv; xi) *Říkadla*
Decca (ADD/DDD) 475 523-2 (5). (i) VPO, Mackerras; (ii) LPO, Huybrechts; (iii) Crossley;
　(iv) London Sinf. (members), Atherton; (v) Sillito; (vi) Bell, Craxton, Pay, Harris, Gatt,
　Eastop; (vii) Christopher Van Kampen; (viii) Gabrieli String Qt; (ix) LA CO, Marriner;
　(x) Urbanová, Beňačková, Bogachov, Novák, Slovak Phil. Ch., VPO, Chailly; (xi) London
　Sinf. Ch.

A multitude of performances and artists here, but a very useful and inexpensive
way of acquiring a lot of Janáček. Mackerras's famous, early-digital accounts of
the *Sinfonietta* and *Taras Bulba* (1981) are well known: brilliant, exciting performances with recording to match, even though some might find the VPO
just too Viennese for this music. The performances of the much rarer *Lachian
Dances* date from 1971, are highly idiomatic and make a welcome appearance
here. The two *String Quartets* come from the composer's last years and are
among his most deeply individual works and profoundly impassioned utterances. The Gabrieli Quartet have the measure of this highly original music and
give just as idiomatic an account of these masterpieces, with the advantage of
vintage (1978) Decca sound, with clarity as well as warmth. The *Suite for String
Orchestra* was Marriner's first record with his new Los Angeles group, which
he made during the orchestra's 1974 tour in England. It is an early and not
entirely mature piece; but when it is played as committedly as it is here (and
ripely recorded), its attractions are readily perceived and it does not want character. Paul Crossley is the impressive soloist in the *Capriccio* and the *Concertino*.
In the account of *Mládí*, the work's youthful sparkle comes across to excellent
effect. Crossley's survey of the piano music is both poetic and perceptive, and
his mastery of keyboard colour and feeling for atmosphere are everywhere evident, and the sound that the engineers have achieved is very truthful and
satisfying. The set brings a number of rarities, including the *Violin Sonata* and
the *Říkadla* for chamber choir and ten instruments, both works very much
worth getting to hear. Finally, Chailly's strong and refined reading of the
Glagolitic Mass makes a splendid finale for this set, with fine detail brought out
in the glowing Decca recording (1998), even if it is not as immediate as some. If
the work's earthiness is a degree underplayed, the emotional depth is fully
brought out, with fine, idiomatic singing and a virtuoso display from Thomas
Trotter in the final organ solo. A distinguished set.

Glagolitic Mass (original version, ed. Wingfield)
Chan. 9310. Kiberg, Stene, Svensson, Cold, Danish Nat. R. Ch. & SO, Mackerras –
　KODÁLY: *Psalmus hungaricus*

The added rhythmic complexities of this original version as interpreted idiomatically by Mackerras encourage an apt wildness which brings an exuberant,
carefree quality to writing which here, more than ever, seems like the

inspiration of the moment. The wildness is also reinforced by having the *Intrada* at the very beginning, before the Introduction, as well as at the end. The chorus sings incisively with incandescent tone, and the tenor soloist, Peter Svensson, has a trumpet-toned precision that makes light of the tessitura and the stratospheric leaps that Janáček asks for. The soprano Tina Kiberg, also bright and clear rather than beautiful in tone, makes just as apt a choice, and only a certain unsteadiness in Ulrik Cold's relatively light bass tone prevents this from being an ideal quartet. Recorded sound of weight and warmth that conveys the full power of the music.

The Cunning Little Vixen (complete); Cunning Little Vixen: Suite (arr. Talich)

Decca 417 129-2 (2). Popp, Randová, Jedlićka, V. State Op. Ch., Bratislava Children's Ch., VPO, Mackerras

Mackerras's thrusting, red-blooded reading is spectacularly supported by a digital recording of outstanding, demonstration quality. The inspired choice of Lucia Popp as the vixen provides charm in exactly the right measure, sparkling and coquettish, spiteful as well as passionate. The supporting cast is first rate too. Talich's splendidly arranged orchestral suite is offered as a bonus in a fine, new recording. Simon Rattle's Covent Garden performance on Chandos is also strongly recommended for anyone wanting this opera sung in English (CHAN 3101 (2)).

(i) From the House of the Dead; (iii) Mládí (for wind sextet); (ii; iii) Ríkadla (for Chamber Ch. & 10 instruments)

Decca 430 375-2 (2). (i) Jedlička, Zahradníček, Zídek, Zítek, V. State Op. Ch., VPO. Mackerras; (ii) L. Sinf. Ch.; (iii) L. Sinf., Atherton

With one exception, the Decca cast is superb, with a range of important Czech singers giving sharply characterized vignettes. The exception is the raw Slavonic singing of the one woman in the cast, Jaroslava Janská, as the boy, Aljeja, but even that fails to undermine the intensity of the innocent relationship with the central figure, which provides an emotional anchor for the whole piece. The chamber-music items added for this reissue are both first rate.

Jenůfa (complete)

Ⓜ Decca 475 8227 (2). Söderström, Ochman, Dvorský, Randová, Popp, V. State Op. Ch., VPO, Mackerras

It was with *Jenůfa* that Janáček scored his first real success in the opera house: the work has a striking and immediate sense of identity, a powerful atmosphere and a strong dramatic argument. This is the warmest and most lyrical of Janáček's operas. And it inspired a performance from Mackerras and his team which is deeply sympathetic, strongly dramatic and superbly recorded. Elisabeth Söderström creates a touching portrait of the girl caught in a family tragedy. The two rival tenors, Petr Dvorský and Wieslav Ochman as the half-brothers Steva and Laca, are both superb; but dominating the whole drama is the Kostelnička of Eva Randová. Some may resist the idea that she is made so sympathetic but, particularly on record, the drama is made stronger and more involving. Chandos's 'Opera in English' series has made a superb performance of this opera available – also with Mackerras conducting – with a superb cast including Janice Watson and Josephine Barstow (CHAN 3106 (2)).

Káta Kabanová; (ii) *Capriccio for Piano & 7 instruments*; *Concertino for Piano & 6 instruments*

Ⓜ Decca 475 7518 (2). Söderström, Dvorský, Kniplová, Krejčík, Márová, V. State Op. Ch., VPO, Mackerras; (ii) Paul Crossley, L. Sinf., Atherton

Káta Kabanová is based on Ostrovsky's play, *The Storm*. Elisabeth Söderström dominates the cast as the tragic heroine and gives a performance of great insight and sensitivity; she touches the listener deeply and is supported by Mackerras with imaginative grip and flair. He draws playing of great eloquence from the Vienna Philharmonic Orchestra. The other soloists are all Czech and their characterizations are brilliantly authentic. But it is the superb orchestral playing and the inspired performance of Söderström that make this set so memorable. The recording has a truthfulness and realism that do full justice to Janáček's marvellous score, vividly transferred to CD. With a double bonus added in the shape of the two concertante keyboard works, in which Paul Crossley is the impressive soloist. These are performances which can be put alongside Firkušný – and no praise can be higher.

(i) *The Makropulos Affair (Věc Makropulos):* complete; (ii) *Lachian Dances*

Decca 430 372-2 (2). Söderström, Dvorský, Blachut, V. State Op. Ch., VPO, Mackerras; (ii) LPO, Huybrechts

Mackerras and his superb team provide a thrilling new perspective on this opera, with its weird heroine preserved by magic elixir well past her 300th birthday. Elisabeth Söderström is not simply malevolent – irritable and impatient rather, no longer an obsessive monster. Framed by richly colourful singing and playing, Söderström amply justifies that view, and Peter Dvorský is superbly fresh and ardent as Gregor. The recording, like others in the series, is of Decca's highest analogue quality. The performance of the *Lachian Dances* is highly idiomatic and makes a good bonus. Mackerras's equally commanding ENO performance (sung in English) is also available at mid-price on Chandos (CHAN 3138 (2)) – one of the finest performances in their 'Opera in English' series.

Osud (complete; in English)

Ⓜ Chan. 3029. Langridge, Field, Harries, Bronder, Kale, Welsh Nat. Op. Ch. & O, Mackerras

Janáček's – most unjustly neglected – opera, richly lyrical, more sustained and less fragmented than his later operas, is not just a valuable rarity but makes an ideal introduction to this composer. Philip Langridge is superb in the central role of the composer, Zivný, well supported by Helen Field as Mila, the married woman he loves, and by Kathryn Harries as her mother – a far finer cast than was presented on a short-lived Supraphon set. Sir Charles Mackerras matches his earlier achievements on the prize-winning series of Janáček opera recordings for Decca, capturing the full gutsiness, passion and impetus of the composer's inspiration. The warmly atmospheric (originally EMI) recording, made in Brangwyn Hall, Swansea, brings out the unusual opulence of the Janáček sound, yet it allows the words to come over with fine clarity. It is now available on Chandos's now extensive (and generally superb) 'Opera in English' series, all at mid-price, with full texts included.

JÄRNEFELT, Armas (1869–1958)

(i) *Berceuse for violin and orchestra. Serenade*; *Suite in E flat*; *Symphonic Fantasy*
BISCD 1753. Lahti SO, Kuusisto (conductor or (i) violin)

Armas Järnefelt is best known for his two popular miniatures, the *Prelude* and *Berceuse*, the remainder of his output having fallen into complete and total oblivion. He was Sibelius's brother-in-law, four years his junior, and almost equally long-lived: he died in 1958, a year later than Sibelius. The Järnefelts were a gifted family: the father was a provincial governor, Aino (who married Sibelius) was a woman of great culture and intelligence; Armas's brother Arvid was a successful novelist, and Eero, to whom Sibelius was close, was a distinguished painter. Armas's career as a conductor rather overshadowed his creative work: he served as chief conductor of the Royal Swedish Opera (1907–32) and spent most of his life in Stockholm. He was a champion of Wagner and introduced several operas to Helsinki during his time there (1904–6).

The bulk of his work comes from the 1890s: the *Serenade* (1893) was written when he was living in Paris and studying with Massenet. This was the period in which, fresh from the success of the *Kullervo Symphony*, Sibelius had embarked on the *Four Legends*. The *Serenade* is a six-movement work lasting half an hour and was his first major opus. The *Symphonic Fantasy*, written in Berlin, comes from January 1895. Its first performance two months later proved to be its last during the composer's lifetime. It met with a generally hostile reception.

It is evident from all the works on this record that Armas Järnefelt was a man of the orchestra; his scoring is sure and colourful and his invention, if not strongly individual, is strong enough to hold the listener. Although his Scandinavian nationalism and his admiration for Wagner are plain to see, his ideas are often appealing and always well laid out for the orchestra. The five-movement *Suite in E flat* from 1897 is probably the most interesting piece here and is well worth getting to know. After the *Berceuse* for violin and orchestra of 1904, the creative fires burned out and his conducting career came to consume him. Jaakko Kuusisto directs the excellent Lahti orchestra with sensitivity and persuasiveness and, as one expects from this label, the sound is vivid and faithful.

JOSQUIN DESPREZ (c. 1450–1521)

Ave Maria (for 4 voices); *Chanson L'Homme armé*; *Missa L'Homme armé super voces musicales*; *Missa L'Homme armé sexti toni*; *Missa La sol fà re mi*; Plainchant: *Pange lingua*. *Missa Pange lingua*; *Praeter rerum seriem*
Ⓑ Gimell CDGIM 206 (2). Tallis Scholars, Phillips

In his notes for this collection Peter Phillips comments that Josquin was as influential in his time as Beethoven was in his. He wrote as marvellously for voices as Beethoven for instruments, and to evoke his name in the same breath as Beethoven's is the best way to put him where he deserves to be. 'In fact,' he said, 'I have come of think of Josquin's sixteen or so authenticated Masses as an equivalent achievement to Beethoven's nine symphonies, each one an intellectual and technical tour de force [see below], each one showing a different side to his personality.'

This two-for-the-price-of-one offer generously combines nearly all the contents of two Josquin CDs, including two of the most familiar settings, both based on the familiar chanson, used by many of his contemporaries, *L'Homme armé*. The recordings of the *Missa Pange lingua* and the ingenious *Missa La sol fà re mi* are also unsurpassed and won a *Gramophone* Award in 1987. The motet, *Ave Maria*, makes a beautiful closing item. The recordings are outstanding, as are the perfectly blended flowing lines of the singing.

(i) *Messe Ave Maris Stella*; *Missa de Beata Virgine*; *Missa Gaudeamus*; *Missa L'Homme armé sexti toni*; *Missa L'Homme armé super voces musicales*; *Missa Pange lingua. Motets à la Vierge*; (ii) *Missa Hercules dux Ferrariae*; Motets: *Inviolata, integra, et casta es, Maria*; *Miserere mei, Deus*. Instrumental pieces: *Chi à Martello Dio Gu'il Toglia*; *Deus, in nomine tuo salvum me fac*
Naive Astrée Auvidis E 8906 (6). A sei voci; (i) Maîtrise des Pays de Loire (members); (ii) Maîtrise Notre-Dame de Paris, Les Saqueboutiers de Toulouse, Ens. Labyrinthes; all directed Fabre-Garrus

Bernard Fabre-Garrus's pacing and flexibility of line are masterly. Five of the six discs include a major Mass setting, together with a group of motets, of which the Paris recording is the most spectacular. This CD (E 8601) offers the

Mass for Hercules, Duke of Ferrara, which is supported throughout by a brass group, who play an introduction and postlude (for sackbuts and drums), and includes also a specially sung and played tribute to the Duke, plus memorable performances of the *Miserere mei, Deus* and an invocation to the Virgin, *Inviolata, integra, et casta es, Maria*. The disc including the beautiful *Missa de Beata Virgine* (in six parts, richly sung by twelve voices) includes five appropriate linking motets *à la Vierge*, including a fine *Ave Maria* and *Stabat Mater* (E 8560). The *Missa Gaudeamus* (E 8612) with its soaring soprano line also stands out as among Josquin's most beautiful Mass settings, while it is fascinating to hear both versions of *L'Homme armé*, where Josquin draws on his cantus firmus so subtly that one has to listen very hard to spot it. Altogether a superb set, faithfully recorded in a warm but not clouding acoustic, and well documented, if in very small print.

Masses: *Missa Fortuna desperata*; *Missa Malheur me bat*

Gimell CDGIM 042. Tallis Scholars, Phillips

The two remarkable Masses offered here are linked by having secular polyphonic songs as their source material. Both were written in three voices, and Josquin paraphrased material from all three vocal parts for his Masses, with *Missa Fortuna desperata* one of the earliest examples of such complex borrowing. The use of these 'quotations' is unpredictable, and not always easy to spot aurally, giving the music extra appeal for the listener interested in discovering its derivations. In the *Credo* of *Missa Fortuna desperata*, for instance, Josquin takes the top part of the chanson and quotes it four times in succession with diminishing speeds, giving the music a powerful impetus. But it is the beauty of the flowing forward momentum which is so compelling in Josquin's writing throughout, and the opening of *Missa Malheur me bat* is particularly rich in its melodic flow. The closing sections of each Mass are comparable. There are three settings of the *Agnus Dei* at the end of the *Missa Malheur* and, even though *Missa Fortuna* has only two, it reaches a comparably deeply satisfying conclusion, and the listener is held powerfully in the music's textural grip. So this makes a particularly rewarding coupling, sung with great conviction and comparable flexibility by the Tallis Scholars, and beautifully recorded. Peter Phillips's notes are exemplary too.

Motetti de Passione . . . B (1503): *Ave verum corpus*; *Christem ducem/Qui velatus*; *Domine, non secundum*; *O Domine Jesu Christe*; *Tu solus, qui facis mirabilia*; *Missa Faisant regretz*

Gaudeamus CDGAU 302. Clerks' Group, Wickham

Josquin's compact but characteristically fluent and appealing four-part Mass setting, *Faisant regretz*, is based on a four-note motif taken from Walter Frye's rondeau for three voices, *Tout a par moy*, which is also included on this CD. This dolorous song must have been very famous in its day, and Josquin ingeniously weaves the very striking motto theme (always easy to recognize) into his vocal texture with great imaginative resource – right through to the *Agnus Dei*. But even more striking in this outstanding collection is the cycle of five motets largely based on the readings in Petrucci, *Motetti de Passione . . . B* of 1503. They are arrestingly chordal in style, the opening declamatory *Tu solus, qui facis mirabilia*, with its bare harmonies, arrestingly so. The extended *Christem ducem/Qui velatus* (a setting of Passiontide hymns by St Bonaventure), which Wickham rightly places last, is the most movingly expressive of all. Superb performances, given an uncanny presence in an ideal acoustic.

KABALEVSKY, Dmitri (1904-87)

The Comedians: Suite
RCA (ADD) 09026 63302-2. RCA Victor SO, Kondrashin – **RIMSKY-KORSAKOV**: *Capriccio espagnol*. **KHACHATURIAN**: *Masquerade Suite*.
TCHAIKOVSKY: *Capriccio italien*

On this classic RCA CD the *Comedians' Galop* follows on almost immediately after the finale of Khachaturian's *Masquerade*, and the impetuous stylistic link is obvious. Kondrashin's performance is affectionate and colourful as well as lively, and the warm resonance of the recording helps prevent the music from sounding too brash. It is irresistibly tuneful and one smiles at its energetic effervescence – a sort of Russian Offenbachian spirit pervades this suite of generally short but varied numbers, with the orchestral colours ear-tickling in invention. The quirky *Gavotte* is one of the *Suite*'s many highlights. The Tchaikovsky and Rimsky-Korsakov couplings are marvellous.

(i) *Piano Concerto 3 (Dedicated to Soviet Youth)*; *Rhapsody for Piano & Orchestra on a Theme of the Song 'School Years'*; (ii) *Poem of Struggle for Orchestra & Chorus*
🅑🅑 Naxos 8.557794. RPO, Yablonsky; with (i) Liu; (ii) Gnesin Academy Ch. (with **RIMSKY-KORSAKOV**: *Piano Concerto*)

The light and cheerful *Third Piano Concerto* receives a sparkling performance here, and it is very well recorded. The *Rhapsody*, premièred in 1964, is based on a popular song Kabalevsky wrote in 1957 called *School Years*. It is unashamedly tuneful and unpretentious and its simple and catchy tunes are irresistible in this lively performance. *The Poem of Struggle*, written in 1931, is more serious, with the composer intending to portray contemporary modern reality. It is no masterpiece, but the rousing chorus at the end is quite effective. Rimsky-Korsakov's *Piano Concerto*, though brief (14 minutes), is a thoroughly entertaining piece with its appealing Russian folksong motif and all the character for which this composer is famous; it makes a fine bonus for the Kabalevsky works.

KARAJAN, Herbert von, conducting Berlin
Philharmonic Orchestra

'In Concert': BEETHOVEN: *Overtures: Coriolan; Egmont.*
ROSSINI: *William Tell.* WAGNER: *Tannhäuser Overture.*
WEBER: *Der Freischütz Overture.* DEBUSSY: *La Mer; Prélude
à l'après-midi d'un faune.* RACHMANINOV: *Piano Concerto 2*
(with Alexis Weissenberg). RAVEL: *Daphnis et Chloé: Suite 2* (with
bonus: Karajan Portrait 'Impressions').
DG DVD 073 4399

Taken from the 1970s, this DVD brings compelling accounts of the master at
work, visually as well as aurally. There is a powerful intensity to the Beethoven
overtures and the opening of *William Tell* is beautifully done, with glorious
playing from the Berliners: the storm music is spectacular and the final *galop*
is as dashing as can be. The horns are glorious in *Der Freischütz* and the famous Berlin brass come into their own in the Wagner *Tannhäuser Overture*, while
the warmth and brilliance of the strings are particularly striking in both. Karajan was always impressive in French repertoire, and this *La Mer* is very good
indeed, if perhaps not quite as intensely compelling as his classic account from
the 1960s. The Rachmaninov concerto is a surprisingly intimate account, not a
showy one, though one marvels at the quality of the orchestral playing, with
Weissenberg, who can be a very fine pianist on his day, the poetic soloist. The
central movement is wonderfully intense, and the finale has plenty of sparkle.
The opening of the *Daphnis Suite* is as haunting as the finale is exciting in its
virtuosic blaze of colour. The sensitive, unobtrusive camerawork adds much to
the enjoyment of these performances. The documentary was made in 1978 (in
German, with English subtitles). There is plenty of fascinating archival material to see; and within the maestro's obviously glamorous, jet-set lifestyle, he
emerges as a musical communicator of warmth – and humour too. A most
revealing issue.

KARAJAN, Herbert von, conducting Berlin
Philharmonic Orchestra, Vienna Philharmonic Orchestra or Orchestre
de Paris

BEETHOVEN (with Oistrakh, Rostropovich, Richter, BPO): *Triple
Concerto.* WAGNER (with BPO): *Der fliegende Holländer:
Overture. Lohengrin: Preludes to Acts I & III. Die Meistersinger
von Nürnberg: Overture. Parsifal: Preludes to Act I & III.
Tannhäuser: Overture & Venusberg Music. Tristan und Isolde:
Prelude & Liebestod.* BRAHMS (with VPO): *Symphony 2.*

MOZART: *Masonic Funeral Music, K.477.* **R. STRAUSS**
(with Rostropovich, BPO): *Don Quixote;* (with VPO): *Metamorphosen;*
(with BPO): *Symphonia domestica.* **SIBELIUS** (with BPO): *En Saga;*
Finlandia; Karelia Suite; Tapiola; Valse Triste; Symphonies 4 & 5.
BRUCKNER: *Symphony 7.* **DEBUSSY**: *La Mer; Prélude*
à l'après-midi d'un faune. **RAVEL**: *Boléro;* (with O de Paris):
Alborada del gracioso; La Valse.
Ⓑ EMI mono/stereo 516091-2 (8)

A self-recommending eight-CD set which includes many of Karajan's finest
EMI recordings, from 1947 to the early 1980s, including a compellingly intense
version of Strauss's *Metamorphosen*. Other highlights include the predictably
fine account of *Don Quixote* with Rostropovitch, the 1975 recording sounding
excellent in this transfer. In the *Symphonia domestica* the sumptuous Berlin
strings produce tone of great magnificence (recorded in 1973). The Wagner
items (recorded in 1974) remain among the most recommendable on CD: the
body of tone produced by the BPO gives breathtaking amplitude at climaxes
and the electricity the conductor generates throughout the programme is
unforgettable. Karajan was a fine Sibelian, and while his accounts of the *Fourth*
and *Fifth Symphonies* (recorded in 1976) did not surpass his earlier, classic, DG
accounts, they are very impressive indeed: the variety of tone-colour and, above
all, the weight of sonority that the Berlin Philharmonic have at their command
are astonishing. This was his third recording of *Tapiola* but his first of *En Saga*,
where he is a brisk story-teller, more concerned with narrative than with
atmosphere at the beginning; but the *lento assai* section and the coda are quite
magical. *Finlandia* is superbly played and realistically recorded. This *Tapiola* is
broader and more spacious than his DG account. And at the storm section,
Karajan's spacious tempo is vindicated; the effect is altogether more electrifying. Karajan's 1977 *La Mer* may not have quite the supreme refinement of his
earlier, DG version, but it has comparable concentration and with the structure
persuasively and inevitably built. The *Prélude* has appropriate languor and
there is a persuasive warmth about this performance, which is beautifully
moulded. The Paris Ravel recordings were taped in 1974 and are outstanding,
as is the Berlin *Boléro* which has fine presence and splendid forward impetus.
The star-studded cast for the Beethoven *Triple Concerto* (recorded in 1969)
makes a breathtaking line-up. This is warm, expansive music-making that
confirms even more clearly than before the strength of the piece. The resonant
recording suffers from a loss of focus in some climaxes but this is not too serious. The Bruckner *Symphony No. 7*, recorded in 1970-71, is really outstanding
and Karajan shows a superb feeling for the work's architecture. The recording
has striking resonance and amplitude; this EMI release has a sense of mystery
which is really rather special. The Brahms *Second Symphony* was recorded in
1949 and has compelling intensity and warmth, with an intense *Adagio* and an
exceptionally fresh and lively finale.

KARAJAN, Herbert von, conducting Vienna
Philharmonic Orchestra

'The Legendary Decca Recordings': **BRAHMS**: *Symphonies 1 & 3; Tragic Overture.* **HAYDN**: *Symphony 103 (Drumroll) & 104 (London).* **MOZART**: *Symphonies 40 & 41 (Jupiter).* **BEETHOVEN**: *Symphony 7.* **DVOŘÁK**: *Symphony 8.* **TCHAIKOVSKY**: *Nutcracker, Sleeping Beauty & Swan Lake: Suites; Romeo and Juliet Fantasy Overture.* **ADAM**: *Giselle.* **GRIEG**: *Peer Gynt: Suites.* **HOLST**: *The Planets.* **J. STRAUSS, Sr**: *Annen-Polka.* **J. STRAUSS**, Jr: *Auf der Jagd; Die Fledermaus: Overture & Ballet Music; Geschichten aus dem Wienerwald: Waltz. Der Zigeunerbaron: Overture.* **JOSEF STRAUSS**: *Delirien Waltz.* **R. STRAUSS**: *Also sprach Zarathustra; Don Juan; Salome: Dance of the 7 Veils; Till Eulenspiegel; Tod und Verklärung*

Ⓜ Decca (ADD) 478 0155 (9)

Karajan's short spell with Decca produced some of his finest recordings with the VPO. In that category here are the Richard Strauss tone-poems, performances full of character and sharply detailed. One marvels at the wide dynamic range of *Also sprach Zarathustra* (1959) as much for the recordings as for the thrilling orchestral virtuosity. *Till* is irrepressibly cheeky and full of wit, and *Salome's Dance* is decadently sensuous. *Don Juan* brings a similar, richly voluptuous response from the Vienna strings. Again, the playing is superb, as beguiling in the love music as it is exhilarating in the chase. The Johann Strauss items also come off magnificently, with an instinctive Viennese lilt in the waltzes and playing of warmth as well as vivaciousness. The rarely heard ballet music to *Die Fledermaus* is especially enjoyable, and his 1961 version of *The Planets* is extraordinarily magnetic and powerful. Tchaikovsky's *Romeo and Juliet* is one of the great performances of the analogue stereo era: the moonlight music is as magical as the fight scenes are dramatic, and the Decca sound captures both beautifully. Of the two Haydn symphonies here, No. 104 comes off better, with Karajan's direct approach, with plenty of earthy vigour in the outer movements and a beautifully shaped slow movement. In Mozart's No. 40, Karajan is articulate and suave, and the performance has genuine dramatic power, even though one feels it moves within carefully regulated emotional limits. Although it is short on repeats, the reading of the *Jupiter* is a strong one, direct and with breadth as well as warmth. Of the performances of the Brahms *Symphonies*, the *Third* is the more successful – the *First* lacks a certain amount of adrenalin, though is not without character and is extremely vividly recorded, while the *Third*, certainly expansive (especially the third movement), is a degree more compelling. The Dvořák *Eighth* is a rich, expansive performance of the first rank. It gets off to a very good start with an especially warm treatment of the lovely opening theme, and it is only later, when an occasional mannerism tends to hold up the flow of the slow movement, that a degree of spontaneity is taken from this otherwise excellent reading. The Beethoven *Seventh* is a straight, matter-of-fact account, reasonably effective, but without the usual compulsion we expect from this conductor. However, Karajan's recording of *Giselle* is lovingly played, a reading of beauty and elegance. The glowing Decca recording is first rate and, as the legend of the Wilis on which *Giselle* is based is a German one, has the distinct impression of Austrian peasantry, and the hunting music will seem to many very appropriate. The Grieg *Peer Gynt Suites* are delightfully and effectively done. Finally, the Tchaikovsky ballet suites are very impressive indeed; tuttis are well focused and the glowing ambience of the Sofiensaal flatters the strings and adds to the woodwind colourings, particularly in the *Nutcracker Suite*, which is less bland here than in Karajan's later re-recording with the BPO. Overall, this disc offers very fine playing from the Vienna Philharmonic and, although the atmosphere is generally relaxed (especially in *Sleeping Beauty*), there is persuasive warmth. The (1959–65) transfers throughout this set are of Decca's best.

KERN, Jerome (1885–1945)

Show Boat (complete recording of original score)
EMI 3 61543-2 [3 61554-2] (3). Von Stade, Hadley, Hubbard, O'Hara, Garrison, Burns, Stratas, Amb. Ch., L. Sinf., McGlinn

In faithfully following the original score, this superb set at last does justice to a musical of the 1920s which is both a landmark in the history of Broadway and musically a work of strength and imagination hardly less significant than Gershwin's *Porgy and Bess* of a decade later. The original, extended versions of important scenes are included, as well as various numbers written for later productions. As the heroine, Magnolia, Frederica von Stade gives a meltingly beautiful performance, totally in style, bringing out the beauty and imagination of Kern's melodies, regularly heightened by wide intervals to make those of most of his Broadway rivals seem flat. The London Sinfonietta play with tremendous zest and feeling for the idiom; the Ambrosian Chorus sings with joyful brightness and some impeccable American accents. Opposite von Stade, Jerry Hadley makes a winning Ravenal, and Teresa Stratas is charming as Julie, giving a heartfelt performance of the haunting number, 'Bill' (words by P. G. Wodehouse). Above all, the magnificent black bass, Bruce Hubbard, sings 'Ol' man river' and its many reprises with a firm resonance to have you recalling the wonderful example of Paul Robeson, but for once without hankering after the past. Beautifully recorded to bring out the piece's dramatic as well as its musical qualities, this is a heart-warming issue.

KHACHATURIAN, Aram (1903-78)

Violin Concerto in D min.

Pentatone SACD Surround Sound PTC 5186 059. Julia Fischer, Russian Nat. O,
Kreizberg - **GLAZUNOV**: *Violin Concerto.* **PROKOFIEV**: *Violin Concerto 1*

Khachaturian's *Violin Concerto* has fair claim to be his most rewarding work, and is certainly preferable to his more inflated *Piano Concerto*. It was written for David Oistrakh, who made a fine mono recording of it, but Julia Fischer has the advantage of first-class surround sound with its vividness and presence. The clarity and freshness of her performance are what immediately strike home in the chattering figuration at the start, with a rare tenderness developing in the lyrical second subject. The yearning lyricism of the slow movement confirms that this was one of the composer's most inspired works in a performance of high contrasts, while the biting clarity of Fischer's performance in the finale brings lightness and sparkle.

Gayaneh (ballet: excerpts); *Spartacus* (ballet; excerpts)

Onyx 4063. Bournemouth SO, Kirill Karabits

Ⓜ Decca (ADD) 460 315-2. VPO, composer (with **GLAZUNOV**: *The Seasons*)

Khachaturian came to Vienna in 1962 to record these impressively idiomatic performances of the most popular numbers from his two ballets, and this Decca record is totally authentic. It is superbly remastered to restore and even improve on the demonstration quality of the original LP, recorded in the Sofiensaal. The performances of these flamboyantly colourful scores are very fresh indeed, and the coupling of *The Seasons*, with Ansermet conducting, is very good too.

However, much more recently, in July 2010, Kirill Karabits virtually upstaged the composer's coupling by carefully selecting the best numbers from each ballet, offering nearly 73 minutes of music (eleven items from *Gayaneh* and six from *Spartacus*). He shows a natural feeling for the Armenian flavour of the composer's lyrical writing and produces great gusto for the exciting numbers, like the *Sabre Dance*. The climax of the masterly *Adagio of Spartacus and Phrygia* could not be more gloriously passionate. The Bournemouth orchestra plays splendidly and the recording (apparently made in the Poole Lighthouse!) is expansive and wide-ranging.

Masquerade Suite

RCA (ADD) 09026 63302-2. RCA Victor SO, Kondrashin - **RIMSKY-KORSAKOV**:
Capriccio espagnol. **KABALEVSKY**: *The Comedians: Suite.*
TCHAIKOVSKY: *Capriccio italien*

Kondrashin certainly knows how to play this music, with warmth as well as sparkle, and even a touch of romantic elegance when Oscar Shumsky plays the violin solo in the *Nocturne*. It is hard not to be all but swept off your feet by the deliciously melancholic *Waltz* which opens this CD, while the *Mazurka* has all the bright energy and colourful orchestration we know from the ballet, *Gayaneh*. The final *Galop* is as boisterous as one could wish and as a whole this is a thoroughly entertaining sub-20 minutes' listening. The resonant recording gives the orchestra a pleasing ambience.

KODÁLY, Zoltán (1882–1967)

(i–ii) *Ballet Music*; *Concerto for Orchestra*; *Dances of Galánta*; *Dances of Marosszék*; *Háry János: Suite*. *Hungarian Rondo*; *Minuetto serio*; *(iii) Variations on a Hungarian Folk Song (The Peacock)*; *Summer Evening*; *Symphony in C*; *Theatre Overture*. (iii–v) *Háry János* (Singspiel: complete). (vi) *The Peacock* (folksong for unaccompanied chorus); (vii; v; iii) *Psalmus hungaricus, Op. 13*.
Ⓑ Decca 478 2303 (4). (i) Dorati; (ii) Philharmonia Hungarica; (iii) LSO, Kertész; (iv) Ustinov (nar.), Komlóssy, Palócz, Melis, Bende, Szőnyi, László, Edinburgh Festival Ch.; (v) Wandsworth School Boys' Ch.; (vi) L. Symphony Ch.; (vii) Kozma, Brighton Festival Ch.

Kodály has been lucky on disc. His vibrantly colourful music has inspired many great conductors to give of their best, as well as giving recording engineers a chance to show their prowess. Following his monumental complete Haydn *Symphonies* survey, Dorati and his orchestra turned to the music of their compatriot, and performed it with the same sense of commitment. He included all the composer's most famous orchestral works, as well as his less well-known works, and this is the first time they have been issued complete. His reading of the popular *Háry János Suite* can stand comparison with the finest, both as a performance and technically as a recording. The *Dances of Galánta* and *Marosszék* have real flair and virtuosity, and while the *Minuetto serio* is a slight piece, it has some charm. If the late *Concerto for Orchestra* never quite fulfils its promise, it contains many attractive ideas, but the equally rare *Theatre Overture* (intended to precede *Háry János*) is thoroughly entertaining throughout its fourteen minutes' duration. Similarly, also intended for *Háry János* is the short *Ballet Music* – and very vivid and colourful it is too. *The Peacock Variations*, it has to be admitted, is not the most polished performance the work has ever received, but it is still most enjoyable, and makes one wonder at its relative neglect. The same might also be said of the *Hungarian Rondo*, a delightful eight-minute work, full of catchy tunes, in richly coloured orchestral dress. Only the *Symphony* disappoints in terms of richness of ideas, but it too is worth exploring. Kertész takes over for the choral items, and he directs a superb version of the *Psalmus hungaricus* – the composer's most vital choral work. Kertész's energy takes one compellingly through all the straight homophonic writing, which in a lesser performance can diminish the work's stature. Here, with the chorus trained by another Hungarian musician, the results are electrifying, and the recording is outstandingly brilliant to match. The light tenor tone of Lajos Kozma is not ideal for the solo part, but again the authentic Hungarian touch helps. Also included in this set is the complete *Háry János* play with music. It was an attempt to re-create in recording terms for English-speaking listeners the curious humour of the original Hungarian play. All of Kodály's music is included, and all the links are provided by Peter Ustinov in many guises. Though perhaps the humour will not be to all tastes, Peter Ustinov – a master raconteur – is a superb and compelling narrator and one cannot imagine a more authentic performance. There are a number of pieces as attractive as those in the well-known suite, and vocal versions of some that many will know already. Superb recording from the late 1960s.

Psalmus hungaricus, Op. 13
Chan. 9310. Svensson, Copenhagen Boys' Ch., Danish Nat. R. Ch. & SO, Mackerras –
JANÁČEK: *Glagolitic Mass*

As the unusual but refreshing coupling for the Janáček *Mass*, the *Psalmus hungaricus* is infected by Mackerras with an element of wildness that sweeps away any idea of Kodály as a bland composer. As in the Janáček, the tenor Peter Svensson is an excellent, clear-toned and incisive soloist, if here rather more backwardly balanced. The glory of the performance lies most of all in the superb choral singing, full, bright and superbly disciplined, with the hushed *pianissimos* as telling as the great *fortissimo* outbursts. It is a mark of Mackerras's understanding of the music that the many sudden changes of mood sound both dramatic and natural. Full, warm and atmospheric recording, with plenty of detail.

KOECHLIN, Charles (1867–1950)

The Jungle Book (Le Livre de la jungle)
Marco Polo 8.223484. Reinland-Pfalz PO, Segerstam

Koechlin's lifelong fascination with Kipling's *Jungle Book* is reflected in this four-movement tone-poem whose composition extended over several decades. *La Course de printemps*, Op. 95, the longest of them, is extraordinarily imaginative and pregnant with atmosphere: you can feel the heat and humidity of the rainforest and sense the presence of strange and menacing creatures. *La Loi de la jungle* is the most static and the least interesting. Leif Segerstam is excellent in this repertoire and, with his refined ear for texture, distils a heady atmosphere; and he is beautifully recorded. Anyone with a feeling for the exotic will respond to this original and fascinating music.

KORNGOLD, Erich (1897–1957)

(i) *Cello Concerto in C, Op. 37*; (ii) *Piano Concerto in C sharp for the Left Hand, Op. 17*; *Symphonic Serenade for Strings, Op. 39*; *Military March in B flat*

Ⓜ Chan. 10433X. BBC PO, Bamert, with (i) Dixon; (ii) Shelley

The *Cello Concerto* is an adaptation of a short piece Korngold composed in 1946 for the film *Deception* starring Bette Davis and Claude Rains. The *Concerto in C sharp for Piano Left Hand* (1924) is altogether a different matter. Composed, like Ravel's *Concerto*, for the one-armed pianist, Paul Wittgenstein, who had lost his right arm during the First World War, it is an extraordinarily imaginative and resourceful work. Although it springs from a post-Straussian world, it is full of individual touches. Howard Shelley gives a radiant performance and is given splendid support. To complaints that the *Military March* (1917) was rather fast, Korngold is said to have replied that it was intended to be played for the retreat! The *Symphonic Serenade for Strings* is very beautiful (as well as beautifully crafted) with a highly inventive Scherzo and an eloquent, rather Mahlerian slow movement. First-rate playing and opulent, well-balanced recording.

Violin Concerto in D, Op. 35

Onyx 4016. Ehnes, Vancouver SO, Tovey – **BARBER**; **WALTON**: *Violin Concertos*

In this inspired and generous coupling, James Ehnes gives one of the finest performances of the *Concerto*, bringing out its full emotional thrust without vulgarity or exaggeration. His playing has always been impressive on disc but here he excels himself in the expressive range as well as the tonal beauty of his performance, with expressive rubato perfectly controlled and some ecstatic playing of the many stratospheric melodies above the stave. The opening oboe solo of the slow movement is radiantly played, and later Ehnes takes it up with ravishing warmth, as does the orchestra. The finale is dazzling, and this unsurpassed, spectacular recording is made the more indispensable by its Barber and Walton couplings.

Symphony in F sharp, Op. 40; (i) Abschiedslieder, Op. 14

Chan. 10431X. BBC PO, Downes, (i) with Finnie

The *Symphony* is a work of real imaginative power. It is scored for large forces – a big percussion section, including piano, celeste, marimba, etc. – and the orchestra is used with resource and flair. The BBC Philharmonic play with enthusiasm and sensitivity for Sir Edward Downes. The *Abschiedslieder* are much earlier and were completed in 1920; there is a great deal of Strauss, Mahler and Zemlinsky here. Linda Finnie is a persuasive soloist, and the balance is eminently well judged. The Chandos sound is wide-ranging and lifelike.

String Quartets 1 in A, Op. 16; 2 in E flat, Op. 26; 3 in D, Op. 34
Chan. 10611 Doric Qt

Korngold's *String Quartets* are of the highest quality. They were written at ten-year intervals; the first (extraordinarily mature) dates from 1920–23, just after the success of his opera, *Die tote Stadt*, and was received with much praise. The first movement is full of energy but immediately introduces a beautiful second subject, while the central *Adagio* is similarly richly lyrical. Indeed, each of the quartets has a beautiful slow movement, the *Second* a *Larghetto* marked *Con molto sentimento*, and the *Third* (dedicated to Bruno Walter) is entitled *Like a Folk Tune*. Each also has a contrasting lighter movement, an engaging *Intermezzo* in Nos. 1, and 2 and a lilting Scherzo in No. 3 (drawing on the score for the film, *Between Two Worlds*). The finales are equally enticing: No. 1 introduces a jaunty march, No. 2 a heady waltz theme, and the lively No. 3 borrows its second subject from the film score for *Devotion* (about the Brontë sisters). These quartets, spontaneously structured, show Korngold at his most melodically memorable and rewarding. They are played most sympathetically here, and are given top-quality Chandos recording.

Die tote Stadt (complete, CD version)
Ⓜ RCA 8869746602 (2). Neblett, Kollo, Prey, Luxon, Bav. R. Ch., Munich R. O, Leinsdorf

At the age of 23 Korngold had his opera *Die tote Stadt* presented in simultaneous world premières in Hamburg and Cologne, some feat. The fantasy story of a bereaved husband meeting a girl exactly like his newly dead wife ventures into dream worlds. The writing might have been sick and morbid but for Korngold's youthfully exuberant score. Many echoes include obvious cribbing from Puccini and Strauss, who similarly knew how to manoeuvre excitingly near cliff edges of vulgarity. *Die tote Stadt* may not be a great opera, but in a performance like this, superbly recorded, it is one to revel in on CD. René Kollo is powerful if occasionally coarse of tone, Carol Neblett sings sweetly in the equivocal roles of the wife's apparition and the newcomer. Hermann Prey, Benjamin Luxon and Rose Wagemann make up an impressive cast.

LALO, Edouard (1823–92)

Andantino; Namouna (excerpts); Rhapsodie norvégienne; Le Roi d'Ys: Overture. Scherzo; (i) Symphonie espagnole, Op. 21
Ⓜ Australian Decca Eloquence (ADD) 480 0049 (2). SRO, Ansermet, (i) with Ricci –
CHABRIER: *España*, etc.

This Lalo compilation shows the composer at his tuneful best. The rare *Namouna* items are most enjoyable, with the composer's ear for felicitous orchestral detail at its most beguiling. The *Sérénade* is very catchy with its piquant use of pizzicato strings, while the rustic-sounding *Fête foraine* is most effective. The *Valse de la cigarette* captivates, while the *Parade de foire* shows the composer creating a wonderfully lolloping melody for the trumpet, among other delights. The orchestral *Scherzo* (adapted by the composer from his *Third Piano Trio*) is another find – an ideal encore. In both the *Rhapsodie norvégienne* and the well-known *Symphonie espagnole*, the composer's flair for providing local colour comes to the fore; the former features a lively *Presto* section, where the fanfares almost suggest a medieval tournament. The popular *Symphonie espagnole* receives a very earthy performance in Ansermet's hands, with Ricci providing much brilliance in the solo part. The rare *Andantino* offers much Gallic charm, while the dramatic overture to *Le Roi d'Ys* has seldom sounded more brilliant than in Ansermet's hands. Indeed, one forgives the minor blemishes of the orchestral playing with such vivid music-making – projected with the warm and detailed sound one takes for granted from this source. The Chabrier items are equally enjoyable.

Cello Concerto 1 in D min.

DG (ADD) 457 761-2. Fournier, LOP, Martinon – **SAINT-SAËNS**: *Cello Concerto 1*. **BLOCH**: *Schelomo*. **BRUCH**: *Kol Nidrei*

Lalo's *Cello Concerto in D minor* is not perhaps the most inspired cello concerto in the repertoire but the music is appealing and Fournier's elegant approach makes the most of the attractive themes. The slow movement has a certain eloquent charm and the *Allegro vivace* finale is enjoyable. Excellent sound from the early 1960s and part of a very attractive collection.

Concerto Russe; Symphonie espagnole

HM PRD 350 017. Poulet, Prague RSO, Válek

A superb disc. Gérard Poulet gives a highly individual account of the *Symphonie espagnole*, to which he brings many inimitable personal touches. But the performance of the *Concerto Russe* is full of warmth and tender lyrical finesse, revealing it as a true masterpiece, with a central movement particularly seductive and with a finale which opens rapturously and with the Russian dance finale scintillating. In both works, Poulet is helped by the strong contribution of Vladimir Válek, whose orchestral backing is full of character, matching the soloist at every turn. The recording is in the demonstration bracket.

Le Roi d'Ys (complete, DVD version)

Dynamic DVD 33592. Piunti, Girard, Martin-Bonnet, Guèze, Van Mechelen, Graus, Tissons, Ch. & O of Opéra Royal de Wallonie, Davin (Director: Jean-Louis Pichon; V/D: Matteo Ricchetti)

Here is an excellent example of a neglected opera, superbly presented and thoroughly recommendable. Lalo's melodramatic overture to *Le Roi d'Ys* is comparatively well known, but not the opera from which it derives, so congratulations to the Belgian Royal Walloon Opera for mounting the work so successfully in 2008, as a co-production with the Opéra Théâtre de Saint-Etienne. First and foremost, it has costumes in the period of the story, and a convincing set which can handle the mystical appearance of the city's Patron Saint Corentin and the opera's spectacular watery climax convincingly. Secondly, the opera is strongly cast, with the two sisters, Margared (Giuseppina Piunti) and Rozenn (Guylaine Girard), carrying their key parts dramatically. Sébastien Guèze, with a pleasingly French tenor voice, is an excellent hero, Mylio, loved by both sisters. Eric Martin-Bonnet as Le Roi holds his own with dignity, and Werner Van Mechelen is a splendid villain (Karnac), who is obsessed with Margared. She doesn't want him, but is furious not to have secured Mylio for herself. She persuades Karnac into helping her to open the locks which will cause the sea to flood the city, and so have her revenge on the happy lovers immediately after their wedding. The score is pleasingly melodic, the opera has plenty of action, and is altogether most entertaining in this excellent video presentation.

LAMBERT, Constant (1905-51)

Horoscope: Suite

ⓑⓑ Hyp. Helios CDH 55099. E. N. Philh. O, Lloyd-Jones – **WALTON**: *Façade*. **BLISS**: *Checkmate* (ballet): *Suite*

The suite from *Horoscope* is Lambert at his very finest. David Lloyd-Jones is very sympathetic to its specifically English atmosphere. He wittily points the catchy rhythmic figure which comes both in the *Dance for the Flowers of Leo* and, later, in the *Bacchanale*, while the third-movement *Valse for the Gemini* has a memorably catchy charm. Excellent playing and first-class sound, perhaps a shade resonant for the ballet pit, but bringing plenty of bloom. A superb bargain.

LANGGAARD, Rued (1893-1952)

(i) *Music of the Spheres. 4 Tone Pictures*

Chan. 9517. Sjöberg, DNRSO, Rozhdestvensky, (i) with Danish Nat. R. Ch.

Rued Langgaard was something of an outsider in Danish music and has been compared with such figures as Ives and Havergal Brian. Although his roots were firmly in the nineteenth century, his musical language is not wholly consistent (one of his later symphonies sounds almost Schumannesque). For much of his career he struggled to gain recognition as an organist and was eventually appointed to Ribe Cathedral in 1940. His music is not especially personal but, at the same time, it must be admitted that the main work recorded here is quite unlike anything else: indeed, the *Music of the Spheres* has a manic intensity which is compelling and on occasion quite disturbing. It was written in 1918-20 and lay neglected after its first performance until the 1960s, when a shortened version of it was recorded by the Stockholm Philharmonic under Blomstedt on EMI. This Chandos recording supersedes the later Danish recording, conducted by Frandsen, yet it still remains difficult to explain the impression it creates. The sonorities are 'advanced' for the period and include tone clusters and a piano struck directly on the strings; and skilful use is make of scraps of simple tunes that are repeated to almost hypnotic effect. Indeed, it is almost surrealistic in vision and its colouring (the dynamics are almost whispered) quite remarkable. The scoring is for two orchestras, one off-stage, with a soprano soloist. This is perhaps the best introduction to Langgaard's music, for the symphonies – while certainly worth exploring – are highly variable in impact and content, though rarely less than interesting. The *Four Tone Pictures*, for voice and orchestra, are evocatively pleasing, and beautifully sung by Gitta-Maria Sjöberg, who also contributes superbly to *The Music of the Spheres*. Rozhdestvensky with his excellent Danish orchestra captures the spirit of the music admirably, and the Chandos recording is richly atmospheric.

LARROCHA, Alicia de (pianist)

BACH: *Beloved Jesu, we are here* (arr. Cohen); *Partita 2 in D min., BWV 1004: Chaconne in D min.* (arr. Busoni). *Sanctify us by thy goodness* (arr. Cohen); *Concerto in the Italian Style, BWV 971; French Suite 6 in E, BWV 817. Concerto 5 in F min., BWV 1056* (with L. Sinf., Zinman). **HAYDN**: *Concerto in D, Hob XVIII:2* (with L. Sinf., Zinman). *Andante con variazioni in F min., Hob XVII:6.* **MOZART**: *Piano Sonatas 11 in A, K. 331/300i; 18 in D, K. 576.* **BEETHOVEN**: *7 Bagatelles, Op. 33.* **MENDELSSOHN**: *Variations sérieuses, Op. 54.* **CHOPIN**: *Berceuse, Op. 57; 24 Preludes, Op. 28. Piano Concerto 2 in F min., Op. 21* (with SRO, Comissiona). **SCHUBERT**: *Piano Sonata in B flat, D.960; Impromptu in A flat, D.899/4.* **LISZT**: *Piano Sonata in B min.* **SCHUMANN**: *Fantasie in C, Op. 17; Allegro, Op. 8; Romance, Op. 28/2. Piano Concerto in A min., Op. 54* (with RPO, Dutoit). **SOLER**: *Sonatas: in G min., SR 42; in D min., SR 15; in F, SR 89.* **TURINA**: *Zapateado.* **GRANADOS**: *El pelele; Danzas espanolas, Book 2, Op. 37: Villanesca; Andaluza; Rondalla aragonesa.* **MONTSALVATGE**: *Sonatina para Yvette.*

MOMPOU: *Prélude VII*. **ALBÉNIZ**: *Tango*; *Iberia, Book 1*.
FALLA: *Fantasía bética*. *Nights in the Gardens of Spain* (with SRO,
Comissiona). **KHACHATURIAN**: *Piano Concerto* (with LPO,
Burgos). **RAVEL**: *Piano Concerto for the Left Hand* (with LPO, Foster).
Decca (ADD) 473 813-2 (7)

Alicia de Larrocha was one of the great pianists of the twentieth century and
her long career began in 1929, when she gave her first public concert at the age
of six. While being especially famous for her performances of the Spanish repertoire, she was far from a specialist pianist, but embraced a wide repertoire
and many of her classic recordings are found in this box set. CD 1 includes
her Bach recordings, and in this repertoire she is strikingly characterful. She
does not apologize for using the piano by attempting to imitate harpsichord
tone; she performs such a work as the *Italian Concerto* in pianistic terms.
Her 14-minute Busoni arrangement of the *Chaconne in D minor* is especially
impressive. In the Bach *F minor Concerto* Zinman's robust accompaniments,
rhythmically strong and alert, are matched by de Larrocha with her firm, clean
articulation, and their partnership is eminently satisfying, particularly in the
famous and beautiful slow movement, which is shaped with a cool, moving
simplicity. In the recording of the Haydn *Concerto* which follows, she seeks to
evoke the fortepiano in her crisp articulation. The outer movements are strongly
characterized, and the rhythmic snap of the 'gypsy' finale is a joy. David Zinman's
accompaniment is excellent and the scale of the recording highly effective, the
resonance giving breadth to the orchestral group.

CD 2 is devoted to recordings of the classical repertoire, and here we have a
very stylish account of Mozart's *Sonata No. 11 in A major* with some impressively characterized variations, and finishing with the famous *Alla turca*
movement. The *F minor Variations* of Haydn are thoughtfully played and sensitively recorded, as is the rest of this CD, which includes a stylish account of
Mozart's *Sonata No. 18*, K.576, in which the slow movement is beautifully
poised, memorable in every way, and the finale sparkles. In the Beethoven
Bagatelles, de Larrocha displays her usual finesse, and her articulation in the
faster pieces is exhilaratingly crisp and clean. Her playing is consistently polished and sympathetic, and each of these miniatures is surely characterized. If
her performance of Mendelssohn's *Variations sérieuses* isn't quite on this level
of inspiration, it is still enjoyably stylish, and the lively passages come off splendidly (though the 1970s sound isn't quite of Decca's vintage quality, unlike the
rest of this CD).

CD 3 comprises her 1974 recording of Chopin's *24 Preludes*. Her highly
poetic way with Chopin is also evident in the recording of the *Second Piano
Concerto*, which is winningly played, with stylish accompaniments and in
excellent sound.

The heart of de Larrocha's performance of Schubert's *B flat major Sonata*,
which opens CD 4, lies in the slow movement, played introspectively and
with great poetic feeling. Her poise and crisp articulation in the final two

movements give much pleasure. Beautiful articulation is again the hallmark of the *Impromptu* which follows. The Liszt *Piano Sonata* receives a strong performance with many perceptive touches. Yet some might find her view just a little too idiosyncratic to be placed in the first flight.

Again, in the Schumann *Fantasy* which begins CD 5, some may find the performance rather too personal for a top recommendation, but there are so many good things in it, not least the excellent recording. Her bold approach works well in the *Allegro* and *Romance*, which again are beautifully played and recorded. In the Schumann *Piano Concerto*, both soloist and conductor are very relaxed indeed. It also has touches of wilfulness, as in the *ritenuto* before the recapitulation of the first movement. Poetry is certainly not absent: the exchanges between the piano and the woodwind soloists are beautifully done, but the lack of overall vitality becomes enervating in the finale, where the approach is spacious, but the basic tempo is too lazy to be convincing.

CD 6 is a delightful collection of lightweight Spanish keyboard music, played with such skill that even the slightest music never becomes chocolate-boxy. The eighteenth-century classicism of the *Sonatas* by Soler makes a splendid foil for the warmer romanticism of Isaac Albéniz and the vivid colours of Granados and Turina (all of them in classic recordings). The short Mompou piece is delightful and the Montsalvatge *Sonatina para Yvette* is no masterpiece but is entertaining and full of colour.

The final CD in the collection boasts one of the very finest of all recorded performances of Falla's *Nights in the Gardens of Spain*. De Larrocha was on top form for this 1970 recording, to which she brought her customary poetry and vitality in this evocative score, and she received admirable support from Comissiona and the engineers. The Khachaturian *Piano Concerto* is a bit slack in the rhythm department in the first movement, but the slow movement, as interpreted by a Spanish pianist and conductor, sounds evocatively like Falla, and the finale too is infectiously idiomatic. The Ravel *Piano Concerto for the Left Hand*, which concludes CD 7, receives a memorable performance in every way, with the Decca engineers bringing out all the sparkle and drama of the playing of this highly individual score. All in all, this boxed set is a fine tribute to a musician who died only recently (in 2010).

LECLAIR, Jean-Marie (1697–1764)

Violin Sonatas, Book 1/1–12

(BB) Naxos 8.57088 8(*1–4*); 8.570889 (*5–8*); 8.570890 (*9–12*) (available separately).
  Adrian Butterfield, Alison McGillivray, Lawrence Cummings

The music of Jean-Marie Leclair is underrated. Its merits are considerable, his lyricism has an appealing directness and charm and his *Allegros* are buoyant and spirited. He wrote well for the flute, but in the main he dedicated himself to the violin, for which he wrote 40 sonatas, and two sets of concertos, Opp. 7 and 10. In 1723 he came to Paris, where his first Book was published. The predominant influence in the music of the time was that of Corelli (whose works were readily available), yet Leclair's native French style is never overwhelmed. However, the twelve *Sonatas* of Book 1 have tended to be neglected in favour of the later works – which, as these recordings show, is totally unjustified, for their invention is strong and fresh, and they happily combine Italian lyricism and melodic memorability with French elegance, but with the dance movements usually given Italian names. Featuring baroque violin, viola da gamba and harpsichord, the performances here are first class, full of life and spontaneous expressive feeling, and they are very well balanced and recorded. Let us hope the present team will also record the later Books.

LECOCQ, Alexandre (1832–1918)

Mam'zelle Angot (ballet, arr. Gordon Jacob)
Ⓜ Australian Decca Eloquence 442 9048 (2). Nat. PO, Bonynge – **HÉROLD**: *La Fille mal gardée*

Mam'zelle Angot is a vivacious score with plenty of engaging tunes, neatly orchestrated in the modern French style. Richard Bonynge offers the first recording of the complete score, and its 39 minutes are consistently entertaining, especially with orchestral playing of such polish and wit. The Kingsway Hall recording is warm and vivid, bringing sharp detail and tangibility, especially at lower dynamic levels. A winner in every way, with an outstanding coupling to match.

LEHÁR, Franz (1870–1948)

Das Land des Lächelns (The Land of Smiles); ***The Merry Widow (Die lüstige Witwe)*** (both complete in German)
Ⓑ EMI mono 4 56385-2 (2) (with bonus disc containing synopsis & libretto with translation via CD-ROM). Schwarzkopf, Gedda, Kunz, Loose, Kraus, Philh. Ch. & O, Ackermann

In her earlier, mono recording as Hanna Glawari in *The Merry Widow* Schwarzkopf has both sparkle and youthful vivacity, and the *Viljalied* – ecstatically drawn out – is unique. Some may be troubled that Kraus as Danilo sounds older than the Baron (Anton Niessner) but it is still a memorably characterful cast.

The Land of Smiles has a comparably glamorous roster, and if here Gedda does not have quite the passionate flair of Tauber in his famous *Dein ist mein ganzes Herz*, his artistry matches an effortless performance. Schwarzkopf and

Kunz sing delectably, and the CD transfers are lively and full of presence. Dialogue is included, but separately cued.

The Merry Widow (in English; complete, DVD version)
Opus Arte DVD OA 0836. Y. Kenny, Skovhus, Kirchschlager, Turay, San Francisco Op. Ch. & O, Kunzel (V/D: Gary Halvorson)

The Merry Widow (*Die lustige Witwe*; in German; complete, CD version)
Ⓜ EMI (ADD) 5 67370-2 (2). Schwarzkopf, Gedda, Waechter, Steffek, Knapp, Equiluz, Philh. Ch. and O, Matačić

It would be hard to imagine a more extravagant production of *The Merry Widow* than Lotfi Mansouri's for the San Francisco Opera, recorded live on DVD in December 2001. Michael Yeargan's sets faithfully echo the 1890s designs at Maxim's in Paris, Thierry Bosquet's costumes are comparably lavish, and the text is unusually full. The dialogue – with Christopher Hassall's translation expanded by Ted and Deena Puffer – is wittier and truer to the Parisian atmosphere than the original German. Yvonne Kenny as the heroine not only sings beautifully but is both vivacious and provocative. Bo Skovhus makes a handsome Danilo, determined not to be putty in her hands, and their final reconciliation to the *Merry Widow Waltz* could not be more moving. Angelika Kirchschlager makes a charming Valencienne, opposite the Camille of Gregory Turay, with Carlo Hartmann as Baron Mirko, Valencienne's husband, strong and characterful, relishing the humour.

Elisabeth Schwarzkopf was surely born to take the role of Hanna, and on CD in stereo Matačić again provides a magical set with a vivid sense of atmosphere, guaranteed to send shivers of delight through any listener. The new transfer certainly retains the full bloom of the original. However, the reissue, with an overall playing time of 79 minutes 40 seconds, is uneconomical, even at mid-price; it would surely have been possible to get the whole opera on a single disc (though it is obviously a case of quality over quantity!). The documentation cannot be faulted, with a full translation included.

LEIGH, Walter (1905-42)

(i) *Agincourt Overture*; (ii-iii) *Concertino for Harpsichord & Strings*; (ii) *The Frogs: Overture & Dance*; (i) *Jolly Roger Overture*; (ii) *A Midsummer Night's Dream: Suite for Small Orchestra*. *Music for String Orchestra*
Lyrita (ADD) SRCD 289. (i) New Philh. O; (ii) LPO; Braithwaite; (iii) with Pinnock

Walter Leigh was a craftsman composer of the finest kind, one who aimed to make his music useful, hence his frequent essays in incidental music. His

personal style remained very English, with frequent but gentle neoclassical overtones. His masterpiece remains his *Harpsichord Concertino*, a deliciously piquant
score which had been recorded three times before this excellent Lyrita recording
(though memories of Kathleen Long's 78-r.p.m. recording, using a piano, are
not erased). Pinnock's sensitive performance is among the finest using harpsichord, though the balance of the solo instrument is rather close. Otherwise the
recording is excellent, as are all the performances. A most worthwhile CD.

LEIGHTON, Kenneth (1929–88)

Symphony 2 (Sinfonia mistica); *Te Deum laudamus*
Chan. 10495. Fox, Nat. Ch. of Wales, BBC Nat. O of Wales, Hickox

This is a hauntingly compelling recording of some of Kenneth Leighton's most
inspired music. Written in the mid-1970s as a response to the death of his
mother, the *Sinfonia Mistica* is, in the composer's words, 'a requiem or a meditation on the subject of death which usually becomes so more real to us in the
second half of life'; yet this music is inspiring rather than depressing. It is
music of a profoundly spiritual nature, and its six movements provide music of
much imagination as well as musical logic. The texts are taken from the great
metaphysical poets such as John Donne and George Herbert, and they are
beautifully sung by Sarah Fox. The orchestral version of his magnificent *Te
Deum laudamus* makes a fine bonus to an outstanding CD. The orchestra and
chorus were inspired to great heights in this recording, and the sound itself is
of demonstration quality.

LEONINUS, Magister (c. 1153–1201)

Organa: Alleluya. Non vos relinquam orphanos; *Alleluya. Dulce
lignum, dulces clavos*; *Alleluya. Spiritus Sanctus procedens*;
Alleluya. Paraclitus Spiritus Sanctus; *Priusquam te formarem*;
Alleluya. Inter natos mulierum; *Viderunt omnes fines terre*;
Alleluya. Dies sanctificatus illuxit nobis; *Alleluya. Pascha nostrum
immolatus est*
(BB) Hyp. Helios CDH 55328. Red Byrd (John Potter, Richard Wistreich), Capella
Amsterdam

Over eight centuries have passed since the construction of the Cathedral of
Notre Dame began and Leoninus, the cathedral's composer, was composing
this music. It is among the first to be successfully written down so that its
pitch and melodic lines could be accurately determined. It is in two parts, with
the top voice moving in unison or octaves, or over a sustained or sometimes

moving second part. Sometimes both voices sing in unison. Much of the writing brings elaborate, rhapsodic melodic lines which are quite beautiful and haunting in these atmospheric, confident and extraordinarily convincing performances, which take us back to the very beginning of written music. Full texts, translations and good documentation, as we expect from Hyperion, make this a particularly precious reissue.

LE ROUX, Gaspard (c. 1660–1707)

Pièces de clavecin: Suites arranged for 2 Harpsichords 1–7
HM HMC 901660. Mitzi Meyerson (Taskin harpsichord, 1769) & Lisa Crawford (Goermans harpsichord after Raskin, 1764)

Little is known about Gaspard Le Roux except that his music was actually published (no commonplace occurrence for keyboard composers at the opening of the eighteenth century) and that he lived and taught in Paris and by 1769 was regarded as a 'famous musicmaster'. Moreover, with his Pièces pour deux clavecins of 1705 he was one of the very first composers to publish music for two harpsichords. His seven Suites offer the usual collection of French dance movements, four in Nos. 2 and 6, seven in Nos. 1, 3, 5 and 7, three in No. 4, while No. 5 includes an impressive Chaconne. The music is attractively inventive and lively, but the two separate keyboard parts were not given to the players; rather, the composer gave some models for the would-be arranger to study at the end of the book so that he could create his own series of duets. In five cases there are basic second harpsichord parts provided, but as Lisa Crawford explains in her interesting notes, the other suites needed substantial changes to the written music in order to work in duet form. However, the problems which arose here have been resourcefully solved, using a variety of approaches, and playing on a pair of eighteenth-century harpsichords Lisa Crawford and Mitzi Meyerson provide here a stimulating and attractive set of duets with great aplomb. They are well recorded and the result is very enjoyable. This disc is a real find – well worth seeking out.

LIADOV, Anatol (1855–1914)

Baba-Yaga, Op. 56; The Enchanted Lake, Op. 62; From the Apocalypse, Op. 66; Kikimora, Op. 63; Mazurka: Village Scene by the Inn, Op. 19; Polonaise, Op. 49; 8 Russian Folksongs, Op. 58; Scherzo in D, Op. 16
Chan. 9921. BBC PO, Sinaisky

The Enchanted Lake and Kikimora are wonderfully atmospheric, and the performances by Vassily Sinaisky and the BBC Philharmonic are pure magic.

Although not the best known, a piece like *From the Apocalypse* is hardly less inspired. The *Eight Russian Folksongs* are especially attractive, with their splashes of local colour, and the dance pieces are equally colourful in their imaginative orchestral dress. The performances are matched by recording of equal richness and luminosity.

LIPATTI, Dinu (piano)

CHOPIN: *Sonata 3 in B min., Op. 58*; *Barcarolle*; *2 Études*; *Mazurka; 13 Waltzes*; *Piano Concerto 1*. **BACH**: *Concerto in D min.*, cond. Ackermann; *Partita in B flat*. **BARTÓK** *Concerto 3* (with Paul Sacher). **BRAHMS**: *Waltzes* (with Nadia Boulanger). **ENESCU**: *Sonata 3*. **GRIEG**: *Concerto* (with Galliera). **LISZT**: *Concerto 1* (with Ansermet); *Années de pèlerinage: Sonetto 104 del Petrarca*. **MOZART**: *Concerto 21 in C, K.467* (with Karajan). **RAVEL**. *Alborada del gracioso*. **D. SCARLATTI**: *Sonatas Kk. 9 & 380*. **SCHUBERT**: *2 Impromptus*. **SCHUMANN**: *Concerto* (with Karajan).
Ⓑ EMI Classics mono 207318 2 (7)

During his short life (1917–50) the great Romanian pianist attained a legendary standing, and the relatively few recordings he made have rarely been out of circulation. The present collection includes rarities such as the *Third Sonata* of Enescu, who incidentally was his godfather as well as sonata partner in wartime Bucharest, and some Brahms *Waltzes* recorded in 1937 with Nadia Boulanger, with whom he studied. Lipatti's Chopin was in a class of its own and exhibits a chaste purity of style that is unique. This is to be found at its apogee in the last recital he gave in Besançon, only a few weeks before his death, and which is accommodated on the last of these CDs. A very special record.

LISZT, Franz (1811–86)

(i–ii) *Piano Concertos 1–2; Fantasia on Themes from Beethoven's 'The Ruins of Athens'; Grand fantasie symphonique on Themes from Berlioz's 'Lélio'; Hungarian fantasia for Piano & Orchestra; Malédiction; Totentanz.* (i) *Ce qu'on entend sur la montagne; Die Ideale; Festklänge; 2 Episodes from Lenau's 'Faust'; Héroïde funèbre; Hamlet; Hungaria; Hunnenschlacht; Mazeppa; Mephisto Waltz 2; Orpheus; Les Préludes; Prometheus; Tasso; Von der Wiege bis zum Grabe;* (i; iii) *Dante Symphony;* (i; iv) *A Faust Symphony.* (i–ii) Concert

Paraphrases: **SCHUBERT**: *Wanderer-Fantasie*. **WEBER**: *Polonaise brillante*.

Ⓑ EMI (ADD) 585573-2 (7). (i) Leipzig GO, Masur; (ii) Béroff; (iii) Leipzig Thomanerchor; (iv) Leipzig R. Ch., male voices

Liszt's orchestral music gets a mixed response. Not everyone responds to his particular style, though undoubtedly his wildly romantic standpoint can be very exciting, and the best of it, by any standards, is remarkable. Masur's comprehensive cycle of tone-poems, symphones and concertos is just about the best he has done for recorded music, and his survey, despite many superb individual recordings (notably from Karajan on DG and, recently, Noseda on Chandos), is the most comprehensive survey available.

Béroff has justly won acclaim for his superb technique and his refined poetic sense, and these recordings show him to be a Lisztian of flair. His accounts of the much-recorded *Concertos* can hold their own with most of the competition: these are exhilarating performances and are given the extra attraction of fine orchestral playing and vivid (late 1970s) sound. The same comments apply to the other piano concertante works: they are all superbly done, with ample brilliance, yet are musical and stylish, with a sense of fun in the virtuosic fireworks. As for the tone-poems, Masur makes the strongest possible case for them. He proves as persuasive an advocate as any on record. The rich sonority of the lower strings, the dark, perfectly blended woodwind tone and the fine internal balance of the Leipzig Gewandhaus Orchestra hold the listener's attention throughout – for in the weaker pieces Liszt benefits from all the help his interpreters can give him. Only in *Orpheus* does Masur let us down: he breezes through it at record speed and misses the endearing gentleness that Beecham brought to it in the early 1960s. In the two *Symphonies*, Masur is again impressive, though even in the *Gretchen* movement of the *Faust Symphony* he moves things on, albeit not unacceptably, and there is no want of delicacy or ardour. The *Faust Symphony* can certainly hold its own, and the same may be said of the *Dante Symphony*. The recordings are well balanced and refined throughout, emerging more freshly than ever on CD. A very considerable achievement.

A Faust Symphony (DVD version)

EuroArts DVD 2072078. Riegel, Tanglewood Festival Ch., Boston SO, Bernstein
(V/D: Humphrey Burton)

Bernstein conducts this riveting 1976 Boston performance, so thrillingly captured on DVD – and one of his very finest recordings, with all the added stimulus of live music-making, and splendidly photographed under the direction of Humphrey Burton. Bernstein seems to possess the ideal temperament for holding together grippingly the melodrama of the long first movement, taking it spaciously but building up the great excitement in the closing pages, while in the lovely *Gretchen* evocation he draws exquisite playing from the Boston Symphony Orchestra – both the woodwind and the strings in the many chamber-music passages. The *Mephistofelean* finale, with its anticipations of the orchestral wildness of Berlioz and the brass sonorities of Wagner, is held together superbly, with the tension building all the time, to be capped by the magnificent entry of the chorus, and sustained to the final profound apotheosis. Kenneth Riegel's impressive tenor contribution to the CD version is surpassed by his ardent singing in this live performance, and the playing of the Boston orchestra is superb throughout, especially in the strings, helped in their sonority and radiance by the unsurpassed acoustic of Symphony Hall.

Festklänge; *Héroïde funèbre*; *Mazeppa*; *Prometheus* (Symphonic Poems)
Chan. 10417. BBC PO, Noseda

For those not wishing to invest in Masur's complete set of Liszt tone-poems, there are single-disc recommendations available. Alas, some classic accounts are currently deleted, most notably Karajan's unsurpassed recordings on DG. However, Gianandrea Noseda has embarked on an impressive new series for Chandos, of which this excellent CD is typical. The highlight here is *Mazeppa*, one of Liszt's very finest in the series alongside *Orpheus* and *Les Préludes*. While Karajan's electrifying version is not surpassed (and probably never will be), Noseda and the BBC Philharmonic Orchestra give it plenty of life and vividly re-create the evocation of the horse galloping across the countryside with the eponymous hero strapped to its back. The other works aren't quite so inspired but offer fine moments: Noseda is suitably exuberant in *Fesklänge*, a showily exciting work, and he catches the sombre atmosphere of the *Héroïde funèbre* eloquently. *Prometheus* is splendid in its melodrama and vivid incident. The BBC orchestra is again on its toes throughout and the Chandos recording is in the demonstration class.

Années de pèlerinage, *2nd Year (Italy) excerpts: Sposalizio*; *Il penseroso*; *Canzonetta del Salvator Rosa*; *Sonetto del Petrarca 47*; *104*; *123*. *Supplement: Venezia e Napoli: Gondoliera*. *2 Legends*: *St Francis of Assisi preaching to the birds*; *St Francis of Paola walking on the water*
Ⓜ DG 477 9374. Kempff

There are many recommendable recordings of the *Années de pèlerinage*, including a fine complete set on DVD by Alfred Brendel (DG 073 41460). But in the early days of mono LP, Kempff made a famous record of some of the more memorable vignettes from the Second Year, adding the engaging *Sposalizio* and *Gondoliera* from the Supplement. Much of that same special choice he included in the present (1975) stereo programme. Out of the catalogue for a long time, it has recently returned as one of DG's 'Originals' and shows that Kempff lost none of his magic and poetry in the intervening years. Few listeners will fail to respond to these evocative and masterly performances, not least the pair of Legends with their delightful evocations of birdsong and Saint Francis walking on the water. The recording is excellent and this is a truly treasurable reissue.

Hungarian Rhapsodies 2, 6, 8 (Capriccio); 9 (Carnival in Pest); 10 (Préludio); 12–14; 15 (Rákóczy)
Ⓑ EMI Masters (ADD) 6 31789-2. Cziffra

As can be heard in the most famous *C sharp minor Rhapsody* (No. 2), Cziffra's reckless impulsiveness is matched by his breathtaking bravura in the closing section. It was an excellent idea to issue this selection from his deleted complete set (from the 1970s), as the recording has fine realism and presence and he was one of the great piano virtuosi of his time.

Piano Sonata in B min.; En rêve; 4 Little Piano Pieces; La lugubre gondola; Nuages gris (Trübe Wolken); Richard Wagner – Venezia; Schlaflos, Frage und Antwort; Unstern! Sinistre, disastro
HM HMC 901845. Lewis

Paul Lewis's version of the Liszt *Sonata* stands out, even among the many dozens of rival recordings, for its power and clarity, enhanced by full, immediate sound. Lewis, with masterly control, brings out the structural strength. For coupling he has an illuminating group of late pieces, including two written for Wagner, not just *La lugubre gondola* (in the second and the more extended version) but *R.W. – Venezia*, building up powerfully over the briefest span. Also two pieces, *Nuages gris* and *Unstern!*, which find the composer at his most adventurous.

LOCATELLI, Pietro (1695–1764)

L'Arte del violino (12 Violin Concertos), **Op. 3**
Ⓜ Hyp. CDS 44391/3. Wallfisch, Raglan Bar. Players, Kraemer

Pietro Locatelli was a younger contemporary of Handel and Vivaldi. It was in 1733 that he wrote *L'Arte del violino*. In its outer movements each of the 12 concertos includes an extended *Capriccio* of enormous technical difficulty, with fast, complicated, sometimes stratospheric, upper tessitura. The slow movements, by contrast, produce a series of flowing ideas that have an inherent Handelian grace. Elizabeth Wallfisch not only throws off the fireworks with ease but produces an appealingly gleaming lyrical line. With excellent, vital and stylish support from Kraemer and his Baroque Raglan Players, this may be counted a stimulating authentic re-creation of a set of concertos which had a profound influence on the violin technique of the time.

LOEWE, Frederick (1901–88), with Alan Jay LERNER (1918–86)

My Fair Lady (Musical)
Sony mono SMK 89997. Andrews, Harrison, Holloway, King and original cast, Ch. & O,
   Allers (with post-recording conversations & playback)

There are many who count *My Fair Lady* as the greatest musical of all, with a 'script' by George Bernard Shaw and brilliantly apt lyrics by Alan Jay Lerner; and who can argue with them, for Frederick Loewe's score was no less inspired. There are 16 numbers here, and not a dud among them, when most modern musicals manage with one or two hits, endlessly reprised.

This is not the later, stereo recording (which is far inferior) but the original mono LP, recorded in 1956 and transferred vividly to CD; moreover it includes the witty original orchestrations by Robert Russell Bennett and Phil Lang, which apparently are no longer in use today in the interests of theatrical economy and a smaller orchestra. As the post-recording conversations reveal at the end of the disc, Julie Andrews was just 21 at the time of the recording; here she is in wonderfully fresh voice (*Show me* is dazzling); so are her colleagues. We need say no more; this is an endlessly enjoyable CD: you feel better having listened to it all the way through and glad to be alive. Why can't composers write tunes like this any more? The documentation is adequate, with a few photographs included, but this reissue was worthy of a more elaborate presentation. Snap it up before it disappears!

LUDWIG, Christa (mezzo-soprano)

'The Art of Christa Ludwig': Lieder: by **BRAHMS**, including *Alto hapsody* (with Philh. Ch. & O, Klemperer). **MAHLER**, including *Das Knaben Wunderhorn*; *Das Lied von der Erde: Der Abschied*. **REGER**. **SCHUBERT**: *Der Hirt auf dem Felsen* (with Gervase de Peyer, clarinet). **SCHUMANN**: *Frauenliebe und-Leben*. **R. STRAUSS**. **WAGNER**: *Wesendonck-Lieder*. **WOLF**. Songs: by **RACHMANINOV**. **RAVEL**: *3 Chansons madécasses*. **SAINT-SAËNS**: *Une flûte invisible* (with Douglas Whittaker). **ROSSINI**: *La regatta veneziana* (with Gerald Moore or Geoffrey Parsons, piano). Arias and excerpts from: **BACH**: *St John & St Matthew Passions*. **BELLINI**: *Norma*. **BIZET**: *Carmen*. **HANDEL**: *Giulio Cesare*. **MOZART**: *Così fan tutte*; *Don Giovanni*. **VERDI**: *Requiem: Lux aeterna*. **R. STRAUSS**: *Der Rosenkavalier*: Act III: *Finale* (with Stich-Randall, Schwarzkopf & Waechter). **WAGNER**: *Tristan: Isolde's Liebestod*
Ⓜ EMI (ADD) 5 17608-2 (5)

The present set is an expansion of an earlier four-disc compilation issued under the same title. The listing above shows just what an extraordinarily versatile artist Christa Ludwig was, with a ravishing voice, readily matched by fine intelligence and natural musical sensitivity, to place her among the special singers of our time, including De los Angeles and Schwarzkopf (to name but two from the same EMI stable). She was as impressive in Schubert as she was in Strauss and Brahms, and her Mahler is very special indeed. This compensates for her below-par Schumann song-cycle. The opera excerpts are no less cherishable and it was a happy idea to close the programme with Isolde's *Liebestod*, *Mi tradi* (from *Don Giovanni*) and the glorious closing scene from *Der Rosenkavalier*. Her voice took naturally to the microphone, so this four-disc set is another source of infinite musical pleasure to be snapped up quickly before it disappears.

LULLY, Jean-Baptiste (1632-87)

Pièces de symphonie (suite of music from the operas: *Acis et Galatée*; *Amadis*; *Atys*; *Béllérophon*; *Persée*; *Phaeton*; *Thésée*)
Ⓜ Australian Decca Eloquence (ADD) 480 2374. ECO, Leppard - **CAMPRA**:
    L'Europe Galante

This is another of Raymond Leppard's enjoyably stylish selections from the high noon of French opera, recorded in 1966. There is plenty to enjoy here, with many numbers such as the lively brass and drum writing in the *Deuxième air pour les combatants*, while the following *Le sommeil* is disarming in its simple charm. The colourfully scored *Thésée Prélude* is short but enjoyable, while that work's more substantial *Overture* is full of lively invention. The *Petit air gay et bourrée pour Les Egyptiens* (from *Phaeton*) is deliciously piquant, with stylish contributions from the woodwind and continuo. The suite ends with a rousing march. Throughout the 20 tracks one marvels at the composer's invention and, although we are more used to this repertoire on period instruments, so stylishly does the ECO perform this music one's ear soon adjusts and one relishes this repertoire on modern instruments. The sound emerges with both warmth and vividness in this, its first transfer to CD.

LUMBYE, Hans Christian (1810-74)

Amelie Waltz; *Britta Polka*; *Champagne Galop*; *Columbine Polka Mazurka*; *Concert Polka* (for 2 violins & orchestra); *Copenhagen Steam Railway Galop*; *Dream Pictures* (fantasy); *The Guards of Amager: Final Galop*; *The Lady of St Petersburg* (polka); *My Salute to*

St Petersburg (march); *Napoli* (ballet): *Final Galop. Polonaise with
Cornet Solo*; *Queen Louise's Waltz*; *Salute to August Bournonville*;
St Petersburg Champagne Galop
ⓑⓑ Regis RRC 1155. Odense SO, Guth

The superb Regis collection (originally on Unicorn) offers 75 minutes of the composer's best music with wonderfully spontaneous performances, demonstrating above all its elegance and gentle grace. It opens with a vigorous *Salute to August Bournonville* and closes with a *Champagne Galop* to rival Johann junior's polka. In between comes much to enchant, not least the delightful *Amelie Waltz* and the haunting *Dream Pictures Fantasia* with its diaphanous opening texture and lilting main theme. But Lumbye's masterpiece is the unforgettable *Copenhagen Steam Railway Galop*. This whimsical yet vivid portrayal of a local Puffing Billy begins with the gathering of passengers at the station – obviously dressed for the occasion in a more elegant age than ours. The little engine then wheezingly starts up and proceeds on its short journey, finally drawing to a dignified halt against interpolated cries from the station staff. Because of the style and refinement of its imagery, it is much the most endearing of musical railway evocations, and the high-spirited lyricism of the little train racing through the countryside, its whistle peeping, is enchanting. This is a superbly entertaining disc, showing the Odense Symphony Orchestra and its conductor Peter Guth as naturally suited to this repertoire as was the VPO under Boskovsky in the music of the Strauss family. The recording has a warm and sympathetic ambience which gives a lovely bloom to the whole concert. This reissue is a bargain if ever there was one.

LUPU, Radu (piano)

Complete Decca Solo Recordings: **BEETHOVEN**: *Piano Concerto 3*
(with LSO, Lawrence Foster). *Piano Sonatas: 8 (Pathétique)*; *14
(Moonlight)*; *19*; *20, Op. 49/1–2*; *21 (Waldstein)*. *2 Rondos, Op. 51*; *32
Variations on an Original Theme in C min., WoO 80*. **BRAHMS**:
3 Intermezzi, Op. 117; *6 Pieces, Op. 118*; *4 Pieces, Op. 119*; *2 Rhapsodies,
Op. 79*; *Piano Sonata 3, Op. 5*; *Theme & Variations in D min.* (arr. from
String Sextet, Op. 18). **SCHUBERT**: *4 Impromptus, D.899*; *4
Impromptus, D.935*; *6 Moments musicaux, D.780. Piano Sonatas:
1 in E, D.157*; *5 in A flat, D.557*; *13 in A, D.664*; *14 in A min., D.784*;
16 in A min., D.845; *18 in G, D.894*; *19 in C min., D.958*; *20 in A,
D.959*; *21 in B flat, D.960*. *2 Scherzi, D.593*. **SCHUMANN**:
Humoreske, Op. 20; *Kinderszenen, Op. 15*; *Kreisleriana, Op. 16*
ⓑ Decca (ADD/DDD) 478 2340 (10)

Radu Lupu was one of Decca's key recording pianists between 1970 and 1993. His early début recording of Beethoven's *Third Concerto* proved to be a small-scale romantic account, individual but lacking real concentration; but the coupling of the 32 *Variations in C minor* proved far more successful and his collection of Beethoven *Sonatas* carried conviction, if at times it was a little mannered. But his recordings of late Brahms were outstanding in every way, producing great intensity and inwardness when those qualities were required, and a keyboard mastery that was second to none. His view of the *F minor Sonata* was also individual – inward, ruminative and always beautifully rounded – and the *Variations* made a rare coupling.

He proved a superb Schubertian. The *Impromptus* were of the same calibre as Brendel's and were beautifully recorded, and his *Moments musicaux*, too, are very fine indeed. In the *Sonatas* he is sensitive and poetic throughout. The *A minor*, D.845, is searching and poetic. He brings tenderness and classical discipline to bear throughout and his playing is musically satisfying in a very Schubertian way. *No. 18 in G major*, D.894, is hardly less fine, a superb reading, relatively straight in its approach but full of glowing perception on points of detail. Moreover, the exposition repeat is observed in the first movement. The analogue recordings from the late 1970s are of Decca's finest. In his account of the *C minor* work, D.958, he finds a simple eloquence that is most moving, and in the two *A major* works, D.664 and D.959, he strikes the perfect balance between Schubert's classicism and the spontaneity of musical thought, and at the same time he leaves the impression that the achievement is perfectly effortless, with an inner repose and depth of feeling that remain memorable long after the performance is ended. He caps the series with a truly memorable performance of the great *B flat Sonata*, D.960, which finds this masterly pianist most eloquent and thoughtful throughout. For his last collection Lupu turns to Schumann and proves to be one of the interpreters whose understanding of this composer can be measured alongside that of Murray Perahia. This is playing of quite exceptional insight and naturalness. His account of the *Humoreske*, Op. 20, is the most poetic and spontaneous since the famous Richter version from the 1950s, and the *Kreisleriana* are hardly less magical. This is playing of great poetry and authority. The recording is excellent, albeit resonant, and this set as a whole is well worth seeking out.

LUTOSŁAWSKI, Witold (1913–94)

Concerto for Orchestra; *Jeux vénétiens*; *Livre pour orchestre*; *Mi-parti*; *Musique funèbre*; *Postlude 1*; *Preludes & Fugues for 13 Solo Strings*; *Symphonic Variations*; *Symphonies 1–2*; (i) *Paroles tissées*; (ii) *3 Poèmes d'Henri Michaux*

Ⓑ EMI (ADD) 2 15318-2 (3). Polish Nat. RSO (or Polish CO), composer; with (i) Devos;
(ii) Kraków R. Ch.

This very recommendable EMI set, conducted by the composer, draws on a six-LP set dating from the late 1970s, including not only the *Concerto for*

Orchestra – the composer's most famous piece, a vibrant and very appealing work for orchestra – but also both the symphonies and the enticing early *Symphonic Variations* with its Szymanowskian palette and luminosity. The two symphonies date from 1947 and 1966/8 respectively. The latter consolidates the new language the composer formed after his change of style in the mid-1950s. The first is written against a musical background influenced by Hindemith, Bartók and Prokofiev, and perhaps by Stravinsky too, but the work has its own individuality. Even today some of this music, notably *Jeux venétiens* and *Mi-parti*, sounds very avant-garde, but the latter piece is hauntingly atmospheric in the composer's hands. The searching *Preludes and Fugues for 13 Solo Strings* (1970–72) show the mature composer. The choral *Poèmes* were written a decade earlier; with their variety of effects, including whispering and syllabic monotones, the writing readily contrasts with the *Paroles tissées* ('woven words') with its mystical feeling and remarkable word-imagery. Together with the elliptical *Postlude* this programme offers a well-planned demonstration of the composer's breadth of achievement, with performances so obviously authoritative and of a high standard, and the recording exceptionally vivid.

McCABE, John (born 1939)

(i) *Flute Concerto. Symphony 4 (Of Time and the River)*
Hyp. CDA 67089. BBC SO, Handley; (i) with Beynon

Completed in 1994, McCabe's *Fourth Symphony*, entitled *Of Time and the River* after Thomas Wolfe's novel, is a magnificent work in two substantial movements – fast to slow, then slow to fast. The idiom is warmer and more approachable than in his earlier music, echoing in its atmospheric orchestration and some of the melodic lines Britten on the one hand and Sibelius on the other, while remaining distinctive and new. Superb performances and vivid recording, not just of the *Symphony* but of the large-scale *Flute Concerto* McCabe wrote for James Galway. Ideal notes as well.

MacCUNN, Hamish (1868–1916)

Concert overture: The Land of the Mountain and the Flood. The Dowie Dens o' Yarrow; The Ship o' the Fiend; Cantata. (i) *The Lay of the Last Minstrel: Breathes There the Man; O Caledonia!. Jeanie Deans* (opera; excerpts)
Hyp. CDA 66815. BBC Scottish SO, Brabbins; (i) with Watson, Milne, MacDougall, Sidhom, Gadd, Danby, Scottish Op. Ch.

The Land of the Mountain and the Flood is a very well-constructed piece, with a memorable tune. Martyn Brabbins and the BBC Scottish Symphony Orchestra, in a brilliant new performance, give it fresh life, and the Hyperion recording has range and sparkle. *The Dowie Dens o' Yarrow* is a very similar piece, with comparable rhythmic impetus and another attractive secondary theme, given to the oboe. The even more atmospheric *Ship o' the Fiend* introduces another endearing lyrical cello theme reminiscent of *The Land of the Mountain and the Flood*.

MacCunn's opera *Jeanie Deans* is a tuneful and colourful piece with plenty of musical vitality. Effie's aria, *Oh! would that I again could see* (she is imprisoned in the Tolbooth), and the following *Lullaby* are touchingly sung here by Lisa Milne, and the choral contribution is very spirited. The excerpt from the cantata *The Lay of the Last Minstrel* brings a suitably vigorous closing chorus, *O Caledonia!*

MacDOWELL, Edward (1860–1908)

(i) *Piano Concertos 1–2. Second Modern Suite, Op. 14*
Hyp. CDA 67165. Tanyel; (i) with BBC Scottish SO, Brabbins

Seta Tanyel gives sparkling performances of these attractive works, relishing the pianistic fireworks typical of this lyrical American composer. The fill-up, involving piano alone, offers a sequence of six colourful and unpretentious genre pieces. Tanyel's characterful playing, full of sparkle and imagination, is well matched by the playing of the BBC Scottish Orchestra under Martyn Brabbins, helped by full-bodied, well-balanced recording.

McEWEN, John Blackwood (1868–1948)

Three Border Ballads: Coronach; *The Demon Lover*; *Grey Galloway*
Chan. 9241. LPO, Mitchell

These three *Border Ballads*, written between 1906 and 1908, are symphonic poems, well stocked with distinctive ideas, and with a strong Lisztian inheritance. *The Demon Lover*, the most ambitious in scale (some might feel too ambitious), has a kind of luscious, melodramatic, post-Wagnerian chromaticism that isn't too far from the world of Scriabin. Even the first to be written, *Coronach*, has a sensuous feeling that one associates with more southern climes, yet the nobility of its main theme also suggests links with Parry and Elgar. The performances here are warmly sympathetic and very well played and recorded, and almost convince one that these works are masterpieces.

A Solway Symphony; (i) *Hills o'Heather. Where the Wild Thyme Blows*

Chan. 9345. (i) Welsh; LPO, Mitchell

McEwen's highly evocative *Solway Symphony* is a triptych of seascapes marked by magically transparent orchestration and crisply controlled argument. Above all, this is warm-hearted music. *Hills o'Heather* is a charming movement for cello and orchestra, while *Where the Wild Thyme Blows* uses slow pedal points to sustain harmonically adventurous arguments. The performances, conducted by Alasdair Mitchell, who edited the scores, are outstanding, a well-deserved tribute to a neglected composer who was far more than an academic. The recording is sumptuously atmospheric.

MACKENZIE, Alexander (1847–1935)

Benedictus, Op. 37/3; *Burns 'Second Scottish Rhapsody', Op. 24*; *Coriolanus* (incidental music): *Suite, Op. 61. The Cricket on the Hearth: Overture, Op. 62. Twelfth Night* (incidental music): *Overture/Suite, Op. 40*

Hyp. CDA 66764. BBC Scottish SO, Brabbins

In the *Burns Rhapsody* Mackenzie uses three Scottish folk tunes quite felicitously, notably 'Scots! Wha hae', which is very emphatic. The second movement has charm, and indeed Mackenzie's own lyrical gift is quite striking, at times even Sullivanesque, as in the *Cricket on the Hearth Overture* (which also shows deft orchestral skill), while the *Benedictus* has a melody typical of its time. The incidental music for *Twelfth Night* is in the form of an overture and is subdivided into six sections, with a Shakespeare quotation for each to identify its mood. The whole programme is presented with commitment and polish by the BBC Scottish Symphony Orchestra and makes a very agreeable 75 minutes of not too demanding listening. Those who respond to this delightful repertoire will also enjoy Mackenzie's highly entertaining *Piano Concerto* (also on Hyperion, CDA 67023), making gorgeous use of Scottish themes, centring around a beautiful lyrical slow movement and featuring a very jolly finale, based on *Green Grow the Rushes O*. It is coupled with a rather heavier rare piano concerto by Tovey. The pianist is Steven Osborne, with the BBC Scottish SO, conducted by Brabbins – and the performance and recording are excellent.

MacMILLAN, James (born 1959)

(i–iii) *Veni, Veni, Emmanuel*; (iv) *After the Tryst*; (i; v) '. . . as others see us . . .'; *Three Dawn Rituals; Untold*

RCA Catalyst 09026 61916-2. (i) Scottish CO, (ii) with Glennie; (iii) with Saraste; (iv) Crouch, Evans; (v) cond. composer

(i) *Veni, Veni, Emmanuel. The tryst*
🅱🅱 Naxos 8.554167. (i) Colin Currie; Ulster O, Yuasa

Veni, Veni, Emmanuel, James MacMillan's most dramatic work, based on the celebrated hymn, here comes in two excellent versions. On RCA the dedicatee, Evelyn Glennie, is the brilliant percussion soloist, dashing from one instrument to another, readily explaining why MacMillan was inspired to write the work for her. After an Introit, five contrasted sections, including a Dance and two Transitions, culminate in the full emergence of the hymn in a *Dance Chorale*, whereupon the soloist processes to the back of the stage while the orchestra plays jingling instruments, until at the back the soloist as a climax plays gigantic tubular bells, a brilliant effect, very well reproduced in both these versions.

Though Glennie has priority, Colin Currie, first percussion finalist in the BBC Young Musician of the Year Contest in 1994, is equally inspired, and is very well supported by the Ulster Orchestra under Takuo Yuasa.

The RCA coupling is much the more generous, with another major work included, the idiosyncratic song-cycle, '. . . *as others see us* . . . ', a sequence of distinctive songs, each representing a historic figure, including Henry VIII, the Duke of Marlborough and poets Byron, Wordsworth and T. S. Eliot, the last an American by birth but later quintessentially English. The piece is rounded off with a song about the feminist, Dorothy Hodgkin. The other pieces, much briefer, equally demonstrate the composer's lively imagination.

The Naxos disc has as coupling *The Tryst*, inspired by a poem of William Soutar, which prompted MacMillan to set the words to a simple melody which has since appeared in many of the composer's works, most strikingly in this vigorous piece, lasting nearly half an hour. Again performances are exemplary, and the recording quality excellent on both discs.

The Confession of Isobel Gowdie; Symphony 3, 'Silence'
Chan. 10275. BBC PO, composer

The *Confession of Isobel Gowdie* was the work which in 1990 at the Proms in London first brought the Scottish composer James MacMillan to wide attention, at once establishing him as one of the most distinctive composers in Britain. His two main sources of inspiration have always been his deep religious faith as a devout Catholic and his strong left-wing sympathies, together with his pride as a Scotsman.

In *The Confession of Isobel Gowdie* he was inspired to write by the tragic story of a woman who in 1662 under torture was forced to confess to witchcraft, which was manifestly untrue. She was strangled and burned at the stake, which has prompted MacMillan to write this major work as a belated requiem for her. The emotional power of the writing is irresistible, as well as the colour and variety of the instrumentation, demonstrating the composer's brilliance of invention. This performance, conducted by the composer, brings out the vividness of the writing as well as the concentration of argument.

It is well coupled with the *Symphony No. 3*, subtitled 'Silence', written in 2002 as a memorial to the Japanese writer, Shusaku Endo, who was horrified by mass violence, torture and genocide. As the subtitle implies, meditation and silence are a central quality of the writing, illustrating the composer's dedication even outside his Catholic faith. Again the composer draws an inspired performance from the BBC Philharmonic, reinforcing the quality of the series of MacMillan's recordings for Chandos, all vividly recorded.

MACONCHY, Elizabeth (1907-94)

(i) *Music for Strings*; (ii) *Overture, Proud Thames*; (iii) *Serenata concertante for Violin & Orchestra*; (iv) *Symphony for Double String Orchestra*

Lyrita (DDD/ADD) SRCD 288. (i–ii) LPO; (iii–iv) LSO; (iii) with Parikian; (i) Wordsworth; (ii–iv) Handley

These works all testify to the strength of Elizabeth Maconchy's imagination, the *Overture*, in the words of the composer, inspired by the river itself 'from its trickling source among green fields to the full tide of life in London'; the *Music for Strings* has the widest variety of tempo and texture in its four movements, with the finale 'an extrovert happy-go-lucky movement'. The *Symphony for Double String Orchestra* is very much in the tradition of British string music, with a flavour not too distant from Tippett's concerto for a similar ensemble. The *Serenata concertante* – a violin concerto in all but name – is grittier and less lyrical, at least until you come to the slow third movement, which builds up in simple lyricism to a grinding climax like that of Walton's *First Symphony*. Handley directs superb, committed performances, vividly recorded, and Barry Wordsworth is equally impressive in the *Music for Strings*.

MAGNARD, Albéric (1865-1914)

Symphonies: 1 in C min., Op. 4; 2 in E, Op. 6; 3 in B flat min., Op. 11; 4 in C sharp min., Op. 21

Ⓑ Hyp. Dyad CDD 22068 (2). BBC Scottish SO, Ossonce

Magnard achieved mixed success in his life, but his dramatic end at the hands of the Germans in 1914 adds a macabre shadow to his story. In 1914, the Germans had invaded the estate of his large house in Baron. The composer fired a shot from an upstairs window and evidently killed two of the German cavalry. However, the retaliation resulted in his death and his house was set on fire, resulting in the loss of several scores. The *First Symphony* (1889-90) was composed in the shadow of Magnard's friend and mentor, Vincent d'Indy, and follows strictly cyclical principles. Yet its ideas still show individuality of character and, despite the debt to Wagner and Franck, the last two symphonies have distinct personalities; they are separated by 17 years. The *Fourth* has an impressive intellectual power and is very well crafted, with no shortage of ideas. For all the appearance of academicism, there is a quiet and distinctive personality here, and dignity too. The superb Hyperion set of these four symphonies, neatly fitting onto two inexpensive CDs, easily outshines earlier rivals, with warm, cleanly focused sound.

MAHLER, Gustav (1860–1911)

Symphonies (i) *1 (Titan)*; (i–ii) *2 (Resurrection)*; (i; iii) *3*; (i; iv) *4*; (i) *5–6 (Tragic)*; *7*; (v) *8 (Symphony of 1,000)*; (i) *9*; *10 (Adagio)*; (vi) *Das Lied von der Erde*

Sony Classical (ADD) 88697-45369-2 (12). (i) NYPO, Bernstein; (ii) with Venora, Tourel, Collegiate Chorale; (iii) with Lipton, Ch.; (iv) with Grist; (v) Spoorenberg, G. Jones, Annear, Reynolds, Procter, Mitchinson, Ruzdjak, McIntyre, Leeds Festival Ch., L. Symphony Ch., Orpington Junior Singers, Highgate School Boys' Ch., Finchley Children's Music Group, LSO Bernstein; (vi) Ludwig, Kollo, Israel PO, Bernstein

Symphony 9 in D min.

DG 477 8620. BPO, Bernstein.

Bernstein's Mahler cycle with the New York Philharmonic, made during the 1960s and early 1970s, was the pioneering set, and the first complete survey on record. Its strengths are well known – not surprisingly, as most of these performances have rarely been out of circulation. They come here with the reminiscences of those who played under Mahler in New York and a memoir by Alma Mahler. The original LPs were housed in a handsome black-leather album, but the CD presentation is also elegant. Bernstein inhabits this world with great intensity and vision, and many will feel that he surpasses his later versions in this respect. Of course, *Das Lied* is another matter, and a special place must be reserved in the Mahler pantheon for Bruno Walter's magisterial set from the early days of mono LP with Ferrier and Patzak.

A valuable appendix to the New York cycle comes from a concert performance of Mahler's *Ninth*, given by Bernstein in Berlin at the Philharmonie, which has a thrilling fervour – quite an emotional experience and outstripping even the intensity and authenticity of Haitink.

Symphony 1 (Titan); (i) *2 (Resurrection)*

Ⓜ Double Decca 448 921-2. LSO, Solti; (i) with Harper, Watts, L. Symphony Ch.

The London Symphony Orchestra play Mahler's *First* like no other orchestra. They catch the magical opening, with its bird-sound calls and evocatively distanced brass, with a singular ambience, at least partly related to the orchestra's characteristic blend of wind timbres. Throughout there is wonderfully warm string-playing and the most atmospheric response from the horns. Solti's tendency to drive hard is felt only in the second movement, which is pressed a little too much, although he relaxes beautifully in the central section. Especially memorable are the poignancy of the introduction of the *Frère Jacques* theme in the slow movement and the exultant brilliance of the closing pages, helped by the wide dynamic and the wonderfully clear inner details of the 1964 Kingsway Hall recording.

Solti's 1964 account of the *Resurrection Symphony* remains a demonstration of the outstanding results Decca were securing with analogue techniques at that time. From the opening growl on the strings, Solti's searing energy is hard to resist in this, one of Mahler's most flamboyantly dramatic works. By contrast, Helen Watts is wonderfully expressive, while the chorus has a rapt intensity that is the more telling when the recording perspectives are so clearly delineated. These recordings are also available separately, No. 1 on 458 622-2 and No. 2 on 475 8501.

(i) *Symphony 3 in D min.*; (ii) *Kindertotenlieder*
Testament mono SBT2 1422. Ferrier; (i) BBC SO, Boult; (ii) Concg. O, Klemperer

In the first days of the Third Programme after the war, the BBC produced its first complete cycle of Mahler symphonies with Bruno Walter conducting the *First*, and later records of his *Fourth* and *Ninth*. Sir Adrian Boult conducted the *Third* with Kathleen Ferrier as soloist in 1947. This was its first performance in England and it was not given again until 1960. These acetates show that Sir Adrian was an *echt*-Mahlerian and completely inside the idiom. Older listeners will be delighted with this (R.L. remembers hearing the broadcast) in spite of the imperfections of the recorded sound. The *Kindertotenlieder* come from a Dutch broadcast made in 1951; Ferrier recorded the cycle with Bruno Walter, who perhaps evinces greater warmth and poetry than Klemperer but no less control. An important document both for Mahlerians and for Ferrier aficionados.

(i) *Symphony 4*; (ii) *Lieder eines Fahrenden Gesellen*
Ⓑ Sony SBK 46535. (i) Raskin, Cleveland O, Szell; (ii) Von Stade, LPO, A. Davis

George Szell's 1966 record of Mahler's *Fourth* represented his partnership with the Cleveland Orchestra at its highest peak, and the digital remastering for CD brings out the very best of the early recording. The performance remains completely satisfying, and the music blossoms, partly because of the marvellous attention to detail (and the immaculate ensemble), but more positively because of the committed and radiantly luminous orchestral response to the music itself. In the finale Szell found the ideal soprano to match his conception. Moreover, in the coupling Frederica von Stade insinuates a hint of youthful ardour into her highly enjoyable account of the 'Wayfaring Lad' cycle.

Symphony 5 in C sharp min.

Ⓜ EMI DVD 4903269-9. BPO, Rattle (with **ADÈS**: *Asyla*)

Ⓑ EMI Masters 9 65935. BPO, Rattle

Rattle's fine version of Mahler's *Fifth* was recorded live in November 2002 at his inaugural concert as music director of the Berlin Philharmonic. The DVD fully captures the atmospheric excitement of the occasion, and the CD too brings out the exuberance of Mahler's writing. The emotional climax of the performance comes as it should in the hushed intensity of the great *Adagietto*. Yet Rattle, looking at the evidence, treats it differently from most latter-day performances which make it expansively elegiac. By contrast he responds to it with the music emerging tenderly, as though from another world. This above all is a songful version, full of tenderness, with phrasing affectionately moulded in spontaneous warmth. It is also a version which demonstrates the joyfulness of much of the writing. The CD issue is inexpensive and the recording is admirable, clear as well as atmospheric, but the DVD has a clear advantage over the CD issue in that it also includes the other work in the concert, Thomas Adès's brilliant showpiece, *Asyla*. The DVD package also contains a second disc with an extended interview with Rattle by Nicholas Kenyon, his biographer.

Symphony 8 (Symphony of 1000)

Ⓜ Decca 475 7521. Harper, Popp, Augér, Minton, Watts, Kollo, Shirley-Quirk, Talvela, V. Boys' Ch., V. State Op. Ch. & Singverein, Chicago SO, Solti

Solti's is a classic recording. Challenged by the tightest possible recording schedule, the American orchestra and European singers responded to Solti at his most inspired with a performance which vividly captures the atmosphere of a great occasion – essential in this of all works. There is nothing cautious about the surging dynamism of the first movement, the electrifying hymn, *Veni Creator spiritus*; and the long second movement, setting the final scene from Goethe's *Faust*, proceeds through its contrasted sections with unrelenting intensity. The hushed prelude in Solti's hands is sharp-edged in *pianissimo*, not at all comforting, while the magnificent recording copes superbly with every strand of texture and the fullest range of dynamic – spectacularly so in the great final crescendo to the words '*Alles vergängliche*'. This is not only one of Solti's best Mahler recordings, it is one of *the* great Mahler recordings in the catalogue. It now comes on a single mid-priced CD as one of Decca's new series of 'Originals'.

Symphony 9

DG 439 024-2. BPO, Karajan

Karajan's 1982 version of the *Ninth* was voted record of the year in the *Gramophone* magazine on its appearance in 1984; and the German critic, Hans Heinz Stuckenschmidt, even went so far as to hail it as the finest performance of all time! It is masterly, wonderfully paced and finely detailed. The Berlin Philharmonic has never sounded like this since the 1980s.

MARCELLO, Alessandro (1669–1747)

6 Oboe Concertos (La Cetra)
Ⓜ Chan. 0744X. Robson, Latham, R. Brown, Coll. Mus. 90, Standage

The six concertos of *La Cetra* reveal a pleasing mixture of originality and convention; often one is surprised by a genuinely alive and refreshing individuality. Standage's set with Collegium Musicum 90 makes the most of Marcello's solo scoring, finding plenty of colour and nuance in these highly inventive works, not only for one or two oboes (or flutes) but for solo violin (Standage himself). Slow movements often possess real poignancy and the fast movements bubble and sparkle. Moreover, he includes an additional *Concerto con l'Eco* that is well worth having. Performances are appealingly stylish and beautifully recorded.

MARCELLO, Benedetto (1686–1739)

Piano Sonatas 3 in G; 5 in D min.; 7 in A min.; 9 in A; 10 in C min.; 2 Minuets in C
RCA 88697814662. Bacchetti (Fazioli piano)

Benedetto Marcello spent his whole life in Venice serving as a nobleman within the Venetian government. His music had been all but forgotten until two manuscripts of his keyboard music were discovered recently in Venice's Marciana Library. It is of the highest quality, as these splendid performances by the Genoese pianist Andrea Bacchetti demonstrate. Bacchetti has already made a number of fine recordings, including two of the Bach *Goldberg Variations*, and his understanding of baroque repertoire is outstanding making this superb set of performances, using a highly suitable Fazioli piano, very rewarding indeed, especially as he is beautifully recorded. He articulates the opening *Allegro* of the *Third Sonata*, with its repeated notes, most winningly, and follows with a simply played *Andante*. The *Largo* slow movements of the *Fifth*, *Ninth* and *Tenth Sonatas*, and the *Cantabile* and *Largo* of No. 7, are all gently expressive in Bacchetti's hands, yet of considerable depth. Allegros are always crisply articulated and bounce along infectiously, and the interplay of the *Presto* movements of the *A minor* and *C minor* works is particularly engaging. The two separate *Minuets* make further attractive contrasts. Altogether a most rewarding collection. Yet Bacchetti tells us that it is difficult for Italian keyboard players to obtain engagements outside Italy, as concert promoters tend to identify Italians with opera only!

MARRINER, Neville, with Academy of
St Martin-in-the-Fields

'Fantasia on Greensleeves': **VAUGHAN WILLIAMS**:
English Folk Song Suite; Fantasia on Greensleeves; The Lark
Ascending. **WARLOCK**: *Capriol Suite; Serenade for Strings.*
BUTTERWORTH: *The Banks of Green Willow; 2 English*
Idylls; A Shropshire Lad. **DELIUS**: *La Calinda; A Song Before*
Sunrise; Intermezzo and Serenade from 'Hassan'; On Hearing the
First Cuckoo in Spring; Summer Night on the River; The Walk to
the Paradise Garden. **ELGAR**: *Elegy for Strings; Serenade for*
Strings; Introduction and Allegro; Sospiri for Strings, Harp &
Organ; The Spanish Lady: Suite.
Ⓑ Double Decca (ADD) 452 707-2 (2)

Neville Marriner made many recordings for Argo/Decca from the 1960s to the
1980s, and this two-CD compilation shows why this is considered a vintage
period for both him and Argo. This exceptionally generous programme focuses
mainly on English pastoral evocations, including Iona Brown's Elysian account
of RVW's *The Lark Ascending*, while that composer's *Fantasia on Greensleeves* is
as beautiful as any, and the piquant tunes in the *English Folk Song Suite* are beautifully brought out. Butterworth's orchestral works are splendidly done, as are the
masterly Warlock items – some of the most attractive music in the repertoire.
There can be no grumbles about the Delius items: these are lovely performances,
warm, tender and eloquent. They are superbly played and recorded in a splendid
acoustic. The recording is beautifully balanced – the distant cuckoo is highly
evocative – though with the relatively small band of strings the sound inevitably
has less body than a full orchestral group, yet in no way is the effect found wanting. If initially some of the Elgar items do not sound totally idiomatic, they are
very characterful performances which grow on one, and they include the rare
snippets arranged by Percy Young from Elgar's unfinished opera, *The Spanish
Lady*. An inexpensive and rewarding programme.

MARTIN, Frank (1890–1974)

(i) *Concerto for Harpsichord. Passacaille*; (ii) *Polyptyque for Violin &*
2 String Orchestras
MDG 601 1539-2. (i) Rudolf Scheidegger; (ii) Willi Zimmermann; Musikkollegium
    Winterthur, Jac van Steen

The rarity here is the *Polyptyque for Violin and Two String Orchestras*, as an earlier
DG record under Thierry Fischer no longer survives. *Polyptyque* comes from the
penultimate year of Martin's life, when he would have been eighty-three. It was

inspired by a polyptych, a set of very small panels he saw in Siena depicting the Passion, and this series of six movements was the result. The first, *'Image des Rameaux'*, portrays the entry of Christ into Jerusalem; its companion, *'Image de la Chambre haute'* evokes Christ answering the anguished questions of his disciples. This pattern of an active movement followed by a reflective one is followed throughout. *Polyptique* is a work of powerful vision and spirituality, written for Yehudi Menuhin and Edmond de Stoutz, who recorded it with their respective orchestras in 1976 on HMV. It is played with consummate artistry by Willi Zimmermann and the Winterthur ensemble under Jac van Steen. The *Harpsichord Concerto* also is marvellously played and has great breadth. It takes only a few seconds longer than Martin's own version with Christiane Jaccottet on the Swiss Jecklin label, but it feels wonderfully natural and unhurried. Martin's own transcription for strings of the noble organ *Passacaille* completes an outstanding addition to his discography.

Concerto for 7 Wind Instruments, Timpani, Percussion & Strings; (i) Petite symphonie concertante; (ii) 6 Monologues from Jedermann

Warner Apex 0927 48687-2. (i) Guibentif, Jaccottet, Ruttimann; (ii) Cachemaille; SRO, Jordan

In the *Petite symphonie concertante*, Armin Jordan has atmosphere and an unhurried sense of pace, and the soloists and orchestra are very well balanced. It is excellently played (with Christiane Jaccottet, who took part in the first performance). The account of the *Concerto for Seven Wind Instruments* is also a fine one. The *Six Monologues* from Hofmannsthal's *Everyman*, written at the height of the Second World War, are subtle and profound. Their concentration of mood is well conveyed by Gilles Cachemaille, and the orchestral detail is well captured. Eminently recommendable and an inexpensive entry into Martin's world.

Symphonie concertante (arr. of Petite symphonie concertante for full orchestra); Symphony; Passacaglia

Chan. 9312. LPO, Bamert

The *Symphony* is a haunting and at times quite magical piece. The two pianos are used effectively and although, as in the *Petite symphonie concertante*, lip service is paid to the 12-note system the overall effect is far from serial. Its main companion here is the transcription Martin made for full orchestra of the *Petite symphonie concertante* the year after its first performance. Harp and piano are used for colouristic effects but completely relinquish any hint of soloist ambitions. The *Passacaglia* is Martin's 1962 transcription for full orchestra of his organ piece. Sensitive playing from the LPO under Matthias Bamert and exemplary Chandos recording.

Der Sturm: Suite. Symphonie concertante; (i) Six Monologues from Jedermann

MDG 901 1614-6. Stavanger SO, Steven Sloane, (i) with Thomas Oliemans

Three key works in eminently acceptable performances. Fischer-Dieskau's famous record of *The Tempest* and the *Everyman Monologues* with the composer himself conducting is one of the classics of the gramophone but enjoys intermittent availability. We do not associate Norwegian artists with this repertoire but these fine musicians prove highly sympathetic interpreters. The four movements from *The Tempest* are ethereal, particularly the other-worldly *Prelude* with its evocation of the Shakespearean seascape. The *Everyman Monologues* are earlier but also rank among Martin's most inspired and challenging pieces; although Martin himself favoured the original voice and piano, the orchestral version has the greater resonance and warmth. Fearing that the *Petite symphonie concertante* would not enjoy many performances, he arranged it for full orchestra without soloists but it never enjoyed the same success. Excellent singing from Thomas Oliemans and fine support from the Stavanger players.

Mass for Double Choir; Passacaille for Organ
Hyp. CDA 67017. Westminster Cathedral Ch., O'Donnell – **PIZZETTI**: *Messa di requiem; De profundis*

The *Mass for Double Choir* is one of Martin's purest and most sublime utterances. The version from the Westminster Cathedral Choir under James O'Donnell is the most outstanding. The boys produce marvellously focused tone of great purity and expressive power, and the tonal blend that O'Donnell achieves throughout is little short of miraculous. This won *Gramophone* magazine's 'Record of the Year' award in 1998, and deservedly so. As a fill-up O'Donnell offers the *Passacaille* for organ, together with two magnificent Pizzetti works.

In terra pax (oratorio)
Ⓜ Decca Eloquence (ADD) 480 2316 (2). Buckel, Höffgen, Haefliger, Mollet, Stämpfli, SRO Ch. & O, Ansermet – **HONEGGER**: *Pacific 231*, etc.

Frank Martin's beautiful score was commissioned by the Swiss Radio in preparation for the announcement of the end of the 1939–45 war, and it was first performed by Ansermet. Martin's music has an appropriate eloquence and spirituality, and he is admirably served by the soloists. The score falls into four short sections, all with biblical texts, and its sincerity and sense of compassion leave a strong impression. With equally interesting couplings, this is well worth having.

MARTINŮ, Bohuslav (1890–1959)

Violin Concertos 1 & 2
Hyp. CDA 677674. Matoušek, Czech PO, Hogwood

The *First Concerto* comes from 1931 and was intended for Samuel Dushkin, who had just premièred the Stravinsky *Concerto*. However, the performance never came off and the manuscript was lost for some time until Harry

Halbreich discovered it in a Washington University library in 1968. The *Second Concerto* was written for Mischa Elman in 1943 and first given in Boston under Koussevitzky. They are both delightful works and Bohuslav Matoušek plays them with much style and virtuosity. As in other issues in the series, Christopher Hogwood reveals total sympathy with the composer's sensibility.

Symphony 1; Concerto for Double String Orchestra, Piano & Timpani
Chan. 8950. Czech PO, Bělohlávek

Symphonies 1–4
BIS CD362/3. Bamberg SO, Neeme Järvi

Symphonies 5; 6 (Fantaisies symphoniques)
Sup. SU 4007-2 Czech PO, Bělohlávek

Symphony 6; Bouquet of Flowers
Sup. 11 1932-2901. Czech PO, Ančerl

Martinů was a latecomer to the symphony, embarking on the *First* in 1942, in his early fifties. He composed the next four at annual intervals and then turned to the *Sixth* in 1953, commissioned and first performed by Charles Munch and the Boston Symphony. The cycle is one of the peaks of symphonic literature; its rhythmic vitality and atmospheric textures are coupled with abundant melodic invention. The opening of the *Sixth* sounds like an Amazonian chorus of insects and birds, with astonishingly vivid colours. Indeed, the colours are in some way enhanced and intoxicating. All six symphonies are the work of an extraordinary imagination; R.L. recalls Robert Simpson, who produced a performance of the *Fifth* with the visiting Czech Philharmonic, saying that the Maida Vale studios positively glowed with light during and after this glorious music. Perhaps the most genial and sunny is the *Fourth*; and this is a good place from which to set out exploring these masterpieces. Its themes are infectiously memorable and its textures transparent and light. The *Second* (1943) has the classicism of Dvořák and springs gloriously to life in Neeme Järvi's BIS recording. The *Third* (1944) is darker but the music's life-enhancing spirit is still strong. Although they took some time before establishing themselves in the LP and CD catalogue, they are now well served: few recordings fall short of excellence. The Czech Philharmonic cycle under Bělohlávek on Chandos has real authenticity of feeling and very good recording quality to commend it. The *Sixth* (*Fantaisies symphoniques*) is arguably the most profoundly original of all these works. The textures are wonderfully transparent – almost luminous – and the mood exalted. Ančerl gave the first Czech performance of No. 6, and this fine recording from 1957 has total naturalness and authority. So if you want a single disc of Martinů's symphonies, this is the one to go for. It has all the sense of discovery and wonder that makes a strong claim on collectors even though the mono sound has its limitations. It comes with a captivating folk cantata, *Bouquet of Flowers*, that should be a popular repertory piece.

Cello Sonatas 1, H 277; 2, H 286; 3, H 340; Variations on a Theme of Rossini, H 290; Variations on a Slovak Theme, H 378
Chan. 10602. Paul Watkins, Huw Watkins

The three *Cello Sonatas* rank high in Martinů's instrumental output. The *First* comes from 1939 and was written for Pierre Fournier, who gave its première in Paris with Rudolf Firkušný only a few days before the Nazi invaders took the city. Martinů fled to New York in March 1941 and composed the *Second Sonata* the following year for Frank Rybka, a Czech musician who had been a pupil of Janáček. In 1943 Martinů met Piatigorsky at Tanglewood, and it was for him that he composed the well-known *Variations on a Theme of Rossini* (*Dal tuo stellato soglio* from Act III of *Mosè in Egitto*). The *Third Sonata* comes nearly a decade later in 1952, written for the cellist-conductor, Hans Kindler, but first given by František Smetana in Prague. The *Slovak Variations* were written in the last few months of his life when he was staying with Paul Sacher in Switzerland.

Paul and Huw Watkins prove committed advocates of this repertoire and their performances can hold their own against their finest rivals. They are as muscular and vibrant as the alternative Hyperion set with Steven Isserlis and Peter Evans, and score over them in including the two sets of *Variations*. The Chandos sound is expertly balanced, natural and lifelike.

String Sextet; 3 Madrigals for Violin & Viola
ⓑⓑ Hyp. Helios CDH 55321. Raphael Ens. - **SCHULHOFF**: *String Sextet*

The *Sextet* for two each of violins, violas and cellos was for many years during the 1950s and '60s Martinů's calling card in the concert hall, but it is now rather a rarity. It comes from 1932 and was written rather quickly – in the course of one week. It is a strikingly assured piece in which the musical argument unfolds with a natural sense of organic growth. Rather to his surprise, it earned Martinů the Elizabeth Sprague Coolidge Medal, winning first prize out of 145 entries. The *Madrigals* are post-war, very typical Martinů, and are despatched with great virtuosity. The Raphael Ensemble give a masterly account of them, and the 1991 recording is truthful and lifelike.

MASSENET, Jules (1842–1912)

Le Cid (ballet music)
ⓜ Australian Decca Eloquence (ADD) 476 2742. Israel PO, Martinon (with **DVOŘÁK**: *Slavonic Dances, Op. 46/1–8; Op. 72/7*) - **MEYERBEER**: *Les Patineurs*

Decca made a house speciality of recording the *Le Cid* and *Les Patineurs* ballet music together over the years, but none is more brilliant than this 1958 recording. In Martinon's hands the tunes fizz and effervesce like the best champagne, while the colourful reflective numbers have picture-postcard atmosphere.

Equally remarkable is the vivid recording, the sort of brilliant yet warm sound for which Decca became famous; and it is superbly transferred to CD. A unique collector's item to be snapped up while it's around.

Scènes alsaciennes; Scènes de féerie; Scènes napolitaines; Scènes pittoresques

ⓑⓑ Naxos 8.553125. New Zealand SO, Ossonce

Best known are the somewhat ingenuous *Scènes pittoresques* and the *Scènes alsaciennes*. The most touching movement is the beautiful *Sous les tilleuls* ('Under the lime trees') with its wilting dialogue between cello and clarinet, played here with an affectionate finesse worthy of a Beecham. With full, sparkling, yet warmly atmospheric recording, this is a first-class disc in every way. A second collection is also available (on Naxos 8.553124) with similarly appealing music: *Hérodiade* (ballet) *Suite*; *Orchestral Suites 1; 2 (Scènes hongroises)* and *3 (Scènes dramatiques)*, though not quite so well recorded.

Manon (complete, DVD version)

DG DVD 073 4431. Netrebko, Villazón, Fischesser, Daza, Corazza, Kataja, Berlin State Op. Ch. & O, Barenboim (Producer: Bernhard Fleischer; V/D: Andreas Morell)

Manon (complete, CD version)

Testament mono SBT 3203 (3). De los Angeles, Legay, Dens, Paris Opéra-Comique O, Monteux

We are particularly well served with outstanding versions of *Manon*. Apart from Renée Fleming's memorable assumption of the role on TDK, Natalie Dessay is wonderfully characterful in her partnership with Villazón on Virgin. But now Villazón (at his finest) is re-partnered with Anna Netrebko, singing gloriously on DG, in a passionate liaison that proves most moving of all. Moreover, whereas David McVicar's production on Virgin from the very beginning underlines the seamy side of the world into which the young Manon enters, the producer of the Berlin version, Bernhard Fleisher, emphazises its glamour, underpinned by luscious costuming (from Susan Hilferty) in 1950s style. But Manon herself is totally charismatic as she moves from innocent ingénue on a bench waiting for a train, to a glamorous blonde of Marilyn Monroe vintage in the Hôtel de Transylvanie. The spectacle of the Cours-la-Reine scene is dazzling, but what one remembers most is the tenderly sensuous love scenes between the two principals, notably the delightful aria when Manon nostalgically serenades her little table, and the great emotional climax when she seduces her lover to make him abandon his plan to enter the Church. With Alfredo Daza a fine, dignified Lescaut and Rémy Corazza most convincing as the villain, Guillot, the close of the opera is handled most movingly. Throughout, Barenboim (who stepped in at the last moment to conduct) achieves first-class orchestral playing and keeps the tension high, and overall the performance is quite unforgettable.

However, no one has recorded the role of Manon in Massenet's opera quite as bewitchingly as Victoria de los Angeles in this historic EMI recording of 1955, girlishly provocative at the start, conveying tragic depth later. The voice is at its most golden, and this vivid new transfer from Testament gives the mono sound extra warmth and immediacy. Henri Legay as Des Grieux also sings with honeyed tones, a believable young lover ensnared, and Pierre Monteux in one of his rare opera recordings is masterly in his timing and phrasing. As a splendid bonus we are also given RCA recordings of Berlioz and Debussy, similarly persuasive, recorded in Boston, also in 1955.

For those who would like a very good modern recording on CD, there is Antonio Pappano's impressive EMI recording (EMI 3 81842-2 (2)). In Act I Gheorghiu instantly establishes the heroine as a vivacious, wilful character with a great sense of fun, and her singing is both imaginative and technically flawless. The aria, *Adieu, notre petite table*, is tenderly affecting, shaded down to a breathtaking *pianissimo* at the end. A fine actress, she develops the character too, while Alagna, always at his happiest in French-language opera, portrays Des Grieux as full of eager innocence as well as passion. The other La Monnaie soloists make a splendid team under Pappano, with José van Dam impressively cast as Des Grieux's father. Pappano himself is as understanding an interpreter of Massenet as he is of Puccini, drawing warmly committed playing and singing from the whole company. Available at mid-price.

Thaïs

Decca 466 7662 (2). Fleming, Hampson, Sabbatini, Bordeaux Op. Ch. & O, Abel

The character of Thaïs in Massenet's opera finds an ideal interpreter in Renée Fleming. After making the heroine's unlikely conversion to virtue totally convincing, she crowns her performance with a deeply affecting account of her death scene, ending with a ravishing *pianissimo* top A. Thomas Hampson as Athanaël, a character working just as improbably in the opposite direction, cannot quite equal her in such total conviction but he is vocally ideal. The others are well cast too, notably Giuseppe Sabbatini as Nicias, and though the Bordeaux Opera Orchestra is not quite as refined as some, Yves Abel draws warmly sympathetic playing from them throughout, with the young French virtuoso, Renaud Capuchon, luxuriously cast in the big violin solo of the *Médi-tation*. Excellent sound. A clear first choice.

Werther

EMI 3 81849-2 (2). Alagna, Gheorghiu, Hampson, Petibon, Tiffin School Children's Ch.,
LSO, Pappano

Though Alagna with his French background is an ideal choice for Werther himself, Gheorghiu with her bright soprano is a less obvious one for the role of the heroine, Charlotte, normally given to a mezzo. But as a magnetic actress she conveys an extra tenderness and vulnerability, with no lack of weight in such a solo as *Laisse couler mes larmes* in Act III. Thomas Hampson is outstanding as Albert and Patricia Petibon is a sweet-toned Sophie. As in Puccini, Pappano is subtle as well as powerful, using rubato idiomatically and with refinement to heighten the drama and point the moments of climax. Good, warm sound.

MATHIAS, William (1934–92)

(i–ii) *Dance Overture, Op. 16*; (iii; ii) *Divertimento for String Orchestra, Op. 7*; (i–ii) *Invocation & Dance, Op. 17*; (iv; ii) *'Landscapes of the mind': Laudi, Op. 62*; *Vistas, Op. 69*. (iii; ii) *Prelude, Aria & Finale for String Orchestra, Op. 25*; (v) *Sinfonietta, Op. 34*

Lyrita (ADD) SRCD 328. (i) LSO; (ii) Atherton; (iii) ECO; (iv) New Philh. O; (v) Nat. Youth O of Wales, Davison

As this collection readily bears out, William Mathias was a composer of genuine talent, versatile as well as inventive. The joyful *Dance Overture* is vividly scored, rather after the manner of Malcolm Arnold, and the *Invocation and Dance* has genuine spontaneity. The *Divertimento* and *Prelude, Aria and Finale* have a family likeness in presenting workmanlike Hindemithian arguments in fast movements and warm lyricism in slow ones, although the *Aria* is restrained and ethereal. The colourful, extrovert *Sinfonietta* was written for the Leicestershire Schools Symphony Orchestra in 1967. Its *Lento* has a delectable blues flavour, and the finale too is popularly based rhythmically, with its lively and sometimes pungent syncopations. Undoubtedly the two most remarkable works here are the two pieces described by their composer as '*Landscapes of the mind*'. *Laudi*, written in 1973, a 'landscape of the spirit', opens with temple bells and then contrasts bold cross-rhythms with gently voluptuous string sonorities, closing with a serene yet sensuous benediction, somewhat after the manner of Messiaen. The even more mystically evocative *Vistas* was inspired by the composer's visit to the USA in 1975. Here an Ivesian influence is unmistakable and, though there are ambiguous bursts of energy, the sections of restrained scoring, with evocatively distant trumpet-calls, are luminously atmospheric. Performances throughout are of the highest calibre, with Atherton at his most perceptive, and the recordings (for the most part engineered by Decca) are outstanding.

MATTHEWS, Colin (born 1946)

(i) *Horn Concerto*; (ii) *Alphabetical Order*

Ⓜ Hallé CDHLL 7515. (i) Watkins; (ii) Goodman (nar.); (i–ii) Hallé O, cond. (i) Elder; (ii) Gardner

We know Colin Matthews mainly from his brilliant orchestrations of Debussy's piano *Préludes*. Now he shows his paces with a highly original *Horn Concerto* which is mostly gently expressive, but also momentarily boldly forceful. It has a superbly confident soloist in Richard Watkins. Now for something entirely different. *Alphabetical Order* is an engagingly friendly but never bland setting, spiced with wit, of Christopher Reid's encapsulation of the alphabet. Narrator Henry Goodman, the Hallé Children's Chorus and the orchestra under Edward Gardner clearly enjoy themselves, and so do we.

MAYERL, Billy (1902–59)

Piano Miscellany
Ⓜ Dutton CDLX 7211. Leslie De'ath

Billy Mayerl was the most popular English composer/performer of light music in the syncopated style in the 1920s and 1930s. It is indeed a very English style; he never went to America, not sure if he would be welcome there, with Gershwin reigning. But that only makes his music the more individual. *Marigold* was his most famous piece and that, alas, is not included here, but much else is, and Leslie De'ath knows just how to play it, with crisp fingers, a swinging rhythm and a light touch. There are two dozen delectable pieces to choose from and the collection is of a quality that you can play right through, or pick and choose. Try the opening and closing Irishry, the charming *Meadowsweet* and *Alpine Bluebell* from 'In my Garden', or the deliciously frivolous *Milkman's Scherzo* and *Clowning*, and the two insect oddities, *Ladybird Lullaby* and *Praying Mantis*. For gentle poetry sample *The Forgotten Forest* and you will surely be hooked. The recording is excellent.

MELOS ENSEMBLE (with Osian Ellis, harp)

RAVEL: *Introduction and Allegro for Flute, Clarinet, Harp & Strings*. **DEBUSSY**: *Sonata for Flute, Viola & Harp*.
ROPARTZ: *Prélude, Marine et Chansons*. **ROUSSEL**: *Sérénade*
Australian Decca Eloquence (ADD) 480 2153

A desert island disc if ever there was one! The ethereal Debussy sonata and the equally heavenly Ravel *Introduction and Allegro* receive immaculate performances that have not been surpassed since the present record appeared in the early 1960s. The magical Roussel *Sérénade* has never been performed better, and the Ropartz rarity gives unfailing delight. Inspired playing and beautifully balanced recorded sound.

MENDELSSOHN, Felix (1809-47)

Violin Concerto in E min., Op. 64

Ⓜ RCA (ADD) SACD 61391-2. Heifetz, Boston SO, Munch – **BEETHOVEN**: *Violin Concerto*

As one might expect, Heifetz gives a fabulous performance. His speeds are consistently fast, yet in the slow movement his flexible phrasing sounds so inevitable and easy that it is hard not to be convinced. The finale is a tour de force, light and sparkling, with every note in place, and Munch's accompaniment throughout is outstanding. The 1959 recording is very good for its period and sounds well on CD, where it is paired with his outstanding Beethoven *Violin Concerto*.

Kyung-Wha Chung follows Heifetz's lead and favours speeds that are faster than usual in all three movements, and the result is comparably sparkling, with the lovely slow movement fresh and songful, not at all sentimental. With warmly sympathetic accompaniment from Dutoit and the Montreal orchestra, given a full-bodied modern recording, the result is one of Chung's happiest records and her coupling of the Bruch *G minor Concerto* and *Scottish Fantasy* may be thought more appropriate than Beethoven (Decca 460 976-2).

Overtures: Calm Sea and a Prosperous Voyage, Op. 27; Fair Melusina, Op. 32; The Hebrides (Fingal's Cave), Op. 26; A Midsummer Night's Dream, Op. 21; Ruy Blas, Op. 95; Trumpet Overture, Op. 101; Overture for Wind Instruments, Op. 24

DG 423 104-2. LSO, Abbado

Each of Mendelssohn's overtures is infused with extraordinary imagination and a rich melodic appeal which has ensured their constant place in the repertoire. Abbado's collection remains one of the most generally recommendable available today. Three of these performances were released with his recording of the symphonies in 1985, but the rest were new, recorded in various venues, but the sound is uniformly excellent. Included is the rare *Overture for Wind* (1824) and the *Trumpet Overture* (1826, more notable for furiously busy strings), and while neither is a forgotten masterpiece, they are entertaining and well worth having. The famous pieces – including the miraculously magical *Midsummer Night's Dream Overture*, the romantically dramatic *Ruy Blas* and the hauntingly evocative *Fingal's Cave* – sound strikingly vivid and spontaneous in Abbado's hands, and the recording, wide in range with plenty of ambience, suits the music admirably.

Symphonies: 3 (Scottish); 4 (Italian). Hebrides (Fingal's Cave) Overture

Ⓜ DG (ADD) 449 743-2. BPO, Karajan

The 20-year-old Mendelssohn visited the Western Highlands of Scotland in 1829 – one of the most beautiful places in Europe. He travelled north by coach at an average speed of four-and-a-half miles per hour to Edinburgh where – remembering its tragic association with past history – he was greatly moved by the ruins of Mary Stuart's Chapel in Holyrood Palace. (He wrote home that 'the chapel is now roofless, grass and ivy grow there, and at that broken altar Mary was crowned Queen of Scotland . . . I believe I found today in that old chapel the beginnings of my Scotch Symphony.') And what an opening indeed, a lovely, nostalgic melody on the strings. Yet the theme is transformed again and again as the work proceeds through slow movement, Scherzo and its exultant finale. Its composer completed the work in 1841 and it is a truly lyrical and evocative masterpiece.

Mendelssohn left Edinburgh three days later, travelling uncomfortably by coach. En route, they called on Sir Walter Scott in Abbotsford. The next day they journeyed on via Stirling, Crief, Perth, Dunkeld, Blair Atholl, Killin, Pitlochry and Fort William, much the same way as one can travel today by modern roads and/or rail. It rained and rained as they passed 'from rock to rock, many waterfalls, beautiful valleys with rivers, dark woods and heath with red heather in blossom – all stern, dark, very lonely'.

On 7 August, Mendelssohn reached Oban and went across by boat to the Island of Mull. And it was the breathtaking sight, seen from Oban harbour, of the wide bay with Mull as backcloth that brought the famous opening theme of the *Hebrides Overture* into Mendelssohn's head. His party stayed in Tobermory on Mull in preparation for their boat journeys to Iona and Staffa. Even today, the voyage to Staffa in a small boat is very uncertain. (It took us three attempts before we could be sure of being able to disembark at the entrance to the cave. It is always wise to phone the Staffa ferry and check if access is possible before leaving Oban.) Mendelssohn was violently seasick on the voyage, but he never forgot the breathtaking sight of the vertical ranks of basalt rock that surround the cave.

On our third (and successful) trip, we took a small portable CD player with us, walked gingerly along the sheer rock face into the cave, waited until everyone else had gone, then sat inside the entrance, with water lapping round us, and played Karajan's recording of the *Overture* right through – a magical experience you too could repeat if you are patient enough to wait for clement weather.

Karajan's Berlin Philharmonic performance is worthy of Mendelssohn's inspiration, and this CD makes a splendid memento of a famous Scottish visit.

(i) *A Midsummer Night's Dream: Overture and Incidental Music*; (ii) *Die erste Walpurgisnacht (Walpurgis Night)*

Ⓜ Australian Decca Eloquence (ADD/DDD) 4801279. (i) Dawson, Schaechter, Frauenchor des Rundfunk, Berlin, Berlin RSO, Ashkenazy; (ii) Lilowa, Laubenthal, Krause, Sramek, Wiener Singverein, VPO, Dohnányi

There is no shortage of excellent accounts of the inspired music to *A Midsummer Night's Dream* with which Mendelssohn 'brought fairies into the orchestra'.

The *Overture*, written in the composer's youth, is magical enough, but it is all but matched by the incidental music, especially the *Nocturne* and *Scherzo*, which were composed much later. Ashkenazy's account dates from 1992 and, with an excellent, warm and vivid recording, superb orchestral playing and lively direction, it is thoroughly recommendable. What makes this CD so appealing, however, is the composer's much rarer dramatic cantata, *Die erste Walpurgisnacht*. Goethe's suitably Gothic text, with its anti-Christian stance, is a bit of an oddity, but it inspired the composer to some especially dramatic writing, again evoking the supernatural world of *A Midsummer Night's Dream*, if in more sinister fashion. Witches and druids are angrily pursued by Christians on the Brocken, and some of the more dramatic moments suggest that had he been given the right libretto Mendelssohn might have made an opera composer. Dohnányi's performance dates from 1976, and is vibrantly performed and recorded. This makes an attractive double package, well worth exploring.

Cello Sonata 2 in D, Op. 58

Testament SBT 1419. Piatigorsky, Pennario (with **CHOPIN**: *Sonata in G min.*
    STRAUSS: *Cello Sonata in F*)

Gregor Piatigorsky was the greatest cellist of his generation and, after Feuermann, the finest interpreter of Bloch's *Schelomo*. The first movement of the *D major Sonata* has something of the atmosphere of the *Italian Symphony*, though it is the middle movements that show Mendelssohn at his best. The playing is of the highest quality. In the Chopin coupling the pianist is Firkušný and, leaving aside the Rostropovich–Argerich set on DG, this has an unsurpassed eloquence.

Octet, Op. 20

Ⓜ Australian Decca Eloquence (ADD) 421 637-2. ASMF Chamber Ens. –
    BOCCHERINI: *Quintet for Cello & Strings*

Mendelssohn's *Octet* is one of the composer's most inspired works – astonishing, considering it was written when the composer was aged just sixteen. Yet not only is the melodic freshness so appealing, but the work's structural maturity completely belies the composer's years. The slow movement is deeply eloquent, while the writing in the Scherzo and in the Presto finale is exhilarating in its wit and bubbling vitality. This 1968 performance by the ASMF is fresh and buoyant, and the recording wears its years lightly. It offers fine judgement in matters of clarity and sonority, and is coupled with a highly desirable and much less well-known work by Boccherini.

Piano Trios: 1 in D min., Op. 49; 2 in C min., Op. 66

Hyp. CDA 67485. Florestan Trio

Dazzling playing from this splendid ensemble puts the Florestan Trio at the very top of the list for these attractive and much-recorded works. The freshness of response and the virtuosity of the pianist, the inimitable Susan Tomes, make this coupling pretty irresistible. Top-quality recorded sound too.

String Quartets: 1 in E flat, Op. 12; 2 in A min., Op. 13; 3 in D; 4 in E min.; 5 in E flat, Op. 44/1–3; 6 in F min., Op. 80; Fugue (1827); Capriccio (1843); Scherzo & Theme & Variations, Op. 81
MDG 307 1055-2 (*Quartets 1–2*); MDG 307 1168-2 (*3–4; Capriccio; Fugue*); MDG 307
1056-2 (*5–6; Scherzo & Theme & Variations*). Leipzig Qt

The excellent Leipzig Quartet, with their warm, richly blended tone and natural finesse, give superbly polished accounts of these delightful works. Their lightness of touch and elegance are balanced by great (but not exaggerated) depth of feeling. They also have a naturalness and warmth that is most satisfying. Their performances serve as a reminder that this is great music which is all too often taken for granted by critics. This is a first-rate recommendation in every respect, with each of the three discs available separately.

But don't make the mistake of buying the five-disc boxed set (MDG 307 1571-200) which includes a beautifully turned and graceful account of the remarkable early *Quartet in E flat* without opus number, which is well worth having. But it also includes the *Octet* and transcriptions of orchestral works (with the group augmented). The orchestral works are inessential, although quite well played and recorded; but the *Octet* is not helped by a recording which tends to coarseness, emphasizing both treble and bass at the expense of a detailed and balanced overall sound picture.

String Quintets 1, Op. 18; 2, Op. 87
BIS SACD 1254. Mendelssohn Quartet with R. Mann

Anyone wanting modern-instrument recordings of two of Mendelssohn's finest chamber works could not better this BIS-SACD. The performances are full of sparkle and vitality: the outer movements have great spirit and energy while the finales with their brilliant contrapuntal writing are played with thrilling virtuosity, and the Scherzo of Op. 87 is like quicksilver, yet the *Intermezzo* of the same work is touchingly simple in its natural warmth. On a DVD/SACD player there is added fullness and resonance in the bass, at the same time producing a very slightly less transparent blend of timbre.

Songs without Words, Books 1–8 (complete); Albumblatt, Op. 117; Gondellied; Kinderstücke, Op. 72; 2 Klavierstücke
Ⓜ DG Double (ADD) 453 061-2 (2). Barenboim

This 1974 set of Mendelssohn's complete *Songs without Words*, delightful music which Barenboim plays with such affectionate finesse, has dominated the catalogue for nearly four decades. The sound is first class. At DG Double price, this sweeps the board in this repertoire.

Elijah

Chan. 8774/5 (2). White, Plowright, Finnie, A. Davies, L. Symphony Ch., LSO, Hickox

Richard Hickox with the London Symphony Chorus and the LSO secures a performance that both pays tribute to the English choral tradition in this work and presents it dramatically as a kind of religious opera. Willard White may not be ideally steady in his delivery, sometimes attacking notes from below, but he sings consistently with fervour. Rosalind Plowright and Arthur Davies combine purity of tone with operatic expressiveness, and Linda Finnie, while not matching the example of Dame Janet Baker in the classic EMI recording, sings with comparable dedication and directness in the solo, *O rest in the Lord*. The chorus fearlessly underlines the high contrasts of dynamic demanded in the score. The Chandos recording, full and immediate yet atmospheric too, enhances the drama.

St Paul, Op. 36

Ⓜ Chan. 10516 (2). Gritton, Rigby, Banks, Coleman-Wright, BBC Nat. Ch. & O of Wales, Hickox

Richard Hickox's version, recorded live in Cardiff with BBC Welsh forces, completely avoids sentimentality, finding a freshness which effectively echoes the Bach *Passions* in punctuating the story of St Paul with chorales and the occasional '*turba*' or crowd chorus. In brushing any Victorian cobwebs away, Hickox tends to favour speeds on the fast side, never sounding hurried but, more importantly, never sounding heavy or pompous as other German versions often do. Choral singing is excellent, and among the soloists, Susan Gritton and Jean Rigby are first rate, though the tenor, Barry Banks, is a little strained and Peter Coleman-Wright sounds rather gritty as recorded, though never wobbly. The warmth and clarity of the recording add to the freshness. It is now offered at mid-price with full texts and translations.

MENOTTI, Gian Carlo (1911–2007)

Amahl and the Night Visitors (opera, complete)

That's Entertainment CDTER 1124. Haywood, Dobson, Watson, Painter, Rainbird, ROHCG Ch. & O, Syrus

Recorded under the supervision of the composer himself, this is a fresh and highly dramatic performance, very well sung and marked by atmospheric digital sound of striking realism. Central to the success of the performance is the astonishingly assured and sensitively musical singing of the boy treble, James Rainbird, as Amahl, while Lorna Haywood sings warmly and strongly as the Mother, with a strong trio of Kings.

MERCURY LIVING PRESENCE
Anthology (recordings not available separately)

BARTÓK: *Music for Strings, Percussion and Celesta*.
MUSSORGSKY (orch. Ravel): *Pictures at an Exhibition*;
SMETANA: *Má Vlast* (Chicago SO, Kubelík). PROKOFIEV: (i) *Love
for Three Oranges: Suite*; *Scythian Suite*; (ii) *Symphony No. 5*
(Dorati with (i) LSO; (ii) Minneapolis SO); *Romeo and Juliet* (ballet) *Suites
Nos. 1 & 2* (Minneapolis SO, Skrowaczewski). MUSSORGSKY: *A Night
on the Bare Mountain* (LSO, Dorati); *Pictures at an Exhibition*
(Minneapolis SO, Dorati plus solo piano version performed by Janis).
CHOPIN: *Études in F & A min.* (Janis). KODÁLY: (i) *Dances of
Galánta*; *Marosszék Dances*; (ii) *Háry János: Suite*. (ii) BARTÓK:
Hungarian Sketches; *Romanian Folk Dances* (Dorati with
(i) Philharmonia Hungarica; (ii) Minneapolis SO). ENESCU: *Romanian
Rhapsodies 1 & 2*. BRAHMS: *Hungarian Dances*; *Variations
on a Theme by Haydn*. LISZT: *Hungarian Rhapsodies 1–6*.
STRAVINSKY: *The Firebird*; *Fireworks*; *Four Études for
Orchestra*; *Scherzo à la Russe*; *Song of the Nightingale*; *Tango*.
TCHAIKOVSKY: *The Nutcracker*. BEETHOVEN:
Wellington's Victory (LSO, Dorati). DVOŘÁK: *Slavonic Dances*;
STRAVINSKY: *Petrushka*; *The Rite of Spring*. TCHAIKOVSKY:
Capriccio Italien; *1812 Overture* (Minneapolis SO, Dorati); *Serenade
for Strings in C* (Philharmonia Hungarica, Dorati). COPLAND:
(i) *Appalachian Spring*; *Billy the Kid*; (ii) *Danzón Cubano*; *El Salón
México* (Dorati with (i) LSO; (ii) Minneapolis SO). SCHUMANN:
Violin Concerto; MENDELSSOHN: *Violin Concerto*; BRAHMS:
Violin Concerto; KHACHATURIAN: *Violin Concerto* (Szeryng,
LSO, Dorati). BARTÓK: *Romanian Folk Dances*. DEBUSSY:
La Plus que lente; NOVÁCEK: *Moto Perpetuo*; BRAHMS:
Hungarian Dances. MARROQUÍN: *Mexican Lullaby*. RIMSKY-
KORSAKOV: *Flight of the Bumble-Bee*. KREISLER: *Allegretto
(in the Style of Boccherini)*; *Caprice Viennois*; *Chanson Louis XIII
and Pavane*; *Liebesleid*; *Liebesfreud*; *Menuet*; *The Old Refrain*;
Praeludium and Allegro; (i) *Recitativo and Scherzo-Caprice*.
Rondino (on a Theme by Beethoven); *Schön Rosmarin*; *Tambourin
chinois*; *Tempo di Menuetto*. LECLAIR: *Violin Sonata No. 3*;
GLUCK: *Melodie*. LOCATELLI: *The Labyrinth* (Szeryng, Charles
Reiner; (i) Szeryng unaccompanied). BACH: *6 Unaccompanied Suites
for Cello*; (i) *2 Sonatas for Cello & Piano*. BRAHMS: *Cello Sonatas
Nos. 1 & 2*; MENDELSSOHN: *Cello Sonata No. 2* (Starker,
(i) with Sebök). DVOŘÁK: *Cello Concerto*. BRUCH: *Kol Nidrei*;
TCHAIKOVSKY: *Variations on a Rococo Theme* (Starker, LSO,

Dorati). (i) BOCCHERINI: *Cello Sonata in A*; VIVALDI: *Cello Sonata in E min.*; CORELLI: *Cello Sonata in D min.*; LOCATELLI: *Cello Sonata in D*; VALENTINI: *Cello Sonata in E*; (ii) BACH: *Cello Sonata in G min.* (Starker with (i) Swedish; (ii) Sebök). BARTÓK: (i) *Violin Concerto No. 2. Second Suite* (Minneapolis SO, Dorati with (i) Yehudi Menuhin). BARTÓK: *Bluebeard's Castle* (with Olga Szönyi, Mihály Székely, LSO, Dorati). BERG: *Wozzeck*: 3 excerpts (with Helga Pilarczyk, LSO, Dorati). (i) CHOPIN: *Piano Concertos 1 & 2*; BEETHOVEN: *Piano Concertos 4*; (ii) *5 (Emperor)* (Bachauer, LSO with (i) Dorati; (ii) Skrowaczewski). BRAHMS: *Piano Concerto No. 2* (Bachauer, LSO, Skrowaczewski); *Variations on a Theme by Paganini*; LISZT: *Hungarian Rhapsody No. 12*; BEETHOVEN: *Piano Sonata No. 9*; RAVEL: *Gaspard de la nuit*; DEBUSSY: *3 Préludes*; STRAVINSKY: *3 Movements from Petrushka* (Bachauer). (i) SCHUMANN: *Cello Concerto in A min.*; LALO: *Cello Concerto in D min.*; (ii) SAINT-SAËNS: *Cello Concerto in A min.* (Starker, LSO with (i) Skrowaczewski; (ii) Dorati). KHACHATURIAN: *Gayaneh* (ballet) *Suite* (LSO, Dorati). SHOSTAKOVICH: *Symphony No. 5* (Minneapolis SO, Skrowaczewski). SUPPÉ: *Overtures: The Beautiful Galatea*; *Boccaccio*; *Light Cavalry*; *Morning, Noon and Night in Vienna*; *Pique Dame*; *Poet and Peasant*; AUBER: *Overtures: The Bronze Horse*; *Fra Diavolo*; *Masaniello*. BERLIOZ: *Overtures: The Corsair*; *Overture: The Roman Carnival*; *Symphonie fantastique*; *Hungarian March*; *Trojan March* (Detroit SO, Paray). LISZT: *Piano Concertos* (i) *1* & (ii) *2* (Janis, Moscow PO with (i) Kondrashin; (ii) Rozhdestvensky); *Hungarian Rhapsody No. 6*; *Sonetto del Petrarca 104*; *Valse oubliée*; SCHUMANN: *Novellette in F*; *Romance in F sharp*; FALLA: *The Miller's Dance*; GUION: *The Harmonica Player*; PROKOFIEV: *Toccata*; SCHUMANN: *Variations on a Theme by Clara Wieck*; MENDELSSOHN: *Song without Words, Op. 62/1*; PINTO: 3 *Scenes from Childhood* (Janis). PROKOFIEV: *Piano Concerto No. 3*; RACHMANINOV: *Piano Concerto No. 1* (Janis, Moscow PO, Kondrashin); *Piano Concerto No. 2* (Janis, Minneapolis SO, Dorati); *Piano Concerto No. 3* (Janis, LSO, Dorati); *Preludes in E flat and C sharp min.* (Janis). SCHUMANN: *Piano Concerto* (Janis, Minneapolis SO, Skrowaczewski); *Arabeske* (Janis). TCHAIKOVSKY: *Piano Concerto No. 1* (Janis, LSO, Menges). HANSON: *For the First Time*; *Merry Mount Suite*; *Mosaics*; (i) Piano Concerto (Eastman-Rochester O, Composer with (i) Mouledous). McBRIDE: *Mexican Rhapsody*; NELSON: *Savannah River Holiday*; MITCHELL: *Kentucky Mountain Portraits*; VARDELL: *Joe Clark Steps Out*; STILL: *Sahdji*; GINESTERA: *Overture to the Creole 'Faust'*; GROFÉ: *Grand*

Canyon Suite; *Mississippi Suite*; **HERBERT**: *(i) Cello Concerto No. 2* (Eastman-Rochester Orchestra, Hanson with (i) Miquelle). **JACOB**: *William Byrd Suite*; **WALTON**: *Crown Imperial*; **HOLST**: *Hammersmith: Prelude and Scherzo*; **BENNETT**: *Symphonic Songs for Band*; **WILLIAMS**: *Fanfare and Allegro*; **HEED**: *In Storm and Sunshine*; **ALLEN**: *Whip and Spur*; **KING**: *The Big Cage*; *Circus Days*; *Invictus*; *Robinson's Grand Entree*; **FILLMORE**: *Americans We*; *Bones Trombone*; *The Circus Bee*; *Rolling Thunder*; **HUFFINE**: *Them Basses*; **JEWELL**: *The Screamer*; **FUCIK**: *Thunder and Blazes*; **FARRAR**: *Bombasto*; **HUFF**: *The Squealer*; **RIBBLE**: *Bennett's Triumphal*; **DUBLE**: *Bravura*; **GOLDMAN**: *Boy Scouts of America*; *Bugles and Drum*; *Children's March*; *Illinois March*; *Interlochen Bowl*; *Onward-Upward*; **HALL**: *Officer of the Day*; **SEITZ**: *March 'Grandioso'*; **REEVES**: *Second Regiment, Connecticut National Guard March*; **ALFORD**: *The Mad Major*; **RODGERS**: *Guadalcanal March*; **SOUSA**: *Ancient and Honorable Artillery Company*; *The Black Horse Troop*; *Bullets and Bayonets*; *The Gallant Seventh*; *The Glory of the Yankee Navy*; *Golden Jubilee*; *The Gridiron Club*; *The High School Cadets*; *The Invincible Eagle*; *The Kansas Wildcats*; *The Liberty Bell*; *Manhattan Beach*; *The National Game*; *New Mexico*; *Nobles of the Mystic Shrine*; *Our Flirtations*; *The Picadore*; *The Pride of the Wolverines*; *Riders for the Flag*; *The Rifle Regiment*; *Sabre and Spurs*; *Sesqui-Centennial Exposition*; *Solid Men to the Front!*; *Sound Off*; 'The Civil War, its Music and its Sounds' (Eastman Wind Ens., Fennell). 'Hi-Fi a la Española and Popovers': **FAITH**: *Brazilian Sleigh Bells*; **LECUONA**: *Andalucia*; *Malagueña*; **GRANADOS**: *Intermezzo*; **BENJAMIN**: *Jamaican Rumba*; **FERNANDEZ**: *Batuque*; **TEXIDOR**: *Amparito Roca*; **FALLA**: *Ritual Fire Dance*; **TURINA**: *The Bullfighter's Prayer*; **GUARNIERI**: *Brazilian Dance*; **DINICU**: *Hora Staccato*; **LISZT**: *Liebestraum*; **CZIBULKA**: *Love's Dream After the Ball*; **SIBELIUS**: *Finlandia*; **DEBUSSY**: *Clair de Lune*; **SHOSTAKOVICH**: *Polka* (Eastman-Rochester Pops Orchestra, Fennell). 'Balalaika Favorites': **BUDASHKIN**: *Fantasy on Two Folk Songs*; **TRAD.**: *At Sunrise*; *Evening Bells*; *My Dear Old Friend, Please Visit Me*; **KULIKOV**: *The Linden Tree*; **OSIPOV**: *Kamarinskaya*; **MIKHAILOV-SHALAYEV**: *Fantasy on Volga Melodies*; **ANDREYEV**: *In the Moonlight*; *Under the Apple Tree*; *Waltz of the Faun*; **SOLOVIEV-SEDOY**: *Midnight in Moscow*; **TCHAIKOVSKY**: *Dance of the Comedians*; **SHISHAKOV**: *The Living Room*; **RIMSKY-KORSAKOV**: *Flight of the Bumble-Bee* (Osipov State Russian Folk Orchestra, Gnutov). **TRAD.**: *Sevillanas*; **GRANADOS**: *Intermezzo*; **TORROBA**: *Allegretto*

(from *Sonatina in A*); *Llamada*; **ALBENIZ**: *Sevilla*; **SOR**:
Obbligato on Étude in B min.; **C. ROMERO**: *Noche en Málaga*;
Romantic Prelude; **TÁRREGA**: *Lágrima*; **VILLA-LOBOS**:
Prelude No. 3; **VISÉE**: *Suite in D min.*; **NARVÁEZ**: *Cuatro
diferencias sobre Guárdame las vacas*; **GALILEI**: *Suite of Six
Dances*; **MILAN**: 3 *Pavanas*; **BACH**: *Bourrée*; *Gavottes I & II*;
Minuet; **DOWLAND**: *King of Denmark's Galliard*; **RAMEAU**:
Gavotte en Rondeau; **SANZ**: *Españoleta* (The Romeros). 'Flamenco!':
TRAD.: *Carabana Gitana*; *Fandangos por Verdiales*; *Farruca y
Rumba*; *Fiesta en Jerez*; *Garrotin*; *Jota*; *Lamento Anduluz*;
Peteneras; *Tanguillos*; *Zorongo*; **GRANADOS**: *Spanish Dance
No. 6*; **TÁRREGA**: *Recuerdos de la Alhambra*; **SINOPOLI**:
Vidalita (Pepe Romero). **RODRIGO**: *Concierto de Aranjuez*
(Angel Romero); *Concierto Andaluz for Four Guitars and Orchestra*
(The Romeros); **VIVALDI**: *Concerto in B min. for Four Guitars*;
Concerto in C for Guitar and Orchestra (Celedonio Romero);
Concerto in G for Two Guitars (Pepe and Celin Romero) (all with
San Antonio SO, Alessandro)
Ⓑ Mercury mono/stereo 478 3566 (51)

Mercury recordings still generate a certain frisson with collectors. The characteristic, up-front sound, distinctive from the early mono recordings (made with
a single microphone) and a mark too of the stereo releases (made with just
three microphones), amazes even today in its sheer vividness. Mercury's bold
'Living Presence' logo and vibrant artwork made a tremendous impact in the
1950s and '60s, and this handsome box set makes a fine tribute to the company, and above all to Wilma Cozart Fine, the remarkable recording director of
Mercury records. This set includes Mercury's first ever recording, Mussorgsky's *Pictures at an Exhibition*, coupled to the second recording they made,
Bartók's *Music for Strings, Percussion and Celesta* (1951) with, both Rafael
Kubelík and the Chicago Symphony Orchestra. The realism of the Mussorgsky
(in spite of some thinness in the top range of the strings) still has the power to
astonish. The performance has great freshness with not a hint of routine anywhere; there are many subtleties, particularly as one picture or promenade is
dovetailed into another. The orchestral virtuosity in *Tuileries*, *Limoges* and the
Chicks' ballet is brilliant but possesses Ravelian delicacy too; similarly the central section of *Baba-Yaga* has a gently sinister quality that is very telling. The
Bartók coupling is most compelling too, with great intensity obtained from the
opening bars and maintained throughout the performance. Kubelík's complete *Má Vlast* dates from the following year and remains one of the freshest
accounts committed to disc.

The rest of the CDs are in stereo, with the indefatigable Antal Dorati featuring in almost half the contents of the box. One forgets how many landmark
LPs he made for Mercury. Included here are his famous explosive recordings of

Tchaikovsky's *1812 Overture* and Beethoven's *Wellington's Victory* (each with a fascinating documentary about the recording), his magical version of the complete *Nutcracker* and, almost above all, his recording of Stravinsky's *Firebird*, which has never been matched in terms of spine-tingling vividness in both sound and music-making. His *Petrushka* and *A Rite of Spring* are hardly less impressive either, and he excelled in virtuoso colourful scores of the nineteenth and twentieth centuries. His performance of Prokofiev's *Scythian Suite* is still the most exciting committed to disc, and the rest of his Prokofiev recordings included here – the *Fifth Symphony* and *The Love for Three Oranges: Suite* – are similarly gripping.

Dorati's flair for colourful music is well displayed in his spontaneous-sounding Liszt *Hungarian Rhapsodies*, Dvořák *Slavonic Dances,* and Brahms *Hungarian Dances* as well as in the Hungarian music of Kodály (the *Háry János Suite* and the *Marosszék* and *Galánta Dances*) and Enescu's *Romanian Rhapsodies*. The *Gayaneh* ballet music of Khachaturian was well suited to this conductor, as was the music of Aaron Copeland; his recording of the latter caused quite a sensation when it first appeared, for its precision of detail and brilliance of colour. The gunshots, with their clean percussive transients in *Billy the Kid* remain electrifying. Bartók's *Bluebeard's Castle* receives a performance with more emphasis on power than mystery and features brilliant playing from the LSO. Mihály Székely as Bluebeard is taut and intense while Olga Szönyi, though more uneven, is strong and incisive. Excerpts from Berg's *Wozzeck* follow on from the Bartók, and excellent they are too.

Dorati also accompanies an array of impressive soloists: Yehudi Menuhin in perhaps his finest version of the Bartók *Violin Concerto No. 2*; János Starker in a full-blooded account of the Dvořák *Cello Concerto* and an excellent account of the delightful Saint-Saëns *Cello Concerto No. 1* (Starker also appears on a disc of baroque solo cello sonatas, the Bach *Cello Sonatas*, Brahms *Cello Sonatas 1 & 2* and Mendelssohn *Cello Sonata No. 2* – all made when this artist was at his peak); Gina Bachauer's impressive performances of the Chopin *Piano Concertos* are included and are notable in that in no other recordings of this repertoire have the orchestral accompaniments been given such a strong profile as they have under Dorati. These two artists are partnered again for a performance of Beethoven's *Fourth Piano Concerto*, and, if it is not among the finest accounts available on CD, it is still very good indeed; and again, in her account of the *Emperor Concerto* (conducted by Skrowaczewski), Bachauer admirably balances romantic power with classical elegance.

Henryk Szeryng appears in rather disappointing performances of the Brahms and Khachaturian *Violin Concertos* (even Dorati is not on top form here), though both are on better form for the Schumann and Mendelssohn *Violin Concertos* (Szeryng is also represented on a disc of 'Violin favourites', with pianist Charles Reiner, all most attractive and appealing). With Byron Janis, Dorati made a superb account of Rachmaninov's *Third Piano Concerto* (with the LSO) and a very fine version of the *Second* (with the Minneapolis SO);

Janis's vivid solo piano account of Mussorgsky's *Pictures at an Exhibition* is also included and coupled with the familiar orchestral version with Dorati. Janis also appears on recordings made in Russia, notably the two *Piano Concertos* of Liszt (conducted by Kondrashin and Rozhdestvensky respectively) – still top recommendations today. He also provides comparably riveting accounts of the Prokofiev *No. 3* and Rachmaninov *No. 1* (both with Kondrashin). He was no less successful in his London recordings of Schumann's *Piano Concerto* (a lovely performance, conducted by Skrowaczewski, another consistently excellent Mercury conductor) and the Tchaikovsky *Piano Concerto* (conducted by Menges), in which Janis dazzles in the same way he does in his Rachmaninov recordings.

Gina Bachauer's performance of Ravel's *Gaspard de la nuit* features the poems which inspired the music (by Aloysius Bertrand) read by Sir John Gielgud, and this partnership is coupled to her sympathetic performances of Debussy and Stravinsky. Her account of Brahms's *Second Piano Concerto* (with Skrowaczewski and the LSO) is very sympathetic if not quite among the best available. Stanisław Skrowaczewski also directs a sometimes wilful but always exciting performance of Shostakovich's *Fifth Symphony* (with the Minneapolis Symphony Orchestra) and his accounts of Prokofiev's *Romeo and Juliet ballet suites* are well characterized and gripping.

Howard Hanson was both an excellent conductor and and excellent composer, and the Mercury box includes a CD of his own highly attractive music, which is melodic, inventive and beautifully coloured, while another disc combines his vibrant performances of Grofé's *Grand Canyon Suite* (with its spectacular *Cloudburst*) and *Mississippi Suite*, coupled to Victor Herbert's pleasing *Cello Concerto No. 2* (with Georges Miquelle). His 'Fiesta in Hi-Fi' recording is remarkable for its vividness, but the dry, up-front sound balance is a drawback (the recordings date from 1956–9). However, the disc features interestingly rare repertoire, including Gineastera's *Overture to the Creole 'Faust'*. Paul Paray made many remarkable recordings for Mercury, galvanizing his Detroit sessions with his distinctive (and now almost extinct) French style of conducting. The three Auber overtures receive scintillating performances which have never been surpassed in terms of sheer *joie de vivre*, and they are coupled with Suppé overtures similarly imbued with a Gallic spirit. His excitingly hard-pressed *Symphonie fantastique* is full of passionate, mercurial neurosis which may be over-the-top for some listeners, but the other Berlioz items come off with comparable electricity. It is a pity that only two of his CDs feature in this set.

Mercury sometimes went 'off-piste' in its choice of repertoire, and the first recording they made in Russia (in fact, the first recording ever made in the Soviet Union by an American company), 'Balalaika Favourites', is irresistible in its vitality and heart-on-sleeve tunes. Indeed, this is one of the unexpected surprises in the Mercury catalogue and is completely captivating. The guitar quartet The Romeros are represented on two CDs, one a varied and colourful programme of mainly Spanish guitar music, balanced by some delightful pieces from the baroque repertoire; the other offers concertos (mainly arrangements of Vivaldi), with Angel Romero having the solo in the justly famous Rodrigo *Concierto de Aranjuez*. Pepe Romero also has a CD all to himself in his 1962 recital 'Flamenco!' and this, like the other CDs featuring The Romeros, offers characteristically vivid sound.

Mercury made several recordings of wind-band music with the Eastman Wind Ensemble under Frederick Fennell, of which Gordon Jacob's *William Byrd Suite* is particularly piquant. The ensemble's discs of Sousa and circus marches, 'Screamers', have a rip-roaring, explosive energy which is almost shattering. 'Hi-Fi a la Española and Popovers', also conducted by Fennell, with the Eastman-Rochester Pops Orchestra, is similarly arresting in its music-making, with Benjamin's engaging *Jamaican Rumba* contrasting with more red-blooded numbers such as Texidor's *Amparito Roca*. An imposing *Finlandia*, along with other more 'classical' pieces, complete the rest of that CD, where Dinicu's *Hora Staccato* will raise an affectionate smile. No doubt designed to show off Mercury's technical prowess, 'The Civil War, its Music and its Sounds' remains striking technically, enjoyable musically and certainly entertaining.

The excellent booklet gives us detailed essays on some of these unique recordings, such as 'The Civil War, its Music and its Sounds' and 'Mercury Living Presence Goes to Russia'. And a bonus CD features a short interview with Wilma Cozart Fine, the label's recording director, whom we had an opportunity to meet personally when she came to England to supervise the transfer of the label's LP recordings to CD.

She told us how, in her relative youth, as just plain Wilma Cozart, but with a university major in music, she went into the company's HQ and offered her services to set up a classical label. She was welcomed with open arms and given a batch of classical tapes for which she was asked to arrange sleeve notes and artwork. She soon returned to suggest that the tapes were of poor quality and would do the company's reputation no good, particularly as in Bob Fine they had a first-class recording engineer who was already making spectacular recordings of popular music. She suggested that at that time several of America's most famous orchestras, including those in Chicago, Minneapolis and Detroit, who were not then under contract to any of the major recording labels, could between them, and with others added later, create a special kind of new classical repertoire.

So it was that she and Bob Fine formed a partnership to make records of the highest quality that were soon to make Mercury famous as a source of classical as well as popular repertoire. Moreover, Fine created a new stereo recording system that used only three microphones to capture the whole orchestra, and the results were astonishingly natural and realistic. The Mercury achievement astonished the recording world, and to set the seal on their relationship Wilma and Bob made it personal when they later married.

MESSAGER, André (1853-1929)

Les Deux Pigeons
Ⓜ Australian Decca Eloquence 476 2448. Welsh Nat. Op. O, Bonynge

Messager's charming gypsy ballet was premièred at the Paris Opéra in 1886 on the same bill as Donizetti's *La Favorita*. But it swiftly established its independence, to remain on the repertoire and be revived (with new choreography by Fredrick Ashton) by the Sadler's Wells Company in 1961. We are familiar with the suite, but this is the first complete recording. The music is light but cleverly scored, after the manner of Delibes; agreeably tuneful, it does not wear out its welcome. Bonynge secures playing from the Welsh Opera Orchestra that is consistently graceful and sparkling, and if the sound is vivid and naturally balanced, it is not quite out of Decca's very top drawer. Superb value at its Eloquence price.

MESSIAEN, Olivier (1908-92)

Turangalîla Symphony
Ⓑ RCA stereo/mono 2CD 74321 84601-2. Leanne Loriod (ondes martenot), Yvonne Loriod (piano), Toronto SO, Ozawa - **ROUSSEL**: *Symphonic 3 & 4* etc.

Messiaen's *Turangalîla Symphony* is on an epic scale, in some ways seeking to embrace almost the totality of human experience. *Turanga* is 'Time' and also implies rhythmic movement. *Lîla* is 'love' and, with strong inspiration from the *Tristan and Isolde* legend, Messiaen's love-music dominates his conception of human experience. The actual love-sequences, both serene and poetically sensuous, feature the ondes martenot with its 'velvety glissandi'. The piano obbligato is also a strong feature of the score.

Ozawa's performance comes from 1967, but you would never guess that from the brilliantly atmospheric sound, which is just as vivid as some of the newer versions, such as Nagano's Erato version (which seems determined to emphasize all the bizarre qualities of the score), and has more warmth and atmosphere. Yvonne Loriod's piano is placed too far forward but her contribution is undoubtedly seminal, and the overall balance is otherwise well managed. The performance itself is brilliantly played: it has plenty of electricity, and a warm sensuality too. It was and remains one of Ozawa's best recordings and is now reissued in a 2-CD set coupled with Roussel.

Couleurs de la Cité Céleste; Hymne au Saint-Sacrement; (i) 3 Petites liturgies de la présence divine
DG 477 7944. R. France PO, Myung-Whun Chung, (i) with Maîtrise de R. France

This was the first of two outstanding single-CD collections of Messiaen's music especially recorded by DG for the centenary of the composer's birth.

(The other is a recital by Pierre-Laurent Aimard – see below). We already know the extraordinary patina of *Couleurs de la Cité Céleste* from the Boulez version, but Myung-Whun Chung's version if anything is even more multicoloured and atmospheric. The *Hymne*, with its long serene opening theme on the strings, in the words of Paul le Flem, 'evokes a mysticism where ecstasy and fervour are combined'. The *Trois petites liturgies* are even more ambitious, intended, in the composer's words, 'to bring a kind of organized act of praise into the concert room', dominated by ecstatic singing from the female chorus, but bringing in a repeated chorale on the strings based on the love theme we know in *Turangalîla*. The scoring includes tuned percussion, the gamelan, ondes martenot and piano and, in the finale, semi-spoken incantations. The work shows the composer at his most imaginative and most haunting, and it is given an inspired performance and superb recording, appropriately in Radio France's Salle Olivier Messiaen.

Piano Music: *Catalogue d'oiseaux*: *Book 3: L'Alouette Lulu. Book 5: La Bouscarle. 4 Études de rythme: Ile de feu I & II. 8 Préludes*
DG 477 7452. Pierre-Laurent Aimard

This is another of the key records of the Messiaen centenary celebrations. Pierre-Laurent Aimard had a personal relationship with the composer and studied with Yvonne Loriod, and his performances have rare authority. He plays all eight of the early *Préludes* (of 1928/9), readily finding Messiaen's special brand of intimate and extrovert impressionism, both highly original and underpinned by a Debussian inheritance. But the titles *Song of ecstasy in a sad landscape*, *The impalpable sounds of a dream* and *A reflection in the wind* are very much Messiaen's own conceptions. The two excerpts from *Catalogue d'oiseaux* are completely contrasted, both unpredictable and both requiring real virtuosity; they are marvellously played. Similarly the extraordinary, exotic, even jazzy rhythms of *Ile de feu* are controlled with amazing sharpness of articulation. The piano recording is wonderfully clear – very much in the demonstration bracket.

Complete Organ Music: (i) *Apparition de l'Église éternelle*; *L'Ascension*; *Le Banquet céleste*; *Les Corps glorieux*; *Diptyque*; *Livre d'orgue*; *Livre du Saint-Sacrement*; *Méditations sur le mystère de la Sainte Trinité*; *Messe de la pentecôte*; *La Nativité du Seigneur*; *Verset pour la fête de la Dédicace*. (ii) *Three posthumous works: Monodie*; *Offrande au Saint Sacrement*; *Prélude* (with birdsong in Messiaen's music)
Ⓑ BIS CD 1770/72 (7). Hans-Ola Ericsson, (i) on Grönlund organ of Lulea Cathedral, Sweden; (ii) on Gerald Woehl organ of Katharinenkirche, Oppenheim, Germany

The outstanding complete survey of Messiaen's organ music by Hans-Ola Ericsson on BIS is of outstanding quality, both musical and technical. It includes recordings of the three posthumous pieces, a 232-page booklet documenting the music and, as an appendix, there are recordings of the bird-calls indicated in Messaien's organ scores. The seven CDs come for the price of three.

Quatuor pour la fin du temps

DG 469 052-2. Shaham, Meyer, Wang, Chung

Messiaen's visionary and often inspired piece was composed during his days in a Silesian prison camp. Among his fellow prisoners were a violinist, a clarinettist and a cellist, who, with the composer at the piano, made its creation possible. This DG recording must take pride of place among its rivals. It is a performance of the highest quality, with a level of concentration and intensity that grips the listener from first to last, and it is superbly recorded. There are notes by both Messiaen and the cellist Étienne Pasquier, who was interned with Messiaen and took part in the première at the German prisoner-of-war camp in January 1941.

MEYERBEER, Giacomo (1791–1864)

Les Patineurs (ballet suite, arr. & orch. Lambert)

Ⓜ Australian Decca Eloquence (ADD) 476 2742. Israel PO, Martinon (with **DVOŘÁK**: *Slavonic Dances, Op. 46/1–8; Op. 72/7*) – **MASSENET**: *Le Cid*

On this vintage LP the sheer vividness of the opening number, with its growling cellos, the swagger of the um-pa-pa rhythm of the strings, and the thundering timpani-strokes are startling even in the SACD age – and, praise be, the transfer is superb. No less remarkable is the quality of the playing, with Martinon inducing the Israeli orchestra to play this repertoire as usually only the French can – the performance explodes with vitality and colour. A unique collector's item, bursting with *joie de vivre*.

Les Huguenots

Ⓜ Decca (ADD) 430 549-2 (4). Sutherland, Vrenios, Bacquier, Arroyo, Tourangeau, Ghiuselev, New Philh. O, Bonynge

Les Huguenots is one of the best – and most spectacular – examples of Meyerbeer's grand operas, written during the golden age of such works. It was premièred in 1836, after the composer had taken some five years composing the score, and it is very far from being an empty showpiece of a work. Indeed, Meyerbeer lavished an inordinate amount of care on this work, carefully researching the historical elements of the story (the St Bartholomew's Eve massacre) and applying an intellectual rigour to the scoring, and filling the opera with both colour and striking orchestral touches. For instance, Marcel's '*Piff-Paff*' aria, with its piquant woodwind and percussion, is both appropriate and quirky, quite unlike anything else in music. Similarly, Raoul's romance in Act I, featuring the viola d'amore, is another nicely individual touch. Of course, there are plenty of rollicking good tunes to admire, plus show-stopping virtuoso arias, exciting choruses, while each of the Acts builds up to an impressively exciting finale.

Les Huguenots was known as 'the night of the seven stars' because of its requirement for seven top-grade artists and, although here the tenor Anastasios Vrenios is somewhat under-powered, seemingly swamped at times, he copes well with the extraordinarily high tessitura, which is more than most rivals have done. Martina Arroyo, too, is below her best as Valentine, but the star quality is unmistakable. Sutherland is predictably impressive. Her '*O beau pays*' is thrillingly done (and complete, unlike her famous early version on 'The Art of the Prima Donna'), with much attention to detail. Tourangeau as the page is another highlight. Originally written for a lyric soprano, Meyerbeer re-wrote the role for contralto Marietta Alboni, and gave her a sparkling aria. '*Non, non, non, vous n'avez jamais*' is a show-stopper of a piece and is deliciously done here by Tourangeau. The rest of the cast is generally excellent, with Gabriel Bacquier and Nicola Ghiuselev fine in their roles. This is by far the most successful recording of this work and with a brilliant recording to match the ambitions of the project. It is well worth investigating by all lovers of French opera and sounds newly minted in its latest CD transfer.

MIASKOVSKY, Nikolai (1881–1950)

Alastor, Op. 14; Lyric Concertino in G, Op. 32/2; Sinfonietta in A min., Op. 68/2
ⓑⓑ Alto ALC 1043. USSR State SO, Svetlanov

What an endearing composer Miaskovsky is! *Alastor* is an early tone-poem from 1910 and is redolent of Glazunov or Arensky – and is marvellously laid out for the orchestra. The charming *Lyric Concertino* with its haunting slow movement comes from the same period as the *Tenth Symphony*, and the *Sinfonietta for Strings* is a post-war work steeped in the gentle, resigned melancholy that characterizes his last years. Very rewarding, and played with total commitment by Svetlanov and his Moscow orchestra. This is a record to which you will return again and again, always with delight.

Divertissement, Op. 80; Silence, Op. 9; Sinfonietta in B min., Op. 32/2
ⓑⓑ Alto ALC 1042. Russian Federation Ac. SO, Svetlanov

Silence is an early tone-poem based on Edgar Allan Poe and dating from 1909. Miaskovsky played it through with his friend Prokofiev. The influence of Wagner and Rachmaninov (particularly *The Isle of the Dead*) is to be felt. The *Sinfonietta for Strings* of 1929 acted as a kind of calling card for the composer during the 1930s and was widely heard in Europe and America. The *Divertissement* comes from 1948, the year in which Zhdanov launched his attack on all the leading Soviet composers of the day, including Miaskovsky. There is a poignant lyricism here and in the first movement an endearing waltz theme that recalls those in Prokofiev's *War and Peace*. Dedicated performances and more than acceptable sound.

Symphonies 1–27. Silence, Op. 9; Sinfonietta in B min., Op. 32/2; Divertissement, Op. 80

Ⓑ Warner Classics 2564 69689-8 (16). Russian Federation Ac. SO, Svetlanov

Miaskovsky is a master symphonist, completely neglected in the concert hall and cold-shouldered by the gramophone companies. Svetlanov believes in this music ardently and his sympathy shines through every bar. The *First Symphony*, also recorded by Rozhdestvensky, is very much in the received tradition, as are its immediate successors; it is in the massive, hour-long *Sixth* of 1922 with a choral finale that Miaskovsky finds his real voice: the delicacy and intense nostalgia of the trio section of the Scherzo is wonderfully affecting and unlike any of his contemporaries. Explore its successors from the interwar years and each has its own distinctive sound-world. No. 21 used to represent the composer in the post-war world but its imposing successor, 22, *'Ballade'*, *in B minor* has richness of vision and breadth of canvas. The pervasive melancholy of No. 25 (a close neighbour of the wonderful *Cello Concerto*) and one of the finest and most expressive, is totally and refreshingly out-of-keeping with the spirit of its times though it is No. 27, which he never lived to hear, that sounds as if it comes from the 1880s rather than 1950. This is a treasure house. However, readers should check that *Symphony* No. 18 is included, as some sets were issued without it!

MILHAUD, Darius (1892–1974)

(i) **Ballade for Piano & Orchestra, Op. 61 Piano Concerto 4, Op. 295;**
(ii) **Symphonies 4, Op. 281; 8 in D (Rhodanienne), Op. 362**

ⒷⒷ Warner Apex 0927 49982-2. (i) Helffer, O Nat. de France, Robertson; (ii) Fr. R. & TV
   PO, composer

An immensely valuable budget reissue. The *Ballade* (1920) was composed for Roussel, and Milhaud made his piano début at its première in New York: its languorous opening seems to hark back to his days in Brazil. The *Fourth Piano Concerto* (1949), written for the virtuoso, Sadel Zkolowsky, is an inventive piece of some substance, with a particularly imaginative and evocative slow movement. Claude Helffer is an admirable exponent of both works, and he and David Robertson readily catch the music's special atmosphere.

   The *Fourth Symphony* was commissioned by French Radio in commemoration of the centenary of the 1848 uprising and revolution, and its four movements offer a vivid portrayal of those events. It is scored for unusually large forces, including two saxophones and a vast array of percussion, all heard to good effect in the first movement, which depicts the uprising with massive polytonal and dissonant clashes; the second laments the fallen, the third describes liberty rediscovered, and the finale is almost festive. The *Eighth Symphony*, written in the late 1950s for a new concert hall at the University of California, is subtitled *Rhodanienne* and evokes the course of the river Rhône from its beginnings in the Alps down to the Camargue. Rich in instrumental resource, it is full of imaginative colours and textures, and the playing of the Orchestre Philharmonique de l'ORTF for Milhaud himself is absolutely first rate. These performances date from 1968, and the sound is much cleaned up for this CD, which commands an unqualified recommendation.

(i) *Le Bœuf sur le toit, Op. 58*; (iv; ii) *Le Carnaval d'Aix, Op. 83b*; (i) *La Création du monde, Op. 81a*; *Saudades do Brasil, Nos. 7–9 & 11*; (ii) *Suite française, Op. 248*; *Suite provençale, Op. 152b*; (iii) *Le Bal martiniquais, Op. 249*; (iii–v) *Paris, Op. 284*; (iii) *Scaramouche, Op. 165b*
🆒 Brilliant 90071/2. (i) O Nat. de France, Bernstein; (ii) Monte Carlo O, Prêtre; (iii) Lee, Ivaldi; (iv) Béroff, (v) Collard

An ideal introduction to this genial composer at a very modest outlay. It brings Bernstein's exhilarating 1971 HMV recordings of *La Création du monde* and *Le Bœuf sur le toit*, still unsurpassed in their flair, together with slightly later recordings by four distinguished French pianists. In the adorable *Carnaval d'Aix*, Michel Béroff is the soloist with the Monte Carlo Orchestra under Georges Prêtre, an ideal conductor in this repertoire. Altogether outstanding value.

Le Carnaval d'Aix, Op. 83b; *Ballade, Op. 61*; *Piano Concertos 1, Op. 127*; *2, Op. 228*; *3, Op. 270*; *4, Op. 295*; *5, Op. 346*; *5 Études for Piano & Orchestra, Op. 63*; *Fantaisie Pastorale, Op. 188*
CPO 777 162-2 (2). Korstick, Basle RSO, Francis

Milhaud recorded the *First Concerto* with Marguerite Long in the days of 78-r.p.m. discs, but there are few alternative versions of the remaining four. Even the captivating *Le Carnaval d'Aix*, based on his ballet *Salade*, which ought to be as popular as *La Création du monde* or the *Suite provençale*, is relatively rare in the concert hall. Together, the pieces on these two CDs comprise Milhaud's complete output for piano and orchestra. At its best it is sunny and irresistible music and always fluently inviting. Very persuasive and strongly recommended.

(i; ii) *Concertino de printemps* (2 versions); (iii) *Piano Concerto 1*; (ii) *Violin Concerto 2*; (iv) *Suite française*; (v) *Scaramouche* (suite for 2 pianos)
Dutton mono CDBP 9711. (i) Astruc with O; (ii) Kaufman, French R. O (members); (iii) Long, O Nat. de France; (iv) NYPO; all cond. composer; (v) Sellick and Smith

Milhaud regarded melody as 'the only living element in music' and turned all his resources to the expression of melodic ideas, often spring-like in their freshness and charm. No more so than in the vivacious *Concertino de printemps* which, in a Dutton scoop, is given here, first in its brilliant (1933) première recording by Yvonne Astruc, and also in an even more breathtaking later version (1949), dazzlingly played by Louis Kaufman. Yet both performances reveal the music's underlying expressive nostalgia, and this is found again in the 'Slow and sombre' middle movement of the *Second Violin Concerto*, which Kaufman also plays superbly, delivering the finale with sparkling virtuosity. He is recorded closely but truthfully.

Marguerite Long (in 1935) scintillates in the small-scale *Piano Concerto*, and the composer delivers the full bonhomie of the *Suite française*, even if here the dated New York recording is brash and two-dimensional. For the most part, however, the splendid Dutton transfers make one forget the early provenance of these always vivid recordings. The performance of *Scaramouche* by Cyril Smith and Phyllis Sellick is unsurpassed, with the light-hearted Brazilian syncopations of the finale especially infectious, and here the 1948 Abbey Road recording sounds very realistic.

Music for 2 Pianos: *Le Bal martiniquais, Op. 249*; *Le Bœuf sur le toit, Op. 58a*; *Carnaval à la Nouvelle-Orléans, Op. 275*; *Kentuckiana, Op. 287*; *La Libertadora, Op. 236a*; *Scaramouche, Op. 165b*; *Songes, Op. 237*
Hyp. CDA 67014. Coombs, Pizarro

Hyperion assemble the bulk of Milhaud's music for two pianos from the popular and irresistible *Scaramouche* through to the duet arrangement of *Le Bœuf sur le toit*. An entertaining and delightful issue which brings some high-spirited pianism from these fine players, and very good recorded sound.

MOERAN, Ernest J. (1894–1950)

(i) *Symphony in G min.*; (ii) *Sinfonietta*; *Overture for a Masque*
Lyrita (ADD) SRCD 247. (i) New Philh. O; (ii) LPO; Boult

First heard in 1937, Moeran's *G minor Symphony* is built confidently on strikingly memorable ideas. This unaccountably neglected and immensely rewarding work is in the best tradition of symphonic writing, and is worthy to rank with the symphonies of Vaughan Williams and Walton. But for all the echoes of these composers, and of Sibelius too, it has a strongly individual voice. Boult's radiant (mid-1970s) performance is both gripping and spacious, the recording very impressive and cast in the Boult mode. Characteristically he refuses to push too hard too soon, but the ebb and flow of tension are superbly controlled to build the most powerful possible climaxes. Rarely, even in Vaughan Williams, has Boult adopted so overtly an expressive style, especially in the glorious slow movement, and the recording quality, although refined, allows the widest dynamic range down to the gentlest *pianissimo* for the hushed, intense opening of that slow movement. The *Sinfonietta* is fresh and appealing too, written a decade later. More extrovert than the symphony, it shows its composer as less ready to write in long paragraphs. It is nevertheless an attractive work and, along with the *Overture*, given Boult's persuasive advocacy it makes an apt coupling. This is a symphony urgently in need of discovery, if you have not already done so.

MOMPOU, Federico (1893–1987)

Cancións y danzas 1, 3, 5, 7–9; *Cants mágics*; *Charmes*; *Dialogues I–II*; *Paisajes*; *Preludios 1, 5 (Palmier d'étoiles), 6* (for the left hand), *7, 9–10*; *3 Variations*
Hyp. CDA 66963. Stephen Hough

The exceptionally generous (77 minutes) and wide-ranging *Gramophone* award-winning recital makes an obvious first choice for those wanting to explore, on a single CD, the fullest possible range of Mompou's piano music. Stephen Hough, who provides illuminating notes, imaginatively describes this as 'the music of evaporation . . . there is no development of material, little counterpoint, no drama or climaxes to speak of; and this simplicity of expression – elusive, evasive and shy – is strangely disarming.' He is completely inside Mompou's fastidious, Satie-esque sound-world and understands the absorbed influences which make this music as much French as Spanish. The recording too is excellent if a little reverberant. Not even Mompou himself equalled, let alone surpassed, Hough in this repertoire.

MONDONVILLE, Jean-Joseph Cassanéa de (1711–72)

Dominus Regnavit (Psalm 92); *Venite Exultemus (Psalm 94)*
(BB) Warner Apex (ADD) 2564 60155-2. Alliot-Lugaz, Borst, Goldthorpe, Huttenlocher, Vocal Ensembles: A Coeur joie de Lille, Animat de Valenciennes. De Chevreuse-Essone, Adam de la Halle; Paillard CO, Paillard – **CORRETTE**: *Laudate Dominum*

Venite Exultemus dates from around 1740 and enjoyed considerable success in its day; given its attractive melodic lines and variety of moods, it is not hard to see why. *Dominus Regnavit*, dating from 1734, has all of these qualities too, with some exciting writing for the chorus in the *Elevaverunt flumina Domine*, depicting the raging of the waves. There is much to enjoy here, including the lovely soprano duet, *Parata sedes*, and the majestic final chorus – a chorus so exhilaratingly enjoyable one feels it should be in the top ten classical hits. This French performance, from the early 1980s, is a decent, idiomatic one and more than a stop gap, but it would be interesting to see what Minkowski would do with this repertoire. The sound is nothing special, but good enough; but it is the quality of musical invention which merits inclusion in this volume, and the Corrette coupling is a joy.

MONTEVERDI, Claudio (1567–1643)

Ab aeterno ordinata sum; Confitebor tibi, Domine (3 settings); Deus tuorum militum; Iste confessor Domini sacratus; Laudate Dominum, omnes gentes; Su le penne de' venti; Nisi Dominus
Ⓑ Hyp. Helios CDH 55345. Kirkby, Partridge, D. Thomas, Parley of Instruments, Goodman or Holman

There are few records of Monteverdi's solo vocal music as persuasive as this. The three totally contrasted settings of *Confitebor tibi* (Psalm 110) reveal an extraordinary range of expression, each one drawing out different aspects of word-meaning. Even the brief trio, *Deus tuorum militum*, has a haunting memorability; it could become to Monteverdi what *Jesu, joy of man's desiring* is to Bach – and the performances are outstanding, with the edge on Emma Kirkby's voice attractively presented in an aptly reverberant acoustic. The accompaniment makes a persuasive case for authentic performance.

(i) *Il ballo delle ingrate*; (ii) *Il combattimento di Tancredi e Clorinda*
Naïve OP 30-196. (i) Ermolli, Dominguez, Carnovich, Franzetti; (ii) Franzetti, Ferrarini, Abbondanza; Concerto Italiano, Alessandrini

This commandingly dramatic account of *Il combattimento*, a totally idiomatic Italianate version from Rinaldo Alessandrini and his Concerto Italiano, offers superb singing from all three principals. Roberto Abbondanza is a splendidly histrionic narrator, and in the death scene Elisa Franzetti singing her farewell is exquisitely moving. Franzetti then returns at the end of *Il ballo delle ingrate* to bid an eloquent plea on behalf of the ungrateful souls, condemned for rebelling against earthly love, to be echoed by Monteverdi's poignant closing chorus from her companions. The latter work was written to be performed at a wedding, with an obvious message for the bride. Daniele Carnovich is a true *basso profondo* and makes a superb Pluto, ready to take the reluctant ladies back to the Underworld, and Francesca Ermolli and Rosa Dominguez are equally fine as Amor and Venus, respectively. The vivid recording is warmly atmospheric.

Vespers 1610
DG Archiv 477 9773 (2). Gabrieli Consort & Players, Paul McCreesh

Like Sir John Eliot Gardiner in his version recorded in the ample acoustic of St Mark's, Venice, Paul McCreesh and the Gabrieli Consort offer a performance of the *Vespers* that attempts to follow liturgical practice. Yet where Gardiner's ample acoustic brings its inconsistencies of balance, McCreesh, recording in the helpful acoustic of Tonbridge Chapel, has a much more controllable acoustic, while still conveying the impression of a live event. The result is a smaller-scale, more intimate reading of this iconic work, very well recorded.

L'Incoronazione di Poppea (CD version)

DG 447 088-2 (3). McNair, Von Otter, Hanchard, Chance, D'Artegna, E. Bar. Sol., Gardiner

With an exceptionally strong and consistent cast in which even minor roles are taken by star singers, Gardiner presents a purposeful, strongly characterized performance. He is helped by the full and immediate sound of the live recording, made in concert at the Queen Elizabeth Hall, London. Sylvia McNair is a seductive Poppea and Anne Sofie von Otter a deeply moving Ottavia, both singing ravishingly. Francesco d'Artegna, a robustly Italian-sounding bass, makes a stylish Seneca, and there are clear advantages in having a counter-tenor as Nero instead of a mezzo-soprano, particularly one with a slightly sinister timbre like Dana Hanchard. So in the sensuous duet which closes the opera, the clashing intervals of the voices are given a degree of abrasiveness, suggesting that, though this is a happy and beautiful ending, the characters still have their sinister side. The text has been modified with newly written ritornellos by Peter Holman, using the original, authentic bass-line, and aiming to be 'closer' to what Monteverdi would have expected than the usual flawed text.

MOZART, Wolfgang Amadeus (1756–91)

(i) Clarinet Concerto, K.622; (ii) Clarinet Quintet, K.581

RCA 82876 60866-2. Richard Stolzman, (i) ECO; (ii) Tokyo Qt

Richard Stolzman gives outstanding performances of the two greatest works in the clarinet repertoire. The *Concerto*, full of spontaneity, brings a comparatively brisk, sparkling tempo in the first movement and a contrasting leisurely *Adagio*, deeply felt, in which Stolzman produces the most beautiful timbre and gently embroiders the reprise of the main theme. The Rondo is high-spirited, with the clarinet roulades delightfully bucolic. By directing the ECO himself, the soloist controls the work's structure as he wants, and then in the *Quintet* the silky-toned Tokyo Quartet provide a seductive backing tapestry, equally full of subtle light and shade, especially striking in the finale. The recording is first class, bright and glowing in both works and admirably balanced.

Flute Concertos 1 in G, K.313; 2 in D, K.314; (i) Flute & Harp Concerto in C, K.299

Ⓑ EMI Masters 9 65937-2. Emmanuel Pahud, (i) Marie-Pierre Langlamet; BPO, Abbado

The fast speeds in these engaging Berlin performances have a light touch, yet no lack of tautness, with the ever-imaginative Emmanuel Pahud set against a modest-sized Berlin Philharmonic playing under Abbado with elegant warmth. Marie-Pierre Langlamet's contribution brings appealing delicacy to the *Flute and Harp Concerto* to make this work especially beguiling. Pahud's cadenzas in the solo concertos are a joy – not too long and often witty, especially in the finale of K.314. Really first-rate recording makes this bargain triptych very recommendable.

(i) *Horn Concertos 1 in D, K.412*; *2–4 in E flat, K.417, 447 & 495*;
(ii) *Piano and Wind Quintet in E flat, K.452*
Ⓑ EMI Masters mono 965 9362. (i) Dennis Brain, Philh. O, Karajan; (ii) Horsley, Brain Wind Ens.

An EMI bargain reissue of Dennis Brain's celebrated (1954) mono record of the *Concertos*, coupled with the delightful *Piano and Wind Quintet*, is self-recommending. Boyd Neel once said that Dennis was the finest Mozart player on any instrument.

Horn Concertos 1–4; *Concert Rondos: in E flat, K.371* (completed John Humphries); *in D, K.514* (completed Süssmayer); *Fragment for Horn & Orchestra in E flat, K.370b* (reconstructed Humphries)
ⒷⒷ Naxos 8.553592. Michael Thompson, Bournemouth Sinf.

This is a particularly valuable – indeed, unique – collection for, as well as offering superb performances of the four regular *Concertos* using revised texts prepared by John Humphries, this outstanding Naxos issue includes reconstructions of two movements designed for an earlier horn concerto dating from soon after Mozart arrived in Vienna. It is fascinating too to have extra passages in No. 4, again adding Mozartian inventiveness. Michael Thompson plays with delectable lightness and point, bringing out the wit in the finales, as well as the tenderness in slow movements. He also draws sparkling playing from the Bournemouth Sinfonietta, very well recorded in clear, atmospheric sound; and these performances make an ideal modern successor to the vintage Dennis Brain versions.

Piano Concertos 1–6; *8–9*; *11–27*; *Concert Rondos 1–2*; (i) *Double Piano Concerto in E flat, K.365*; (i; ii) *Triple Piano Concerto in F, K.242*
Ⓑ Sony (ADD/DDD) 82876 872302 (12). Perahia; (i) Lupu; ECO

The Perahia cycle is a remarkable achievement; in terms of poetic insight and musical spontaneity the performances are in a class of their own. There is a wonderful singing line and at the same time a sensuousness that is always tempered by spirituality. About half the recordings are digital and of excellent quality and, we are glad to report, the earlier, analogue recordings have now been skilfully remastered with first-class results. This is an indispensable set in every respect.

(i) *Piano Concertos 9 in E flat (Jeunehomme), K.271; 14 in E flat, K.449. Piano Sonata 8 in A min., K.310*

ⓑⓑ Alto (ADD) ALC 1047. Brendel, (i) I Solisti di Zagreb, Antonio Janigro

It would be wrong not to include in our book an example of Alfred Brendel's early recordings from the LP era. Here (on a pair of Vanguard recordings from 1966 and 1968) he is teamed with Janigro and I Solisti di Zagreb, who provide stylish, well-paced and warm accompaniments with fine string playing. Our original *Penguin Guide* review commented: 'Brendel's performance of No. 9 is quite outstanding, elegant and beautifully precise; the performance of No. 14 is also first rate and has a memorably vivacious finale. This is an outstanding reissue, truthfully remastered with natural sound and a particularly realistic piano image.'

Piano Concerto 20 in D min., K.466; (i) *Piano Concerto for 3 Pianos in F, K.242*; (ii) *Rondo in C, K.373*; *Adagio in E, K.261. Symphony 32 in G, K.318*

Opus Arte DVD OA 1004D. Martha Argerich, New Japan PO, Christian Arming; with
(i) Paul & Rico Gulda; (ii) Renaud Capuçon

Martha Argerich and her musical companions radiate a delight in music-making that makes this concert, recorded in Tokyo, a highly enjoyable and satisfying musical experience. The camerawork is devoid of gimmickry and places the listener to good advantage throughout. What a fine and expressive player Renaud Capuçon is! In the *D minor Concerto* Argerich is magisterial.

Piano Concertos 20 in D min., K.466; 21 in C, K.467; 23 in A, K.488; 27 in B flat, K.595; Rondo for Piano & Orchestra in D, K.382

ⓑⓑ EMI (ADD) 6 31796-2 (2). Barenboim, ECO

Barenboim recorded the complete Mozart concertos twice, first with the ECO for EMI and later for Warner Classics with the Berlin Philharmonic, in each case directing the orchestra from the keyboard. Both have their considerable merits, but the sense of spontaneity in the EMI recordings brings the message that this is music hot off the inspiration line and is hard to resist, even though it occasionally leads to over-exuberance and idiosyncrasies. These are as nearly live performances as one could hope for on record, and the playing of the English Chamber Orchestra is splendidly geared to the approach of an artist with whom the players have worked so regularly.

The coupling of Nos. 20 and the beautiful *23 in A major* was the first of the series to be recorded, and Barenboim's playing has all the sparkle and sensitivity one could ask for. The orchestral accompaniment is admirably alive, and one's only reservation concerns the somewhat fast tempi he adopts for finales. There need be no reservations about his account of K.467, which is accomplished in every way, but K.595 is rather more controversial. He indulges in great refinement of touch and his reading of the slow movement is overtly romantic. Even so, this inexpensive double gives much pleasure, for the recording is spacious and truthful.

**(i) *Piano Concerto 27 in B flat, K.595*; *Rondo in A min., K.511*;
(ii) *Double Concerto in E flat, K.365***

ⓑⓑ Naxos 8.111294. Schnabel, (i) LSO, Barbirolli; (ii) Karl-Ulrich Schnabel, LSO, Boult

Schnabel's account of the *B flat Concerto* with Barbirolli conducting the LSO was one of the mainstays of the pre-war HMV catalogue, and it is good to hear its virtues so vividly restored. Good, too, to have the 1936 version of the *Double Concerto* with Schnabel's son, Karl-Ulrich, and Boult. The *A minor Rondo* was a post-war recording, marvellously played, and one of the products of his 1946 visit to London. Mandatory listening.

Violin Concertos 1–5; (i) _Sinfonia concertante for Violin and Viola, K.364_

DG 477 7371. Giuliano Carmignola, O Mozart, Claudio Abbado; (i) with Danusha Waskiewicz

The Italian virtuoso, Giuliano Carmignola, was a semi-finalist at the 1974 International Tchaikovsky Competition; members of the Orchestra della Scala who were present alerted Abbado to his talent. They played the Mozart concertos together with the period-instrument Orchestra Mozart and established a close rapport. Carmignola's partner in the *Sinfonia concertante*, Danusha Waskiewicz, is hardly less accomplished. These recordings were made at Bologna in 2007 and must be ranked among the finest in this repertoire, whether on period or modern instruments. Impeccable recording.

Symphony in F, K.19a; _Symphonies 1 in E flat, K.16_; _4 in D, K.19_; _5 in B flat, K.22_; _6 in F, K.43_; _7 in D, K.45_; _7a in G (Alte Lambacher), K.45a_; _in B flat, K.45b_; _8 in D, K.48_; _9 in C, K.73_; _10 in G, K.74_; _in F, K.75_; _in F, K.76_; _in D, K.81_; _11 in D, K.84_; _in D, K.95_; _in C, K.96_; _in D, K.97_; _in C, K.102_; _12 in G, K.110_; _13 in F, K.112_; _14 in A, K.114_; _in D, K.120 & 121_; _15 in G, K.124_; _16 in C, K.128_; _17 in G, K.129_; _18 in F, K.130_; _19 in E flat, K.132_; _20 in D, K.133_; _21 in A, K.134_; _in D, K.161_; _22 in C, K.162_; _23 in D, K.181_; _24 in B flat, K.182_; _25 in G min., K.183_; _26 in E flat, K.184_; _27 in G, K.199_; _28 in C, K.200_; _29 in A, K.201_; _30 in D, K.202_; _31 in D (Paris), K.297_; _32 in G, K.318_; _33 in B flat, K.319_; _34 in C, K.338_; _35 in D (Haffner), K.385_; _36 in C (Linz), K.425_; _38 in D (Prague), K.504_; _39 in E flat, K.543_; _40 in G min., K.550_; _41 in C (Jupiter), K.551_.

ⓑⓑ EMI 585589-2 (12). ECO, Tate

Jeffrey Tate's Mozart *Symphonies* survey is one of the finest things he has done for the gramophone. Recorded over a long period, from 1984 to 2003, his inspiration remained constant. Tate entered at the deep end by taking on

Nos. 40 and 41 first, and they remain impressive accounts. In the *Jupiter*, the apt scale of the ECO allows the grandeur of the work to come out fully: on the one hand, it has the clarity of a chamber orchestral performance, but on the other, with trumpets and drums, its weight of expression never underplays the scale of the argument, which originally prompted the unauthorized nickname. In both symphonies, exposition repeats are observed in outer movements, particularly important in the *Jupiter* finale, which with its miraculous fugal writing bears even greater argumentative weight than the first movement, a point firmly established by Tate. Those who like a very plain approach may find his elegant pointing in the slow movements excessive, but Tate's keen imagination on detail, as well as over a broad span, consistently conveys the electricity of a live performance. The recording is well detailed, yet has pleasant reverberation. Both the *Linz* and the *Prague* receive strong but elegant performances, bringing out the operatic overtones in the latter, not just in the *Don Giovanni*-like progressions in the slow introductions, but also in the power of the development section and in the wonder of the chromatic progressions in the slow movement, as well as the often surprising mixture of timbres. In the *Linz*, Tate is attractively individual, putting rather more emphasis on elegance and finding tenderness in the slow movement, taken like the *Adagio* of the *Prague* at a very measured speed.

Moving backwards to the earlier symphonies, from No. 25 onwards (itself very well done), Tate's detailed articulation and fine detail are always telling. In all these works, he provides a winning combination of affectionate manners, freshness and elegance. (Readers should note: the alternative movements, originally included in this middle batch of symphonies, have been excised on this bargain-box release.) The three-disc set which comprises 16 early symphonies, from Nos. 13 to 24, written before his first out-and-out masterpiece among the symphonies (No. 25) include some of the rarer, early, unnumbered works, usually adaptations of early opera overtures, and all of them colourful pieces. The first three CDs in the box set are new recordings (2003) and concentrate on his earliest symphonies, and again include many of the unnumbered symphonies (here given supplementary numbers, from 42 to 52); these early works are full of vitality (even if with a couple of them their authenticity is doubtful). Tate finds a fresh exhilaration in these scores where the young Mozart was finding his feet, exploring possibilities all the time. There is a surprising amount of variety in these very early works, often pointing to his future brilliance in the opera house. The recordings are fresh and warm throughout this set, which is strongly recommended, especially at super-bargain price.

Symphonies 40; 41 (Jupiter)
Ⓜ DG 478 3621. VPO, Bernstein

Bernstein's electrifying account of No. 40 is keenly dramatic, individual and stylish, with the finale delightfully airy and fresh. If anything, the *Jupiter* is even finer: it is both exhilarating in its tensions and it observes the repeats in both halves of the finale, making it almost as long as the massive first movement. Bernstein's electricity sustains its length, and one welcomes it for establishing the supreme power of the argument, the true crown of Mozart's symphonic output. Pacing cannot be faulted in any of the four movements and, considering the problems inherent in making live recordings, the 1984 sound is first rate, lacking only the last degree of transparency in tuttis. This mid-price reissue takes its place again at the top of the list of recommendations for this coupling.

(i) *Clarinet Trio in E flat (Kegelstatt), K.498*; (ii) *Piano Trios 2 in G, K.496*; *3 in B flat, K.502*; *4 in E, K.542*; *5 in C, K.548*; *6 in G, K.564*

Ⓑ EMI 3 44643-2(2). Barenboim, (i) Matthias Glander, Felix Schwartz; (ii) Nikolaj Znaider, Kyril Zlotnikov

Mozart composed piano trios as early as his set of six (K.10–15), but it is the present works, covering a period of two years when Mozart was also occupied with *Figaro* and *Don Giovanni*, that are representative of his mastery. Barenboim's partners, the Danish violinist Nikolaj Znaider and Belarusian cellist Kyril Zlotnikov, are a natural and most musical team and their playing radiates an infectious pleasure in music-making. The recordings are well balanced and have excellent clarity.

Piano Quartets 1 in G min., K.478; *2 in E flat, K.493*

Ⓜ Decca Eloquence (ADD) 480 3521. Lamar Crowson with the Pro Arte Qt

Mozart's piano quartets are among the finest of all his chamber works. These beautifully intimate recordings, perfectly balanced, were recorded in 1965 but have been splendidly remastered and sound wonderfully natural. Lamar Crowson plays with great sensitivity and constantly delights the ear, particularly in the slow movement and finale of K.478. This disc has many competitors but none are finer, and this reissue is most competitively priced.

String Quartets 1–23; *Divertimenti, K.136–8*

Ⓑ DG 477 8680 (6). Amadeus Qt

The Amadeus Quartet accommodate the 23 *String Quartets* plus the 3 *Divertimenti*, K.136–8, comfortably on six discs. They were recorded between 1963 and 1977, and the new transfers are of good quality. It goes without saying that there are good things among them. They play with great polish and fluency and there are many who have remained loyal to them over the years. But there is a blandness which at times pervades the music-making (as in K.387) and a number of interpretative points to question, in K.421 and K.465 for instance, while the curious mannerism of sometimes swelling out on individual notes is noticeable from time to time. There are, of course, also some fine performances, the *Hunt Quartet*, K.458, for instance and all three *Prussian Quartets*. There appears to be no alternative complete box, but plenty of smaller collections to choose from.

String Quartets: 14 in G (Spring), K.387; 15 in D min., K.421; 16 in E flat, K.428; 17 in B flat, K.458 (Hunt); 18 in A, K. 464; 19 in C (Dissonance), K.465
EuroArt Unitel DVD 2072328 (2). Hagen Qt

These are beautifully alive and sensitively phrased performances that give much pleasure. They were recorded in 1998 in the elegant environment (and excellent acoustic) of the Grosser Saal of the Salzburg Mozarteum and they are impeccably presented visually. A most satisfying issue, which can be recommended with enthusiasm.

String Quartets 20 (Hoffmeister); 21–23 (Prussian Quartets 1–3)
Ⓜ CRD (ADD) CRD 3427/8. Chilingirian Qt

The Chilingirian Quartet give very natural, unforced, well-played and sweet-toned accounts of the last four *Quartets*. They are very well recorded too, with cleanly focused lines and a warm, pleasing ambience; indeed, in this respect these two discs are second to none.

String Quintets: 1 in B flat, K.174; 2 in C min., K.406; 3 in C, K.515; 4 in G min., K.516; 5 in D, K.593; 6 in E flat, K.614. Divertimento for String Trio in E flat, K.563
Ⓜ Decca (ADD) 470 950-2 (3). Grumiaux Trio, with Gérecz, Lesueur

Grumiaux's distinguished set of the *String Quintets* is coupled with his unsurpassed (1967) version of the rather less well-known but equally inspired *Divertimento for String Trio* – an ideal linking. Beautifully played, the remastering of these fine analogue recordings is outstandingly natural – a tribute to the Philips engineers, even though this reissue is now assigned to Decca.

Così fan tutte (complete, DVD version)
Medici Arts DVD 207 2368 (2). Frittoli, Kirchschlager, Skovhus, Schade, Corbelli, Bacelli, V. State Op. Ch. & O, Muti (Director: Roberto de Simone; V/D: Brian Large)

Così fan tutte (CD version)
EMI (ADD) 5 67382-2 (3). Schwarzkopf, Ludwig, Steffek, Kraus, Taddei, Barry, Philh. Ch. & O, Boehm

It is a pleasure to welcome the Medici Arts 1996 *Così* from the Vienna State Opera. Roberto de Simone is one of those rare stage directors who do not seek to impose their own personality over that of the composer. This is a most stylish production, with attractive costumes and sets that are a viewing pleasure, especially the sea vista at Naples. When Guglielmo and Ferrando leave, they do so on a convincing backstage boat simulation, while the famous *Trio* which follows reveals Mozart's exquisite part-writing clearly, instead of smoothing it into vocal homogeneity. Throughout, the singing (and acting) cast is in every way excellent, with Barbara Frittoli as convincing a Fiordiligi as Angelika

Kirchschlager is an engaging Dorabella, and both feistily resist the temptation to stray, until their attempting seducers spectacularly feign arsenic poisoning. Monica Bacelli is a knowingly vivacious and ever-resourceful Despina (especially when disguised as the doctor) and she sings both her arias with real charm. Alessandro Corbelli, too, is a conniving Don Alfonso, yet not overplaying his role. Muti's conducting is splendidly alive and fresh. What more could you want?

Boehm's classic set has been splendidly remastered as one of EMI's 'Great Recordings of the Century' and remains a clear first choice among CD versions. Its glorious solo singing is headed by the incomparable Fiordiligi of Schwarzkopf and the Dorabella of Christa Ludwig; it remains a superb memento of Walter Legge's recording genius and remains unsurpassed by other recordings made before or since. The documentation is generous and includes a full libretto and sessions photographs.

Don Giovanni (CD version)

Decca (ADD) 478 1389 (3). Della Casa, Danco, Siepi, Corena, Dermota, V. State Op. Ch., VPO, Krips

Krips's version was recorded in 1955 for the Mozart Bicentenary and has been one of the top recommendations of this work ever since. Freshly remastered, it sounds better than ever; few, if any, allowances have to be made for the date of the stereo recording. Its intense, dramatic account of the Don's disappearance into hell has rarely been equalled and never surpassed on CD. And there are many equally memorable sequences: the finale to Act I is electrifying. As a bass Don, Siepi (a wonderful, truly great singer) is marvellously convincing, but there is hardly a weak link in the rest of the cast. The early stereo recording is pretty age-defying, full and warm, with a lovely Viennese glow which is preferable to many modern recordings. However, special mention should also be made of Giulini's classic EMI set with Schwarzkopf, Sutherland and Cappuccilli – all singing on top form, supremely conducted and recorded, and another indispensable recording (EMI 5 67869-2 (3)).

Die Entführung aus dem Serail (DVD version)

DG DVD 073 4075. Gruberová, Grist, Araiza, Orth, Talvela, Holtzmann, Bav. State Op. Ch. & O, Boehm (Director: August Everding)

Karl Boehm conducted his beautifully paced account of Entführung at the Bavarian State Opera in April 1980, just over a year before he died. It was always a favourite opera with him. And the performance has a winning glow, with an excellent cast of soloists. Edita Gruberová as Konstanze is at her freshest: clear and agile, tender in Traurigkeit, brilliant in Marten aller Arten. Though Reri Grist as Blonde has an edge on the voice, hers is a charming and characterful assumption, most of all when confronting the powerful Osmin of Martti Talvela, a giant of a figure with a voice to match. Francisco Araiza too is at his peak, with Norbert Orth exceptionally strong as Pedrillo. August Everding's stylized production, with smoothly sliding scenery by Max Bignens, sets each scene deftly and atmospherically in the Pasha's palace. The 1980 sound is exceptionally bright and clear for its age.

Die Entführung aus dem Serail (CD version)

Ⓜ DG (ADD) 429 868-2 (2). Augér, Grist, Schreier, Neukirch, Moll, Mellies, Leipzig R. Ch., Dresden State O, Boehm

Boehm's is a delightful account, superbly cast and warmly recorded. Arleen Augér proves the most accomplished singer on record in the role of Konstanze, girlish and fresh, yet rich, tender and dramatic by turns, with brilliant, almost flawless coloratura. The others are also outstandingly good, notably Kurt Moll, whose powerful, finely focused bass makes him a superb Osmin, one who relishes the comedy too. The warm recording is beautifully transferred, to make this easily the most sympathetic version of the opera on CD, with the added attraction of being at mid-price. Admirers of opera sung in English should also investigate Menuhin's sparkling performance on Chandos, with an outstanding cast (Dobbs, Eddy, Gedda, Fryatt, Mangin, Kelsey), full and vividly recorded in 1967 and an absolute joy from beginning to end (Chan. 3081 (2)).

Idomeneo (complete, DVD version)

Arthaus DVD 101 079. Lewis, R. Davies, Goeke, Betley, Barstow, Oliver, Fryatt, Wicks, Glyndebourne Ch., LPO, Pritchard (Director: John Cox; V/D: Dave Heather)

Idomeneo (CD version)

DG 431 6742 (3). Rolfe Johnson, Von Otter, McNair, Martinpelto, Robson, Hauptmann, Monteverdi Ch., E. Bar. Sol., Gardiner

It was at Glyndebourne that this *opera seria* was first heard in Britain, and over the years John Pritchard made a speciality of conducting the piece, always a vigorous and dramatic interpreter of what misguidedly used to be regarded as undramatic. Like Pritchard as conductor, Richard Lewis in the title-role was a veteran still in superb voice. John Cox's production of 1974 is brilliantly devised to bring out the limited dimensions of the stage in the old Glyndebourne opera house, with concentric circles framing the whole stage, giving a long perspective to highly atmospheric scenes at the end of the tunnel. It works beautifully, not least when the sea monster appears at the end of Act II. The snag with this version for some will be the elderly edition Pritchard uses, with the role of Idamante taken by a tenor rather than a mezzo, thus upsetting the balance of the great quartet in Act III. Nevertheless, it is included in this book as it is a beautifully crafted reading, with Leo Goeke's tenor as Idamante well contrasted with the fine Idomeneo of Ryland Davies. Josephine Barstow at her peak is a formidable Elettra and Bozena Betley a sweet Ilia. The incidental roles are very well taken by vintage Glyndebourne performers, Alexander Oliver, John Fryatt and Dennis Wicks.

With its exhilarating vigour and fine singing, Gardiner's aim has been to include all the material Mozart wrote for the original (1781) production, and he recommends the use of the CD programming device for listeners to select the version they prefer. Gardiner's Mozartian style is well sprung and subtly moulded rather than severe. The principals sing beautifully, notably Anne Sofie von Otter as Idamante and Sylvia McNair as Ilia, while Anthony Rolfe Johnson as Idomeneo is well suited here, with words finely projected. The electrifying singing of the Monteverdi Choir adds to the dramatic bite. There is also an excellent version of this opera sung in English on the Chandos label, with a fine cast and superbly conducted by David Parry (CHAN 3103 (2)).

Le nozze di Figaro (complete, DVD version)

Opus Arte DVD OA 09990. Schrott, Persson, Röschmann, Finley, Shaham, ROHCG Ch. & O, Pappano (Director: David McVicar; V/D: Ferenc van Damme)

Le nozze di Figaro (CD version)

Decca (ADD) 478 1720 (3). Gueden, Danco, Della Casa, Dickie, Poell, Corena, Siepi, V. State Op. Ch., VPO, Kleiber

An outstanding new-styled DVD *Figaro* from David McVicar to lead the top choices. It is set in the 1830s, which simply means that the costumes are brought forward a few decades, but are still a pleasure to look at. The Count's palace is on a realistically impressive scale, with a huge staff, and its elegance contrasts with the scruffy room to be allotted to Figaro and Susanna after they are married, where the opera opens. Erwin Schrott is a lively, resourceful and above all very good-looking Figaro, but the delightful Susanna (Miah Persson), charmingly dressed, is his match and they both sing splendidly. So does Gerald Finley, even if he portrays a truly unattractive, permanently disgruntled, jealous Count, and one wonders what Rosina originally saw in him. But his anger gives a spice to the action, especially in Mozart's marvellous extended finale to Act II which, with wonderful music, keeps the viewer continually wondering what is coming next. The dignified Countess (Dorothea Röschmann) sings her pair of key arias beautifully and affectingly. While she conveys her deep unhappiness at her husband's unfaithful behaviour, she is appealingly spirited and stands her own ground, obviously enjoying Cherubino's attempts to win her favours. Rinat Shaham is very personable, and her singing of 'his' two arias in that role is another of the highlights of the production. Altogether this is very recommendable indeed. The sets are appealing and the action moves forward with a swing, with the performance conducted with his usual flair by Antonio Pappano.

Erich Kleiber's famous set was one of Decca's Mozart Bicentenary recordings of the mid-1950s. It remains a memorably strong performance with much fine singing, and few sets have matched its constant stylishness. Hilde Gueden's Susanna might be criticized, but her golden tones are certainly characterful and her voice blends enchantingly with Lisa Della Casa's. Suzanne

Danco and Della Casa are both at their finest. A dark-toned Figaro in Cesare Siepi – simply one of the most magnificent singers of the twentieth century – adds much contrast to the performance. While it is true that the recitatives are rather slow by modern standards, this is not inconsistent with Kleiber's overall approach, which lets the music's intrinsic sparkle emerge completely naturally and without any force. For those who prefer a more 'authentic' approach to this score, René Jacobs's outstanding version with the Concerto Cöln on Harmonia Mundi is strongly recommended. Vividly recorded and conducted, and with a very strong cast (Gens, Ciofi, Kirchschlager, McLaughlin, Keenlyside, Regazzo), it is perhaps the most outstanding of modern versions available today (HM HMC90 1818/20).

Die Zauberflöte (DVD version)

TDK DVD DVWW-CLOPMF. Cotrubas, Schreier, Gruberová, Talvela, Boesch, Sieber, Hiestermann, V. State Op. Konzertvereinigung, VPO, Levine (Stage Director: Jean-Pierre Ponnelle; V/D: Brian Large)

Die Zauberflöte (CD version)

DG 477 5789 (2). Röschmann, Miklósa, Strehl, Pape, Müller-Brachmann, Kleiter, Azesberger, Zeppenfeld, Arnold Schoenberg Ch., Mahler CO, Abbado

Jean-Pierre Ponnelle's production of *Die Zauberflöte*, with his own charming toytown sets and costumes, was the one revived more than any other in the history of the Salzburg Festival. From the start, with James Levine at his most brilliant and perceptive as conductor, it struck an ideal medium between the pantomime element and the weightier implications of the Masonic background to the story. With Brian Large as video director exploiting the evocative setting in the Felsenreitschule with its series of layers of cliff recesses, it makes an ideal entertainment on film in this 1982 recording, with the possible reservation that an unusually large amount of spoken dialogue is included which, with well-chosen chapter headings, can easily be reduced on DVD.

As DG's wording on the box makes clear, this is Abbado's very first *Magic Flute* on record and indeed – as they claim – it is a triumphant success. Its freshness and charm, with ravishing playing from the Mahler Chamber Orchestra, reminds us of our first encounter with the celebrated Fricsay recording (still available on DG 435 741-2 (2)). But Abbado's cast is finer still, for here René Pape's magnificent Sarastro dominates the opera, just as intended. He and the superb chorus bring just the right touch of gravitas, so all the pantomime fun with Papageno and Papagena is nicely balanced. Moreover, Erika Miklósa's Queen of the Night's second aria, *Der Hölle Rache*, is quite as dazzling as Rita Streich's celebrated version, and it is slightly fuller in tone. Dorothea Röschmann and Christoph Strehl are a perfectly matched Pamina and Tamino, for both have lovely voices: Strehl is ardent and Röschmann is infinitely touching when she mistakenly thinks Tamino is lost to her for ever. The smaller parts are also without flaw. Kurt Azesberger is a splendid Monostatos, and even the speaker, George Zeppenfeld, has a honeyed tone. But most magical of all are the little vocal ensembles, wonderfully warm and refined, especially the numbers featuring the Three Ladies (Caroline Stein, Heidi Zehnder and Anne-Caroline Schlüter), who blend so delightfully but not suavely, and the Three Boys (from the Tölzer Knabenchor), who are just as memorable. Although the moments of drama are not lost, this is above all an affectionately relaxed performance, with Abbado continually revelling in the lyrical beauty of Mozart's wonderful score. It is, of course, a live performance, so it has the extra communicative tension that brings; but the audience are (mercifully) angelically quiet, although we are aware of their presence during the fun created by the ever-reluctant Papageno. The recording is first class and, while there is a great deal of dialogue, it can be programmed out.

MUSSORGSKY, Modest (1839–81)

Pictures at an Exhibition (orch. Ravel)
Ⓜ RCA (ADD) 09026 61401-2. Chicago SO, Reiner – **RESPIGHI**: *Fountains of Rome; Pines of Rome*

There are many fine recordings of Mussorgsky's celebrated *Pictures*, but Reiner has the advantage of the rich acoustics of Chicago's Symphony Hall and a 1957 sound-balance which is highly atmospheric, if less sharply focused than some. The final climax of *The Great Gate of Kiev* shows the concentration of the playing, but this is also obvious throughout and the remastering is fully worthy of the performance. Reiner's recording is also available in an excellent new SACD transfer (RCA 82876 61394-2), where the couplings include *Night on a Bare Mountain*, Tchaikovsky's *Marche slave* and the engaging *Marche miniature*, Borodin's *Polovtsian March*, Kabalevsky's *Colas Breugnon Overture*, and Glinka's *Ruslan and Ludmilla Overture*, all splendidly played and recorded.

Boris Godunov (DVD version)
Decca DVD 075 089-9 (2). Lloyd, Borodina, Steblianko, Leiferkus, Kirov Op. Ch. & O, Director: Gergiev (Tarkovsky, V/D Humphrey Burton)

In 1990 the Covent Garden production of *Boris Godunov*, directed by the Russian Andre Tarkovsky, and rehearsed by Stephen Lawless, was adopted by the Mariinsky Theatre in St Petersburg. This two-disc DVD offers the resulting film, originally shown on BBC television, a magnificent presentation of the opera in the edition prepared by David Lloyd-Jones using the original 1872 version of the score. Valery Gergiev conducts an outstanding Kirov Opera cast, joined in the title role by Robert Lloyd from Covent Garden, giving one of his greatest performances ever, strong and resonant and movingly acted. It is astonishing how the different incidental parts are cast from strength with star singers, each rising superbly to the challenge of a major scene – Pimen, Varlaam, Rangoni and the Simpleton (who sings his *pathétique* solo twice – in the first scene of Act IV and at the end). Olga Borodina is magnificent as Marina in the Polish scenes opposite the powerful Grigory of Alexei Steblianko, and even such a small part as Feodor, Boris's young son, is taken with passionate intensity by a then rising star, Larissa Diadkova. Musically it would be hard to imagine a finer performance, even though the recording balance sometimes has voices too distant and unrelated to close-up pictures. Visually it is superb too, with the complex, episodic story told with extraordinary clarity, set on a simple but very grand stage, with a floor in false perspective adding to the grandeur. Costumes are authentic and often colourful, with Tarkovsky's often stylized production bringing unforgettable moments, as when Rangoni comes and sits centre stage at the end of the love scene between Marina and Grigory, and turns to give the most sinister stare as the curtain falls. Altogether an outstanding set.

Khovanshchina (complete, DVD version)

Arthaus DVD 100 310 (2). Ghiaurov, Atlantov, Marusin, Kocherga, Burchuladze, Semtschuk, Slovak Philharmonic Ch., V. Boys' Ch., V. State Op. Ch. & O, Abbado (Stage/ Director Kirchner

The Arthaus DVD recording was made in 1989, with Nicolai Ghiaurov leading an outstanding cast in what is essentially the Shostakovich version of the opera with the finale prepared by Stravinsky. Rimsky-Korsakov's marvellous orchestration is rejected as too sumptuous these days, and his corrections of Mussorgsky's harmony are seen as too academically correct. And with the beautiful, tragic music of Abbado's ending, the strength and dignity of the Old Believers is reinforced. Indeed Abbado, who has for so long been Mussorgsky's most eloquent champion among Western conductors of his generation, is electrifying throughout. There is an intensity here, and a mastery both of pace and climax. The playing of the Vienna orchestra is exquisite in the quieter episodes and sumptuous in tone, as is the moving contribution of the chorus. The recording, too, is superbly balanced and defined, and visually the production is good to look at. The camera is expertly directed, and always where the viewer wants it. This is a mandatory choice for all lovers of Russian opera.

NIELSEN, Carl (1865–1931)

(i) *Clarinet Concerto*; (ii) *Flute Concerto*; (iii) *Violin Concerto, Op. 33*

Chan. 8894. (i) Thomsen; (ii) Christiansen; (iii) Sjøgren; Danish Nat. RSO, Schønwandt

Niels Thomsen's powerfully intense account of the late *Clarinet Concerto* is completely gripping. Michael Schønwandt gives sensitive and imaginative support, both here and in the two companion works. Toke Lund Christiansen is hardly less successful in the *Flute Concerto*. Kim Sjøgren and Schønwandt give a penetrating and thoughtful account of the *Violin Concerto*; there is real depth here, thanks in no small measure to Schønwandt. The recording is first class.

Violin Concerto, Op. 33

Ⓜ Sony SMK 89748. Lin, Swedish RSO, Salonen – **SIBELIUS**: *Violin Concerto*

Cho-Liang Lin brings as much authority to Nielsen's *Violin Concerto* as he does to the Sibelius, and he handles the numerous technical hurdles with breathtaking assurance. Salonen is admirably supportive and gets first-class playing from the Swedish Radio Symphony Orchestra. An admirable coupling, very well balanced and recorded.

Symphonies 1–2; (i) 3; (ii) Aladdin (suite). Maskarade Overture

Ⓑ Double Decca 460 985-2 (2). San Francisco SO, Blomstedt; (i) with Kromm, McMillan; (ii) San Francisco SO Ch.

(i) Symphonies 4–6; (ii) Little Suite; (ii–iii) Hymnus amoris, Op. 12

Ⓑ Double Decca 460 988-2 (2) (i) San Francisco SO, Blomstedt; (ii) Danish Nat. RSO, Schirmer; (iii) with Bonney, Pedersen, Mark Ainsley, M. & B. Hansen, Danish Nat. R. Ch., Copenhagen Boys' Ch.

These two Double Decca issues offer an admirable and inexpensive way of collecting Blomstedt's complete cycle of Nielsen's symphonies which is self-recommending. All six performances are among the finest available. The engaging *Aladdin Suite* is also winningly played, and the *Overture* to Nielsen's comic opera, *Maskarade*, is appropriately high-spirited. Ulf Schirmer too shows a natural affinity for Nielsen. On the second issue he gives a persuasive account of Nielsen's first published opus, the endearing *Little Suite for Strings* and the early cantata, *Hymnus amoris*, one of his warmest and most open-hearted scores. To put it briefly, this remains the best all-round modern set of the symphonies, and the bonuses add to its attractions.

Complete Piano Music: 5 Pieces. Op. 3; Symphonic Suite, Op. 8; Humoresque-Bagatelles, Op. 11; Piano Music for Young and Old, Op. 53; Chaconne, Op. 32; Theme & Variations, Op. 40; Suite, Op. 45; 3 Piano Pieces, Op. 59

Hyp. CDA 76591/2. Martin Roscoe

Apart from Grieg, no Scandinavian composer has written for the piano with more individuality or understanding than Nielsen. Even though the early Op. 3 *Pieces* are Schumannesque, they speak with distinctive and touching personal accents, and all five are strong on both humour and character. Nielsen's greatest piano music is clustered into a period of four years (1916–20), with his final thoughts in the medium, the *Three Pieces*, Op. 59, of 1928 being composed in the immediate wake of the *Clarinet Concerto*, music that already breathes the air of other planets. Apart from Leif Ove Andsnes, no pianist of international standing has championed it on record and, with the exception of John Ogdon and John McCabe, it has almost been the exclusive preserve of Nordic artists. The *Suite* is not only Nielsen's greatest keyboard work but arguably the mightiest ever written in Scandinavia. Martin Roscoe is right inside this music and guides us through its marvels with great subtlety and authority. Hyperion give him vivid and natural recorded sound and there are outstanding notes by Daniel Grimley.

Aladdin (complete incidental music), *Op. 34*
Chan. 9135. Ejsing, Paevatalu, Danish Nat. R. Chamber Ch. & SO, Rozhdestvensky

Until now the *Aladdin* music has been known only from the 20-minute, seven-movement suite, but the complete score runs to four times its length. Some numbers are choral, and there are songs and a short piece for solo flute. Thirteen of the movements are designed to accompany spoken dialogue and, although not all of it is of equal musical interest and substance, most of it is characteristically Nielsenesque, and much of it is delightful. The two soloists, Mette Ejsing and Guido Paevatalu, are very good and the Danish Radio forces respond keenly to Rozhdestvensky's baton. This is not top-drawer Nielsen but, given such a persuasive performance and excellent recording, one is almost lulled into the belief that it is.

Maskarade (complete)
Dacapo (ADD) SACD 6.220507/8 (2). Hansen, Plesner, Landy, Johansen, Serensen,
  Bastian, Brodersen, Haugland, Danish Nat. R. Ch. & SO, Frandsen

Nielsen's second and last opera now comes realistically remastered on SACD, and must be considered a triumphant success in its new format, with the rear speakers (used discreetly) adding to the atmospheric feeling. But it still sounds admirable through a normal stereo set-up. Frandsen's performance is distinguished by good – sometimes very good – singing and alert orchestral support. Above all, the sound is musical, the images are well located and firm, and the overall presentation is vivid. But the deleted Decca set remains first choice.

NØRGÅRD, Per (born 1932)

Symphony 1 (Sinfonia austera); *Symphony 2*
Chan. 9450. Danish Nat. SO, Segerstam

Per Nørgård is the leading Danish composer of his generation. The *Sinfonia austera*, Nørgård's *First Symphony*, comes from 1955 and has a strong atmosphere with something of Holmboe's sense of power and forward movement, impressive and compelling. The *Second* (1970) is different in kind, static in feeling and hypnotic in effect. The 'infinite series' which shaped his *Voyage into the Golden Screen* dominates the whole piece. There are some striking and imaginative effects here. Very good performances too from Leif Segerstam and the Danish National Symphony Orchestra.

Symphony 6 (At the End of the Day); Terrains vagues
Chan. 9904. Danish Nat. SO, Dausgaard

Written in 1998–9 to celebrate the millennium in the Danish National Orchestra's first concert in January 2000, Nørgård's *Sixth Symphony* is a powerful and violent piece that makes no compromises. One takes it on trust even at a first hearing that, as the composer claims, it is tautly structured; from the opening onwards it demonstrates a vivid feeling for orchestral colour, presented with an energy too often missing in new music of the late twentieth century. Nørgård has said that this was to be the last of his symphonies, and the hushed close suggests something valedictory, but the vitality of invention not just in the symphony but in the substantial orchestral work with which it is coupled, written even more recently, suggested that he might change his mind, which he did with his *Seventh Symphony* (2006). Neither work makes for easy listening, but in this superbly engineered recording the power of the writing comes over most persuasively, demanding attention.

NORRINGTON, Roger, with London Philharmonic
Choir and London Philharmonic Orchestra

'Music for the Last Night of the Proms': ARNE: Rule Britannia
(with Sarah Walker). **WALTON**: *Crown Imperial*. **STANFORD**: *Songs of the Sea* (with Thomas Allen). **VAUGHAN WILLIAMS**: *Serenade to Music* (with Felicity Lott, Lisa Milne, Rosa Mannion, Yvonne Kenny, Ann Murray, Diana Montague, Della Jones, Catherine Wyn Rogers, Anthony Rolfe Johnson, John Mark Ainsley, Toby Spence, Timothy Robinson, Stephen Roberts, Christopher Maltman, Michael George, Robert Lloyd). **ELGAR**: *Pomp and Circumstance March 1*. **PARRY**: *Jerusalem*. **WOOD**: *Fantasia on British Sea Songs*.
Ⓜ Australian Decca Eloquence 480 0476-8

It is easy to respond to the popular music of the last night of the Proms, particularly *Rule Britannia* and *Jerusalem*, heard here in Elgar's wonderfully rich arrangement; and, on the words, 'Bring me my arrows of desire', the sweeping strings bring a truly gulp-inducing moment. Sarah Walker is the vibrant mezzo in Arne's *Rule Britannia*, heard in Sir Malcolm Sargent's expert arrangement. It is easy, too, to overlook the skill of Sir Henry Wood's *Fantasia on British Sea Songs*, with their catchy tunes dressed in colourful orchestrations. Thomas Allen is in top voice for Stanford's briny *Songs of the Sea*, with the opening

Drake's Drum making an unforgettable impression – surely one of the most telling sea-song settings in all English music. *Crown Imperial* comes off very well too, with one of Walton's finest tunes as its centrepiece and truly breathtaking Waltonian brass chords in the coda. In composing the first *Pomp and Circumstance March,* Elgar was very proud of the 'damned good tune' which was to become 'Land of hope and glory', and rightly so. In complete contrast, Vaughan Williams's *Serenade to Music* – one of the most haunting of the composer's vocal works, has an astonishingly distinguished line-up of solo singers and brings another dimension to the programme. The (studio) sound is excellent and this surprisingly little-known CD is one of Sir Roger Norrington's most successful recordings, resurrected on Australian Decca Eloquence.

OCKEGHEM, Johannes *(c. 1410–97)*

Alma redemptoris Mater; Ave Maria; Credo 'De village'; Fors seulement; Gaude Maria; Intemerata Dei Mater (2 versions); Masses: *Au travail suis; Celeste beneficium; Cuiusvis toni; De plus en plus; Ecce ancilla Domini; Fors seulement; L'Homme armé; Mi-mi; Prolationum; Quinti toni; Sine nomine* (2 settings *à 3* & *à 5*); *Requiem. Salve Regina; S'elle m'amera/Petite camusette.*
ⓑ ASV Gaudeamus CD GAX 550 (5). Clerks' Group, Wickham

This admirable bargain box collects together the survey by Edward Wickham's Clerks' Group of Ockeghem's major religious works, including twelve Mass settings and the *Requiem.* A treasure chest. All the performances are of the highest order and have refreshing enthusiasm. The recording is first class too.

Alma redemptoris Mater; Ave Maria; Missa L'Homme armé
ⓑⓑ Naxos 8.554297. Oxford Camerata, Summerly (with **JOSQUIN DESPREZ**:
   Memor esto verbi tui)

On Naxos, the soaring opening *Ave Maria,* gloriously sung, immediately sets the seal on the inspirational power of Ockeghem's music. It is followed by the plainchant, *Alma redemptoris Mater* and then by its polyphonic setting, simple and flowing and harmonically rich. The robust ballad, *L'Homme armé* ('The armed man must be feared') must have been hugely popular in its day since so many composers used it as a basis for a Mass. In Ockeghem's setting the work's dramatic and emotional peak is readily found in the extended *Sanctus,* resolved in the sublime melancholy of the *Agnus Dei.* It is sung superbly here and is marvellously paced. Josquin's setting of sixteen verses from Psalm 119, *Memor esto verbi tui,* with its expressively fertile imitative devices, makes an eloquent postlude and the recording, made in the Chapel of Hertford College, Oxford, could hardly be better. It dates from February 1997, thus aptly commemorating the 500th anniversary of Ockeghem's death.

OFFENBACH, Jacques (1819–80)

(i) *Cello Concerto (Concerto militaire)*. *Les Fées du Rhin: Overture, Ballet & Grande Valse*. *Orphée aux enfers: Overture*. *Le Voyage dans la Lune: Ballet des Flocons de neige*

DG 477 6403. Les Musiciens du Louvre, Minkowski, (i) with Pernoo

Long before he scored his big success as a composer of operettas with *Orpheus in the Underworld*, Offenbach was renowned as the 'Liszt of the Cello', an outstanding virtuoso. This 45-minute *Concerto militaire* is the most important of his compositions from that period, here recorded complete for the first time. After the composer's death, the score, badly edited, had the three movements sold separately, and it has been thanks to the outstanding detective work of the editor, Jean-Christophe Keck, that the *Concerto* has now been fully restored. Both the first movement and the finale introduce military themes, with timpani prominent in both, and with the main theme of the finale anticipating the style of Offenbach's operettas. That finale, 20 minutes long, offers a wide range of invention, including one funeral procession episode. The sound, recorded live in Grenoble, tends to be plummy, but there is ample detail to bring out the fine quality of the performance by both the soloist, Jérôme Pernoo, and the orchestra of period instruments under Marc Minkowski. The sparkling fill-ups add to the attractions of the disc, with the ballet from *Les Fées du Rhin* offering the first version of what later became the *Barcarolle* in the *Tales of Hoffmann*.

Gaîté Parisienne

Ⓜ Australian Decca Eloquence (ADD) 476 2724. ROHCG O, Solti - **GOUNOD**: *Faust: ballet music*. **RESPIGHI**: *Rossiniana*

Solti's 1959 *Gaîté Parisienne* is the most brilliant committed to disc. While I.M. feels that the music-making is just that bit too hard driven, there is no doubting the sheer virtuosity of this remarkable orchestra and their bravura is infectious. Solti is far from unstylish here, but rather than allowing Offenbach's brand of champagne to bubble up to the surface gradually, Solti tends to whack you over the head with it! Exciting music-making, never dull, and vintage Decca sound.

Overtures: *Barbe-Bleue*; *La Belle Hélène*; *La Grande Duchesse de Gérolstein*; *Le Mariage aux lanternes*; *Orfée aux enfers* (with **ADAM**: *Si j'étais Roi*. **BOIELDIEU**: *Le Calife de Bagdad*; *La Dame Blanche*. **HÉROLD**: *Zampa*)

Ⓜ Australian Decca Eloquence mono 476 2757. LPO, Martinon

Martinon's LP collection of Offenbach overtures is quite the best ever committed to disc and now it has made it on to CD. Under Martinon, these overtures explode like a shaken bottle of ice-cold champagne, with the *Can-can* finales of *Orfée* and *La Grande Duchesse* going like the devil. While no one has captured the whirlwind Offenbach spirit as Martinon does, it is for the elegance that one especially relishes this collection, with the simple, folk-like tunes of *Barbe-Bleue* so beautifully phrased, and so gentle, it makes the sharply pointed strings in the lively finale even more effective. Nowhere is this rhythmic sharpness more apparent than in the deliciously crisp finale of the rare *Le Mariage aux lanternes*, a work of Mozartian charm. The engaging oboe tune in *La Belle Hélène* is beautifully phrased, and in that opera's famous waltz you can see how Offenbach once beat Johann Strauss in a waltz-writing competition. In the rollicking good tune at 1 minute 27 seconds in *La Grande Duchesse* ('I love the military'), the strings play with carefree vivacity as well as polish. Decca has handsomely coupled the Offenbach items with Martinon's contemporary LP of once popular French overtures, with the orchestra giving of their very best. *The White Lady* is especially enjoyable, with a delightful bassoon passage underpinning the second subject. The early 1950s sound is vivid, but rather too bright: the original LXT LP (before it was re-cut) was undoubtedly warmer and sounded better balanced, but this transfer is well ahead in sound compared to the edgy Ace of Clubs and Eclipse LP versions, last seen around 30 years ago. This reissue needs to be snapped up before it disappears again.

La Belle Hélène (complete, DVD & CD versions)

TDK DVD DV-OPLBH; CD Virgin 5 45477-2 (2). Lott, Beuron, Sénéchal, Le Roux, Naouri, Todorovitch, Ch. & Musiciens du Louvre, Grenoble, Minkowski (Stage Director: Laurent Pelly)

The new production of *La Belle Hélène* staged by Laurent Pelly, with costumes by Chantal Thomas, retains all the mythological characters, but they appear to Hélène as in her dream of being the most beautiful woman in the world and falling in love with the virile young Paris. Her double bed, to which she retires at the beginning, becomes the focus of the action until Act III, which takes place on the beach at Naples, from where she finally sails away with Paris. The whole production fizzes and has touches of romantic naughtiness which only the French can bring off with real style. There is an additional 'Behind the Scenes' sequence, narrating the background to this brilliantly successful production.

Favouring brisk speeds and light textures, using the period instruments of Les Musiciens du Louvre, Marc Minkowski gives a winning sparkle to this delectable send-up of the classical story. He also has the benefit of offering a more complete, more authentic text than any predecessor. It was recorded after the highly successful stage production at the Châtelet Théâtre in Paris in September 2000, when Felicity Lott was hailed as an outstanding star in the role of Hélène. That is true, even if vocally there are moments when her voice is not at its sweetest, not as rounded as it might be; but her feeling for the idiom and her characterization are unerring. Outstanding in the cast is the seductively honeyed tenor of Yann Beuron as Paris. His 'Judgement of Paris' solo in Act I has rarely been matched, with exquisite *pianissimo* singing in the final stanza, enhanced by Minkowski's persuasive rubato. An excellent supporting cast, including such stalwarts of the repertory as Michel Sénéchal and François Le Roux. Although the CDs are in every way recommendable, the live performance on DVD is sheer delight, adding an extra dimension to Offenbach's scintillating score.

Les Contes d'Hoffmann (The Tales of Hoffmann; complete, CD version)
Decca (ADD) 417 363-2 (2). Sutherland, Domingo, Tourangeau, Bacquier, R. Suisse
    Romande & Lausanne Pro Art Ch., SRO, Bonynge

Offenbach's final work, *Les Contes d'Hoffmann*, was a posthumous triumph for the composer. In this marvellous *opéra comique*, Offenbach fully captured the sense of the grotesque in the E. T. A. Hoffmann stories as well as a sense of irony and humour. Of course Offenbach was nothing if not a man of the theatre, so the work is highly theatrical and entertaining, brimming with good tunes, rollicking choruses and many instantly memorable numbers. Offenbach longed to write one serious masterpiece and in this story of disillusioned love at its centre he achieved it, sadly dying before the work was performed. It survived in somewhat corrupt forms, but Bonynge's solution to the textual problems is undoubtedly the most successful. This recording, from 1971, is one of the supreme achievements of the many Sutherland/Bonynge/Decca recordings. Joan Sutherland gives a virtuoso performance in four heroine roles, not only as Olympia, Giulietta and Antonia, but also as Stella in the Epilogue, which is given even greater weight by the restoration of the *Quartet*, a magnificent, thrilling climax. Bonynge opts for spoken dialogue, and puts the Antonia scene last, as being the more substantial. His direction is unfailingly sympathetic, while Sutherland is impressive in each role, notably as the doll Olympia and in the pathos of the Antonia scene. As Giulietta she hardly sounds like a *femme fatale*, but still produces beautiful singing. Domingo gives one of his finest performances on record (his famous *Kleinzach* aria in the Prologue goes with a real swing) and so too does Gabriel Bacquier. Huguette Tourangeau is outstanding as La Muse and Nicklausse. It is a memorable set in every way, with a superb supporting cast, with such people as Hugues Cuénod adding much character and an authentic flavour to the performance as a whole. The Decca recording is outstanding, rich, full and vividly atmospheric.

'The World of Offenbach': Overtures: La Belle Hélène; La Fille du tambour-major; Orpheus in the Underworld. Excerpt: Le Papillon; Les Contes d'Hoffmann; La Grande-Duchesse; de Gérolstein; La Périchole; Robinson Crusoé
Ⓑ Decca Australian Eloquence 480 5318. Crespin, Sutherland, Domingo, Sumi Jo,
    Tourangeau; Various Orchestras, cond. Ansermet, Bonynge, Lombard

Opening and closing delightfully with the *Barcarolle*, and vividly recorded, this is an unmissable and generous 'lucky dip' to match and even surpass 'The World of Borodin', creating an unforgettably entertaining 74 minutes. The overtures and operetta excerpts are equally diverting, marvellously sung, and are topped off with Sumi's Jo's sparkling *Valse tyrolienne*.

ORFF, Carl (1895–1982)

Carmina Burana (DVD version)
RCA DVD 74321 852859. Popp, Van Kesteren, Prey, Bav. R. Ch., Munich R. O, Eichhorn
   (Video Producer: Jean-Pierre Ponnelle)

Carmina Burana (CD version)
Ⓑ Sony (ADD) SBK 47668. Harsanyi, Petrak, Presnell, Rutgers University Ch., Phd. O,
   Ormandy

This fine RCA recording of *Carmina Burana*, conducted by Kurt Eichhorn in 1975, with outstanding soloists, has been issued previously on CD, and here it is treated to an imaginative staging for DVD by Jean-Pierre Ponnelle. The main background set is a ruined church, against which the singers are seen in medieval costume, with action, sometimes surreal, invented to illustrate each section of the work, a technique which seems to anticipate the virtual reality of our digital age. So the roasted swan episode is introduced by a drunken monk, with a large swan in the background actually being roasted on a spit, and Lucia Popp is in a medieval wimple looking and sounding enchanting. Hermann Prey is the superb baritone soloist, taking the main burden, and the choir is bright and lively. As a supplementary item comes a long interview with Orff himself – in German with English subtitles – in which he talks animatedly about key childhood experiences and how he came to write *Carmina Burana*.

On CD, Ormandy and his Philadelphians have just the right amount of panache to bring off this wildly exuberant picture of the Middle Ages by the anonymous poets of former days, and there is no more enjoyable analogue version. It has tremendous vigour, warmth and colour and a genial, spontaneous enthusiasm from the Rutgers University Chorus, men and boys alike, that is irresistible. The soloists are excellent, but it is the chorus and orchestra who steal the show; the richness and eloquence of the choral tone is a joy in itself. This is quite splendid – one of Ormandy's most inspired recordings and, even if you already have the work in your collection, this exhilarating version will bring additional stimulation.

ORMANDY, Eugene, with Philadelphia Orchestra

HOLST: *The Planets (suite)* (with Mendelssohn Club of Philadelphia Ch.). **DEBUSSY**: *La Mer*
EuroArts DVD 2072268 (Producer: Tobius Möller; V/D: Kirk Browning)

This superb DVD brings a frisson of pleasure to see and hear Ormandy conduct the Philadelphia Orchestra in their old home, the Academy of Music where he (and Stokowski before him) made so many of their recordings. It is, of course, not like an academy but a very handsome auditorium, here displaying warmly glowing acoustics. The programme was made for showing on TV in Munich, and Ormandy (who was 78 at the time) makes a charming introductory speech in fluent German. He was born in Hungary, emigrating to the USA at the age of 22. He first conducted the orchestra in 1931, taking over at short notice after Stokowski had left and Toscanini was the interim maestro. He then became the orchestra's principal conductor in 1938 and continued until 1980, 'an artistic tenure unique in the history of American orchestras'.

Ormandy recorded *The Planets* on disc for RCA, but the recording was fiercely brilliant and did little justice to the orchestral sound. Not so here. This live recording, superbly played, not only demonstrates the famous string-sound, but also the richness of the orchestra's overall sonority, heard at its most overwhelming in the glorious performance of the big tune at the centre of *Jupiter*, which Ormandy takes at a nobly expansive pace, pointing the different layers of the climax tellingly. This follows a powerful *Mars* and a fleet *Mercury*, with Holst's imaginative orchestration then demonstrating every orchestral section, the strings and solo horn in a peaceful *Venus* with rapt translucent textures, the crisply vigorous brass in *Uranus*, the massed horns in the outer sections of *Jupiter*. The performance is at its finest in the restrained melancholy of *Saturn*, deeply felt and somehow personal in its communication, while the ethereal singing of the superb Mendelssohn Club Choir in *Neptune* is truly mystic in Ormandy's hands, and beautifully tapers off at the close. The comparably atmospheric *La Mer* also shows the orchestra's richness of colour and texture and descriptively moves towards a fine climax, without being quite as memorable as *The Planets*. This is however an indispensable DVD that will give enormous satisfaction for the sheer quality of the orchestral playing. The sound is not sharply detailed but naturally balanced, and the cameras range over the orchestra most tellingly so that the listener really feels involved with the playing.

PAGANINI, Niccolò (1782–1840)

Violin Concertos 1–6; 24 Caprices, Op. 1; Duo merveille;
Introduction & Variations on 'Di tanti palpiti' from Rossini's
Tancredi; Introduction & Variations on 'Nel cor più non mi sento'
from Paisiello's La molinara; Maestoso sonata sentimentale;
Perpetuela; La primavera; Sonata with Variations on a Theme by
Joseph Weigl; Sonata Napoleone; Le streghe (Variations on a
Theme by Süssmayr), Op. 8; Variations on 'God Save the King';
Variations on 'Non più mesta' from Rossini's La Cenerentola.
Ⓑ DG 463 754-2 (6). Accardo, LPO, Dutoit

Paganini's music, while rarely embracing deep emotional depths, occupies a secure place in the repertoire on account of its virtuoso brilliance - often thrillingly exciting when played in the right hands - combined with a seemingly endless supply of good tunes. The Accardo/Dutoit Paganini cycle remains a secure first choice: the *Concertos* are brilliantly and imaginatively played and well recorded. Indeed, these accounts do not fall down in any department. The individual discs are contained in an excellently packaged DG bargain box.

PALESTRINA, Giovanni Pierluigi da
(1525-1594)

Lamentations of Jeremiah, Book 3 (complete)
Hyp. CDA 67610. Westminster Cathedral Ch., Baker

This is the Third Book of Palestrina's settings for Maundy Thursday, Good Friday and Holy Saturday, very beautifully sung at Westminster Cathedral and superbly recorded. The variety of the music is much wider than one might have expected, and in Lectio III for Good Friday (*Aleph. Ego vir videns paupertatem meam*) the trebles rise up into the heavens ecstatically. A memorable disc indeed, showing Palestrina at his most inspirational.

Missa Hodie Christus natus est. Motets: Alma redemptoris mater; Canite tuba; Deus tu conversus; Christe, redemptor omnium; Hodie Christus natus est; Magnificat Primi toni; O admirabile commercium; O magnum mysterium; Tui sunt coeli
Hyp. CDA 67396. Westminster Cathedral Ch., Baker

Vividly set against the cathedral acoustic, warm but clear, this performance of the Christmas music brings out better than most rival versions the exuberance of the cries of 'Noë' (Nöel) that dramatically punctuate the piece, reflecting individual joy in welcoming the birth of Christ. The nine other items, all relating to Advent and Christmas, culminate in the *Magnificat Primi toni* with its rich textures, framed before and after by the plainsong antiphon, *Hodie Christus natus est*.

'**The Essential Palestrina**': *Missa Assumpta est Maria* (with *Plainchant: Assumpta est Maria)*; *Motet: Assumpta est Maria. Missa Brevis; Missa Papae Marcelli; Missa Sicut lilium inter spinas. Motet: Sicut lilium inter spinas*
Ⓑ Gimell CDGIM 204 (2). Tallis Scholars, Phillips

This highly recommendable and well-documented box joins together two CDs recorded by the Tallis Scholars between 1981 and 1989. As is their practice, this group records the Masses together with the motets on which they are based, even if they are by other composers. Their account of the most celebrated of Palestrina's works, the *Missa Papae Marcelli*, brings a characteristically eloquent and moving performance. A most rewarding collection, excellently recorded.

PARRY, Hubert (1848–1918)

(i) *The Birds: Bridal March*. (ii) *English Suite*; *Lady Radnor's Suite* (both for strings); *Overture to an Unwritten Tragedy*; *Symphonic Variations*
Lyrita (ADD) SRCD 220. (i) LPO; (ii) LSO; Boult

Before Chandos, Hyperion and Dutton began championing British music in the 1980s, it was Lyrita who promoted English music and they produced many fine, classic – even pioneering – recordings. The superb quality of this particular disc was typical of the high standards they almost always achieved. Not that this is the greatest of great music but, when performed and recorded as persuasively as it is here, it does make one feel that its neglect is our loss. The *Bridal March* comes from Parry's equivalent to Vaughan Williams's *Wasps*, a suite of incidental music for *The Birds*, also by Aristophanes. Here the rich, *nobilmente* string melody asserts itself strongly over any minor contributions from the woodwind aviary. The two *Suites* of dances for strings have some charming genre music and the *Overture* is very strongly constructed. But best of all is the set of variations with its echoes of Brahms's *St Antony* set and its foretastes of *Enigma*: a big work in a small compass. Boult's advocacy is irresistible and the CD transfer demonstrates the intrinsic excellence of the analogue recordings, with gloriously full string-sound.

Symphonies 1–5; Symphonic Variations
Ⓜ Chan. 9120-22 (3). LPO, Bamert

The rehabilitation of Parry has long been overdue. Chandos have now done this remarkable British nineteenth-century 'English Renaissance' musician full justice by recording the complete set of his symphonies. Bamert proves a masterly interpreter and takes us convincingly through the symphonic terrain of a highly influential composer of whom Elgar declared, 'He is our leader – no cloud of formality can dim the healthy sympathy and broad influence he exerts upon us. Amidst all the outpourings of modern English music the work of Parry remains supreme.'

Parry began work on his *First Symphony* in 1880. Only a few weeks previously he had made his acquaintance with Brahms's *First*, and it had an obvious influence on him, not least in the grand main theme of his own finale. Bamert immediately demonstrates his response to the composer's music in the way the opening *Con fuoco* sails off with a powerful thrust in the first movement. His control of the overall structure with its interrelated thematic material is most convincing, through the eloquent *Andante* and the Scherzo with its double trio, until he brings the finale to an impressively up-beat conclusion.

The *Second Symphony* opens confidently (with distinct Mendelssohnian associations) and Brahms's influence reappears in the main lyrical idea of the finale. In between there is a reminder of Dvořák in a Scherzo and of Schumann in the romantic warmth of the *Andante*. But for all its eclecticism and occasional long-windedness, notably in the finale, Parry finds his own voice, and the music has a genuine vital flow. Bamert's advocacy holds the listener's attention and the orchestra responds with obvious relish.

The *Third Symphony* is the most immediately approachable of the symphonies, with bold melodies, often like sea-shanties, and its forthright structure. Yet it is No. 4 which proves even more rewarding, a larger-scale and more ambitious work which, amazingly, was never performed at all between the first performance of the revised version in 1910 and the present recording. The bold opening, in its dark E minor, echoes that of Brahms's *First Piano Concerto*, leading to an ambitious movement lightened by thematic transformation that can take you in an instant into infectious waltz-time. The elegiac slow movement and jolly and spiky Scherzo lead to a broad, noble finale in the major key. Bamert again proves a masterly interpreter, bringing out the warmth and thrust of the writing – akin to that of Elgar, but quite distinct. The sound is rich and full to match the outstanding playing.

The *Fifth* and last of Parry's symphonies is in four linked movements, terser in argument than the previous two in the series and often tougher, though still with Brahmsian echoes. After the minor-key rigours of the first movement, *Stress*, the other three movements are comparably subtitled *Love*, *Play* and *Now*, with the Scherzo bringing echoes of Berlioz, and the optimistic finale opening with a Wagnerian horn-call.

(i) *Blest Pair of Sirens*; *I was Glad* (anthems); (ii) *Invocation to Music (An Ode in Honour of Henry Purcell)*; (iii) *The Lotus-Eaters*; (iv) *The Soul's Ransom*

Ⓑ Chan. 241-31 2-for-1 (2). (i) L. Symphony Ch., LSO, Hickox; (ii) Dawson, Davies, Rayner Cook; (iii–iv) Jones; (iv) Wilson-Johnson; (ii–iv) LPO Ch., LPO, Bamert

Here is an outstanding collection of some of Parry's finest choral music, with two of his most popular anthems, admirably conducted by Richard Hickox, used on the second disc to frame what is perhaps his most influential and powerful work, the *Invocation to Music*, a superb setting of Robert Bridges's *Ode in Honour of Purcell*. Parry's inspiration was at its peak, and the flowing, richly melodic lyrical style was to anticipate the Elgar of the *Coronation Ode* and even *Gerontius*. The soloists here are splendid, with the passionate central soprano and tenor duet, *Love to Love calleth*, followed by the magnificent bass *Dirge*, and the very Elgarian chorus, *Man, born of desire*, later to be capped by the glorious closing apotheosis, *Thou, O Queen of sinless grace*, which Matthias Bamert moves on arrestingly to its final climax.

The first disc pairs *The Lotus-Eaters*, a setting for soprano, chorus and orchestra of eight stanzas from Tennyson's choric song of that name, with *The Soul's Ransom*. Subtitled *Sinfonia Sacra*, and using biblical texts, with its sequence of solos and choruses it forms a broadly symphonic four-movement structure (lasting around 45 minutes) with references back not only to Brahms and the nineteenth century but to much earlier choral composers, notably Schütz. Della Jones is the characterful soloist in both works, to be joined by David Wilson-Johnson in the latter piece. The singing throughout is first class, warmly sympathetic, as is the orchestral playing, and Matthias Bamert is in his element in this repertoire, as is the Chandos recording team.

The Chivalry of the Sea

Ⓜ Dutton CDLX 7172. BBC Ch. & SO, Lloyd-Jones (with **KELLY**: *Elegy 'In Memoriam Rupert Brooke'*. **ELKINGTON**: *Out of the Mist*) – **ELGAR**: *The Spirit of England*. **GURNEY**: *War Elegy*

Parry wrote this cantata in 1916 to commemorate the loss of HMS *Invincible* when she exploded with many victims at the Battle of Jutland. The piece, which has many fine qualities, is saddled with a very poor poem, full of oddly archaic language, by the then Poet Laureate, Robert Bridges. Nonetheless, what matters is the quality of Parry's music, not just elegiac but including vigorous passages and one sequence in sea-shanty rhythm. It comes on a fascinating disc, offering first recordings of five war-inspired works.

PÄRT, Arvo (born 1935)

Cantus in Memory of Benjamin Britten; Festina lente (for string orchestra & harp); Fratres; Summa (for string orchestra)
Telarc CD 80387. Manning, Springuel, Gleizes, I Fiamminghi, Werthen

For all the repetitions involved in Pärt's minimalist progressions there are no more hypnotic examples of his curiously compelling, ritualistic writing than this sequence of six settings of a very simple monastic chorale which he calls *Fratres*. We hear it first slowly swelling up from a *piano-pianissimo* on strings, with unobtrusive decorative percussion, then sink away again. Then follow variants featuring first a solo violin, then for a carefully blended wind octet, for eight cellos used in their higher register, then returning to a string group and quickening to achieve the flavour of an elegant baroque dance, further adapted to the more economical texture of a string quartet, and finally rustling on the cello with the piano tolling a bell-like accompaniment until a closing climax builds and abates. The Britten tribute and *Festina lente for strings and harp ad libitum* are used as interludes. The playing here has great atmosphere and concentration, while Telarc's glowing sound adds to the sensuous playing beauty.

PAVAROTTI, Luciano (tenor)

'The Great Decca Recordings': Arias from: **PUCCINI**: *La bohème* (with BPO, Karajan); *Tosca* (with Nat. PO, Rescigno); *Turandot* (with LPO, Mehta). **DONIZETTI**: *L'elisir d'amore* (with ECO, Bonynge); *La favorita* (with Teatro Comunale di Bologna O, Bonynge); *La Fille du régiment* (with ROHCG O, Bonynge). **R. STRAUSS**: *Der Rosenkavalier* (with VPO, Solti). **BIZET**: *Carmen*. **GOUNOD**: *Faust* (with V. Volksoper O, Magiera). **BELLINI**: *I Puritani* (with LSO, Bonynge). **VERDI**: *Aida* (with V. Volkesoper O, Magiera); *Requiem* (with VPO, Solti); *Rigoletto* (with LSO, Bonynge); *Il trovatore* (with Nat. PO, Bonynge). **LEONCAVALLO**: *Pagliacci* (with Nat. PO, Patanè). **PONCHIELLI**: *La Gioconda* (with New Philh. O, Magiera). Songs: **LEONCAVALLO**: *Mattinata* (with Philh. O, Gamba). **BELLINI**: *Vanne, o rosa fortunate*. **ROSSINI**: *La danza* (with Teatro Comunale di Bologna O, Bonynge). **CURTIS**: *Torna a Surriento* (with Nat. PO, Bonynge). **FRANCK**: *Panis angelicus*. **SCHUBERT**: *Ave Maria* (with Nat. PO, Adler). **DENZA**: *Funiculì Funiculà* (with Teatro Comunale di Bologna O, Guadagno)
Ⓑ Decca (ADD) 476 7148 (2)

An excellent anthology, originally released to coincide with the *Gramophone* 'Artist of the Year' award, which Pavarotti received in 1991. Included are items from Pavarotti's vintage period with Bonynge and Sutherland: *La Fille du régiment* with those astonishing high Cs (nine of them!) thrills as always and in his equally successful role in *L'elisir d'amore*, *Una furtiva lagrima* does not descend into sentimentality as it so often does. His ability to sing a beautiful *legato* line is well displayed in the *I Puritani* number, while all the show-stoppers – *La donna è mobile* and the like – are unlikely to disappoint (his splendid *Nessun dorma* must now be opera's most famous recording). The Puccini and Verdi items provide more meaty weight and contrast with the lighter, popular numbers, which include such little gems as Rossini's *La danza*, Leoncavallo's *Mattinata* and the irrepressible *Funiculì Funiculà*. With warm and vivid Decca sound, and texts and translations, it all adds up to a very attractive programme.

'Pavarotti's 30th Anniversary Concert' (1991) (with June Anderson, Piero Cappuccilli, Paolo Coni, Enzo Dara, Giovanni Furlanetto, Raina Kabaivanska, Patrizia Pace, Giuseppe Sabbatini, Shirley Verrett, O del Teatro Communale di Bologna, Leone Magiera or Maurizio Benini): Excerpts from: **PUCCINI**: *Tosca* (with Kabaivanska); *La Bohème* (with Sabbatini, Cappuccilli). **MOZART**: *Don Giovanni* (with Furlanetto, Pace). **DONIZETTI**: *L'elisir d'amore* (with Dara, Pace). *La favorita* (with Coni, Verrett); *Lucia di Lammermoor* (with Anderson and others).

CILEA: L'Arlesiana. **VERDI**: *Il trovatore* (with Verrett); *La forza del destino* (with Cappuccilli); *La traviata* (with everyone)
Decca DVD 071 140-9

Pavarotti and James Levine (piano) *in Recital* (1992) (DVD version (Director: Brian Large) bonus: '*Pavarotti and the Italian Tenor*', with Leone Magiera, piano): Arias from: **MOZART**: *Così fan tutte*. **VERDI**: *I Lombardi*. **MASSENET**: *Werther*. **FLOTOW**: *Martha*. **PUCCINI**: *Tosca*; *Turandot*. Songs by **ROSSINI**; **BELLINI**; **RESPIGHI**; **MASCAGNI**; **SIBELLA**; **DENZA**; **TOSTI**
Decca DVD 074 3071

'**Pavarotti in Central Park**' (26 June 1993, with NYPO (members), Leone Magiera): Excerpts from: **VERDI**: *Luisa Miller* (including *Overture*); *I vespri siciliani: Overture*. *La traviata: Prelude to Act III*. **DONIZETTI**: *Lucia di Lammermoor*. **MASSENET**: *Werther*. **CILEA**: *L'Arlesiana*. **PUCCINI**: *Tosca*; *Turandot*. Songs by **LEONCAVALLO**; **MASCAGNI**; **DI LAZZARO**; **SIBELLA**; **DENZA**; **DE CRESCENZO**; **DE CURTIS**; **DI CAPUA**. **STRAYHORN**: *Take the A Train*. **TRAD.**: *I can go to God in prayer*. **ELLINGTON**: *It don't mean a thing if it ain't got that swing* (both with Harlem Boys' Ch.). Also: **MERCADANTE**: *Flute Concerto in E min.: Rondo russo*. **BIZET/BORNE**: *Fantasia on 'Carmen'* (with Andrea Griminelli, flute)
Decca DVD 071 180-9

Pavarotti in Three Concerts (complete, DVD collection)
Decca DVD 074 3221

Pavarotti made his stage début at the Teatro Municipale, in the town of Reggio Emilia, in a performance of *La Bohème*. He had a star-studded cast with him on 29 April 1991 to celebrate the 30th anniversary of that first appearance, and there is plenty to enjoy here. Pavarotti himself sets the adrenalin running by opening with *Recondita armonia*, and the *Tosca* duet which follows with Raina Kabaivanska retains the passionate atmosphere. If Mozart's *Là ci darem* (Furlanetto and Pace) then falls a little flat, both these artists show their paces later, Patrizia Pace with Enzo Dara in the duet from *L'elisir d'amore* and Furlanetto in the stirring *Lucia di Lammermoor* sextet.

One of the slight snags with a concert like this is the outsize personality of Pavarotti himself, but he does not dwarf Piero Cappuccilli in the duet from *La forza del destino*, or the dark mezzo of Shirley Verrett in the famous *Ai nostri monti* from *Il trovatore*. For a final encore the whole cast join in to sing the exhilarating opening scene of *La traviata*, concluding a very happy occasion.

One does not think of Pavarotti as a recitalist in songs with piano, and here he acknowledges that by including several popular arias, which are very well received by the audience. He is not a Mozartian stylist, but he sings the aria from *Così* pleasingly enough; but one of the highlights of the programme is a warm-hearted *M'appari* from Flotow's *Martha*. Predictably at home in Bellini and Rossini, Pavarotti then surprises with his imaginative response to the three well-chosen Respighi items, especially the engaging *Pioggia*. Sibella's *La Girometta* (the name of a young girl) is another hit with the audience. On the whole this is enjoyable because of the strength of Pavarotti's personality and the way he conveys his enjoyment. Needless to say James Levine accompanies flawlessly. But many items are short and the vociferous applause becomes a problem. In the bonus section 'Pavarotti and the Italian Tenor', he talks and illustrates the background of singing in Italy and then introduces some of his celebrity predecessors with the help of old movie clips and photos, and the silent film of Caruso miming the *Prologue* to *Pagliacci* to his 78-r.p.m. record is rather effective.

Pavarotti gave his concert in New York's Central Park in 1993 to an audience of half a million people. He is well up to form in the usual favourites and, as always, has a few novelties, with the popular numbers featuring the excellent Harlem Boys' Choir. Interestingly, he repeats some of the successes of his New York recital, notably Sibella's *La Girometta*, Denza's *Occhi di fata* and Mascagni's *Serenata*, and his encores include *Pourquoi me réveiller* from Massenet's *Werther* and Di Capua's *O sole mio*, besides the usual three Puccini arias, *Recondita Armonia*, *E lucevan le stelle* (from *Tosca*) and of course *Nessun dorma*, which he can sing marvellously ten times out of ten.

PEARS, Peter (tenor)

'Anniversary Tribute': **BRITTEN**: Excerpts from: *Albert Herring* (with ECO, composer); *Billy Budd* (with LSO, composer); *Death in Venice* (with ECO, Bedford); *A Midsummer Night's Dream* (with Veasey, LSO, composer); *Owen Wingrave* (with Harper, Baker, Fisher, Douglas, Luxon, Vyvyan , Shirley-Quirk, ECO, composer); *Peter Grimes* (with Studholme, Kells, Nilsson, Pease, Claire Watson, Jean Watson, Evans, Keene, Kelly, Ch. & ROHCG O, composer); *The Rape of Lucretia* (with ECO, composer); *The Turn of the Screw* (with Hemmings, Mandikian, Dyer, Vyvyan, Cross, E. Op. Group O, composer; *War Requiem* (with Vishnevskaya, Bach Ch., Melos Ens., L. Symphony Ch. & LSO, composer). *Canticle II: Abraham and Isaac* (with Proctor, composer (piano)); *Canticle V: The Death of St Narcissus* (with Ellis (harp)); *Holy Sonnets of John Donne, Op. 35*; *Sechs Hölderlin-Fragments, Op. 61*; *Seven Sonnets of Michelangelo* (with composer (piano)); *Serenade for Tenor, Horn & Strings* (with Brain, Boyd Neel O, composer). Britten Folksong settings: *The foggy, foggy dew*; *A brisk young widow*; *O Waly, Waly*; *Le roi s'en va-t'en chasse*; *The ploughboy*. **IRELAND**: *The Land of Lost Content*;

The Trellis. **BRIDGE**: *'Tis but a week; Goldenhair; When you are old; So perverse; Journey's end*. **IRELAND**: *Love and Friendship; Friendship in Misfortune; The One Hope*. **RAINIER**: *Cycle for Declamation*. **SCHUBERT**: *Ganymed*. Excerpts from: *Winterreise; Die Schöne Müllerin*. **SCHUMANN**: *Dichterliebe* (with Britten (piano)). **DOWLAND**: *In darkness let me dwell; I saw my lady weep*. **ROSSETER**: *What then is love but mourning*. **PILKINGTON**: *Rest, sweet nymphs*. **MORLEY**: *It was a lover and his lass* (with Bream (lute)). Excerpts from: **HANDEL**: *Acis and Galatea* (with Philomusica of L., Boult). **PURCELL**: *The Fairy Queen* (with ECO, composer). **SCHÜTZ**: *Matthäus-Passion* (with Luxon, Shirley-Quirk, Dickinson, Heinrich-Schütz-Chor, Norrington). **BACH**: *Christmas Oratorio; Matthäus-Passion* (with Stuttgart CO, Münchinger); *Mass in B min.* (with Bav. RSO, Jochum). *St John Passion* (with Shirley-Quirk, Howells, Wandsworth Boys' Ch., ECO, Britten). **ELGAR**: *The Dream of Gerontius* (with King's College, Cambridge, Ch., L. Symphony Ch., LSO, Britten). **SCHUMANN**: *Szenen aus Goethes Faust* (with Hill, Cable, Elwes, Jenkins, Noble, Aldeburgh Festival Singers, ECO, Britten). **BERLIOZ**: *L'Enfance du Christ* (with St Anthony Singers, Goldsbrough O, C. Davis). **LUTOSLAWSKI**: *Paroles tissées* (with L. Sinf., composer). **VAUGHAN WILLIAMS**: *On Wenlock Edge* (with Britten (piano), Zorian Qt). **TIPPETT**: *Boyhood's End; The Heart's Assurance* (with Noel Mewton-Wood (piano)); *Songs for Ariel* (with Britten (piano)). **DELIUS**: *To Daffodils*. **MOERAN**: *The Merry Month of May*. **VAN DIEREN**: *Dream Pedlary; Take, O take those lips away*. **WARLOCK**: *Piggésnie; Along the Stream*. **GRAINGER**: *Bold William Taylor*. **BUSCH**: *Two Songs of William Blake; If thou wilt ease thine heart; Come, O come, my life's delight* (with Tunnard (piano)). **A. BUSH**: *Voices of the Prophets* (with composer (piano)).
Decca mono/stereo 478 2345 (6)

Peter Pears was one of the most important and influential tenors of the last century, especially through his relationship with the composer, Benjamin Britten. He recorded a vast range of repertoire, and this valuable collection, released in time for the centenary of the singer's birth, demonstrates just how wide his repertoire was. Of course, his role as Britten's muse for over thirty years not only shaped the works themselves, but also their performance. With Britten, they recorded all his major works for Decca and of course they are all classic, definitive performances. It must have been a challenge what to include and what not to include from this vast source, and it is a tribute to Decca's Raymond MacGill that this set has been planned so intelligently. Extracts from most of Britten's operas are included here, as well as an extract from the legendary recording of the *War Requiem*, and also the early recording of the *Serenade for Tenor, Horn and Strings*, clearly dubbed from an LP, but a performance fresher and even more haunting than his later remakes. In the following *Seven Sonnets of Michelangelo* and *The Holy Sonnets of John Donne*, Pears presents this music with compelling intensity. Pears's voice may well not strike everyone as the most beautiful of sounds, but so astute is his characterization and formidable his musical intelligence that he is able to portray the comic flavour of *Albert Herring* with as much conviction as the haunting melancholy of *Death in Venice*. Even late in his recording career, in such items as *Canticle V* (recorded in 1976), there is something compelling in his delivery, even if it can't match the freshness of the earlier recordings. Tippett was one of the many other twentieth-century composers Pears became associated with, and here he offers a compelling version of his *Boyhood's End* and *The Heart's Assurance*. Pears's account of Vaughan Williams's *On Wenlock Edge* is masterful (also dubbed from an LP recording, dating from 1945). Richard Rodney Bennett's *Tom O'Bedlam's Song*, written especially for Pears, receives a superb performance and is one of the many highlights found in this collection. Britten's interest in folksong resulted in some very Britten-esque arrangements of folk music, which may not be every one's cup of tea, but the examples included here are all very distinctive and enjoyable. However, all lovers of English song will find much to relish here, with items such as Ireland's *The Trellis* and the cycle, *The Land of Lost Content*, especially beautiful; but the songs of Frank Bridge and Peter Warlock, Delius and Moeran are no less compelling. Pears's superb insight into musical expression made him a natural singer of Lieder, and excerpts from his classic recordings of Schubert and Schumann songs are included, as well as a première release of Schubert's *Ganymed*. Indeed, there are many rarities sprinkled throughout this collection, many appearing on CD for the first time. Rainier's *Cycle for Declamation* is hardly something one comes across every day, but its inclusion here is welcome. Another joy of this set is the superb accompaniments of Benjamin Britten; but in a selection of baroque songs, by Dowland, Rosseter, Pilkington and Morley, Julian Bream accompanies most sensitively on the lute, adding another very appealing colour to this collection. Pears sings this repertoire most beautifully and they are among the highlights of this set. In these large-scale readings (by today's standards) of Bach and Purcell, Pears brings his unique insight into these famous works and makes one long to hear the complete performance. All in all, a superb tribute to one of the most characterful and important singers of the twentieth century.

PENDERECKI, Kzysztof (born 1933)

(i) *Anaklasis*; (ii-iii) *Capriccio for Violin & Orchestra*; (iii-iv) *Cello Concerto*; (iii) *De natura sonoris I & II*; *The Dream of Jacob*; *Emanationen for 2 String Orchestras*; *Fonogrammi*; (iii; v) *Partita for Harpsichord & Orchestra*; (iii) *Threnody for the Victims of Hiroshima*; (i) *Symphony*; (iii–vi) *Canticum canticorum Salomonis*

ⓑ EMI Gemini (ADD) 3 81508-2 (2). (i) LSO; (ii) Wilkomirska; (iii) Polish Nat. RSO; (iv) Palm; (v) Blumenthal; (vi) Kraków Philh. Ch.; all cond. composer

For those who admire such athematic music this inexpensive anthology, in authoritative performances under the composer's own direction, makes a splendid introduction to Penderecki's music. *Anaklasis* is an inventive piece for strings and percussion, and *De natura sonoris* is also brilliant in its use of contrasts. Wilkomirska proves a superb soloist in the *Capriccio* and so does Palm in the *Cello Concerto*. The beautiful and touching *Threnody for 52 Strings* is the composer's best-known piece, and it is here given a magnificent performance. *The Dream of Jacob* of 1974 is as inventive as the rest, but sparer. Penderecki's music relies for its appeal on the resourceful use of sonorities and his sound-world is undoubtedly imaginative, albeit limited. The choral work is a setting of a text from the *Song of Solomon* for large orchestra and sixteen solo voices. But the *Symphony* is the most ambitious work here. It was commissioned by a British engineering firm and first performed in Canterbury Cathedral. That setting influences the range of sumptuous orchestral colours devised by the composer, though you could argue that this work is a series of brilliant orchestral effects rather than a symphonic argument. However, with such a committed performance it is certainly memorable. The 1970s recordings are excellent and this EMI Gemini is an undoubted bargain.

Symphony 7 (Seven Gates of Jerusalem)

ⓑ Naxos 8.557766. Pasichniyk, Mikolaj, Marciniec, Tesarowicz, Carmei, Warsaw Nat. Ch. & PO, Wit

Only after the first performance of this magnificent work, designed to celebrate the third millennium of the city of Jerusalem, did Penderecki decide to include it among his symphonies. It is a massive cantata in seven movements, setting Psalms in Hebrew, with Penderecki handling colossal forces with thrilling mastery. He was right to underline the symphonic element in this way, as the sequence of movements brings together the choral and symphonic elements in his work very effectively. The figure '7' is used obsessively, not least in seven-note themes.

The very opening is shattering in its impact, setting Psalm 48, while the longest of the seven movements is the fifth, *Lauda Zion*, setting Psalm 147, a Scherzo introduced by timpani and percussion. With striking and immediately attractive themes it brings a colossal climax as powerful as anything Penderecki has written. At its peak it is interrupted by the sixth movement, setting a declamation of words from the Book of Ezekiel, representing the word of God, reinforced by a distinctive bass trumpet solo. The seventh movement then rounds the work off with a triumphant setting of Psalm 48. Performances under Antoni Wit are superb, strong and intense, with an excellent chorus and team of soloists.

PERGOLESI, Giovanni Battista (1710-36)

'Pergolesi Year' *Bicentenary Collection* (as below; complete)
DG 477 8464 (3). Swiss Radio/TV Ch., O Mozart, Abbado

(i) *Salve Regina in C min.*; (ii) *Stabat Mater*; (iii) *Violin Concerto in B flat*
DG 477 8077. (i) Kleiter; (ii) Harnisch, Mingardo; (iii) Carmignola; O Mozart, Abbado

(i-ii) *Missa S. Emido* ; (i) *La conversione e morte di San Guglielmo
duca d'Aquitania: E dove che le luci . . . Manca la guida al piè*;
(iii) *Laudate pueri Dominum*; (ii) *Salve Regina in F min.*
DG 477 8463. (i) Cangemi; (ii) Mingardo; (iii) Harnisch, Romano; Swiss Radio/TV Ch.,
   O Mozart, Abbado

(i) *Chi non ode e chi non vede*; (ii-iii) *Confitebor tibi, Domine*; (i) *Dixit
Dominus*; (ii) *Salve Regina in A min.*
DG 477 8465. (i) Harnisch; (ii) Kleiter; (iii) Bove; Swiss Radio/TV Ch., O Mozart, Abbado

For his 'Pergolesi Year' sequence with a superb team of soloists, the Swiss
Radio Chorus and the splendid Bologna Orchestra Mozart, Abbado has chosen
the richest of Pergolesi's sacred works to make one realize that the composer
wrote some of the greatest music of its kind in the early eighteenth century.
The first CD centres on the famous *Stabat Mater*, and Abbado's account
(his second recording) with splendid soloists (the fresh-voiced Rachel Harnisch and Sara Mingardo with her dark, sonorous timbre) brings great intensity
and ardour to this piece, and he secures alive playing with something of a
period-instrument character from the modern-instrument orchestra – this
without diminishing religious sentiment. As a bonus he offers Pergolesi's only
Violin Concerto (in B flat), an engaging work, splendidly played by Giuliano
Carmignola.

   The second collection opens with the most ambitious work included in the
series, the *Missa S. Emidio*, for soloists, two five-part choirs and two orchestras, in which Pergolesi sets only the *Kyrie eleison* and *Gloria*, yet which offers
30 minutes of superbly varied music in 12 memorable sections, alternating
expressive antiphonal passages, rich solos and imitative writing, with beautiful solos from Veronica Cangemi and Sara Mingardo with her remarkably
resonant lower register. Mingardo follows up with the *Salve Regina in F minor*,
a performance of deep feeling. The recitative and aria, *Manca la guida*, is an
early work, taken from a religious opera describing the spiritual battle between
Good and Evil, which Cangemi sings with an equally expressive response, and
the collection ends with the spectacular *Laudate pueri Dominum* with its
resounding trumpets and horns and the bright-voiced soprano line alternating
with the almost Handelian chorus and the work ending with a lively fugato to
match the opening.

   One of the highlights of the third collection is Harnisch's account of the aria
of unrequited love, *Chi non ode e chi non vede*, with its changing tempi and

expressive anguish ('Merciless Cupid you should either ease my distress or soften her severity'), while Julia Kleiter and Rosa Bove are hardly less memorable in the rare setting of Psalm 110, *Confitebor tibi Domine*, with its arresting choral opening, while the chorus is even more eloquent in the closing *Gloria Patri* and *Sicut erat*. Kleiter returns for the *A minor Salve Regina*, and the spectacular *Dixit Dominus* makes a splendid finale. This was written for two choruses of similar size and two orchestras, one of strings alone, the second with two each of oboes, flutes, horns and trumpets added. With Rachel Harnisch returning as celestial soloist, the result has great variety and power. These three CDs come either separately or in a boxed set and are very recommendable indeed.

Stabat Mater (DVD version)

EMI DVD 5 99404 9. Frittoli, Antonacci, Filharmonica della Scala, Muti (DVD Producer: Carlo Assalini)

Stabat Mater (CD version)

Naïve OP 30441. Bertagnolli, Mingardo, Concerto Italiano, Alessandrini

Muti's dedicated performance has two first-class soloists in Barbara Frittoli and Anna Caterina Antonacci, who make a fine team, both in their expressive vocal interchanges and in matching their vibratos. Muti's tempi are spacious, and the use of modern instruments and the resonant acoustic ensure a warm and beautiful sound from the comparatively modest-sized orchestral group, while the soloists are clearly focused and well balanced in relation to the overall visual imagery. This moving performance is greatly enhanced by the backcloth of the beautiful cupola frescoes of Gaudenzio Ferrari on which the camera frequently dwells with poignant effect to illustrate the Crucifixion and the poignant image of Mary standing at the foot of the Cross. Subtitles are available if required, and there is also an option to follow the score, with the visual images forming a shadowy backcloth. Bonuses include a long and intellectual exposition of the historical development of Italian music by Muti, and a whimsical commentary, 'Pergolesi and his Double', confirming that a great deal of the music attributed to Pergolesi was written by others hoping to take advantage of his reputation. But the *Stabat Mater* is authentic and is splendidly performed here.

Both the soprano, Gemma Bertagnolli, and the contralto, Sara Mingardo (with her remarkably resonant lower register), have extraordinarily colourful voices, which blend beautifully at the work's sustained opening, but which only display their full richness in their solos, notably *Cujus animam gementem* and *Fac, ut portem Christi mortem*. This is a totally Italianate performance of both high drama and moving pathos. The closing *Quando corpus morietur*, in which both singers join in sustained legato, is very moving indeed, followed by a passionately final affirmation of faith. Alessandrini's instrumental support could not be more telling, and the recording is made in an ideal acoustic.

PEROTINUS, Magister (c. 1160–1225)

Organa: *Alleluya, Nativitas*; *Sederunt principes*
Lyrichord (ADD) LEMS 8002. Oberlin, Bressler, Perry, Barab (with **LEONIN**: Organa)

Perotinus extended the simple polyphony of Leonin from two to three and four
parts, and the ear is very aware of the intervals which characterize the organum: unison, octave, fourths and fifths. The music is more florid, freer than
the coupled works, written several decades before. The performances here are
totally compelling and the recording excellent.

PIATIGORSKY, Gregor (cello)

CHOPIN: *Sonata in G min., Op. 65* (with Rudolf Firkušný (piano)).
MENDELSSOHN: *Sonata 2 in D, Op. 58*; **STRAUSS**: *Sonata
in F, Op. 6* (both with Leonard Pennario (piano))
Testament SBT 1419

Gregor Piatigorsky was a legendary cellist whose artistry and virtuosity (in that
order) were inspiring. In the 1930s he was slightly overshadowed by Casals,
and in the post-war years he had Fournier, Tortelier and Rostropovich clam-
ouring for attention. The three performances on this Testament release are
masterly in every way: elevated in feeling and effortless in their virtuosity. The
Chopin with Rudolf Firkušný, recorded in the mid-1960s by RCA, is arguably
the finest recorded account (challenged only by the 1980 Rostropovich-Arger-
ich, currently withdrawn), while the Mendelssohn and Strauss with Pennario
are hardly less commanding.

PIERNÉ, Gabriel (1863–1937)

(i) *Andante*; *Berceuse*; *Canzonetta*; *Chamber Sonata*; *La Danseuse
espagnole*; *Fantaisie impromptu*; *Violin Sonata*; (ii) *Giration* (ballet);
Sérénade; *Pastorale variée*; (ii–iii) *Nuit divine*; (ii) *Pastorale for Wind
Quintet*; *Pièce for Oboe & Piano*; *Piano Quintet*; *Préludio e
fughetta*; *Solo de concert*
Timpani 2C 1110 (2). (i) Koch, Ivaldi; (ii) Instrumental Soloists of Luxembourg PO, Ivaldi;
    (iii) with Rémy Franck (narrator)

Those readers remembering the 78-r.p.m. era may recall Gabriel Pierné's once
famous novelty, the *Parade of the Little Lead Soldiers*. He made his initial reputation with orchestral morceaux of this kind. With the arrival of the *Violin*

Sonata at the turn of the century he began to write music of more depth. It is a work of feeling, the lyrical inspiration of the first movement is appealing, and the dreamy, folksy *Andante tranquillo* is hardly less endearing. Influences of Pierné's mentor, César Franck, are plain. But the work is impressive on its own terms, especially when played with such warmth and conviction as it is by Philippe Koch and Christian Ivaldi, and vividly recorded. The *Piano Quintet* of 1916/17 is also strongly influenced by the comparable Franck work. The performers play throughout with great conviction. However, with the wind music on the second disc, the ear is endlessly diverted. The pieces for plangent oboe, or bubbling bassoon (with piano) are delightful, as is the *Pastorale variée* for wind septet (including trumpet), while the *Giration* ballet (of 1933) is whimsically inventive and engagingly scored. These works are all played with pleasing elegance and are beautifully recorded. At times one is reminded of the music of Françaix. However, the last, rather sentimental, item on the disc, *Nuit divine*, includes the recitation of a poem by d'Albert Samain for which no translation is provided! Otherwise presentation and documentation are impeccable.

PIZZETTI, Ildebrando (1880–1968)

Clitennestra: Preludio. Concerto dell'estate; 3 Symphonic Preludes (from 'L'Edipo Re'). La Festa delle Panatenee: 3 Pezzi per orchestra
ⓑ Naxos 8.572013. Thessaloniki State SO, Myron Michailidis

The *Concerto dell'estate* has not been recorded since the days of LP, when it was very successfully recorded by Lamberto Gardelli for Decca. It is a work of inventive skill and resource, and has no lack of charm, as have its companions on this disc. The performances from Thessalonika under Myron Michailidis are good without being top-drawer.

3 Symphonic Preludes from 'L'Edipo Re' di Sofocle; La Pisanella; Preludio a un altro giorno; Rondò veneziano
ⓑ Hyp. CDH 55329. BBC Scottish SO, Vänskä

After a long period of neglect, Pizzetti's music is making something of a cautious comeback. This well-filled programme makes an excellent introduction to Pizzetti. It is natural that he should be overshadowed by his contemporary, Respighi, who has so rich and colourful a palette. *La Pisanella* is a delight and was one of his few works to make it into the 78-r.p.m. catalogue. But Pizzetti is also a master of the orchestra and richly inventive. Osmo Vänskä conducts with authority and flair, and obviously believes in these all too rarely performed scores. The *Rondò veneziano* of 1929 was first performed by Toscanini; the three *Preludes* from the opera *L'Edipo Re di Sofocle* are full of interest, and *La pisanella* is a sunny and glorious work. Osmo Vänskä plays all these pieces with appropriate feeling, but the string sound lacks real body and richness, particularly at the bass end of the spectrum.

Messa di requiem; De profundis
Hyp. CDA 67017. Westminster Cathedral Ch., O'Donnell – **MARTIN**: *Mass for Double Choir*, etc.

Pizzetti's 'serene and lyrical *Requiem*' (as his biographer, Guido Gatti, puts it) is a work of surpassing beauty which will be a revelation to those who have not encountered it before, particularly in this fervent and inspired performance. It comes with the *De profundis* he composed in 1937 to mark the healing of his breach with Malipiero. This Westminster Cathedral version is simply sublime and a must for anyone who loves or cares about choral music.

Assassinio nella cattedrale (Murder in the Cathedral) (complete, DVD version)
Decca DVD 0743253. Raimondi, Cordella, Valleggi, Antonio de Gobbi, Elia Fabbian, Marrocu, Zaramella, Soloists & Ch. of Conservatorio Piccinni di Bari, Bari Province SO, Piergiorgio Morandi

Assassinio nella cattedrale is the only Pizzetti opera ever to have been professionally staged in England. It is based on Alberto Castelli's translation of T. S. Eliot's play, which Pizzetti shortened and adapted: he omits the knights' justification of the murder of the archbishop in Eliot's epilogue. The Sadler's Wells production in 1962 was not well received: Pizzetti's restraint and nobility were ill attuned to the psyche of that much-overrated decade. A 1960 mono set with Karajan and the Vienna Opera with no less a Becket than Hans Hotter was issued on two DG CDs but quickly disappeared.

This performance, recorded in the Basilica di San Nicola in Bari, should do much to put this wonderful score back on the map. Raimondi has tremendous presence as the Archbishop and is in magnificent voice (he must now be approaching 70) and acts majestically. The remainder of the cast is hardly less inspired, and the production is visually sumptuous. The opera is short: its First Act is just over 40 minutes long while the *Intermezzo* (Becket's Christmas morning sermon in 1190) and the Second Act together run to under 50. But it is totally compelling, musically and dramatically. The musical flow is dignified and stately, as befits the subject-matter, and the orchestral palette is subtle in its colouring. There are moments when its melodic lines suggest that the lessons of Mussorgsky and *Pelléas* have been observed, as has late Verdi, and the choral writing has an almost symphonic sweep. *Assassinio nella cattedrale* has been absurdly neglected on the stage (as indeed has Pizzetti generally) but this superbly paced and intensely felt reading brings home the beauty and nobility of this score. Recommended with enthusiasm.

PONCHIELLI, Amilcare (1834–86)

La Gioconda (complete, CD version)
Ⓜ EMI (ADD) 5 56291-2 (3). Callas, Cossotto, Ferraro, Vinco, Cappuccilli, Companeez, La Scala, Milan, Ch. & O, Votto

Maria Callas gave one of her most vibrant, most compelling, most totally inspired performances on record in the title-role of *La Gioconda*, with flaws very much subdued. The challenge she presented to those around her is reflected in the soloists – Cossotto and Cappuccilli both at the beginning of distinguished careers – as well as the distinctive tenor Ferraro and the conductor Votto, who has never done anything finer on record. The recording still sounds well, though it dates from 1959. This is a mid-priced set with a synopsis.

POULENC, Francis (1899–1963)

'**Francis Poulenc and Friends**': (i) *Double Piano Concerto in D min.*; (ii) *Concerto in G min. for Organ, Timpani & Strings*; (iii) *Dialogues des Carmélites*; *La voix humaine*; *Les Mamelles de Tirésias*; *La Courte Paille*; (iv) *Flute Sonata*; (v) *Pastourelle*; *Toccata*; (vi) *3 Mouvements perpétuels*; (vii) *Banalités*; *Chansons villageoises*; *Chansons gaillardes*; (viii) *Sarabande*
EMI DVD DVB 3102019. Composer, with (i) Février, O Nat. de l'ORTF, Prêtre; (ii) Grunewald, Philh. O de l'ORTF, Prêtre; (iii) Duval; (iv) Rampal, Veyron-Lacroix; (v) Tacchino; (vi) Février; (vii) Bacquier, Février; (viii) Gendron, Ivadli

An indispensable item for admirers of this inspiriting and life-loving composer. Much of this DVD derives from a concert in the Salle Gaveau to mark Poulenc's sixtieth birthday, where he is seen in conversation with Bernard Gavoty. (He is as entertaining a speaker as he is witty a composer.) The two *Concertos* come from 1962 and 1968 respectively, the former at about the time when these artists recorded it commercially. Poulenc's score is both witty and at times profound, though he is by no means as elegant or polished at the keyboard as, say, Britten or for that matter his partner here, Jacques Février. It is good to see and hear the delightful Denise Duval, who sings with great artistry; small wonder that Poulenc adored her so much. The picture quality is variable but acceptable and, though the camerawork in the first movement of the *D minor Concerto* is a bit fussy, it is otherwise exemplary both in the other movements and elsewhere in this compilation.

(i) *Les Animaux modèles*; (ii–iii) *Les Biches* (ballet: complete); (ii) *Bucolique*; (i; iv) *Concert champêtre* (for harpsichord & orchestra); (i; v) *Double Piano Concerto in D min.*; (vi) *2 Marches et un intermède* (for chamber orchestra);

Les Mariés de la Tour Eiffel (La Baigneuse de Trouville; Discours du général); (ii) Matelote provençale; Pastourelle; (vi) Sinfonietta; Suite française

🅑🅑 EMI (ADD/DDD) 5 69446-2 (2). Prêtre, with (i) Paris Conservatoire O; (ii) Philh. O; (iii) Amb. S.; (iv) Van der Wiele; (v) composer, Février; (vi) O de Paris

Les Biches comes here in its complete form, with the choral additions that Poulenc made optional when he came to rework the score. The music is a delight, and so too is the group of captivating short pieces, digitally recorded at the same time (1980): *Bucolique, Pastourelle* and *Matelote provençale*. High-spirited, fresh, elegant playing and sumptuous recorded sound enhance the claim of all this music. The *Suite française* is another highlight. It is well played and recorded in a pleasing, open acoustic. Poulenc himself was a pianist of limited accomplishment, but his interpretation with Jacques Février of his own skittish *Double Concerto* is infectiously jolly. In the imitation pastoral concerto for harpsichord Aimée van der Wiele is a nimble soloist, but here Prêtre's inflexibility as a conductor comes out the more, even though the finale has plenty of high spirits. The *Sinfonietta*, too, could have a lighter touch. *Les Animaux modèles* is based on the fables of La Fontaine, with a prelude and postlude, but here the recording is rather lacking in bloom, and the *Deux marches* are also a trifle over-bright. Still, these are all relatively minor quibbles and the two-CD set is tempting for the complete *Les Biches* alone. With nearly 156 minutes' playing time, this pair of CDs is well worth exploring.

Les Biches (ballet: suite)
Chan. 9023. Ulster O, Y. P. Tortelier **MILHAUD**; *Le Bœuf; La Création*) - **IBERT**: *Divertissement*

Yan Pascal Tortelier and the Ulster Orchestra give an entirely winning account of Poulenc's ballet suite. Here the opening has delightfully keen rhythmic wit, and the playing is equally polished and crisply articulated in the gay *Rag-Mazurka* and infectious finale. The lovely *Adagietto* is introduced with tender delicacy, yet reaches a suitably plangent climax. Top-drawer Chandos sound and splendid couplings ensure the overall success of this admirable compilation.

(i–ii) *Clarinet Sonata*; (i; iii) *Elégie for Horn & Piano*; (i; iv) *Flute Sonata*; (i; v) *Oboe Sonata*; (i–vi) *Sextet for Piano, Flute, Oboe, Clarinet, Bassoon & Horn*; (i; v–vi) *Trio for Piano, Oboe & Bassoon*; (i; vii) *Violin Sonata*; (i; viii) Piano Duet: *Le Bal masqué: Capriccio for 2 Pianos. Elégie; L'Embarquement pour Cythère; Sonata for Piano, 4 Hands: Sonata for 2 Pianos* (i) Solo Piano Music: *À l'exposition. Bourrée, au Pavilon d'Auvergne. Badinage; Eventail de Jeanne: Pastourelle. Feuillets d'album; Français d'après Claude Gervaise (16ème siècle); Homage à J. S. Bach: Valse-improvisation sur le nom de Bach. Hommage à Albert Roussel: Pièce brève sur le nom d'Albert Roussel. Humoresque*; *5 Impromptus* (revised, 1939 edition); *15 Improvisations*; *2 Intermezzi*; *Mélancolie*; *3 Mouvements perpétuels*; *Napoli*; *8 Nocturnes*; *3 Novelettes*; *3 Pastorales*; *Petites pièces enfantines: 6 Villageoises*. *3 Pièces*; *Presto in B flat*; *3 Promenades*; *Les Soirées de Nazelles*; *Suite française d'après Claude Gervaise (16ème siècle)*. *Suite pour piano*; *Thème varié*; *Valse*.

Ⓑ Decca 475 7097 (5). (i) Pascal Rogé (piano), with (ii) Michel Portal (clarinet); (iii) André Cazalet (horn); (iv) Patrick Gallois (flute); (v) Maurice Bourgue (oboe); (vi) Amaury Wallez (bassoon); (vii) Chantal Juillet (violin); (viii) Jean-Philippe Collard piano)

Poulenc has the capacity to charm and enchant and, at the same time, speak to the listener. His lightness of touch and elegance often mask a vein of deeper feeling, into which he can briefly move to striking and original effect. No one is more closely attuned to Poulenc's world than Pascal Rogé, and his presence ensures the authenticity of feeling which runs through all these performances: his playing is both imaginative and inspiriting. The first disc to be issued in 1988 won the *Gramophone*'s Instrumental Award. Rogé is a far more persuasive exponent of this repertoire than any previous pianist on record, although his masterly companion, Jean-Philippe Collard, is no less superb in the music for piano duet, and the Decca recording serves them very well indeed. The music has many unexpected touches and is teeming with character. Who but Poulenc would have written a frivolous *Valse-improvisation* to celebrate the name of B-A-C-H, and he is equally felicitous in the delicious *Third Impromptu* or the gentle melancholy of the *Badinage*. The *Mouvements perpétuels* are among the composer's most seductive piano miniatures and the *Napoli Suite* also has much charm. But he is perhaps at his most touching in his suite of pieces paying a tribute to Claude Gervaise, which is thoroughly imbued with personal nostalgia.

The chamber music is hardly less appealing. The playing of Maurice Bourgue in the *Oboe Sonata* is both masterly and touching, and all these artists are on top form. The performances have a wonderful freshness and convey a real sense of delight. The *Sextet* has an irresistible charm and, whether in the melting lyrical episode in the first movement or the sparkling articulation of the finale, these artists have an unfailing elegance. The reverberance of the Salle Pleyel is a slight drawback, but the internal balance both of the players and of the recording engineers is excellent, and altogether this is an enchanting set.

Complete *Mélodies*

Ⓜ Decca 475 9085 (4). Lott, Dubosc, Kryger, Le Roux, Cachemaille, Rogé

At mid-price, this collection repackages Decca's four CDs of Poulenc songs accompanied by the ever-sensitive Pascal Rogé. For those who prefer fine modern recording, this provides consistently refined and idiomatic performances, making it an ideal alternative to the EMI collection of vintage recordings originally issued to celebrate the Poulenc Centenary. Felicity Lott is a stylist par excellence and her sympathy for and affinity with the songs of Poulenc is long-standing. Her recordings with Pascal Rogé, whose understanding of this repertoire is *sans pareil*, centre on the theme of childhood, and range from *La courte paille* – written for Denise Duval, Poulenc's favourite soprano, to sing for her young son – to the *Cinq poèmes de Max Jacob* which evoke the childhood memories of Brittany. Dame Felicity is in excellent form throughout and brings the right blend of feeling and style to everything here. *Hier*, the third of the *Trois poèmes de Louise Lalanne*, is marvellously characterized and quite haunting. Catherine Dubosc was a memorable Blanche in the *Dialogues des Carmélites* and she is thoroughly at home in the Poulenc idiom. She is perhaps less successful in varying her character in each song (her approach to very different moods tends to be a little uniform). Like her fellow artist, the baritone Gilles Cachemaille, she is rather forwardly balanced. François le Roux, a high baritone who can cope with the demanding tessitura of the songs written for the composer's friend, Pierre Bernac, takes on the major share of his disc, notably the fine cycle, *Tel jour, telle nuit*. He also sings superbly the three extra songs for *Le bestiaire*, only recently published. On the fourth CD, Gilles Cachemaille, a warmer but less versatile baritone, and Urszula Kryger provide contrast in an equally varied selection. Throughout this series Pascal Rogé is the intensely poetic accompanist.

Songs: 'C'; *Le Carafon*; *Chanson d'Orkenise*; *Fêtes galantes*; *Les gars qui vont à la fête*; *Hôtel*; *Le Reine de Cœur*

Ⓜ Decca 475 7712. Crespin, Wustman (with recital of French song) – **RAVEL**: *Shéhérazade*. **BERLIOZ**: *Les Nuits d'été*. **DEBUSSY**: *Songs*

Crespin sparkles in this repertoire and these readings are exceptionally vivid. There is bravura in the quirkily amusing *Le Carafon* ('The little water jug') and *Fêtes galantes* and *Les gars qui vont à la fête* are similarly exhilarating. Indeed, Crespin fully understands the distinctive humour of these songs as well as the whimsy in such numbers as *Hôtel* – not to forget the gorgeous vein of melancholy which runs through 'C'. All of it is utterly French in style and spirit, and Crespin understands the style completely. A superb bonus, beautifully recorded (in 1967), for her legendary Berlioz and Ravel recordings.

Dialogues des Carmélites (complete, DVD version)

Arthaus DVD 100 004. Schmidt, Fassbender, Petibon, Henry, Dale, Chœurs de l'Opéra du Rhin, Strasbourg PO, Latham-Koenig

Poulenc set great store by this opera and this DVD is a remarkably gripping and wholly convincing production which may well serve to persuade those who have not seen the light about this piece. In Anne-Sophie Schmidt it has a Blanche who looks as good as she sounds, and a cast which has no weak member. The production conveys the period to striking effect and the claustrophobic atmosphere of the nunnery. The camerawork is imaginative without ever being intrusive and the production is so well managed that the *longueurs* which normally afflict the closing scene in the opera house pass unnoticed. Of the other roles Hedwig Fassbender (Mère Marie de l'Incarnation), Patricia Petibon (Sœur Constance), Didier Henry (Le Marquis de la Force) and Laurence Dale (as the Chevalier de la Force) are exemplary both as singers and as interpreters. This production is excellent dramatically – and *looks* good. The stage director is Marthe Keller, who was the eponymous heroine of Honegger's *Jeanne d'Arc au bûcher* on DG. The Strasbourg orchestra play well for Jan Latham-Koenig and, even disregarding its compelling visual presence, it has the strongest musical claims as well. Subtitles are in English, German and Flemish.

PRAETORIUS, Michael (1571–1621)

Dances from Terpsichore

Hyp. CDA 67240. Parley of Instruments, Renaissance Violin Band, Holman

Terpsichore is a huge collection of some 300 dance tunes used by the French court dance-bands of Henri IV. They were enthusiastically assembled by the German composer, Michael Praetorius, who also harmonized them and arranged them in four to six parts; however, any selection is conjectural in the matter of orchestration. This 70-minute collection from Peter Holman and his various instrumental groups must be regarded as the most authentic and comprehensive now available. Praetorius makes it clear in the preface to *Terpsichore* that he regards these as French dances, and Holman convincingly suggests that they were intended primarily for performance on a French-style violin band, or a lute combination (a group of four lutes play together here), and that is the instrumentation that he very refreshingly offers.

PROKOFIEV, Serge (1891–1953)

Cinderella (ballet: complete)

Decca Ⓑ 455349-7 (2). Cleveland O, Ashkenazy (with Glazunor: *The Seasons*)

Cinderella, along with *Romeo and Juliet*, is one of Prokofiev's finest scores and one of the great ballets of the twentieth century. Ashkenazy gets excellent results from the Cleveland Orchestra. There are many imaginative touches in this score – as appealing, indeed, as the story itself – and the level of invention is astonishingly high. When it was transferred to CD, this recording's fine definition was enhanced and the coupled account of Glazunor's *Seasons* is equally successful, with superb playing by the RPO.

Piano Concertos 1–5
Ⓑ Double Decca (ADD) 452 588-2 (2). Ashkenazy, LSO, Previn

Ashkenazy is a commanding soloist in both the *First* and *Second Concertos*, and his virtuosity in the *First* is quite dazzling. If he is curiously wayward in the opening of the *Second*, there is no question that this too is a masterly performance. The *Third Concerto* is keen-edged and crisply articulated, and the only reservation here concerns the slow movement, which at times is uncharacteristically mannered. Ashkenazy is authoritative in No. 4 and gives an admirable account of No. 5: every detail of phrasing and articulation is very well thought out, and yet there is no want of spontaneity or any hint of calculation. Throughout, Previn and the LSO accompany sympathetically and the remastered recordings make the most of the vintage, mid-1970s, Kingsway Hall sound. Although there may be even finer recordings of individual concertos, as a complete, consistent set this remains unbeatable.

Piano Concerto 3 in C, Op. 26
Ⓜ DG 447 438-2. Argerich, BPO, Abbado - **RAVEL**: *Piano Concerto in G*, etc.

Martha Argerich made her outstanding recording of the Prokofiev *Third Concerto* in 1967, while still in her twenties. There is nothing ladylike about the playing, but it displays countless indications of sensuous, feminine perception and subtlety, and Abbado's direction underlines that from the very first, with a warmly romantic account of the ethereal opening phrase on the high violins. This is a much more individual performance than almost any other available and it brings its own special insights. The recording, always excellent, sounds even more present in its current transfer.

Violin Concerto 1 in D, Op. 19
Pentatone Surround Sound SACD PTC 5186 059. Fischer, Russian Nat. O, Kreizberg - **GLAZUNOV; KHACHATURIAN**: *Violin Concertos*

On Pentatone, the unique triptych of three warmly compelling concertos from this brilliant young German virtuoso, Julia Fischer, superbly recorded in full, bright, clear sound, could hardly be bettered. Central to her choice is her love of the Khachaturian, but her approach to the Prokofiev is just as warm. With fine shading, she takes a thoughtful, meditative view of the yearning melodies, the element in the work that, as she says, most attracts her, but her bravura playing is just as impressive.

Violin Concertos 1–2
Ⓜ Decca (ADD) 425 003-2. Chung, LSO, Previn - **STRAVINSKY**: *Violin Concerto*

Kyung-Wha Chung's performances emphasize the lyrical quality of these concertos with playing that is both warm and strong, tender and full of fantasy. Previn's accompaniments are deeply understanding, while the Decca sound has lost only a little of its fullness in the digital remastering. The Stravinsky coupling is equally stimulating.

Peter and the Wolf
ⓑⓑ Naxos mono 8.111290. Eleanor Roosevelt, Boston SO, Koussevitzky – **SIBELIUS**: *Symphony 2*

This disc offers Koussevitzky's second recording of *Peter and the Wolf*, with a former First Lady, Eleanor Roosevelt, as narrator. This account of *Peter* (whether you take to the narration or not) is supremely natural and should provide a model for young conductors. It comes with a powerful Sibelius *Second Symphony*.

Romeo and Juliet (complete ballet), *Op. 64*
ⓑ EMI (ADD) 9 67701-2 (2). LSO, Previn

There are many who would claim *Romeo and Juliet* as Prokofiev's greatest score, alongside *War and Peace*. Its boisterously violent depiction of the feud between the Montagues and the Capulets is movingly set against the delicate portrayal of Juliet herself and the poignant, bittersweet lyricism of her love for Romeo, while the work's final climax is powerfully conceived. Previn and the LSO made their recording in conjunction with live performances at the Royal Festival Hall in 1973 when their partnership was at its zenith, and the result reflects the humour and warmth which went with these live occasions. Previn's pointing of rhythm is consciously seductive, whether in the fast, jaunty numbers, or in the soaring lyricism of the love music. The Kingsway Hall recording quality is full and immediate, yet atmospheric too, and the remastering highly successful.

Symphonies 1 (Classical) in D, Op. 25; 2 in D min., Op. 40; 3 in C min., Op. 44; 4 in C, Op. 47 (original, 1930 version); 4 in C, Op. 112 (revised, 1947 version); 5 in B flat, Op. 100; 6 in E flat min., Op. 111; 7 in C sharp min., Op. 131
Ph. 475 7655 (4). LSO, Gergiev

After the symphonies of Sibelius, Shostakovich and Carl Nielsen, the seven of Prokofiev are the greatest of the twentieth century. They are heard at their finest in these performances, recorded at London's Barbican Centre in May 2008. The refinement and delight of the *Classical Symphony*, deliberately Haydnesque in its economy and exuberant high spirits, ensures its popularity and marks its blend of pastiche and originality. After the Revolution, Prokofiev settled in the West and was swept up into the atmosphere of post-war Paris and the modernism of Stravinsky. The *Second Symphony* (1924) inhabits an altogether different landscape and its first movement exhibits both a high decibel level and a degree of dissonance. It bears a passing if remote resemblance to Beethoven's *C minor*

Sonata, Op. 111, namely a sonata-form first movement followed by a theme and set of variations. Its provenance suggests a kinship to the Honegger of *Pacific 231* and *Rugby*. I [R.L. writing] first heard the piece in Charles Bruck's mono recording and was bowled over by its dynamism, ferocity and the lyricism and inventiveness of the variations. But no recording we know matches the commitment and eloquence of this newcomer.

During his Paris days Prokofiev wrestled with an opera based on Valery Bryusov's *The Fiery Angel* but he realized that its chances of production were negligible. And so he drew on it extensively for his next symphony, perhaps the darkest and most atmospheric of all his works. Koussevitzky, who commissioned and premièred it and the next two symphonies, hailed it as 'the best symphony since Tchaikovsky's *Sixth*'! The *Fourth* also has stage connections – with the ballet, *The Prodigal Son*, a twenty-minute score, well held together and full of characteristic and fetching melodic invention. (The Scherzo is taken over from the ballet unaltered and also served as a piano piece.) The work languished in neglect after the Boston performances (1930). Later, and long after his return to the Soviet Union, Prokofiev revised and extended the work without really improving it. The present set will allow you to make up your mind for yourself.

The *Fifth Symphony* (1944) is in many ways the most popular of the later symphonies, and Gergiev has many rivals. One indispensable set is the very first, by Koussevitzky and the Boston Symphony, which you should snap up if you can find it, and another is by Ormandy and the Philadelphia Orchestra. Not that there is anything lacking in the playing of the LSO here; the strings surpass themselves in the slow movement and the wind and brass excel throughout. The *Sixth* (1946) and greatest of the symphonies, finds Gergiev at his most searching. Ansermet conducted the première recording in the early days of LP (one of his best records, available on Australian Eloquence 480 0834, coupled with characterful performances of the *Classical* (in two versions) and *Fifth Symphonies*); and Mravinsky's matchless intensity makes his an indispensable document. After the dark years of the late 1940s, the *Seventh Symphony* (1953) offers a brighter and more innocent world; its accessibility can easily deceive listeners into underestimating its achievement. Throughout, Gergiev and his players give their all, and readers will be held under their spell. The sound is well detailed and expertly balanced. The set firmly displaces earlier recommendations.

Symphony 5, Op. 100
Orfeo mono 427041. VPO, Mitropoulos – **SCHUMANN**: *Symphony 2*

Telarc CD 80683. Cincinnati SO, Paavo Järvi

Dmitri Mitropoulos was an outstanding conductor and anything he did will be special. Prokofiev's *Fifth* was recorded with the Vienna Philharmonic at the 1954 Salzburg Festival, and the sound is light years removed from Telarc's Järvi version. Moreover, the ORF (Austrian Radio) balance is not ideal either. However, there is only one word for the performance – electrifying. Readers should try to hear this powerful reading.

However, Karajan, whose Berlin Philharmonic account also remains in a class of its own and is coupled with the *Rite of Spring* (DG 463 613-2), obviously takes precedence for this work.

Quintet in G min., Op. 39

Ⓜ Australian Decca Eloquence (ADD) 480 2152. Melos Ens. – **SEIBER**: *A Portrait of the Artist as a Young Man*. **SHOSTAKOVICH**: *Piano Quintet*

Prokofiev's *Quintet* for oboe, clarinet, violin, viola and double-bass is a product of his Parisian exile in the 1920s, and in its quirky style and odd layout of six movements it is characteristic. The score essentially derives from an earlier ballet score, and there are certainly passages you could very well dance to. But in its fairly light-hearted way the composer mixes his tuneful humour with a degree of bitterness and sarcasm and a dash of the grotesque, to form this agreeable work, very well played and vividly recorded.

(i) Alexander Nevsky, Op. 78; (ii) Lieutenant Kijé, Op. 60; Scythian Suite, Op. 20

DG (ADD) 447 419-2. (i) Obraztsova; L. Symphony Ch., LSO; (ii) Chicago SO; Abbado

Abbado's performance of *Alexander Nevsky* culminates in a deeply moving account of the tragic lament after the battle (here very beautifully sung by Obraztsova), made the more telling when the battle itself is so fine an example of orchestral virtuosity. The chorus is as incisive as the orchestra. A fine account of *Lieutenant Kijé* and what is among the best versions of the *Scythian Suite* to appear in recent years make this a very desirable reissue. However, one must not forget Fritz Reiner's electrifying account of *Nevsky* on RCA (09026 63708-2), coupled with an exciting account of the Khatchaturian *Violin Concerto*.

The Fiery Angel (complete, DVD version)

Arthaus DVD 100 390. Gorchakova, Leiferkus, Pluzhnikov, Ognovanko, soloists; Kirov Op. Ch. & O, Gergiev

The presence of vision in the finely directed DVD serves to underline an implicit ambiguity in the opera – whether Madiel and the spirits conjured up in Act II are real or are just Renata's paranoid delusions. Here the use of mimed figures, unseen by the protagonists but perceived by the audience, was a brilliant solution. The frenetic, highly charged atmosphere of the final Convent scene benefits by vision particularly in this splendid production. The sound has marvellous presence and detail.

War and Peace (DVD version)

TDK DVD DV OPWP (2). Guryakova, Gunn, Brubaker, Kotcherga, Obraztsova, Gerello, Zaremba, Margita, Poretsky, Paris Nat. Op. Ch. & O, Bertini (Director: Zambello, Hugues R. Gall)

War and Peace (CD version)

Chan. 9855 (4). Morozova, Williams, Lavender, Balashov, Dupont, Stephen, Ionova, Ewing, Opie, Russian State Symphonic Cappella, Spoleto Festival O, Hickox

Bertini's account was recorded at the Opéra Bastille in March 2000 and was the opera's first (and much heralded) staging in France. It has plenty in its favour, including a good cast, with an excellent Natasha in Olga Guryakova. There is a fine Bolkonsky in Nathan Gunn and an ideal Pierre Bezhukov (Robert Brubaker), who both looks and sounds exactly right. Perhaps Anatoli Kotcherga is not quite as memorable a Kutuzov as Nikolai Okhotnikov on the Kirov set, but he is commanding nevertheless. Gary Bertini conducts his fine chorus and orchestra well and, generally speaking, there are few serious weaknesses. In addition to the 210 minutes of the opera itself, the Paris recording includes two features on the production, running to 79 minutes or so. No one investing in the set is likely to be greatly disappointed, for the viewer is held from start to finish.

Recorded live at the 1999 Spoleto Festival in full and open Chandos sound, Richard Hickox's formidable version of Prokofiev's epic opera offers a strong, thrustful performance with a cast more consistent than those on rival sets. With a warm understanding of the idiom, helped by a substantial Russian element among the singers, not least the chorus, Hickox keeps the 13 scenes moving well at speeds often on the fast side. Pointing the dramatic contrast between personal tragedy and great public events, the surging lyricism of Prokofiev's inspiration is sharply set against bitingly rhythmic writing, whether in the party scenes of the first part or the wartime scenes of the second half. The glorious tunefulness of the patriotic numbers has just the gulp-in-the-throat quality needed, whether it's General Kutuzov's big aria, nobly sung by Alan Ewing, or the big choruses fervently sung by the Russian choir.

Ekaterina Morozova is a moving Natasha, Slavonic in timbre, weighty but still girlish enough, with an edge to the voice that rarely turns squally. She is well matched in the beautiful opening scene by Pamela Helen Stephen as her cousin, Sonya, while Roderick Williams is a fresh, virile Andrei, and Justin Lavender a vulnerable-sounding Pierre, who convincingly erupts in anger. Alan Opie is a characterful Napoleon, with the battle scene of Borodino thrillingly vivid, not least in shattering cannon shots. Other versions may have starrier individual contributions, but this one has no weak link, and the recording is not just full and brilliant but, beautifully balanced, captures the sweetness of the Spoleto strings very persuasively. The four-disc layout (for the price of three) means breaks come at the ends of scenes.

PUCCINI, Giacomo (1858–1924)

La Bohème (DVD and CD versions)

EMI DVD 2 17417-9. Gheorghiu, Vargas, Arteta, Tézier, Luisotti (Producer: Franco Zeffirelli)

DG 477 6600 (2). Netrebko, Villazón, Cabell, Daniel, Children's Ch. & Bav. R. Ch. & SO, De Billy

Zefirelli's extraordinary set, especially built for the Met. production of *La Bohème*, has already been used for over 300 performances over the years. It is still unsurpassed, and visitors walking on stage in the Act II street scene have felt they were actually in Paris itself. The opera opens and closes just as seductively in the house-top garret, while the snow in Act III is astonishing tangible. One wishes opera settings could always be realistic like this, instead of too often following producers' crazily eccentric whims, with no connection to the music. Gheorghiu's return to the Met. for this production was rightly celebrated. She sings gloriously, of course, but her portrayal of Mimì has matured, notably so in her acting in the opening scene, her first meeting with Rudolfo (Ramón Vargas), also singing ardently. Clearly this lovers' meeting is not quite as innocent as it seems, although Rudolfo is equally complicit in hiding the key. Before that, the horseplay between the four Bohemians has been tingling with zest. Then the Café Momus of Act II is dazzling, with the interplay of a huge animated cast dominated by Ainhos Arteta's sparklingly unpredictable Musetta. Marcello (Ludovic Tézier) joins Act III in the snow to sing in the memorable quartet, and the opera's closing Act could not be more moving. Nicola Luisotti conducts Puccini's greatest score with passion and much tenderness, and the recording projects the voices and orchestra with admirable realism. Altogether a triumph, and wonderfully enjoyable to watch and listen to.

The new DG recording on CD is the companion CD *La Bohème* for our time. The singing of the two stars, the glorious-voiced Anna Netrebko and the thrilling Rolando Villazón, is unforgettable. One needs to say little more, except that Nicole Cabell as Musetta and Boaz Daniel as Marcello are equally memorable, as is the vividly alive and expressive orchestral playing under Betrand de Billy. The recording has splendid reality and projection. The set comes in a handsome box with libretto.

La Fanciulla del West (complete, CD version)

Decca (ADD) 421 595-2 (2). Tebaldi, Del Monaco, MacNeil, Tozzi, St Cecilia Ac., Rome, Ch. & O, Capuana

This is one of the most successful of all Tebaldi's Puccini recordings for Decca. Here she gives one of her most warm-hearted and understanding performances on record, and Mario Del Monaco displays the wonderfully heroic quality of his voice to great – if sometimes tiring – effect. Cornell MacNeil as the villain,

Sheriff Rance, sings with great precision and attack, but unfortunately lacks a villainous-sounding voice to convey the character fully. Jake Wallace's entry and the song *Che faranno i viecchi miei* is one of the high spots of the recording, with Tozzi singing beautifully. Capuana's expansive reading is matched by the imagination of the production, with the closing scene wonderfully effective in spectacular sound.

On DVD, Slatkin conducts a bitingly dramatic account of Puccini's American opera with an understanding cast in Giancarlo del Monaco's ultra-realistic production for the Met. in New York. In 1992, Sherrill Milnes was still an outstanding Rance, at once handsome and sinister, while Plácido Domingo is just as warmly expressive, both lyrical and heroic, as he is in the Covent Garden DVD of nine years earlier. As Minnie, the pretty and buxom Barbara Daniels with her bright, big soprano gives a characterful performance, even if her cheating in the poker game is no more convincing than usual. As Jake Wallace, the camp minstrel, Yanni Yannissis in his Act I solo is strong if a little tremulous. Bright, clear recording, bringing out the emotional tug behind Slatkin's reading, powerfully so at the very end (DG 073 4023).

Madama Butterfly (complete, CD version)

EMI 216487-2 (2). Gheorghiu, Kaufmann, Shkosa, Capitanucci, St Cecilia Ch. & O, Pappano

The linking in Puccini of the leading soprano, Angela Gheorgiu, and EMI's star opera conductor, Antonio Pappano, makes for a resounding success. Pappano's natural feeling for the phrasing and dynamic shading of Puccini's great melodies is here enhanced by having an Italian chorus and orchestra, the St Cecilia forces of which Pappano is chief conductor. They follow his every nuance, and the wide-ranging recording brings out the subtlety of so many *pianissimos* which in earlier recordings came out as *mezzofortes*. Butterfly's first entry from afar in Act 1 is ravishing. The moment when Butterfly through her telescope identifies Pinkerton's ship returning is all the more overwhelming, while the passion of the great climaxes both in the love duet of Act 1 and in the tragic suicide aria of the closing pages underpins the superb singing of Gheorghiu. This may not be a role which she would ever take live on stage, at least not in a large opera-house, but, intelligent singer that she is, she has plainly thought through the role, bringing out emotional details from full-throated passion to tender expressiveness. Her vehemence in rebutting Sharpless's hints at Pinkerton's infidelity are as moving as her tenderness in so much of her singing, and the great aria, *Un bel dì*, has rarely been so richly or securely sung in a complete *Butterfly*, when too many divas are not quite steady under pressure.

Gheorghiu is well-matched with the Pinkerton of Jonas Kaufmann, equally secure and well focused. His may not be a very Italianate tenor-tone, but he seems totally comfortable in the Italian text and, like Gheorghiu, brings out many detailed subtleties. The firm Sharpless of Fabio Capitanucci and the well-balanced Suzuki of Enkelejda Shkosa add to the success of the set. With its refined digital recording it stands as an excellent first choice in a very competitive field.

Manon Lescaut (complete, DVD version)

EMI DVD 2 17420 9. Mattila, Giordani, Croft, Travis, Met. Op. Ch. & O, Levine (Stage
  Director: Gina Lapinsky; V/D: Brian Large)

Whether in the very realistic opening Amiens inn scene or in Geronte's sumptuous apartment in Act II, the Met. production is characteristically spectacular, with superb costumes to match the sets, while the deportation in Act III is frighteningly realistic. The only let-down is the American wasteland of Act IV, which always seems an unrealistic ending, but that is Puccini's miscalculation, not the Met.'s. Karita Mattila is a beautiful Manon, but we see her age as the opera progresses. She sings very affectingly indeed and is matched by the ardent Des Grieux of Marcello Giordani, with a tenor voice of comparably rich quality. Dale Travis makes a splendidly unlikeable Geronte. James Levine conducts with a flowing, passionate lyricism; indeed, the performance of the famous *Intermezzo* is an unforgettably passionate highlight. Very good sound completes this DVD's many virtues.

James Levine again conducts a very desirable CD version of this opera. With Luciano Pavarotti as a powerful Des Grieux, Levine brings out all the red-blooded drama of Puccini's first big success, while not ignoring the warmth and tender poetry. Pavarotti tackles his little opening aria, *Tra voi belle*, with a beefy bravado that misses the subtlety and point of Domingo, for example. But then he characteristically points word-meaning with a bright-eyed intensity that compels attention, and there is little harm in having as passionate a portrait of Des Grieux as Pavarotti's. The rest of the cast is strong too, with Dwayne Croft a magnificent Lescaut who brings out the character with wry humour. The veteran Giuseppe Taddei is superbly cast as Geronte, very characterful and still full-throated, while Cecilia Bartoli makes the unnamed singer in the Act II entertainment into far more than a cipher (Decca 440 200-2 (2)).

La Rondine (complete, DVD version)

EMI DVD 6 31618-9. Alagna, Gheorghiu, Brenciu, Oropesa, Ramey, Met. Op. Ch. & O,
  Armiliato (Director: Brian Large)

(i–iii) *La Rondine* (complete); (i; iii) *Le Villi: Prelude*; *L'abbandono*; *La tregenda*; *Ecco la casa . . . Torna al felice*; (i; iv) Song: *Morire?* (CD version)

Ⓜ EMI 6 40738-2 (2). (i) Alagna; (ii) Gheorghiu, Mula-Tchako, Matteuzzi, Rinaldi;
  (iii) L. Voices, LSO, Pappano; (iv) Pappano (piano)

It seems remarkable that EMI should have issued so close to each other two separate recordings, both with Gheorghiu and Alagna, of Puccini's little-known but delightfully tuneful opera. The first performance has the advantage of Pappano's conducting, with his ability to transform the work with his natural feeling for Puccini. But Marco Armiliato directs the Met. production sensitively and with hardly less lyrical warmth and vividness. Moreover the Metropolitan Opera sets are wonderfully elegant. The partnership of Gheorghiu, most moving in the Violetta-like role of the heroine, Magda, and Alagna as the stranger she falls in love with, brings ardently beautiful singing from both artists, and their passion, expressed both tenderly and passionately, is, if anything, finer, more mature in the second, live, Metropolitan Opera set. Consistently, Gheorghiu makes you share the courtesan's wild dream of finding her young student lover. As Ruggero, the hero, Alagna winningly characterizes in his freshest voice. What will especially delight Puccinians in both sets is that he is given an extra aria about Paris, *Parigi e un citta*, which transforms his otherwise minimal contribution in Act I. The role of the poet, Prunier, is also memorable, thanks to the casting of the clear-toned William Matteuzzi on CD in what is normally a comprimario role. But Marius Brenciu on the DVD gives an attractively dapper characterization of this elusive character; while, under Pappano, Inva Mula-Tchako is well cast in the soubrette role of Lisette, bright, clear and vivacious, Lisette Oropesa at the Met. all but steals the part with her humour and charm. In the third Act Gheorghiu and Alagna put a seal on their Met. performance, wonderfully touching, when they have to make their final farewell, and their singing is totally memorable. The earlier set, however, adds excerpts from *Le Villi*, warm and dramatic, including two orchestral showpieces. Alagna also gives a ringing account of Roberto's aria, as he does of the song, *Morire?* (with Pappano at the piano), the source of the extra aria for Ruggero included in the main opera.

Tosca (complete, CD version)
Ⓜ EMI mono 5 62890-2 (2). Callas, Di Stefano, Gobbi, Calabrese, La Scala, Milan, Ch. & O, De Sabata

There has never been a finer recording of *Tosca* than Callas's first with Victor de Sabata conducting and Tito Gobbi as Scarpia. He makes the unbelievably villainous police chief into a genuine three-dimensional character, and Di Stefano, as the hero Cavaradossi was at his finest. The conducting of De Sabata is spaciously lyrical as well as sharply dramatic, and Walter Legge's mono recording is superbly balanced. The new transfer brings enhanced sound that could almost be stereo, with the voices caught gloriously, and the mid-priced set includes a full libretto and translation.

However, Callas had a stereo successor in Gheorghiu (in partnership with Pappano) and her singing is also very compelling: she constantly sheds new light on one phrase after another. And her performance includes an account of the aria *Vissi d'arte* of velvet beauty. Gheorghu's is undoubtedly another great performance significantly expanding on what we already know of her, as magnetic as Callas, rich and beautiful as well as dramatic (EMI 5 85644-2).

Il Trittico: (i) *Il Tabarro*; (ii) *Suor Angelica*; (iii) *Gianni Schicchi*
(CD version)

EMI 5 565 872-2 (3). (i; iii) Gheorghiu, Alagna; (i) Guelfi, Guleghina, Shicoff; (ii) Gallardo-Domâs, Manca di Nissa; (ii–iii) Palmer; (iii) Van Dam, Roni; (i–ii) L. Voices; (ii) Tiffin Boys' Ch.; (i; iii) LSO; (ii) Philh. O; Pappano

No previous recordings of the three one-Acters in Puccini's triptych bring quite such warmth or beauty or so powerful a drawing of the contrasts between each – in turn Grand Guignol melodrama, pure sentiment and high comedy. Pacing each opera masterfully, Pappano heightens emotions fearlessly to produce at key moments the authentic gulp-in-the-throat, whether for the cuckolded barge master, Michele, for Sister Angelica in her agonized suicide and heavenly absolution, or for the resolution of young love at the end of *Gianni Schicchi*.

Angela Gheorghiu and Roberto Alagna, as well as making a tiny cameo appearance in *Il Tabarro* as the off-stage departing lovers, sing radiantly as Lauretta and Rinuccio in *Gianni Schicchi*, with the happy ending most tenderly done. Maria Guleghina, well known for her fine Tosca, makes a warm, vibrant Giorgetta, and the touch of acid at the top of the voice adds character. Even more remarkable is the singing of the young Chilean soprano, Cristina Gallardo-Domâs as Sister Angelica. This is a younger, more tender, more vulnerable Angelica than usual, the dynamic shading brings *pianissimos* of breathtaking delicacy, not least in floated top-notes. The casting in the middle opera is as near flawless as could be. The Zia Principessa is sung with chilling power by Bernadette Manca di Nissa, her tone firm and even throughout. Felicity Palmer with her tangy mezzo tone is well contrasted as the Abbess. And she is just as characterful as the crabby Zita in *Gianni Schicchi*. Among the men, Carlo Guelfi makes a superb Michele in *Il Tabarro*, incisive, dark and virile. Neil Shicoff makes a fine Luigi, his nervy tenor tone adding character. As Gianni Schicchi, José Van Dam is in fine voice, with his clean focus bringing out the sardonic side of Schicchi, and his top Gs wonderfully strong and steady still. The recording is comfortingly sumptuous and atmospheric, very wide in dynamic range, with magical off-stage effects.

Warner provide a recommendable DVD of a traditional production of this opera from La Scala. Piero Cappuccilli as the barge master is well supported by the believably hard-voiced Sylvia Sass as Giorgetta, and the melodrama is brought off effectively. In the title-role of *Suor Angelica*, Rosalind Plowright is at her finest, both vocally and when commanding our sympathy; Dunja Vejzovic's Princess is not as intimidating as she should be, but she sings well enough. The set for *Gianni Schicchi* is unrealistically spacious but Cecilia Gasdia is a rich-voiced Lauretta and, at the centre of the story, Juan Pons is a firm and believable Schicchi, although the staging of his final solo as a devil from hell is totally misguided in just the way that producers refuse to let well alone. But the veteran Gianandrea Gavazzeni conducts throughout with vitality and warmth, and altogether this has much to offer (Warner 5050467 0943-2).

Turandot (complete, DVD version)

TDK DVD DVWW-CLOPTUR. Marton, Carreras, Ricciarelli, V. Sängerknaben, V. State Op.
   Ch. & O, Maazel (Director: Harold Prince; V/D: Rodney Greenberg)

Turandot (complete, CD version)

Decca (ADD) 414 274-2 (2). Sutherland, Pavarotti, Caballé, Pears, Ghiaurov, Alldis Ch.,
   Wandsworth School Boys' Ch., LPO, Mehta

Maazel's spectacular 1983 Vienna State Opera version, recorded live, is outstanding in every way and is unlikely to be surpassed by modern versions
(although Chen Kaige's extravagant, stylized 'Chinese' version on Unitel, with
Maria Guleghina very impressive in the title-role, has been highly praised elsewhere). But the Vienna State Opera set also has splendidly vivid oriental
costumes, using masks on the chorus and most of the principal characters.
Indeed it is exotically telling, with the set equally theatrical, its central staircase
ideal for the enormously compelling scene where Turandot (Eva Marton) asks
the three questions and José Carreras replies, with just the right degree of hesitation to keep the tension high. Marton was surely born to take the part of the
heroine, singing with great power, and conveying her final change of heart most
believably. Carreras also sings gloriously, creating the role of Calaf as both
heroic and warmly sympathetic. Katia Ricciarelli is a very touching Liù, her
voice creamily beautiful, and Ping, Pang and Pong (again exotically costumed
and masked) bring an almost Gilbertian touch to their bizarre charcterizations.
The Vienna State Opera Chorus sing gloriously in the big scenes and the orchestra play with the utmost vividness under Maazel's thrilling direction. Very
highly recommended.

   Joan Sutherland gives an intensely revealing interpretation, making the icy
princess far more human and sympathetic than ever before, while Pavarotti
gives a performance equally imaginative, beautiful in sound, strong on detail.
To set Caballé (as Liù) against Sutherland was a daring idea, and it works
superbly well; Pears as the Emperor is another choice that works surprisingly
well. Mehta directs a gloriously rich and dramatic performance, superlatively
recorded, still the best-sounding *Turandot* on CD.

PURCELL, Henry (1659–95)

England, my England (film)

Isolde Films TP DVD 151. Callow, Ball, Redgrave, Shrapnel, Graham, Varcoe, Dawson,
   Argenta, Monteverdi Ch., E. Bar. Sol., Gardiner (TV Director: Tony Palmer)

When little is known about the life of Henry Purcell except the date of his death
and his burial in Westminster Abbey, Tony Palmer has created a fantasy not just
about the period but about its many great figures, from Milton and Locke to
Pepys, Newton and Wren. The Great Plague and the Fire of London figure

prominently, but over everything is the figure of Simon Callow, not just as Charles II but as himself, both tackling Shaw's play, *In Good King Charles's Golden Days*, at the Royal Court Theatre and quoting the jaundiced comments of John Osborne, co-author of the script, likening the 1680s to the 1880s. Michael Ball plays the part of the composer himself.

The musical side is presented splendidly, with John Eliot Gardiner directing his Monteverdi Choir and English Baroque Soloists with a starry line-up of soloists. The result is a kaleidoscope of impressions, carefully put together, which adds up to a most moving whole. The film ends with the finale of Benjamin Britten's *Variations and Fugue on a Theme of Purcell, The Young Person's Guide*, reflecting Palmer's own career. Not surprisingly, the film, first shown on Christmas Day 1995 on Channel Four, became an instant prize-winner.

Complete Sacred Music

Hyp. CDS 44141/51 (11). Soloists, King's Cons., King

The different categories of work here, Services, Verse Anthems, Motets (or Full Anthems) and devotional songs, cover the widest range of style and expression, with Robert King's own helpful and scholarly notes setting each one in context. Generally the most adventurous in style are the Full Anthems, with elaborate counterpoint often bringing amazingly advanced harmonic progressions. Yet the Verse Anthems too include some which similarly demonstrate Purcell's extraordinary imagination in contrapuntal writing. So though Volume 6 is confined to Verse Anthems and devotional songs, they too offer passages of chromatic writing which defy the idea of these categories as plain and straightforward. As the title suggests, the devotional song, *Plung'd in the Confines of Despair*, is a particularly fine example. Although all the earlier volumes are full of good things, Volume 7 is especially recommendable and contains the *Music for the Funeral of Queen Mary* of 1695, with drum processionals, the solemn *March* and *Canzona for Brass* and *Funeral Sentences*; it has the *B flat Morning Service*, two settings of the Coronation anthem, *I Was Glad* (one of them previously unrecorded), a magnificent Full Anthem, three Verse Anthems and two splendid devotional songs. Volume 8, too, is full of fine music. The opening Verse Anthem, *In Thee, O Lord, Do I Put my Trust*, opens with a very striking, slightly melancholy *Sinfonia*, with a six-note figure rising up from a ground bass which sets the expressive mood. The closing anthem, so appropriate from an island composer, *They that Go Down to the Sea in Ships*, is characteristically diverse, with Purcell helping the Lord 'maketh the storm to cease' and at the end providing a joyful chorus of praise. King's notes and documentation closely identify each item, adding to one's illumination.

There are plenty of key items in the final three volumes, including (in Volume 9) *In Guilty Night* and the dialogue cantata *Saul and the Witch of Endor*, with Susan Gritton, Rogers Covey-Crump and Michael George. An outstanding series, full of treasures, with King varying the scale of forces he uses for each item. Often he uses one voice per part, but he regularly expands the ensemble with the King's Consort Choir or turns to the full New College Choir, which includes trebles. The individual discs are no longer available separately, but all 11 CDs come neatly packaged in cardboard sleeves.

Sonatas of 3 Parts: 1-12; 4 Parts: 1-10; Chacony; 3 Pavans; 3 Parts on a Ground
Chan. 0572/3. Purcell Quartet

In these *Sonatas* Purcell turns to a new concerted style which had been developed in Italy. Interspersed among the *Sonatas* are three earlier and highly chromatic *Pavans* and the famous *Chacony*. The playing is authoritative and idiomatic, and the artists are firmly focused in a warm but not excessively reverberant acoustic. This is Purcell at his finest.

Complete Ayres for the Theatre: ***Abdelazar; Bonduca; Music in: Amphitryon; Distress'd Innocence; The Double Dealer; The Fairy Queen & Sonata while the Sun Rises; The Gordian Knot Unty'd; The Indian Queen and Symphony; King Arthur; The Man-Hater; The Married Beau; The Old Batchelor; The Prophetess or the History of Dioclesian; Timon of Athens; The Virtuous Wife. Overtures: to Sir Anthony Love; in G min.***
Hyp. CDS 44381/3. Parley of Instruments, Goodman

When Purcell died suddenly in 1695 he left much unpublished music. The most unexpected of these volumes was '*A Collection of Ayres, Compos'd for the Theatre and upon other Occasions*. These Ayres formed the first printed edition devoted entirely to the incidental music used in London theatres. The presentation here does not offer the suites as they would have been heard in the theatre. The overtures which begin each collection would have come halfway through the sequence of movements, placed between the movements which warned the audience that the play was about to begin (the 'first music' and 'second music') and those that marked the division of the play into Acts (the 'act tunes'). These overtures are mostly structured in the two-section form established by Lully, opening usually with dotted rhythms. The suites for Purcell's semi-operas, *King Arthur*, *The Fairy Queen* and *The Indian Queen*, interpolated some of the theatrical dances and song tunes (heard here without the words).

Roy Goodman's aim in this recording is to present *Ayres for the Theatre* complete and to produce the effect of a concert performance of the suites under Purcell's direction, primarily on strings, but using oboes and bassoons in some of the movements of *Dioclesian* and *King Arthur*. As Peter Holman comments in the notes, 'Purcell's music offers no shortage of minuet-like airs, but horn-pipes are equally common, and throughout there is a preponderance of breezy, tuneful airs, some of which achieved the status of popular tunes. There are also many beautiful, soulful airs distinguished by Purcell's unfailing ear for string sonorities.' *Abdelazar*, of course, includes the rondeau made famous by Benjamin Britten's variations.

The performances by Goodman and the authentic Parley of Instruments are thoroughly alive, stylish and responsive to the composer's ready invention. The recording is in every way pleasing, clear, yet full-bodied.

Funeral Music for Queen Mary (with (i) *Queen's epicedium*); *March & Canzona on the Death of Queen Mary*. Funeral Sentences: *Man that is born of a woman*; *In the midst of life are we in death*; *Thou knowest, Lord, the secrets of our hearts*. Anthems: *Hear my prayer*; *Jehovah quam multi sunt*. (ii) *3 (Organ) Voluntaries: in D min.*; *in G*; *in C*

🅱🅱 Naxos 8.553129. Oxford Camerata, Summerly; with (i) Lane; (ii) Cummings

On the Naxos CD this glorious, darkly intense funeral music is given an outstandingly fresh and clear rendition, vividly recorded, matching even the finest rival versions. The sharpness of focus in the sound means that Purcell's adventurous harmonies with their clashing intervals are given extra dramatic bite in these dedicated performances, marked by fresh, clear soprano tone in place of boy trebles. The choice of extra items – full anthems with their inspired counterpoint rather than verse anthems – is first rate. Aptly, the extended solo song for soprano (with simple organ accompaniment), *The Queen's epicedium*, is also included with the funeral music, sung with boyish tone by Carys-Ann Lane.

Airs & Duets

Lyrichord LEMS 8024. Dooley, Crook, Instrumental Ens., Brewer (harpsichord)

Jeffrey Dooley (counter-tenor), a pupil and protégé of the late Alfred Deller, has a truly beautiful voice and takes naturally to this repertoire. Among his solo items *Be welcome, then, great sir* and the *Divine Hymn (Lord, what is man)* are quite ravishing, while *Hark! the ech'ing air* is delectably sprightly. Particularly engaging is *One charming night* from *The Fairy Queen*, with a pair of recorders. The tenor Howard Crook also has a disarmingly personable vocal line, and his solos, including *Beauty, thou scene of love* and the sombre *Here let my life*, are hardly less memorable, with the famous *If music be the food of love* splendidly sung. But it is when these two voices join together in duet that one's senses are truly ravished, from the opening *Let the fifes and the clarions* and the similarly light-hearted *Sacharissa's grown old* to *Many, many such days* (with its bassoon obbligato), and not forgetting *Sound the trumpet*. The celebration of the queen, *Hail, gracious Gloriana, hail!*, makes a well-chosen finale. The simple instrumental accompaniments are managed most stylishly, and this concert cannot be too highly recommended.

Dido and Aeneas (complete, CD version)

Ⓜ Decca (ADD) 466 387-2. Baker, Herincx, Clark, Sinclair, St Anthony Singers, ECO, Lewis

Janet Baker's 1962 recording of Dido is a truly great performance. The radiant beauty of the voice is obvious enough, but the opening phrase of 'When I Am

Laid in Earth' and its repeat a few bars later is a model of graduated *mezza voce*. Then, with the words 'Remember Me', delivered in a monotone, she subdues the natural vibrato to produce a white tone of hushed, aching intensity. Anthony Lewis and the ECO (Thurston Dart is a model continuo player) produce the crispest and lightest of playing which never sounds rushed. Herincx is a rather gruff Aeneas, but the only serious blemish is Monica Sinclair's Sorceress. She over-characterizes in a way that is quite out of keeping with the rest of this production. Like most vintage Oiseau-Lyre recordings, this was beautifully engineered. And it is a welcome reissue on the Decca Legends label.

The outstanding mezzo, Sarah Connolly, is central to the success of the fine new 'authentic' Chandos version of Purcell's operatic masterpiece, with period instrumentalists of the OAE accompanying, led by the violinist Margaret Faultless and with Elizabeth Kenny and Steven Devine directing. Connolly's characterization is deeply moving, with fine tonal contrasts in *Dido's Lament*. Gerald Finley too makes the most of the limited role of Aeneas with highly expressive singing. One young singer to note is Lucy Crowe as Belinda, with John Mark Ainsley as the Sailor, making up a cast with no weak link. First-rate recording, finely balanced to an apt scale (Chan. 0756).

The Fairy Queen (complete, DVD version; combined with excerpts from Shakespeare's *A Midsummer Night's Dream*)

Opus Arte DVD OA1031D. Vocal cast: Crowe, Sampson, Lyon, Foster-Williams, Glyndebourne Ch., OAE, Christie. Actors: Sally Dexter, Joseph Millson, Desmond Barrit, Jotham Annan (V/D: Françoise Roussillon)

Arthaus DVD 100 200. Kenny, Randle, Rice, Van Allan, ENO Ch. & O, Kok (Director: David Pountney)

The Fairy Queen (complete, CD version)

ⓜ DG Al Fresco 477 6733 (2). Harrhy, J. Smith, Nelson, Priday, Penrose, Stafford, Evans, Hill, Varcoe, Thomas, Monteverdi Ch., E. Bar. Sol., Gardiner

Recorded live at the Coliseum in London in 1995, the first DVD ENO production of *The Fairy Queen*, conducted by Nicholas Kok, was in essence a sparkling fantasy, thanks to the brilliant stage direction of David Pountney and the choreography of Quinny Sacks. The sequence of masques was treated as a series of circus turns and, thanks also to the fantastic costumes of Dunya Ramicova, the atmosphere of the circus is never far away, helping to hold together an episodic sequence of scenes, originally designed to back up a garbled version of Shakespeare's *A Midsummer Night's Dream*. Titania – Yvonne Kenny at her finest – and Oberon – the exotic Thomas Randle – stand out the more sharply as otherworldly figures, thanks to their glamorous costumes. A fun entertainment, as unstuffy a presentation of Purcell's problematic masterpiece as could be, vividly filmed and recorded, but not really covering all the work's inherent production problems.

Many will feel that these are finally resolved by the director of the splendid new Opus Arte Glyndebourne production which won a *Gramophone* award in 2010. The reconciling of Purcell's score and its original play, performed by a full cast, is finally realized with a most imaginative production from Jonathan Kent that is gorgeous visually and most entertaining to watch; and the Purcell masques fit readily with the spoken narrative. The whole presentation combines charm and period musicality (with the admirable William Christie in charge). Among the singers, Carolyn Sampson (as usual) stands out. But the whole cast is excellent. In most respects visually and dramatically this is a triumph.

Gardiner's CD performance, concentrating on the music, is also a delight from beginning to end for, though authenticity and completeness reign, scholarship is worn lightly and the result is consistently exhilarating, with no longueurs whatever. The fresh-toned soloists are first rate, while Gardiner's regular choir and orchestra excel themselves, with Purcell's sense of fantasy brought out in each succeeding number. Beautifully clear and well-balanced recording. Reissued at mid-price on DG's Al Fresco label.

RACHMANINOV, Sergei (1873–1943)

Piano Concertos 1–4; Rhapsody on a Theme of Paganini, Op. 43
Hyp. CDA 67501/2. Hough, Dallas SO, Litton

Piano Concertos 2 in C min., Op. 18; 3 in D min., Op. 30
Avie AV 2192. Simon Trpčeski, RLPO, Petrenko

The vintage 1970s recordings by Ashkenazy, the LSO and Previn have long been our primary recommendation for the Rachmaninov concertos (Double Decca 444 839-2), but more recently Stephen Hough and Andrew Litton, recorded live on a Hyperion two-CD set, offer magnetic performances that reflect the thoughtfulness and care with which this masterly pianist approaches even the most frequently performed works, his interpretations refreshingly based on indications in the score rather than performing tradition. With Litton equally a devotee of the composer, this is strongly recommendable, even if the recording quality does not quite match another outstanding series of recordings by Simon Trpčeski and the Royal Liverpool Philharmonic Orchestra under their new conductor, Vasily Petrenko.

Trpčeski's playing combines dazzling brilliance with warmly natural phrasing with the natural ebb and flow so characteristic of the composer's richly romantic melodic lines. Petrenko's tempi are not dissimilar to Previn's and his partnership with his soloist is all-embracing. The first-movement climax of the *C minor Concerto* is handled with complete spontaneity and the slow movement has an Elysian close. The opening theme of the *D minor Concerto* has an affecting simplicity; conversely, the more virtuosic of the composer's two cadenzas is effectively used at the first-movement climax. Then the slow movement brings a wonderful surge of expressive feeling from the strings. Both works close thrillingly and the listener is left thoroughly satisfied, particularly as the well-balanced Avie recording is so natural, yet makes a splendid impact.

The Isle of the Dead, Op. 29; The Rock, Op. 7; Symphonic Dances, Op. 45
Avie AV 2188. RLPO, Petrenko

This is the first time Rachmaninov's three masterly symphonic poems have appeared on a single disc, and the arresting performances by Vasily Petrenko and the Royal Liverpool Philharmonic Orchestra provide a truly unforgettable triptych, marvellously played and given full-blooded, demonstration-quality recording. There are excellent notes too, by Anthony Bateman, and he reveals that in 1893 Tchaikovsky saw the score of *The Rock* and was so impressed by its vivid, darkly colourful orchestration that he planned to conduct it on a European tour. But alas, his death in November of that year prevented that. It is no wonder that Tchaikovsky admired the work, for it is very Russian and is tragically based on Chekhov's short story, 'On the Road'. This tells of two travellers, a world-weary old man (lower strings) and a beautiful young woman (a tripping flute), who meet for one night during a snowstorm. Their dialogue reaches a passionate climax, but they part in the morning, without resolving the man's problems. As a symbol for the work Rachmaninov chose the opening lines of a gloomy poem by Mikhail Lermontov, 'Upon the breast of a gigantic rock a golden cloudlet rested for one night.'

The Isle of the Dead is also broodingly atmospheric, inspired by a painting by Arnold Böcklin depicting Charon, the ferryman of Greek mythology who rowed the souls of the dead across the river Styx to their final resting place. Charon's oars are depicted by an insistent five-note motif in the lower strings. The *Dies irae* (a medieval chant that seemed to haunt the composer) eclipses the work's secondary ardent theme representing life.

There are three *Symphonic Dances* which together form a kind of sinfonia. The work was written in America in 1940 and dedicated to Eugene Ormandy. The first movement opens with incisive chords, then develops a bold, jaunty rhythm for its immediately catchy main theme. But the languorous secondary theme is even more memorable, introduced on the melancholy alto saxophone and taken up richly (lusciously, as phrased by the Liverpool strings), moving to a climax. But again it is to be interrupted ominously by the *Dies irae*. The central waltz is spectral, apprehensive, even ghoulish in feeling, but has a more romantic centrepiece, before the music disintegrates. The finale is then completely taken over by the *Dies irae*. A tolling bell announces its appearance as a demonic dance, alternating with its transformation into a rather more exultant religious chant, which eventually provides a positive resolution. The Liverpool performance is tremendously compelling, and this is one of the finest non-concertante Rachmaninov CDs in the catalogue.

Symphonies 1–3; *The Isle of the Dead, Op. 29*; *The Rock, Op. 7*; *Symphonic Dances, Op. 45*; (i–ii) *The Bells, Op. 35*

Ⓑ DG 477 9505 (4). Russian Nat. O, Pletnev; with (i) Marina Mascheriakova, Sergei Larin, Vladimir Chernov; (ii) Moscow State Chamber Ch. (with **TANEYEV**: (ii) *John of Damascus, Op. 1*)

In the *First Symphony* Mikhail Pletnev produces a range of sonority and clarity of articulation that we recognize from his keyboard playing, and there is a poetic vision alongside a splendid command of architecture. The symphony is quite outstanding in his hands, and so is *The Isle of the Dead*, which has a sense of inevitability and forward movement that recall both Rachmaninov himself and Koussevitzky. Pletnev also brings a fresh mind to the *Second Symphony*, with his approach very much controlled, giving a strong sense of onward current, less of the heart-on-sleeve emotion in the slow movement that we remember from Previn's passionately committed performance (valid in a quite different way). *The Rock* too is imaginatively presented and fills out the disc impressively.

In the *Third Symphony* we are again reminded of the clarity and lightness of articulation experienced in Pletnev's pianism, and the work's feeling throughout is held in perfect control. It is a performance of quality, although it must be said that ensemble is endangered by some frenetically fast speeds in the exhilarating finale. Yet Pletnev can easily persuade you that his interpretative idiosyncrasies in the outer movements are spontaneous and right, and the opulent sound-world of this wonderful symphony is beautifully served by the Russian players (and in particular the strings). The coupling with the *Symphonic Dances* is similarly persuasive in a individually Russian way.

Again, *The Bells* comes in a performance that shows the music in an entirely new light. Pletnev has his finger on the composer's pulse and always has special insights to bring to his music. He goes beyond the work's vivid colours and lush sonorities and, without in any way indulging in over-characterization, gets singing and playing of impressive subtlety and intensity. The coupling of Taneyev's *John of Damascus* is particularly valuable, and this fourth CD was given a Rosette by us when issued separately. The Taneyev work is a noble piece whose long neglect on the gramophone is at last rectified, and it is given a truly memorable performance; as with the rest of this seductive DG collection, the sound is first class.

Symphony 2 in E min., Op. 27

Unitel Classics DVD 2072258. Phd. O, Ormandy (with **STRAVINSKY**: *The Firebird: Suite*)

Ormandy pioneered the recording of the three Rachmaninov symphonies in stereo, and in most ways his performances remain unsurpassed. The original set is still available on Sony (SB2K 63257). But now comes a DVD to show us how his performances really sounded. Here is the *echt*-Philadelphia sound that was captured only fitfully on 78s and LPs. This Rachmaninov *Second* wipes the floor with any competitor: the rich, sumptuous string sonority, the wonderful, expressive wind and brass, and the total unanimity of attack that is still a source of amazement. Ormandy recorded the symphony some five times, the present issue in 1979 as part of his eightieth birthday celebrations. He is amazingly youthful and ardent, and the Stravinsky is no less dazzling. The sound is gorgeous throughout and the visual direction under Kirk Browning all one could wish for. Even among the finest of the fine, this stands out.

Morceaux de fantaisie, Op. 3; *Sonata 2 in B flat min., Op. 36*; *Variations on a Theme of Chopin, Op. 22*
Elan 82248. Rodriguez

Préludes, Op. 32/1–13; *Sonata 1 in D min., Op. 28*
Elan 82244. Rodriguez

This is some Rachmaninov playing! Santiago Rodriguez is the real thing. For a moment one imagines that Rachmaninov himself is at the keyboard. Rodriguez has something of Pletnev about him: wonderful authority and immaculate technical control, tremendous electricity as well as great poetic feeling. Outstanding in every way and well worth seeking out.

Vespers, Op. 37
HM Chant du Monde RUS 788050. St Petersburg Capella, Chernuchenko

Rachmaninov's *Vespers* – more correctly the *'All-night Vigil'* – rank not only among his most soulful and intensely powerful music but they are also the finest of all Russian choral works. The St Petersburg Capella offers singing of an extraordinarily rapt intensity. The dynamic range is enormous, the perfection of ensemble and blend and the sheer beauty of tone such as to exhaust superlatives. The recording does them justice and is made in a suitably atmospheric acoustic.

RAMEAU, Jean-Philippe (1683–1764)

Ballet music: *Les Fêtes d'Hébé*; *Hippolyte et Aricie*
Erato 3984 26129-2. Les Arts Florissants, Christie

This is all delightfully fresh and inventive music and Rameau's scoring is ever-resourceful and, as presented here, constantly sparkling and ear-tickling. Most entertaining, and beautifully recorded.

370 **RAMEAU, Jean-Philippe**

Pygmalion (Acte de ballet); *Le Temple de la Gloire* (excerpts); *Air gay*.
Grands Motets: *Deus noster refugium*; *In convertendo, Dominus*;
Quam dilecta tabernacula
Virgin 2CD 5 22027-2 (2). Soloists, including Fouchécourt, Piau, Gens, Le Concert
Spirituel, Niquet

Pygmalion falls in love with a female statue he has sculpted. The statue is then (courtesy of Venus) brought to life by that very love – a moment of sheer orchestral magic in Rameau's delightful score. The Virgin recording is robustly operatic, immediately obvious in the Overture, with its boldly repeated notes, superbly articulated, which may (or may not) have been intended by Rameau to simulate the sculptor's chisel. Jean-Paul Fouchécourt gives a strong characterization of Pygmalion and, apart from Sandrine Piau as the statue, her two female colleagues are suitably histrionic. The excerpts from *Le Temple de la Gloire* are quite brief (about 8 minutes). For the reissue, the coupling is three of Rameau's most impressive Grands Motets, beautifully sung and with refined accompaniments. *Deus noster refugium* is a colourful setting of Psalm 46, while *Quam dilecta tabernacula* opens with a particularly lovely soprano solo, pure yet sensuous, followed by an impressive fugue. *In convertendo, Dominus* is an even more complex setting of Psalm 126 with great variety between the movements and an interpolation from Psalm 69 as the fifth movement.

Hippolyte et Aricie (CD version)

Ⓑ Erato 2564 66305-2 (3). Padmore, Panzarella, Hunt, Naouri, James, Les Arts
Florissants, Christie

William Christie has the benefit of using the text specially prepared for the complete Rameau Edition by Sylvie Bouissou, restoring fully the original 1733 score. Christie, using rather larger forces than his competitor on DG, produces warmer textures and timbres, consistently bringing out the sensuous beauty of much of the writing as well as its dramatic point. At speeds fractionally broader than Minkowski's, he bounces rhythms more infectiously, and allows himself more flexible phrasing without undermining the classical purity of style. Though Anne-Maria Panzarella as Aricie is not as golden in tone as Véronique Gens on the alternative DG set, she is fresh and bright, responding immediately to Christie's timing, which more consistently seems geared to stage presentation, with a conversational quality given to passages of recitative. Mark Padmore is a more ardent Hippolyte than his opposite number and Lorraine Hunt a weightier, more deeply tragic Phèdre, with Eirian James a warm Diane, and Laurent Naouri as Thésée weightier than Russell Smythe on DG. The Erato sound too is weightier and more immediate than that of the DG set. Altogether this is a most welcome reissue.

Les Indes Galantes (DVD version)

Opus Arte DVD OA 0923 D (2). Panzarella, Agnew, Berg, Croft, Petibon, Les Arts
Florissants Ch. & O, Christie (V/D: Thomas Grimm)

Described as an Opera-ballet in four Acts, *Les Indes Galantes* was Rameau's biggest stage success in his own lifetime, and one can understand why from this spectacular production, staged at the Paris Opéra in 2004. The director, Andrei Serban, presents the piece with the sort of lavish effects and movement that would have delighted eighteenth-century audiences. Sets are stylized and costumes are basically in period, but with random updating for members of the chorus, as when they appear as French sailors. Act II, set in Peru at the time of the Incas, brings the most striking spectacle, with the eruption of a volcano – cue for the backcloth of Andean peaks to wobble and sway amid fiery lightning – for which Rameau devised vividly descriptive music. His inspiration is at white heat throughout, with William Christie and a large and stylish team of singers and players revelling in each number, often deliberately over-acting in the more melodramatic moments of this fantastic drama. Outstanding amongst the soloists are Nathan Berg as Huascar (crushed by a boulder from the sky after his Act II aria), Anna Maria Panzarella as Emilie and Paul Agnew as Valère, with João Fernandez memorably in drag as Bellone. The final curtain brings an exuberant encore after the credits, with Christie hilariously joining in the dance. Extras include a feature about Rameau with Christie, Serban and the choreographer, Bianca Li, among those interviewed.

Une Symphonie imaginaire
DG 47903974. Les Musiciens du Louvre, Minkowski

What a splendid idea of Marc Minkowski's it was to create this 'imaginary' symphony, based on Rameau's theatre music. The result is a highly entertaining suite of dance movements, rather in the tradition of Beecham's Handel suites, but with somewhat more authentic orchestrations! And what a colourful composer Rameau was! Right from the opening number, the colourful *Zaïs Overture*, with its scurrying strings and woodwind writing punctuated with dramatic percussion, grabs your attention straight away. One marvels at Rameau's imagination and sheer entertainment value throughout. Minkowski has selected some obvious highlights, including an orchestrated version of the famous *La Poule* (an anonymous transcription), plus many of the dance numbers which we have enjoyed from complete opera recordings. There are plenty of fast, exciting numbers, such as the brilliant *Tambourins* from *Dardanus* (try getting that out of your mind after playing it), many with a piquant rustic flavour (the *Musette* and *Rondeau* from *Les Fêtes d'Hébé* and the ensuing *Tambourin* are delightful and similarly hard to dislodge from one's memory), and the lively *Danse des Sauvages* from *Les Indes galantes* offers plenty of exhilaration. No less impressive is the beauty of many of the slow numbers – the *Air gracieux* from *La Naissance d'Osiris* and the *Air tendre* from *Les Fêtes d'Hébé* are hauntingly beautiful. But there are several such examples. The playing is brilliant throughout and numbers such as *Orage* (from *Platée*) give the strings an opportunity to show off their prowess to the full. Minkowski directs this delightful Rameau concoction with Gallic brilliance and elegance, all caught in exceptionally vivid sound. What a distinctive and original composer Rameau was – highly recommended. DG also offer on their website as a bonus Mozart, symphony no. 14 in G minor.

Le Temple de la Gloire: Suites 1 & 2
Ⓜ Australian Decca Eloquence (ADD) 480 2373. ECO, Leppard – **CHARPENTIER**: *Médée: Suite*. **GRÉTRY**: *Suite of Ballet Music*

Even though the authentic movement has revolutionized performances of this repertoire, it is a joy to return to these very stylish Raymond Leppard recordings again. This is an enchanting CD, superbly recorded. Rameau's score has much character: the opening, with its brass effects, is most impressive, while the *Air for the Demons* is especially evocative and the *Air tendre* has a haunting beauty of its own. Raymond Leppard gives us an object lesson in how to perform this music on modern instruments; his springy rhythms and, especially, his use of the continuo to colour the texture are most imaginative. Rameau was relatively unknown when this recording was made (1966) and it was recordings like this which alerted us to the many delights this composer offers. With equally appealing couplings, this CD should be snapped up immediately.

RAUTAVAARA, Einojuhani (born 1928)

Adagio Celeste (for string orchestra); Book of Visions; Symphony 1
Ondine SACD ODE 1064-5. Belgian Nat. O, Franck

This is recorded in spacious four-channel SACD, which admirably suits Rautavaara's rich orchestral textures, and immediately so in the sumptuously powerful string cantilena which opens the *First Symphony*, written in two movements in 1955, but with a third added in 2003. Rautavaara acknowledged his debt to Shostakovich in this work, partly because of its string writing, but also because of the 'grotesque and ironic' Scherzo which closes the work.

The *Adagio Celeste* then follows. Inspired by a poem by Lassi Nummi which begins, 'Then, that night, when you want to love me in the deep of night, wake me,' it makes an ecstatic interlude between the *Symphony* and the imaginatively scored four chapters of the *Book of Visions*, each telling a *Tale*: darkly of *Night*, feverishly of *Fire*, warmly and sensuously of *Love*, and dramatic and apprehensive in *Fate*. The performances throughout are superbly played by this fine orchestra and, whether using two or four speakers, the sound is richly opulent, and in the demonstration bracket for its superb recording of the strings.

Angels and Visitations; (i) Violin Concerto. Isle of Bliss
Ondine ODE 881-2. (i) Oliveira; Helsinki PO, Segerstam

Rautavaara's wholly original *Violin Concerto* is hauntingly accessible and grips the listener completely. It moves from an ethereal opening cantilena, through a series of colourful events and experiences until, after a final burst of incandescent energy, it makes a sudden but positive homecoming. The lively opening of the *Isle of Bliss* is deceptive, for the music centres on a dreamy, sensual romanticism and creates a rich orchestral tapestry with a sense of yearning ecstasy, yet overall it has a surprisingly coherent orchestral structure. *Angels and Visitations* is close to the visions of William Blake and (as the composer tells us) brings a sense of 'holy dread'. The extraordinary opening evokes a rustling of angels' wings which is then malignantly transformed, becoming a ferocious multitude of bumble-bees. It is a passage of real imaginative power, in some ways comparable to the storm sequence in Sibelius's *Tapiola*. Elmar Oliveira is the inspired soloist in the *Violin Concerto*, floating his line magically and serenely in the opening *Tranquillo* and readily encompassing the work's adventurous shifts of colour and substance. Segerstam provides a shimmering backing and directs a committed and persuasively spontaneous orchestral response throughout all three works. The recording is superbly balanced, spacious and vivid in detail.

(i) *Harp Concerto. Symphony 8*
Ondine ODE 978-2. (i) Nordmann; Helsinki PO, Segerstam

The *Concerto* (2001) is predominantly reflective and highly imaginative in its use of texture. In addition to the soloist, Rautavaara adds two harps in the orchestra in order, as he puts it, to create 'a really full and lush harp sound when needed'. The French soloist, Marielle Nordmann, a pupil of Lily Laskine, gives a performance of great distinction and subtlety. Rautavaara speaks of the musical growth of the *Eighth Symphony* as characterized by slow transformation, a strong narrative element and 'the generation of new, different aspects and perspectives from the same premises, the transformation of light and colour'. As always with this composer there is a strong feeling for nature. Perhaps the most haunting movement is the third, the quiet radiance of which stays with the listener. Excellent playing from the Helsinki Philharmonic under Leif Segerstam and state-of-the-art recording.

Symphony 7; Cantus arcticus; (i) *Dances with the Winds (Concerto for Flutes & Orchestra)*
BIS CD 1038. (i) Alanko; Lahti SO, Vänskä

The *Seventh Symphony* is both powerful and atmospheric. There is a good deal of Sibelius in its first movement and there is a pervasive sense of nature. Rautavaara betrays some affinities with the minimalists but offers greater musical substance. The BIS recording is excellent, with state-of-the-art sound, and Vänskä's performance has impressive power and atmosphere; he keeps the music moving and casts a strong spell. Both shorter pieces, the familiar *Cantus arcticus* and the *Dances with the Winds*, a concerto in which the solo flautist plays four members of the flute family, are from the 1970s, and these fine performances have appeared before in other couplings.

RAVEL, Maurice (1875-1937)

Alborada del gracioso; *Une barque sur l'océan*; *Boléro*; (i) *Daphnis et Chloé* (complete). *Ma Mère l'Oye* (complete); *Menuet antique*; *Ouverture de féerie*; *Pavane pour une infante défunte*; *Rapsodie espagnole*; *Le Tombeau de Couperin*; *La Valse*; *Valses nobles et sentimentales*.
EMI (ADD) 5 00892-2 (3). O de Paris, Martinon; (i) with Paris Op. Ch.

Like his version of *Daphnis et Chloé*, Martinon's *Ma Mère l'Oye* is exquisite, among the finest ever put on record. The *Valses nobles et sentimentales* and *La Valse* are very good indeed, though *La Valse* has a rather harsh climax; but there is much ravishing delicacy of orchestral playing, notably in *Le Tombeau de Couperin* and the rare *Ouverture de féerie* (*Shéhérazade*). The sound is warm and luminously coloured and the refined virtuosity of the Orchestre de Paris is a constant source of delight. All in all, these represent some of the finest and most idiomatic versions of this repertoire in the catalogue. However, Karajan's EMI collection (EMI 476859-2) and Reiner's collection (RCA 74321 88692-2) are comparable and distinguished classics of the gramophone.

(i) *Piano Concerto in G*. *Gaspard de la nuit*
Ⓜ DG 447 438-2. Argerich; (i) BPO, Abbado – **PROKOFIEV**: *Piano Concerto 3*

Argerich's half-tones and clear fingerwork give the *G major Concerto* unusual delicacy, but its urgent virility – with jazz an important element – comes over the more forcefully by contrast. The compromise between coolness and expressiveness in the slow minuet of the middle movement is tantalizingly sensual. Her *Gaspard de la nuit* abounds in character and colour. The remastered recordings sound first class.

Piano Concerto in G; *Piano Concerto in D for the Left Hand*
Chan. CHSA 5084. Jean-Efflam Bavouzet, BBC SO, Y. P. Tortelier (with **MASSENET**: 2 *Impromptus*; 2 *Pièces*; *Toccata*; *Valse folle*) – **DEBUSSY**: *Fantaisie*

Bavouzet's accounts of the two Ravel *Piano Concertos* are very special, quite wonderfully atmospheric, indeed magical; the delicacy and finesse of the pianism are dazzling. His refinement of nuance and clarity of articulation are a source of wonder, and jazz influences are infectiously conveyed. The slow movement of the *G major* is ravishing and the *Left Hand Concerto* is wonderfully atmospheric, particularly at the opening. Beautifully balanced and finely detailed recording. The coupled Debussy *Fantaisie*, which influenced Ravel, is no less revealing, and the Massenet encores are delectable.

Daphnis et Chloé (ballet: complete)
RCA (ADD) SACD 82876 61388-2. New England Conservatory & Alumni Ch., Boston SO, Munch

Charles Munch's Boston account of *Daphnis et Chloé* is one of the great glories of recorded music. The playing in all departments of the Boston orchestra is simply electrifying. The sound here may not be as sumptuous as the Dutoit on Decca (though it is still very fine by any standards), but the richness of colour lies in the playing, and there is a heady sense of intoxication that at times sweeps you off your feet, and the integration of the chorus is impressively managed. Try the *Danse de supplication de Chloé* and the ensuing scene in which the pirates are put to flight, and you will get a good idea of how dazzling this is, with the ballet ending in tumultuous orchestral virtuosity. The SACD transfer offers rather more ambience than the CD, and the effect is quite glorious.

Daphnis et Chloé: Suite 2

Sony DVD 88697202449. BPO, Karajan - **DEBUSSY**: *La Mer; Prélude à l'après-midi d'un faune*

A magical account of *Daphnis*. Perhaps Karajan's DG recording on LP during the mid-1960s was even more sumptuous, but this superbly controlled and beautifully recorded performance still captivates, and it is expertly directed for the cameras. It was recorded at the Philharmonie in 1987, two years before Karajan's death.

Valses nobles et sentimentales; La Valse

VAI DVD 4226. Chicago SO, Charles Munch (with **BERLIOZ**: *Royal Hunt and Storm*. **RAMEAU**, arr. **D'INDY**: *Dardanus suite*. **BEETHOVEN**: *Symphony 8*. **BERLIOZ**: *Le Carnaval romain*. **WAGNER**: *Die Meistersinger: Prelude to Act III*, cond. Pierre Monteux)

Charles Munch's *Valses nobles* is one of the very finest accounts of the piece we have heard. The sound on this black-and-white telecast of 1963 is far from ideal but the performance has immense charm and character. The *Valses nobles* is perfectly paced, much more relaxed than we hear nowadays and with plenty of time for the artists to breathe. This is a model of Ravel style and, watching Munch, one realizes how naturally his charm captivates his players. The DVD is self-recommending as it includes some fine Berlioz from both Munch and Monteux (recorded in 1961) and a splendidly characteristic Beethoven *Eighth* from the latter.

(i) String Quartet in F; (ii) Violin Sonata in G

Hyp. CDA 67759. (i) Dante Quartet; (ii) Krysia Osostowicz, Simon Crawford-Phillips - **DEBUSSY**: *String Quartet*

The Dante performance of the Ravel *Quartet* matches the finest available, admirable in ensemble, attack and beauty of timbre, and very well balanced. Krysia Osostowicz has an impeccable sense of style and she herself gives an authoritative account of the Ravel *Sonata* in partnership with Simon Crawford-Phillips.

(i) *Frontispice* (for five hands). *Introduction and Allegro*; *Rapsodie espagnole*; *Shéhérazade*; *Sites auriculaires: Entre cloches*. *La Valse*
⑱ Regis RRC 1356. Stephen Coombs & Christopher Scott (pianos); (i) with Yuki Matsuzawa

Ravel often composed his orchestral music at the piano before he orchestrated it and, as we wrote about this disc when it was first issued in 1990, this recital is quite outstanding in every way: in terms of imaginative vitality, sensibility and wit. The recording too is beautifully clear and atmospheric. Obviously Stephen Coombs and Christopher Scott are a first-class team, and they are effectively joined by Yuki Matsuzawa's fifth hand in the rare *Frontispice*. But the highlights of the recital are the sensuously idiomatic *Rapsodie espagnole*, full of Spanish subtlety, and *La Valse* with its thrilling climax, which are used to frame the programme.

Histoires naturelles
Testament mono SBT 1311. Souzay, Bonneau - **FALLA**: *7 Canciones populares españolas*. **FAURÉ**: *Après un rêve*, etc.

Souzay made this record of the *Histoires naturelles* in 1951, only half a dozen years after his début in Paris, and it still remains arguably the finest recorded account of Ravel's imaginative cycle. Magnificently transferred, the sound belies its age and comes with some Fauré songs that are among the classics of the gramophone.

Shéhérazade (song-cycle)
Ⓜ Decca 475 7712. Crespin, SRO, Ansermet (with recital of French song) -
BERLIOZ: *Les Nuits d'été*. **DEBUSSY**; **POULENC**: *Songs*

Ravel's magically sensuous writing finds the ideal interpreter in Régine Crespin, supported as she is here by the maestro magician, Ansermet. The sheer richness of the singer's tone does not prevent this fine artist from being able to achieve the delicate languor demanded by an exquisite song like *The enchanted flute*. Indeed, her operatic sense of drama brings almost a sense of self-identification to the listener as the slave-girl sings to the distant sound of her lover's flute (while her master sleeps). This is ravishing. The warm, rich sheen of the glorious Decca recording spins a tonal web around the listener which is quite irresistible. This CD is one of the great glories of recorded music.

(i) *L'Enfant et les sortilèges*; (ii) *L'Heure espagnole* (complete operas)
DG (ADD) 449 7692 (2). Ogéas, Collard, Berbié, Sénéchal, Gilma, Herzog, Rehfuss, Maurane, RTF Ch. & Boys' Ch., RTF Nat. O; (ii) Berbié, Sénéchal, Giraudeau, Bacquier, Van Dam, Paris Op. O; Maazel (with **RIMSKY-KORSAKOV**: *Capriccio espagnol*; **STRAVINSKY**: *Le Chant du rossignol*)

Maazel's recordings of Ravel's two one-Act operas were made in the early 1960s and, though the solo voices in *L'Enfant* are balanced rather closely, the remastered sound in both operas is wonderfully vivid and atmospheric, and each performance is splendidly stylish. The singing is delightful: neoclassical crispness of articulation goes with refined textures that convey the ripe humour of the one piece, the tender poetry of the other. The inclusion of Maazel's superb, early-stereo accounts of Rimsky's *Capriccio* (with the Berlin Philharmonic) and *Le Chant du rossignol* glitteringly played by the Berlin Radio Orchestra, two classics of the gramophone, makes this reissue more desirable than ever. Readers may also be interested to learn that Ansermet's equally vividly characterized early-stereo account of *L'Enfant et les sortilèges* is available on Australian Decca Eloquence. The vividness of the sound still amazes today, and it is coupled with his mono *L'Heure espagnole* and some Ravel songs gorgeously sung by Suzanne Danco (480 0124 (2)). Bour's pioneering magical (1947) mono version of *L'Enfant et les sortilèges* on Testament (SBT 1044) also should never be forgotten and in some ways is the greatest performance of this sublime score on disc.

RAWSTHORNE, Alan (1905-71)

(i) *Oboe Concerto*; (ii) *Cello Concerto*. *Symphonic Studies*
Ⓑ Naxos 8.554763. RSNO, Lloyd-Jones, with (i) Stéphane Rancourt; (ii) Alexander Baillie

Rawsthorne belongs to the same generation as Rubbra, Frankel and Constant Lambert, and his distinctive voice with its richly inventive harmonic idiom is too rewarding to disappear from view, although his profile has been less in evidence in recent years. The *Symphonic Studies* (1939) sums up all his characteristic strengths: melodic inventiveness, structural resource and lucid and individual-sounding orchestration. The lyrical post-war *Oboe Concerto* (1946), written for Evelyn Rothwell, and the eloquent *Cello Concerto* (1965) are both full of memorable ideas, and Alexander Baillie has the full measure of the latter's breadth and sweep. David Lloyd-Jones is a masterly and persuasive advocate of this music.

Piano Concertos 1-2; (ii) *Overture: Street Corner*. *Symphonic Studies*
Lyrita (ADD) SRCD 255. (i) Binns, LSO, Braithwaite; (ii) LPO, Pritchard

Both of Rawsthorne's *Piano Concertos* are among the most memorable written by twentieth-century British composers, providing a Prokofiev-like contrast between jagged figuration and lyrical warmth. Without losing the necessary edge in the writing, Malcolm Binns (creating their stereo début in 1979) brings out the expressiveness of the music, particularly in the *First Concerto* with its hushed slow movement and interlude in the middle of the final *Tarantella*. There is plenty of vigour in both dance finales (the second has its quota of Latin-American rhythms). *Street Corner* is one of Rawsthorne's once familiar

shorter pieces, but it is not often heard now in spite of its considerable inventive appeal. The *Symphonic Studies* is by general consent Rawsthorne's most
original and masterly composition and well withstands the test of time. The
LPO under Pritchard plays with evident enjoyment and the 1977 recording has
a fine sense of space and splendid detail.

Symphonies (i) *1*; (ii) *2 (Pastoral)*; (iii) *3*
Lyrita (ADD/DDD) SRCD 291. (i–ii) LPO; (i) Pritchard; (ii) Chadwell, cond. Braithwaite;
  (iii) BBC SO, Del Mar

Here is a chance to get to grips with the symphonies of another neglected British composer whose music is distinguished by impeccable craftsmanship and
first-rate invention, as is readily demonstrated by the *First*, played with evident
enjoyment by the LPO under Sir John Pritchard. But, of the three, the *Second
(Pastoral) Symphony* is the most readily approachable, since its thematic material catches the ear, especially in the expressive ideas of the *Poco lento* and the
gay country-dance Scherzo. Like Vaughan Williams (and Mahler), Rawsthorne
uses a soprano soloist in the finale, with a succinct text by Henry Howard, Earl
of Surrey (1516–47), giving brief impressions of three of the four seasons: spring,
summer and winter. The music has a powerful atmosphere, and Tracy Chadwell
copes successfully with the rather angular vocal line to catch the essential melancholy of the poem.

Though the actual thematic material of the *Third Symphony* is initially hard
to identify (it is possibly too consistent in style and cut for conventional ideas
of sonata form), the formal layout is never in doubt. The first movement culminates in a calm recapitulation which resolves earlier tensions most satisfyingly,
and the separate sections of the *Sarabande* slow movement build up into one
of the most passionate climaxes that Rawsthorne ever wrote. A Scherzo with
nebulous, rather Waltonian motifs flying around is followed by a finale that
daringly keeps changing gear between fast and slow. It is questionable whether
Rawsthorne maintains the flow of argument with sufficient momentum in this
movement, but there is no doubting whatever the beauty and effectiveness of
the hushed epilogue. All three works receive superb performances, and the
recording is outstanding, with the sense of space and splendid detail we expect
from Lyrita.

String Quartets 1–3; *Theme and Variations for Two Violins*
ⓑⓑ Naxos 8.570136. Maggini Qt

The Maggini continue their survey of British quartets with this comprehensive
recording of the three *Quartets* of Rawsthorne, plus the work which in many
ways helped to spawn them, the *Theme and Variations for Two Violins* of 1937.
What links all these works is Rawsthorne's obsession with variations form,
very clearly demonstrated in that early duet. *The First Quartet*, of 1939, similarly
consists of a theme and variations, while the *Second Quartet* (1954) similarly

concludes with a variation movement, and the *Third Quartet* (1965) has a Chaconne as its darkest and most intense movement. Those last two works increasingly demonstrate the influence of Bartók, without disturbing the distinctive clarity of Rawsthorne's musical idiom. Ideal performances, vividly recorded.

RESPIGHI, Ottorino (1879–1936)

(i) *Ancient Airs and Dances*; (ii) *3 Botticelli Pictures*; (iii) *The Birds (suite)*; (iv) *Feste romane*; (v) *The Fountains of Rome*; (vi) *The Pines of Rome*

Ⓜ Double Decca (ADD) 443 759-2 (2). (i) LPO, López-Cobos; (ii) Argo CO, Heltay; (iii) LSO, Kertész; (iv) Montreal SO, Dutoit; (v) SRO, Ansermet; (vi) Cleveland O, Maazel

An inexpensive anthology, useful for including three of Respighi's most charming, rarer works – *The Birds, Ancient Airs and Dances* and *Three Botticelli Pictures* – among his more famous 'Roman Trilogy'. *The Birds* is one of the most engaging pieces of Respighi's music and deserves to be better known. Kertész's recording dates from the late 1960s and remains impressive, both as a performance and for the vintage Decca sound. *The Dove* is evocative in its minor-keyed elegance, and the strings play deliciously in *The Hen*, as they do delicately in *The Nightingale*. *The Cuckoo* is very naturally evoked and makes the music sound more substantial than it really is.

Now that Dorati's classic Mercury recording of the *Ancient Airs and Dances* is not available, the 1978 version here, conducted by López-Cobos, takes its place. If it is not quite so subtle it is superbly recorded, and the Kingsway Hall acoustic, with its characteristic warmth, gives the orchestra an enticing bloom. The music-making has striking intensity – and the third movement of the *Second Suite* and the central movements of the *Third* demonstrate this readily. The LPO strings produce playing of considerable fervour, and there is plenty of sparkle in the lighter sections throughout.

The third rarity in this collection is the *Three Botticelli Pictures*, a delicate and affecting piece, striking in its orchestral colour and freshness of invention. The music is fastidiously scored for small forces, and the effect is one of refinement and great skill in the handling of pastel colourings. It is both beautifully played (the opening *Spring* is exhilarating) by the Argo Chamber Orchestra under László Heltay and recorded (1978).

Respighi's Roman Trilogy is presented here with three different conductors and orchestras: Ansermet, with his ear for detail and orchestral colour, yields up vivid results in the *Fountains of Rome* (the opening of the Triton Fountain is startling), while the rarer and ultra-flamboyant *Feste romane* is full-bloodedly presented under Dutoit. Maazel's *Pines of Rome* is a strong, direct performance, and memorable in impact. If not in the league of the very best available, the recording is excellent.

Belkis, Queen of Sheba: Suite. Metamorphosen modi XII
Chan. 8405. Philh. O, Simon

The ballet-suite *Belkis, Queen of Sheba* is a score that set the pattern for later Hollywood biblical film music. Indeed, from the richly exotic *The Dream of Solomon* to the final *Orgiastic Dance*, via the explosive *War Dance* and the seductive *Dance of Belkis at Dawn*, this is hardly subtle music, though Respighi's orchestral palette is as imaginative as always. The *Metamorphosen*, on the other hand, is a taut and sympathetic set of variations. It has been ingeniously based on a medieval theme, and though a group of cadenza variations relaxes the tension of argument in the middle, the brilliance and variety of the writing have much in common with Elgar's *Enigma*. Superb playing from the Philharmonia, treated to one of the finest recordings that even Chandos has produced. Indeed, this mid-1980s CD received one of the many *Gramophone* Engineering Awards that Chandos won in the 1980s and '90s and sounds just as spectacular today.

Burlesca; 5 Études-Tableaux (Rachmaninov, arr. Respighi); Preludio, corale e fuga; Rossiniana
Chan. 10388. BBC PO, Noseda

Few composers can rival Ottorino Respighi in his exploitation of orchestral sound, not least in his arrangements of other composers' music. This splendid disc offers two important examples of his arrangements, not just the score he concocted from Rossinian fragments, but (most impressive of all) the total re-creation of five of Rachmaninov's *Études-Tableaux*, turning them into totally new works, at times barely recognizable against the piano originals.

It is true that *Rossiniana* does not match its dazzling predecessor, *La Boutique fantasque*, in colour or memorability, but here Respighi chose Rossini pieces that are not quite so memorable, with the longest of the four movements a solemn lament. Of the Rachmaninov arrangements there can be no reservations whatever, leaving one open-mouthed at Respighi's ingenuity and imagination. The other two works date from much earlier, with the *Burlesca* ripe with horn-writing and the *Prelude, Chorale and Fugue* even more remarkable. Written as a student exercise when Respighi was only 21, it already demonstrates his mastery over orchestral colours. Performances of all four works are outstanding, with the Chandos sound bringing out the full richness of Respighi's writing.

The Fountains of Rome; The Pines of Rome
Ⓜ RCA (ADD) 09026 61401-2. Chicago SO, Reiner - **MUSSORGSKY**: *Pictures at an Exhibition*

Reiner's legendary recordings of *The Pines* and *Fountains of Rome* were made in Symphony Hall, Chicago, on 24 October 1959, and these extraordinarily atmospheric performances have never been surpassed since for their spectacle or their sultry Italian warmth. The turning on of the Triton fountain brings an unforced cascade of orchestral brilliance. Reiner's classic recording has now been given RCA's SACD face-lift and sounds more vividly brilliant than ever. The coupling of the Mussorgsky *Pictures* is hardly less compelling.

Rossiniana (arr. Respighi)
Ⓜ Australian Decca Eloquence (ADD) 476 2724. SRO, Ansermet – **OFFENBACH**: *Gaîté Parisienne*. **GOUNOD**: *Faust: ballet music*

It is perhaps curious that this work is usually catalogued under Respighi, whereas *La Boutique fantasque*, which Respighi also based on Rossini's music, is more often found under Rossini. *Rossiniana* is not as inspired as that score, but there is still much to enjoy. Ansermet's performances are the very opposite of the Solti items on this CD, and it is the delicate colour and balance of these scores (rather than immaculate orchestral playing) that Ansermet fans will most admire. The final *Tarantella* is especially enjoyable here. Vintage Decca sound.

String Quartet in D min.; *Quartetto dorico*. (i) *Il tramonto (The Sunset)*
BIS CD1454. New Hellenic Qt, (i) with Stella Doufexis

The New Hellenic is reputedly the finest quartet in Greece, and their accounts of these two Respighi rarities are certainly accomplished. The *D minor Quartet* comes from 1909, at the end of the composer's studies with Rimsky-Korsakov in Russia and Bruch in Germany. Respighi was an accomplished violinist and violist, playing in the Imperial Opera as the latter and in the Mugellini Quartet as the former. His knowledge of string technique is evident in the early *Quartet* and in the later *Dorian Quartet* of 1924, written when he was being drawn towards ecclesiastical modes. *Il tramonto (The Sunset)*, a setting of Shelley, is more familiar in its orchestral form, but Stella Doufexis blends in with the more intimate texture to good effect. The recording is up to the high standards of the house.

RICCI, Ruggiero (violin)

SIBELIUS: *Violin Concerto in D min.* (with LSO, Fjeldstad).
TCHAIKOVSKY: *Violin Concerto* (with LSO, Sargent); *Scherzo*; *Sérénade mélancolique* (with LSO, Fjeldstad). **SARASATE**: *Carmen Fantasy*; *Zigeunerweisen*. **SAINT-SAËNS**: *Havanaise*; *Introduction and Rondo Capriccioso, Op. 28* (with LSO, Gamba). **KHACHATURIAN**: *Violin Concerto* (with LPO, Fistoulari)
Australian Decca Eloquence (ADD) 480 2083 (2)

Ricci was a prolific recording virtuoso who made many dashing recordings for Decca from the 1950s to the 1970s. Not all listeners responded to his close vibrato, but he had a considerable international reputation. These two CDs contain some of his most successful discs, and his admirers will be glad to have them available again, though they must be approached with some caution. Though there have been finer accounts of the Sibelius *Violin Concerto*, Ricci's, dating from the late 1950s, still remains a formidable one. He has the clean, clear-cut and effortless technique that is a prime necessity for this concerto. The reading is straightforward, with no lack of intensity (the finale has real electricity). A considerable contribution to the success of the performance is made by Fjeldstad with the LSO (the same conductor who made Curzon's classic recording of the Grieg *Piano Concerto* around the same time). Although Ricci is well forward, he is sufficiently detached from the orchestra to give an impression of depth. The same conductor accompanies the two delightful Tchaikovsky movements that might almost be part of an early Tchaikovsky violin concerto. The *Sérénade* was written in 1875, three years before the well-known concerto. It is slighter than the slow movement of the actual concerto but has a similar wistful sweetness, entirely characteristic of the composer, and is most appealing melodically. The *Scherzo*, arranged from a group of pieces written for violin and piano, is short, genial, pithy and very attractive. Ricci plays both pieces admirably and the accompaniment and recording are again excellent. As for the performance of the main Tchaikovsky *Concerto*, Ricci is especially impressive in the finale, where the soloist's brilliance comes into its own – inspiring an electricity in Sargent's conducting which was often lacking in his studio recordings. If the slow movement isn't quite as impressive as either his earlier, mono recording or his later, Phase 4 version with Fournet (it lacks a warm lyricism, not helped by his close vibrato), it remains a vital reading, and the Decca sound is excellent. The second disc comprises colourful violin show-pieces of Sarasate and Saint-Saëns which show off Ricci's extrovert style very well. His brilliance is dazzling, making the most of the bright colours and seductive melodies. The Saint-Saëns items are justly admired, but part of the success of these performances is also thanks to the lively, precise accompaniments of Piero Gamba and the LSO – all brightly captured in stereo by Decca in the late 1950s. The Khachaturian *Violin Concerto* (one of the composer's very best works) completes this disc. Fistoulari matches Ricci's brilliance in terms of extrovert, bright playing and, with vivid Decca stereo sound (1956), one can see why this recording was originally so popular. For Ricci's admirers this two-CD set makes a suitable companion to Decca's five-CD 'Originals Masters' box (475 108-2), which includes some of Ricci's most impressive chamber-music recordings, including the delightful Weber *Violin Sonatas*, as well as his classic Paganini *Caprices* (for which he was well suited) and his mono recording of Paginini's *First* and *Second Violin Concertos* (with excellent accompaniments from Anthony Collins) and a characterful performance of Lalo's *Symphonie espagnole* (with Ansermet). A second volume of concertos has also been released on Australian Decca Eloquence (480 2080), which includes a rare mono performance of the Beethoven *Violin Concerto* (with the LPO and Boult), a brilliant Mendelssohn (with the Netherlands RPO and Fournet), the Bruch No. 1 (with the LSO and Gamba – a full-blooded reading) and the much rarer *Concerto* of Dvořák (with the LSO and Sargent).

RIES, Ferdinand (1784–1838)

Piano Concerto, Op. 132; Grand Variations on 'Rule Britannia', Op. 116; Introduction et Variations Brillantes, Op. 170
ⓑ Naxos 8.570440. Hinterhuber, RLPO, Grodd

Perhaps these are not the greatest recordings of the greatest music, but it is entertaining rarities like these that make record collecting so much fun. These three works are associated with Ferdinand Ries's successful period of living in England, from 1813 until the early 1820s. Beethoven's influence in this 35-minute *Piano Concerto* is obvious and it is a thoroughly entertaining work, subtitled 'Farewell to England'. Written in 1823, it is very much in the same vein as Hummel's concertos of the period: very tuneful, with melodic classicism tempered with more dramatic overtones. The finale is a toe-tapping delight. It would be wonderful to hear such music in the concert hall, but I suspect that all we ever shall get is this recording – which luckily is first rate. The *Grand Variations on 'Rule Britannia'* is an absolute hoot, with its bold introduction leading up to its famous theme, which is treated to some brilliant variations. The *Introduction et Variations Brillantes* is a similarly brilliant treatment of 'Soldier, soldier, will you marry me?' Sparkling performances to match the music, and the recording is first rate.

RIMSKY-KORSAKOV, Nikolay (1844–1908)

Capriccio espagnol; Christmas Eve: Suite. Dubinushka; The Flight of the Bumblebee; May Night: Overture. Russian Easter Festival Overture; Sadko; The Snow Maiden: Suite. Symphony 2 (Antar); The Tale of Tsar Saltan: Suite
ⓑ Australian Decca Eloquence stereo/mono 480 0827 (2). SRO, Ansermet

This two-CD Rimsky-Korsakov set surely shows Ansermet at his very finest. The opening of the *Christmas Eve Suite* has a chilled, icy, magical atmosphere, and this colourful tone-poem builds up to a magnificent polonaise – an adrenalin-inducing moment – where Ansermet's rhythmic bite is at its best. The *Snow Maiden Suite* is similarly colourful, with Ansermet bringing out all the brilliance of the woodwind and percussion in particular. Neither the *Russian Easter Festival Overture* nor *Capriccio espagnol* is as inspired as this, though the rhythmic point in *Capriccio espagnol* (the only mono recording on this CD) is unfailingly enjoyable. The opening of *Dubinushka* is delightfully and jauntily pointed, with the bass drum (as always from this source) beautifully captured, adding to the piquant effect. *Sadko* has marvellous atmosphere and intensity – as well as drama – and there is plenty of felicitous music, as well as playing, in the score. *May Night*, with its vibrant strings, comes off well, as does all the brilliance in the *Tale of Tsar Saltan Suite*. Even if Ansermet's bee in the *Flight of the Bumblebee* is a rather leisurely creature, it is invested with plenty of buzz from all departments of the orchestra. The longest work in this collection is the still rare *Antar*, which Ansermet helped to pioneer on LP – he recorded its first stereo release in astonishingly early stereo, dating from June 1954, yet sounding amazingly full, if not as expansive as the later recordings on this CD.

Capriccio espagnol, Op. 34
RCA (ADD) 09026 63302-2. RCA Victor SO, Kondrashin – **KABALEVSKY**:
  The Comedians: Suite. **KHACHATURIAN**: *Masquerade Suite*.
  TCHAIKOVSKY: *Capriccio italien*

Kondrashin's 1958 performance is among the finest ever recorded, ranking alongside Maazel's famous Berlin Philharmonic account, but with the advantage of slightly more sumptuous string-textures. Like the coupled Tchaikovsky *Capriccio*, it has great flair and excitement, with glittering colour and detail in the variations and the *Scena e canto gitano*. The orchestral zest is exhilarating, yet there is warmth too, and the resonant recording still sounds very good indeed.

Scheherazade, Op. 35 (DVD version)
Medici Arts DVD 2072276. Phd. O, Ormandy (with **GLINKA**: *Ruslan and Ludmilla Overture*. **HANDEL**: *Concerto in D*. **WOLF-FERRARI**: *Il segreto di Susanna Overture*. **STRAUSS**: *Der Rosenkavalier Suite*)

Scheherazade (symphonic suite), Op. 35 (CD version)
RCA SACD 82876 66377-2 (2). Chicago SO, Reiner – **STRAVINSKY**: *Chant du rossignol*

Now here is something rather special. Ormandy recorded it at the Academy of Music, Philadelphia, in 1977–8. Television concerts by Karajan and the Berlin Philharmonic are available in abundance, from Beethoven to Strauss, but the other great partnerships of the period also producing a unique sonority, flair and virtuosity are scantily represented. Here we have a performance of *Scheherazade* which is perfect in every way, with a superb violin soloist in Norman Carol. The visual side of things is expertly managed, as is the sound.

Reiner's magnificent (1956) *Scheherazade* stands out among the many superb RCA recordings made in Chicago in the 1950s. In the new SACD transfer the sensation of sitting in the concert hall is uncannily real, and the recording itself has extraordinary lustre. Reiner's first movement opens richly

and dramatically and has a strong forward impulse. Sidney Harth, the orchestral leader, naturally balanced, plays most seductively. Reiner's affectionate
individual touches in the gloriously played slow movement have much in common with Beecham's version, and they sound similarly spontaneous. The
finale, brilliant and exciting, was recorded in a single take and has a climax of
resounding power and amplitude, and the acoustics throughout provide the
orchestra with plenty of body and arresting brass sonorities. The Stravinsky
coupling also shows the conductor and orchestra at their finest, and this is a
CD that should be in everyone's collection.

Cantatas: (i) *Inz Gomera, Op. 60*; *The Song of Alexis, Man of God, Op.
20*; (ii–iii) *The Song of Oleg the Wise, Op. 58*; (iii–iv) *Switsezianka (or
The Girl in the Lake), Op. 44*
HM Chant du Monde RUS 288175. (i) Fedotova, Sizova; (ii) Didenko; (iii) Kortchak; (iv)
Mitrakova; Moscow Ac. Ch., Moscow SO, Ziva

These splendid secular choral cantatas are a real find, and show an endearing
new facet to Rimsky's genius. Try the opening *Song of Alexis, Man of God*, superbly
sung by a fine Russian chorus, and you will surely be hooked immediately. The
composer re-uses music written to accompany pilgrims in *The Maid of Pskov*, to
evoke the legend of Saint Alexis, who renounced marriage with a princess in
order to lead a hermit's life. Its noble melody is based on a Russian folksong. *The
Song of Oleg the Wise*, set to a poem by Pushkin, for tenor (who tells the story) and
bass (Oleg) is melodramatically operatic, and *Inz Gomera*, based on Homer, even
more so with its powerful orchestral *Prelude* depicting Poseidon's tempest, before
the luminously seductive writing for the female voices.

Switsezianka (using a poem by Lev May) is the familiar folk tale of the watery
nymph who captivates her young swain and insists on his fidelity, with a dire
penalty if he forgets her. She then returns in an even more beautiful form to
test his faithfulness and he immediately forgets his vows, succumbs to temptation, and is swallowed up by the frothing waters of the lake. Rimsky's highly
atmospheric scena, using soprano and tenor soloists, climaxes as a splendid
quartet of performances, with fine Russian singers throughout. The recording
is first class and so is the documentation, with full translations included,
which are easy to follow even without the original Russian.

ROREM, Ned (born 1923)

(i) *Flute Concerto*; (ii) *Violin Concerto*. *Pilgrims*
ⓑⓑ Naxos 8.559278. (i) Khaner; (ii) Quint; RLPO, Serebrier

Ned Rorem is already a celebrated composer of the newer generation in
America; he writes tonally and without the need to shock his listeners into

submission. On this well-planned Naxos disc we are transported into his refined, often elegiac sound-world by the opening *Pilgrims* for string orchestra, which evokes a quiet feeling of 'remembrance'.

Each of the two *Concertos* is programmatic, the work for flute offering a series of vignettes with often virtuosic embroidery. It is superbly played by Jeffrey Khaner. The arresting opening drum-command introduces the haunting five-note motif on which the six movements all draw. So the work is almost a set of variations, ending with a catchy *False Waltz* and on to the refined mood of the closing *Résumé and Prayer*. The result is highly imaginative and full of variety, if perhaps a little over-extended. The *Violin Concerto* opens dramatically and ardently and is a true interplay between soloist and accompaniment, its second movement an unlikely *Toccata-Chaconne* built over a jagged timpani rhythm. But the heart of the work is lyrically heart-warming in its gentle beauty, first a simple *Romance without Words*, followed by the serene *Midnight*, 'a microsonic variation'. Philippe Quint is a deeply responsive soloist, playing with silvery timbre: the composer could not have asked for better, and throughout Serebrier directs the accompanying RLPO most sympathetically. First-class recording.

ROSSINI, Gioachino (1792–1868)

String Sonatas 1–6 (complete)
Ⓑ Double Decca (ADD) 443 838-2 (2). ASMF, Marriner (with **CHERUBINI**: *Étude for 2 French Horns & Strings* (with Tuckwell). **BELLINI**: *Oboe Concerto in E flat* (with Lord). **DONIZETTI**: *String Quartet*)

We have a very soft spot for the sparkle, elegance and wit of these ASMF performances of the Rossini *String Sonatas*, amazingly accomplished products for a 12-year-old. Marriner offers them on full orchestral strings but with such finesse and precision of ensemble that the result is all gain. The 1966 recording still sounds remarkably full and natural, and the current CD transfer adds to the feeling of presence. The new Double Decca format has other music added. Apart from the Donizetti *Quartet*, which has an appropriately Rossinian flavour, the two minor concertante works are well worth having, with both Barry Tuckwell (in what is in essence a three-movement horn concertino) and Roger Lord in excellent form.

Overtures: *Armida*; *Il barbiere di Siviglia*; *Bianca e Faliero*; *La cambiale di matrimonio*; *La Cenerentola*; *Demetrio e Polibio*; *Edipo a Colono*; *Edoardo e Cristina*; (i) *Ermione. La gazza ladra*; *L'inganno felice*; *L'italiana in Algeri*; *Maometto II*; *Otello*; (i) *Ricciardo e Zoraide. La scala di seta*; *Semiramide*; *Le siège de Corinthe*; *Il Signor Bruschino*; *Tancredi*; *Torvaldo e Dorliska*; *Il Turco in Italia*;

Il viaggio a Reims; William Tell; Sinfonia al Conventello; Sinfonia di Bologna
Ⓜ Decca (ADD) 473 967-2 (3). ASMF, Marriner, (i) with Amb. S.

Marriner's reissued Trio spans all Rossini's overtures, but one must remember that the early Neapolitan operas, with the exception of *Ricciardo e Zoraide* and *Ermione*, make do with a simple Prelude, leading into the opening chorus. *Ricciardo e Zoraide*, however, is an extended piece (12 minutes 25 seconds), with the choral entry indicating that the introduction is at an end. *Maometto II* is on a comparable scale, while the more succinct *Armida* is an example of Rossini's picturesque evocation, almost like a miniature tone-poem. Twenty-four overtures plus two sinfonias make a delightful package in such sparkling performances, which eruditely use original orchestrations. The well-known popular overtures stand competition with the best. Indeed, *William Tell* has almost Toscaninian thrust in the final gallop, but it is the frothy, infectious music-making which one enjoys most. Full, bright, atmospheric recordings, spaciously reverberant with no artificial brilliance.

For a single-disc recommendation of Rossini's most popular overtures, Reiner's Chicago version from 1958 (RCA 82876 65844-2) is hard to beat, and they emerge on CD as sparkling and vivacious as ever. Giulini's Philharmonia recordings on EMI, from the early 1960s, are equally recommendable and very inexpensive (CfP 2 28281-2). For those who insist on digital recording, Chailly's two-CD bargain set on Decca (443 850-2 (2)) is strongly recommended, stylish performances in demonstration sound, with London's finest musicians (National Philharmonic Orchestra).

William Tell: ballet music
Ⓜ Australian Decca Eloquence (ADD) 480 2388 (2). Paris Conservatoire O, Fistoulari
   (with **SAINT-SAËNS**: *Bacchanale*. **VERDI**: *Aida: ballet music*) – (see also under **FISTOULARI**)

With such stylish pointing of strings, Rossini's ballet music to *William Tell* sounds freshly minted, with the distinctive sound of the Paris orchestra adding to the drama of proceedings. Outstanding couplings, too.

Stabat Mater
Chan. 8780. Field, D. Jones, A. Davies, Earle, L. Symphony Ch., City of L. Sinfonia, Hickox

Richard Hickox rightly presents Rossini's *Stabat Mater* warmly and with gutsy strength. Rossini's *Stabat Mater* is full of rollicking good tunes and operatic theatricality – and includes an exhilarating final chorus, among many memorable moments. All four soloists here are first rate, not Italianate of tone but full and warm, and the London Symphony Chorus sings with fine attack as well as producing the most refined *pianissimos* in the unaccompanied quartet, here as usual given to the full chorus rather than to the soloists. Full blooded and atmospheric sound.

Il barbiere di Siviglia (complete, DVD version)

Warner NVC Arts DVD 4509 99223-2. Ewing, Rawnsley, Cosotti, Desderi, Furlanetto, Glyndebourne Ch., LPO, Cambreling (Producer: John Cox; V/D: Dave Heather)

Il barbiere di Siviglia (complete, CD version)

Ⓜ EMI mono 4 56444-2 (2). Callas, Alva, Gobbi, Ollendorf, Philh. Ch. & O, Galliera

The NVC DVD offers the finest recording of *Il barbiere* since the famous Callas/Gobbi set on CD; moreover it has the inestimable advantage of video, which greatly enhances the humour. Maria Ewing is an absolutely delightful Rosa, her prettiness matching her coquettish charm and superb vocal bravura. John Rawnsley's ebulliently self-assured Figaro dominates the proceedings as he should, and Max René Cosotti's golden-toned Almaviva completes the vocal cast with distinction although, as Basilio, Ferruccio Furlanetto's *La calunnia* is also a joy. Claudio Desderi is an old hand at *opera buffa* and his Bartolo is as vocally fluent as his demeanour is amusingly angry. All told, a marvellous cast, superb singing, and sparklingly stylish orchestral playing from the LPO under Cambreling make this 1981 Glyndebourne recording a set to treasure.

Gobbi and Callas were at their most inspired in 1957 when the famous EMI mono recording was made in Kingsway Hall, whose acoustics ensured a recording with an attractive ambience. It has been nicely refurbished and, while the set is not absolutely complete in its text, the performance comes up so crisp and sparkling that it can be confidently recommended even above Cecilia Bartoli's Decca version which, also full of fun, is on three CDs (425 520-2) against EMI's pair. Callas remains supreme as a minx-like Rosina, summing up the character superbly in *Una voce poco fa*. The sound comes up very acceptably in this fine new transfer, clarified, fuller and more atmospheric, presenting a uniquely characterful performance with new freshness and immediacy.

La Cenerentola (CD version)

Decca 478 3456 (2). Bartoli, Matteuzzi, Corbelli, Dara, Costa, Banditelli, Pertusi, Teatro Comunale di Bologna Ch. & O, Chailly

On the Decca CDs Cecilia Bartoli makes an inspired Cenerentola. Her tone-colours are not just more sensuous than those of her rivals; her imagination and feeling for detail add enormously to her vivid characterization, culminating in a stunning account of the final rondo, *Non più mesta*. William Matteuzzi is an engaging prince, sweeter of tone and more stylish than his direct rivals, while the contrasting of the bass and baritone roles is ideal between Alessandro Corbelli as Dandini, Michele Pertusi as the tutor, Alidoro, and Enzo Dara as Don Magnifico. Few Rossini opera-sets have such fizz as this, and the recording is one of Decca's most vivid.

Bartoli also appears in this, practically her signature role, in a fizzing Houston Opera production on DVD (Decca 071 444-9: Dara, Giménez, Corbelli, Pertusi, Houston Grand Opera Choir and Symphony Orchestra, Campanella). Bruno

Campanella conducts very spiritedly and visually the production could not be more winning; and the camera placing is a great credit to Brian Large.

Le Comte Ory (CD version)

DG 477 5020 (2). Flórez, Miles, Bonfadelli, Todorovitch, De Liso, Pratico, Prague Ch., Bologna Theatre O, López-Cobos

This is one of the most delectable of all Rossini's comic operas, an essay in French that set a new pattern for the composer. Jesús López-Cobos, the most skilled of Rossini conductors, even matches in rhythmic lift and comic timing the magic example of Vittorio Gui on the classic Glyndebourne recordings of the 1950s. The big ensemble that ends Act I is even faster than Gui, yet it is just as effervescent. The presence of an audience plainly helps, and the performance gains enormously too from the brilliant characterization of the central character of the predatory Count himself, played by Juan Diego Flórez, tackling the most formidable florid passages with ease and imagination. As the object of his desires, the Countess Adele, whose husband is away at the Crusades, Stefania Bonfadelli sings with equal fluency, a coloratura soprano with a mezzo-ish tinge in the lower register who can reach a top E flat with ease. Alastair Miles as the Count's tutor sings strongly, making him rather a severe character, with Marina de Liso light and sparkling as the page, Isolier. The closely focused recording is full and firm, if not always kind to the orchestra, with the voices very well caught, and vociferous applause at the end of each Act adding to the sense of presence.

Warner have also issued an excellent DVD of this wonderful opera (0630 18646-2), with bright, colourful sets and a superb cast (Marc Laho as Ory, Annick Massis as the Countess and Diana Montague as Isolier), conducted with sparkle by Andrew Davis.

La gazza ladra (complete, DVD version)

Arthaus DVD 102 203. Feller, Condo, Kuebler, Cotrubas, Cologne Op. Ch., Gürzenich O, Cologne, Bartoletti (TV Director: José Montes-Baquer)

Recorded live at the Cologne opera in 1987, this sparkling performance is a winner. One forgets the improbabilities of the plot, so agreeably enjoyable is the performance, with Cotrubas a charming Ninetta; and her suitor, Giannetto, sung by David Kuebler, is ardent but tender when he needs to be. All the roles are done with character and obvious enjoyment, including the ensembles and choruses. The orchestra is lively and alert, with Rossini's tuneful invention a constant source of delight. The production is the crowning glory of this performance, with beautiful sets and costumes, all brightly and sympathetically lit.

Chandos have recorded an equally winning version of this opera, sung in English, with a superb cast including Majella Cullagh as the heroine, Ninetta, and Christopher Purves as the Major, her employer, and David Parry draws sparkling playing from the orchestra, chorus and soloists alike (CHAN 3097 (2)).

William Tell (complete, CD version in French)

EMI 028 826 2 (3), Finley, Lemieux, Byström, Osborn, St Cecilia Ac., Pappano

Opening with an arresting account of the Overture, then offering consistently thrilling singing from the chorus, and a vividly energetic orchestral response, Pappano's new live recording of *William Tell* (in the original French version) tends to sweep the board. The performance is cast from strength: Gerald Finley is an excellent Tell, Malin Byström is an impressive Matilde and the high-lying tenor role of Arnold is accomplished with flair by John Osborn. But it is the ensembles that one remembers most, especially the splendour of the powerful closing affirmation of Swiss liberty.

L'italiana in Algeri (complete, DVD version)

DG DVD 073 4261. Horne, Montarsolo, Ahlstedt, Merritt, Kesling, Milas, Met. Op. Ch. & O, Levine (V/D: Brian Large)

Marilyn Horne is the great star focus of the 1986 production from the Met. She had a great affinity with the role of Isabella. 'I don't know where she leaves off and I begin: the character comes to easily to me,' she comments. She is predictably brilliant in the coloratura passages, with her commanding presence not getting in the way of a sense of fun. Her lover, Lindoro, is sung more than capably by Douglas Ahlstedt, though his tone is not consistently beautiful (some high-lying passages are a bit strained). Mustafà, sung by the veteran Paolo Montarsolo, has a bit of wobble in his voice, but he has the relish of an old pro who knows his role inside out. His wife Elvira is charmingly sung by Myra Merritt. All the various comic roles are well done, especially with such seasoned singers as Spiro Milas in the role of Haly, the captain of the Algerian pirates. The production by Jean-Pierre Ponnelle is brightly attractive, and the direction is at the service of the performance. Levine conducts with characteristic energy, though his style is more suited to Verdi than to the charm of Rossini. The bonuses include an interview with Marilyn Horne talking about Rossini, plus a couple of extra arias from *Samson et Dalila* and *The Ghosts of Versailles*.

There have been many fine recordings of this score on CD, but Berganza's Decca version from the 1960s is still very recommendable (475 8275). The fine cast (Alva, Corena, Panerai, Maggio Musicale Fiorentino Ch. & O) under Varviso offers Rossinian sparkle in abundance and the music blossoms readily. Teresa Berganza makes an enchanting Italian Girl, and the three principal men are all characterful. The recording is vintage Decca, vividly remastered, and adds greatly to the sparkle of the whole proceedings. The reissue includes a libretto with translation, and this is a fine bargain.

Semiramide (complete, CD version)

Decca (ADD) 475 7918-2 (3). Sutherland, Horne, Rouleau, Malas, Serge, Amb. Op. Ch., LSO, Bonynge

This is simply one of the great opera recordings in the catalogue. The partnership of Joan Sutherland and Marilyn Horne – both at their supreme peak – delivers one ravishing number after another. Rossini concentrates on the love of Queen Semiramide for Prince Arsace (a mezzo-soprano) and musically the result is a series of fine duets. In Sutherland's interpretation, Semiramide is not so much a Lady Macbeth as a passionate, sympathetic woman and, with dramatic music predominating over languorous cantilena, one has her best, bright manner. Marilyn Horne is well contrasted, direct and masculine in style, and Spiro Malas makes a firm, clear contribution in a minor role. Rouleau and Serge are variable but more than adequate, and Bonynge keeps the whole opera together with his alert, rhythmic control of tension and pacing. Vintage Decca sound is the icing on the cake.

Tancredi (complete, DVD version)
TDK DVD DVWW OPTANC. Barcellona, Takova, Giménez, Maggio Musicale Fiorentino, Frizza (V/D: Andrea Bevilacqua)

Tancredi (1813) was Rossini's first mature opera and it secured his popularity at home and abroad as the leading composer of Italian opera. Recordings have already revealed it to be a score of some power, but now we have a superb performance on DVD. The cast is terrific, with Raúl Giménez coping with Rossini's florid and high-flying writing, and Marco Spotti's bass firm and positive. The women are equally impressive: Darina Takova is agile and she gets round her fiendishly difficult writing with aplomb. She is sweetly affecting in her yearning numbers and looks marvellous on the stage. Daniela Barcellona, in the trouser role of Tancredi, is very fine indeed, providing appropriate contrast to Takova. Riccardo Frizza's conducting maintains the forward impulse of the rather complicated story with both musical spontaneity and theatrical drama. One's admiration for this Rossini opera is also enhanced: apart from the impressive arias and duets, the exciting rum-ti-tum choruses and grand finales are irresistible – no wonder he became so popular! The (alas) sad ending is touchingly and exquisitely done. The production, by Pier Luigi Pizzi, is unfussy and effective, with the greys and blacks of the stylish set sympathetically lit to provide an excellent backdrop to the drama. Simple costumes but, again, very effective. The production works for the opera, the music and the singers. Decent sound. Thoroughly recommended.

Il viaggio a Reims (complete, DVD version)
Opus Arte DVD OA 0967 D. Belyaeva, Ouspenski, Youdina, Shtoda, Kiknadze, Safiouline, Guigolachvili, Voropaev, Kitchenko, Tsanga, Kamenski, Sommer, Tanovtski, Iliouchnikov, Chmoulevitch, Mariinsky Theatre Ac., Mariinsky Theatre O, Gergiev (Director: Alain Maratrat; V/D: Vincent Bataillon)

In a co-production with the Théâtre Châtelet in Paris, the singing team and orchestra from the Mariinsky Theatre in St Petersburg offer a sparkling account of Rossini's festival opera under their director, Valery Gergiev. Originally written for a one-off celebration, *Il viaggio a Reims* was almost entirely forgotten until recent years, and it proves to be a delight from beginning to end, with a feast of fine numbers. Some of these were quickly used by Rossini in one of his earliest Paris operas, *Le Comte Ory*, but there is much besides. Maratrat's production updates the action to the 1930s, with the men in the cast wearing trilbies. That includes Gergiev himself, who conducts his orchestra on stage. With such a well-coordinated team it is hard to pick out individual stars among the young singers, but Vladislav Ouspenski as Baron von Trombonok, Anastasia Belyaeva as Madame Cortese, Daniil Shtoda as Count Libenskof and Edouard Tsanga as Lord Sidney all give memorable performances.

For those wanting a CD version of this score, DG offers one of the most sparkling and totally successful live opera recordings available, with Claudio Abbado (with the COE) in particular more free and spontaneous sounding than he generally is on disc, relishing the sparkle of the comedy, and the line-up of soloists could hardly be more impressive (Ricciarelli, Terrani, Cuberli, Gasdia, Araiza, Giménez, Nucci, Raimondi, Ramey, Dara), with no weak link. Abbado's brilliance and sympathy draw the musical threads compellingly together with the help of superb, totally committed playing from the Chamber Orchestra of Europe (DG 477 7435 (2)).

ROUSE, Christopher (born 1949)

(i) *Flute Concerto*. *Phaeton*; *Symphony 2*
Telarc CD 80452. Houston SO, Eschenbach, (i) with Wincenc

The remarkable five-movement *Flute Concerto*, commissioned by the present soloist, followed two years after Rouse's *Trombone Concerto*. The beautiful first and last movements, with their serene, soaring solo line, are connected thematically and share the Gaelic title *Anhran* ('Song'). They frame two faster, much more dissonant and rhythmically unpredictable movements. The kernel of the work is the gripping central *Elegia*, written in response to the terrible murder of the two-year-old James Bulger by two ten-year-old schoolboys. Rouse introduces a rich, Bach-like chorale which moves with a wake-like solemnity towards a central explosion of passionate despair. Throughout, the solo writing demands great bravura and intense emotional commitment from the flautist, which is certainly forthcoming here.

The *Second Symphony* is a three-part structure, with the outer movements again using identical material to frame the anguished central slow movement. In the composer's words, that forms a 'prism' through which the mercurial opening material is 'refracted' to yield the angry, tempestuous finale. The desperately grieving *Adagio* is another threnody for a personal friend and colleague, Stephen Albert, killed in a car accident in 1992. *Phaeton* is a savage, explosive early work

(1986), which could hardly be more different from the tone-poem of Saint-Saëns. Helios's sun chariot, immediately out of his son's control, charges its way across the heavens with horns roistering, and is very quickly blown out of the sky by Zeus's thunderbolt. Performances here are excellent, very well played and recorded, and the *Flute Concerto* is unforgettable.

Alas, the supreme RCA recording of Rouse's *Trombone Concerto, Gorgon* and *Iscariot* (with the Colorado SO, Alsop, 09026 68410-2) is deleted but can probably be found on the internet. Well worth seeking out – it is an electrifying sonic experience, breathtaking in its impact and one of the great digital recordings of the last century.

ROUSSEL, Albert (1869–1937)

Bacchus et Ariane (ballet: complete), *Op. 43*; *Le Festin de l'araignée (The Spider's Feast), Op. 17*
Chan. 9494. BBC PO, Y. P. Tortelier

The exhilarating (1931) score for *Bacchus et Ariane* teems with life and is full of rhythmic vitality. What a marvellously inventive and resourceful score it is! Tortelier offers the best version yet and the BBC Philharmonic play with tremendous zest. They also give a sensitive and atmospheric account of *Le Festin de l'araignée*. They offer us the complete banquet, not just the chosen dishes on the set menu! This magical score weaves a strong spell. Splendid recording and performances of rewarding and colourful music that deserves to be more widely heard – although it has to be said that neither of the two works here is long absent from the catalogue, and rightly so.

Le Marchand de sable qui passe (incidental music): *Suite, Op. 13*; *Divertissement for Piano Quintet, Op. 6*; *Sérénade for Flute, Harp, & String Trio*; *Trio for Flute, Viola & Cello, Op. 40*; *Impromptu for Harp, Op. 21*; *Duo for Bassoon & Double-Bass*
Praga PRD 350018. Czech Nonet, with Englichová (harp), Wiesner (piano)

This is an enchanting disc, revealing another side to Roussel in the elegance and refinement of his writing for small instrumental groups. The incidental music for *Le Marchand de sable qui passe*, scored for string quintet, harp, flute, clarinet and horn, is hauntingly atmospheric, recalling Ravel's *Introduction and Allegro*. Although the textures and colouring are quite individual, the ethereal melody of the *Scène finale* has a magic comparable with the closing scene of Ravel's *Ma Mère l'Oye*. The piquant *Sérénade* and *Flute Trio* are hardly less delicate in feeling; both have subtly restless slow movments, the latter closing with whimsically capricious high spirits. The *Duo for Bassoon and Double-Bass* (written for Serge Koussevitzky) brings an interlude of bucolic humour, and the miniature *Divertissement* for piano quintet is also capriciously light-hearted and worthy of Jean Françaix, although still Rousselian. The performances have an Elysian charm and sophistication of feeling and are beautifully recorded.

Symphony 1 (Le Poème de la forêt); Le Marchand de sable qui passe: Incidental music; Résurrection: Symphonic Prelude
🅑🅑 Naxos 8.570323. RSNO, Denève

Symphony 2; Pour une fête de printemps; Suite in F
🅑🅑 Naxos 8.570529. RSNO, Denève

Symphony 3 in G min.; Bacchus et Ariane, Op. 43
🅑🅑 Naxos 8.570245. RSNO, Denève

Symphony 4; Concert pour petit orchestre; Petite suite; Rapsodie flamande; Sinfonietta
🅑🅑 Naxos 8.572135. RSNO, Denève

The Roussel symphonies have often maintained a somewhat tenuous hold on the catalogue, but all at once there is a wide choice available, and collectors must make up their own minds about which of the alternatives are most desirable. The most recent digital set on Naxos is, on balance, perhaps the best, and is certainly well on its way to being the most comprehensive. The *First Symphony* is a highly atmospheric, impressionistic piece and, although with no programme, each movement represents a season, starting with Winter. The influence of Debussy is felt, along with d'Indy as well as Franck. It is music to wallow in, and much of it is exquisitely coloured and all of it is highly atmospheric. *Résurrection* is the composer's earliest work. Again, Roussel's ability to capture a mysterious atmosphere is on full display – qualities which also make his music for the play *Le Marchand de sable qui passe* ('The Sandman') so appealing. The four movements include an atmospheric 'Prélude', a lovely, imaginative 'Scène 2', a beautifully languorous 'Interlude et Scène 4' and a wistful 'Scène finale'. None of the music is particularly fast or lively, but it is never dull.

Unlike the majority of performances in this cycle, the *Second Symphony* is taken at quite a slow pace, but not unsympathetically slow. All the brooding colours of this densely impressionistic score are brought out, allowing the listener to wallow in much gorgeous orchestral detail. *Pour une fête de printemps* delightfully paints a picture of French rural life, while the composer's vibrant *Suite in F* finds the composer in his best neo-baroque mode; this work is undoubtedly complex in structure, but overall it leaves an impression of exhilaration, with these three baroque dances full of incident (though memories of Paul Paray's Mercury recording are not erased).

With the third CD, one comes to the *Third Symphony* and the ballet, *Bacchus et Ariane* – two of the most colourful and vibrant scores of the twentieth century. This is undoubtedly exciting music, and Denève catches the mood perfectly. The pounding rhythms of the opening of the *Symphony No. 3* are perhaps the best captured on CD and the imposing slow movement builds up to a fine climax, and the following *Vivace* and *Allegro con spirito* have all the dash one could ask for. The same can almost be said of *Bacchus et Ariane*. Denève characterizes the ballet superbly and it ends in the fine blaze of colour, as it should.

The *Fourth Symphony*, with its mysterious opening, launches into an arresting *Allegro con brio* every bit as thrilling as the opening of the *Third Symphony*, with the *Fourth* again offering another powerful slow movement, followed by two lively and exhilarating fast movements, of much quirky appeal and colour. This final CD is especially valuable for including many rarities: a delightful *Flemish Rhapsody* with an especially imposing beginning and three three-movement works: the delightful *Petite suite*, with its exhilarating opening *Aubade*, a magically wistful *Pastorale*, and again a quirkily rhythmic *Mascarade* finale, makes for very enjoyable listening. Similarly entertaining is the *Concerto pour petit orchestre* in which rhythmic interest is just as entertaining as the orchestral colours themselves. The *Sinfonietta* lasts for just under 10 minutes, yet its three movements are perfectly crafted and are not a second too long or too short. This last CD falls a little short, for although the sound of this Naxos cycle is generally first rate, here the engineers do not always follow the main melodic lines in the *Symphony*'s textures.

(i) *Symphonies 3 in G min., Op. 42; 4 in A, Op. 53*; (ii) *Bacchus et Ariane Suite 2*

Ⓑ RCA stereo/mono 2CD 74321 84601-2 (2). Radio France PO, Janowski; (ii) Boston SO, Munch - **MESSIAEN**: *Turangalîla Symphony*

Janowski has a natural feeling for the Roussel idiom and his performances of the symphonies are well worth having. Perhaps the Scherzo of the *Third* is a shade too fast, but in all other respects his readings cannot be faulted. The digital recording has plenty of presence, body and detail, and this coupling is made especially recommendable by the presence not only of Ozawa's *Turangalîla* but also of the mono recording of Munch's second suite from Roussel's ballet. In the new transfer the sound is little short of amazing in its colour and bloom and has striking luminosity. The Boston Orchestra was still under Koussevitzky's spell at the time and the playing is quite electrifying. This is indispensable, even if a few bars are missing - perhaps owing to the original tapes being damaged, or Munch himself having made a cut in performance.

RÓZSA, Miklós (1907-95)

Film Scores: (i-ii) *Ben Hur* (extended excerpts); (iii) *Julius Caesar* (3 excerpts); (i; iv) *Quo Vadis* (extended excerpts)

Ⓜ Australian Decca Eloquence (ADD) 480 3790 (2). (i) composer; (ii) Nat. PO & Ch.; (iii) Nat. PO, Herrmann; (iv) RPO & Ch.

With its gaudy primary colours and red-blooded conviction, Rózsa's score for *Ben Hur* is a potent mixture of orchestral spectacle and choral kitsch. There is an appealing lyrical theme for the love story, an exciting sequence for the galley slaves rowing into battle, and a stirring *Parade* for the famous chariot race. Towards the end, the religiosity, with its lavish spectacle of chorus and orchestra, overwhelms the listener in an ocean of sumptuous vulgarity.

Quo Vadis provides more of the same, with an exciting *Chariot Chase*, an exotic *Assyrian Dance*, stirring marches and red-blooded, epic 'Hollywood' choral contributions in such items as the *Fertility Hymn*. In *The Burning of Rome*, the composer pulls out all the stops with this colourful orchestral palette, and if by the end of it all one feels a little exhausted, the journey was never dull. The rather darker music for the three short items from *Julius Caesar* is equally effective, with *Caesar's Ghost* with its eerie tremolo strings, vividly captured by Decca, especially memorable. It is all presented here with great conviction, and the Decca Phase Four techniques create maximum impact, with rich sonorities and a sparklingly brilliant upper range.

Hungarian Serenade; 3 Hungarian Sketches; Overture to a Symphony Concert; Tripartita

Chan. 10488. BBC PO, Gamba

Miklós Rózsa wrote a substantial amount of orchestral music unrelated to his film scores. His style remained as telling in these orchestral scores, however, and this disc appropriately begins with his entertaining *Overture to a Symphony Concert*. It is an imaginative, optimistic score, with the composer's Hungarian roots emerging in a work conceived during the hopeful days of the abortive 1956 Hungarian uprising, when the composer was living in exile. The *Hungarian Serenade* is a delightfully tuneful piece, piquant in its orchestral and harmonic colourings. *Tripartita* shows the composer experimenting with a more gritty style in 1971/2, with its finale reminiscent of Walton. Nevertheless, it is exciting and accessible music. The earlier *Three Hungarian Sketches* are each descriptive movements which are vibrant with local colour and melody. Rumon Gamba and the BBC Philharmonic play these scores with brilliance, and the Chandos sound is quite superlative.

RUBBRA, Edmund (1901–86)

Symphonies 1–8 (Hommage à Teilhard de Chardin); (i) 9 (Sinfonia Sacra). 10–11

Ⓜ Chan. 9944 (5). BBC Nat. O of Wales, Hickox, with (i) Dawson, D. Jones, Roberts, BBC Nat. Ch. of Wales)

The first movement of Rubbra's *First Symphony* is fiercely turbulent; a French dance tune, a *Perigourdine*, forms the basis of the middle movement; but the pensive, inward-looking finale, which is as long as the first two movements put together, is the most powerful and haunting of the three. Richard Hickox and his fine players do make the score of the *Second Symphony* more lucid than Handley's Lyrita recording from the 1970s. The performance is meticulously prepared and yet flows effortlessly, and the slow movement speaks with great eloquence.

The *Third Symphony* (1939) has a pastoral character and a certain Sibelian feel to it (woodwind in thirds), though Rubbra is always himself. In the final movement there is even a hint of Elgar in the fourth variation. The opening of the *Fourth Symphony* is of quite exceptional beauty and has a serenity and quietude that silence criticism, and there is a constant elevation of feeling and continuity of musical thought. Rubbra's music is steeped in English polyphony and it could not come from any time other than our own.

Hickox's reading of the *Fifth Symphony* is easily the finest and most penetrating; the slow movement has great depth and, thanks to a magnificent recording, a greater clarity than either of its predecessors. Tempi are unerringly judged and he brings depth and gravitas to the very opening of the work.

The heart of the *Sixth Symphony* is the serene *Canto* movement, which is not dissimilar in character to the *Missa in honorem Sancti Dominici*. It is arguably the finest of the cycle after No. 9, and Hickox and his fine players do it proud. The *Seventh Symphony* (1956) receives a performance of real power from Hickox and his Welsh orchestra. This is music that speaks of deep and serious things and its opening paragraphs are among the most inspired that Rubbra ever penned.

The *Eighth Symphony* is a tribute to Teilhard de Chardin, a Jesuit and palaeontologist (1881–1955), who fell out with the Church over his approach to evolution. It has something of the mystical intensity that finds its most visionary outlet in the *Ninth Symphony*, which is arguably Rubbra's finest work and an unqualified masterpiece. Subtitled *The Resurrection*, it was inspired by a painting of Donato Bramante and has something of the character of the Passion, which the three soloists relate in moving fashion. Hickox offered a particularly imaginative account of the *Eleventh Symphony*, a work in one movement (1979) of which this was the début recording. Like so much of Rubbra's music, it has an organic continuity and inner logic that are immediately striking and, in common with the *Tenth Symphony* (also in one movement), its textures are spare and limpid.

(i) *Sinfonia concertante. A Tribute*; (ii) *The Morning Watch*; (iii) *Ode to the Queen*

Chan. 9966. BBC Nat. O of Wales, Hickox; with (i) Shelley; (ii) BBC Nat. Ch. of Wales;
   (iii) Bickley

Originally coupled to the Hickox Rubbra symphony cycle (now issued in a midprice box, see above), these make a valuable supplement to that set. The form in which we know the *Sinfonia concertante* is the revision Rubbra made in the 1940s. Its beautiful opening almost anticipates the *Piano Concerto in G major*, but it is the searching and thoughtful finale, a prelude and fugue, composed in memory of his teacher, Gustav Holst, which makes the strongest impression. Howard Shelley is a superb advocate and it is difficult to imagine a better performance. *The Morning Watch* is Rubbra at his most inspired. The text comes from the seventeenth-century metaphysical poet, Henry Vaughan, and the music matches its profundity and eloquence. It was originally to have formed part of a choral fifth symphony, and it is a score of great nobility which took an amazing half-century to be recorded. *A Tribute* – a lovely piece – is dedicated to Vaughan Williams, and the *Ode to the Queen* was commissioned by the BBC to celebrate the Coronation of the present Queen and is Rubbra's only song-cycle with full orchestra.

Admirers of this composer should also investigate a bargain Chandos release (with the Bournemouth Sinfonietta, conducted by Schönzeler) which includes his charming *Improvisations on Virginal Pieces by Giles Farnaby* – this pre-war work's charms are very effectively uncovered, revealing its textures to their best and most piquant advantage (Chan. 6599). It is coupled with a decent version of the *Tenth Symphony* and *A Tribute*.

Missa cantuariensis, Op. 59; Missa in honorem Sancti Dominici, Op. 66

Chan. 10423. St Margaret's, Westminster, Singers, Hickox

These Masses were recorded in the presence of the composer and are given with the greatest eloquence and finesse. They were composed in 1946 and 1948 and are among the most beautiful *a cappella* choral works of the twentieth century. A must for all collectors of choral music, even those who do not normally respond to Rubbra.

RUTTER, John (born 1945)

(i–ii) *Suite antique* (for flute & orchestra); (iii) *5 Childhood Lyrics* (for unaccompanied choir); (ii–iii) *Fancies*; *When Icicles Hang* (for choir & orchestra)

Coll. COLCD 117. (i) Dobing, Marshall; (ii) City of L. Sinfonia; (iii) Soloists, Cambridge Singers; composer

This whole collection is imbued with Rutter's easy melodic style and the touches of offbeat rhythm which he uses to give a lift to his lively settings. The *Antique Suite* (for flute, harpsichord and strings) opens with a serene Prelude, but includes a typically catchy Ostinato, a gay Waltz and a chirpy closing

Rondeau. *Fancies* has a delightful *Urchins' Dance*, after the fairy style of Men-delssohn, and its *Riddle Song* has a most appealing lyrical melody. But the mood darkens for the closing *Bellman's Song*. Among the *Childhood Lyrics*, the settings of Edward Lear's *Owl and the Pussy-cat* and *Sing a Song of Sixpence* are particularly endearing. The evocative *When Icicles Hang* brings characteristi-cally winning scoring for the orchestral woodwind (Rutter loves flutes) and another fine melody in *Blow, Blow, Thou Winter Wind*. The work ends happily in folksy style. Splendid performances throughout. The performances here are excellent and so is the recording.

Christmas carols: *Angels' Carol*; *Candelight Carol*; *Carol of the Children*; *Christmas Lullaby*; *Donkey Carol*; *Dormi Jesu*; *Jesus Child*; *Love Came Down at Christmas*; *Mary's Lullaby*; *Nativity Carol*; *Sans Day Carol*; *Second Amen*; *Shepherd's Pipe Carol*; *Star Carol*; *There is a Flower*; *The Very Best Time of Year*; *What Sweeter Music?*; *Wild Wood Carol*. Arrangements: *Angel Tidings*; *Away in a Manger*; *I Wonder as I Wander*; *Silent Night*
Hyp. CDA 67245. Polyphony, City of L. Sinfonia, Layton

John Rutter's delightful carols will always be especially remembered and are treasured by us. 'They were my calling cards,' he says. 'You have to remember that the Christmas carol is one of the very few musical forms which allows classically trained musicians to feel it's permissible to write tunes!' And, as is shown again and again here, Rutter never had difficulty in coming up with a memorable melodic line, whether it be the *Shepherd's Pipe Carol*, with its characteristic flute writing, which opens the programme, or the deliciously perky *Donkey Carol*, with its catchy 5/8 syncopated rhythm, which closes it.

The 22 carols included here were composed in a steady stream over a period of three decades, with the charming *Dormi Jesu* dating from as recently as 1999. Rutter's writing is notable not only for its tunefulness and winning use of cho-ral textures, but also for his always engaging orchestrations.

Gloria; (i) *Magnificat*. *Te Deum*
ⒷⒷ Naxos 8.572653. Choirs of St Albans Cathedral; Ensemble DeChorum, Winpenny (organ), Lucas; (i) with Elizabeth Cragg (soprano)

Framed by superb accounts of the *Gloria* and *Te Deum*, each with a magnificent brass contribution from members of the Ensemble DeChorum, and given splendidly resonant sound-quality by the ambience of the Cathedral and Abbey Church of St Albans, this is one of the most attractive Rutter collections yet. His religious choral music is the most widely performed of any contemporary English composer, not only in the United Kingdom and the Commonwealth, but in North America too. Listening to the *Gloria* one can understand why. With its Waltonesque opening and thrilling use of the brass, it communicates immediately, and the central *Andante* is touchingly elegiac, while the closing Amens are exultant. It makes you feel good.

In the *Magnificat* Rutter characteristically uses a recognizable four-note motif to fit the word itself, and the lovely second movement, *Of a Rose, a lovely Rose*, is memorable enough to be extracted for separate performance. Some might feel that for a *Magnificat* the setting is a little soft-centred, as both the lovely *Et Misericordia* and the *Esurientes* are gently lyrical, each featuring a diminutive solo treble, but the closing *Gloria Patri et Filio* is triumphant.

Rutter tells us that the *Te Deum* is not easy to set to music because it is not the work of a single author, but a compilation of three separate texts. Yet it has been associated with rejoicing and ceremony for centuries – indeed, Henry V, in Shakespeare's play, orders it to be sung (in an earlier setting) to celebrate the victory at Agincourt. Rutter's solution is to make the final section (of a piece which is only eight minutes long) hymn-like, but he then lifts the spirits with scoring for brass, timpani, percussion and organ. The performances here are quite splendid in every respect, with moving solo singing, a dedicated choral contribution, and excellent support from the Ensemble DeChorum and Tom Winpenny (organ) admirably directed by Andrew Lucas.

(i–iv) *Requiem*. Anthems: (i; iv) *Arise, shine*; (i) *Come Down, O Love Divine*; (i; v) *Musica Dei donum*; (i; iv) *2 Blessings for Choir & Organ*. Organ Pieces: (iv) *Toccata in 7*; (iv; vi) *Variations on an Easter Theme for Organ Duet*

ⓑⓑ Naxos 8.557130. (i) Clare College, Cambridge, Ch.; (ii) L. Sinfonia; (iii) with Thomas; (iv) Rimmer (organ); (v) Jones; all cond. Brown; (vi) with Collon

John Rutter's melodic gift, so well illustrated in his carols, is used in the simplest and most direct way to create a small-scale *Requiem* that is as beautiful and satisfying in its English way as the works of Fauré and Duruflé. The penultimate movement, a ripe setting of *The Lord is my Shepherd* with a lovely oboe obbligato, sounds almost like an anglicized *Song of the Auvergne*. This work was used in America at the first anniversary of 9/11, and the Clare College Choir crossed the Atlantic to perform it – a great tribute to the composer.

The newest Naxos recording of the *Requiem* tends to trump all previous versions, even the composer's own very fine account. Recorded in the expansive acoustic of Douai Abbey, Berkshire, it is very beautifully sung indeed, joyful in the *Sanctus* and darkly dramatic in the *Agnus Dei* with its steady drum beat. Elin Manahan Thomas is an ideal soloist, singing the *Pie Jesu* with touching simplicity and rising up celestially in the *Lux aeterna*. Christopher Hooker's oboe obbligato in *The Lord is my Shepherd* is comparably sensitive. The extra items are equally successful. The *Two Blessings*, with their easy melodic flow, are rather like Rutter's carols, and the pair of thematically linked organ voluntaries, the first immediately rhythmically catchy, the duet *Variations*, sonorous and unpredictable, round off the programme most satisfyingly. Both are very well played indeed, and the recording is first class.

'A Song in Season': *Carol of the Magi*; *I am with you always*;
The King of Blis; *Look to the day*; *Look at the world*; *Lord, thou
hast been our refuge*; *Most glorious Lord of life*; *O Lord, thou hast
searched me out*; *To every thing there is a season*; *Veni, Sancte
Spiritus*; *Wells Jubilate*; *Winchester Te Deum*
Coll. COLCD 135. Cambridge Singers, RPO, composer, John Birch (organ)

John Rutter's melodic gift never deserts him, and it blossoms here as readily as
ever. This very appealing programme, the most recent in the Rutter discology,
is framed by a pair of resplendent celebratory commissions, the exultant *Wells
Jubilate* and *Winchester Te Deum*, both written for important celebrations at
their respective venues, while the anthem, *Lord, thou hast been our refuge*,
brought another occasion of splendour at St Paul's Cathedral. The rest of the
programme is slightly (but only slightly) less spectacular and includes a characteristic *Carol of the Magi* with a fine cello obbligato warmly played by Tim
Gill, and the endearing *O Lord, thou has searched me out* with a lovely cor anglas
obbligato played by Leila Ward. *Lord, thou hast been our refuge* has an extended
concertante trumpet part, brilliantly played by Brian Thomson. The performances by Rutter's own choir are full of ardent joy and rich, flowing lyricism, and
the recording is first class.

SÆVERUD, Harald (1897–1992)

Symphony 6 (Sinfonia dolorosa), Op. 19; Galdreslåtten, Op. 20; Kjæmpevise-slåtten, Op. 22; Peer Gynt Suites 1 & 2
BIS CD 762. Stavanger SO, Dmitriev

The *Sixth Symphony* (*Sinfonia dolorosa*) is a short but intense piece from the war
years, dedicated to a close friend who perished in the resistance, and the
Kjæmpevise-slåtten ('Ballad of Revolt') comes from the same years. It is an
inspiriting work, an outraged, combative reaction to the sight of the Nazi occupation barracks near his Bergen home. The *Peer Gynt* music, written for a
post-war production of Ibsen's play, could not be further removed from Grieg's
celebrated score. It is earthy and rambunctious and makes Grieg sound positively genteel. So, too, does the delightful, inventive and wholly original
Galdreslåtten. Eminently satisfactory performances from the Stavanger orchestra under Alexander Dmitriev, brought vividly to life by the BIS recording team.

Symphony 7 (Salme), Op. 27; (i) Bassoon Concerto, Op. 44. Lucretia (suite), Op. 10
BIS CD 822 (i) Rønnes; Stavanger SO, Dmitriev

The one-movement *Seventh* (1945) is a deeply felt work, a hymn of thanksgiv-
ing for peace. The *Lucretia Suite* derives from the incidental music Sæverud

wrote in 1936 for André Obey's play. Much of it is highly imaginative (the evocation of night in the fourth movement, for example), and the charming middle movement, *Lucretia Sleeping*. The *Bassoon Concerto* (1965) was revised towards the end of his long life in collaboration with Robert Rønnes, the soloist here. Absolutely first-class performances and recordings.

SAINT-SAËNS, Camille (1835–1921)

Cello Concerto 1 in A min.
DG (ADD) 457 761-2. Fournier, LOP, Martinon – **LALO**: *Cello Concerto 1.* **BLOCH**: *Schelomo.* **BRUCH**: *Kol Nidrei*

Fournier brings his customary nobility to this *Concerto*, and he is well supported by Martinon, who provides stylish accompaniments with the Lamoureux Orchestra. The Saint-Saëns *Concerto* is a stronger work than the Lalo on this CD and contains much that is memorable, especially so in the delicious *Allegretto con moto* middle movement – a piece of the utmost piquancy and deliciousness that it is almost edible! The richly lyrical finale is another highlight, but the whole work is really most enjoyable. The recording, from 1960, has never sounded better than on this new DG Originals transfer, and the collection is excellent in every way.

Piano Concertos 1–5; Africa Fantaisie, Op. 89; Allegro appassionato; Op. 70; Rapsodie d' Auvergne, Op. 73; Wedding Cake Caprice-valse, Op. 76
Hyp. CDA 67331/2. Hough, CBSO, Oramo

Marvellous performances of these delightful and ever inventive works from Stephen Hough, full of joy, vigour and sparkle, with Oramo and the CBSO accompanying spiritedly and with the lightest touch. This recording is in the demonstration bracket, and this Hyperion set includes no fewer than four engaging encores. An easy first choice for this repertoire. Saint-Saëns was both a very appealing tunesmith and a natural craftsman, and it is difficult to think of a pair of CDs that are more diverting than this set.

Violin Concertos 1–3
Hyp. CDA 67074. Graffin, BBC Scottish SO, Brabbins

Though Saint-Saëns's *Third Concerto* is relatively well known, with its charming *Andantino* set between two bravura movements, and the *First Concerto*, in a single movement, has not been neglected either, the *Second Concerto* is the earliest and longest, yet arguably the most memorable – full of the youthful exuberance of a 23-year-old. The French violinist Philippe Graffin, with rich, firm tone, gives performances full of temperament, warmly supported by Martin

Brabbins and the BBC Scottish Symphony Orchestra, and the recording cannot be faulted.

Danse macabre, Op. 40; (i) *Havanaise*; *Introduction and Rondo capriccioso*. *La Jeunesse d'Hercule, Op. 50*; *Marche héroïque, Op. 34*; *Phaéton, Op. 39*; *Le Rouet d'Omphale, Op. 31*

Ⓜ Decca (ADD) 425 021-2. (i) Kyung-Wha Chung, RPO; Philh. O; Dutoit

Beautifully played performances, recorded in the Kingsway Hall with splendid atmosphere and colour. Charles Dutoit shows himself an admirably sensitive exponent of this repertoire, revelling in the composer's craftsmanship and revealing much delightful orchestral detail. *La Jeunesse d'Hercule* is the most ambitious piece, twice as long as its companions; its lyrical invention is both sensuous and elegant. The *Marche héroïque* is flamboyant but less memorable, and *Phaéton*, a favourite in the Victorian era, now sounds slightly dated. But the delightful *Omphale's Spinning Wheel* and the familiar *Danse macabre* show the composer at his most creatively imaginative. Decca have now added Kyung-Wha Chung's equally charismatic and individual 1977 accounts of what are perhaps the two most inspired short display-pieces for violin and orchestra in the repertoire. Altogether a splendid collection.

Symphonies: in A; *in F (Urbs Roma)*; *1–2*; (i) *3 (Organ Symphony)*

Ⓑ EMI (ADD) 6 31804-2 (2). French Nat. R. O, Martinon; (i) with Bernard Gavoty (organ)

Saint-Saëns's *A* and *F major Symphonies* were totally unknown and unpublished until the time of their recording and have never been dignified with numbers. Yet the *A major*, written when the composer was only 15, is a delight and may reasonably be compared with Bizet's youthful work in the same genre. More obviously mature, the *Urbs Roma Symphony* is perhaps a shade more self-conscious, and more ambitious too, showing striking imagination in such moments as the darkly vigorous Scherzo and the variations movement at the end. The first of the numbered symphonies is a well-fashioned and genial piece, again much indebted to Mendelssohn and Schumann, but with much delightfully fresh invention. The *Second* is full of excellent ideas.

Martinon directs splendid performances of the whole set, well prepared and lively. The account of the *Third* ranks with the best; freshly spontaneous in the opening movement, and with the threads knitted powerfully together at the end of the finale. Here the recording could do with rather more sumptuousness. Elsewhere the quality is bright and fresh, with no lack of body. This is an enterprising reissue and is well worth seeking out.

Symphony 3 in C min., Op. 78

Ⓜ RCA (ADD) SACD 82876 61387-2. Zamkochian (organ), Boston SO, Munch –
DEBUSSY: *La Mer*. **IBERT**: *Escales*

It is easy to see why Saint-Saëns's so-called 'organ' symphony is so popular – in a great performance such as the one listed here it can be a thrilling aural experience. Munch's Boston recording dates from 1960, yet sounds spectacular on CD. The performance is stunning, full of lyrical ardour and moving forward in a single sweep of great intensity. The couplings show Munch and his Bostonians at their peak, if not quite so outstandingly recorded. We believe that for the symphony recording the producer moved out the audience seats used in the stalls, and then had the orchestra moved forward to sit in the auditorium. The result was to use the hall's superb acoustics to maximum effect.

Samson et Dalila (complete, DVD version)

Arthaus DVD 100 202. Domingo, Verrett, Wolfgang Brendel, San Francisco Op. Ch. & O,
   Rudel (Director: Nicolas Joel; V/D: Kirk Browning)

Samson et Dalila (complete, CD version)

EMI 5 09185-2 (2). Domingo, Meier, Fondary, Ramey, Courtis, L'Opéra-Bastille Ch. & O,
   Myung-Whun Chung

Recorded in 1981 at the San Francisco Opera House, this DVD of Saint-Saëns's biblical opera offers a heavily traditional production with realistic sets and costumes like those in a Hollywood epic. Sporting a vast bouffant wig like a tea-cosy (ripe for Dalila's shears in Act II), Plácido Domingo is in magnificent, heroic voice, with Shirley Verrett also at her peak as Dalila, at once seductive and sinister. Other principals are first rate too, and the chorus, so vital in this opera, sings with incandescent tone in a rip-roaring performance under Julius Rudel, culminating in a spectacular presentation of the fall of the Temple of Dagon. Most enjoyable.

In the EMI CD set, Domingo with Chung gives a deeper, more thoughtful performance than on DVD, broader, with greater repose and a sense of power in reserve. When the big melody appears in Dalila's seduction aria, *Mon cœur s'ouvre*, Chung's idiomatic conducting encourages a tender restraint, where others produce a full-throated roar. Meier may not have an ideally sensuous voice for the role of the heroine, with some unwanted harshness in her expressive account of Dalila's first monologue, but her feeling for words is strong and the characterization vivid. Generally Chung's speeds are on the fast side, yet the performance does not lack weight, with some first-rate singing in the incidental roles from Alain Fondary, Samuel Ramey and Jean-Philippe Courtis. Apart from backwardly placed choral sound, the recording is warm and well focused.

SALIERI, Antonio (1750–1825)

Overtures: *Angiolina, ossia Il matrimonio per sussuro*; *Cublai, gran kan de' Tartari*; *Falstaff, ossia Le tre burle*; *La locandiera*. *Sinfonia Il giorno onomastico*; *Sinfonia Veneziana*; *26 Variations on 'La folia di Spagna'*

Chan. 9877. LMP, Bamert

The music here brings a profusion of ear-tickling ideas, and the secondary themes for Salieri's concise, lively overtures are most engaging. Tuttis, with trumpets, are invariably bright and rather grand, but the lighter scoring shows a nice feeling for woodwind colour and there is much elegant phrasing for the violins. Perhaps the most striking work is the kaleidoscopic set of 26 *Variations on 'La follia'*, which occupies 18 minutes, continually changing colour and mood, often dramatically, sometimes bizarrely, but usually entertainingly (although there is an element of repetition). The London Mozart Players play all this music most winningly, with vigour, polish and charm, and the Chandos recording is state of the art.

SALLINEN, Aulis (born 1935)

(i–ii) *Cello Concerto, Op. 44*; (iii) *Chamber Music I, Op. 38*; (i; iii) *Chamber Music III, Op. 58*; (iii) *Some Aspects of Peltoniemi Hintrik's Funeral March*; (iv) *Sunrise Serenade* (for 2 trumpets & chamber orchestra), *Op. 63*; (ii) *Shadows, Op. 52*; *Symphonies 4, Op. 49*; *5 (Washington Mosaics), Op. 57*
Finlandia 4509 99966-2 (2). (i) Noras; (ii) Helsinki PO; (iii) Finland Sinf.; Kamu; (iv)
    Harjanne, Välimäki, Avanti CO, Saraste

This Finlandia Double brings an extensive survey of Sallinen's music and provides an inexpensive entry into the composer's world. Apart from the symphonies, the *Cello Concerto* of 1976 is the most commanding piece here. Sallinen's ideas resonate in the mind. Arto Noras has its measure and plays with masterly eloquence. The performances under Okko Kamu are very impressive and the recording quite exemplary. Overall, excellent value.

SATIE, Eric (1866–1925)

Embryons desséchés; *6 Gnossiennes*; *3 Gymnopédies*; *Je te veux*;
Nocturne 4; *Le Piccadilly*; *4 Préludes flasques*; *Prélude et tapisserie*;
Sonatine bureaucratique; *Vieux sequins et vieilles cuirasses*
Ⓜ Decca 475 7527. Pascal Rogé

Pascal Rogé gave Satie his compact disc début with this fine recital, which is splendidly caught by the microphones. So this is a perfect candidate for Decca's series of Originals. Rogé has a real feeling for this repertoire and he conveys its bitter-sweet quality and its grave melancholy as well as he does its lighter qualities. He produces, as usual, consistent beauty of tone, and this is well projected by the recording.

SCARLATTI, Domenico (1685–1757)

Keyboard Sonatas, Kk.1; *3*; *8–9*; *11*; *17*; *24–5*; *27*; *29*; *87*; *96*; *113*; *141*;
146; *173*; *213–14*; *247*; *259*; *268*; *283–4*; *380*; *386–7*; *404*; *443*; *519–20*; *523*
Virgin 5 61961-2 (2). Pletnev (piano)

This carefully chosen selection of some of Scarlatti's finest and most adventurous
sonatas stretches over two CDs, giving the fullest opportunity to demonstrate
the extraordinary range of this music in a recital-length programme playing for
140 minutes. In the opening *D major Sonata*, Kk.443, Pletnev establishes a firm
pianistic approach, yet the staccato articulation reminds us that the world of
the harpsichord is not so far away. However, in the *G major Sonata*, Kk.283,
and in the following Kk.284 his fuller piano sonority transforms the effect of
the writing. The second CD opens with the almost orchestral Kk.96 *in D*, with
its resonant horn calls, and later the lovely, flowing *C minor Sonata* and the
even more expressive Kk.11 *in F sharp minor* bring a reflective, poetic feeling
which could not have been matched in colour by the plucked instrument. The
performances throughout are in the very front rank.

Keyboard Sonatas, Kk.20; *24*; *27*; *30*; *87*; *197*; *365*; *426–7*; *429*; *435*;
448; *455*; *466*; *487*; *492*; *545*; *in G min.*
BIS CD 1508. Sudbin (piano)

Yevgeny Sudbin finds, besides much to charm the ear, an infinite expressive
depth in many of the minor key works, which are played here with appealing expressive freedom. (Sample Kk.87 or Kk.197 in *B minor* or the delicacy of
Kk.466 in *F minor*.) From the very opening *B flat major* work we are aware that
this is a modern piano, but how well it suits these innovative and infinitely
diverse *Sonatas*. There is sparkle and brilliance here too, and Sudbin can be
both strong and delectably light-fingered. He is recorded splendidly, and this
can be placed among the finest and most generous of recent single-disc Scarlatti collections (76 minutes).

SCHARWENKA, Franz Xaver (1850–1924)

Piano Concertos 2 in C min., Op. 56; *3 in C sharp min., Op. 80*
Hyp. CDA 67365. Tanyel, Hanover R. Philharmonie des NDR, Strugala

These two *Concertos* bristle with technical challenges of which Seta Tanyel
makes light. She is fully equal to their technical demands and takes them comfortably in her stride. The *Second Concerto* comes from 1880, and the debt to
both Chopin and Hummel can be clearly discerned. The composer himself
gave the first performance of the *Third* in Berlin in 1899 to much acclaim –
understandably so, given the quality of the central *Adagio*. Tanyel not only copes

with the virtuoso demands of Scharwenka's writing but is a very musical player. Excellent support from Tadeusz Strugala and the Hanover Radio Orchestra, and a first-class (1996) recording.

SCHMIDT, Franz (1874-1939)

Symphonies 1-4
Chan. 9568 (4). Detroit SO, Neeme Järvi

Chandos have now boxed their individual releases of the symphonies into a four-CD set, discarding the fill-ups. The *First Symphony* was composed during Schmidt's early- to mid-20s and, as one might expect, is derivative, even if his orchestration is masterly. Right from the start, one is left in no doubt that Schmidt is a born symphonic composer with a real feeling for the long-breathed line and the natural growth and flow of ideas. He began work on the *Second Symphony* on leaving the Vienna Philharmonic in 1911 and finished it two years later. The *Third* (1927-8) is a richly imaginative score in the romantic tradition, though it yields pride of place among the symphonies to the elegiac, valedictory *Fourth* (1933-4), whose nobility and depth of feeling shine through every bar. The Detroit Symphony Orchestra under Neeme Järvi play with a freshness and enthusiasm that are totally persuasive. They almost sound Viennese, and the recordings are very good indeed.

Das Buch mit sieben Siegeln (The Book with 7 Seals)
ⓑⓑ EMI Gemini 5 85782-2 (2). Oelze, Kallisch, Andersen, Odinius, Pape, Reiter, Bav. R. Ch. & SO, Welser-Möst; Winklhofer (organ)

This EMI bargain version of Schmidt's *Book with Seven Seals* was recorded live in the Herculessaal in 1997 and is played by the magnificent Bavarian Radio Orchestra with the Bavarian Radio Chorus under Franz Welser-Möst, who shows great sympathy for the score. The soloists are excellent. However, no texts are included.

SCHOECK, Othmar (1886-1957)

(i) Concerto for Cello & Strings, Op. 61. (ii) Cello Sonata; Six Song Transcriptions
BIS CD 1597. Christian Poltéra, with (i) Malmö SO, Tuomas Ollila; (ii) Julius Drake

Although best known for his songs, some three hundred in number plus the remarkable cycle, *Lebendig begraben*, and several operas, the Swiss composer Othmar Schoeck composed concertos for violin, horn and, in the last decade of his life, the *Cello Concerto*, which Pierre Fournier premièred in 1948. This has a strong vein of melancholy and a poignant eloquence redolent of the previous century. It is a work characterized by great lyrical intensity and depth of feeling, beautifully conveyed here by his countryman Christian Poltéra with the Malmö Symphony Orchestra. Poltéra also gives us the three-movement *Cello Sonata*, left incomplete on the composer's death. Deeply satisfying music, impeccably played and equally impeccably recorded.

SCHOENBERG, Arnold (1874–1951)

Pelleas und Melisande; *Verklaerte Nacht*
Ⓜ DG 457 721-2. BPO, Karajan

There are many listeners who cannot come to terms with Schoenberg's later extravagances, but these early symphonic poems have an unforgettable Straussian opulence. They have never been presented as ravishingly as by Karajan and the Berlin Philharmonic on this splendidly recorded disc. The sensuality of the famous nocturnal piece brings a gorgeous tapestry of sound, while the emotional element of the lovers' tryst is presented at full power. *Pelleas und Melisande* too has an unequalled combination of expressive intensity, precision and refinement.

Erwartung
Ⓜ Decca 478 3408 (2). Silja, VPO, Dohnányi – **BERG**: *Wozzeck*

Schoenberg's searingly intense monodrama makes an apt and generous coupling for Dohnányi's excellent version of Berg's *Wozzeck*. As in the Berg, Anja Silja is at her most passionately committed, and the digital sound is exceptionally vivid. With Solti's fine version of *Moses and Aaron* awaiting reissue this is strongly recommendable.

(i) *Serenade for Septet & Bass Voice, Op. 24. Suite, Op. 29*
Ⓜ Australian Decca Eloquence 480 2154. Melos Ens., (i) with John Carol Case (with **BERG**: *4 Pieces for Clarinet & Piano*)

The *Serenade for Septet and Bass Voice* is one of the most accessible of the works which Schoenberg wrote after adopting serial technique. Not that his application of serialism is strict here, except in the rather angular sounding settings of a Petrarch sonnet, which is perhaps the least attractive of the movements. Conversely, the most immediately attractive is a *Song Without Words* that seems to have very little relationship with serialism at all. It would be unfair to draw generalizations from this, for above all the work shows that twelve-tone music can express far more than gloomy neurotic self-torture. The performance here emerges superbly on this, its first appearance on CD. Indeed, it is nothing less than dazzling in its sharply vivid brilliance, and it does much to help one accept the argument. John Carol Case does wonders with the cruel vocal line. In the *Suite*, Schoenberg deliberately found inspiration in Viennese dance-rhythms, and modelled the structure on the serenades and divertimentos of the Mozart/Haydn period. But those associations are misleading, for Schoenberg was virtually incapable of producing genuinely light music, and this piece only nags at one if one tries to treat it trivially. It is as formidable as most of the composer's other works of the mid-1920s, and it deserves close study. The Melos performance is more relaxed than the composer's own metronome marks would strictly allow but, with superb playing from De Peyer and Crowson, the conviction of the writing should be apparent to the listener who has not yet fathomed its logic. As in the recording of the *Serenade*, the recording is outstanding. These pieces are coupled with Berg's *Four Pieces for Clarinet and Piano*, written in 1913 and dedicated to his master, Schoenberg. Lasting around seven minutes, these virtuosic works offer much variety of texture and imagination, with the composer drifting back to traditional tonality more often than one would expect from Berg. Again, outstanding performance and recording.

(i-ii) *Gurrelieder*; (iii) *Chamber Symphony 1, Op. 9*; (ii) *Verklaerte Nacht*

Ⓑ Decca 473 728-2 (2). (i) Jerusalem, Dunn, Fassbaender, Brecht, Haage, Hotter, St Hedwig's Cathedral Ch., Berlin, Düsseldorf State Musikverein; (ii) Berlin RSO; (iii) Concg. O; Chailly

Chailly's magnificent recording of Schoenberg's massive *Gurrelieder* remains highly recommendable. Siegfried Jerusalem as Waldemar is not only warm and firm of tone, but imaginative too. Susan Dunn makes a sweet, touchingly vulnerable Tove, while Brigitte Fassbaender gives darkly baleful intensity to the message of the Wood-dove. Hans Hotter is a characterful speaker in the final section. The impact of the performance is the more telling with sound both atmospheric and immediate, bringing a fine sense of presence, not least in the final choral outburst. For this bargain Double Decca issue, Decca have added well-played and -recorded accounts of the *Chamber Symphony No. 1* – one of the first works to show the composer at full stretch – and his most popular work, *Verklaerte Nacht*.

Pierrot lunaire, Op. 21

Ⓜ Chan. 6534. Manning, Nash Ens., Rattle (with **WEBERN**: *Concerto for 9 Instruments, Op. 24*)

With *Pierrot lunaire* we come to Schoenberg at his most taxing, with its vocal writing that combines speech and a vocal line. Yet if anyone can convince the listener that it can provide a unique atmosphere it is Jane Manning. She steers a masterful course between the twin perils, on the one hand actually singing, on the other simply speaking. Her sing-speech brings out the element of irony and darkly pointed wit that is essential. Rattle again proves a natural Schoenbergian, drawing strong, committed performances from the members of the Nash Ensemble and, apart from some intermittently odd balances, the sound is excellent.

SCHREKER, Franz (1878–1934)

Ekkehard (Symphonic Overture), Op. 12; Fantastic Overture, Op. 15; Interlude from 'Der Schatzgräber'; Nächtstuck (from 'Der ferne Klang'); Prelude to a Drama; Valse lente
Chan. 9797. BBC PO, Sinaisky

This sequence of six pieces presents a good cross-section of his output, demonstrating Schreker's development from the *Symphonic Overture, Ekkehard*, and the charmingly unpretentious *Valse lente*, to the later works, which remain sumptuously late-romantic but which were regarded as daringly modern by early audiences. Both the *Nachtstück* from *Der ferne Klang* (1909) and the *Prelude to a Drama* (1913) – the drama in question being the opera, *Die Gezeichneten* – are powerfully imaginative. Perhaps the most seductive piece is the *Valse lente*. Schreker had a wonderful sense of fantasy, a feeling for colour, and impressive mastery of the orchestra. The textures are lush and overheated. Sinaisky draws seductively beautiful playing from the BBC Philharmonic, heightened by gloriously rich Chandos sound, and the whole disc serves to advance Schreker's cause.

Prelude to a Grand Opera; Prelude to 'Das Spielwerk'; Romantic Suite, Op. 14; (i) 5 Gesäng
Chan. 9951. (i) Karneus; BBC PO, Sinaisky

The *Romantic Suite* comes from 1903, when Schreker was in his mid-twenties, though its third movement began life independently as an *Intermezzo for Strings* a year earlier. It is a rather beautiful piece, as, for that matter, is the first-movement *Idylle*, written at much the same time as when he was making the first sketches for *Der ferne Klang*. There is a lot of Strauss here and, in the mercurial Scherzo, Reger – the latter is a highly inventive movement. Only the finale, *Tanz*, is routine. The *Five Songs*, imaginatively sung by the Swedish mezzo, Katarina Karneus, have plenty of atmosphere and mystery, and are well worth getting to know. The disc covers the whole of Schreker's career: the Prelude to *Das Spielwerk* is a wartime piece, while the *Vorspiel zu einer grossen Oper* comes from the last months of his life. It is darker than his earlier pieces but, despite its expert orchestration, remains somewhat overblown. The playing of the BBC Philharmonic under Sinaisky is superb and the recording is in the demonstration class. Intelligent liner notes.

SCHUBERT, Franz (1797-1828)

Symphonies 1-6; *8 (Unfinished)*; *9 (Great)*; *Grand Duo in C, D.812*
(orch. Joachim); *Rosamunde Overture (Die Zauberharfe), D.644*
Ⓑ DG 477 8687 (5). COE, Abbado

Abbado's is an outstanding set in every way. Rarely has he made recordings of the central Viennese classics which find him so naturally sunny and warm in his expression. The playing of the Chamber Orchestra of Europe is both beautiful and deeply committed, consistently refined and elegant, but with ample power when necessary. Speeds are often on the fast side but never feel breathless, and the recording is refined, with fine bloom on the string-sound. Textually, too, the Abbado set takes preference over its rivals. Abbado asked a member of the orchestra, Stefano Mollo, to carry out research on the original source-material in Vienna for the symphonies not yet included in the 'Neue Schubert-Ausgabe'. As a result of his work, there are certain fascinating differences from what we are used to. The box contains the five separate discs (including Joachim's orchestration of the *Grand Duo* – originally for piano duet) and a booklet with a modest note by Wolfgang Stähr.

Symphonies (i) *8 (Unfinished)*; (ii) *9 in C (Great)* (CD version)
Ⓜ Decca Australian Eloquence 480 4725. (i) VPO; (ii) LSO; Josef Krips

Symphonies 8 (Unfinished); *9 in C (Great)* (DVD version)
TDK DVD DVWW-COWANDS6. NDR SO, Günter Wand

Krips first recorded the *Unfinished* in the very early days of mono LP, a gentle, glowing performance; and here in 1969 with the VPO he directs an unforced, flowing and wonderfully satisfying account, helped by excellent playing and splendid Sofiensaal recording, produced by Christopher Raeburn. This may lack some of the dramatic bite of more histrionic accounts, but the atmospheric opening of both movements is immediately gripping, and concentration is maintained consistently up to the beautifully shaped final coda, establishing the work's claim to be the first truly great romantic symphony. It makes a splendid coupling for Krips's much earlier LSO recording of the *Ninth*, which has long been counted by us as one of his very finest records, perhaps the finest. The performance similarly has a direct, unforced spontaneity which shows Krips's feeling for Schubertian lyricism at its most engaging. The playing is polished, yet flexible, dramatically strong without ever sounding aggressive. In the final two movements Krips finds an airy exhilaration which makes one wonder why some other conductors can ever keep the music earthbound as they do. The pointing of the Trio in the Scherzo is delectable, and the feathery lightness of the triplets in the finale makes one positively welcome every one of its many repetitions. As a whole this represents the Viennese tradition at its finest. Great care has been taken with the remastering, which in No. 9 retains the glowing Kingsway Hall bloom and expansiveness of the original LP.

Munch also gives a magnificent performance of the *Great C major Symphony* with the Boston Symphony Orchestra, but one whose character is very different from the Krips version. In sheer dramatic tension it even outshines Toscanini. This is very much the Toscanini approach – in the introduction and *Allegro* of the first movement even faster than his – but one must emphasize that it is far from being an unsympathetic or rough-riding account of the work. True there is more excitement than repose, and at the big climax of the slow movement Munch reinforces the dissonances with an accelerando. Yet throughout, he and his players show an implicit sympathy; indeed, in the hushed slow-movement passage immediately after the climax, the rubato is controlled in an exact and precise manner, yet somehow remains spontaneous-sounding. The remastered 1958 recording still has plenty of edge, yet in the impressive new SACD transfer the sound is filled out by the warm reson-ance of the Boston acoustic. This is even more striking in the expansive lower strings at the opening of the *Unfinished Symphony*, recorded three years earlier. Here Munch's performance has a fine, lyrical impulse, with sensitive wind-playing in the second movement; but (especially compared with Krips) there is a certain heaviness of approach (not unattractive) which is quite different from the Munch account of the *Ninth Symphony* (RCA SACD (ADD) 88697 04603-2).

Recorded live, Günter Wand's performances of the two greatest Schubert symphonies have immense concentration and visionary atmosphere. But to have his magically evocative and ravishingly played account of the *Unfinished* as well as the *Great C major* on a single DVD makes for an unforgettable listening and watching experience. The cameras continually and perceptively follow the performance detail, showing Wand as a direct, unostentatious con-ductor, often achieving remarkable results with the minimum of gesture. The interpretation of the *Ninth* solves the work's problems of tempo changes by achieving a warmly natural musical flow, expanding spontaneously to high drama at key moments. The sound in the Musik- und- Kongresshall, Lübeck, is first class too, and this must be counted among the finest orchestral DVDs yet to appear.

Arpeggione Sonata, D.821 (arr. for cello)

Ⓜ Decca (ADD) 475 8239. Rostropovich, Britten – **DEBUSSY**: *Cello Sonata*.
SCHUMANN: *5 Stücke im Volkston*

Though one may accuse Rostropovich of a degree of self-indulgence in his per-formance of the *Arpeggione Sonata*, we are completely won over by the artist's warmth and obvious love for this music. There is great concentration of feeling in this performance from the word go, and the richly atmospheric Decca sound remains superb in this transfer. Indeed, the lilting way in which Britten and Rostropovich treat the rhythms is very infectious and provides both the intim-acy of chamber-music playing with the sparkle of a live performance. As for this music itself, it is crammed full of Schubert's most memorable tunes and is essential listening both for fans of this composer and of chamber music in general. Outstanding couplings too.

Octet in F, D.803

Onyx ONYX 4006. Mullova, Moraguèz, Postinghel, Cokri, Chamorro, Krüger, M. Fischer-Dieskau, Stoll

The newest Onyx version of the Schubert *Octet* is not only the best since the celebrated 1958 Vienna Octet version on Decca, it actually surpasses it. These artists find a greater depth than their predecessors in a work that we all think we know well. There is not only grace, pathos and tenderness here, but also a thoughtful attention to details of phrasing and internal balance. Tempi are generally on the slow side, but the listener's attention is compelled throughout. Musically a most satisfying and revealing account – and a moving one too, very well recorded indeed.

The Vienna Octet's earlier (1958) recording on Decca of the Schubert *Octet* has stood the test of time. It has a magical glow, with the group at its peak under the leadership of Willi Boskovsky. The horn has a Viennese fruitiness which helps to make the performance more authentic. And these fine players never put a foot wrong throughout. The recording betrays its age only in the upper registers but is basically full and modern-sounding. The delightful and unusual Spohr coupling (see below) makes this a fine pairing (Decca 466 580-2). This recording is also available on a desirable Double Decca CD, with an equally classic version of the *Trout Quintet* (with Curzon), the *Arpeggione Sonata* and the *Fantasy* for violin and piano (452 393-2 (2)).

(i) *Piano Quintet in A (Trout)*. *Moments musicaux, D.780*

Ⓜ Decca 458 608-2. András Schiff; (i) with Hagen Qt

András Schiff and the Hagen Quartet give a delectably fresh and youthful reading of the *Trout Quintet*, full of the joys of spring, but one which is also remarkable for hushed concentration, as in the exceptionally dark and intense account of the opening of the first movement. The Scherzo brings a light, quick and bouncing performance, and there is extra lightness, too, in the other middle movements. This version observes the exposition repeat in the finale, and with such a joyful, brightly pointed performance one welcomes that. The *Moments musicaux* are also beautifully played by Schiff and very well recorded to make a considerable bonus.

Piano Trios 1–2; *Adagio in E flat (Notturno) for Piano Trio, D.897*; Sonata in B flat for Piano Trio, D.28

MDG 342 1166-2 (*Trio 1*); 342 1167-2 (*Trio 2; Notturno; Sonata*). V. Piano Trio
(available separately)

The performances by the Vienna Piano Trio are outstanding in every way. Their playing is wonderfully fresh and spring-like, and the contribution of the pianist,

Stefan Mendl, is ear-catchingly crisp. This is true chamber-music-making by a beautifully matched team, dramatic and expressive by turns, with remarkable ongoing spontaneity, yet full of incidental subtleties. The recording is in the demonstration class, perfectly balanced. The two CDs are available separately; the first includes the alternative version of the finale, which Schubert composed first, as an appendix.

String Quintet in C, D.956

Testament mono SBT 2031. Hollywood Qt, with Kurt Reher (with **SCHOENBERG**: Verklaerte Nacht, with Reher and Dinkin)

The Hollywood Quartet's 1951 version of Schubert's magical *Quintet* (with Kurt Reher as second cello) stands apart from all others. Over half a century on, its qualities of freshness and poetry, as well as an impeccably confident technical address, still impress as deeply as ever. The coupled 1950 account of *Verklaerte Nacht* was the first version ever to appear on record in its original sextet form, and arguably it remains unsurpassed and possibly unequalled. This almost flawless performance enjoyed the imprimatur of Schoenberg himself, who supplied the sleeve-note for it (reproduced in the excellent booklet), the only time he ever did so. The sound throughout both works is remarkably good and very musical. This disc is the product of consummate artistry and remains very special indeed.

Alfred Brendel plays and introduces Schubert (on DVD): Volume 1: *Piano Sonatas 14 in A min., D.784; 15 in C, D.840; Wanderer Fantasy in C min., D.760*
Medici Arts DVD 2057 808

Volume 2: *Piano Sonatas 16 in A min., D.845; 17 in D, D.850*
Medici Arts DVD 2057 818

Volume 3: *Piano Sonata 18 in G, D.894; Impromptus 1–4, D.899; 5–8, D.935*
Medici Arts DVD 2057 828

Volume 4: *Piano Sonata 19 in C min., D.958; Moments musicaux 1–6, D.780; 3 Klavierstück, D.946*
Medici Arts DVD 2057 838

Volume 5: *Piano Sonatas 20 in A, D.959; 21 in B flat, D.960*
Medici Arts DVD 2057 848

Alfred Brendel has always placed Schubert at the centre of his repertoire, alongside Beethoven. He made his first Schubert LPs in the late 1950s on the Vox and Turnabout labels in the early days of stereo, and these recordings, with their fresh, natural eloquence, remain very recommendable. He recorded second (analogue) and third (digital) cycles for Philips later, and then in 1976/7 presented these late sonatas with thoughtful spoken introductions on TV, via Radio Bremen, throwing much light on their compositional substance and giving his own assessment of the music and its structure. Here they are on five DVDs. The commentary is in German but good translations are provided and in each case the performances follow, separately banded and naturally and forwardly recorded in a sightly resonant ambience.

Brendel tells us that Schubert composed without the aid of a piano keyboard – what he heard was in his imagination. Brendel divides his music into two periods, the second of which begins in 1822 with the *Wanderer Fantasy*, which transformed piano writing in a quite unprecedented way (notably so in the use of tremolandos, a quite new device). Its bravura demanded exceptional pianistic ability (almost certainly beyond Schubert himself) and indeed a dynamic range that anticipated a piano of the future. Brendel goes on to stress the importance of the pedal in creating an orchestral effect, demonstrated in the unfinished *C major Sonata*, D.840, of 1825, the first of three sonatas written during that year.

The *A minor*, D.845, brings the widest range of emotion and introduces a two-part theme, in Brendel's words contrasting 'soloist and chorus' (almost like a pianistic 'concertino' and 'ripieno'), which he illustrates, and also includes masterly variations on a graceful theme for its slow movement. The *D major*, D.850, with its disarming opening brings another mellow slow movement marked simply *Con moto* but which is even more notable for the childlike theme of its finale, 'a portrait of a child painted by a grown-up', he suggests.

The *G major*, D.894, he reflects, demands a poet of the piano, 'who must be able to create intimacy'. Schumann's description of the second set of *Impromptus* as 'a crypto sonata', Brendel suggests, was miguided. They are each individually 'a series of musical adventures' with sound-painting and atmosphere dissolving into colour with *Nos. 2 in A flat* and *3 in G flat* (with its Rosamunde theme) especially poetic. He plays them with only a slight pause between them, giving a sense of their being linked.

The last three sonatas, D.958, D.959 and D.960, written in 1828, only weeks before Schubert's death, are compared with Beethoven's final three sonatas, and 'reveal a greater concentration', as if the composer was aware of the short time he had left to him. The penultimate *Sonata in A*, D.959, has an 'unexpectedly bizarre' and unpredictably rhapsodic first movement and might be compared with Beethoven's Op. 31/1. Yet all four movements are linked by two key motifs, each a pair of adjacent notes which dominate the texture. The last and greatest sonata of all, *21 in B flat*, was written only two months before Schubert's death. He was sick with typhoid fever, and the magical theme which dominates the first movement has 'an air of leave-taking', while the *Andante* 'is the most beautiful of all his elegies for the piano'. Brendel plays the work with serene intensity and comments that, in spite of suggestions that at his death Schubert's imagination still had much more to offer, 'whether he would have been able to create anything more beautiful than this *B flat Sonata* is open to question'.

He is photographed simply by the cameras, and the video director, Peter Hamin, plays no visual tricks, focusing either on his personal image or his hands. There are excellent additional notes in the booklet by Jeremy Siepman. Brendel's later Schubertian style is bolder than Imogen Cooper's (for instance), vibrant with poetic intensity yet fully concerned with the works' intellectual depth.

Imogen Cooper on CD: Volume 1: *Piano Sonatas 16 in A min., D.845; 17 in D, D.850; 20 in A, D.959; 11 Ecossaises, D.781; 3 Klavierstück, D.946*
Ⓜ Avie AV 2156 (2)

Volume 2: *Piano Sonatas 18 in G, D.894; 19 in C min., D.958; 16 German Dances, D.783; 4 Impromptus, D.935; 6 Moments musicaux, D.780*
Ⓜ Avie AV 2157 (2)

Between 1986 and 1990 Imogen Cooper made a series of outstanding recordings of the later Schubert *Piano Sonatas* for the Priory/Ottavo label entitled 'The Last Six Years'. In 2009 she embarked on a new Schubert cycle published by Avie, but this time the performances are recorded live in the Queen Elizabeth Hall and in consequence they are even more spontaneous in feeling. They are also beautifully recorded; indeed the piano could not be more naturally captured, nor the feeling of live music-making conveyed to the listener. She displays a very special feeling for the composer's lyricism, and the warm colouring and fine shading of timbre are as pleasing to the ear as the many subtle nuances of phrasing, and her bold sonority at higher dynamic levels is particularly satisfying.

On the first disc of Volume 1 the *A major Sonata* brings a truly Schubertian *Andantino*, ravishingly gentle in its cantabile variations, contrasting with the sparkling Scherzo and song-like finale. The eleven *Ecossaises* which follow are more robust miniatures, while most memorable among the three *Klavierstück* is the second, a *Barcarolle in E flat*, which stands out for its lyrical charm. On the second disc the *A minor Sonata* (the first of Schubert's sonatas to be published) brings an enchanting set of variations (deftly contrasted here), while Imogen Cooper plays the child-like finale of the *D major* work, with its 'ticktock' accompaniment, with captivating delicacy.

The *C minor Sonata*, which opens Volume 2, is cast in a key which was special to Beethoven (who had died the year before) and its great *Adagio* has a grave beauty which is undoubtedly a tribute to that master. Then the finale trips along in tarantella style which recalls Beethoven's *Sonata*, Op. 31/3. By contrast, the opening of the *G major Sonata* has a mood of calm, opening with a cantabile, questioning main theme, its mood all but echoed in the closing, lighthearted Allegretto. The *German Dances* are engagingly light-hearted, but the *Moments musicaux* and four *Impromptus* show Cooper at her finest and most spontaneous, especially the two pieces in *A flat major* presenting the composer at his most beguiling.

Piano Sonata 21 in B flat, D.960; Allegretto in C min., D.915; 6 Moments musicaux, D.780
EMI 5 03423-2. Kovacevich

Stephen Kovacevich made a memorable recording of the great *B flat major Sonata* for Hyperion which (in our 1988 edition) we called 'one of the most eloquent accounts on record of this sublime sonata'. One could well say the same of the later (1994) EMI version, though, if anything, it explores an even deeper vein of feeling than its predecessor. Indeed, it is the most searching and penetrating account of the work to have appeared in recent years and, given the excellence and truthfulness of the recording, must carry the strongest and most enthusiastic recommendation. For this reissue EMI have added the six *Moments musicaux*, which he recorded six months later, also at Abbey Road, and which have comparable insights.

Rosamunde Overture (Die Zauberharfe), D.644, & Incidental Music, D.797 (complete)
Ⓜ Australian Decca Eloquence (ADD) 466 677-2. Yachmi, V. State O Ch., VPO, Münchinger

Münchinger's performance of the delightful *Rosamunde* music glows with an affectionate warmth and understanding which places this as one of his very best records. Sometimes with this conductor, particularly with his own Stuttgart orchestra, he could seem a little stiff and un-spontaneous. But with the VPO it was a different matter (he also, with the same orchestra, made a magnificent recording of Haydn's *Creation*, also available on Decca). There is an unforced spontaneity about this performance, as well as strength here, and the 1970s recording is rich and naturally balanced. The vocal numbers are superbly done and the VPO – with its glowing strings – is at its magnificent best.

Die schöne Müllerin; Schwanengesang; Winterreise
Ⓜ DG (ADD) 477 7956 8 (3). Fischer-Dieskau, Moore

Dietrich Fischer-Dieskau and Gerald Moore had each recorded these three great cycles of Schubert several times already before they embarked on this set in 1971–2 as part of DG's Schubert song series. It was no mere repeat of earlier triumphs. If anything, these performances – notably that of the darkest and greatest of the cycles, *Winterreise* – are even more searching than before, with Moore matching the hushed concentration of the singer, who is in wonderfully fresh voice, in some of the most remarkable playing that even he has put on record.

Collectors wanting to jump in at the deep end might choose instead the 21-disc coverage in Fischer-Dieskau's monumental survey of nearly all the Schubert Lieder suitable for the male voice. No fewer than 405 songs are included, plus the three cycles above (DG 477 5765).

23 Favourite Lieder, including: *An die Musik*; *An Sylvia*; *Auf der Bruck*; *Die Forelle*; *Du bist die Ruh'*; *Erlkönig*; *Das Fischermädchen*; *Heidenröslein*; *Lachen und Weinen*; *Ständchen*; *Die Taubenpost*; *Der Wanderer*

Ⓜ DG 477 6358. Terfel, Martineau

Bryn Terfel's disc of Schubert was one of his finest recordings to confirm his exceptional gift for projecting his magnetic personality with keen intensity in Lieder, not just in opera. Terfel emerges as a positive artist, giving strikingly individual and imaginative performances of these 23 favourite songs. As you immediately realize in three favourites, *Heidenröslein*, *An Sylvia* and *Du bist die Ruh'*, Terfel is daring in confronting you face to face, very much as the young Fischer-Dieskau did, using the widest range of dynamic and tone. Full, firm sound.

'A Schubert Evening'

ⒷⒷ EMI Gemini (ADD) 5 86251-2 (2). Janet Baker, with Moore or Parsons

This very generous collection combines a pair of recitals recorded by Dame Janet Baker at two different stages in her career, in 1970 and a decade later. The first collection includes a number of comparative rarities, ranging from the delectably comic *Epistel* to the ominous darkness of *Die junge Nonne*. With Gerald Moore (who returned to the studio out of retirement especially for the occasion) still at his finest, this is a hugely satisfying collection. A very high proportion of favourite Schubert songs is included in the second, 1980 group. With a great singer treating each with loving, detailed care the result is a charmer of a recital. Dame Janet's strongly characterized reading of *Die Forelle* makes it a fun song, and similarly Parsons's naughty springing accompaniment to *An Sylvia* (echoed later by the singer) gives a twinkle to a song that can easily be treated too seriously. One also remembers the ravishing *subito piano* for the second stanza of *An die Musik*. There are no texts, but this remains an unmissable reissue.

SCHULHOFF, Ervin (1894–1942)

String Sextet

Ⓑ Hyp. Helios CDH 55321. Raphael Ens. – **MARTINŮ**: *String Sextet; 3 Madrigals for Violin & Viola*

Like Martinů, Schulhoff was born in Bohemia and was first a student in Prague. He studied briefly with Reger and Debussy no less, and was highly prolific (there are eight symphonies, though the last two were not complete). The *Sextet* of 1924 is an effective piece, with traces of Mahler and early Schoenberg. Its première at Donaueschingen in 1924 took place in the same week as Schoenberg's *Serenade*. Schulhoff lived in Germany during the inter-war years, returning to Prague at the time of the Nazi invasion. A man of the Left, he had taken Soviet citizenship, which afforded him protection until Hitler invaded Russia. As a Jew, he was arrested and he died in the notorious Würzburg concentration camp.

SCHUMAN, William (1910–92)

(i) *Violin Concerto*. *New England Triptych*
🅑🅑 Naxos 8.559083. Bournemouth SO, Serebrier, (i) with Quint (with IVES: *Variations*)

Schuman's powerfully expressive *Violin Concerto* (1959) underwent more than one transformation during its gestation, with the original three movements becoming two. After a strong, rhythmically angular opening (with the soloist immediately introducing the work's dominating motif) the first movement soon slips into a magically lyrical *molto tranquillo*. Later there is a sparkling scherzando section and an extended cadenza, before the brilliant conclusion. Lyrical feeling also seeps through the finale, although there is plenty of vigour and spectacle too, and a fugue, before the bravura *moto perpetuo* display of the closing section. Altogether a splendidly rewarding work, given a first-rate performance here by Philip Quint and the strongly involved Bournemouth players under Serebrier. They are no less persuasive in the *New England Triptych*, a folksy, immediately communicative work. First-class recording in an attractively spacious acoustic. The coupling, which Schuman orchestrated, could not be more apt.

Symphonies 3; *5*; *Judith (Choreographic Poem)*
Naxos 8.559317. Seattle SO, Schwarz

Symphonies 4; *9 (Le fosse ardeatine)*; *Circus Overture*; *Orchestra Song*
Naxos 8.559254. Seattle SO, Schwarz

Symphony 6; *New England Triptych (3 Pieces for Orchestra after William Billings)*; *Prayer in a Time of War*
Naxos 8.559625. Seattle SO, Schwarz

Symphonies 7; *10 (The American Muse)*
Naxos 8.559255. Seattle SO, Schwarz

Symphony 8; *Night Journey* (with **IVES**, arr. **SCHUMAN**: *Variations on 'America'*)
Naxos 8.559651

🅑🅑 Naxos 8.505228 (5). Seattle SO, Schwarz

Gerard Schwarz and the Seattle orchestra have recorded all the Schuman symphonies. Nos. 1 and 2 appear to not be available at present, although recordings exist.

Nos. 3–10, recorded between 2004 and 2010, are all included in this box. Schuman is said to have composed early in the morning and then turned to musical education and administration for the rest of the day. The two-movement *Third Symphony* has a baroque model, offering a 'Passacaglia and Fugue' balanced by a 'Chorale and Toccata'. The *Fourth Symphony* followed its better-known predecessor within a few months, and its première was conducted by Koussevitzky. The *Fifth* is for strings alone and is contrapuntally stimulating, as is the comparatively sober *Sixth*. Dating from 1960, the *Seventh* was commissioned for the 75th season of the Boston Symphony and marks Schuman's return to the symphony after a gap of 11 years. The *Eighth* (1962) is a large-scale work, using an expanded orchestra with an impressive array of percussion. The *Ninth* was written in 1967, when Schuman had visited Rome and seen the memorial *Le fosse ardeatine* that commemorates a random massacre by Nazi forces. It is a dark and powerful score. The *Tenth* was commissioned for the bicentennial celebrations of 1976.

Of the shorter works, *Judith* (1949), a 'choreographic poem', powerfully tells the story of the Jewish widow who offered herself to General Holofernes, then, when he was about to seduce her, beheaded him. The *New England Triptych* is based on melodies from the time of the American Revolution, and *Prayer in a Time of War* anticipated America's participation in the Second World War. *Night Journey* is drawn from Schuman's ballet about Jocasta and Oedipus, while his resplendent arrangement of Ives's *Variations on 'America'* is both spectacular and patriotic.

William Schuman is a major voice in American symphonic music, and no one investigating these works will be disappointed, as they are exceptionally well played and recorded.

SCHUMANN, Robert (1810–56)

Cello Concerto in A min., Op. 129 (DVD version)
DG DVD 073 4351. Maisky, VPO, Bernstein – **HAYDN**: *Cello Concertos 1–2; Violin Concerto G, in C: Adagio*, arr. for cello (V/D: Humphrey Burton)

Maisky and Bernstein make a splendid partnership in Schumann's *Cello Concerto*, ardent and commanding, with a warmly expressive slow movement. Visually this could hardly be better managed, and the recording is first class. What a joy too are Maisky's glorious performances of Haydn's pair of *Cello Concertos*, which he directs himself, alongside the transcription of part of the *Violin Concerto* with the Vienna strings playing beautifully on modern instruments.

Piano Concerto in A min., Op. 54
Ⓜ EMI 5 03419-2. Andsnes, BPO, Jansons – **GRIEG**: *Piano Concerto*

Though Kovacevich's coupling of the Schumann and Grieg *Concertos* remains thoroughly recommendable and very tempting (Philips 475 7773), Andsnes's

Schumann is of the highest poetic feeling and distinction. Like the Grieg, it brings glorious playing from both soloist and orchestra under Jansons, a performance similarly combining spontaneity and concentration, dedication and warmth, with no hint of self-consciousness or routine. The pianistic virtuosity is commanding but never overrides tenderness. A performance of both subtlety and nobility, recorded in particularly lifelike and well-balanced sound. A classic version for our time.

(i) *Piano Concerto in A min.*; *Konzertstück, Op. 92. Arabeske, Op. 18*; *Carnaval, Op. 9*; *Davidsbündlertänze, Op. 6*; *Fantasie in C, Op. 17*; *Humoreske, Op. 20*; *Kinderszenen, Op. 15*; *Kreisleriana, Op. 16*; *Nachtstücke, Op. 23*; *Novellette, Op. 99/9*; *Papillons, Op. 2*; *3 Romanzen, Op. 28*; *Sonata 2 in G min., Op. 22*; *Symphonic Studies, Op. 13*; *Waldszenen, Op. 82*

Ⓑ DG (ADD) 477 8693 (5). Wilhelm Kempff; (i) with Bav. RSO, Kubelik

Recorded between 1967 and 1973, this anthology celebrates Kempff's special feeling for Schumann. He is in his element in pieces like the *Arabesque*, the relatively little-known first and third *Romances*, and the *Novellette*, where he inspires an element of fantasy, of spontaneous recreation, and he is also at his most inspirational in the *Fantasie in C. Davidsbündlertänze*, the *Nachtstücke* and *Papillons* are also extremely fine. On the other hand, the comparatively extrovert style of the *Carnaval Suite* suits him less well. However, Kempff's thoughtful, intimate readings of two of the *Études symphoniques* and *Kreisleriana* are marvellously persuasive, giving a clear illusion of live performance spontaneously caught, and again well recorded. Similarly, if the sharper contrasts of the *Humoresque* are toned down by charm and geniality, the *Waldszenen* are glowingly relaxed, and both are comparably personal and individual.

The *Concerto* was one of the last works to be recorded. It opens with a very solid account of the opening chords, and then Kempff proceeds characteristically to produce an unending stream of poetry. His tempi are generally leisurely and he is richly supported by Kubelik and the Bavarian Radio Orchestra. The *Konzertstück* too, not one of Schumann's most inspired pieces, is played most persuasively, with Kempff's magic leading the ear on.

Symphonies 1–4 (DVD version)
DG DVD 073 4512. VPO, Bernstein

Symphony in G min. (Zwickau); *Symphonies 1–32; 3 (Rhenish), Op. 97*; *Symphony 4* (original, 1841 version and revised, 1851 version); (i) *Konzertstück for 4 Horns & Orchestra in F, Op. 86. Overture, Scherzo & Finale, Op. 52* (CD version)
DG 457 591-2 (3). (i) Montgomery, Edwards, Dent, Maskell; ORR, Gardiner

Schumann's symphonies offer searing nineteenth-century romanticism with their flowing melodies and fresh, vibrant inspiration. Apart from Bernstein's set with the VPO, there have been several fully recommendable accounts of these works over the years, with classic versions from Sawallisch (EMI), Karajan (DG) and Solti (Decca), all very different but all very recommendable and worth considering. However, John Eliot Gardiner offers the most revelatory insights of all and includes not just the four regular symphonies but a complete survey of Schumann as symphonist. He seeks specifically to explode the myth that Schumann was a poor orchestrator, pointing out how quick he was to learn from his own mistakes. Gardiner makes an exception over the 1851 revision of the *Fourth Symphony*, in which Schumann thickened the woodwind writing with much doubling. Illuminatingly, both versions of that symphony are included, with the contrasts well brought out. Gardiner himself, like Brahms, prefers the slimmer, more transparent first version, suggesting that the 1851 changes made it safer and less original. Yet, paradoxically, in performance Gardiner is even more inspired in the later version, which here emerges as bitingly dramatic, working up to a thrilling coda. Like other cycles, this one offers the *Overture, Scherzo and Finale* of 1841 as a necessary extra; but still more fascinating is the *Konzertstück* of 1849 for four horns, with the ORR soloists breath-taking in their virtuosity on nineteenth-century instruments. Also included is the early, incomplete *Symphony in G minor* of 1832 (named after Schumann's home town of Zwickau). Under Gardiner, the two completed movements emerge as highly original in their own right. This set is undoubtedly one of Gardiner's finest achievements.

Bernstein's outstanding complete DVD set of the Schumann symphonies (on a single disc) shows him at his very finest – electrifying in controlling tension, spirited and genial in bringing out Schumann's rich lyricism, powerful in creating the music's drama. John Rockwell of the *New York Times* suggested that in these later Schumann performances 'the orchestral playing is surer and more idiomatic ... warm, full and Germanic'. 'Bernstein,' he concludes, 'catches the romantic secret of this music in a way that most conductors have not.' Throughout the set he achieves glorious orchestral textures from the VPO to completely negate any suggestion that the composer's scoring is thick and unwieldy. Indeed, he always uses the original scores, and the very *First Symphony* sounds wonderfully fresh and spring-like, the performance joyously light-hearted. In the *Second* Bernstein obviously identifies completely with the *Adagio*, playing it with great tenderness, and then the orchestra jubilantly explodes into the closing *molto vivace*. In the *Third* the very opening is exuberant and the brass produces remarkable sonority in the fourth movement's opening evocation of Cologne Cathedral. Most remarkable of all is the *Fourth*, played with enormous zest, and in the extraordinary 'Wagnerian' transition, from Scherzo to finale, Bernstein out-Furtwänglers Furtwängler in bringing a feeling of actual creative growth as the brass, with unforgettable power, makes its way remorselessly to the main allegro, which then dashes off bitingly and exhilaratingly, and accelerates spontaneously into the unstoppable coda. Throughout, the Vienna Philharmonic give of their all, and watching Bernstein enjoying himself doing the same is an experience in itself. Fortunately, Humphrey Burton's video direction is worthy of the occasion, and the audio producer, John McClure, can take similar credit for the superbly balanced sound in the Musikverein.

Symphony 2 in C, Op. 61

Orfeo mono 427041. VPO, Mitropoulos - **PROKOFIEV**: *Symphony 5*

Mitropoulos was an artist of the strongest personality and integrity. Schumann's greatest symphony, together with Prokofiev's *Fifth*, comprised his début with the Vienna Philharmonic at the 1954 Salzburg Festival. He holds the *Second Symphony* together but achieves great intensity in its heavenly slow movement. The ORF (Austrian Radio) balance is not ideal but, given the quality of this electrifying performance, the sound is of lesser importance.

Fünf Stücke im Volkston

Ⓜ Decca 475 8239. Rostropovich, Britten - **SCHUBERT**: *Arpeggione Sonata*.
  DEBUSSY: *Cello Sonata*

Though simpler than the Debussy *Sonata* with which it is coupled, this is just as elusive a work. Rostropovich and Britten show that the simplicity is not quite as square and solid as might at first seem and that, in the hands of masters, these *Five Pieces in Folk Style* have rare charm, particularly the last with its irregular rhythm. The excellent recording justifies the reissue under the 'Classic Sound' logo.

Piano Quartet, Op. 47; Piano Quintet, Op. 44; Piano Trios 1–3, Opp. 63, 80 & 110

Ⓑ Decca Duo 456 323-2 (2). Beaux Arts Trio (augmented)

Philips compiled a particularly generous measure for this Duo of Beaux Arts/Schumann performances from the 1970s, which now reappears on the Decca label. The illustrious trio (with associates) give splendid readings of the *Piano Quartet* and *Quintet*. The vitality of inspiration is brought out consistently, and with that goes their characteristic concern for fine ensemble and refined textures. The *Piano Trios* are hardly less successful.

String Quartets 1–3, Op. 41/1–3

ⒷⒷ Naxos 8.570151. Fine Arts Qt

Having all three of Schumann's Opus 41 *Quartets* on a single Naxos disc makes a superb bargain. These fine works (notably the last and most impressive, No. 3) are the products of Schumann's extraordinary year of chamber inspirations, 1842, which also saw the composition of the *Piano Quintet* and *Piano Quartet*. The Fine Arts Quartet, founded as long ago as 1946, remains a magnificent interpreter, here vividly recorded in sessions in Holland in 2006.

'Abegg' Variations, Op. 1; Arabeske, Op. 18; Blumenstück, Op. 19; Bunte Blätter, Op. 99; Carnaval, Op. 9; Davidsbündlertänze, Op. 6; Études symphoniques, Op. 13; Fantasy in C, Op. 17; Fantasiestücke, Op. 12; Faschingsschwank aus Wien, Op. 26; Humoreske, Op. 20; Kinderszenen, Op. 15; Kreisleriana, Op. 16; Nachtstücke, Op. 23; Novelletten, Op. 21/1, 2 & 8; Papillons, Op. 2; 3 Romanzen, Op. 28; Sonatas 1–2; Waldszenen, Op. 82

Ⓑ Decca 470 915-2 (7). Ashkenazy

Vladimir Ashkenazy's survey of Schumann's piano music comes from the late 1980s through to the mid-1990s. Of course there are individual performances here that have been equalled by other artists – Lupu's unforgettable accounts of the *Humoresque* and *Kreisleriana* and Brendel's strong, poetic *Fantasiestücke* and *Kinderszenen* for instance (434 732-2). But this is not to minimize the achievement of these thoughtful and intuitive performances or the artistry and excellence which Ashkenazy brings to bear on a composer for whom he obviously he has a great feeling. The recordings are very natural, and readers wanting a complete Schumann coverage will find this set very rewarding.

Humoreske, Op. 20; Kinderszenen, Op. 15; Kreisleriana, Op. 16 – see **LUPU**, Radu

SCHÜTZ, Heinrich (1585–1672)

(i) *Christmas Oratorio (Weihnachtshistorie)*; (ii) *Historia der Auferstehungshistorie*

Da Capo 8.226058. (i) Adam Riis, Else Torp, Jakob Bloch Jespersen; (ii) Johan Linderoth; Ars Nova Copenhagen, Concerto Copenhagen, Sirius Viols, Paul Hillier

The splendid Ars Nova Copenhagen, directed by the sensitive Paul Hillier, provide here totally compelling recordings of Schütz's inspired settings of the *Christmas Oratorio* and the *History of the Resurrection*. The *Oratorio* tells the Christmas story, beginning with Joseph and Mary's journey to Bethlehem (to be taxed), where Mary 'brought forth her first-born son in a manger'. The flight into Egypt follows, Herod's slaughter of the innocents, and the family's return from Egypt to safety in Nazareth.

Schütz sets the story with touching simplicity as an ongoing narration from the Evangelist (here the infinitely touching tenor, Adam Riis), accompanied by a simple organ continuo. One is gripped by the combination of purity and vividness of the music. The narration is regularly interrupted by eight *Intermedia* involving an Angel, the Host of Angels, Shepherds, Wise Men, High Priests and Herod. Each has a richly scored accompaniment appropriate to the text.

The words of the Shepherds, for instance, are given a pastoral sinfonia featuring a pair of recorders; the High Priests are accompanied by four trombones, and Herod is accompanied by two high trumpets; and the solo singing is very fine, especially the radiant-voiced soprano, Else Torp.

The *Resurrection Historia*, by contrast, draws on very simple plainsong for its vocal style, and features ten texts continuing the Bible story after the crucifixion, with the anointing of Jesus, the earthquake, the rolling back of the stone, and Mary Magdalene's meeting with the restored Jesus, whom she does not at first recognize. Schütz's text tells us that the disciples, too, doubt, even after Jesus has joined them for their supper and later shown his hands and feet. Then, blessing them with the words, 'Receive ye the Holy Spirit,' his final command is, 'If ye remit the sins of anyone, they are remitted, and if ye retain the sins of anyone they are retained,' and the key Christian teaching is made clear. Schütz then ends his work with an eloquent chorus giving ample thanks to God.

SCOTT, Cyril (1879–1970)

Aubade, Op. 77; (i) *Violin Concerto*; (ii) *Festival Overture*. *3 Symphonic Dances*
Chan. 10407. BBC PO, Brabbins; with (i) Charlier; (ii) Sheffield Philharmonic Ch.

These are all most persuasive performances, given Chandos's top-quality recording which makes the *Three Symphonic Dances* glow with colour and all but lose their capacity to seem over-long. The *Festival Overture* is more of an atmospheric evocation than an occasional piece, lustrously orchestrated, with the finale suddenly reinforced by organ and chorus. The *Violin Concerto* is a one-movement, rhapsodical work, elusive structurally, but lyrically appealing. It has a distinctly improvisatory character, which Olivier Charlier and Brabbins catch with admirable spontaneity. But easily the best work here is the *Aubade*, richly sensuous in its scoring and voluptuous in its manipulation of texture. It is superbly played.

(i) *Cello Concerto*. *Symphony 1*
Chan. 10452. BBC PO, Brabbins, (i) with Watkins

This is in some ways the most revealing of the issues in Brabbins's Cyril Scott series for Chandos, with works from opposite ends of his long career, the *Symphony No. 1* of 1899 and the *Cello Concerto* of 1937. The *Symphony* is more traditional than Scott's later symphonies, with its clean-cut thematic material. It was written when Scott had been studying in Frankfurt with other British composers of the time, including Quilter, Balfour Gardiner and Grainger. This was before Scott acquired a French flavour in his music, and the result is very attractive. The *Cello Concerto*, beautifully played with Paul Wakins as soloist, is in a conventional three movements, with the fast outer movements separated by a reflective *Pastoral* for unaccompanied cello, before the jolly, sparkling finale. A first-rate disc, very well recorded.

Piano Concertos 1 in C; 2; Early One Morning (poem for piano & orchestra)

Lyrita (ADD) SRCD 251. Ogdon, LPO, Herrmann

Cyril Scott's lush *First Piano Concerto* dates from 1913 and its extravagant style belongs to the pre-war era. Those for whom Scott's name conjures memories of a piece called *Lotus Land* might feel that its atmosphere is well expressed by that title. Ogdon and Herrmann make a coherent whole out of Scott's essentially rhapsodical piece. The *Second Concerto* dates from Scott's later years, and although it has undoubted atmosphere, its shifting moods and rhapsodic chromaticism may not suit all tastes. The spirit of Delius is certainly evoked in this work, and it is even more apparent in the poem, *Early One Morning*. For all one's reservations, however, Scott's music has a haunting quality that makes one want to return to it. The composer is splendidly served by his performers here, who create a feeling of spontaneity even when the music itself eddies gently with comparatively little forward movement. The recording, from the mid-1970s, is quite excellent in its CD format.

SCRIABIN, Alexander (1872–1915)

(i) Piano Concerto in F sharp min., Op. 20; (ii) Prometheus (The Poem of Fire), Op. 60; Rêverie; Symphonies Le Poème de l'extase, Op. 54; (iii) 1 in E, Op. 26. 2 in C min., Op. 29; 3 (The Divine Poem), Op. 43

Ⓜ BIS CD 1669-70 (3). (i) Pöntinen; (ii) Derwinger; (iii) Blom, Magnusson; (ii–iii) Stockholm Philharmonic Ch.; Royal Stockholm PO, Segerstam

Segerstam is very much at home in this repertoire and he gets very good results from this fine orchestra. Both Love Derwinger in *Prometheus* and Pöntinen in the *F sharp minor Concerto* are intuitive interpreters of the *art nouveau* Russian master. BIS offer this as three CDs for the price of two. The recordings come from 1989–91 and enjoy the excellent acoustic of the Stockholm Konserthus.

Piano Music: Allegro appassionato & miscellaneous works; Piano Sonatas 1–10; Études; Impromptus; Mazurkas; Poèmes; Préludes; Waltzes

Cap. AH 193 (8). Lettberg (plus DVD documentary)

The present set encompasses Scriabin's complete solo piano output, recorded in collaboration with Deutschlandradio Kultur between 2004 and 2007. Maria

Lettberg can withstand comparison with the most exalted company. She is completely attuned to the hyper-refined sensibility and ecstatic rapture of Scriabin's world and, whether it be in the Chopinesque foothills of the *Préludes* or the mesmeric power of the late *Sonatas*, she characterizes this repertoire to something like perfection. In addition to the eight CDs there is a DVD entitled 'Alexander Scriabin: Mysterium' which includes paintings and animations by Andrea Schmidt and interviews which examine the composer's musical beliefs and his mysticism. Strongly recommended.

SEIBER, Mátyás (1905–60)

3 Fragments from 'A Portrait of the Artist as a Young Man'
Ⓜ Australian Decca Eloquence (ADD) 480 2152. Pears, Dorian Singers, Melos Ens. –
  SHOSTAKOVICH: *Piano Quintet*. **PROKOFIEV**: *Quintet in G min*.

Seiber's haunting work here makes its début on CD. He was particularly attracted to Joyce, and enshrined in his *Chamber Cantata* for speaker, singers and instrumentalists is something of the strange opposition of peace and violence that typifies *A Portrait of the Artist as a Young Man*. Peter Pears is perfectly cast for the speaker's part, and the instruments and voices blend magically around his clear and deliberate declamation. There is a haunting beauty in the opening and closing *Lento* movements; and the dramatic writing, especially the percussion in the central *Feroce*, is superbly captured in this warmly vivid recording, dating from 1960, but sounding superb in this transfer. A fascinating 'collector's piece' in every way.

SHEPPARD, John (c. 1515–c. 1559)

Aeterne rex altissime; *Audivi vocem de coelo*; *Beata nobis gaudia*; *Dum transisset Sabbatum* (1st & 2nd settings); *In manus tuas* (2nd & 3rd settings); *Gaude, gaude, gaude Maria*; *Hostis Herodes impie*; *Impetum fecerunt unanimes*; *In manus tuas* (3rd setting); *Libera nos, salva nos* (2nd setting); *Sacris solemniis*; *Sancte Dei pretiose*; *Spiritus Sanctus procedens* (2nd setting). Second Service: *Magnificat*; *Nunc dimittis*. *Te Deum laudamus*. *Western Wynde Mass*
Ⓜ Hyp. Dyad CDD 22022 (2). The Sixteen, Christophers

Ave maris stella; *Cantate Mass*. Motets: *Deus tuorum militum* (1st setting); *Filiae Hierusalem, venite*; *Haec dies*; *In manus tuas Domine* (1st setting); *In pace, in idipsum*; *Iusti in perpetuum vivent*; *Jesu salvator saeculi, redemptis*; *Jesu salvator saeculi, verbum*;

Laudem dicite Deo; *Libera nos, salva nos* (1st setting); *Paschal Kyrie*; *Reges Tharsis et insulae*; *Salvator mundi, Domine*; *Spiritus Sanctus procedens* (1st setting); *Verbum caro factum est*

Ⓜ Hyp. Dyad CDD 22021 (2). The Sixteen, Christophers

The first collection listed (CD 22022) is especially attractive as it includes Sheppard's *Western Wynde Mass*. However, this is a less elaborate setting of this famous theme than some others, notably that of John Taverner, for until the closing *Agnus Dei* Sheppard consistently places the melodic line on top, whereas Taverner moves the tune about within the lower parts. Nevertheless, Sheppard's setting has an appealingly simple beauty, while the extended *Te Deum laudamus* is even richer in its harmonic progressions.

However, in the past we have given our Rosette to the companion set (CDD 22021), for it includes Sheppard's glorious six-voiced *Cantate Mass*, much more complex than *Western Wynde* and, with its glowingly textured polyphony, surely among his most inspired works. The Sixteen consistently convey the rapturous beauty of Sheppard's writing, above all in the ethereal passages in the highest register, very characteristic of him. There are not many more beautiful examples of Tudor polyphony than this.

SHOSTAKOVICH, Dmitri (1906–75)

Testimony (film, directed by Tony Palmer)

TP DVD 145. Kingsley, Shrapnel, Rigby, Shirley-Quirk, Golden Age Singers, Chilingirian Qt, Shelley, LPO, Barshai

Described by *Films and Filming* as 'the best British film of the year', Tony Palmer's study of Shostakovich is typically revelatory. Palmer follows the line presented by the unauthorized biography, *Testimony*, that the composer was hostile to the Soviet regime, whatever compromises he had to make. Ben Kingsley movingly presents the composer with great sympathy, highlighting Shostakovich's experiences in the 300-day siege of Leningrad, when human flesh was eaten so as to avoid starvation, though Shostakovich himself did not have to endure that. The snarling of Zhdanov, artistic chief, and the boasting of Stalin are equally well conveyed by John Shrapnel and Terence Rigby respectively. The musical side could hardly be finer, with Rudolf Barshai drawing dramatic playing from the LPO, backed up by the Chilingirian Quartet in the *String Quartet No. 8*. Six of the symphonies are quoted, notably the *Leningrad Symphony* with its portrayal of the Nazi invasion in the nagging ostinato of the first movement. Also very effective are the vocal contributions of John Shirley-Quirk and the Golden Age Singers in the quotations from the *Symphony No. 13* with its setting of Yevtushenko. A great film, one of the finest that even Tony Palmer has made.

(i–ii) *Alone: Suite, Op. 26*; (i; iii) *The Bolt: Suite, Op. 27a* (1934 version); (iv) *The Bolt: Suite, Op. 27a* (1931 version); (v) *Chamber Symphony (String Qt 4), Op. 83a*; *Chamber Symphony (String Quartet 8), Op. 110a*; (vi) *Cello Concertos 1–2*; *Piano Concertos:* (i–ii; vii) *1 in C min. for Piano, Trumpet & Strings*; (viii–ix) *2 in F, Op. 102*; *Violin Concertos:* (x) *1 in A min., Op. 99*; (xi) *2 in C sharp min., Op. 129*; (i–ii) *The Counterplan: Suite*; (viii) *Festive Overture, Op. 96*; *5 Fragments, Op. 42*; *Funeral & Triumphal Prelude*; (i; iii) *The Gadfly* (excerpts); (iv) *The Golden Age: Suite, Op. 22a*; (i–ii) *The Great Citizen: Funeral March*; (iv) *Hamlet: Suite, Op. 32a*; (i–ii) *Hamlet* (excerpts), *Op. 116*; *Jazz Suites 1 & 2*; (i; iii) *Moscow-Cheryomushki: Suite, Op. 105*; (viii) *October, Op. 131*; (ii; xii) *Overture on Russian and Kirghiz Folk Themes, Op. 115*; (i–ii) *Pirogov: Scherzo & Finale. Sofia Perovskaya: Waltz*; (v) *Symphony for Strings, Op. 118a*; *Symphony for Strings & Woodwinds, Op. 73a*; (i–ii) *Tahiti Trot (Tea for Two)*; *The Tale of the Silly Little Mouse* (arr. Cornall), *Op. 56*; (xiii) *The Execution of Stepan Razin*; (viii; xiv) *The Song of the Forests*

Ⓑ Decca 475 7431 (9). (i) Chailly; (ii) Concg. O; (iii) Phd. O; (iv) Gothenberg SO, Järvi; (v) COE, Barshai; (vi) H. Schiff, Bav. RSO, Maxim Shostakovich; (vii) Brautigam, Masseurs; (viii) RPO, Ashkenazy; (ix) Ortiz; (x) Mullova, RPO, Previn; (xi) Kremer, Boston SO, Ozawa; (xii) Haitink; (xiii) Vogel, Leipzig Ch. & RSO, Kegel; (xiv) Kotliarov, Storojev, New London Children's Ch., Brighton Festival Ch.

This feast of Shostakovich includes Chailly's three famous CDs of ballet and film suites and the supremely delightful *Jazz Suites* – some of the most appealing music Shostakovich ever wrote. All sorts of intriguing repertoire is here, and Shostakovich's ready fund of melody and his exotic orchestral palette, spiced with touches of wit, make for a kaleidoscope of memorable vignettes. The *Romance* from *The Gadfly* is included (in its original orchestration). *Hamlet* (there are two versions of the music here) brings music of more pungency and dramatic power, while the composer's instantaneous and irresistible arrangement of Youmans's 'Tea for Two', the *Tahiti Trot*, almost upstages everything. One of the most substantial film scores, *Alone*, brings a wide range of picaresque and touching evocations. Other highlights include the opening number from *Moscow-Cheryomushki*, which has great energy and élan, and the luscious violins in the *Tango* from *The Bolt* are a joy. Chailly plays this repertoire superbly and receives magnificent orchestral playing from both the Concertgebouw and Philadelphia orchestras, with Decca sound to match.

The *Cello Concertos* with Heinrich Schiff are superbly recorded and the *First* can hold its own with the finest. The *Second* is a haunting piece, essentially lyrical; it is gently discursive, sadly whimsical at times, and tinged with smiling melancholy that hides deeper troubles. The (Philips) recording is enormously impressive. There's a perfectly enjoyable account of the *Piano and Trumpet Concerto* from Ronald Brautigam and his excellent trumpet partner, Peter Masseurs, vividly accompanied by Chailly. The *Second Piano Concerto* with Cristina

Ortiz is very successful: she gives a sparkling account of the jaunty first move-ment and brings out the fun and wit in the finale with fluent, finely pointed playing. The *First Violin Concerto* is disappointing, although it is all very expert; the performance is ultimately routine and wanting in atmosphere. Gidon Kre-mer's DG account of the *Second Violin Concerto* is played with his customary aplomb, but the recording is not really in the demonstration bracket.

The *Chamber Symphony* is an arrangement for full strings of the *Eighth Quartet* and the *Symphony for Strings* is a similar transcription of the *Tenth*. These are strong performances and are excellently recorded (DG). With two substantial choral rarities – Ashkenazy's *The Song of the Forests* (a freshly tune-ful and enjoyable work that would have pleased the Soviet authorities) and Kegel's dramatic (1972) recording of the red-blooded *The Execution of Stepan Razin* – this bargain set is well worth considering. Texts and translations included.

Ballet Suites 1–5; *Festive Overture, Op. 96*; *Katerina Ismailova: Suite*
Ⓜ Chan. 7000/2 (2). RSNO, Järvi

This highly entertaining set generally represents Shostakovich in light-hearted, often ironic mood, throwing out *bonnes-bouches* like fireworks and with a sparkling vividness of orchestral colour. The *Ballet Suites* were the composer's way of satirically but anonymously re-using material from earlier works which lay unperformed for political reasons. There are plenty of good tunes. The *Fifth Suite* draws entirely on music from a 1931 ballet, *The Bolt*. This is the most extended of the five *Suites*, offering nearly half an hour of music, full of wry, quirky ideas, typical of the young Shostakovich. The *Suite* from *Katerina Ismailova* ('Lady Macbeth of Mtsensk') consists of entr'actes which effectively act as emotional links between the scenes, and the writing is both illuminating and characterful. Järvi is entirely at home in all this music and clearly relishes its dry humour. The playing is equally perceptive and full of flair. The recording is spectacular and resonantly wide-ranging in the Chandos manner.

(i) *Piano Concertos 1–2*; *The Unforgettable Year 1919: The Assault on Beautiful Gorky*. (ii) *The Gadfly: Suite: Barrel Organ Waltz*; *Romance*. (iii) *Jazz Suites 1*; *2*; *Waltz 2*. *Tahiti Trot (Tea for Two)*
Ⓑ CfP 382234-2. (i) Alexeev, ECO, Maksymiuk; (ii) ASMF, Marriner; (iii) Phd. O, Jansons

Alexeev recorded the Shostakovich *Piano Concertos* in the early 1980s and they have become classics of the early digital era. The digital recording is in every way excellent and scores over most of its competitors in clarity and presence. Artistically, Alexeev has more personality than his rivals, and he has the advan-tage of sensitive and idiomatic support from the ECO and Maksymiuk. Alexeev does not always observe the composer's dynamic indications, but in nearly every other respect comes closest to both the spirit and letter of the scores (there are two small departures from the score in No. 1, but they are really too trivial to mention). No. 1 is very lively and characterful and No. 2 is the best we have had since Bernstein's pioneering record. The one-movement concerto from a film score called *The Unforgettable Year 1919* is a sort of Soviet *Warsaw Concerto*, and it is hard not to be swept up by its heart-on-sleeve emotions, and it is very enjoyable. For this reissue, EMI have added Jansons's sumptuously recorded *Jazz Suites* and two excerpts from *The Gadfly* – both works showing the composer at his most irresistibly tuneful.

Violin Concerto 2, Op. 129
BBC Legends BBCL 4267. David Oistrakh, LSO, Ormandy (with **TCHAIKOVSKY**:
   Violin Concerto; **BLISS**: *Fanfare;* LPO, Maxim Shostakovich)

The *Second Concerto* was written for Oistrakh's sixtieth birthday but Shostakovich got the wrong date and produced it a year earlier. (He composed another new work for the following year's sixtieth, the *Violin Sonata.*) This 1967 Festival Hall performance under Eugene Ormandy was its première in the West, and its freshness and urgency tell. Oistrakh's playing is thrilling both in this and the Tchaikovsky, recorded in 1972 with the LPO. Well-detailed and vivid sound.

Symphonies 1–12; (i) 13; (ii) 14; 15; (iii) Violin Concerto 2, Op. 129; (iv) The Execution of Stepan Razin, Op. 119; The Sun Shines on our Motherland, Op. 90
Melodiya MELCD 10 01065 (11). Moscow PO, Kondrashin; with (i) Eisen, RSFSR Ac. Ch.;
   (ii) Tselovalnik, Nestorenko; (iii) D. Oistrakh; (iv) Gromadsky

Our last encounter with Kondrashin's cycle was on 12 boxed LPs, and it remains mandatory listening. The *Fourth*, its première recording, has wonderful intensity, as indeed does the *Eighth*, though we prefer Mravinsky's 1960 broadcast on BBC Legends. (The first movement of the *Sixth* still strikes us as a bit fast.) But on balance this all has the ring of authenticity that one expects from a conductor who was so closely associated with the composer and who gave the premières of *Symphonies 4* and *13*.

Symphony 1 in F min. (complete, plus rehearsal)
Medici Arts DVD 2072158. Schleswig-Holstein Music Fesival O, Bernstein

As Bernstein says before he begins the rehearsal which goes with this performance, Shostakovich's *First Symphony* is a quirky, unpredictable piece which pokes fun at authority with an 'Up yours' attitude, yet which begins to falter as its young composer finds himself being taken over by the expressive power of the music he is writing. So this is no ordinary rehearsal. The orchestral players learn much more than they expected about what the composer is trying to convey, and so do we. The performance of the symphony itself has extraordinary power, a palette of colour and revelation of detail far beyond what we hear during an ordinary account. It is also thrilling, marvellously played and very vividly recorded. Bernstein has such a friendly spirit of communication as he unlocks the music's main secrets that, by watching and listening to this DVD, it is possible to get inside this very remarkable and original work that was its composer's symphonic début.

Symphony 5 in D min., Op. 47
BBC (ADD) BBCL 4169-2. LSO, Stokowski (with **VAUGHAN WILLIAMS**: *Symphony 8*)

Stokowski made the first and greatest mono recording of the Shostakovich *Fifth* on 78s, unforgettable for its intensity of vision, especially in the slow movement. But the present version, recorded live in the Royal Albert Hall in the 1964 Prom season, is its more recent match. It vividly demonstrates that, even in his eighties, Stokowski was unsurpassed in this great work, his own favourite among the series. The biting tensions of the opening are masterfully concentrated with the pure, sinuous lines of the second subject in a performance of exceptional dedication and refinement, with each movement bringing fresh revelations, and the slow movement unforgettable in its lyrical passion. Excellent stereo sound, remarkably vivid for a radio broadcast of the period. The Vaughan Williams coupling is hardly less revelatory.

Symphony 7 in C (Leningrad), Op. 60
MDG Surround Sound SACD 937 1203-6. Bonn Beethoven O, Kofman

This superbly realistic and spectacular new recording from the unlikely source of the Bonn Beethoven Orchestra rather sweeps the board. Roman Kofman has the full measure of this remarkable work. He builds the famous first-movement ostinato with unremitting concentration into an overwhelming climax, and his reading creates a satisfying combination of passion and irony in the work as a whole, with raptly beautiful playing and great intensity from the strings in the *Adagio*, and jubilant triumph at the work's close. The recording is very much in the demonstration class, whether using two speakers or four.

Symphony 8 in C min., Op. 65
BBC (ADD) BBCL 4002-2. Leningrad PO, Mravinsky (with **MOZART**: *Symphony 33 in B flat, K.319*)

Mravinsky's BBC recording comes from the Festival Hall concert given during the Leningrad orchestra's tour in 1960 at which Shostakovich himself was present. The CD transfer reproduces the occasion with great realism and a wide dynamic range. This reading has tremendous intensity and authenticity of feeling. It comes with a bonus – the first half of the concert, which was given over to an elegant performance of Mozart's *Symphony 33*. Even among modern recordings this more than holds its own and the sound is very good indeed. Mandatory listening.

Symphony 10 in E min., Op. 93
Ⓜ DG 477 5909. BPO, Karajan

Already in his 1967 recording Karajan had shown that he had the measure of this symphony: this newer version is, if anything, even finer. In the first movement he distils an atmosphere as concentrated as before, bleak and unremitting, while in the *Allegro* the Berlin Philharmonic leave no doubts as to their peerless virtuosity. Everything is marvellously shaped and proportioned, and the early (1981) digital sound is made firmer by this 'original-image'-bit reprocessing.

24 Preludes and Fugues, Op. 87
Medici Arts DVD 3085248. Tatiana Nikolayeva

During the Bach bicentenary year in 1950, Shostakovich heard the *Forty-Eight* played by the young Tatiana Nikolayeva with such admiration that he composed his own *Preludes and Fugues* for her. Some forty years on, she recorded them in Scotland for BBC Television, and her mastery still shines through. Authoritative performances, well recorded and with discreet, intelligent camerawork, this is a set to cherish. There is a short but admirable feature by the artist, setting out the circumstances of their composition.

Piano Quintet. Op. 57
Ⓜ Australian Decca Eloquence (ADD) 480 2152. Melos Ens. - **PROKOFIEV**:
   Quintet. **SEIBER**: *Portrait of the Artist as a Young Man*

Shostakovich's *Piano Quintet*, written in 1940, is one of his most deeply moving works. It includes two intensely serious movements, a slow opening prelude and fugue and a slow Intermezzo, alternating with characteristically offbeat movements – a rumbustious Scherzo and a wayward finale. This performance, dating from 1964, may not be the most profound the work has received, but it is very well played and recorded, and is coupled to two other works of great interest.

SIBELIUS, Jean (1865–1957)

Belshazzar's Feast, Op. 51: Suite. Canzonetta, Op. 62a; Kuolema: Scene with Cranes; Valse triste, Op. 44/1–2. Night Ride and Sunrise, Op. 55; Pan and Echo, Op. 53a; 2 Pieces, Op. 45; Valse romantique, Op. 62b
ⓑⓑ Naxos 8.570763. New Zealand SO, Inkinen

Sibelius's output is much larger than one may think from the (understandable) repetition of his most famous works. This inexpensive CD shows just how marvellous his lesser-known music is. This is the Finnish conductor Pietari

Inkinen's second Sibelius anthology with the excellent New Zealand orchestra and, for the most part, he again stays off the beaten path. The *Canzonetta* and *Valse romantique* are little more than salon pieces, but his delicacy of feeling gives them status. *Pan and Echo* and the engaging *Suite* from *Belshazzar's Feast* are more substantial and, like the masterly *Night Ride and Sunrise*, are played with splendid idiomatic feeling. Once again the favourite *Valse triste*, in its charm, shows just why it is a favourite. First-class recording completes the listener's pleasure in an anthology that is worth every penny of its modest cost.

(i) *Belshazzar's Feast* (complete score), *Op. 51. The Countess's Portrait (Grefvinnans konterfej)*; (ii) *Jedermann (Everyman)* (incidental music), *Op. 83*

BIS CD 735. (i) Paasikivi; (ii) Lehto, Tiilikainen, Pietiläinen, Lahti Chamber Ch.; Lahti SO, Vänskä

The incidental music to Hugo von Hofmannsthal's morality play, *Everyman*, is fragmentary, wisps of sound; all of it is atmospheric and the best of it (the *Largo* section from track 12 onwards) finds Sibelius at his most inspired. The complete score for Hjalmar Procopé's *Belshazzar's Feast* brings us some seven minutes of extra music. The scoring is different from and less effective than the concert suite. *Grefvinnans konterfej (The Countess's Portrait)* is a short, wistful piece for strings which comes from 1906. Dedicated, sensitive performances from the Lahti Symphony Orchestra, and excellent recording. An indispensable disc for all Sibelians.

Violin Concerto in D min., Op. 47

Ⓜ Sony SMK 89748. Cho-Liang Lin, Philh. O, Salonen – **NIELSEN**: *Violin Concerto*

Cho-Liang Lin's playing is distinguished not only by flawless intonation and an apparently effortless virtuosity but also by great artistry. He produces a glorious sonority at the opening, and the slow movement has tenderness, warmth and yet restraint, with not a hint of over-heated emotions. Lin encompasses the extrovert brilliance of the finale and the bravura of the cadenza with real mastery. The Philharmonia Orchestra rises to the occasion under Esa-Pekka Salonen and the recording is first class.

The Bard, Op. 64; En Saga, Op. 9; The Oceanides, Op. 73; Pohjola's Daughter, Op. 49; Tapiola, Op. 112

BIS CD 1283. Lahti SO, Vänskä

RCA's set of the Sibelius tone-poems with Sir Colin Davis and the LSO are in a special class, as indeed is Karajan's magisterial and definitive *Tapiola* on DG; but, as with so many records by the major companies, one can never be sure if they are in currency and, if they are, how long they will survive in the catalogue. BIS never delete anything and Osmo Vänskä and the Lahti orchestra are authoritative interpreters who convey the atmosphere and mystery of these extraordinary scores. They are magnificently recorded too and, though Vänskä exaggerates *pianissimo* markings, they are a sound recommendation.

Symphonies 1 in E min., Op. 39; 2 in D, Op. 43; 5 in E flat, Op. 82; 7 in C, Op. 105 (DVD version)

Unitel Classica DVD 702208 (2). VPO, Bernstein (DVD Director: Humphrey Burton)

These are among the very finest DVD recordings Leonard Bernstein made in America and Europe to climax his career. They date from 1988 (Nos. 2 and 5), 1990 (No. 7) and 1991 (No. 1, with which he identifies completely). This is the most passionately intense performance of all, quite unsurpassed in every respect. It opens with the most haunting clarinet solo, beautifully played, which Bernstein then follows by building to an overwhelming climax. The timpani in echoing the main theme dominates the first movement's *Allegro energico*. The *Andante* is utterly Sibelian in colour and feeling, and the climax of the great lyrical tune of the finale is unforgettable.

Bernstein's comment that 'There's more to a Sibelius symphony than just nationalism, the special fascination of this music comes from the suspense in its construction', is borne out fully in his account of the *Second Symphony*, which with its richly scored opening and intensely felt and flexible *Tempo andante, ma rubato* then races through the Scherzo and builds to the increasingly magnificent climaxes of the finale. When that great climbing tune first appears, Bernstein's facial expression bursts into unrestrained joy, as if he's saying, 'This is what we have been waiting for.' And the tension is maintained in the interludes which move the music along between the increasingly powerful appearances of the main theme. The coda is overwhelming. Incidentally, Sibelius once criticized young contemporary composers for not using the bass of the orchestra adequately. Here he underpins everything on a richly resonant bass, whether on strings, brass (and especially the tuba) or even the timpani.

Symphonies 1–7; Finlandia, Op. 26; Karelia Suite, Op. 11; Kuolema: Valse triste, Op. 44/1; Legend: The Swan of Tuonela, Op. 22/2; Rakastava, Op. 14; Tapiola, Op. 112

Exton OVCL-00279 (*Symphonies 1 & 3; Rakastava*); OVCL 00292 (*Symphony 2; Swan of Tuonela; Tapiola*); OVCL 00282 (*Symphonies 4 & 5; Finlandia*); OVCL 00293 (*Symphonies 6 & 7; Karelia Suite; Valse triste*); discs available separately. Royal Stockholm PO, Ashkenazy

Hitherto we have recommended Sir Colin Davis's splendid RCA seven-disc bargain box with the LSO for a complete coverage of the symphonies plus key orchestral works, and this remains very compelling. The excellence of the LSO playing is matched by consistently fine RCA recording (82876 55706-2). But now, for those willing to pay rather more for four full-priced CDs, there is an even more recommendable coverage, with the additional advantage that all four discs are available separately. These performances come from a cycle Vladimir Ashkenazy gave in Stockholm in 2006–7, and very impressive they are. Ashkenazy has a pretty unerring feeling for the inner pulse of Sibelius. The opulence of the *First* and *Second Symphonies* is caught superbly; by comparison, the tonal palette of the *Third* is lithe and muscular and powerful in its movement towards classicism. The *Fourth*, too, is an intense and powerful reading which casts a remarkable spell. The desolate closing paragraphs of the finale, with the repeated oboe phrase (which Sibelius once told his son-in-law, the conductor Jüssi Jalas, represented Peter's thrice denial of Christ), are portrayed with real eloquence. The *Fifth* has a sense of mystery and the majestic breadth required, and he handles the transition into the Scherzo section of the first movement with impressive control. The *Sixth* and *Seventh* are hardly less masterly. *Rakastava* occupies a very special place in all Sibelius for its purity and sense of innocence, and Ashkenazy plays it with great feeling and restraint. For many collectors the extremely vivid and natural sound of this Stockholm recording will be a decisive factor: it has great presence and realism. But Ashkenazy and his orchestra penetrate the spirit of all these wonderful scores.

Symphonies 1 in E min., Op. 39; 4 in A min., Op. 63
Ⓜ LSO Live SACD LSO0601. LSO, C. Davis

Colin Davis's accounts of the *First* and *Fourth Symphonies* come from 2006 and 2008 and were recorded at the Barbican Centre. Sir Colin has always been a particularly thoughtful interpreter of the *Fourth* and we recall hearing him conducting it with great natural authority when he was with the BBC Scottish Orchestra in the 1960s. His reading has deepened over the years and is much broader in tempo and more profound in feeling. The *Fourth* was always one of the triumphs of his Boston survey on Philips. Along with the 1937 Beecham and the 1954 Karajan/Philharmonia set on Columbia, which earned the composer's imprimatur, it was one of the most inward and searching readings he had then committed to disc. The present reading runs to a little under 40 minutes and has an even greater sense of breadth than his 1994 account on RCA. Sir Colin allows himself more space, but there is even more imaginative and poetic depth. He takes us completely inside this world; we become enveloped by it and feel we inhabit it. The *First Symphony*, too, has all the ardour and excitement of his earlier recordings. In short, Sibelius conducting of real stature, to which the LSO respond wholeheartedly.

Symphony 2 in D, Op. 43
ⓑⓑ Naxos mono 8.111290. Boston SO, Koussevitzky (with **GRIEG**: *The Last Spring*) –
   PROKOFIEV: *Peter and the Wolf*

Taped during his last recording sessions in November 1950, Koussevitzky's performance of Sibelius's *Symphony No. 2* is given with an electricity that transcends studio conditions, yet has great colour and emotional intensity. As a *bonne bouche* there is a rapt and expressive account of Grieg's *The Last Spring*, notable for the warmth and intensity of the Boston strings. No wonder one critic spoke of them as one of the glories of Western civlization!

Symphonies (i) *2 in D, Op. 43*; (ii) *5 in E flat, Op. 82*
Testament SBT 1418. (i) RPO; (ii) Hallé O; Barbirolli

Two of the finest Sibelius performances that Sir John ever recorded. The inspired *Second* with the RPO on top form, produced by the legendary Charles Gerhardt, comes from 1962 and was recorded in the admirable acoustics of Walthamstow Town Hall. This was previously issued for *Reader's Digest* and was subsequently released on RCA. The *Fifth*, on the other hand, is not the commercial recording he made for EMI but a Prom recorded in the Royal Albert Hall in August 1968.

SIMPSON, Robert (1921-97)

Symphonies (i) *1*; (ii) *2*; (i) *3*; (ii) *4*; (i) *5*; (iii) *6–7*; (i) *8*; (ii) *9*; (iii) *10*; (iv) *11*; ***Variations on a Theme by Nielsen***
Hyp. CDS 44191/7 (7). (i) RPO; (ii) Bournemouth SO; (iii) RLPO; (i–iii) cond. Vernon Handley; (iv) City of L. Sinfonia, Matthew Taylor

Born in Leamington Spa, Robert Simpson read medicine in London for two years before embarking on a musical career. He studied with Herbert Howells from 1942 to 1946, and championed such composers as Nielsen and Reger. In 1951 he obtained a doctorate in music from Durham University, presenting his *First Symphony* as his 'thesis'. The same year he joined the BBC Music Division, thus beginning a 30-year association with the Corporation, during which time he worked with various musical luminaries of his generation, notably Deryck Cooke and Hans Keller (and, for an equal length of time, with R.L.). In 1980 he resigned his position in protest at the BBC's reduction of its orchestras and his disillusionment with its policies. After many years of living in rural Buckinghamshire, Simpson moved to the west coast of Ireland in 1986 but his last years were affected by a severe stroke.

Simpson is one of the few twentieth-century composers to have responded creatively to late Beethoven (Michael Tippett is another) so that, although the world of feeling his music encompasses may be complex, his language retains a basic simplicity of utterance. His is not music in which beauty of incident is cultivated as a desirable end, but rather it is the continuity of the musical argument that is crucial; and beauty comes as a by-product. The 11 *Symphonies* (and the 15 *String Quartets*, all recorded by Hyperion) have a power and integrity that is almost unique among his contemporaries (perhaps the Dane, Vagn Holmboe, whom he much admired, is a similar master). Vernon Handley is a masterly interpreter; and the composer Matthew Taylor, for whom the *Eleventh* and the *Nielsen Variations* were written, is an equally impressive advocate. For anyone interested in the progress of the symphony in England in the twentieth century, this is a self-recommending set. All these recordings are available separately, and should prove an admirable investment.

SMETANA, Bedřich (1824-84)

Der Fischer, Rybár; Hakon Jarl; Jubel Overture; March for the Shakespeare Festival; Prague Carnival; Richard III; Venkovanka, the Peasant Woman; Wallenstein's Camp (symphonic poems)
Chan. 10413. BBC PO, Noseda

This is simply the finest compilation of Smetana's colourful symphonic poems ever put on disc. We have previously had a fine collection of the key works by the Bavarian Radio Orchestra under Kubelik, but that has now been reissued as a double set, paired with a less attractive version of *Má Vlast* (DG 459 418-2). In any case, apart from Gianandrea Noseda's splendidly vivid and imaginative performances (especially the darkly atmospheric *Richard III*, the highly dramatic *Hakon Jarl* and the spectacularly military evocations of *Wallenstein's Camp*), the Chandos disc triumphs by its demonstration-quality, state-of-the-art recording. Not to be missed.

Má Vlast
Ⓜ Sup. 11 1208-2. Czech PO, Kubelik

In 1990, Rafael Kubelik returned to his homeland after an enforced absence of 41 years, to open the Prague Spring Festival with this vibrant performance of *Má Vlast*. He had recorded the work twice before in stereo, but this Czech version is special, imbued with passionate national feeling, yet never letting the emotion boil over. As in the bold opening of *Vyšehrad*, with the harp strongly profiled, the intensity of the music-making is immediately projected, and the trickling streams, which are the source of *Vltava*, have a delicacy almost of fantasy. *Šárka*, with its bloodthirsty tale of revenge and slaughter, is immensely dramatic, contrasting with the pastoral evocations of the following piece; the Slavonic lilt of the music's lighter moments brings the necessary contrast and release. The recording is vivid and full, but not sumptuous; yet this suits the powerful impulse of Kubelik's overall view, with the build-up to the exultant close of *Blaník* producing a dénouement of great majesty.

The Bartered Bride: Overture; Polka; Furiant. Má vlast: Vltava
Ⓜ Decca (ADD) 475 7730. Israel PO, Kertész – **DVOŘÁK**: *Slavonic Dances*, etc.

Kertész's performance of the *Bartered Bride Overture* is one of the most exhilarating on CD. It has enormous freshness and exuberance, and the separate entries in the overture are beautifully positioned in the very vivid sound. The dances are exceptionally lively too, and *Vltava* flows with equal spontaneity, generating quite a surge of electricity in the climaxes.

Piano Trio in G min., Op. 15
Hyp. CDA 67730. Florestan Trio (with **Petr EBEN**: *Piano Trio*. **MARTINŮ**: *Piano Trio 1: 5 pièces brèves*)

The Florestan give exemplary accounts of the two classic Czech trios after Dvořák by Smetana and Martinů and, despite the masterly Suk Trio, it is difficult to imagine them surpassed. Petr Eben (1929–2007) was the doyen of the generation after Martinů. He was sent to Buchenwald during the Nazi occupation but survived and, after studies in Prague, taught in the music history department at Charles University, then briefly taught in Manchester (1978–9). His *Trio* of 1986 pits the two string players against the piano, and is full of vitality and intelligence: at times one is reminded of a blend of Martinů and Lutoslawski, though Robert Philip's excellent note suggests Ives.

The Bartered Bride (complete; in English)

Ⓜ Chan. 3128 (2). Gritton, Clarke, Robinson, Rose, Davies, Howard, Montague, Moses, Bonner, Leggate, Hesketh-Harvey, ROHCG Ch., Philh. O, Mackerras

What makes this translated version so successful is not just the brilliant conducting of Sir Charles Mackerras and the scintillating playing of the Philharmonia Orchestra, with an exceptionally strong team of soloists working well together, but also the extra impact of the comedy made by a performance in the vernacular. The echoes of G&S, with double-rhymes given a jolly, Gilbertian ring, distracting in many operas, for once seem entirely appropriate, adding to the joy of the piece. Kecal the marriage broker has many patter numbers, in which Peter Rose is wonderfully agile, characterfully establishing himself as the key figure in the story. Even the chorus has rapid tongue-twisters to cope with, crisply performed by the Covent Garden Chorus. Susan Gritton is a radiant heroine, producing golden tone and rising superbly to the challenge of the poignant numbers when it seems that Jeník has betrayed her. Paul Charles Clarke as Jeník is less successful when his tenor grows uneven under pressure, though his characterization is first rate. The other two tenor roles are both superbly taken by Timothy Robinson as the stuttering simpleton, Vašek, and Robin Leggate as the ringmaster in Act III. Strong casting too for Mařenka's parents, Neal Davies as Krušina and Yvonne Howard as Ludmila, clearly establishing their contrasted responses to the proposed marriage of Mařenka and Vašek.

SMITH, Alice Mary (1839–84)

Symphonies in A min.; in C min.; (i) Andante for Clarinet & Orchestra
Chan. 10283. LMP, Shelley; (i) with Malsbury

Alice Mary Smith was the first British woman to have composed a symphony and have it performed. And what a fine work the *C minor Symphony* is, attractively tuneful throughout and with a fine grasp of orchestration and form. It has a particularly delightful second-movement *Allegretto amorevole*, with a folksy principal melody of real memorability. The Scherzo opens with rollicking horns, and even the Victorian *maestoso* finale lightens up after a while.

The *A minor Symphony* is immediately Mendelssohnian in its richly lyrical forward impetus, and the romantic *Andante* opens with the horns and then offers a flowing cantilena. The third movement is a little like a Laendler, while the finale is boisterous and confident.

Her *Andante for Clarinet and Orchestra*, delicately scored and persuasively played here by Angela Malsbury, again demonstrates Smith's easy melodic gifts, very song-like and pleasing. Howard Shelley and the London Mozart Players are admirable advocates throughout, and this CD is most enjoyable.

SMYTH, Ethel (1858–1944)

(i) *Concerto for Violin, Horn & Orchestra. Serenade in D*
Chan. 9449. (i) Langdon, Watkins; BBC PO, De la Martinez

The *Concerto for Violin, Horn and Orchestra* is a highly successful piece in every respect. The first movement begins with an ambitious string melody, then the soloists enter alternately with the endearing secondary idea (one of the composer's very best tunes) which is imaginatively developed in a free fantasia of flowing and dancing melody and varying moods; only at the recapitulation do the soloists share the opening theme. The romantic central *Elegy* brings a touchingly beautiful and nostalgic exchange between the two soloists.

The *Serenade in D major* might well be Brahms's. Not only does the rich string-writing of the first movement have a glorious sweep, but the harmonic thinking and progressions are *echt*-Brahms. Yet Smyth's invention is of high quality, for all its eclecticism. With superb performances and warm, sumptuous recording, both these colourful and tuneful works will give great pleasure. This is easily the most impressive Smyth offering yet to have appeared on CD, and it is conducted with understanding and commitment.

SOLER, Antonio (1729–83)

Sonatas for Harpsichord (complete)
ⓑⓑ Naxos 8.553462/3/4/5 (Vols. *1–4*); 8.554434 (Vol. *5*); 8.554565/6 (Vols. *6–7*); 8.555031/2 (Vols. *8–9*); 8.557137 (Vol. *10*); 8.557640 (Vol. *11*); 8.557937 (Vol. *12*); 8.570292 (Vol. *13*). Rowland (harpsichord)

The Catalan composer Padre Antonio Soler was a monk who spent most of his life at the Escorial, a famous monastery near Madrid. There his duties included that of choir master, the provision of choral music for services and the writing of secular music for the royal family (who often visited the monastery). Yet he found time to compose 150 keyboard *Sonatas* (he apparently managed to survive on four hours' sleep each night, rising in time for early morning Mass). Between 1752 and 1757 he is reputed to have studied with Domenico Scarlatti, and most of his own sonatas show this influence. They are single-movement works in binary form (two sections), often exuberant, bravura pieces, some with dance rhythms; others are slow movements (some of these extended and marked *cantabile* and *espressivo*). But he also wrote more ambitious sonatas. *63 in F* and *67 in D* (in Volume 12) are three-movement works, each beginning with a slow movement, and are part of a group of six *Sonatas* dating from 1777, while *97-9* are part of a group of three *Sonatas* in four movements (Op. 8), written in 1783. The variety of Soler's invention is remarkable, sometimes drawing on local folk themes. The outstanding Scottish keyboard player Gilbert Rowland has recorded this repertoire over a long period, beginning in the late 1990s and concluding in 2005, playing with great vitality and variety of characterization, bringing every sonata fully to life. He is truthfully recorded, in a perfect acoustic, and you can dip into any one of these 13 discs (all available separately) and be sure of receiving musical refreshment.

SPOHR, Ludwig (1784-1859)

Octet in E, Op. 32
Decca (ADD) 466 580-2. V. Octet - **SCHUBERT**: *Octet in F, D.803*

Spohr's *Octet* is a particularly charming work, and the variations on Handel's *Harmonious Blacksmith*, which form one of the central movements, offer that kind of naïvety which, when done as stylishly as here, makes for delicious listening. The playing is expert throughout, with the five strings blending perfectly with the two horns and clarinet, and altogether this is a winning performance. The 1960 recording is fresh and open and leaves little to be desired.

STAINER, John (1840-1901)

The Crucifixion
ⓑⓑ Naxos 8.557624. Gilchrist, Bailey, Clare College, Cambridge, Ch., T. Brown; S. Farr (organ)

It is good to have an outstanding digital recording of *The Crucifixion*, with excellent soloists (the tenor, James Gilchrist, outstandingly eloquent); and Clare College Choir, directed by Timothy Brown, sings very beautifully, catching the music's devotional simplicity movingly, without sentimentality. Stephen Farr's organ contribution is supportive but not intrusive. The recording, made in Guildford Cathedral, is first class. With the congregational hymns included,

this must now take pride of place, although we still have a soft spot for the old
St John's version with Owen Brannigan and Richard Lewis.

STANFORD, Charles (1852–1924)

(i) *Piano Concerto 2 in C min., Op. 126*; (ii) *Becket, Op. 48: The
Martyrdom (Funeral March)*; (iii) *The Fisherman of Lough Neagh
and What He Saw (Irish Rhapsody 4), Op. 141*
Lyrita SRCD 219. (i) Binns, LSO; (ii-iii) LPO; (i; iii) Braithwaite; (ii) Boult

Stanford's *Second Piano Concerto*, although in three rather than four movements, is a work on the largest scale, recalling the Brahms *B flat Concerto*.
Yet Stanford asserts his own melodic individuality and provides a really memorable secondary theme for the first movement. The piece is enjoyable and
uninflated, especially when played with such spontaneous freshness. The
recording is surely a demonstration of just how a piano concerto should be
balanced. The *Funeral March* comes from incidental music commissioned at
the request of Tennyson for Irving's production of his tragedy, *Becket*. It has an
arresting opening but is otherwise a fairly straightforward piece, strongly
melodic in a Stanfordian manner. Like the more familiar *Irish Rhapsody*, it is
splendidly played and recorded.

(i) *Piano Concerto 2, Op. 126*; *Down Among the Dead Men. Irish
Rhapsodies: 1 in D min., Op. 78*; *2 in F min. (Lament for the Son
of Ossian), Op. 84*; (ii) *3 for Cello & Orchestra, Op. 137. 4 in A min.
(The Fisherman of Lough Neagh and What He Saw), Op. 141*; *5 in
G min., Op. 147*; (iii) *6 for Violin & Orchestra, Op. 191*
Chan. 10116 (2). Ulster O, Handley, with (i) Fingerhut; (ii) Raphael Wallfisch; (iii)
  Mordkovitch

Stanford's set of *Irish Rhapsodies* (two of them, concertante pieces with highly
responsive soloists) are the more impressive when heard as a set. They originally appeared with the symphonies but sometimes seemed stronger and more
concentrated than these more ambitious works. They are splendidly played
and recorded. The *Rhapsody No. 1* features and makes rather effective use of
one of the loveliest of all Irish tunes, the *Londonderry Air*. The *Second* has a
melodramatic flair which is most enjoyable. The *Third* is very Irish indeed and
makes use of several good tunes, beautifully played by both the orchestra and
the cellist, Raphael Wallfisch. The *Fourth*, the most famous, is also the most
distinctive and individual work by the composer, bringing together sharply
contrasted, colourful and atmospheric Irish ideas under the title *The Fisherman
of Loch Neagh and What He Saw*. The *Fifth* dates from 1917, reflecting perhaps
in its martial vigour that wartime date. Even more characteristic, though, are
the warmly lyrical passages, performed passionately by Handley and his Ulster

Orchestra, played with splendid thrust and commitment. The *Sixth* is a concertante work, with its nostalgia nicely caught by the soloist here, Lydia Mordkovitch, who is obviously involved. All the *Rhapsodies* are superbly played and recorded. Margaret Fingerhut is a first-rate soloist, both in the *Second Piano Concerto* and in her apt and entertaining account of the *Down Among the Dead Men Variations*, for Stanford was a dab hand at this format. Again, superb performances and recording.

Symphonies 1–7
Chan. 9279/82 (4). Ulster O, Handley

Now available in a box of four CDs, with the fill-ups which accompanied the original CDs now issued on two separate CDs, this is obviously the most attractive way to approach this generally impressive if uneven symphonic canon. Handley and his Ulster Orchestra are completely at home in this repertoire, and the vintage Chandos recording is consistently of this company's best quality. Like Parry's symphonies, this is mandatory listening for anyone interested in British music.

Stanford's mature musical studies had been in Berlin and Hamburg, and he came back to England, profoundly influenced by the German symphonic style (the Scherzo of the *First Symphony* (1876) even has the character of a Laendler). His work was duly performed and then, like the *Second*, put in a cupboard. Now we can discover for ourselves that, although he could assemble a convincing structure, his melodic invention was not yet strong enough to achieve real memorability.

The *Second Symphony*, until this recording, had lain neglected for over a century. The influences of the German masters are strong but the work still has its own individuality, for the most part in the scoring. The *Third* and most celebrated of the seven symphonies of Stanford is a rich and attractive work, none the worse for its obvious debts to Brahms. The ideas are best when directly echoing Irish folk music, as in the middle two movements, a skippy jig of a Scherzo and a glowing slow movement framed by harp cadenzas.

The *Fourth Symphony*, like the *Third*, is a highly confident piece and an effective symphony, even if it runs out of steam before the close of the finale despite attractive invention. The *Fifth* is colourfully orchestrated and full of easy tunes, illustrating passages from Milton's *L'Allegro* and *Il Penseroso*. The last two movements readily live up to Stanford's reputation as a Brahmsian, representing the *Penseroso* half of the work, and the slow epilogue brings reminders of Brahms's *Third*.

The *Sixth Symphony* is not the strongest of the set, but it has a rather lovely slow movement, with a pervading air of gentle melancholy. The first movement has some good ideas, but the finale is too long in the way that Glazunov symphonies tend to overuse their material. Nevertheless Vernon Handley makes quite a persuasive case for this work.

The *Seventh Symphony* sums up its composer as a symphonist – structurally sound, yet now not so heavily indebted to Germany, and with the orchestration often ear-catching. It is not a masterpiece, but it could surely not be presented with more conviction than here by Handley and his excellent orchestra.

STANLEY, John (1712–86)

6 Concertos in 7 Parts, Op. 2 (1742)
ⓑ Hyp. Helios CDH 55361. Parley of Instruments, Roy Goodman

London born, at the age of two John Stanley was supposedly blinded in a domestic accident with a broken china basin. But it seems likely that he remained partially sighted, for he gained a reputation as an organist (playing at the Temple Church) and established himself as a successful composer. Later in his life he followed Handel as director of oratorios at Covent Garden, and in 1779 he succeeded William Boyce as Master of the King's Musick. His six *Concertos* of seven parts appeared in 1742. They owe much to Handel and are clearly modelled on the latter's Opus 6, while two of the set (Nos. 3 and 6) have keyboard figuration suitable for the organ. They are played as organ concertos here by Peter Holman (following the example of Handel's Op. 4). All are works of quality and well worth having on disc – like Handel, Stanley writes jolly fugues. As might be expected, the performances here are first rate and they are excellently recorded.

STENHAMMAR, Wilhelm (1871–1927)

(i) *Symphonies 1 in F; 2 in G min., Op. 34; Serenade for Orchestra, Op. 31* (with *Reverenza* movement); *Excelsior Overture, Op. 13; The Song (Sången): Interlude, Op. 44; Lodolezzi Sings (Lodolezzi sjunger): Suite; Piano Concertos* (ii) *1;* (iii) *2 in D min., Op. 23;* (iv) *Ballad: Florez och Blanzeflor;* (v) *2 Sentimental Romances;* (vi) *Midwinter, Op. 24; Snöfrid, Op. 5*
BIS (DDD/ADD) CD 714/716. (i) Gothenburg SO, Järvi; (ii) Derwinger; (iii) Ortiz; (iv) Matthei; (v) Wallin; (vi) Gothenburg Ch.; (ii–v) Malmö SO, P. Järvi

Paavo Järvi's performances are now repackaged at a distinctly advantageous price. The *First Piano Concerto* makes use of Stenhammar's own orchestration, which came to light only recently in America; and this is the most comprehensive compilation of Stenhammar's orchestral music now on the market. All the performances and recordings are of high quality, and the only serious criticism to make affects the first movement of the *Second Symphony*, which Järvi takes rather too briskly. In the *Second Piano Concerto* Cristina Ortiz is a good soloist.

Piano Sonatas: in G min.; in A flat, Op. 12; 3 Fantasies; Nights of Late Summer, Op. 33
Hyp. CDA 67689. Sturfält

Stenhammar's *G minor Sonata* is an ambitious, romantic work with an unforgettable main theme dominating its first movement, and in many ways it is an equivalent in its youthful ardour of the Brahms *F minor* work. The *Three Fantasies*, Op. 11, of 1895 are Brahms-influenced, the first again boldly passionate; but the composer's own personality comes through, and notably so in the charming *Dolce scherzando* and the closing *Molto espressivo*. But the *A flat major Sonata* (composed in the same year) is a highly individual work, balancing serious lyricism with drama, and closing with a vibrant, unpredictable finale. Martin Sturfält suggests it has an affinity with Beethoven. The five pieces which make up the *Nights of Late Summer* are not overtly descriptive: their feeling is personal, although the exception is the closing, charming, *Poco allegretto*, which has almost a tang of Grieg. Sturfält plays all this music with much feeling and understanding, and great spontaneity, as at a live recital, and the recording (produced by Andrew Keener) is very real indeed. This is a disc well worth exploring.

STERNDALE BENNETT, William
(1816–75)

Piano Concertos 1 in D min., Op. 1; 2 in E flat, Op. 4; 3 in C min., Op. 9; 5 in F min.; Adagio; Caprice
Lyrita SRCD 204 (*Nos. 1 & 3; Caprice*); SRCD 205 (*Nos. 2 & 5; Adagio*). Binns, LPO or Philh.O, Braithwaite

Perhaps it was hearing Mendelssohn play his *G minor Concerto* in 1832 that prompted the sixteen-year-old Sterndale Bennett to write his Opus 1, a *Concerto in D minor* and a work of extraordinary fluency and accomplishment. The *Second Concerto* proves to be another work of great facility and charm. It takes as its model the concertos of Mozart and Mendelssohn, and the brilliance and delicacy of the keyboard writing make one understand why the composer was so highly regarded by his contemporaries. David Byers, who has edited the concertos, speaks of Bennett's 'gentle lyricism, the strength and energy of the orchestral tuttis'; and they are in ample evidence, both here and in the *Third Piano Concerto*, composed when he was eighteen. The *F minor Concerto* of 1836 is eminently civilized music with lots of charm; the *Adagio*, which completes the disc, is thought to be an alternative slow movement for Bennett's *Third Concerto* (1837). Whether or not this is the case, it is certainly a lovely piece. No praise can be too high for the playing of Malcolm Binns, whose fleetness of finger and poetic sensibility are a constant source of delight, and for the admirable support he receives from Nicholas Braithwaite and the LPO. The engineers produce sound of the highest quality. A most enjoyable pair of discs, available separately.

STOKOWSKI, Leopold (conductor)

'Decca Recordings 1965–1972': Orchestral transcriptions: **BACH**: *Toccata and Fugue in D min., BWV 565; Well-Tempered Clavier: Prelude in E flat min., BWV 853. Chorales: Mein Jesu: was für Seelenweh, BWV 487; Wir glauben all'an einen Gott, BWV 680. Easter Cantata: Chorale: Jesus Christus, Gottes Sohn, BWV 4. Passacaglia and Fugue in C min., BWV 582.* **RACHMANINOV**: *Prelude in C sharp min.* (all with Czech PO). **BYRD**: *Earl of Salisbury Pavan; Galliard* (after Tregian). **CLARKE**: *Trumpet Voluntary* (with Snell, trumpet). **SCHUBERT**: *Moment musical in F min., D.780/3.* **CHOPIN**: *Mazurka in A min., Op. 17/4.* **TCHAIKOVSKY**: *Chant sans paroles, Op. 40/6.* **DUPARC**: *Extase* (with LSO). **DEBUSSY**: *La cathédrale engloutie.* **TCHAIKOVSKY**; *Symphony 5, Op. 64.* **BERLIOZ**: *Symphonie fantastique* (with New Philh. O). *Damnation de Faust: Ballet des sylphes.* **SCRIABIN**: *Poème de l'extase.* **ELGAR**: *Enigma Variations* (with Czech PO). **FRANCK**: *Symphony in D min.* **RAVEL**: *L'Éventail de Jeanne* (with Hilversum R. PO). *Daphnis et Chloé: Suite 2* (with L.Symphony Ch.). **STRAVINSKY**: *Firebird Suite* (1919 version). **DEBUSSY**: *La Mer; Prélude à l'après-midi d'un faune.* **MESSIAEN**: *L'Ascension: 4 Méditations symphoniques* (all with LSO)
Decca (ADD) 475 145-2 (5)

Leopold Stokowski was undoubtedly one of the very greatest conductors of the twentieth century. Like many of the maestros of the era – Karajan, Munch, Klemperer, Barbirolli – he created an orchestral sound that was uniquely his own; and all self-respecting record collectors should sample the Stokowski experience. The complete set of which this was only the first volume comprises the majority of the conductor's Decca recordings made for their hi-fi-conscious Phase 4 system which, by close microphoning and the use of a 20-channel mixer, created exceptionally vivid projection and detail, though often at the expense of a natural acoustic. In this set, none was more spectacular than the 1968 Kingsway Hall *Symphonie fantastique*, with the New Philharmonia Orchestra, in which the brass have satanic impact in the *Marche au supplice* and the finale. The performance is as idiosyncratic as it is charismatic, and is thrilling in every way. Stokowski's warmth of phrasing is aptly romantic, but generally the most surprising feature is his meticulous concern for the composer's markings. The *Ballet des sylphes* makes a ravishing encore.

Elgar's *Enigma Variations* also shows Stokowski at his most persuasive, richly phrased by the Czech players and completely spontaneous-sounding. Equally, the Czech account of Scriabin's *Poème de l'extase* (edited from more than one performance) has all the passionate commitment of the live concert hall, with the ebb and flow of tension and the flexibility of the phrasing again captured compellingly.

Among the LSO recordings, *La Mer* has surprisingly slow basic tempi, but the effect is breathtaking in its vividness and impact, and the *Prélude à l'après-midi d'un faune* is richly languorous, yet has wonderful intensity. The account of the second *Daphnis et Chloé Suite* is comparably glowing, with sumptuous playing, and the multi-channel technique is used here to produce exactly the proper disembodied, ethereal effect for the off-stage chorus. Stokowski takes the choral parts from the complete ballet and adds a *fortissimo* chord at the very end; but after such involving music-making (the end is electrifying), few will begrudge him that idiosyncrasy .

The *Firebird Suite* is similarly sumptuous, and the gentler music shows the wonderful luminosity Stokowski could command from a first-class orchestra. Rich-textured violins dominate the beginning of the final climax, which reaches white-hot intensity. Messiaen's *L'Ascension* is tonally hardly less opulent, yet Stokowski is characteristically persuasive in developing the smooth flow of the music. Some may feel that the final sweet meditation for strings alone, *Prayer of Christ Ascending to the Father*, lacks true spirituality, but it is played very beautifully.

The most controversial performance here is of Tchaikovsky's *Fifth Symphony*. Although there is no doubting the electricity of the music-making, Stokowski tends to languish rather than press forward. Yet he also creates some thrilling climaxes and he certainly holds the listener throughout. However, he makes a number of small cuts in the outer movements and (astonishingly) dispenses with the pause before the finale. In the César Franck *Symphony*, the Hilversum orchestra plays with tremendous energy. The problem – and an endearing quality of this performance – is that Stokowski's reading, though moulded with conviction, underlines vulgarities in the score that most conductors try to minimize.

The transcriptions – for which Stokowski was famous and without which no anthology would be complete – range from thrilling Technicolor Bach to the extraordinarily imaginative arrangement of Debussy's *La cathédrale engloutie*, which has a wholly different sound-world from the original, piano version. The sheer force of Stokowski's orchestral personality makes all this music very much his own.

STRAUSS Family

STRAUSS, Johann Sr (1804–49)

STRAUSS, Johann Jr (1825–99)

STRAUSS, Josef (1827–70)

STRAUSS, Eduard (1835–1916)

Boskovsky Decca Strauss Edition: **Johann STRAUSS**, Jr: Galops: *Aufs Korn*; *Banditen*. Marches: *Egyptischer*; *Franz Joseph I Rettungs-Jubel*; *Napoleon*; *Persischer*; *Russischer*; *Spanischer*. *Perpetuum* *mobile*. Polkas: *Annen*; *Auf de Jagd*; *Bitte schön!*; *Champagne*; *Demolirer*; *Eljen a Magyar!*; *Explosionen*; *Freikugeln*; *Im Krapfenwald'l*; *Leichtes Blut*; *Lob der Frauen*; *Ohne Sorgen!*; *Pizzicato* (with Josef); *Neue Pizzicato*; *So angst sind wir nicht*; *'S gibt nur a Kaiserstadt, 's gibt nur a Wien!*; *Stürmisch in Lieb' und Tanz*; *Tik-Tak*; *Tritsch-Trasch*; *Unter Donner und Blitz (Thunder & Lightning)*; *Vergnügungszug*. Quadrilles: *Fledermaus*; *Orpheus*; *Schützen* (with Joseph & Eduard). Waltzes: *Accelerationen*; *An der schönen, blauen Donau (Blue Danube)*; *Bei uns z'Haus*; *Carnevals-Botschafter*; *Du und Du*; *Erinnerung an Covent-Garden*; *Freet euch des Lebens*; *Frülings-stimmen (Voices of Spring)*; *Geschichten aus dem Wienerwald (Tales from the Vienna Woods)*; *Kaiser (Emperor)*; *Künstlerleben (Artist's Life)*; *Lagunen*; *Liebeslieder*; *Mephistos Höllenrufe*; *Morgenblätter (Morning Papers)*; *Nordseebilder*; *Rosen aus dem Süden (Roses from the South)*; *Seid umschlungen, Millionen!*; *Schneeglöckchen*; *1,001 Nacht*; *Wein, Weib und Gesang (Wine, Woman & Song)*; *Wiener Blut (Vienna Blood)*; *Wiener Bonbons*; *Wo die Citronen blüh'n!*. **Johann STRAUSS, Sr**: Galops: *Sperl*; *Wettrennen*. *Radetzky March*. Polka: *Piefke und Pufka*. Waltz: *Loreley-Rhein-Klänge*. **Josef STRAUSS**: Polkas: *Auf Ferienreisen*; *Brennende Liebe*; *Eingesendet*; *Die Emancipierte*; *Extempore*; *Feuerfest*; *Frauenherz*; *Heiterer Mut*; *Im Fluge*; *Jokey*; *Die Libelle*; *Moulinet*; *Rudolfsheimer*; *Die Schwätzerin*. Waltzes: *Aquarellen*; *Delirien*; *Dorfschwalben aus Osterreich (Village Swallows)*; *Dynamiden*; *Mein Lebenslauf ist Lieb' und Lust*; *Sphärenklänge (Music of the Spheres)*; *Transactionen*. **Eduard STRAUSS**: Polkas: *Bahn Frei!*; *Mit Extrapost*. Waltz: *Fesche Geister*.

Ⓑ Decca (ADD) 455 254-2 (6). VPO, Boskovsky

So popular was and is the music of the Strauss family, it is easy to forget how remarkable it is. Not only did the family provide a seemingly limitless fund of memorable tunes, they crafted them into works of perfection, and wrapped them up in supremely effective orchestrations. Willi Boskovsky's Decca recordings stand out as supreme achievements, both for him and for the Decca Record Company. Following a sequence begun in the days of mono LPs by Clemens Krauss, Boskovsky showed a unique feeling for the Straussian lilt, while the playing he drew from the VPO was consistently persuasive.

Boskovsky had the ability, like Johann Strauss himself, to lead the orchestra from the violin, and the results here could hardly be more idiomatic, with both conductor and orchestra fully steeped in the tradition of playing this repertoire. Not only do these performances glow with atmosphere, they are tingling with life and energy, with all the many details in both the melodic line and harmonic invention vividly brought out. All the popular waltzes are supremely done, but there are so many delightful rarities here as to make one wonder at their relative neglect. The engaging *Die Libelle* is a magical portrayal of a dragonfly, while the polka, *Elijen a Magyar!*, is exhilarating in its high-spirited effervescence. Only the earliest recordings betray their age but they are still fine by any standards. Indeed, the Decca engineers fully rose to the occasion throughout these sessions (notably so when special effects were required, as in the *Explosion* and *Thunder and Lightning Polkas*, while the gunshot in *Auf der Jagd* is startling) with the Sofiensaal providing the ideal ambience, with plenty of warmth and bloom. These six vintage CDs (offering 86 titles) span Willi Boskovsky's long recording career, from the late 1950s to the late 1970s. In 1979, he directed the first of the now famous VPO New Year Concerts (recorded digitally by Decca, and available on 448 572-2 (2)) and that recording tradition continues to the present day. Boskovsky's achievement in this repertoire remains unique for the unfailing sparkle of the performances.

As a supplement to the above set – and for those, like us, who can't resist this repertoire – readers will almost certainly enjoy Antal Dorati's arrangement of the lesser-known Strauss items he used to form the ballet, *The Graduation Ball*. This delightfully inventive score is now available in Dorati's sparkling (1976) Decca recording with the Vienna Philharmonic Orchestra on Australian Decca Eloquence (476 752-2), coupled with Bonynge's equally enjoyable National Philharmonic version of *Le Beau Danube*, another Strauss confection (with an especially exhilarating finale), this time arranged by Désormière.

Polka: *Unter Donner und Blitz*. Waltzes: *An der schönen, blauen Donau*; *Kaiser*; *Morgenblätter*; *Rosen aus dem Süden*; *Treasure*; *Wiener blut*. **Josef STRAUSS**: *Dorfschwalben aus Osterreich*. **R. STRAUSS**: *Der Rosenkavalier Waltzes* (with **WEBER**: *Invitation to the Waltz*)
Ⓜ RCA 82876 671615-2. Chicago SO, Reiner

Reiner's collection was recorded in 1957 and 1960, but the new SACD transfer restores the voluptuousness to the sound. Although the *Thunder and Lightning Polka* has an unforgettable explosive exuberance (and the sound is startlingly vivid and full), these performances are memorable for their Viennese lilt, especially the *Emperor Waltz* and Josef's *Village Swallows*. Reiner is especially persuasive in the introductory interchanges of Weber's *Invitation to the Waltz*, while the *Der Rosenkavalier* Waltz sequence brings a passionate surge of adrenalin.

Die Fledermaus (with gala performance)
Ⓜ Decca (ADD) 475 8319 (2). Gueden, Köth, Kmentt, Wächter, Berry, Zampieri, Resnik,
  V. State Op. Ch., VPO, Karajan (with guests: Tebaldi, Corena, Nilsson, Del Monaco,
  Berganza, Sutherland, Björling, L. Price, Simionato, Bastianini, Welitsch)

Karajan's 1960 Decca set was originally issued – very handsomely presented and with much blazing of publicity trumpets – as a so-called 'Gala performance' – with various artists from the Decca roster appearing to do their turn at the 'cabaret' included in the Orlofsky ball sequence. This was a famous tradition of performances of *Die Fledermaus* at the New York Met. in the early years of the last century. The party pieces now have a vintage appeal, and even Tebaldi's *Viljalied* (rather heavy in style) sets off nostalgia for an earlier era. There is a breathtaking display of coloratura from Joan Sutherland in *Il Bacio*, a Basque folksong sung with delicious simplicity by Teresa Berganza, and Leontyne Price is wonderfully at home in Gershwin's *Summertime*. But the most famous item is Simionato and Bastianini's *Anything you can do I can do better*, sung with more punch than sophistication, but endearingly memorable, half a century after it was recorded.

The performance of the opera itself has all the sparkle one could ask for. If anything, Karajan is even more brilliant than he was on the old EMI mono issue, and the Decca recording is scintillating in its clarity. Hilde Gueden is deliciously vivacious as Rosalinde, a beautifully projected interpretation. She and others do fall short in the singing, with her confidence a drawback in showing how tentative Erika Köth is as Adèle, with her wavering vibrato (her *Mein Herr Marquiss* is well below the standard of the best recorded performances) and Waldemar Kmentt (Eisenstein) a tight, German-sounding tenor, and Giuseppe Zampieri as Alfred no more than adequate, it does take some of the gilt off the gingerbread. But the rest of the cast are very good, and this recording oozes a charm and glamour from a bygone era. The reissue, as one of Decca's 'Originals', handsomely reproduces the original frontispiece on the CD box and includes full text and translation (though not of the gala items).

Der Zigeunerbaron (original version; complete)

ⓑⓑ Naxos mono 8.11329/30. Schwarzkopf, Gedda, Kunz, Köth, Prey, Philh. Ch. & O, Ackermann (with excerpts from earlier recordings of *Der Zigeunerbaron* by Elisabeth Rethberg (1930); Lotte Lehmann, Richard Tauber (1928); *Schatz-Walzen*: Berlin State Op. Ch. & O, Leo Blech (1929))

This superb Philharmonia version of *The Gypsy Baron* from the mid-1950s, now reappearing on Naxos, has never been matched in its rich stylishness and polish. Schwarzkopf as the gipsy princess sings radiantly, not least in the heavenly *Bullfinch Duet* (to the melody made famous by MGM as 'One day when we were young'). Gedda, still youthful, produces heady tone, and Erich Kunz as the rough pig-breeder gives a vintage, *echt*-Viennese performance of the irresistible *Ja, das schreiben und das lesen*. Mark Obert-Thorn's transfer is immaculate, and the bonus items are a pleasure in themselves.

STRAUSS, Richard (1864–1949)

An Alpine Symphony; *Also sprach Zarathustra*; *Aus Italien*; *Le Bourgeois gentilhomme: Suite, Op. 60*; (i) *Burleske for Piano and Orchestra*; (ii) *Concertos for Horn, 1 & 2*; (iii) *Concerto for Oboe*;

(iv) *Concerto for Violin in D minor. Dance Suite* (from harpsichord pieces by François Couperin); *Don Juan*; (v) *Don Quixote*; (vi) *Duett-Concertino. Ein Heldenleben*; *Josephslegende*; *Macbeth*; *Metamorphosen*; (vii) *Panathenäenzug, Op. 74*; *Parergon zur Sinfonia*; *Symphonia domestica*; *Der Rosenkavalier: Waltzes* (arr. Kempe); *Salome: Dance of the Seven Veils. Schlagobers: Waltz. Till Eulenspiegels lustige Streiche*; *Tod und Verklärung*.

Ⓑ EMI 573614-2 (9). Dresden State O, Kempe; with (i) Frager; (ii) Damm; (iii) Clement; (iv) Hoelscher; (v) Paul Tortelier; (vi) Weise, Liebscher; (vii) Rösel

Rudolf Kempe's Richard Strauss survey, recorded in the mid-1970s, has stood the test of time and is a formidable achievement, especially in its latest bargain-box incarnation. The Dresden orchestra is a magnificent body and the strings produce gloriously sumptuous tone, strikingly in evidence in *Metamorphosen*. Kempe had recorded the *Alpine Symphony* before with the RPO, and there is little to choose between the two so far as interpretation is concerned: he brings a glowing warmth to this score. His *Aus Italien* is more convincing than any previous version: the sound, with its finely judged perspective, is again a decisive factor here. He gives a most musical account of the delightful *Dance Suite* based on Couperin keyboard pieces, although here one may wish for more transparent textures. Perhaps one could also quarrel with the balance in *Don Quixote*, which gives Tortelier exaggerated prominence and obscures some detail. The performance, however, is another matter and must rank with the best available. *Macbeth* is also very convincing and is well paced. Ulf Hoelscher's eloquent account of the early *Violin Concerto* is more than welcome, as is the *Symphonia domestica*. Kempe's version of this work is no less desirable than Karajan's, a little more relaxed without being in any way less masterly. His *Also sprach Zarathustra* is completely free of sensationalism that mars so many newer performances. *Le Bourgeous gentilhomme* receives a superb performance – and what a delightful score it is. Both *Don Juan* and *Till Eulenspiegel* have received more electrifying performances elsewhere, though Kempe's are by no means second rate, just not quite at the level of inspiration of the rest of his Strauss recordings. The *Burlesque* is well worth having (it is beautifully recorded) and there are few satisfactory alternatives in the *Parergon to the Symphonia domestica* or the *Panathenäenzug*, both written for the one-armed pianist, Paul Wittgenstein, and played impressively here. Peter Damm's performances of the *Horn Concertos* are first class. Similarly, while Manfred Clement's *Oboe Concerto* is a sensitive reading, his creamily full timbre may not appeal to those brought up on Goossens. There can be no reservations whatsoever about the *Duet Concertino*, where the sounds from the bassoon and clarinet are beguilingly succulent, while the interwining of both wind soloists with the dancing orchestral violins in the finale has an irresistible, genial finesse. Throughout, the superb playing of the Dresden orchestra under Kempe adds an extra dimension to the music-making.

An Alpine Symphony; Also sprach Zarathustra; Death and Transfiguration; Don Quixote; Ein Heldenleben, Op. 40; Metamorphosen; Symphonia domestica
Sony DVD 886971954469. BPO, Karajan

There have been many wonderful post-war Strauss interpreters, from Clemens Krauss to George Szell and Rudolf Kempe; but Karajan had a special way with the composer, as we are reminded in these DVD performances, sensitively handled by the video director and, of course, stunningly played. The *Metamorphosen* is moving, even if Karajan's pioneering set with the Vienna Philharmonic had even greater immediacy of feeling. The *Death and Transfiguration* is also marvellously played and has genuine grandeur and nobility. These performances belong in any good collection. Unaccountably (and unforgivably), the two soloists in *Don Quixote* are not credited either in the skimpy booklet, on the sleeve, or on the screen.

Also sprach Zarathustra, Op. 30; Ein Heldenleben, Op. 40
Ⓜ RCA (ADD) 82876 61389-2. Chicago SO, Reiner

These were the first stereo sessions the RCA engineers arranged with Fritz Reiner, after the company had taken over the Chicago orchestra's recording contract from Mercury, and the series of records they made with Reiner and his players in Orchestra Hall remain a technical peak in the history of stereo recording and the impressive feeling of space it conveyed. Later reissues have improved on its definition, but none has done so with the stunning success of the present transfer. *Ein Heldenleben* shows Reiner in equally splendid form. There have been more incisive, more spectacular and more romantic performances, but Reiner achieves an admirable balance, and whatever he does is convincing. If anything, the recording sounds even better than *Also sprach*, and the warm acoustics of Orchestra Hall help convey Reiner's humanity in the closing pages of the work.

Le Bourgeois gentilhomme (incidental music): Suite
Dux DUX0764. Wroclaw PO, Jacek Kaspszyk – STRAVINSKY: *Pulcinella Suite*

Richard Strauss, like Stravinsky, experimented with neoclassicism, drawing on the music of François Couperin and, most importantly, Lully's incidental music to Molière's *Le Bourgeois gentilhomme*. He used Lully as a source for an arietta in the first Act of *Der Rosenkavalier*, so it is not surprising that his rich-textured 'baroque' orchestral style has something in common with his orchestral writing in that opera, especially the two fully scored 'Menuettes', and the expansive finale. So Strauss's orchestral suite makes a fine diverse contrast to Stravinsky's *Pulcinella*. Both offer ear-tickling listening, and it is remarkable that they have not been coupled on disc before. Jacek Kaspszyk obviously has great sympathy for both scores and presents all this music with spirit and warmth. The recording too, engineered by Classic Sound's Neil Hutchinson, is first rate, and the concert-hall acoustic is just right for the music.

Don Juan
Ⓜ Decca (ADD) 475 8225. V. State Op. Ch., VPO, Karajan – **HOLST**: *The Planets*

Karajan's Decca recording of *Don Juan*, recorded in the Sofiensaal in 1960, is still among the finest versions. The sound of the Vienna Philharmonic is more leonine than that of the Berlin Philharmonic but does not lack either body or attack, and this *Don* has great zest and passion.

Ein Heldenleben, Op. 40 (DVD version)
RCO Live DVD RCO 04103; or Surround Sound (CD) RCO 04005. Concg. O, Jansons
(DVD with documentary introducing Mariss Jansons as the orchestra's conductor; V/D: Hans Hulscher)

Ein Heldenleben, Op. 40 (CD version)
Testament SBT1430. BPO, Karajan – **BEETHOVEN**: *Symphony 4*

Jansons's magnificent Concertgebouw performance of *Ein Heldenleben* comes in a superb SACD recording in natural surround sound which, with four speakers, captures the richness of the Concertgebouw acoustic and gives the orchestra the most sumptuous and detailed presentation in a live performance that combines adrenalin flow, refinement of detail and glorious playing. The DVD offers the special visual treat of the Concertgebouw as a backcloth for great music-making in first-class sound (though not quite as opulent as the CD), plus a vivid pictorial survey of the performance which is both rewarding and interesting in a score as diverse and detailed as *Ein Heldenleben*, as the camera follows the orchestra's involvement.

Karajan's *Heldenleben* was recorded at the Royal Festival Hall when the Berlin Philharmonic came to London in April 1985. The performance can only be described in superlatives, and the Testament sound is similarly impressive. In his sleeve-note Richard Osborne speaks of its wonderful sonority, 'lambent in its beauty, never cloying or opaque'. How right he is! The Beethoven *Fourth* is superbly played too and, if perhaps not an appropriate coupling, is a very welcome one.

4 Last Songs; Orchestral Lieder
Ⓜ EMI (ADD) 5 66908-2. Schwarzkopf, Berlin RSO or LSO, Szell

For the Legends version of Schwarzkopf's raptly beautiful version of the *Four Last Songs* (1965), EMI have added not just the old coupling of Strauss orchestral songs but also seven extra items which she recorded in 1968, also with George Szell conducting, but with the LSO instead of the Berlin Radio Orchestra. There are few recordings in the catalogue which readily capture the magic of Schwarzkopf's singing in all its variety of tone and meaning, perfectly matched by inspired playing. The current remastering seems to add even more lustre to the voice and orchestra alike. The Legends release, although without texts, includes a bonus DVD of Schwarzkopf in the Act I finale of *Der*

Rosenkavalier, with Hertha Töpper and the Philharmonia Orchestra under Mackerras (1961).

Ariadne auf Naxos (CD version)

Ⓜ EMI 2 08824-2 (2). Janowitz, Geszty, Zylis-Gara, King, Adam, Schreier, Dresden State O, Kempe

Kempe's relaxed, languishing performance of this most atmospheric of Strauss's operas is matched by opulent (1969) EMI recording. Janowitz sings with heavenly tone-colour (marred only when hard pressed at the climax of the Lament) and Zylis-Gara makes an ardent and understanding composer. Sylvia Geszty's voice is a little heavy for the fantasic coloratura of Zerbinetta's part, but she sings with charm and assurance. James King sings the part of Bacchus with forthright tone and more taste than many tenors. Those who remember Karajan's mono set with Schwarzkopf will not find this ideal, but there is warmth and atmosphere here in plenty. The reissue comes with full libretto.

Elektra (CD version)

Decca (ADD) 475 8231 (2). Nilsson, Collier, Resnik, Stolze, Krause. V. State Op. Ch., VPO, Solti

Both Nilsson and Solti are the great stars of this electrifying performance – one of the great operatic triumphs of the stereo era. Nilsson is incomparable in the name-part, with the hard side of Elektra's character brutally dominant. Only when – as in the Recognition scene with Orestes – she tries to soften the naturally bright tone does she let out a suspect flat note or two. As a rule, she is searingly accurate in approaching even the most formidable, exposed top notes. One might draw a parallel with Solti's direction – sharply focused and brilliant in the savage music which predominates; and even if he lacks the languorous warmth one ideally needs in the Recognition scene, if only for contrast, he is magnetic throughout. The rest of the cast is hardly less impressive, Regina Resnik as Klytämnestra is supremely impressive, as is Marie Collier as Chrysothemis. Tom Krause makes a dramatic Oreste, matching the interpretation of this performance as a whole. The brilliance of the 1967 recording is brought out all the more in the newest digital transfer, aptly so in this work. Indeed, the fullness and clarity are amazing for the period.

Die Frau ohne Schatten (CD version)

Decca 436 243-2 (3). Behrens, Varady, Domingo, Van Dam, Runkel, Jo, VPO, Solti

In the Heldentenor role of the Emperor, Plácido Domingo, the superstar tenor, gives a performance that is not only beautiful to the ear beyond previous recordings but which has an extra feeling for expressive detail, deeper than that which was previously recorded. Hildegard Behrens as the Dyer's Wife is also a huge success. Her very feminine vulnerability is here a positive strength. And the voice has rarely sounded so beautiful on record. Julia Varady as the

Empress is equally imaginative, with a beautiful voice, and José Van Dam with his clean, dark timbre brings a warmth and depth of expression to the role of Barak, the Dyer, which goes with a satisfyingly firm focus. Reinhild Runkel in the key role of the nurse is well in character, with her mature, fruity sound. Eva Lind is shrill in the tiny role of the Guardian of the Threshold, but there is compensation in having Sumi Jo as the Voice of the Falcon. With the Vienna Philharmonic surpassing themselves, and the big choral ensembles both well disciplined and warmly expressive, this superb recording is unlikely to be surpassed for many years. Solti himself is inspired throughout.

Intermezzo (complete, DVD version)

Warner NVC Arts DVD 50-51442-8857-2-9. Lott, Pringle, Caley, Gale, Glyndebourne Festival Op. Ch., LPO, Kuhn (Stage Director: John Cox; V/D: David Buckton)

This is as perfect a realization of Strauss's conversation piece as one could possibly imagine, and it is even more enjoyable for being performed in Andrew Porter's brilliant English translation. Felicity Lott looks ravishing and sings delightfully as Christine, John Pringle is perfectly cast as her husband, Robert, and Ian Caley makes a winningly ingenuous foil as the young baron. John Cox's 1920s sets and the costumes are ideal (notably Lott's dresses) and the production values are what every stage director should seek, and few find. Moreover, the clever alignment with the composer's own domestic situation is neatly achieved. Gustav Kuhn directs the complex orchestral accompaniments with great skill and the LPO is in sparkling form. If only all opera productions were as beautifully realized as this!

Der Rosenkavalier (complete, DVD version)

DG DVD 073 0089 (2). Lott, Von Otter, Bonney, Moll, Hornik, V. State Op. Ch. & O, Carlos Kleiber (Producer: Otto Schenk; V/D: Horant Hohlfeld)

Carlos Kleiber has spoken of Felicity Lott as his ideal Marschallin, and she is probably currently as unrivalled in this role as was Schwarzkopf in the 1950s (whose famous recording with Karajan (EMI 5 67605-2) remains highly recommendable on CD). Lott does not wear her heart on her sleeve, and her reticence makes her all the more telling and memorable. The other roles are hardly less distinguished, with Anne Sofie von Otter's Octavian splendidly characterized and boyish, while Barbara Bonney's Sophie floats her top notes in the Presentation of the Rose scene with great poise and impressive beauty and accuracy. Kurt Moll's Ochs, a splendidly three-dimensional and subtle reading, is one of the other highlights of the performance. Otto Schenk's production deserves the praises that have been lavished on it, and Rudolf Heinrich's sets are handsome. Carlos Kleiber draws some ravishing sounds from the Vienna Philharmonic and his reading of the score is as Straussian and as perfect as you are likely to encounter in this world. The sound is very natural and lifelike, not too forward and with a good perspective.

Salome (complete, DVD version)

DG DVD 073 4339. Stratas, Beirer, Varnay, Weikl, soloists, VPO, Boehm (Producer: Götz Friedrich)

Salome (complete, CD version)

Decca (ADD) 475 7528 (2). Nilsson, Collier, Hale, Hoffmann, Stolze, Waechter, VPO, Solti

We have long treasured Karl Boehm's 1976 performance, and it is splendid that it is now available in so excellent a DVD version. It is now almost certainly the best *Salome* either on CD or DVD (Birgit Nilsson notwithstanding). Teresa Stratas really looks the part as well as singing it (she has been acclaimed as the finest singing-actress of her day) and the rest of the cast is superb. Astrid Varnay's depiction of Herodias is masterly, as is Hans Beirer's Herod. Above all, Götz Friedrich's production evokes the atmosphere and dramatic intensity of Strauss's opera, and one can only echo the New York critic who declared it 'one of the most successful musical-theatrical performances I have ever seen'. Friedrich serves the score to perfection; his production is miles removed from the 'dustbin on Mars' sets favoured by many directors nowadays.

Recorded in Decca's 'Sonic Stage' in 1962, Solti's analogue recording of *Salome* remains one of the classics of the gramophone. The balance between the voices and orchestra is most convincingly achieved, with the great orchestral climaxes handled superbly by the engineers. Birgit Nilsson is splendid throughout and this is one of her finest performances on record: she is hard-edged as usual but, on that account, more convincingly wicked; the determination and depravity are latent in the girl's character from the start. In the final scene she rises to new heights, compelling one to accept and even enjoy the horror of it, while the uncleanness is conveyed more vividly than in almost any other performance – live or recorded. One's spine tingles even as one squirms. The end of the opera provides a famous master-stroke of Decca engineering – where Salome kisses the head of John the Baptist in delighted horror ('I have kissed thy mouth, Jokanaan!') – it is made all the more spine-tingling with the close-up effect of the voice almost whispering in one's ear. Of this score Solti is a master; he has rarely sounded so abandoned in a recorded performance. Waechter makes a clear, young-sounding Jokanaan. Gerhardt Stolze portrays the unbalance of Herod with frightening conviction, and Grace Hoffmann does all she can in the comparatively ungrateful part of Herodias.

STRAVINSKY, Igor (1882–1971)

Sony had access to the immensely valuable series of recordings made by Stravinsky himself. They were all issued individually over the years, but the 22 discs now come complete in a handsome box with full documentation at a super-bargain price. How long they will remain available we cannot predict, but the box will undoubtedly be available in the marketplace or on line as a collector's item and is certainly worth seeking out.

The Stravinsky Edition: Vols. 1–7: Ballets, etc.: (i) *The Firebird*; *Fireworks*; (iii) *Histoire du soldat*; (i) *Petrushka*; (iii–iv) *Renard the Fox*; (i) *The Rite of Spring*; (i) *Scherzo à la russe*; (ii) *Scherzo fantastique*; (v) *The Wedding (Les Noces)*; (vi) *Agon*; (i) *Apollo*; (i) *Le Baiser de la fée*; (i) *Bluebird (pas de deux)*; (vii) *Jeu de cartes*; (viii) *Orphée*; (i; ix) *Pulcinella*; (ii) *Scènes de ballet*. Ballet Suites: (i) *Firebird*; *Petrushka*; *Pulcinella*

Vols. 8–9: Symphonies: (i) *Symphony in E flat*; (ii) *Symphony in C*; (i) *Symphony in 3 Movements*; (ii; x) *Symphony of Psalms*; (i) Stravinsky in rehearsal: *Apollo*; *Piano Concerto*; *Pulcinella*; *Sleeping Beauty*; *Symphony in C*; *3 Souvenirs*

Vol. 10: Concertos: (i; xi) *Capriccio for Piano & Orchestra* (with Robert Craft); *Concerto for Piano and Wind*; (i; xii) *Movements for Piano & Orchestra*; (i; xiii) *Violin Concerto in D*

Vol. 11: Miniatures: (i) *Circus Polka*; *Concerto in D for String Orchestra*; *Concerto for Chamber Orchestra, 'Dumbarton Oaks'*; (ii) *4 Études for Orchestra*; (i) *Greeting Prelude*; (ii) *8 Instrumental Miniatures*; *4 Norwegian Moods*; *Suites 1–2 for Small Orchestra*

Vols. 12–13: Chamber music and historical recordings: (iii) *Concertino for 12 Instruments*; (xiv–xv) *Concerto for 2 Solo Pianos*; (xv–xvi) *Duo concertante for Violin & Piano*; (xvii–xviii) *Ebony Concerto* (for clarinet & big band); (iii) *Octet for Wind*; (iii; xix) *Pastorale for Violin & Wind Quartet*; (xv) *Piano Rag Music*; (xviii) *Preludium*; (iii; xx) *Ragtime* (for 11 instruments); (xv) *Serenade in A*; (iii) *Septet*; (xii) *Sonata for Piano*; (xxi) *Sonata for 2 Pianos*; (xviii) *Tango*; (xxii) *Wind Symphonies*

Vols. 14–15: Operas and Songs: (iii; xxiii) *Cat's Cradle Songs*; (xxiii–xxiv) *Elegy for J. F. K.*; (ii; xxv) *Faun and Shepherdess*; (iii; xxvi) *In memoriam Dylan Thomas*; (iii; xxvii) *3 Japanese Lyrics* (with Robert Craft); (xxvii; xxix) *The Owl and the Pussycat*; (iii; xxvii) *2 Poems by K. Balmont*; (i; xxx) *2 Poems of Paul Verlaine*; (i; xxiii) *Pribaoutki (Pleasant Songs)*; (i; xxiii) *Recollections of my Childhood*; (xxviii; xxxi) *4 Russian Songs*; (xxxvii) *4 Russian Peasant Songs*; (iii; xxiii) *3 Songs from William Shakespeare*; (i; xxvii) *Tilim-Bom* (A Story for Children); (xxxii) *Mavra*; (xxxiii) *The Nightingale*

Vols. 16–17: (xxxiv) *The Rake's Progress*

Vols. 18–19: Oratorio and Melodrama: (i; xxxv) *The Flood* (with Robert Craft); (i) *Monumentum pro Gesualdo di Venosa (3 Madrigals recomposed for instruments)*; (vii) *Ode*; (xxxvi) *Oedipus Rex*; (i; xxxvii–xxxviii) *Perséphone*

Vols. 20–21: Sacred Works: (x) *Anthem (The dove descending breaks the air)*; (x) *Ave Maria*; (i; x xxxix;) *Babel*; (iii; x; xxvi; xxviii) *Cantata*; (xl) *Canticum sacrum*; (ii; x) *Credo*; (iii; x) *Introitus (T. S. Eliot in memoriam)*; (xli) *Mass*; (i; x) *Pater noster*; (i; xlii) *A Sermon, a Narrative & a Prayer*; (i; xliii) *Threni*; (i; x) *Chorale*; (xlvi) *Epitaphium Variations on: Vom Himmel hoch, da komm ich her* (arr.); *Zvezdoliki*

Vol. 22: Robert Craft Conducts: (i; xliv) *Abraham and Isaac*; (iii) *Danses concertantes*; (i; xlv) *Double Canon: Raoul Dufy in memoriam*; (i; xlvii) *Requiem Canticles*; (i) *Song of the Nightingale* (symphonic poem). (i) *Orchestral Variations: Aldous Huxley in memoriam*.

ⓑ Sony 88697 103112 (22). (i) Columbia SO; (ii) CBC SO; (iii) Columbia CO; (iv) Shirley, Driscoll, Gramm, Koves; (v) Allen, Sarfaty, Driscoll, Barber, Copland, Foss, Sessions, American Chamber Ch., Hills, Columbia Percussion Ens.; (vi) LA Festival SO; (vii) Cleveland O; (viii) Chicago SO; (ix) Jordan, Shirley, Gramm; (x) Festival Singers of Toronto, Iseler; (xi) Entremont; (xii) Rosen; (xiii) Stern; (xiv) Soulima Stravinsky; (xv) Igor Stravinsky; (xvi) Szigeti; (xvii) Goodman; (xviii) Columbia Jazz Ens.; (xix) Baker; (xx) Koves; (xxi) Gold, Fizdale; (xxii) NW German RSO; (xxiii) Berberian; (xxiv) Howland, Kreiselman, Russo; (xxv) Simmons; (xxvi) Young; (xxvii) Lear; (xxviii) Albert; (xxix) Craft; (xxx) Gramm; (xxxi) Di Tullio, Remsen, Almeida; (xxxii) Belinck, Simmons, Rideout, Kolk; (xxxiii) Driscoll, Grist, Picassi, Smith, Beattie, Gramm, Kolk, Murphy, Kaiser, Bonazzi, Washington, DC, Op. Society Ch. & O; (xxxiv) Young, Raskin, Reardon, Sarfaty, Miller, Manning, Garrard, Tracey, Tilney, Sadler's Wells Op. Ch., Baker, RPO; (xxxv) Harvey, Cabot, Lanchester, Reardon, Oliver, Tripp, Robinson, Columbia SO Ch., Smith; (xxxvi) Westbrook (nar.), Shirtey, Verrett, Gramm, Reardon, Driscoll, Chester Watson, Washington, DC, Op. Society Ch. & O; (xxxvii) Gregg Smith Singers, Smith; (xxxviii) Zorina, Molese, Ithaca College Concert Ch., Fort Worth Texas Boys' Ch.; (xxxix) Calicos (nar.); (xl) Robinson, Chitjian, LA Festival Ch. & SO; (xli) Baxter, Albert, Gregg Smith Singers, Columbia Symphony Winds & Brass; (xlii) Verrett, Driscoll, Hornton (nar.); (xliii) Beardslee, Krebs, Lewis, Wainner, Morgan, Oliver, Schola Cantorum, Ross; all cond. composer; (xliv) Frosch; (xlv) Baker, Igleman, Schonbach, Neikrug; (xlvi) Gleghorn, Bioch, Remsen; (xlvii) Anderson, Bonazzi, Bressler, Gramm, Ithaca College Concert Ch., Gregg Smith; cond. Craft

On these 22 super-bargain-price CDs you have the unique archive of recordings which Stravinsky left of his own music. Almost all the performances are conducted by the composer, with a few at the very end of his career – like the magnificent *Requiem Canticles* – left to Robert Craft to conduct with the composer supervising. In addition there is a handful of recordings of works otherwise not covered, mainly chamber pieces. With some recordings of Stravinsky talking and in rehearsal (included on the CDs devoted to the symphonies) it makes a vivid portrait.

Stravinsky may not have been a brilliant conductor, but in the recording studio he knew how to draw out alert, vigorous performances of his own music, and every one of these items illuminates facets of his inspiration which other interpreters often fail to notice. There are few if any rival versions of *The Rite of Spring* – nowadays, astonishingly, his most frequently recorded work – to match his own recording of 1960 in its compelling intensity and inexorable sense of line. Of the major ballets, *Petrushka* and *The Firebird* are valuable, but *The Rite* is required listening: it has real savagery and astonishing electricity. The link between *Jeu de cartes* from the mid-1930s and Stravinsky's post-war opera, *The Rake's Progress*, is striking; Stravinsky's sharp-edged conducting style underlines it, while the curiously anonymous-sounding *Scènes de ballet* certainly have their attractive movements. *Orpheus* has a powerful atmosphere, though one of Stravinsky's most classically restrained works, a good performance, with the composer's own authority lending it special interest. However, its invention is less memorable and distinguished than *Apollo*, one of Stravinsky's most gravely beautiful works. *Agon* is one of the most stimulating of Stravinsky's later works. The orchestra responds with tremendous alertness and enthusiasm to Stravinsky's direction. The recording of *Le Baiser de la fée* is a typical CBS balance with forward woodwind. However, if the recorded quality does not inspire too much enthusiasm, the performance certainly does. Stravinsky's recording of *Pulcinella* includes the vocal numbers which, when sung well, add to the variety and sparkle of the piece, while in the orchestra the clowning act of the trombone and the humour generally is strikingly vivid and never too broad. Similarly with the chamber scoring of the suite from *The Soldier's Tale*, the crisp, clear reading brings out the underlying emotion of the music with the nagging, insistent little themes given an intensity that is almost tear-laden. There is a ruthlessness in the composer's own reading of *Les Noces* which exactly matches the primitive robustness in this last flowering of Russian nationalism in Stravinsky. The earlier parts are perhaps too rigid, but as the performance goes on one senses the added alertness and enthusiasm of the performers. *Renard* is a curious work, a sophisticated fable which here receives too unrelenting a performance. The voices are very forward and tend to drown out the instrumentalists.

In the early *Symphony in E flat*, the young Stravinsky's material may be comparatively conventional and the treatment much too bound to the academic procedures taught him by his master, Rimsky-Korsakov, but at least in this performance the music springs to life. Each movement has its special delights to outweigh any shortcomings. The performance is obviously as near definitive as it could be. The composer's account of the *Symphony in Three Movements* is an object lesson for every conductor who has tried to perform this work. Stravinsky shows how, by vigorous, forthright treatment of the notes, the emotion implicit is made all the more compelling. The Columbia Symphony plays superbly and the recording is full and brilliant. Stravinsky's career never quite equalled the intensity of the pre-war 78-r.p.m. performance of the *Symphony of Psalms*. That had many more technical faults than this later, stereo version, and it is only fair to say that this new account is still impressive. It is just that with so vivid a work, it is a shade disappointing to find Stravinsky as an interpreter at less than maximum voltage. Even so, this closing section of the work is very beautiful and compelling. The CD transfers of the American recording are somewhat monochrome by modern standards, but fully acceptable.

The iron-fingered touch of Philippe Entremont has something to be said for it in the *Capriccio for Piano and Wind*, but this performance conveys too little of the music's charm. The *Movements for Piano and Orchestra* with the composer conducting could hardly be more compelling. Stern's account of the *Violin Concerto in D* adds a romantic perspective to the framework, and at one time, no doubt, Stravinsky would have objected. But an expressive approach to Stravinsky is permissible in a soloist, when the composer is there to provide the bedrock under the expressive cantilena. Plainly this has the forthright spontaneity of a live performance.

The *Dumbarton Oaks Concerto*, with its obvious echoes of Bach's *Brandenburgs*, is one of the most warmly attractive of Stravinsky's neoclassical works, all beautifully played and acceptably recorded. The *Octet for Wind* of 1924 comes out with surprising freshness and, throughout, the unexpected combination of neo-Bach and neo-Pop is most refreshing. *Ragtime* could be more light-hearted, but Stravinsky gives the impression of knowing what he wants. The *Ebony Concerto*, in this version conducted by the composer, may have little of 'swung' rhythm, but it is completely faithful to Stravinsky's deadpan approach to jazz.

In *Le Rossignol* the singing is not always on a par with the conducting, but it is always perfectly adequate and the recording is brilliant and immediate. *Mavra* is sung in Russian and, as usual, the soloists – who are good – are too closely balanced, but the performance has punch and authority, and on the whole the CD quality is fully acceptable. The songs represent a fascinating collection of trifles, chips from the master's workbench dating from the earliest years. There are many incidental delights, not least those in which the magnetic Cathy Berberian is featured.

The Rake's Progress is one of the highlights of the set and has never since been surpassed. Alexander Young's assumption of the title-role is a marvellous achievement, sweet-toned, accurate and well characterized. In the choice of other principals, too, it is noticeable what store Stravinsky set by vocal precision. Judith Raskin makes an appealing Anne Truelove, sweetly sung if not particularly well projected dramatically. John Reardon too is remarkable more for vocal accuracy than for striking characterization, but Regina Sarfaty's Baba is marvellous on both counts. The Sadler's Wells Chorus sings with even greater drive under the composer than in the theatre, and the Royal Philharmonic play with warmth and a fittingly Mozartian sense of style to match Stravinsky's surprisingly lyrical approach to his score. The CDs offer excellent sound.

The *Cantata* of 1952 is a transitional piece between Stravinsky's tonal and serial periods. However, of the two soloists, Alexander Young is much more impressive than Adrienne Albert, for her voice is entirely unsuitable, with an unformed choirboy sound somehow married to a wide vibrato. For the sake of Stravinsky, one endures her. The *Canticum sacrum* includes music that some listeners might find tough (the strictly serial choral section). But the performance is a fine one and the tenor solo from Richard Robinson is very moving. The Bach *Chorale Variations* has a synthetic modernity and recalls the espresso bar, though one which still reveals underlying mastery. The *Epitaphium* and the *Double Canon* are miniatures, dating from the composer's serial period, but the *Canon* is deliberately euphonious.

The *Mass* is a work of the greatest concentration, a quality that comes out strongly if one plays this performance immediately after *The Flood*, with its inevitably slack passages. As directed in the score, trebles are used here, and it is a pity that the engineers have not brought them further forward: their sweet, clear tone is sometimes lost among the lower strands. In *The Flood*, originally written for television, it is difficult to take the bald narration seriously, particularly when Laurence Harvey sanctimoniously keeps talking of the will of 'Gud'. The performance of *Oedipus Rex*, too, is not one of the highlights of this set. *Perséphone*, however, is full of that cool lyricism that marks much of Stravinsky's music inspired by classical myths. As with many of these vocal recordings, the balance is too close, and various orchestral solos are highlighted.

Of the items recorded by Robert Craft, the *Requiem Canticles* stands out, the one incontrovertible masterpiece among the composer's very last serial works and one of the most deeply moving works ever written in the serial idiom. Even more strikingly than in the *Mass* of 1948, Stravinsky conveys his religious feelings with a searing intensity. The *Aldous Huxley Variations* are more difficult to comprehend but have similar intensity. Valuable, too, is the ballad, *Abraham and Isaac*.

Le Baiser de la fée (Divertimento)

Pentatone SACD Surround Sound PTC 5186 061. Russian Nat. O, Jurowski –
TCHAIKOVSKY: *Suite 3*

In the Stravinsky *Divertimento* the deft scoring of the Tchaikovsky material is a constant delight, much of it on a chamber-music scale; and its delicacy, wit and occasional pungency are fully appreciated by Jurowski. His performance is as near ideal as one can imagine, electric in tension to give the illusion of live music-making. He steers a nice course between bringing out the romantic warmth of the Tchaikovsky sources (songs and piano music) and the neoclassical element in Stravinsky's style of the 1920s. So the chugging rhythms on the horns in the most memorable section of the second movement convey jollity in their springing step, while the pointing of contrasts in the *Pas de deux*, the longest of the four movements, brings yearning warmth in the big lyrical moments and wit in the faster sections. Exceptionally vivid sound, recorded by Pentatone's Dutch engineers in Moscow, which reproduces superbly in surround sound.

Le Chant du rossignol (Song of the Nightingale)

RCA SACD 82876 66377-2 (2). Chicago SO, Reiner – **RIMSKY-KORSAKOV**: *Scheherazade*

Le Chant du rossignol, which Stravinsky made from the material of his opera, deserves a much more established place in the concert repertoire. It is a highly appealing work, full of colour and imagination. In its new SACD format, Reiner's 1956 recording brings astonishingly vivid sound, full of presence, an excellent coupling for his strong and dramatic reading of *Scheherazade*. If this transitional work – composed over two separate periods – can seem lacking something in thrust in a mediocre performance, Reiner's virile, sharply focused reading relates it more clearly to *The Rite of Spring*. The virtuosity of the playing and the clarity of direction are arresting, while the glittering detail of the orchestral palette in the work's five cued closing sections is most evocative.

Violin Concerto in D

Ⓜ Decca (ADD) 425 003-2. Chung, LSO, Previn – **PROKOFIEV**: *Violin Concertos 1-2*

Kyung-Wha Chung is at her most incisive in the spicily swaggering outer movements which, with Previn's help, are presented here in all their distinctiveness, tough and witty at the same time. In the two movements labelled *Aria*, Chung brings fantasy as well as lyricism, conveying an inner, brooding quality. The pairing with Prokofiev is now reissued in Universal's 'Critics' Choice' series – and worthily so.

(i) *The Firebird* (ballet: complete; choreography: Mikhail Fokine); (ii) *Les Noces* (choreography: Bronislava Nijinska) (DVD version)

Opus Arte DVD OA 0832 D. (i) Benjamin, Cope, Rosato, Drew; (ii) Yanowsky, Pickering and members of Royal Ballet; ROHCG O, or 4 pianos, cond. Carewe. (V/D: Ross MacGibbon)

A moving and well-directed visual record, totally free from attention-seeking camerawork, brings these two marvellous ballets in their original choreography back to life, as if one had the privilege of visiting Diaghilev's Ballets Russes. The dancing is of the highest standard, led by Leanne Benjamin's Firebird, and costumes and sets are visually equally memorable. There are two important bonuses, in addition to the rehearsal footage. Those who have treasured their TV recordings of Stravinsky's own appearance with the New Philharmonia Orchestra at the Royal Festival Hall in 1965 when he was 83 will cherish the DVD transfer, which has much-enhanced definition, both visually and aurally. Finally there is a hilarious description by David Drew of Nijinska's visit to Covent Garden to mount *Les Noces* in the late 1960s.

(i) *The Firebird*; (ii) *The Rite of Spring* (ballets: complete)

Ⓜ Sony SMK 89875. Columbia SO, composer

Stravinsky's own 1961 version of *Firebird* is of far more than documentary interest, when the composer so tellingly relates it to his later work, refusing to treat it as merely atmospheric. What he brings out more than others is the element of grotesque fantasy, the quality he was about to develop in *Petrushka*, while the tense violence with which he presents such a passage as *Katshchei's Dance* clearly looks forward to *The Rite of Spring*. That said, he encourages warmly expressive rubato to a surprising degree, with the line of the music always held firm. But the revelatory performance here is *The Rite of Spring*, for Stravinsky's own 1960 recording has never been surpassed as an interpretation of this seminal twentieth-century score. Over and over again, one finds passages which in the balancing and pacing (generally fast) give extra thrust and resilience, as well as extra light and shade. The digital transfer may be on the bright side, but brass and percussion have thrilling impact, sharply terraced and positioned in the stereo spectrum.

Readers who require the best in digital sonic splendour in *The Rite* could do worse than investigate Chailly's powerfully impressive Cleveland version, now on a bargain Double Decca CD (473 73102), coupled with equally colourful accounts of *The Firebird Suite*, an impressive account of the *Jeu de cartes* ballet, a vividly characterized *Petrushka* and a beautifully recorded and played version of *Apollo* music. Indeed, these recordings from the 1980s and '90s have rarely been equalled sonically, never mind surpassed. With Dorati's electrifying account of *The Firebird* on Mercury now no longer available on CD, Ansermet's recording on Australian Decca Eloquence should not be forgotten. It was Ansermet's last recording and, with the New Philharmonia Orchestra used, rather than his own Suisse Romande Orchestra, the orchestral playing is as magnificent as the Decca recording, which captures with astonishing vividness all the magic Ansermet brings to this score (Australian Decca Eloquence 480 3780 (2)).

Petrushka (1911 score; complete)
Ⓜ RCA (ADD) SACD 82876 67897-2. Boston SO, Monteux - **FRANCK**: *Symphony*

As he conducted the ballet's première, it is good to have Monteux's recording at last satisfactorily remastered, with the sound now vivid and the Boston ambience more of an advantage than a drawback. This 1959 performance has great flair and it is better played than the conductor's earlier account with the Paris Conservatoire Orchestra.

Pulcinella Suite
Dux DUX0764. Wroclaw PO, Jacek Kaspszyk - **R. STRAUSS**: *Le Bourgeois gentilhomme: Suite*

Diaghilev, inspired at the time by the Italian *commedia dell'arte*, commissioned the ballet *Pulcinella* (1920), with its narrative based on the antics of the eponymous Neapolitan clown. The result stimulated the most striking example of Stravinsky's neoclassical style which, with its witty stylization, vivid orchestration, and piquant harmonic palette, created a delightful semi-baroque orchestral pastiche. The *Suite* opens boldly, then continues with a delicious oboe (siciliana) *Serenata*, followed by a delicately graceful *Scherzino* and *Tarantella*. The brass enter boisterously for a *Toccata*, then comes a pensive *Gavotte*, leading to a pair of charming variations. The very Stravinskian *Vivo* has a strident trombone contrasting jokingly with a more contained double-bass solo, and the suite closes with a gracious *Minuetto* and an exhilarating, bravura finale. Stravinsky's scoring is wonderfully inventive and is played with much sparkle and point by this excellent Polish orchestra. This makes a perfect foil for the more sumptuous Richard Strauss coupling and also very entertaining listening.

(i) *The Soldier's Tale. Concertino for Twelve Instruments*; *Pastorale*; *Octet for Wind Instruments*; *Ragtime*; (ii) *Septet* (with **SCHOENBERG**: *Chamber Symphony*. **BERG**: *Adagio* (*Chamber Concerto*))

Ⓜ Australian DG Eloquence (ADD) 480 3300. Boston Chamber Players; with (i) Gielgud, Courtenay, Moody; (ii) Kalish (piano)

This DG performance dates from 1972, though the narration was recorded in 1975. The performance of the music is superb and is recorded with crystal clarity and very sharply characterized. However, it is the speech which makes this performance so completely memorable. Directed by Douglas Cleverdon, the reading hits exactly the right balance between 'characterful' performances and 'over-the-top' performances. Sir John Gielgud, with his distinctive timbre, pitches the style just right with a superb, detached, sardonic wit, and Tom Courtenay and Ron Moody are equally adept at adding colour to the story. Of the orchestral items, the *Pastorale* is an early piece, a vocalise for voice and piano written in 1907, which Stravinsky arranged for Dushkin in 1934. The *Octet* comes from 1923, and the *Septet* from 1953, when Stravinsky was moving towards serialism, albeit gently. All these pieces are musically rewarding and full of the composer's wit and intelligence, and they are given exemplary performances by the distinguished group, and the sound emerges as fresh as paint. The fill-ups are very apt. For a concert tour of Spain, Webern arranged Schoenberg's *Chamber Symphony* for the quintet of instruments used in *Pierrot Lunaire*. Here members of the Boston Symphony Orchestra give a powerfully convincing performance, beautifully recorded. Berg's own transcription of the middle movement of the *Chamber Concerto* makes another apt work for this collection.

(i) *Oedipus Rex*; (ii) *Symphony of Psalms*

Ⓜ Sony (ADD) 88697 00819. (i) Kollo, Krause, Troyanos, Harvard Glee Club, Boston SO; (ii) English Bach Festival Ch., LSO; Bernstein

Recorded in 1972, not long before Bernstein transferred allegiance from CBS to DG, these two performances of the two supreme masterpieces of Stravinsky's inter-war years make a formidable coupling. With Michael Wagner as an excellent narrator (naturally pronouncing it 'Eddipus' in the American way) the casting is exceptionally strong in this severely stylized opera, a work which increasingly reveals its emotional heart. René Kollo in the title-role is especially moving, with the chorus shading the repetitions of the closing pages beautifully. The recording of the *Symphony of Psalms* with British forces was recorded in conjunction with live performances at the English Bach Festival: strong and intense, ending with a tender account of the final *Laudate Dominum*, one of the most beautiful inspirations in all Stravinsky.

STRIGGIO, Alessandro (*c.* 1536/7–92)

CD: Motet: *Ecce beatam lucem*. *Missa Ecco sì beato giorno*. Intermedi & madrigals: *Fuggi, spene mia; O giovenil ardire; Altr'io che queste spighe; D'ogni gratia et d'amor; O de la bella Etruria invitto Duce; Caro dolce ben mio; Miser'oimè*. ANON.: *Spem in alium* (Plainchant). GALILEI: *Contrapunto Secondo di BM*. TALLIS: *Spem in alium*. DVD: *Ecce beatam lucem; Missa Ecco sì beato giorno*. TALLIS: *Spem in alium*. Documentary: 'The Making of Striggio'
Decca CD & DVD 478 2734 (2). I Fagiolini, Robert Hollingworth

Alessandro Striggio, the natural son of a Mantuan nobleman, joined the court of Duke Cosimi I de' Medici in Florence. Seven books of his madrigals were published, besides many others in anthologies, and he divided his time between work for the Medici and his court connection in Mantua. He also wrote occasional music for Medici marriages and their entertainments. His forty-part motet *Ecce beatam lucem* was performed for a visit of two papal envoys in 1561 and again in 1568 in Munich for a wedding feast, probably with instrumentation. By 1566 Striggio had composed the often spectacular Mass based on *Ecco si beato giorno* in forty parts which follows on here. It is very impressive indeed; moreover after the *Bendictus*, beautifully sung here by a single treble voice, he expands the doubled *Agnus Dei*, in its second appearance to sixty voices. Striggio was a string virtuoso and so an example of the music he played, written by Vincenzo Galilei, is used as a prelude to his other, shorter vocal works, mostly madrigals for five voices. Tallis's more familiar *Spem in alium* is a tribute to Striggio. The performances here are without peer and the recording first class. The programme is made the more enticing by the inclusion of a DVD which offers a documentary about the composer plus surround-sound performances of the combined motet and Mass, and the complementary work by Tallis.

SUK, Josef (1874–1935)

Asrael Symphony
Ondine ODE1132-5. Helsinki PO, Ashkenazy

As far as CD is concerned (though not the concert hall), Suk's masterpiece is coming into its own. It started life as a tribute to Dvořák, Suk's father-in-law, who died in 1904, but Suk's grief was compounded by the death of his wife,

Dvořák's daughter. It is a profoundly moving score and Václav Talich in his performance from the early 1950s comes closer to its spirit than any other (Supraphon mono 11 1902-2). However, Vladimir Ashkenazy's sensitive version with his Finnish orchestra remains first choice for its authenticity of feeling and impressive modern recording. Talich remains the one to have on purely musical grounds, but most collectors will prefer the superior Ondine recording.

SULLIVAN, Arthur (1842–1900)

(i) *Pineapple Poll* (ballet; arr. Mackerras); (ii) *Henry VIII: March and Graceful Dance*; *Victoria and Merrie England*

Ⓜ Australian Decca Eloquence (DDD/ADD) 480 1284. (i) Philh. O, Mackerras; (ii) RPO, Nash

Mackerras's arrangement of Sullivan's tunes to create the ballet *Pineapple Poll* is highly ingenious. Not only are the tunes themselves sparkling, they have been arranged in such a way as to form a superb ballet, and also make a delightful hour or so of undemanding but sophisticated light listening. He recorded the work several times (his first recording is discussed in a collection under Mackerras) but this Decca version is the most sumptuous. He conducts with warmth as well as vivacity, and the elegantly polished playing of the Philharmonia gives much pleasure. The record was made in the Kingsway Hall, and the CD transfer, though brightly vivid, has a pleasing bloom. Indeed the quality is in the demonstration bracket, with particularly natural string-textures. The *Henry VIII March* has a rather imposing beginning and builds up to a rousing climax, while the following *Graceful Dance* is both light and charming. *Victoria and Merrie England* may not show Sullivan at his finest, but there is plenty of characteristic writing to enjoy, and all these performances are brightly played and vividly recorded. At any rate, they make a fine bonus to the outstanding *Pineapple Poll*.

Symphony in E (Irish); *In memoriam Overture*; *The Tempest: Suite, Op. 1*

Chan. 9859. BBC PO, Hickox

Sullivan's *Irish Symphony* is hardly a masterpiece, but it has its fine moments, not least the *Allegretto* third movement, beginning with a deliciously folk-like tune on the oboe, which expands to a robust statement from the entire orchestra. It was once used as the theme music to an early 1970s television adaptation of *Tom Brown's Schooldays*. The impressive opening of the symphony builds to an enterprising allegro; the slow movement has great charm and the finale is bright and vivacious with particularly fetching orchestration. Hickox offers also the imposingly solemn *In memoriam Overture* and the *Suite* from *The Tempest*, composed at the age of 18, yet with much attractive invention (the *Overture to Act IV* is especially delightful), a taste of things to come. Hickox's performances are typically excellent, as is the Chandos sound.

The Savoy Operas

The Gilbert and Sullivan operas have been too often dogged by musical snobbery. For so long have these works been part of the musical landscape (in English-speaking countries, at least) that is has become difficult for some to realize their true excellence. However, they have endured and the authors of this book are all great enthusiasts, completely discounting the original disparaging remarks in the Edward Sackville-West/Desmond Shawe-Taylor *Record Guide*, which stated: 'Every musical boy has some jovial uncle who has rammed Gilbert and Sullivan down his throat ever since childhood.' We hope that we don't exaggerate our enthusiasms here, but suggest that readers will discover the quality of these works for themselves. For indeed their pleasures remain fresh and delightful and are a tribute to both the musicality of Arthur Sullivan and the wit of W. S. Gilbert.

For many years, the two great stereo series of Gilbert and Sullivan opera recordings were on EMI (with Sargent conducting) and Decca (mainly with Isidore Godfrey). If we generally prefer the Decca recordings, it is mainly because of Godfrey's splendid affinity with the G&S idiom – a conductor steeped in the performing tradition. Indeed, after thirty years in the opera house, travelling up and down the country, he conducted every performance like a 'first night'. The Decca recordings too are generally the more vivid and theatrical, but there is much to recommend in the EMI series also, for they are extremely well cast.

Not too long ago, Decca put out their entire G&S stereo series in a boxed set – as well as making them available individually – using all the original and very charming artwork. Alas, the boxed set has been deleted and so too have several of the individual titles. The Decca set included rarities such as *The Grand Duke*, *The Sorcerer* and *Utopia Ltd*, with a host of orchestral items as fill-ups. The EMI recordings have been gathered together in a bargain box and include none of those rarities, but all the most famous G&S operas, together with a good sprinkling of other items, such as the charming *Symphony in E* (*Irish*) and the *Cello Concerto*. This remains an excellent recommendation, for the casting is generally superb, and even if Sargent doesn't always show all the theatrical sparkle of these scintillating works, his musicianship is never in doubt (EMI 5 74468-2 (16)).

Of newer recordings, Sir Charles Mackerras's outstanding versions on Telarc are thoroughly recommendable. Mackerras was a masterful G&S conductor, and his recordings of *HMS Pinafore*, *The Mikado*, *The Pirates of Penzance*, *Trial by Jury* and *Yeomen of the Guard* are available at bargain price in a boxed set on Telarc 80500 (5), exhilarating performances, full of life and zest. A single CD of highlights from these recordings is also available (Telarc 80431).

The Gondoliers
Decca (ADD) 473 632-2 (2). Reed, Skitch, Sandford, Round, Styler, Knight, Toye, D'Oyly
  Carte Op. Ch., New SO of L., Godfrey

Isidore Godfrey's conducting here is vividly alive and this is one of the best of his G&S recordings on Decca. For this recording, the company provided a large and first-class orchestra and a superbly spacious recording. The solo singing throughout is consistently good. Jeffrey Skitch and Jennifer Toye are a well-matched pair of lovers, and the two gondoliers and their wives are no less effective. Thomas Round sings *Take a pair of sparkling eyes* very well indeed. The ensemble singing is perfectly balanced and always both lively and musical. The *Cachucha* is captivating and goes at a sparkling pace. Everywhere one can feel the conductor's guiding hand – an instance is the splendidly managed broadening of the orchestral ritornello which forms the closing bars of Act 1. The dialogue is for the most part well spoken, and Kenneth Sandford, who is a rather light-voiced Don Alhambra, makes much of his spoken part as well as singing his songs with fine style. John Reed is a suitably dry Duke of Plaza-Toro and he is well partnered by Gillian Knight. All in all this was, and remains, a considerable achievement.

HMS Pinafore (DVD version)
Decca (ADD) 473 638-2 (2). Reed, Skitch, Round, Adams, Hindmarsh, Wright, Knight,
  D'Oyly Carte Op. Ch., New SO of L., Godfrey

I.M. played the horn in the D'Oyly Carte Orchestra for some months early in his career and came to admire greatly the way Isidore Godfrey nightly brought an uncanny freshness to each performance, and especially to *HMS Pinafore* (I.M's favourite). There is a marvellous spontaneity about the invention, and some-how the music has a genuine briny quality. *Pinafore* also contains Dick Deadeye, the strangest character in all the Savoy Operas, who seems to have popped suddenly to the surface – somewhat in Freudian fashion – from Gilbert's sub-conscious, a more powerful figure than any of the matronly ladies at whom Gilbert liked to poke fun. It would be difficult to imagine a better recorded per-formance than this classic set from the 1960s. It is complete with dialogue and, while there is controversy about this (we personally find that we never tire of the best lines), here the dialogue is vital in establishing the character of Dead-eye, since much of his part is spoken rather than sung. Indeed, the dialogue is spoken extremely well here. Donald Adams is a totally memorable Deadeye and his larger-than-life personality underpins the whole piece. Among the others, Jeffrey Skitch is a first-class Captain; Jean Hindmarsh is totally convin-cing as Josephine (it was a pity that she stayed with the company for so short a time) and she sings with real charm. Thomas Round is equally good as Ralph Rackstraw. Little Buttercup could be slightly more colourful, but this is a small blemish, and among the minor parts George Cook is a most personable Bill Bobstay. The choral singing is excellent, the orchestral playing up to standard, and Godfrey conducts with marvellous spirit and lift. The recording has splendid atmosphere.

Iolanthe

Decca (ADD) 473 641-2 (2). Reed, Sansom, Newman, Knight, Adams, Round, Styler, Sandford, D'Oyly Carte Op. Ch., Grenadier Guards' Band, New SO of L., Godfrey

For this 1960 recording of *Iolanthe*, the set was given added panache by the introduction of the Grenadier Guards' Band into the *March of the Peers*. Mary Sansom is a convincing Phyllis, and she is completely at home with the dialogue, while Alan Styler makes a vivid and charming personal identification with the role of Strephon, an Arcadian shepherd. Kenneth Sandford is splendid in the *Sentry Song* and John Reed is very good as the Lord Chancellor: dryly whimsical, he provides a characteristically individual characterization. Godfrey's conducting is light and infectious, and there is much to delight the ear in the famous Trio of Act II with the Lord Chancellor and the two Earls, superbly sung by Donald Adams and Thomas Round.

The Mikado

Decca (ADD) 473 644-2 (2). Ayldon, Wright, Reed, Sandford, Masterson, Holland, D'Oyly Cart Op. Ch., RPO, Nash

This was another triumph in Decca's re-recording of the Savoy Operas in stereo. Indeed, this recording had the effect of adding a coat of bright new paint to the score, and the G&S masterpiece emerges with a pristine sparkle. Musically, this is one of the finest versions the D'Oyly Carte Company have ever put on disc. The choral singing is first rate, with much refinement of detail. The glees, *Brightly dawns* and *See how the fates*, are robust in the D'Oyly Carte manner, but more polished than usual. The words are exceptionally clear throughout, without sizzling sibilants. This applies to an important early song in Act I, *Our great Mikado*, which contains the seeds of the plot and is sometimes delivered in a throaty, indistinct way. Not so here: every word is crystal clear. Of the principals, John Reed is a delicious Ko-Ko, a refined and individual characterization, and his famous *Little list* song has an enjoyable lightness of touch.

(However, one has to recall here Martyn Green's famous and hilarious portrayal of Ko-Ko. One remembers his performance, just before he retired, in the huge Blackpool Opera House. He had built a peg ladder into the side of the proscenium arch and ran up it like a rabbit to deliver from the top corner his immortal plea to Katisha: 'Shrink not from me.' Needless to say, it brought the house down.)

Kenneth Sandford gives his customary vintage projection of Pooh Bah – a pity none of his dialogue has been included. Valerie Masterson is a charming Yum-Yum; *The sun whose rays* (considered by many to be Sullivan's finest aria) has rarely been sung with more feeling and charm, and it is followed by a virtuoso account of *Here's a how-de-do* which one longs to encore (as used to happen in the theatre). Colin Wright's vocal production has a slightly nasal quality, but one soon adjusts to it and his voice has the proper bright freshness of timbre for Nanki-Poo. John Ayldon's Mikado provides a laugh of terrifying bravura. Katisha (Lyndsie Holland) is commanding, and her attempts to interrupt the chorus in the finale of Act I are superbly believable and dramatic. With excellent sound throughout, this is all very enjoyable indeed.

The Pirates of Penzance

Decca (ADD) 473 650-2 (2). Reed, Adams, Potter, Masterson, Palmer, Brannigan, D'Oyly
    Carte Op. Ch., RPO, Godfrey

Isidore Godfrey's second recording of *The Pirates of Penzance* is helped by a more uniformly excellent cast than on the earlier, mono version and, this time, all the dialogue is included. The theatrical spontaneity is well maintained, and the spoken scenes with the Pirate King are particularly effective. Donald Adams has a great gift for Gilbertian inflexion and some of his lines give as much pleasure as his splendidly characterized singing. Christine Palmer's Ruth is not quite so poised, but her singing is first rate – her opening aria has never been so well done. John Reed, while not eclipsing memories of Martyn Green, shows his usual flair with his unlikely portrayal of the First Lord of the Admiralty. Valerie Masterson is an excellent Mabel, and if her voice is not creamy throughout its range, she controls it with great skill to delight us often. Her duet with Frederick, *Leave me not to pine alone*, is enchanting, sung very gently. Godfrey has prepared us for it in the overture and it is one of the highlights of this set. Godfrey's conducting is as affectionate as ever, more lyrical here, without losing rhythmic buoyancy, and one can hear him revelling in the many touches of colour in the orchestration, which the RPO presents with great sophistication. But perhaps the greatest joy of this set is Owen Brannigan's Sergeant of Police, a part this artist was surely born to play. It is a marvellously humorous performance, yet the humour is never clumsy, and the famous *Policeman's Song* is so fresh that it is almost like hearing it for the first time. The recording is superbly spacious and clear throughout, with a fine sense of atmosphere.

(i) The Yeomen of the Guard; (ii) Trial by Jury

Decca (ADD) 473 665-2 (2). (i–ii) Hood, Reed, Sandford, Adams; (i) Harwood, Knight,
    Potter, Lawlor; (ii) Round; D'Oyly Carte Op. Ch.; (i) RPO, Sargent; (ii) ROHCG O, Godfrey

Sir Malcolm's breadth of approach is at once apparent in the overture. The spinning song which follows also begins deliberately; it has a striking lyricism, with much play in the echo effects, but not quite the lightness of touch that Godfrey would manage. This is not to imply that Sargent's result is less effective, only that it is not quite what one expected from a traditional D'Oyly Carte reading on Decca. As soon as the chorus enters (*Tower warders*), the degree of

Sargent's 'grand operatic' approach makes a remarkable impact; indeed, one has seldom heard the choruses in *Yeomen* expand with such power, nor indeed has the orchestra (especially the brass) produced such a regal sound. As the work proceeds the essential spaciousness of Sargent's reading begins to emerge more and more, and the ensemble singing is especially lovely. There is no lack of drama either, and the only aspect of the work which is played down is the humorous side. The interjections of Jack and Wilfred in the Act 1 finale are obviously seen as part of the whole rather than a suggestion of the humour that somehow seems to intrude into the most serious human situations. The pathos of the famous *Jester's Song* in the Second Act is beautifully conveyed, but the only moment to raise a real smile is the duet which follows, *Tell a tale of cock and bull*. But with consistently fine singing throughout from all the principals and especially from Elizabeth Harwood (as Elsie), supported by a perfectly balanced recording, this *Yeomen* is unreservedly a success. *Trial by Jury* is lovingly conducted by Godfrey, and this immaculate and very well-recorded CD gives an illusion of an ideal performance from a perfectly placed seat. The balance and dynamic range are both judged to perfection, and the orchestral score tells without ever being too loud. John Reed plays the part of the Judge to perfection, even if he does sound perhaps a little too youthful.

SUPPÉ, Franz von (1819–95)

Overtures: Die Frau Meisterin; Die Irrfahrt um's Glück; Light Cavalry; Morning, Noon and Night in Vienna; Pique Dame; Poet and Peasant; Tantalusqualen; Wiener-Jubel (Vienna Jubilee)
(B) EMI 5 09029-2. ASMF, Marriner

Marriner's collection of Suppé *Overtures* has been out of the catalogue too long and now goes straight to the top of the list. The sound has opulence, bloom, a wide amplitude, realistic definition and a natural presence. The performances admirably combine exuberance, fine ensemble and style. At Encore price this is a reissue not to be missed on any account.

SUTHERLAND, Joan (soprano), with Orchestra and Chorus of the Royal Opera House, Covent Garden, Franscesco Molinari Pradelli

'The Art of the Prima Donna': Arias from: **ARNE**: *Artaxerxes*. **HANDEL**: *Samson*. **BELLINI**: *Norma*; *I Puritani*; *La sonnambula*. **ROSSINI**: *Semiramide*. **GOUNOD**: *Faust*; *Roméo et Juliette*. **VERDI**: *Otello*; *Rigoletto*; *La traviata*. **MOZART**: *Die*

Entführung aus dem Serail. **THOMAS**: *Hamlet*. **DELIBES**:
Lakmé. **MEYERBEER**: *Les Huguenots*.
Ⓜ Decca (ADD) 478 3071 (3). Bonus CD: Joan Sutherland discusses her life and career
with Jon Tolansky

Joan Sutherland is an operatic phenomenon. The number of recordings from
her that we have recommended in this book is a remarkable tribute to her art
and, of course, to the support and guidance from her conductor/husband,
Richard Bonynge. Throughout the 1960s, she made a number of two-LP sets
comparable in achievement to this early collection, including 'Command Performance' and 'The Age of Bel Canto'. These are, alas, not currently available,
though her enticing collection of 'Romantic French Arias' is (discussed below).
Her very first recital LP, which features her début recording of the Mad scene
from *Lucia di Lammermoor*, conducted by Nello Santi (with the Paris Conservatoire Orchestra) is now available on Regis 1364. That 1959 recording, which
also includes arias from *I vespri siciliani* and *Linda di Chamounix*, contains
some of the most treasurable examples of coloratura singing on record and will
surely return to the catalogue on Eloquence. Some of it has re-appeared in a
six-CD set, 'The Art of Joan Sutherland' (Decca 475 6302), which contains
many rarities and is well worth seeking out.

'The Art of the Prima Donna' was issued in 1960 and has never been out of
the catalogue. We have included the full original review (by E.G.) from 1960 as
it remains as true today as it was then. Only E.G.'s remarks about the sound do
we now need to challenge, as these performances now sound first class in their
latest CD transfer: bright, warm and vivid, and showing the best traditions of
Decca. E.G. wrote: 'No more ambitious recital has ever been attempted on
record, and it is a matter of speculation whether even Melba or Tetrazzini in
their heyday managed to produce sixteen consecutive recordings quite so dazzling as these performances. Indeed it is to the Golden Age that one naturally
turns rather than to current singers when making any comparisons. Sutherland herself by electing to sing each one of these fabulously difficult coloratura
arias in tribute to a particular soprano of the past, from Mrs Billington in the
eighteenth century, through Grisi, Malibran, Pasta and Jenny Lind in the nineteenth, to Lilli Lehmann, Melba, Tetrazzini and Galli-Curci in this, is asking to
be judged on the standards of the Golden Age. On the basis of recorded reminders she comes out of any comparisons with flying colours. It is not a question
of claiming that she is a Lilli Lehmann, a Melba and a Ponselle all in one, but
of going naturally to the very best Golden Age exponent in each case and meas-
uring Sutherland beside her. In any close comparison there are obviously many
points of interpretation on which a particular Golden Ager scores against Sutherland. But Sutherland so often emerges triumphant, that one is tempted to
claim for her a greater consistency and certainly a wider range of sympathy
than even the greatest Golden Agers displayed. No doubt we shall be told that
acoustic recordings do not show the true powers of the great artists of the past,
but it is on the basis of those recordings that for years past we have been

bombarded with the most glowing claims for greatness (many of them quite justifiable). Perfectly fair then to use such recordings to assess Sutherland.

'Sutherland has more than any other comparable singer in recent years taken the trouble (with the invaluable guidance of her husband, Richard Bonynge) to toil away in apprenticeship at the comparatively dreary techniques of bel canto singing, and now her reward comes in being able to stand up in technical comparison. Add to that the great advantage of living in an age when considerations of taste and style on the one hand and the dramatic side of operatic performance on the other are more closely regarded, and Sutherland may well be taken as having the best of both worlds. It is an absurd mistake for example to think of Sutherland versus Callas. If anything Sutherland is very much of the school of Callas, benefiting from her example in intensity of dramatic portrayal (which the Golden Agers, primarily concerned with technical matters, rarely attempted). Listen to the three great Bellini arias, *'Casta Diva'*, from *Norma*, *'Quia la voce'* from *I Puritani* and *'Come per me'* from *Sonnambula*, and the sense of presence, of profound intensity of interpretation is inescapable. Sutherland has learnt that from Callas, but she has in addition a far more complete technical equipment, and above all a voice of tonal beauty that one can only describe as heavenly. We have had plenty of agile coloraturas with tweety voices and less-than-agile coloraturas with fuller-toned voices, but rarely have we had the ideal combination. I have already mentioned the Bellini arias as outstanding, and besides the three I have noted there is the *Polonaise* from *Puritani*, *Son 'vezzosa verg'*, the florid decorations exquisitely pointed. *'Bel raggio'* from *Semiramide* is even more breathtaking, and the *'Caro nome'* is one of the finest ever recorded, with a long-held trill at the end and phrasing that is at once precise and conceived as a whole. At one point for example Sutherland phrases the first four semiquavers of each sequential group legato and puts a staccato on the last two alone, a magical effect when executed with such apparent ease. The 'Willow Song' from *Otello* displays the dark colour that Sutherland can adopt on occasion, a deeply moving performance comparable with De los Angeles's fine recording (another singer who demands comparison with the Golden Age). The top A sharp at the end is wonderfully clean and accurate, but unfortunately the recording catches Sutherland's intake of breath before it, and so spoils the knife-edge effect one ideally asks.

'Here for the first time we have Sutherland in warhorse arias from the French repertoire too. The Mad scene from Thomas's *Hamlet* has some superb moments in it, notably the frisking dotted section taken with a lilt that makes Callas's much slower version seem tame and dull. The "Bell Song" from *Lakmé* with its melismatic meanderings allows Sutherland to display the widest range of tone-colour from a dreamy softness to the brightness of golden tone. The "Waltz Song" from *Romeo and Juliet* is taken much slower than Melba, but it allows the grace-notes to come out in a way one rarely hears and with delicious precision. Most spectacular of all the French arias is the Queen's aria from Meyerbeer's *Les Huguenots* in which the cabaletta is something one can barely imagine any voice coping with. Yet Sutherland rides triumphantly through the fantastic arpeggios and runs.

'Then there are the two English arias, the little-known one from Arne's *Artaxerxes*, once a standard test-piece for eighteenth-century coloraturas, and Handel's "Let the Bright Seraphim", in which the da capo is taken, so allowing Sutherland to make some even more dazzling additions than at first. Finally in *"Martern aller Arten"* Sutherland shows her powers in coping with a completely different style, strong and forthright, where in Bellini and Donizetti she is yielding and flexible. It makes one look forward to her Constanza on stage.

'The recording is exceptionally good with the Decca brilliance never spilling over into hardness. The sound is softened by reverberation. At times a bathroom effect is none too distant, but the beauty of Sutherland's voice makes one very tolerant.'

The set is handsomely produced in booklet from, with full texts and translations and many colour photographs.

SWEELINCK, Jan (1562–1621)

Allemand (Gratie); *Esce mars*; *Die flichtig Nimphae*; *Fantasia Crommatica*; *Mein junges Leben hat ein Endt*; *Paduana Lachrymae*; *Pavan Philippi*; *Toccata a 3 G2*; *Toccata C2*; *Toccata Noni Toni*; *Toccata Primi Toni*; *Toccata Secundi Toni*; *Unter der Linden grune*; *Von der Fortuna werd ich getrieben*
Chan. 0758. Woolley (harpsichord)

Robert Woolley, using two harpsichords, has produced a glorious CD of some of Sweelinck's most inspired keyboard music. There are all sorts of delights here, from the beautiful variations on *Mein junges Leben hat ein Endt*, to the substantial *Fantasia Crommatica* which ends the recital – and what an impressive piece it is too. Sweelinck's music is full of imagination, taking influences from all over Europe and mixing them together to form an original voice. *Die flichtig Nimphae* is very charming indeed, but there is an unforced elegance about all the music on this CD which is quite captivating. This CD is superbly recorded and Robert Woolley is a masterful exponent of this repertoire.

SZELL, George (conductor)

'Decca & Philips Recordings, 1951–1969': BEETHOVEN: *Symphony 5*. MOZART: *Symphony 34*. BRAHMS: *Symphony 3*. DVOŘÁK: *Symphony 8*. SIBELIUS: *Symphony 2* (with Concg. O).

BEETHOVEN: *Egmont: complete incidental music* (with Pilar Lorengar, Klaus-Jürgen Wussow, VPO). **MENDELSSOHN**: *A Midsummer Night's Dream: Overture & Incidental Music*. **SCHUBERT**: *Rosamunde: Overture and Ballet Music 2*; *Entr'actes to Acts I & III* (with Concg. O). **HANDEL**: *Music for the Royal Fireworks: Suite* (arr. Harty); *Water Music: Suite* (arr. Harty/ Szell); *The Faithful Shepherd: Minuet* (arr. Beecham); *Serse: Largo* (arr. Reinhardt). **TCHAIKOVSKY**: *Symphony 4* (with LSO).
Ⓜ Decca mono/stereo 475 6780 (5)

Szell made some excellent recordings for Decca and Philips, and some of the best are found here. One of them brings a famous story about the Decca recording sessions for his Tchaikovsky *Fourth Symphony* with the LSO in 1962. Apparently the producer, John Culshaw, didn't think Szell was creating as much tension as expected. So during the playback at the recording session, he set controls at a lower level than usual, with the treble response cut back a little. Szell reacted immediately and marched back to the orchestra – all fired up – and produced the electrifying performance we have here, one of the great Tchaikovsky recordings of the stereo era. Goodness knows why it has been out of the catalogue for so long, as it has consistently been highly praised by us and others. So this reissued set is worth getting for this performance alone.

Many readers, like us, will have a nostalgic feeling for the Handel–Harty suites of Handel's *Fireworks* and *Water Music* from which earlier generations got to know this marvellous music, before the days of 'authenticity'. Szell's accounts (1961) – with the two extra Handel lollipops – are recommendable indeed. The orchestral playing throughout is quite outstanding, and the strings are wonderfully expressive in the slower pieces. The horns excel, and the crisp new transfers seem to add to the sheer zest of the music-making.

The problem with performing Beethoven's incidental music for Goethe's *Egmont* within the original dramatic context is at least partially solved on Decca by using a text by the Austrian poet, Franz Grillparzer. The music is interspersed at appropriate points, including dramatic drum-rolls in Egmont's final peroration, this last scene being from Goethe's original. The Decca presentation (1969), with Klaus-Jürgen Wussow the admirably committed narrator, is dramatic in the extreme. Szell's conducting is dramatic indeed, the music vividly characterized, the tension lightened in certain places with subtlety, and the whole given remarkably dramatic impact. The songs are movingly sung by Pilar Lorengar. Full texts and translations are included and the stereo sound is rich and vivid. The Philips account of the *Fifth Symphony* (1966) is not quite as intense as the Cleveland recording (CBS/Sony) but is still a fine one, with excellent playing and decent sound. The Sibelius *Symphony No. 2* (1964) is a classically conceived performance, tautly held together and superbly played and recorded – no reservations about this. The Mendelssohn items are no less successful, with superlative playing from the Concertgebouw Orchestra. Here the lightness and clean articulation of the violins in the *Overture* are a delight; the nimble wind-playing in the Scherzo sparkles and there is a fine horn solo in the *Nocturne*. The recording dates from 1957 and sounds admirably clear, without loss of bloom. In the Schubert, originally coupled with the Mendelssohn, the *Overture* has engaging rhythmic spring, and the *Ballet* and *Entr'actes* combine polish with charm. The Mozart *Symphony No. 34* is vibrantly recorded (1966), with bright, lively outer movements and a slow movement of considerable charm. The two mono recordings here, Brahms's *Third Symphony* and Dvořák's *Eighth*, are both full-blooded, vital readings. The snag is the thin, early Decca sound (1951), particularly in the Brahms, which really does lack body, with the violins inclining to aggressive shrillness under pressure. Nevertheless, this box set is well worth exploring, not least for Szell's Tchaikovsky.

SZYMANOWSKI, Karol (1882–1937)

Violin Concertos 1, Op. 35; 2, Op. 61; Nocturne; Tarantella
🅑🅑 Naxos 8.557081. Kaler, Warsaw PO, Wit

Naxos offer an exceptionally clear recording of these four concertante works by Szymanowski, not just the two *Violin Concertos*, but orchestrated versions of the *Nocturne* and *Tarantella*. As on other Naxos discs, Ilya Kaler gives pure, clear readings with flawless intonation and careful use of vibrato. Having a Polish conductor and orchestra as his accompanists adds to the idiomatic feel of each, with the magical orchestral sounds beautifully conjured up, particularly in No. 1, the more radical of the two concertos. Kaler plays the two relatively brief concertante pieces just as sympathetically, with the *Tarantella* a flamboyant virtuoso vehicle, making a splendid climax to an excellent disc.

(i) *Violin Concertos 1–2*; (ii) *Symphonies 3 (Song of the Night)*; (iii) *4 (Symphonie concertante)*; (iv) *Demeter*; (v) *Litany to the Virgin Mary*; (vi) *Stabat Mater*
🅑🅑 EMI (ADD) 2CD 2 06870-2 (2). Polish R. Nat. SO, with (i) Kulka; cond. Maksymiuk; (ii) Ochman, Kraków Polish R. Ch.; (iii) Paleczny; (ii–iii) cond. Semkow; (iv; vi) Rappé; (v–vi) Gadulanka; (vi) Hiolski & Ch., cond. Wit

These committed performances are from the 1970s and early 1980s and are atmospheric and sensitive. Kulka's accounts of the two *Violin Concertos* are highly finished and convey much of the ecstasy, longing and sensuousness of these luminous scores. The pianist in the *Symphonie concertante*, Piotr Paleczny, is no mean artist and has all the finesse and imagination as well as the requisite command of colour. *The Song of the Night* has great refinement and atmosphere, and the other vocal and choral works are similarly idiomatic. The sound generally is naturally recorded and balanced.

Symphonies 2; (i) *3 (Song of the Night)*
ⓑⓑ Naxos 8.570721. (i) Minkiewicz; Warsaw Philharmonic Ch. & O, Wit

These are notably warm and idiomatic performances, again showing Antoni Wit as a conductor to reckon with, creating orchestral colour and passion with equal intensity. The excellent, clear-voiced tenor soloist, Ryszard Minkiewicz, and the chorus make a passionate impression during No. 3, and altogether this pair of performances could not be more idiomatic. The recording too is first class.

(i–iii) *Stabat Mater, Op. 53*; (ii) *Demeter, Op. 37b*; (i) *Litany to the Virgin Mary, Op. 59*; (i) *Penthesilea, Op. 18*; (i) *Veni Creator, Op. 57*
ⓑⓑ Naxos 8.570724. Warsaw Philharmonic Ch. & O, Wit; with (i) Hossa; (ii) Marciniec; (iii) Brk

Naxos have replaced the performers of their previous (identical) collection of Szymanowski's choral music with a new team, and in particular using fine soloists. The *Stabat Mater* is not only one of Szymanowski's greatest achievements but one of the greatest choral works of the twentieth century. This new account has the advantage of highly sensitive conducting and an excellent response from the choir and orchestra. The *Liturgy to the Virgin Mary* is another late work of great poignancy, but *Demeter* has exotic, almost hallucinatory textures. It is all heady and intoxicating stuff, and not to be missed by those with a taste for this wonderful composer. The recording is excellent.

String Quartets 1 in C, Op. 37; 2, Op. 56
Hyp. CDA 67684. Royal Qt (with **RÓŻYCKI**: *Quartet in D min., Op. 49*)

The inspired *First Quartet* of 1915–16 comes from the period of the *First Violin Concerto* and the *Third Symphony* and shares their mystical harmonic soundworld. The *Second* (1927) comes from the years after the composition of *King Roger*, and is as fastidiously conceived as its predecessor. Both are masterpieces which should figure alongside Bartók in public esteem; and both are well served by this fine Polish ensemble. They include as a makeweight a quartet by Szymanowski's immediate contemporary but more conservative colleague, Ludomir Różycki (1884–1953), well worth hearing but not in the same league as its companions.

TALLIS, Thomas (*c.* 1505–85)

The Complete Vocal & Instrumental Music of Tallis:

Vol. 1: *Music for Henry VIII* (SIGCD 001); Vol. 2: *Music at the Reformation* (SIGCD 002); Vol. 3: *Music for Queen Mary* (SIGCD 003); Vol. 4: *Music for the Divine Office* – *1* (SIGCD 010); Vol. 5: *Music for the Divine Office* – *2* (SIGCD 016); Vol. 6: *Music for a Reformed Church* (SIGCD 022); Vol. 7: *Music for Queen Elizabeth* (SIGCD 029); Vol. 8: *Lamentations & Contrafacta* (SIGCD 036); Vol. 9: *Instrumental Music & Songs* (SIGCD 042 (2))

Volumes 1–9: Ⓜ Signum SIGCD 060 (10). Chapelle du Roi, Alistair Dixon, with soloists, instrumentalists & Charivari Agréable

Alistair Dixon and his Chapelle du Roi (plus other contributors) have now completed their distinguished integral coverage of the music of the great Elizabethan composer, Thomas Tallis. The complete series is currently available in a mid-priced box with full documentation, but the discs are all available separately and are discussed individually below.

Just looking at the titles of the individual volumes underlines the dramatic period of English history through which Tallis lived and composed, successfully moving from a Latin liturgy to English settings, then back again. Finally, during the reign of Elizabeth I, in the best spirit of English compromise he created new from the old in setting English words to music originally written to serve Latin texts. Even the famous *Spem in Alium* was heard anew as *Sing and glorify*, although generations later it reverted to its original Latin format.

The first disc augurs extremely well for the project. The programme is framed by three Marian votive antiphons, the first two comparatively immature and rather similar. *Salve intemerata*, however, is masterly in its concisely integrated part-writing (with some soaring treble solos, beautifully sung here). The *Mass* sharing its name uses much of the same material: the *Gloria* and *Sanctus* are particularly fine. The *Alleluia* and *Euge celi porta* are less ambitious but still serenely beautiful, four-part plainchant settings used as part of the Ladymass.

Most, possibly all, of the music in Volume 2 dates from the 1540s and reflects the remarkable diversity of musical response that came directly from the profound change in reformed religious procedures that developed in England within a single decade. Much liturgical music was still sung in Latin, notably the splendid *Magnificat* and the deeply felt *Sancte Deus*, but already there are settings in English, including three fine early anthems, an extended English *Benedictus* and a remarkable five-part *Te Deum*, all very different from the music in Volume 1 of this series. The surprisingly homophonic setting of the Latin *Mass* is forward-looking, too, and very telling.

Volume 3 returns to the Latin rite, and all the works here date from the reign of Mary Tudor (1553–8). The collection opens with the Psalm setting, *Beati immaculati*, and includes also the glorious, large-scale votive antiphon, *Gaude gloriosa*, magnificently sung. The key work here, however, is the seven-part *Mass Puer natus est nobis*, which is incomplete. Here the *Gloria, Sanctus* and *Agnus Dei* are performed with the plainchant Propers for the third Mass of Christmas. As usual the singing is splendid, but there is a good deal of monodic chant here, beautifully phrased certainly, but which will reduce the appeal of this volume for some collectors.

Volume 4 in this ever-rewarding series is the first to concentrate on music for the cycle of eight services, Matins, Lauds, Prime, Terce, Sext, None, Vespers and Compline, sung daily in Latin Christendom. The riches of the polyphony here are unending. *Dum transisset sabbatum* and the six-part *Videte miraculum* are particularly fine, while the seven-part *Loquebantur variis linguis* with its recurring *Alleluias* spins an even more complex contrapuntal web. Even the simplest of the settings here, *Quod chorus vatum*, is moving by its comparative austerity.

Volume 5 of Alistair Dixon's invaluable survey continues the music that Tallis wrote for the Divine Office begun in Volume 4. But the special interest of this CD is the inclusion of the organ music, simply written and based on plainchant melismas. Tallis generally used the organ as a substitute for voices, interchanging instrumental with sung text. In this aurally appealing alternation, the organist played the odd-numbered verses, usually providing – as in *Veni Redemptor genitum* – a piquant introduction to contrast with the sonorous vocal entry. The organ used for the recordings, in the private chapel at Knole, is the oldest playable organ in England, so its choice seems admirable, and Andrew Benson-Wilson's contribution to the success of this CD is considerable, since all the organ music is most appealing.

Volume 6 is devoted to music which Tallis composed for use in the reformed services promulgated by *The Booke of the Common Prayer*, which came into effect in 1549, here presented in the normal liturgical sequence. Much of the music is simple and homophonic, but it has an unadorned beauty of its own. The anthems are richer in the interplay of parts but are still brief, and the collection ends with the nine even briefer psalm-tune harmonizations which Tallis contributed to Archbishop Matthew Parker's *Psalter*, published in about 1567.

Elizabeth was the fourth monarch to sit on the throne in Tallis's lifetime, and Tallis was by then in his sixties. Both composer and monarch appear to have been determined that the new Elizabethan Latin motets should seek new expressive approaches, while drawing on the best of the past. Their success is confirmed by the fact that cathedral musicians fitted English words to much of Tallis's music. *Absterge Domine* therefore also becomes *Discomfort them O Lord*. The two Psalm settings included, *Domine, quis habitatbi* (Psalm 15) and the shorter but no less impressive *Laudate Dominum* (Psalm 117), are both memorable. The most celebrated of these motets is of course *Spem in Alium*, with its incredibly dense part-writing still able to astonish the ear. It is sung gloriously here, its ebb and flow and rich climaxes splendidly controlled.

Tallis's two richly expressive settings of the *Lamentations of Jeremiah* are given in Volume 8 in serene and dedicated performances, followed by what are known as *contrafacta*, English versions by the post-Reformation English Church of Latin motets rewritten by Tallis. The music itself, usually in five parts, seems to adapt very well to its linguistic transformation; the first piece here, *Wipe Away my Sins (Absterge Domine)*, described as 'A Prayer', is particularly beautiful. *With all our hearts and mouths* and the lovely *Arise, O Lord* both derive from Tallis's first setting of *Salvator mundi*, while *I Call and Cry to Thee (O sacrum convivium)*, very popular in its day, was to lay the basis for Tallis's English anthems.

The fascination of the final volume in Signum's comprehensive survey is the virtually unknown instrumental music, consisting of a small collection of works for viols and some fine pieces for keyboard, which we hear variously on virginals, harpsichord or organ. In his excellent notes, John Milsom suggests that while Tallis's official duties involved him only as a church musician, he may have written some of this music for the Tudor Court, and the keyboard pieces could conceivably have been written for Queen Elizabeth I, who was a celebrated amateur performer. Certainly they are attractive enough.

The consort manuscripts give no indication of the instrumentation, but viols (as used here) seem a likely choice, and Tallis's pair of *In nomines* are the first known examples of this form (settings using the *Gloria tibi Trinitas* as a basis). As far as is known, Tallis did not write for the lute, so the impressively complex work based on the plainsong, *'Felix namque'*, is almost certainly an arrangement by an unknown lutenist. This is heard alongside the less virtuosic keyboard version written two years earlier. *Mr Tallis's Lesson* (which we hear both on harpsichord and on organ) is a very agreeable pedagogic piece based on a decorated canon, and was no doubt intended as a study for the composer's choirboy pupils.

As for the songs, they make a wonderful closing section. The very touching *When shall my sorrowful sighing slack* might well have been composed by Dowland, and *Ye sacred muses*, a tribute to Byrd, is fully worthy. They are sung most sympathetically by Stephen Taylor (counter-tenor), and the instrumental pieces from Charivari Agréable, Laurence Cummings (virginals and harpsichord) and Andrew Benson-Wilson (organ), are expertly played, while Lynda Sayce gives a virtuoso account of the arrangement of *Felix namque*.

The bonus disc includes a complete setting of the *Litany*, omitted from Volume 6, two brief organ *Versets*, and a further performance of the earlier, less complex version of *Felix namque*. As with the other organ pieces, Benson-Wilson uses the organ at the private chapel in Knole in Kent (owned during Tallis's lifetime by both Archbishop Cranmer and Henry VIII). All in all, Volume 9 makes a fitting conclusion to a splendid project, admirably realized, and as before full texts and translations are included.

TANEYEV, Sergei (1856–1915)

Suite de concert for Violin & Orchestra, Op. 28
Hyp. CDA 67642. Ilya Gringolts, BBC Scottish SO, Volkov - **ARENSKY**: *Violin Concerto*

Neither the Arensky *Concerto* nor the *Suite de concert* is much heard in the concert hall and most music lovers will have come to know them from records: the Taneyev in Oistrakh's wonderful Columbia LP with Nicolai Malko and the Philharmonia Orchestra from the mid-1950s. The *Suite de concert* is Taneyev's only work for violin and orchestra and its elegance and virtuosity are heard to splendid effect here. At no time does Ilya Gringolts allow his brilliance to draw attention to itself and away from this inventive and fastidiously crafted score. Apart from its musical resource (particularly in the imaginative *Märchen* movement and the masterly theme and variations) there is an impressive and congenial personality that radiates warmth and learning. Gringolts tosses off its formidable difficulties with fluency, virtuosity and lyrical intensity, and he is expertly and sensitively partnered by Ilan Volkov and the BBC Scottish Orchestra. The balance between soloist and orchestra is truthful and most musically judged, though the orchestral texture would perhaps benefit from greater transparency.

Also available (on Chan. 10491) is Lydia Mordkovitch's account of the *Suite de concert* with the RSNO, Järvi). Above all, she concentrates on bringing out an incredible range of colours from her instrument, and if her intonation isn't always immaculate, her sheer intensity carries the day. The *Tarantella* finale is excitingly done. One attraction of this release is the colourfully tuneful *Fantasy on Russian Themes* by Rimsky-Korsakov, in which the composer's gift for conjuring up a magical atmosphere is superbly realized by the soloist. Järvi conducts both works with his usual expertise, and the Chandos recording is warm and richly detailed.

String Trios: in E flat, Op. 31; in B min.; in D
Hyp. CDA 67573. Leopold String Trio

If you enjoy the Tchaikovsky *Quartets*, you'll almost certainly enjoy these *Trios*, although there is no movement quite as memorable as the Tchaikovsky *Andante cantabile*. The Op. 31 *Trio*, which opens the disc, is the finest, with consistently memorable invention. Taneyev, like Mendelssohn, is particularly good at Scherzi, and both Scherzi, in Opus 31 and the *D major* work, are prime examples. The (reconstructed) two-movement *B minor Trio* opens rather lugubriously, but its second-movement *Theme and Variations* is quixotically inventive, yet far from frivolous, with fine, expressive writing to balance the characteristic scherzando writing. The *D major Trio* was written three decades before the others: it has a friendly opening movement and a very touching *Adagio*. The Leopold String Trio are right inside all this music, play and balance impeccably, and they are very realistically recorded.

TÁRREGA, Francisco (1852–1909)

16 Preludios; Alborada (Capricho); Capricho árabe (Serenata); Estudio brilliante de Alard; Recuerdos de la Alhambra; Las Dos Hermanitas (Dos Valses); Gavota (Maria); 3 Mazurkas: Adelita; Marieta; Mazurka in G. Pavana; Polkas: Rosita; Pepita. Gran vals; Vals; Isabel (Johann Strauss II); Paquito; Vals in D.
ⓑ Naxos 8.572365. Mats Bergström (guitar)

Francisco Tárrega was the most influential Spanish virtuoso guitar player and composer of the nineteenth century, a charismatic romantic who, with a cigarette always in his mouth, apparently captivated his audiences. His memorable fluttering *Recuerdos de la Alhambra*, inspired by a visit to the Alhambra Palace in Granada, is justly famous (it is played superbly here), but his highly regarded 16 *Preludios*, delectable tiny miniatures, have comparable charm and individuality. No. 9 here surprisingly draws on Mendelssohn's *Hebrides Overture*, while the *Serenata, Capricho árabe*, is more exotic and the *Alborada (Capricho)* is also highly individual. The mazurkas, engaging dance pieces, a pavane, a gavotte, waltzes and polkas, are mostly named to catch the personality of their dedicatees. *Isabel* draws on two themes from Johann Strauss's *Kiss Waltz*.

The Swedish guitarist Mats Bergström is a superb artist, playing with much feeling and with infinitely subtle shading of dynamic, while his *Estudio brillante* brings a closing burst of virtuosity. This may be comparatively lightweight music, but it gives enormous pleasure. The recording is quite perfect, made within an ideal ambience, and this is one of the two finest guitar recitals in the catalogue (the other is Julian Bream's electrifying collection of the music of Albéniz and Granados).

TARTINI, Giuseppe (1692-1770)

(i-ii) *Cello Concerto in A*; *Violin Concertos:* (ii-iii) *in D min., D.45*; (iv; ii) *in E min., D.56*; *in G, D.82*; (iv-v) *Violin Sonatas* (for violin & continuo): *in A*; *in G min.*; *in F, Op. 1/1, 10 & 12*; *in C, Op. 2/6*; *in G min. (Devil's Trill)*
Warner Apex 2564 61693-2 (2). (i) Zannerini; (ii) Sol. Ven., Scimone; (iii) Toso; (iv) Amoyal; (v) Farina, Moses

Here is a collection to make the listener understand why Tartini was so admired in his day. Spanning both halves of the eighteenth century as he did, he possesses the lyrical purity of Corelli and Vivaldi with a forward-looking sensibility that is highly expressive. Indeed, his invention is almost romantic at times and there are moments of vision which leave no doubt that he is underrated. The orchestral playing is committed, and the fresh, warm, analogue recording from the 1970s is pleasingly transferred. Tartini's *Sonatas* take their virtuosity for granted; even the *Devil's Trill* does not flaunt its bravura until the finale with its extended trills – considered impossibly difficult in his day. These works call for playing of the greatest technical finesse and musicianship. Pierre Amoyal plays them superbly; he makes no attempt to adapt his style to period-instrument practice. Instead his performances have a sweetness of tone and expressive eloquence to commend them and, though he is forwardly placed, the (unimportant) harpsichord continuo just comes through to give support. The violin is beautifully recorded. A most desirable pair of CDs.

Violin Concertos, Op. 1/1, 4–5 & 12; in C

Ⓑ Hyp. CDH 55334. Wallfisch, Raglan Bar. Players, Kraemer

Tartini's Op. 1 was published in Amsterdam in 1728, but only included Nos. 1, 4 and 5 of the present set. No matter what their provenance, they are all most engaging works in three movements, although the first includes an additional and modestly paced *Fugue à la brève*. The performances here are splendid. Elizabeth Wallfisch may be playing a period instrument, but her timbre is smooth and polished, with no edginess, and the *Adagio* or *Cantabile* slow movements could not be sweeter. She is splendidly athletic in *allegros*, as are her alert accompanying group and they are very well balanced in the recording.

(Unaccompanied) *Violin Sonatas: in A min., B:a3; in G min. (Sonata de Diavolo), B:g5; L'arte del arco, B:f11: 14 Variations on the Gavotte from Corelli's Op. 5/10; Pastorale for violin in scordatura, B:a16*

HM HMU 907213. Manze

Andrew Manze plays those genuinely fiendish trills in the finale of the *Devil's Trill Sonata* quite hair-raisingly. Manze calls the opening *Largo* an 'infernal siciliana' (yet presents it with great poise and refined espressivo), and the central movement (hardly less remarkable) becomes a 'demonic moto perpetuo'. Yet Corelli's gavotte is played with engaging delicacy, the bravura left for the variations. The *A minor Sonata* also includes a set of variations, which again offers an amazing range of musical and technical opportunities, as does the colourful hurdy-gurdy finale of the *Pastorale* which ends so hauntingly. Manze's playing is totally compelling and confirms that the music is 'complete' without a continuo. The recording is very real and immediate.

TAVENER, John (born 1944)

(i) *The Protecting Veil*; (ii–iii) *The Last Sleep of the Virgin*; (iv–v) *Angels*; *Annunciation*; *The Lament of the Mother of God*; (iv; vi) *Hymns of Paradise*; *God is with us*; (iii–iv; vi) *Thunder entered her*

Ⓑ EMI 2-CD 2 37691-2. (i) Isserlis, LSO, Rozhdestvensky; (ii) Chilingirian Qt; (iii) Simcock (handbells); (iv) Winchester Cathedral Ch., Hill; (v) Kingelborg; (vi) Kendall

This EMI Double joins Steven Isserlis's outstanding account of *The Protecting Veil* to a choral collection. David Hill conducts the Winchester Cathedral Choir with David Dunnett at the organ, all very atmospherically recorded. Though some of the longer and more meditative pieces rather outstay their welcome, each one presents a sharply definitive vision, culminating in a magnificent Christmas proclamation, 'God is with us.' 'Quiet and intensely fragile' is Tavener's guide to performances of the bonus item here, *The Last Sleep of the Virgin.*

Ex Maria Virgine (A Christmas Sequence for Choir & Organ)

ⒷⒷ Naxos 8.572168. Clare College, Cambridge, Ch., Timothy Brown; McVinnie or Jacobs (organ)

This makes an ideal CD for those collectors who are unfamiliar with Tavener's music, for it covers the full range of his diverse choral writing, and indeed his imaginative organ effects. The title work, *Ex Maria Virgine*, was dedicated to Prince Charles and Camilla on their marriage. It has ten sections, displaying much choral variety, throbbing to 'Nowell! Out of your sleep', producing a chorale lullaby for 'Sweet was the song', vigorously extolling the 'King of the Angels' in *Ave Rex Angelorum*, then 'Ding-donging merrily on high', before gently 'Rocking' Mary's babe to sleep. *Unto us is born a son* is both peaceful and fiercely triumphant, while *Verbum caro* plangently rises to a glorious close. The other motets here picture the *Nativity*, move radiantly through *O Thou Gentle Light*, closing with a portrayal of the *Angels*, set among delicate organ filigree. Throughout, the singing of Clare College Choir under Timothy Brown rises richly (and falls meditatively) for every occasion, and the two organists, James McVinnie and Simon Thomas Jacobs, make the very most of their many opportunities. Much of this music shows the composer at his most inspired, and the recording, produced by John Rutter in Norwich Cathedral, is outstandingly fine.

Requiem; *Eternal Memory*; *Mahāshakti*

EMI 50999-2 35134-2. Palmer, Knight, Thomas, Kennedy, RLPO & Ch, Petrenko

John Tavener's second setting of the *Requiem*, commissioned to celebrate Liverpool as the European City of Culture in 2008, is the more moving when the composer had been told he was under sentence of death through persistent ill-health. He explains his theme, quoting the idea, 'Our glory lies where we cease to exist,' thinking to write about the after-life. The result is a characteristic example of Tavener's 'spiritual minimalism', with evocative choruses and repeated mantras for the soprano in ostinato above the choir. Various movements echo those in the traditional *Requiem*, the *Kyrie* following the opening-movement *Primordial White Light* and *Kali's Dance* which is the equivalent to the traditional *Dies irae* in its bite. The closing movement, *Ananda*, rounds the work off in a moving crescendo of choral sound, finally fading to nothing.

Mahāshakti is for solo violin, tam-tam and strings and is also highly evocative in its celebration of celestial feminine energy; and *Eternal Memory* is a deep meditation on the memory of death, including a brisk passage for solo strings. Excellent sound, though the chorus could be a little closer. Performances otherwise are first rate from soloists, chorus and orchestra under the inspired direction of Vasily Petrenko.

TAVERNER, John (c. 1495–1545)

Missa Corona spinea. Motets: Gaude plurium; In pace
Ⓑ Hyp. Helios CDH 55051. The Sixteen, Christophers

The Sixteen, using professional singers (and secure female trebles), are magnificent and they sing gloriously throughout. Taverner's inspiration is consistent and his flowing melismas are radiantly realized, with fine support from the lower voices; indeed, the balance and blend are nigh on perfect. The two motets are no less beautifully sung, and the recording, made in St Jude's Church, Hampstead, is outstanding both in clarity and in its perfectly judged ambience. A superb disc and an astonishing bargain.

Mass: The Western Wynde; Alleluia, Veni, electa mea; O splendor gloria; Te Deum
Ⓑ Hyp. Helios CDH 55056. The Sixteen, Christophers

Western Wynde Mass is beautifully sung and recorded by Harry Christophers' Sixteen in what must be regarded as an ideally paced and proportioned performance. But what makes this inexpensive Helios reissue doubly attractive is the collection of other works included. *O splendor gloria* carries the exulted mood inherent in its title (referring to Christ and the Trinity) and the *Alleluia* is equally jubilant. Most remarkable and individual of all is the masterly five-part *Te Deum*, a profoundly poignant setting, harmonically and polyphonically, even richer than the *Mass*, and using those momentary shafts of dissonance that can make music of this period sound so forward-looking. The recording is superb and this CD is obviously the place to start for those wanting to explore this excellent Helios series.

TCHAIKOVSKY, Peter (1840–93)

(i) Andante cantabile; (i–ii) Violin Concerto. Symphonies: (i) 4; (iii) 5
DG DVD 073 4511. (i) NYPO; (ii) Belkin; (iii) Boston SO; Bernstein

This superb collection not only shows Bernstein at his most inspired, communicating his own great pleasure in the music, but also his ability to implant his own charismatic personality on *any* orchestra. Here there is virtually no difference between the electrifying results in Boston and New York. For instance, although the interpretations of the two symphonies are different, the *Fourth* relatively straightforward, the *Fifth* with Bernstein responding literally to Tchaikovky's marking, 'con alcuna licenza', the rich sweep of string-tone is common to each venue, but especially so in the Boston *Fifth*, where the second subject of the first movement and the glorious climax of the *Andante cantabile* are both almost overwhelming. Each work, too, has an electrifying coda, the kind that sends the audience and orchestra home thrilled and satisfied in equal measure, feeling again what wonderful symphonies these are, even if Tchaikovsky himself had nagging doubts about the uninhibited splendour of the closing peroration of the *Fifth*. Koussevitzky in Boston had felt his mission with Tchaikovsky was 'to open the gate of heaven and let the people experience ecstasy', and Bernstein followed his mentor's 'theme song'.

Capriccio italien, Op. 45; 1812 Overture, Op. 49; Fate, Op. 77; Festival Overture on the Danish National Anthem, Op. 15; Francesca da Rimini, Op. 32; Hamlet, Op. 67a; Manfred Symphony, Op. 58; Marche slave, Op. 31; Overture in F; Romeo and Juliet (Fantasy Overture); The Tempest, Op. 18; The Voyevoda, Op. 78.
DG Trio 477 053-2 (3). Russian Nat. O, Pletnev

Pletnev has a quite special feeling for Tchaikovsky's music, gauging its highly charged emotional content and dramatic flair to perfection, and never losing sight of the disciplined mind which oversaw the musical design. There is no shortage of great performances of *Romeo and Juliet* and *Francesca da Rimini*, and Pletnev's account with his Russian National Orchestra certainly ranks among them. But the special value of this set is that it offers rarities like *The Voyevoda* and the *F major Overture* in performances which are unlikely to be bettered for a very long time. When it first appeared, we placed his *Manfred* among the finest in the catalogue, and that judgement still holds. An essential purchase, particularly at so competitive a price.

Capriccio italien, Op. 45
RCA (ADD) 09026 63302-2. RCA Victor SO, Kondrashin – **KABALEVSKY**: *The Comedians: Suite.* **KHACHATURIAN**: *Masquerade Suite.* **RIMSKY-KORSAKOV**: *Capriccio espagnol*

Kondrashin's 1958 recording of Tchaikovsky's *Capriccio italien* has never been surpassed. The arresting opening still surprises by its impact, the brass fanfares – first trumpets, then horns, then full tutti – sonically riveting. The music is alive in every bar and a model of careful preparation, with the composer's dynamic markings meticulously terraced. Kondrashin's pacing throughout is absolutely right and the closing section is highly exhilarating. This is a stereo demonstration disc if ever there was one. And the couplings are pretty good too.

(i) *Piano Concertos 1 in B flat min., Op. 23; 2 in G, Op. 44* (with two additional recordings of *Andante*; ed. Siloti & ed. Hough); *3 in E flat, Op. 75; Concert Fantasia in G, Op. 56.* (Piano solo) *None but the lonely heart, Op. 6/6; Solitude, Op. 73/6*
Hyp. CDA 67711/2. Hough; (i) Minnesota O, Vänskä

This set is undoubtedly a key Tchaikovsky issue, and it includes one of the finest, most imaginative accounts of the great *B flat minor Concerto* ever put on record. Stephen Hough is not only a commanding soloist, playing with a sensitive balance of virtuosity and lyrical warmth, but time and again both he and the Minnesota Orchestra under Osmo Vänskä bring out magical detail in Tchaikovsky's score which reveals the work as far more than a barnstorming popular warhorse. After an arresting opening from the horns, the main theme of the *Allegro con spirito* is played with unexpectedly rhythmic subtlety and lift, while the delicacy of the touching string *pianissimos* in the 'Romeo and Juliet' allusion in the second subject of the first movement is matched by Hough's searching originality in the long cadenza, which is made an integral part of the recapitulation. The *Andantino semplice* is exquisitely delicate and then scintillating, with delectable bravura, and the closing climax of the brilliant finale carries all before it. The piano dominates the proceedings and the only minor criticism here lies in the balance of the strings, which might have been placed more forwardly, but their playing does not lack lyrical intensity.

The performers also relish the original structure of the *Concert Fantasia*, opening with its colourful Russian dance and with a large-scale cadenza taking the place of the development, giving an opportunity for considerable bravura from the soloist, which Stephen Hough tackles with much élan. Tchaikovsky holds back his main lyrical theme for the second movement, *Contrastes*, which is played very tenderly, and then an abundance of virtuosity from all concerned returns to finish the piece off spectacularly. This work was justly popular in the composer's lifetime. Perhaps this recording will encourage its return to the repertoire.

The *Second Concerto* has seldom been successful, either on record or in the concert hall. In the best-known, early, mono recording on DG, by Cherkassky, the first movement was taken at a phlegmatic four-in-a-bar tempo and the result was leaden. Vänskä does not make this mistake and presents the music with thrilling vitality and flair, with the secondary theme providing sensitive contrast. The slow movement has a truly memorable main theme, which Hough phrases beautifully, and then the scoring turns into chamber music with the piano joined by solo violin and cello.

At early performances the work was 'edited' by Siloti, who cut the *Andante* by over six minutes in all. Here we have what Tchaikovsky wrote originally: the complete movement with its variations on the main theme plays for nearly 14 minutes, and not a minute too long in such a sensitive performance. The finale, with its catchy rondo theme, then explodes into sparkling exuberance, to close the performance with rumbustious vitality.

The single-movement *Third Concerto* began life as a symphony but, with only the first movement completed, Tchaikovsky resourcefully then turned it into a concerto, using three themes, including a catchy toccata-like dance motif and a calmer lyrical tune, plus a long cadenza. There is plenty of bravura writing for the pianist, and the work undoubtedly has its moments when as well played as it is here; but, although undoubtedly enjoyable, it is overall less successful than the *Concert Fantasia*. As a bonus Stephen Hough has arranged two of Tchaikovsky's songs, each full of characteristic Russian melancholy, to make a pair of appealing encores.

(i) *Violin Concerto in D, Op. 35*; *Sérénade mélancolique*; *Valse-Scherzo*; (ii) *Souvenir d'un lieu cher*

Pentatone SACD PTC 5186 095. Fischer; (i) Russian Nat. O, Kreizberg; (ii) Kreizberg (piano)

There are almost countless recordings of this lovely concerto and one could recommend many of them: Repin, Vengerov, Chung, Bell, Milstein and, of course, Heifetz. But we have chosen Julia Fischer as she offers the ideal coupling of the *Sérénade mélancolique*, *Valse-Scherzo* and the *Souvenir d'un lieu cher*, for this includes the 'Méditation', the composer's first idea of a slow movement for the concerto, later replaced by the *Canzonetta*. It comes here with the original piano accompaniment, played by the conductor. Moreover Fischer is characterful in every phrase she plays, with sparkle and a sense of fantasy in virtuoso passages and with an inner intensity when playing the intimate lyrical sections. She is greatly helped by the conducting of Yakov Kreizberg with the Russian National Orchestra which is both taut and sympathetic, with an ideal balance for the soloist, allowing the widest range of dynamic, and the SACD sound is impressively spacious and realistic.

(i) *1812 Overture*. *Capriccio italien*

Ⓜ Decca (ADD) 475 8508. (i) Bronze French cannon, bells of Laura Spelman Rockefeller Memorial Carillon, Riverside Church, New York City; Minneapolis SO, Dorati (with separate descriptive commentary by Deems Taylor) – **BEETHOVEN**: *Wellington's Victory*

Just as in our listing of this famous Mercury record (now on Decca's 'Originals') we have placed *1812* first, so in the credits the cannon and the glorious sounds of the Laura Spelman Carillon take precedence, for in the riveting climax of Tchaikovsky's most famous work the effects completely upstage the orchestra. On this remastered CD the balance is managed spectacularly, with the 'shots' perfectly timed, while the Minneapolis orchestra are clearly enjoying themselves, both in *1812* and in the brilliant account of *Capriccio italien*. Deems Taylor provides an avuncular commentary on the technical background to the original recording.

Hamlet (Fantasy Overture), Op. 67a; *Romeo and Juliet (Fantasy Overture)*; *The Tempest (Symphonic Fantasy)*

DG 477 9355. Simón Bolívar SO of Venezuela, Dudamel

The Simón Bolívar Orchestra of Venezuela is founded on the government's decision to provide classical music at the centre of the syllabus of every school in the country. Each has its own orchestra and the very best players have a chance to compete to play with the country's central orchestra as recorded here. Thus an almost unbelievably high standard of musical and technical excellence has been achieved, mainly through the direction of its young maestro, Gustavo Dudamel. This is their astonishing recording début, one of the finest Tchaikovsky discs in the catalogue.

Dudamel really understands the composer, and especially the structure of his works, the control of their melodic lines, their flexibility and the way each section relates to what follows. Moreover, he conducts with complete spontaneity and encourages his young players to revel in the music's passion, which they do grippingly. *Hamlet,* darkly atmospheric from the very opening, is played with resonant dramatic power and feeling, superseding Stokowski's famous Everest recording in every respect. *Romeo and Juliet* is treated like a symphonic poem, beginning and ending poignantly with Friar Laurence's music and flaring into the spectacular fight sequences between the two opposing families. The introduction of the great love theme is perfectly timed, and when it reaches its climax the strings play as if their very lives depended on it. The coda creates a true sense of despair and the closing crashing chords are perfectly managed.

The performance of *The Tempest,* an early work (1873), hitherto underestimated and neglected, springs to life with the beautifully played opening horn theme picturing the magic island, followed by a very Russian main theme, soon expanded by the brass. But the work's atmosphere is hauntingly captured, with Caliban and Ariel making striking appearances and the lovers' music infinitely touching and tender. Again, the passion of the playing sweeps the music along thrillingly to make a great climax, but the piece ends gently and nostalgically (introducing the horn theme), as it began. The recording is splendidly colourful and full-blooded and this memorable triptych represents one of the finest Tchaikovsky issues for many years.

Manfred Symphony; The Voyevoda (symphonic poem)
ⓑ Naxos 8.570568. RLPO, Petrenko

We first heard Tchaikovsky's *Manfred Symphony* in the 1950s, conducted by Kletzki, live in Preston, Lancashire. But he offered only the first movement and the work (written in 1885, between the *4th* and *5th Symphonies*) has continued to remain something of a Cinderella in the concert hall. However, it has received several fine recordings, including those by Jansons, Ashkenazy and Pletnev, and even one by Toscanini, though severely truncated. Now comes a clear first choice from Vasily Petrenko and the Royal Liverpool Philharmonic which has received the finest recording of all, and which we have come increasingly to admire since it appeared in 2009. Throughout, Petrenko creates electrifying tension and achieves striking refinement of detail, while the orchestra clearly responds to his inspirational, flexibly romantic, and very Russian style.

The opening movement has great character, with the Manfred theme powerfully characterized. The first appearance of Astarte, Manfred's beloved, brings ravishingly delicate string-playing, and the coda where the horns are instructed by Tchaikovsky to (lift up their instruments and) play *pavillons en l'air* is thrilling. But it is in the central movements that the performance rises to the greatest lyrical heights. The spray of the Waterfall Scherzo glitters iridescently and the lovely melting string melody representing the Alpine Fairy has never sounded more luscious. Similarly, the pastoral *Andante*, which can produce longueurs, flows with tenderness and warmth combined, Tchaikovsky's melodic inspiration never flagging. The spectacular finale (with its rivetingly powerful organ entry) pictures the subterranean hall of Arimanes in the form of a globe of fire surrounded by spirits, with Nemesis and the Destinies. For the summoning of the spirit of Astarte, who announces Manfred's coming death, Petrenko creates a moving rallentando as Manfred's soul (in Byron's poem) 'hath ta'en its earthless flight; / Whither? I dread to think – but he is gone'.

The Voyevoda, written in 1891, is a much less successful work. Tchaikovsky himself destroyed the score after its first performance, but it was later reconstructed from the orchestral parts. It tells of a provincial governor who surprises his wife *in flagrante delicto* with her lover and instructs his servant to shoot her. In error the servant shoots his master instead, bringing a sudden end to the music. The work has characteristic moments and, though no masterpiece, when played as convincingly as it is here makes a fascinating bonus for the outstanding performance of *Manfred*.

The Nutcracker (ballet: complete)
EMI 6 31621-2 (2). BPO, Rattle

The Nutcracker (ballet: complete); *Suites 3 in G; 4 in G (Mozartiana)*
Ⓜ Australian Decca Eloquence 480 0557 (2). SRO, Ansermet

Ansermet's 1958 *Nutcracker* is simply one of the best performances of this score committed to disc. This was undoubtedly one of the finest things Ansermet did in the early days of stereo, and the Decca recording still sounds remarkably rich and vivid, with a freshness and sparkle to match the composer's approach. Ansermet's feeling for orchestral colour and detail tells throughout, and the short dances of Act II have much piquancy of characterization. Indeed, the whole performance feels as magical as the story itself, and all admirers of this score (one of the composer's finest) should acquire this release. The two very appealing *Suites* which fill up the second disc are not quite in this league of performance but they are affectionately played and enjoyable, if not ideally polished. Tchaikovsky wrote *Mozartiana* to bring 'little-known Mozart pieces' before the public. They are much better known now; if Tchaikovsky's orchestration is a little anachronistic, it has a certain charm. The *Third Suite* has a warmly moulded Tchaikovskian *Elégie* as its slow movement and includes a superb set of variations as its finale, one of the composer's least-known masterpieces, characteristically inventive. There is rich use of orchestral colour throughout, and a superb polacca for its finale, introduced with characteristic Tchaikovskian sleight-of-hand.

In terms of finesse and sheer beauty of texture the Berlin Philarmonic

Orchestra is in a different league from the Suisse Romande group. Rattle's performance of Tchaikovsky's wonderful score is fully worthy of it, in its detail, atmosphere and vividness, with some wonderful solo contributions from the BPO woodwind, and with the strings luscious in the *Waltz of the Flowers*. The EMI recording is excellent too, but there is an extra magic in Ansermet's performance, and the Decca sound was ahead of its time, and fully worthy of it. Moreover, the Decca set costs very much less and has highly attractive couplings. We have enjoyed it greatly since it first appeared and continue to do so.

The Nutcracker; *Sleeping Beauty*; *Swan Lake* (ballets: complete)
Ⓑ Decca (ADD) 460 411-2 (6). Nat. PO, Bonynge

Tchaikovsky's three great ballets are undisputed masterpieces of the genre – the only question for debate is, which of the three is the greatest. The answer, one is tempted to say, is whichever one is listening to at the time, for each is imbued with more inspiration and magic than most composers achieve in a lifetime. Richard Bonynge conducted all three in the 1970s and they remain firm recommendations, especially as they are now all available in an attractive bargain box set. In *The Nutcracker*, Bonynge's approach is highly sympathetic and he secures brilliant playing from the National Philharmonic. Though it might be said that the opening is a little literal and lacking in a bit of atmosphere, from the *Transformation Scene* onwards the playing catches fire, and the latter part of the ballet finds the conductor on top form, with all the Characteristic Dances performed with style and brilliance. *Swan Lake* receives a strong and vigorous performance with the forward impulse of the music-making immediately striking. Decca have matched the interpretation with a somewhat dry acoustic, producing a leonine string-tone, though the remastering has increased the feeling of sumptuousness. The brightly lit sound-picture provides robust detail in place of glamour, but that goes with Bonynge's theatrical interpretation. The brass sounds are open and vibrant, and the 'fairy castle' fanfares have here more of the atmosphere of a medieval tournament. There is a consistent freshness in this performance and many of the spectacular moments are thrilling. Again, in *The Sleeping Beauty* one is struck by Bonynge's rhythmical pointing, which is always characterful. If the upper strings still lack sumptuousness, the overall sound is excellent by any standards. Bonynge is especially good at the close of Act II when, after the magical *Panorama*, the Princess is awakened. There is a frisson of tension here and the atmosphere is most evocative. As at the end of *Swan Lake*, the finale of *Sleeping Beauty* and the 'Apothéose' are almost overwhelming in impact.

Orchestral Suite 3 in G, Op. 55
Pentatone SACD PTC 5186 061. Russian Nat. O, Jurowski - **STRAVINSKY**: *Le Baiser de la fée*

Tchaikovsky's *Third Orchestral Suite* is the most inspired of the four, and Vladimir Jurowski brings out the surging lyricism of all four movements. So the touching *Elégie* is warmly moulded, with phrasing that seems totally idiomatic. The rhythmic lightness of the second movement's *Waltz* leads into a dazzling account of the third-movement Scherzo, taken at a genuine *presto*, yet with no feeling of breathlessness. But the work's climax is the closing set of variations on a particularly attractive theme. When Tchaikovsky was in England to receive his honorary degree at Cambridge University (where he met and befriended Grieg) his skill with variations was singled out among his many talents. The attractive breadth of structural, yet derived, ideas, and the felicitous changes of orchestral colour show him at his most inspired, leading to a thrilling build-up to the polacca climax at the conclusion. Exceptionally vivid sound, recorded by Pentatone's Dutch engineers in Moscow, spectacular in surround sound.

Swan Lake (highlights)
Ⓜ Australian Decca Eloquence (ADD) 442 9032. Concg. O, Fistoulari

This is a key recording, much admired in the early stereo era. Fistoulari was a great conductor of ballet music, and we have long admired this 1960 collection of highlights from *Swan Lake* which at the time of its first issue was revelatory. It is a real collector's item and this is its CD début. It is essentially a relaxed reading, but the Concertgebouw Orchestra plays superbly and there is a wonderful sense of the theatre, combined with spontaneous music-making. For its date the recording is outstanding, too. At a little over 46 minutes' playing time, this is very much a case of quality over quantity.

Symphonies 1–6; Capriccio italien; Manfred Symphony
Ⓑ Chan. 10392 (6). Oslo PO, Jansons

Jansons's Tchaikovsky series, which includes *Manfred*, is self-recommending. The full romantic power of the music is consistently conveyed and, above all, the music-making is urgently spontaneous throughout, with the Oslo Philharmonic Orchestra always committed and fresh, helped by the richly atmospheric sound. If you want all six symphonies, this is a supreme bargain. Of course the complete Karajan set, made in the 1970s, displays the same superlative qualities we expect from this combination and is hardly less illuminating (DG 429 679-2). But Karajan does not include *Manfred* and the Jansons set is not displaced.

Symphonies 4–6 (DVD version)
DG Unitel DVD 073 4384. BPO, Karajan

Symphonies 4–5 (DVD version)
Sony DVD 888579849. VPO, Karajan

The *Fourth* and *Fifth* were recorded by Sony in 1984 at the Grossesaal of the Musikverein with the Vienna Philharmonic at a time when Karajan's relationship with the Berlin Philharmonic was under some strain. The *Fourth* is one of the most commanding and compelling accounts of this great work we have heard, and one's attention is riveted throughout. Karajan's famous 1950s account of the *Fourth* with the Philharmonia Orchestra bore witness to his special relationship with this music, and this makes an equally strong impression. Excellent video presentation enhances its impact.

The alternative performances on DG were made in 1973 and show this extraordinary partnership at their most characteristic. None of Karajan's Tchaikovsky performances was routine; and these recordings, made at the Philharmonie, have exemplary power and feeling. The Sony versions have marginally more focused camerawork, but these earlier versions, which Karajan himself oversaw in production, are hardly less satisfying.

Symphonies (i) *4*; (ii) *5*; (iii) *6 (Pathétique)* (CD versions); (i) *Serenade for Strings (Waltz and Finale* only)

Ⓑ Andromeda ANDRCD 9107 (2). (i) VPO; (ii) O Sinfonica di Torino della RAI; (iii) BPO; all cond. Furtwängler

The recordings made between 1950 and 1952, this fascinating historic Furtwängler box is a curiosity well worth investigating. The Sackville-West/Desmond Shawe-Taylor *Record Guide* thought that in No. 4 Furtwängler's conducting 'lacks the fire he once brought to Tchaikovsky's symphonies', although they thought the strings 'remarkably fine'. Certainly we find the climax of the first movement very impressive, although the finale, brilliantly played, lacks the last degree of free-flowing adrenalin.

The *Fifth*, however (deriving from acetates), is fully acceptable, with a superbly passionate slow movement. It was recorded live in Turin in 1951 and the inexperienced Italian audience provide unwanted clapping in the brief silence before the work's final peroration. (This reminds us of a true story related in Sir Henry Wood's autobiography, when at a Prom performance, at that same moment in the last movement he heard two ladies in the front row share the comment 'We always fry ours in dripping'!)

The Berlin Philharmonic are on top form in the *Pathétique* (of which Furtwängler was a master) and this is comparable with his 1938 performance included in the conductor's 21-disc EMI anthology (see above), although the present recording does not quite match the earlier one.

The excerpts from the *String Serenade* used to be available on a single HMV 78 disc, once treasured by I.M., and here, as in the other works, the transfers are generally well managed, although the violin timbre is inclined to be shrill. But for the conductor's admirers this will be an indispensable set.

Variations on a Rococo Theme for Cello & Orchestra, Op. 33

DG (ADD) 447 413-2. Rostropovich, BPO, Karajan - **DVOŘÁK**: *Cello Concerto*

Rostropovich uses the published score rather than the original version which more accurately reflects the composer's intentions. But this account, with Karajan's glowing support, is so superbly structured in its control of emotional light and shade that one is readily convinced that this is the work Tchaikovsky conceived. The recording (made in the Jesus-Christus Kirche) is beautifully balanced and is surely one of the most perfect examples of DG's analogue techniques.

Eugene Onegin (complete)

Decca (ADD) 417 413-2 (2). Kubiak, Weikl, Burrows, Reynolds, Ghiaurov, Hamari, Sénéchal, Alldis Ch., ROHCG O, Solti

Solti, characteristically crisp in attack, has plainly warmed to the score of Tchaikovsky's colourful opera, allowing his singers free rein in rallentando and rubato to a degree one may not expect of him. The Tatiana of Teresa Kubiak is most moving – rather mature sounding for the ingénue of Act I, but with her golden, vibrant voice rising most impressively to the final confrontation of Act III. The Onegin of Bernd Weikl may have too little variety of tone, but again this is firm singing that yet has authentic Slavonic tinges. The rest of the cast is excellent, with Stuart Burrows as Lensky giving one of his finest performances on record. Here, for the first time, the full range of expression in this most atmospheric of operas is superbly caught, with the Decca CDs vividly capturing every subtlety, including the off-stage effects. For those wishing to see this opera on DVD, there is Graham Vick's much-acclaimed Glyndebourne production from 1994. Not only is the production convincing, but the cast is too. However, it is Elena Prokina's magnificent portrayal of Tatiana that is the crowning glory of this release. The video direction is admirably discreet, with no intrusive camerawork and with the eye being directed where one feels it ought to be (Warner DVD 0630 14014-2).

Iolanta (complete, CD version)

Melodiya MEL CD 10 01697 (2). Sorokina, Atlantov, Nesterenko, Mazurok, Bolshoi Theatre Ch. & SO, Ermler

About two years before this book went to print we had the good fortune to see a first-rate production of this opera at the London Guildhall School of Music and discovered that it is a small-scale masterpiece. It tells of Iolanta, daughter of King René, who is blind from birth but who, by her father's orders, lives in ignorance of her affliction. Her doctor says a cure is possible, but only if she is told of her blindness and is eager to be cured. But the King refuses to take this course. Two knights arrive at the palace, Robert and Vaudémont. Robert was betrothed to Iolanta during his childhood, but he has not seen her and does not know that she is blind. In any case he wants to marry the Countess of Lotharingia. Because of some confusion over a red-and-white rose, Vaudémont then discovers Iolanta's secret and, deeply touched, professes his love for her. The king is furious at his discovery, but the path is set for Iolanta, with the help of the doctor, and through her own determination to regain her sight, to join her new lover and husband. All ends happily.

Tchaikovsky was captivated by the story; his brother, Modest, wrote the libretto and the opera was first performed in 1892. Tchaikovsky's music is delightful, full of melody and even with a reminder of Tatiana in the early music for the heroine. The performance here is understandably very Russian, with Tamara Sorokina a characterful Iolanta, if somewhat shrill in her upper range. However, Vladimir Atlantov is a strong, passionate Vaudémont with a fine tenor voice, and Evgeny Nesterenko a commanding King René. The choral and orchestral support under Mark Ermler is excellent, and the opera's closing scene, when Iolanta first sees light, is truly memorable, for Tchaikovsky, as always, identified with his heroine's plight. The 1976 recording is faithful and this is a delightful surprise that will give much pleasure. It is well worth seeking out as a Russian import. The set is attractively packaged, although, alas, without a translation.

Queen of Spades (*Pique Dame*) (complete, DVD version)

Decca DVD 070 434-9. Grigorian, Gulegina, Leiferkus, Gergalov, Filatova, Borodina, Kirov Op. Ch. & O, Gergiev (Producer: Yuri Temirkanov; V/D: Brian Large)

Pushkin's dark story of a gambler's growing obsession with discovering the secret that will bring him riches is taut and concentrated. It unfolds with gripping psychological intensity, all the more powerful for its understatement, Though Modest Tchaikovsky's libretto differs in many respects from Pushkin's story.

Dating from 1992, the Philips DVD, with the conductor Valery Gergiev looking very young, is a live recording of the Kirov Company's grandly traditional production. It is handsome to look at and is very well staged. Yuri Temirkanov (Gergiev's predecessor at the Kirov) produces and does not lose sight of the Rococo component in this wonderful opera. Yet it is a straightforward and clean-cut presentation, deftly using massive choruses to match the opulent costumes and scenery, and nearly all the cast is first rate. The cast differs slightly from the CD performance, though that too is thoroughly recommendable (Ph. 438 141-2 (3)).

TELEMANN, Georg (1681–1767)

Concertos: for 2 Corni da caccia in F, TWV 52:F3; for Violin & 3 Corni di caccia in D, TWV 54:D2. Overtures: for 2 Corni di caccia in D, TWV 55:D17; for 2 Corni di caccia & 2 Oboes in F, TWV 55:F3

MDG 605 1045-2. Deutsch Natural Horn Soloists, New Düsseldorf Hofmusik

The Deutsch Natural Horn Soloists are a superb group. They play here expertly, using hand horns without valves and demonstrating the most thrilling bravura, whether in partnership with oboes, where the interplay of the *Réjouissance* in the *F major Overture* (or *Suite*) is a real hit number, or in the *Concerto in F*, which reminds one a little of Handel's *Water Music*. In the *Concerto* scored for three horns, the solo violin in the *Grave* slow movement gives expressive contrast before sharing the exuberant finale. With excellent recording, this is outstanding in every way, but not to be played all in one go!

Concertos, Overtures: (i) *5 Concertos for 2 Flutes, with Lute, Bassoon & Strings* (Cap. 10 284); (ii) *Chamber Concerto for Alto Recorder in G min., TWV 43:G3*; (iii) *Double Concerto in E min. for Recorder & Flute*; (iv) *Concerto for 3 Trumpets & 2 Oboes in D*; (ii) *Sonata in A for Recorder, 2 Scordato Violins & Continuo, TWV 43:A7*; (v) *Tafelmusik II: Trio in E min. for Recorder, Oboe & Continuo* (Cap. 49 431); (vi) *Overtures (Suites): in C, TWV 55:C3 (Hamburg Ebb and Flow) & C6*; *Overture in E min., TWV 55:C5* (Cap. 10 625); *Overtures: in D* (connected with a *Tragicomical Suite*); *in F (Alster Echo), TWV 55:F11*; *in D, TWV 55:D15* (Cap. 49 428); (vii) *Overtures (Suites): in D, TWV D18*; *TWV 55:D6 & D7*; *in F* (Cap. 49 429).

Cap. 49 426 (5). (i) Dresden Bar. Soloists, Haupt; (ii) Huntgeburth, Berlin Bar. Company; (iii) Höller, Hünteler, Capella Colonsiensis, G. Fischer; (iv) Friedrich & soloists, Budapest Strings; (v) Passin, Gütz, Leipzig Bach Coll.; (vi) Capella Colonsiensis, Linde; (vii) Deutsch Bach Soloists, Winschermann

If you want a representative collection of Telemann at his best, this Capriccio box (with the five CDs in a slip case) is hard to better. The *Concertos* for a pair of flutes are continually inventive, and the two compilations of miscellaneous concertos and chamber music offer plenty of variety, not only in the music but also in the performances, although all are authentic in the best possible way. The *Suites* (*Overtures*) are all among the composer's best, including the two most famous, both pictorial or progammatic, the *Alster Echo* and the *Hamburg Water Music*. The performances and recordings are excellent, as is the documentation. As far as we know, the discs are not currently available separately.

Flute Concertos in D, TWV:51:D2; in G, TWV:51:G2; Concerto for 2 Flutes, Violone in A min., TWV:53:a; Concerto for Flute, Oboe d'amore & Viola d'amore in E, TWV:53:E; Tafelmusik: Concerto for Flute & Violin in A, TWV:53:A2

Ⓜ EMI 5 03435-2. Pahud, Berlin Bar. Soloists, Kussmaul

An enchanting disc. Everything Emmanuel Pahud plays seems to turn to gold, and he has admirable support from his solo colleagues (including Albrecht Meyer (oboe d'amore) and Wolfram Christ (viola d'amore)). Throughout allegros are wonderfully nimble and light-hearted. The Berlin Baroque Soloists, directed by Rainer Kussmaul, accompany with wonderful finesse and warmth, and the recording is in the demonstration bracket.

Alster (Overture) Suite; La Bouffonne Suite; Triple Horn Concerto in D; Grillen-Symphonie

Chan. 0547. Coll. Mus. 90, Standage

The *Triple Horn Concerto* opens the programme with the hand-horns rasping boisterously. Then comes *La Bouffonne Suite*, with its elegant *Loure* and the extremely fetching *Rigaudon*, while the work ends with a touchingly delicate *Pastourelle*, beautifully played here. The *Grillen-Symphonie* ('cricket symphony') brings a piquant dialogue between upper wind and double-basses in the first movement, while the second has unexpected accents and lives up to its name *Tändelnd* ('flirtatious'). The horns (four of them) re-enter ambitiously at the colourful *Overture* of the *Alster Suite*, add to the fun in the *Echo* movement and help to simulate the Hamburg glockenspiel that follows. The entry of the Alster Shepherds brings a piquant drone effect, but best of all is the wailing *Concerto of Frogs and Crows*, with drooping bleats from the oboe and then the principal horn. Standage and his group make the very most of Telemann's remarkable orchestral palette and play with great vitality as well as finesse.

(i) *Viola Concerto in G*; (ii) *Suite in A min. for Recorder & Strings*; *Tafelmusik*, Part 2: (iii) *Triple Violin Concerto in F*; Part 3: (iv) *Double Horn Concerto in E flat*

ⓑⓑ Naxos 8.550156. (i) Kyselak; (ii) Stivín; (iii) Hoelblingova, Hoelbling, Jablokov; (iv) Z. & B. Tylšar; Capella Istropolitana, Edlinger

It is difficult to conceive of a better Telemann programme for anyone encountering this versatile composer for the first time and coming fresh to this repertoire, having bought the inexpensive Naxos CD on impulse. Ladislav Kyselak is a fine violist and is thoroughly at home in Telemann's splendid four-movement *Concerto*; Jiři Stivín is an equally personable recorder soloist in the masterly *Suite in A minor*; his decoration is a special joy. The *Triple Violin Concerto* with its memorable *Vivace* finale and the *Double Horn Concerto* also show the finesse which these musicians readily display. Richard Edlinger provides polished and alert accompaniments throughout. The digital sound is first class.

Tafelmusik (Productions 1–3; complete)

ⓑ DG 477 8714 (4). Col. Mus. Ant., Goebel

This is one of the most rewarding of all Telemann recordings. The playing of the Cologne Musica Antiqua is distinguished by dazzling virtuosity and unanimity of ensemble and musical thinking. They also have the advantage of very vivid and fresh recording quality; the balance is close and present without being too forward, and there is a pleasing acoustic ambience. At its bargain price this is very enticing indeed.

Kapitänsmusik, 1724

CPO SACD 777 176-2. Podkoscielna, Post, Vieweg, Abele, Telemannisches Coll. Michaelstein, Rémy

In Hamburg, Telemann often had to compose celebratory occasional pieces called *Kapitänsmusik*, consisting of an oratorio and serenata. The one on this CD was first performed in 1724 and this is the first time it has been performed complete since that time. The oratorio part has sacred texts, while the serenata part has secular texts, but both find the composer providing some extraordinarily good music. This music shows Telemann at his most flamboyantly creative, with some brilliantly florid, virtuosic writing, performed with comparable vigour by the soloists and the orchestra. The lively arias in both the oratorio and serenata are very exciting, and the opening of the serenata with its minor-keyed woodwinds is deliciously piquant and memorable, as is the aria which follows. One marvels time and time again at Telemann's inventive orchestration, especially in his use of woodwind colouring, and this whole CD is one of flamboyant invigoration. Superbly recorded in SACD surround sound, warm yet sharply vivid. Full texts and translations are provided.

THOMAS, Ambroise (1811–96)

Mignon (complete)
Sony (ADD) SM3K 34590 (3). Horne, Vanzo, Welting, Zaccaria, Von Stade, Méloni,
   Battedou, Hudson, Ambrosian Op. Ch., Philh. O, Almeida

Thomas's once-popular adaptation of Goethe has many vocal plums, and here a very full account of the score is given, with virtually all the alternatives that the composer devised for productions after the first, not least one at Drury Lane in London, where recitatives were used (as here) instead of spoken dialogue; an extra aria was given to the soubrette Philine and other arias were expanded. The role of Frédéric was given to a mezzo-soprano instead of a tenor, and here the appropriately named Frederica von Stade is superb in that role, making one rather regret that she was not chosen as the heroine. However, Marilyn Horne is in fine voice and sings with great character and flair, even if she hardly sounds the frail figure of the ideal Mignon. Nonetheless, with Alain Vanzo a sensitive Wilhelm, Ruth Welting a charming Philine and colourful conducting from Almeida, this is an essential set for lovers of French opera. The 1977 recording has a pleasingly warm ambience and the voices are naturally caught in the present transfer.

TIPPETT, Michael (1905–98)

(i) *Concerto for Double String Orchestra*; (ii) *Fanfare for Brass*;
(i) *Fantasia Concertante on a Theme of Corelli*; *Little Music for String Orchestra*; (iii) *Suite in D for the Birthday of Prince Charles*
Ⓜ Australian Decca Eloquence (ADD) 476 7960. (i) ASMF, Marriner; (ii) Philip Jones Brass
   Ens.; (iii) LSO, Colin Davis

A splendid Tippett anthology and an ideal introduction to this composer. Beginning with the striking *Fanfare for Brass*, it moves on to the charming *Suite for the Birthday of Prince Charles*, full of attractive ideas and a distinct 'Robin Hood' atmosphere – the subject of the composer's early folksong opera, parts of which were used in the score. Next comes Marriner's classic Argo recording, featuring some of Tippett's most inspired and approachable music. On any count, the *Concerto for Double String Orchestra* is one of the most beautiful works for strings written in the twentieth century. The *Corelli Fantasia* is a similarly sumptuous work, and the *Little Music* is very appealing too. Superb 1970s recordings and altogether an outstanding compilation.

'Tippett Collection': (i) *Concerto for Orchestra*; (ii) *Concerto for Double String Orchestra*; (ii–iii) *Triple Concerto for Violin, Viola, Cello & Orchestra*; (i) *Fantasia Concertante on a Theme of Corelli*; (iv) *Fanfare for Brass*; (i) *Little Music for Strings*; (v) *Suite for the Birthday of Prince Charles*; *Symphonies:* (i) *1–2*; (i; vi) *3*; (v) *4*; (vii) *Sonata for 4 Horns*; (viii) *String Quartets 1–3*; (ix) *Piano Sonatas 1–3*; (x) *Midsummer Marriage*: *Ritual Dances*.

Ⓑ Decca 475 6750 (6). (i) LSO, C. Davis; (ii) ASMF, Marriner; (iii) with Pauk, Imai, Kirshbaum; (iv) Philip Jones Brass Ens.; (v) Chicago SO, Solti; (vi) with Harper; (vii) Tuckwell Horn Qt; (viii) Lindsay Qt; (ix) Crossley; (x) ROHCG O, Pritchard

For those wanting to explore Tippett's music in depth, for the centenary of his birth Decca provided an even more extensive collection, which includes the four *Symphonies*, the first three conducted by Sir Colin Davis with the LSO fully committed, and the *Fourth* by Sir Georg Solti, who also offers the agreeable if less substantial *Suite for the Birthday of Prince Charles*. Tippett himself described the *Third* as a hybrid symphony; he consciously follows the example of Beethoven's *Ninth* in the transition to the final, vocal section, in which the soprano sings three blues numbers, and Heather Harper almost manages to mute the relative crudities of Tippett's text. Solti's brilliantly played account of the *Fourth Symphony* is comparably powerful, although there are depths and tenderness in this score yet to be uncovered. Certainly these recordings and performances have a special place in the catalogue, although (as Hickox has since shown) there are other dimensions to these scores which are not uncovered here.

(i) *The Rose Lake*; (ii) *The Vision of St Augustine*
RCA 82876 64284-2. LSO; (i) C. Davis; (ii) with Shirley-Quirk, L. Symphony Ch., composer

As Sir Colin Davis's superb recording with the LSO demonstrates from first to last, *The Rose Lake* is arguably the most beautiful of all Tippett's works. It was in 1990 on a visit to Senegal that the 85-year-old composer visited a lake, Le Lac Rose, where at midday the sun transformed its whitish-green colour to translucent pink. It led to this musical evocation of the lake from dawn to dusk, centred round the climactic mid-moment when the lake is in full song. The 12 sections, sharply delineated, form a musical arch, with the lake-song repre-sented in five of them on soaring unison strings in free variation form.

That culminating masterpiece is well coupled with Tippett's own 1971 recording, never previously available on CD, of his *Cantata, The Vision of St Augustine*. First heard in 1965, it is a work which can now be recognized as the beginning of his adventurous Indian summer. His reading is expansively atmospheric rather than tautly drawn, bringing out the mystery of the piece.

The Midsummer Marriage (complete)

Lyrita SRCD 2217 (2). Remedios, Carlyle, Burrows, Herinx, Harwood, Watts, Ch. & O of
  ROHCG, C. Davis

This outstanding (originally Philips) 1970 recording of Tippett's masterpiece is a work that should be in the standard repertoire, alongside Britten's *Peter Grimes*, for the music consistently has that inspired melodic flow which distinguishes all great operas. That Tippett's visionary conception, created over a long period of self-searching, succeeds so triumphantly on record – if anything, with greater intensity than in the opera house – is a tribute above all to the exuberance of the composer's glowing inspiration, his determination to translate the beauty of his vision into musical and dramatic terms. Any one minute from this 154-minute score should be enough to demonstrate the unquenchable energy of his writing, his love of rich sounds. There are few operas of any period which use the chorus to such glorious effect, often in haunting offstage passages, and, with Sir Colin Davis a burningly committed advocate and with a cast that was inspired by live performances in the opera house, this is a set hard to resist, even for those not normally fond of modern opera. The so-called 'difficulties' of the libretto, with its mystical philosophical references, fade when the sounds are so honeyed in texture and so consistently lyrical, while the story – for all its complications – preserves a clear sense of emotional involvement throughout. The singing is glorious, the playing magnificent and the recording outstandingly atmospheric, and the Lyrita transfer brings an extraordinary sense of realism, the feeling of sitting in the stalls inside an opera house with quite perfect acoustics – even though the recording was made in Wembley Town Hall.

TOMKINS, Thomas (1572–1656)

Music for viols: **Almain in F** (for 4 viols); **Fantasias 1, 12 & 14** (for 3 viols); **Fantasia** (for 6 viols); **Galliard: Thomas Simpson** (5 viols & organ); **In Nomine II** (for 3 viols); **Pavane in A min.** (for 5 viols & organ); **Pavane in F**; **Ut re mi (Hexachord fantasia)** (both for 4 viols). (Keyboard:) (i) **Fancy for two to play. Pavan & Galliard: Earl Strafford**. (Organ:) **In nomine**; **Miserere**; **Voluntary**. Verse anthems: **Above the stars**; **O Lord, let me know mine end**; **Thou art my King**

Ⓑ Naxos 8.550602. Rose Consort of Viols, Red Byrd; Roberts; (i) with Bryan

This well-planned Naxos programme is carefully laid out in two parts, each of viol music interspersed with harpsichord and organ pieces and ending with an anthem. It gives collectors an admirable opportunity to sample very inexpensively the wider output of Thomas Tomkins, an outstandingly fine Elizabethan musician whose music is still too little known. Perhaps the most remarkable piece here is the *Hexachord fantasia*, where the scurrying part-writing ornaments a rising and falling six-note scale (hexachord). The two five-part verse anthems and *Above the stars*, which is in six parts, are accompanied by five viols, with a fine counter-tenor in *Above the stars* and a bass in *Thou art my King*.

Music for harpsichord and virginals: ***Barafostus Dreame***; ***2 Fancies***; ***Fancy for 2 to Play***; ***Fortune my Foe***; ***Galliard of 3 Parts***; ***Galliard Earl Strafford***; ***2 Grounds***; ***In nomine***; ***Lady Folliott's Galliard***; ***Miserere***; ***Pavan***; ***Pavan Earl Strafford with its devision***; ***Pavane of 3 Parts***; ***A Sad Pavane for these Distracted Times***; ***Toy made at Poole Court***; ***What if a Day***; ***Worcester Brawls***
Metronome METCD 1049. Cerasi (virginals and harpsichord)

Carole Cerasi offers here the finest available collection of the keyboard music of the last of the great English virginalists, Thomas Tomkins. Indeed, it is the repertoire played on the virginals that stands out, especially her exquisitely spontaneous performance of *A Sad Pavane for these Distracted Times*, and her equally sensitive response to the dolorous *Fortune my Foe* (the two most extended pieces here). In contrast, the charmingly good-humoured *Toy made at Poole Court* is given the lightest rhythmic lift. She uses a modern copy of an early 17th-century Ruckers and it could hardly be more realistically recorded. The harpsichord pieces (using a copy of an instrument by Bartolomeo Stephanini) are more robust and often have exuberant decoration, as in the disc's title-piece, *Barafostus Dreame*. *Earl Strafford's Galliard* is another splendid example of her exciting bravura on the latter instrument, and the closing *Ground* with extended variations is a tour de force. The recording venue has a pleasing ambience and the balance is ideal if you set the volume level carefully.

TORELLI, Giuseppe (1658–1709)

Concerti musicali, Op. 6/1–12; *Sonata a 4 in A min.*
Signum SIGCD 157. Charivari Agréable, Kah-Ming Ng

This set is given the sobriquet 'the original Brandenburg concertos'. Up to a point that is acceptable, but Bach's Margrave of Brandenburg was a different person from Torelli's employer, the Margrave of Brandenburg-Ansbach. However, Torelli did dedicate his *Concerti musicali* to Sophie Charlotte, Electress of Brandenburg, although nothing came of the dedication. But the *Concerti musicali* are a real discovery and they are most attractively presented here. Originally intended for strings alone, the Charivari have included oboes, recorders and bassoon and a continuo featuring chamber organ as well as theorbo and harpsichord. The result is most enjoyable: allegros are jolly and slow movements expressive and appealing, and Kah-Ming Ng brings the music to life vividly and spontaneously, helped by lively, truthful recording.

(i) *Violin Concertos, Op. 8/8, 9 & 11*; (i–ii) *Double Violin Concertos, Op. 8/2, 4, 5, 6*; (iii) *Sinfonias for Trumpet in D (G 8)*; (iii–iv) *for 2 Trumpets in D (G 23)*; *Concerto for 2 Trumpets in D*
Chan. 0716. (i) Standage; (ii) Weiss; (iii) Steele-Perkins; (iv) Blackadder; Col. Mus. 90

While Torelli's earlier *Concertos* remain in the world of the concerto grosso, by the time he came to write Op. 8 (published in 1709) he had moved away to give his soloists independence. The lustrous, busy opening of Op. 8/2 is immediately enticing, but these are all attractive works, particularly *No. 4* (where the pointed theme of the finale reminds one of 'All we like sheep') and *No. 11*, with its *Largo e staccato* central movement anticipating Vivaldi. The solo *Concerto in E minor*, Op. 8/9, is also a particularly fine work. Not surprisingly, the period performances here are first class. The rather more conventional *Trumpet Concertos* are also in confident hands, and the accompaniments throughout are characteristically stylish and the Chandos recording first rate.

TOSCANINI, Arturo, with NBC Symphony Orchestra

BIZET: *La Jolie Fille de Perth: Suite*. **COPLAND**: *El salón México*. **GOLDMARK**: *Rustic Wedding Symphony* (2 movts only). **KALINNIKOV**: *Symphony 1*. **MASSENET**: *Scènes alsaciennes (Suite 7)*. **MEYERBEER**: *Dinorah Overture*. **SOUSA**: *El Capitán*; *Semper fidelis*. **SMITH**: *Star-Spangled Banner*. **MOZART**: *Sinfonia Concertante, K.364* (with Mischakoff, Cooley).
Testament mono SBT 1404 (2)

Most of these live radio recordings were made by Toscanini at the height of the Second World War, and the fervour of the playing plainly reflects that, most strikingly in the patriotic marches by Sousa and the American National Anthem. What is striking is that Toscanini in these recordings demonstrates little of the rigidity that marred so many of his NBC recordings for RCA. The ebb and flow of rhythm and phrasing in the rare Kalinnikov *Symphony* could not be more winning, and Toscanini's timing in the Spanish-American rhythms of *El salón México* is perfect, with just the right degree of hesitation. Nor is the Mozart *Sinfonia concertante* rigid, with two of his NBC principals as soloists. With such colourfully tuneful rarities as the *Dinorah Overture* and the *Scènes alsaciennes*, along with the delightful *Jolie Fille de Perth Suite*, this makes a very winning collection. The sound too is full-bodied and generally less dry than in his commercial NBC recordings of the period, here very well transferred.

TREDICI, David Del (born 1937)

Final Alice
Ⓑ Australian Decca Eloquence 442 9955. Hendricks, Chicago SO, Solti

How rare it is to be able to recommend a late-twentieth-century work that is so immediately appealing. Commissioned to celebrate the Bicentennial of the United States in 1976, this instalment of Del Tredici's sequence of Lewis Carroll settings has much to fascinate the ear, particularly in a virtuoso performance like this. Familiar texts are neatly assembled, with a minimum of violence to the original, to present a dramatic cantata for just one voice and orchestra. Barbara Hendricks proves a characterful and urgent guide, a vibrant narrator as well as a fine singer. Solti and his superb orchestra plainly enjoy the fun from first to last: it is good to welcome an extended work which sustains its length without pomposity and with immediate warmth of communication. The recording is outstandingly brilliant and its première release on CD is enormously welcomed.

TUBIN, Eduard (1905–82)

Symphonies: (i) *1 in C min.*; *2 (The Legendary)*; *3 in D min.*; (ii) *4 in A (Sinfonia lirica)*; (iii) *5 in B min.*; (ii) *6*; (iv) *7*; (ii) *8*; (iv) *9 (Sinfonia semplice)*; *10.* (ii) *Suite from the ballet, Kratt*; (iv) *Toccata for Orchestra*
Ⓜ BIS CD 1402/06 (5). (i) Swedish RSO; (ii) Bergen PO; (iii) Bamberg SO; (iv) Gothenburg SO; Järvi

Neeme Järvi's survey of the Tubin *Symphonies* is here packaged, shorn of some of its couplings and presented in an attractive and competitive format (five CDs for the price of three). These are marvellous works, rich in invention and with the real breadth of the symphonist about them. Anyone who is attuned to the symphonies of Sibelius or Prokofiev will find themselves at home in this world. The opening of the *Second Symphony* is magical: there are soft, luminous string chords that evoke a strong atmosphere of wide vistas and white summer nights, but the music soon gathers power and reveals a genuine feeling for proportion and of organic growth. If there is a Sibelian strength in the *Second Symphony*, the *Sixth*, written after Tubin had settled in Sweden, has obvious resonances of Prokofiev – even down to instrumentation – and yet Tubin's rhythmic vitality and melodic invention are quietly distinctive. The first two movements of the wartime *Third Symphony* are vintage Tubin, but the heroic finale approaches bombast. The *Eighth* is his masterpiece; its opening movement has a sense of vision and mystery, and the atmosphere stays with you. This is the darkest of the symphonies and the most intense in feeling, music of

great substance. The *Fourth* is a highly attractive piece, immediately accessible, the music well argued and expertly crafted. The opening has a Sibelian
feel to it, but the closer one comes to it, the more individual it seems. The
Ninth Symphony is in two movements: its mood is elegiac and a restrained melancholy permeates the slower sections. Its musical language is direct, tonal
and, once one gets to grips with it, quite personal. If its spiritual world is clearly
Nordic, the textures are transparent and luminous, and its argument unfolds
naturally and cogently. The *Fifth* makes as good a starting point as any to
investigate the Tubin canon. Written after he had settled in Sweden, it finds
him at his most neoclassical; the music is finely paced and full of energy and
invention. The *Seventh* is a marvellous work and it receives a concentrated and
impressive reading. As always with Tubin, you are never in doubt that this is a
real symphony which sets out purposefully and reaches its goal. The ideas
could not be by anyone else and the music unfolds with a powerful logic and
inevitability. The *Tenth Symphony* is a one-movement piece that begins with a
sombre string idea, which is soon interrupted by a periodically recurring horn
call – and which resonates in the mind long afterwards. The recordings are
absolutely first class.

TURINA, Joaquin (1882–1949)

(i) *Danzas fantásticas*; (ii) *La oración del torero, Op. 34*; *La
procesión del Rocio, Op. 9*; (i; iii) *Rapsodia sinfónica*; (i) *Sinfonia
sevillana*

Ⓑ Regis RRC 1299. Bátiz, with (i) LPO; (ii) Mexico City PO; (iii) Wibaut

The three LPO items were recorded in 1983 and originally released on HMV.
The three *Danzas fantásticas* are understandably better known than the other
two works included on the original LP. The *Sinfonia* is a programmatic triptych
with an attractive nocturnal slow movement; the scoring of the outer movements (as in the *Danzas*) is gaudy but effective. The *Rapsodia* is a pleasant if not
especially memorable piece for piano and orchestra. Bátiz is a sympathetic
exponent of this repertoire and, with the LPO, he brings out the Latin colours
and atmosphere. Two further colourful pieces have been added to this bargain
release, with the Mexico City Philharmonic, also conducted by Bátiz. They are
similarly well played and well recorded. An undoubted bargain.

TURNAGE, Mark-Anthony (born 1960)

Blood on the Floor (DVD version)

Arthaus DVD 100 430. Ens. Modern, Rundel (Director: Doris Götzl; V/D: Barrie Gavin)

With Peter Rundel conducting a group of German musicians, *Blood on the Floor* is a powerful piece, inspired by a painting of Francis Bacon. A complete performance is here introduced by a feature film. Characteristically, the idiom is abrasive with a jazz element important, making it attractive despite the unpleasantness of the subject with its element of drug addiction. It would be hard to imagine a better performance, very well played and recorded.

An Invention on 'Solitude' Cortège for Chris; 2 Elegies Framing a Shout; 3 Farewells; 2 Memorials; Sleep On; True Life Stories: Tune for Toru

Black Box BBM 1065. Nash Ens. (members)

Anyone coming new to Turnage could not do better than start here, for all this music is intensely expressive and instantly communicative. Its overriding character is thoughtful and contemplative, although *An Invention on 'Solitude'* is the exception for, while inspired by the Brahms *Clarinet Quintet*, the writing, for the same combination, 'fluctuates between stillness and violence'. The *Cortège for Chris* (Christopher Van Kempen, the Nash Ensemble's cellist who died in 1998) features both cello and clarinet, as well as a ruminative piano, while the *Two Memorials* are commemorated with haunting soliloquizing from the solo saxophone.

The *Three Farewells* are strangely obsessive: each has a hidden text, the second, *Music to Hear* for viola and muted cello, a Shakespeare sonnet. The finale, *All will be well*, was written as a wedding piece, and the composer observes ironically 'the marriage didn't last'. Not surprisingly, some of the most peaceful and serene writing comes in *Sleep On*, for cello and piano, a triptych framed by a lovely *Berceuse* and a restful *Lullaby*. The solo saxophone returns for the first of the *Two Elegies* and, after being exuberantly interrupted by the *Shout* – a spiky and restlessly energetic boogie – the piano (with the saxophone) 'searches for and finds repose'.

The reflective closing *Tune for Toru* (a gentle piano piece) was written in response to the death of the Japanese composer Toru Takemitsu and readily finds the stillness the composer was searching for in his *Invention on 'Solitude'*. Superbly responsive performances throughout and vividly real recording, within an attractively spacious acoustic.

VAŇHAL, Jan (1739–1813)

Symphonies: in C min., Bryan Cm2; in D, Bryan D4; in G min., Bryan Gm2

Chan. 9607. LMP, Bamert

The *G minor Symphony*, the second of Vaňhal's symphonies in that key, is an absolute delight, full of good ideas and comparable with the *Sturm und Drang* of Haydn's *No. 39* or Mozart's *No. 25* in the same key. The *C minor Symphony* (1770) is also a work of originality, with an occasional foreshadowing of Beethoven. Matthias Bamert and the London Mozart Players give an excellent account of themselves, and are recorded with clarity and warmth.

VARÈSE, Edgar (1883–1965)

Tuning Up; *Amériques* (original version); *Arcana*; *Dance for Burgess*; (i) *Density 21.5*. *Déserts*; (ii) *Ecuatorial*; (iii–iv) *Un grand sommeil noir* (original & orch. Beaumont versions). *Hyperprism*; *Intégrales*; *Ionisation*; (v–vi) *Nocturna*. *Octandre*; (v) *Offrandes*. *Poème électronique*

Ⓑ Decca 460 208-2 (2). Concg. O or Asko Ens.; Chailly; with (i) Zoon (ii) Deas
   (iii) Delunsch; (iv) Kardoncuf; (v) Leonard; (vi) Prague Philharmonic Male Ch.

This comprehensive coverage of the music of Varèse was given a 1999 *Gramophone* Award for Twentieth-Century Music. He first came to public notice in the 1930s when Percy Scholes chose him to represent the last word in zany modernity in his 'Columbia History of Music', but this mockery backfired. *Octandre* (one movement then recorded) sounds quirkily original now as it did then (it is played marvellously here). The witty opening *Tuning Up* sets the mood for writing which is ever ready to take its own course, regardless of tradition, and set new musical paths. *Amériques*, which follows, is heard in its original (1921) version, lavishly scored, with reminiscences of music by others, not least the Stravinsky of *The Rite of Spring*. It makes fascinating listening. *Ionisation*, less ear-catching, stands as a historic pointer towards developments in percussion writing. *Poème électronique* originated at the 1958 Brussels World Fair, where it was played through more than 400 loudspeakers inside the Philips pavilion. The montage of familiar and electronic sounds (machine noises, sonorous bells, etc.) comes from the composer's original four-track tape. But all the works here are sharply distinctive and show the composer as a true revolutionary, usually decades ahead of his time. The vocal pieces are among the most fascinating aurally, not least *Ecuatorial*, a setting in Spanish, with bass soloist, of a Mayan prayer, brightly coloured and sharp, with brass, percussion, organ, piano and ondes martenot. *Un grand sommeil noir* is a rare surviving early song, lyrically Ravelian in feeling, heard here in both the original version with piano, and in an orchestration by Antony Beaumont. *Nocturnal*, Varèse's haunting last piece, was left unfinished. Completed by Professor Chou, it is as extravagant and uninhibited as ever, featuring male chorus and a solo soprano voice, used melodically to evoke a mysterious dream-world. All the performances here are superbly definitive and this set would be hard to surpass. The recording acoustic, too, is open, yet everything is clear.

VAUGHAN WILLIAMS, Ralph (1872–1958)

Fantasia on Greensleeves; (i) *Fantasia on a Theme of Thomas Tallis*
Ⓜ EMI Masters (ADD) 6 31788-2. Sinfonia of London; (i) with Allegri Qt, Barbirolli (with
   DELIUS: *Brigg Fair*) – **ELGAR**: *Introduction and Allegro for Strings*, etc.

Barbirolli's inspirational performance of the *Tallis Fantasia* now rightly takes
its place among EMI's 'Great Recordings of the Century'. For many of us it is
the composer's supreme masterpiece, and Barbirolli's ardour, combined with
the magically quiet playing of the second orchestra, is unforgettable. The
recording (made in the dead of night to ensure background silence) has magnificent definition and sonority, achieving dramatic contrasts between the
main orchestra and the distanced solo group, which sound wonderfully ethereal. For the reissue EMI have added Delius's *Brigg Fair* to the original Elgar
couplings, making this Masters reissue an unbeatable bargain.

The Lark Ascending
Ⓜ EMI 5 62813-2. Kennedy, CBSO, Rattle – **WALTON**: *Viola Concerto; Violin
   Concerto*

Vaughan Williams's *Lark Ascending* is of a modest length but, like the *Tallis Fantasia*, it is one of his most moving works. The millions of listeners to Classic FM
picked the work as their first choice from the whole classical repertoire. Nigel
Kennedy's spacious and evocative account of this inspirational piece is beautifully recorded, and it makes an ideal coupling for the two Walton *Concertos*.

Symphonies: (i) *A Sea Symphony (1)*; *A London Symphony (2)*;
(ii) *A Pastoral Symphony (3)*. *4 in F min.*; *5 in D*; *6 in E min.*;
(iii) *Sinfonia antartica (7)*. *8 in D min.*; *9 in E min.* (iv) *Concerto
accademico in D min.* (v) *Tuba Concerto. 3 Portraits from
'The England of Elizabeth'*; *The Wasps Overture*.
Ⓑ RCA (ADD) 82876 55708-2 (6). LSO, Previn, with (i–iii) Harper, (i) Shirley-Quirk, L.
   Symphony Ch; (iii) Amb. S., R. Richardson (speaker); (iv) Buswell; (v) Fletcher

Previn recorded the Vaughan Williams *Symphonies* over a five-year span from
1968 to 1972, and his achievement in this repertoire represented a peak in his
recording career at that time. Here the nine symphonies plus their original fill-
ups have been neatly compressed on to six CDs. The most striking performances
are those which were recorded last, *Nos. 2, 3* and *5*; for these Previn achieves
an extra depth of understanding, an extra intensity, whether in the purity of
pianissimo or the outpouring of emotional resolution. For the rest there is only
one performance that can be counted as disappointing, and that is of the symphony one might have expected Previn to interpret best, the taut and dramatic
Fourth. Even that is an impressive account, if less intense than the rest. Otherwise, the great landscape of the whole cycle is presented with richness and

detail in totally refreshing interpretations, brilliantly recorded and impressively transferred to CD. The extra items are worth having too, notably the two *Concertos* with responsive soloists.

(i) *A Sea Symphony*; (ii) *Fantasia on Christmas Carols*; *Hodie (A Christmas Cantata)*

Ⓑ EMI 9 68934-2 (2). (i) Marshall, Philh. O; (i–ii) Roberts, L. Symphony Ch.; (iii) Gale, Tear, Choristers of St Paul's; (ii–iii) LSO; all cond. Hickox

Richard Hickox has recorded the *Sea Symphony* twice; the second version with Susan Gritton and Gerald Finley as soloists and with the advantage of SACD surround sound may be preferred by some readers (Chan. CHSA 5047). But this earlier (1990) EMI version is hardly less impressive and the two-disc set includes also the *Christmas Carol Fantasia* and the rare *Hodie*. Hickox directs a strong, warmly expressive reading of the *Symphony*. His relatively brisk speeds and his ability to mould melodic lines with an affectionate rubato – notably with the bright-toned, finely drilled London Symphony Chorus – never sounds breathless, and he relishes the sea-sounds that Vaughan Williams gives to the orchestra. The different sections in the longer outer movements are given strong cohesion, and the finale, 'The Explorers', ends in warmth rather than mystery on *O my brave soul!* Margaret Marshall is a bright, fresh soprano, and if Stephen Roberts is a little lacking in weight in the baritone solos, his singing is thoughtful and well detailed. Hickox also directs an urgent, freely expressive reading of the big Christmas cantata, *Hodie*, helped by refined and incisive choral singing from the combined choirs; and the *Christmas Carol Fantasia* proves an ideal bonus coupling, also warmly done.

A London Symphony (original, 1913 version)

Chan. 9902. LSO, Hickox (with **BUTTERWORTH**: *The Banks of Green Willow*)

A London Symphony was Vaughan Williams's own favourite among his symphonies (and I.M.'s too). It was the one he had revised most often, first between 1918 and 1920, and later even more radically in the 1930s, with the definitive score finally published in 1936. What this revelatory recording demonstrates is that the 20 minutes or so of music that was excised included many passages that represent the composer at his most magically poetic. There is even a case for saying that in an age which now thrives on expansive symphonies – the examples of Bruckner, Mahler and Shostakovich always before us – the original offers the richer experience. Vaughan Williams undoubtedly made the work structurally tauter, but discursiveness in a symphony is no longer regarded as a necessary fault.

No one could make the case for this 1913 version more persuasively than Hickox. He draws ravishing sounds throughout from the LSO, with an unerring feeling for idiomatic rubato and a powerful control of massive dynamic contrasts. In this original version the first movement is no different, but each of the other movements here includes substantial sections completely eliminated later, some of them echoing Ravel of *Daphnis and Chloé*, including an extended one in the Scherzo. The sumptuous Chandos sound, with an extraordinarily wide dynamic range, adds to the impact of the performance, which comes with a short but valuable and beautifully played fill-up.

Symphony 6; Fantasia on a Theme of Thomas Tallis

BBC Legends (ADD) **BBCL** 4256-2. L New, Boult (with **BAX**: *Mediterranean*.
   BERG: *Lyric Suite*. **HADLEY**: *One Morning in Spring*)

Sir Adrian made the first recording of the *Sixth Symphony* in the days of 78s, but this performance comes from the 1972 Cheltenham Festival and its companions from the late 1960s, so the recordings are in stereo. As is well known, he conducted the British première of *Wozzeck* which was much admired by the composer, and the *Three Pieces* from the *Lyric Suite* come from the Maida Vale Studios and the BBC Symphony Orchestra. A most desirable issue which collectors should seek out.

(i) Dona nobis pacem; (ii) Sancta Civitas

ⓑⓑ Naxos 8.572424. Bach Ch., Bournemouth SO, Hill, with (i) Pier; (ii) Staples; (i–ii) Brook;
   (ii) Winchester Cathedral Choristers, Winchester College Quiristers

Naxos here offers an ideal coupling of two parallel Vaughan Williams masterpieces, each seriously neglected. Both date from the inter-war period, when the composer was expressing disillusion after his experiences in the First World War. Both with Latin titles, they mark a departure from the composer's earlier pastoral style towards expression far more abrasive, a style which also erupted in the ballet-score *Job* and the *Fourth Symphony*.

In vivid, atmospheric sound, David Hill directs his forces in performances which bring out all the savagery of the writing, not least in the violent use of timpani. Though *Dona nobis pacem*, written in 1936, is described as a cantata and *Sancta Civitas* of 1923–5 an oratorio, they both last just over half an hour, and are among RVW's most atmospheric works, with a distant chorus evocatively used in *Sancta Civitas*. *Dona nobis* foretells the horror of the Second World War in its six movements with texts from the Bible as well as from Walt Whitman and John Bright, while *Sancta Civitas* depicts the battle between good and evil as expressed in the Book of Revelation. Not just the choruses but also the three soloists are outstanding: the American soprano Christina Pier in *Dona nobis pacem*, the tenor Andrew Staples in *Sancta Civitas*, and baritone Matthew Brook in both. A first-rate disc, made the more attractive at super-bargain price.

(i) On Wenlock Edge (song-cycle from A. E. Housman's A Shropshire Lad); (ii) 10 Blake Songs for voice & oboe; (i) 4 Hymns. (iii) Songs: Merciless Beauty; The New Ghost; The Water Mill

ⓑ EMI 9 68939-2 (2). Ian Partridge, with (i) Music Group of London; (ii) Janet Craxton; (iii)
   Jennifer Partridge – **WARLOCK**: *Capriol Suite; The Curlew; Songs*

This is an outstandingly beautiful record, with Ian Partridge's intense artistry and lovely, individual tone-colour used with compelling success in Vaughan Williams songs, both early and late. The Housman cycle has an accompaniment for piano and string quartet which can sound ungainly but which here, with playing from the Music Group of London, matches the soloist's sensitivity; the result is both atmospheric and moving. The *Ten Blake Songs* come from just before the composer's death: bald, direct settings that with the artistry of Partridge and Craxton are darkly moving. The tenor's sister accompanies with fine understanding in two favourite songs as a welcome extra. The other (much rarer) items make an attractive bonus, with the *Four Hymns* distinctively accompanied by viola and piano. The Warlock anthology, provided as coupling, is hardly less desirable.

VERDI, Giuseppe (1813–1901)

Complete Prelines, Overtures & Ballet Music
Chan. 9510 (4). BBC PO, Downes

Verdi overtures provide an astonishing variety of tunes and colour, and his ballet music, written for Paris productions of his operas, includes some of the most scintillatingly tuneful music he ever wrote. Edward Downes's Verdi survey covers virtually all the overtures, preludes and ballet music, the latter full of charm when played so elegantly and recorded so beautifully. Original versions are included when available, so we get the first (1857) score of the *Prelude* to *Simon Boccanegra* and the brief (1862) prelude to *La forza del destino*, as well as the familiar, expanded, 1869 overture. The outstanding novelty is Verdi's extended (1871) overture written for the Italian première of *Aida*. The shorter *Prelude* heard at the opera's Cairo première was substituted at the last moment and the 1871 piece was never heard of again. The ballet music was, of course, an essential requirement if a work was to be performed at the Paris Opéra. Verdi often rose to the occasion and produced charming, tuneful music, felicitously scored. In the suite from *Il trovatore* (an unlikely subject for a balletic diversion) the delightful third section, *La Bohémienne*, is worthy of Delibes in its use of graceful violins and piquant woodwind. Not surprisingly, Downes has the full measure of this music. The finer overtures are played with bold characterization and dramatic fire. *Nubucco*, with its dignified sonority, and *Giovanna d'Arco* both show the BBC Philharmnonic brass at their finest in quite different ways, and *Luisa Miller* is another very strong performance. The strings play most beautifully in the *Traviata Preludes*. With such richly expansive recording, showing Chandos engineering at its most spectacular, the effect is less bitingly leonine than in Karajan's two-disc survey. But even if not all this music is top-class Verdi, the Chandos set offers much to enjoy, and the spontaneity and elegance of the music-making are never in doubt.

Ballet music from: *Don Carlos*; *Otello*; *I vespri siciliani*

Ⓜ Australian Decca Eloquence (ADD) 480 045. Cleveland O, Maazel (with **LEONI**:
The Prayer and the Sword: Incidental music)

Although there have been excellent comprehensive collections of Verdi's ballet music from Downes (Chandos) and Almeida (Philips), this selection is the most exciting committed to disc. First, the playing is superlative, with the orchestra responding to Maazel's electrifying direction with style and brilliance, making the most of Verdi's tuneful and witty music. Secondly, it is treated to vintage Decca sound, making this one of the great recordings of 'light' music in the catalogue. Listen, for instance, to the oboe at the beginning of the third of the *Four Seasons* from *I vespri siciliani* or the woodwind playing in the final movement – exhilarating in its energy and bravura. Moreover, it is coupled with some charmingly attractive and very rare music by Leoni.

Requiem Mass (CD version)

EMI 6 98936 2 (2). Harteros, Ganassi, Villazón, Pape, St Cecilia Ac. Ch. & O, Pappano

Following Antonio Pappano's award-winning version of *Madama Butterfly*, EMI shrewdly persuaded him to record the Verdi *Requiem* similarly with the St Cecilia Chorus and Orchestra in Rome, of which he is chief conductor. Having Italian forces performing this work adds to the warmth of this superb version. In every way it is a worthy successor to such classic recordings as Toscanini's uniquely intense account from the days of mono, Giulini's dedicated EMI version with the Philharmonia and the most starry quartet of soloists, as well as Barbirolli's Rome version, a labour of love.

As in Puccini, Pappano has a natural feeling for phrasing and pacing in Verdi, and with forces close to him the result is spectacular, given even greater impact when the recording was made in the recently opened Parco della Musica in Rome, giving air and space to the sound. The dynamic range is very wide indeed, arguably too wide, when the murmured opening of the chorus is barely audible in the first few bars. Nevertheless, a fine achievement by the EMI engineers. The *Dies irae* is wonderfully thrilling. The women soloists may not be quite so starry a duo as Schwarzkof and Ludwig for Giulini, but Anja Harteros and Sonia Ganassi make a splendid match, firm and true; while it would be hard to imagine a finer account of the tenor's role than that of Rolando Villazón, subtle beyond anything one might have expected from an Italianate tenor in the old days, with shading of dynamic beautifully handled. Similarly, René Pape is a highly intelligent bass-baritone, not as dark in colour as a full bass, but for that very reason better matched with the other soloists.

It is a sign of the times that the St Cecilia Chorus could hardly offer a sharper contrast with the slipshod Italian opera choruses of old, with the ensemble consistently excellent. The orchestra too bears witness to the fine standards latterly achieved by Italian orchestras, traditionally individualistic and undisciplined. Altogether a set to rival and even outshine the finest of the past.

Aida (complete, CD version)

EMI (ADD) 769300-2 (2). Freni, Carreras, Baltsa, Cappuccilli, Raimondi, Van Dam, V. State Op. Ch., VPO, Karajan

On EMI, Karajan's is a performance of *Aida* full of splendour and pageantry, while yet it is fundamentally lyrical. On this point there is no feeling of Freni lacking power even in a role normally given to a larger voice, and there is ample gain in the tender beauty of her singing. Carreras makes a fresh, sensitive Radames, Raimondi a darkly intense Ramfis and Van Dam a cleanly focused King, his relative lightness no drawback. Cappuccilli gives a finely detailed performance of Amonasro, while Baltsa as Amneris crowns the whole performance with her fine, incisive singing. Despite some over-brightness on cymbals and trumpet, the Vienna orchestra's sound for Karajan, as transferred to CD, is richly atmospheric, both in the intimate scenes and, most strikingly, in the scenes of pageantry, reflecting the Salzburg Festival production which was linked to the recording. The set has been attractively repackaged and remains first choice on CD, irrespective of price.

Un ballo in maschera (complete, DVD version)

Decca DVD 074 3227 (2). Pavarotti, Ricciarelli, Quilico, Blegen, Berini, Met. Op. Ch. & O, Patanè (Producer: Elijah Moshinsky; V/D: Brian Large)

This 1980 live performance is another of the productions from the New York Met. to show Pavarotti at his very finest, both as a singer and as actor (his dying scene of forgiveness is especially telling). He is in splendid voice as Riccardo and is partnered by Katia Ricciarelli as Amelia, also at her finest, and looking ravishing. Their great love duet in Act II is gloriously sung and Patanè rises to the occasion and creates a richly romantic orchestral outburst, all but anticipating Puccini. Among the others in this superb cast, Judith Blegen is a delightful Oscar with sparkling coloratura and Blanca Berini an unforgettable fortune-teller (Ulrica), virtually stealing the scenes in which she appears (with her eyes as well as her voice). Louis Quilico makes an effectively agonized Renato, Amelia's unfortunate husband. The costumes are traditional, the sets practical. Patanè conducts throughout with flair and Brian Large's video direction could hardly be bettered. Highly recommended.

For those looking for a CD version, a bargain DG set, with Domingo, Ricciarelli, Bruson, Obraztsova, Gruberová, La Scala, Milan, Choir and Orchestra, conducted by Claudio Abbado, is strongly recommended. The Abbado reading is admirably paced and, with a splendid feeling for the sparkle of the comedy – and a superb cast, who all characterize beautifully – it is hard to fault (453 148-2 (2)).

Don Carlos (complete, DVD version)

Warner DVD 0630 16318-2. Alagna, Hampson, Van Dam, Mattila, Meier, Halfvarson, Théâtre du Châtelet Ch., O de Paris, Pappano

This fine Warner issue provides one of the clearest instances where DVD scores on almost every level over the equivalent CD set. Here you have the full three and a half hours of music on a single disc, as against three CDs on EMI. The sound on the DVD may be marginally less full than on the CD, but it would take someone with an exceptional ear to feel short-changed. The chorus is rather less crisply disciplined in places, but it rises splendidly to the big challenge of the *Auto-da-fé* scene of Act III. And where too many DVDs skimp on the number of index points, this one follows the normal CD practice of having them at every crucial point. All that, plus the advantage of having a visual presentation of Luc Bondy's production. The sets are simple and stylized, the production never gets in the way of the music, with the costumes of Moidele Bickel (coloured black, white or crimson) close enough to seventeenth-century fashion not to distract from the drama. The score is tautly and warmly presented, as on CD, by Antonio Pappano, and the principals are as fine a team as have ever been assembled for this opera on disc – here using the original French text and the full five-Act score, complete with Fontainebleau scene. Karita Mattila gives the most masterly performance as the Queen, with one inspired passage after another, culminating in a supreme account of her Act V aria. Roberto Alagna is in superb voice too, firm and heroic, well matched against Thomas Hampson, noble as Rodrigo. José van Dam may not have the deep bass normal for the role of Philip II, but having a more lyrical voice brings compensating assets, and he contrasts well with the Grand Inquisitor of Eric Halfvarson. An outstanding issue. For those wishing for a CD version, Pappano's excellent recording is available on EMI 5 56152-2 (3).

Falstaff (complete, CD version)

EMI 3 77349-2 (2). Gobbi, Schwarzkopf, Zaccaria, Moffo, Panerai, Philh. Ch. & O, Karajan

This 1956 Karajan recording presents not only the most pointed account orchestrally of Verdi's comic masterpiece (the Philharmonia Orchestra at its very peak) but one of the most vividly characterful casts ever gathered for a recording. If you relish the idea of Tito Gobbi as Falstaff (his many-coloured voice, not quite fat-sounding in humour, presents a sharper character than usual), then this is clearly a first choice. The rest of the cast too is a delight, with Schwarzkopf a tinglingly masterful Mistress Ford, Anna Moffo sweet as Nannetta and Rolando Panerai a formidable Ford. On CD the digital transfer is sharply focused.

La forza del destino (1862 version; complete, CD version)

Ⓜ RCA (ADD) 74321 39502-2 (3). L. Price, Domingo, Milnes, Cossotto, Giaiotti, Bacquier, Alldis Ch., LSO, Levine

Leontyne Price recorded the role of Leonora in an earlier RCA version made in Rome in 1956, but the years between that and this recording from the mid-1970s have hardly touched her voice. The roles of Don Alvaro and Don Carlo are ideally suited to the team of Plácido Domingo and Sherrill Milnes so that their confrontations are the cornerstones of the dramatic structure. Fiorenza Cossotto makes a formidable rather than a jolly Preziosilla, while on the male side the line-up of Bonaldo Giaiotti, Gabriel Bacquier, Kurt Moll and Michel Sénéchal is far stronger than on any rival set. The sound is full and vivid, and this strong, well-paced version with an exceptionally good and consistent cast is strongly recommended.

Luisa Miller (complete, DVD version)

DG DVD 073 4027. Scotto, Domingo, Milnes, Morris, Giaiotti, Met. Ch. & O, Levine
  (Director: Nathaniel Merrill; V/D: Roland Ott)

Recorded at the Met. in New York in 1979, James Levine's version of *Luisa Miller* consistently demonstrates his Verdian mastery, and not just in the best-known masterpieces. This production is superbly cast, with Renata Scotto agile, bright and characterful in the title-role, with Plácido Domingo singing gloriously as the enamoured Rodolfo and Sherrill Milnes comparably fine as Luisa's father. This opera is unusual in not having the principal baritone as the villain, but here James Morris as Wurm and Bonaldo Giaiotti as Count Walter provide the necessary bite. Not only in Levine's conducting but in the sets and costumes of Nathaniel Merrill's production the attractive rustic element of the piece is effectively brought out.

For a CD version, you can't go too far wrong with Maag's Decca version (475 8496-2 (2)), with Caballé, Pavarotti, Milnes, Reynolds, L. Op. Ch. and the Nat. PO. Caballé gives a splendid (if not flawless) portrait of the heroine, and Pavarotti is full of creative, detailed imagination. As Federica, Anna Reynolds underlines the light and shade, consistently bringing out atmospheric qualities. With strong conducting by Maag, this recording has been vividly transferred to CD, now on Decca's 'Originals' label.

Macbeth (complete, CD version)

Ⓜ Ph. 475 8393 (3). Bruson, Zampieri, Shicoff, Lloyd, Deutsche Oper, Berlin, Ch. & O,
  Sinopoli

Even more than his finest rivals Sinopoli presents this opera as a searing Shakespearean inspiration, scarcely more uneven than much of the work of the Bard himself. In the Banqueting scene, for example, Sinopoli creates extra dramatic intensity by his concern for detail and his preference for extreme dynamics, and Renato Bruson and Mara Zampieri respond vividly. Zampieri's voice may be biting rather than beautiful, occasionally threatening to come off the rails, but, with musical precision an asset, she matches exactly Verdi's request for the voice of a she-devil. Neil Shicoff as Macduff and Robert Lloyd as Banquo make up the excellent quartet of principals, while the high voltage of the whole performance clearly reflects Sinopoli's experience with the same chorus and orchestra at the Deutsche Oper in Berlin. The recording is vivid, well balanced and focused, but atmospheric.

For a DVD version of this opera, TDK's live Parma version (Nucci, Valayre, Iori, Iuliano, Pascoli, Parma Teatro Regio Ch. & O, Bartoletti; Director: Liliana Cavani, V/D: Andrea Bevilacqua; TKK DVD DVWW-OPMACPA) goes straight to the top of the list because of Leo Nucci's unforgettably powerful portrayal of Macbeth. Sylvie Valayre as Lady Macbeth, if not Callas, is physically attractive and resourcefully seductive in dominating in their joint Machiavellian plotting. Her voice has a certain amount of intrusive vibrato but is strong and clear, and her acting is vivid yet not overly melodramatic. Her sleepwalking scene (seemingly filmed separately) is most tellingly done and very well sung. Roberto Iuliano is an excellent Macduff. The rest of the cast give good support, especially the chorus, who sing superbly throughout, with Bartoletti preventing the closing sequence (with both principal characters dead) from being an anticlimax. The production is acceptable, although having the audience visible from either side of the stage is disconcerting. Moreover, the witches' scenes are extraordinarily conceived, with the witches apparently doing their laundry, so that when Macbeth arrives he has to push his way through the washing! However, even with these distractions, this is all very compelling, especially the banquet scene in Act II, when Macbeth loses his reason; here both the principal characters are at their finest.

Nabucco (complete, CD version)

Ⓜ Decca (ADD) 478 1717 (2). Gobbi, Souliotis, Cava, Prevedi, V. State Op. Ch. & O, Gardelli

A masterly performance on Decca, with dramatically intense and deeply imaginative contributions from Tito Gobbi as Nabucco and Elena Souliotis as the evil Abigaille. Souliotis made this the one totally satisfying performance of an all-too-brief recording career, wild in places, but no more than is dramatically necessary. Though Carlo Cava as Zaccaria is not ideally rich of tone, it is a strong characterization, and Gardelli, as in his later Verdi recordings for both Decca and Philips, showed what a Verdian master he is, whether in pointing individual phrases or whole scenes, simply and naturally. Vivid and atmospheric 1965 sound completes a fine set, now reissued as one of Decca's 'Originals'. The one minor blemish is that the Viennese chorus, although richly expansive, lacks bite in *Va pensiero*.

Otello (complete, DVD version)

DG DVD 0734040. Vickers, Freni, Glossop, Malagu, Bottion, Deutsche Oper Ch., BPO, Karajan (Director: Karajan; V/D: Georges Wakhevitch)

Filmed in Munich and Salzburg in 1972/3, Karajan's disc offers a vivid production taken from the Salzburg Festival, superbly cast. Jon Vickers sings gloriously in the title-role, a heroic tenor who sings cleanly and accurately and with great passion, totally unstrained. Though Mirella Freni's soprano might seem a little lightweight for Desdemona, it is sweetly beautiful, a totally charming portrayal of the wronged heroine, with Peter Glossop at his peak as the most sinister

Iago, again totally unstrained. The co-ordination that Karajan obtains from his fine team, not just soloists but chorus and orchestra too, is a model for any rival, with Wakhevitch adding to the impact in the visual element, often set in the open air, with a stormy seascape at the start, and architectural sets. The film was made in conjunction with an audio recording, and the only slight snag is that there is a minor cut in the big central ensemble of Act III.

Of the many very fine versions on CD, perhaps the top choice is Plácido Domingo's third recording of *Otello* (DG 439 805-2 (2) – Studer, Leiferkus, Ch. & O of the Bastille Opera, Chung) which proves to be more freely expressive and even more involved than his previous ones; the baritonal quality of his tenor has here developed to bring an extra darkness, with the final solo, *Niun mi tema*, poignantly tender. Cheryl Studer gives one of her finest performances as Desdemona, the tone both full and pure, while Sergei Leiferkus makes a chillingly evil Iago, the more so when his voice is the opposite of Italianate, verging on the gritty, which not everyone will like. With plenty of light and shade, Myung-Whun Chung is an urgent Verdian, adopting free-flowing speeds yet allowing Domingo full expansiveness in the death scene. The Chorus and Orchestra of the Bastille Opera excel themselves, setting new standards for an opera recording from Paris, and the sound is first rate.

Rigoletto (complete, CD version)
Decca (ADD) 414 269-2 (2). Sutherland, Milnes, Pavarotti, Talvela, Tourangeau, Amb. Op. Ch., LSO, Bonynge

Just over ten years after her first recording of this opera, Sutherland appeared in it again, this time with Pavarotti, who is an intensely characterful Duke: an unmistakable rogue but a charmer too. Thanks to him and to Bonynge above all, the Quartet becomes a genuine musical climax. Sutherland's voice has acquired a hint of a beat, but there is little of the mooning manner that disfigured her earlier assumption, and the result is glowingly beautiful as well as supremely assured technically. Milnes makes a strong Rigoletto, vocally masterful rather than strongly characterful.

Simon Boccanegra (complete, DVD version)
TDK DVD DVWW OPSIBOW. Hampson, Gallardo-Domâs, Furlanetto, Dvorský, Daniel, V. State Op. Ch & O, Gatti (Director: Peter Stein; V/D: Anton Reitzenstein)

It is rare that you have a quintet of principals who sing with such clear and rock-steady tone as those chosen for Peter Stein's Vienna State Opera production of *Simon Boccanegra* in 2002. Thomas Hampson as Boccanegra is at his peak, singing and acting magnificently. He is deeply moving opposite Cristina Gallardo-Domâs as Maria in their great recognition scene, one of the most touching moments in all Verdi. Hampson is well matched by Ferruccio Furlanetto with his dark, finely controlled bass as Fiesco, his adversary, and by Boaz Daniel as Paolo. The great Council Chamber scene is not only sung superbly, starting with Hampson in his address, *Plebe, Patrizi*, but Gatti builds up to the 'gulp' moment unerringly. At this point the set is less minimally stylized and more realistic than in other scenes of this great opera, setting the seal on a fine version, well recorded.

Abbado's 1977 recording of *Simon Boccanegra* (DG 449 752-2 (2) – Freni, Cappuccilli, Ghiaurov, Van Dam, Carreras, La Scala, Milan, Ch. & O) makes a fine choice for those wanting a CD version of this opera as it is one of the most beautiful Verdi sets ever made. The playing of the orchestra is brilliantly incisive as well as refined, so that the drama is underlined by the extra sharpness of focus. The cursing of Paolo after the great Council Chamber scene makes the scalp prickle, with the chorus muttering in horror and the bass clarinet adding a sinister comment, here beautifully moulded. Cappuccilli, always intelligent, gives a far more intense and illuminating performance than the one he recorded for RCA earlier in his career; and Ghiaurov as Fiesco sings beautifully too. Freni as Maria Boccanegra sings with freshness and clarity, while Van Dam is an impressive Paolo. With electrically intense choral singing as well, this is a set to outshine even Abbado's *Macbeth*, and it is superbly transferred to CD – now at mid-price.

La traviata (complete, DVD version)

Decca DVD 071 431-9. Gheorghiu, Lopardo, Nucci, ROHCG Ch. & O, Solti (Director: Richard Eyre; V/D: Humphrey Burton & Peter Maniura)

As this DVD rightly claims, this famous Solti performance of *La traviata* captures one of the most sensational débuts in recent operatic history. Singing Violetta for the first time, Angela Gheorghiu made the part entirely her own. But the DVD can also claim a special plaudit for the magical opening, when the camera focuses closely on Solti while he conducts the *Prelude*, with every movement of his hands and the concentration in his eyes creating the music in front of us. He holds the tension at the highest level throughout, with the strings playing marvellously, and recorded with absolute realism. Then the curtain goes up and Bob Crowley's superb stage spectacle spreads out before our eyes. The singing is glorious, and this is one of the DVDs that should be a cornerstone in any collection.

Defying the problems of recording opera live at Covent Garden, the Decca engineers here offer one of the most vivid and involving versions ever of *La traviata*. As on stage, Gheorghiu brings heartfelt revelations, using her rich and vibrant, finely shaded soprano with consistent subtlety. Youthfully vivacious in Act I, dazzling in her coloratura, she already reveals the depths of feeling which compel her later self-sacrifice. In Act II she finds ample power for the great outburst of *Amami, Alfredo*, and in Act III almost uniquely uses the second stanza of *Addio del passato* (often omitted) to heighten the intensity of the heroine's emotions. Frank Lopardo emerges as a fresh, lyrical Alfredo with a distinctive timbre, passionate and youthful-sounding too. Leo Nucci, a favourite baritone of Solti, provides a sharp contrast as a stolid but convincing Germont.

There is a wealth of additional performances to choose from for those who just want a CD version. Joan Sutherland recorded the role twice, first in the early 1960s with John Pritchard and, excellent though that version is, her digital re-make in the late 1970s is even finer, cast with Pavarotti on superb form and with Bonynge's finely sprung conducting, it is pretty unbeatable (Decca 430 491-2 (2)). Of course, Callas's many fans will prefer her 1955 version with Giulini, in a vividly dramatic performance, though with sound which is far from ideal (EMI 5 66450-2 (2)).

Il trovatore (complete, CD version)

Ⓜ RCA (ADD) 74321 39504-2 (2). L. Price, Domingo, Milnes, Cossotto, Amb. Op. Ch., New Philh. O, Mehta

The soaring curve of Leontyne Price's rich vocal line is immediately thrilling in her famous Act I aria, and it sets the style of the RCA performance, full-bodied and with dramatic tension consistently high. The choral contribution is superb: the famous *Soldiers'* and *Anvil Choruses* are marvellously fresh and dramatic. When *Di quella pira* comes, the orchestra opens with great gusto and Domingo sings with a ringing, heroic quality worthy of Caruso himself. There are many dramatic felicities, and Sherrill Milnes is in fine voice throughout; but perhaps the highlight of the set is the opening section of Act III, when Azucena finds her way to Conte di Luna's camp. The ensuing scene with Fiorenza Cossotto is vocally and dramatically electrifying.

Arias from: (i) *Aida*; (i; ii) *Don Carlo*; (ii) *Ernani*; *Macbeth*; (i) *Otello*; (ii) *Nabucco*

Ⓜ EMI Legends (ADD) 557760. Callas, with (i) Paris Conservatoire O; (ii) Philh. O; Rescigno

Classic Callas recordings, which should be in every opera lover's collection. The Philharmonia recordings, made in 1958, marked Callas's only visit to record at Abbey Road Studios. Much of the content shows the great diva at her very finest. Dismiss the top-note wobbles from your mind, and the rest has you enthralled by the vividness of characterization as well as musical imagination. It is sad that Callas did not record the role of Lady Macbeth complete. Here *La luce langue* is not as intense as the Act I aria and Sleepwalking scene, which are both unforgettable, and she holds the tension masterfully in the long *Don Carlos* scene. Abigaille, Elvira and Elisabetta all come out as real figures, sharply individual. Finely balanced recordings and sounding good in their Legends transfer. The Paris recordings (with the orchestra's distinctive timbre) are exciting too, with the Desdemona from *Otello* commandingly taken, Aida's *Ritorna vincitor* vehemently done, and *O don fatale* done as theatrically as you can imagine. With the bonus DVD of arias filmed in 1965 with the O Nat. de l'ORTF under Prêtre – compelling stuff – this one of the best Callas collections about, though no texts are included.

VICTORIA, Tomás Luis de (c. 1548-1611)

'The Victoria Collection': *Requiem (Officium defunctorum)*
(with Alonso Lobo: *Versa est in luctum*); *Lamentations of Jeremiah*
(for Maundy Thursday, Good Friday & Holy Saturday) (with Juan
Gutiérrez de Padilla: *Lamentations for Maundy Thursday); Tenebrae*
Responsories
Ⓑ Gimell GIMBX 304 (3). Tallis Scholars, Peter Phillips

Tomás Luis de Victoria's *Requiem*, the *Tenebrae Responsories* and the *Lamenta-*
tions, with their mystical intensity of expression, represent the peak of Spanish
Renaissance music, even though their composer spent his earlier years (1565-
87) in Rome. This admirable three-disc collection contains some of his most
beautiful and celestially serene settings. The *Requiem* (or *Officium defunctorum*)
is one of his very finest works. In their outstanding performance the Tallis
Scholars achieve great clarity of diction: they are 12 in number, and as a result
the polyphony is clear and so are the words. The presentation embraces also
Alonso Lobo's motet, *Versa est in luctum*, written for the funeral of Phillip II
of Spain, which Victoria greatly admired, and appended to his score. The *Lam-*
entations of Jeremiah for the services on Maundy Thursday, Good Friday and
Holy Saturday have a serene but poignant simplicity which Peter Phillips captures movingly, with spacious tempi. As they proceed the number of voices
Victoria uses gradually increases, with the final Jerusalem sections always
expanding the scoring, so there is a crescendo not only within each Lament but
within each set of three and then over the nine. This disc also includes the
six-voice *Lamentations for Maundy Thursday* by Juan Gutiérrez de Padilla
(*c.*1590-1664), born in Málaga, but who moved to New Spain (Mexico), where
he became Maestro de Capella at Puebla Cathedral. The music (to quote Peter
Phillips) 'is spiced up with the augmented intervals beloved of every Iberian
composer'.

    The *Responsories* are so called because of the tradition of performing them
in the evening in increasing darkness, as the candles were extinguished one
by one. The Tallis Scholars' performance is restrained but flawless in both
blend and intonation. They are beautifully recorded throughout, and this well-
documented set is offered at a special bargain price to commemorate (in 2011)
the quatercentenary of Victoria's death.

VILLA-LOBOS, Heitor (1887-1959)

(i-ii) *Bachianas brasileiras 3*; *Mômoprecóce*; (iii) *Guitar Concerto*;
(iv) *Fantasia for Soprano Saxophone & Chamber Orchestra*;
(i) Piano music: *A prole do bebê (suite)*; *A lenda do caboclo*; *Alma*

brasileira (Chôros 5); Ciclo brasiliero; Festa no sertão; Impressões seresteiras

ⓑ EMI Gemini 3 81529-2 (2). (i) Ortiz; (ii) New Philh. O, Ashkenazy; (iii) A. Romero, LPO, López-Cobos; (iv) Harle, ASMF, Marriner

In many ways this is one of the finest Villa-Lobos collections in the catalogue, certainly the most varied. His rather melancholy piano-piece *A lenda do caboclo* ('Legend of a half-caste') gives a clue to the unique identity of this music, for the composer's mother was Hispanic, his father of Indian descent. No. 3 of the *Bachianas Brasileiras*, which dates from 1938, is the only one of the series to involve the piano. The *Mômoprecóce* began life in 1920 (while the composer was living in Paris) as a set of piano pieces called *Carnaval das Crianças* and it was reworked in its concertante form later. Like so much of Villa-Lobos's music, the score is rowdy and colourful. Cristina Ortiz, herself Brazilian, is a natural choice for this repertoire. She plays with appropriate vigour, reflective feeling and colour, and Ashkenazy gives splendid support. The late-1970s recording is excellent, with the CD transfer adding a little edge to the high violins. Ortiz is equally impressive in the solo piano pieces (again very well recorded), which she plays with flair and at times with touching tenderness, as in Villa-Lobos's portraits of the *Clay* and *Rag Dolls*, the third and sixth members of *A prole do bebê* ('Baby's family'), Angel Romero makes the most of the comparatively slight *Guitar Concerto*, bringing out its Latin feeling. The *Fantasia for Soprano Saxophone* is a more substantial piece with three well-defined movements, contrasted in invention. John Harle is a perceptive soloist with a most appealing timbre and this is one of the highlights of the set. The recordings in both these concertante works (made in 1984 and 1990 respectively) are well up to the best Abbey Road analogue standards.

(i) **Chôros** *1*; (ii) **Chôros** *4* (for 3 horns & trombone); (iii) **Chôros** *6, 8* & *9*

BIS CD1450. (i) Fabio Zanon; (ii) Dante Venque, Ozéas Arantes, Samuel Hamzem, Darrin Coleman Milling: (iii) São Paulo SO, John Neschling

The series of *Chôros* on which Villa-Lobos embarked in the 1920s, employ various instrumental combinations. The *First* (1920) is for solo guitar and the *Fourth* (1926) for three horns and bass trombone. The *Sixth* (also 1926) is the first for orchestra, and both the *Eighth* (1925) and *Ninth* (1929) employ Brazilian percussion instruments; the resulting sonorities, such as the *caracaxa* (child's rattle) have great exotic appeal. Villa-Lobos absorbed into his system much of the contemporary music of the day, Debussy, *The Rite of Spring*, *Le bœuf sur le toit* and works of Les Six. Yet it is the richly textured exoticism, evoking the sounds of the Brazilian forest, the boundless vitality of the dance, which resonates in the memory. Villa-Lobos creates his own sound-world and there is an infectious life and atmosphere here. John Neschling, born in Rio de Janeiro, and a pupil of Swarowsky and Bernstein, gets an enthusiastic response from his fine São Paolo players, and the BIS recording team does them proud. A good entry point into this composer's world.

VIVALDI, Antonio (1678-1741)

'Ultimate Vivaldi': Disc 1: *The Four Seasons*; *Triple Violin Concerto in F, RV 551*; *Quadruple Violin Concerto in B min., RV 580* (Accardo & soloists, I Solisti di Napoli). Disc 2: *Concertos for Bassoon, RV 498* (Gatt); *Flute, RV 441* (Bennett); *Oboe, RV 456* (Black); *2 Oboes, RV 535* (with Nicklin); *2 Oboes, Bassoon, 2 Horns & Violin, RV 574* (as above, with T. & I. Brown; Davis); *Piccolo Concerto in C, RV 443* (Bennett). Disc 3: *Cello Concertos, RV 401; 411; 412; 413; 418; 424* (Schiff, ASMF, Marriner). Disc 4: *Concertos for Guitar, RV 93; 356; 425; for 2 Guitars, RV 532; for 4 Guitars, RV 580* (Los Romeros (members), ASMF, I. Brown). Disc 5: *Double Concerto for Guitar & Viola d'amore, RV 540*, arr. Malipiero (Fernández, Blume, ECO, Malcolm). *Glorias: in D, RV 588 & 589* (soloists, St John's College, Cambridge, Ch., Wren O, Guest).
ⓑⓑ Decca (ADD) 475 8536 (5)

This is undoubtedly the highlight of Decca's super-budget 'Ultimate' composer series. There is no better Vivaldi collection in the catalogue, led by Salvatore Accardo's outstanding version of *The Four Seasons* and including a superb collection of miscellaneous concertos with outstanding wind soloists from Marriner's Academy (plus the excellent Heinrich Schiff in the *Cello Concertos*), and members of Los Romeros (originally by Philips) in the works for guitar (originally for mandolin, lute or violins). The selection is capped by splendid accounts from St John's of the two *Glorias*, including the more famous, RV 589. But it is a pity there are no accompanying liner notes.

(i) *The Four Seasons, Op. 8/1-4*; (ii) *Bassoon Concerto in A min., RV 498*; (iii) *Double Concerto for 2 Oboes in D min., RV 535*; (iv) *Piccolo Concerto in C, RV 443*
Ⓜ Decca (ADD) 475 7531. (i) Loveday; (ii) Gatt; (iii) Black, Nicklin; (iv) Bennett; ASMF, Marriner

Marriner's 1969 recording of *The Four Seasons* with Alan Loveday has been our top recommendation for four decades, and it is still unsurpassed. It has an element of fantasy that makes the music sound utterly new; it is full of imaginative touches, with Simon Preston subtly varying the continuo between harpsichord and organ. The opulence of string-tone may have a romantic connotation, but there is no self-indulgence in the interpretation, no sentimentality, for the contrasts are made sharper and fresher. Indeed, its stylish success on modern instruments makes one wonder what the fuss about period performance is all about. It now comes back into the catalogue with three bonus concertos which are hardly less enjoyable.

L'estro armonico, Op. 3; (i) *Bassoon Concerto in A min., RV 498*; (ii) *Flute Concerto in C min., RV 441*; (iii) *Oboe Concerto in F, RV 456*; (i; iii–iv) *Concerto in F for 2 Oboes, Bassoon, 2 Horns and Violin, RV 574*

Ⓑ Double Decca 443 476-2 (2). (i) Gatt; (ii) Bennett; (iii) Black; (iv) Nicklin, T. Brown, R. Davis, I. Brown, Hogwood, Tilney, Heath; ASMF, Marriner

Those who have not been won over by the more abrasive sound of period instruments will find Marriner's set no less stylish than those of his period-performance rivals. As so often, he directs the Academy in radiant and imaginative performances of baroque music and yet observes scholarly good manners. The delightful use of the continuo – lute and organ, as well as harpsichord – the sharing of solo honours and the consistently resilient string-playing of the ensemble make for compelling listening. The 1972 recording, made in St John's, Smith Square, is immaculately transferred, and as a bonus come four of Vivaldi's most inventive concertos, each with its own special effects.

La stravaganza, Op. 4

Ⓑ Double Decca (ADD) 444 821-2 (2). ASMF, Marriner

Marriner's performances make this music irresistible. The solo playing of Carmel Kaine and Alan Loveday is superb and, when the Academy's rhythms have such splendid buoyancy and lift, it is easy to accept Marriner's preference for a relatively sweet style in the often heavenly slow movements. The contribution of an imaginatively varied continuo (theorbo and organ) adds much to the colour of Vivaldi's score. The recordings, made in St John's, Smith Square, in 1974, are of the highest quality, with CD transfers in the demonstration class.

(i) *La cetra (12 Violin Concertos), Op. 9*; (ii) *Double Oboe Concerto in D min., RV 535*; (iii) *Piccolo Concerto in C, RV 443*

Double Decca (ADD) 448 110-2 (2). (i) Iona Brown; (ii) Black, Nicklin; (iii) Bennett; (ii–iii) cond. Marriner; ASMF

For *La cetra* Iona Brown acts as director in the place of Sir Neville Marriner. So resilient and imaginative are the results that one detects virtually no difference from the immaculate and stylish Vivaldi playing in earlier Academy Vivaldi sets. There is some wonderful music here; the later concertos are every bit the equal of anything in *The Trial between Harmony and Invention*, and they are played gloriously. The recording too is outstandingly rich and vivid, even by earlier Argo standards with this group, and the Decca transfer to CD retains the demonstration excellence of the original analogue LPs, with yet a greater sense of body and presence. For the Double Decca reissue, two of Vivaldi's most engaging wind concertos have been added, winningly played by three Academy soloists. The sound is just as fine as in the concertos for violin.

(i) *Mandolin Concerto in C, RV 425*; (i–ii) *Double Concerto for 2 Mandolins in G, RV 532. Concerti con molti strumenti: Concerto for Violin & 2 Flutes diritti; 3 Oboes & Bassoon* (dedicated to Sua Altezza Reale di Sassonia), *RV 576*; *Concerto for 2 Violins in tromba marina, 2 Flutes diritti, 2 Mandolins, 2 Salmoè, 2 Theorbos & Cello, RV 558*; *Concerto for Violin solo, 2 Oboes & Bassoon* (dedicated to S. Pisandel) (Dresden version), *RV 319*; *Concerto for 2 Violins & 2 Cellos in D, RV 564*; *Concerto in C for 3 Violins, Oboe & 2 Flutes diritti, 2 Viole all'inglese, Salmoè, 2 Cellos, 2 Harpsichords & 2 Violins in tromba marina, RV 555*.

Virgin 5 45527-2. (i) Scaramuzzino; (ii) Maurer; soloists, Europa Galante, Biondi

Another excellent disc from Fabio Biondi and his outstanding period-instrument group. The two simple *Mandolin Concertos* are played intimately and are perfectly balanced. The *Concertos con molti strumenti* offer an extraordinary range of tone-colour, especially the extravagantly scored *C major Concerto*, RV 555. In the *Largo* of this work the violin plays an obbligato line to the two solo harpsichords, which are given alternating arpeggios in a pendulum style, embroidering them *a piacimento* ('as they please'). Toussaint Loviko, who provides the excellent notes, tells us that Vivaldi's girl musicians were hidden by grilles curtained with black gauze, so they were able to exchange instruments at will and were thus able to surprise their listeners.

Concertos for Strings in C, RV 115; *in C min., RV 120*; *in D, RV 121 & 123*; *in D min., RV 129*; *in F, RV 141*; *in F min., RV 143*; *in G min., RV 153, 154 & 156*; *in A, RV 158 & 159*.

Naïve OP 30377. Concerto Italiano, Alessandrini

Rinaldo Alessandrini and his Concerto Italiano offer 12 concertos played with great brio and expressive sensibility, and you have only to sample the first or the last of the concertos here, RV 159 and RV 123, to hear how deeply expressive are the brief slow movements, and how infectious are the *Allegros*. First-class recording ensures that this new series gets the strongest recommendation.

'Concerti con molti istromenti': Concerto funèbre in B flat for Oboe, Chalumeau, Violin, 3 Viole all'inglese, RV 579; *Concerto in C for 2 Recorders, Oboe, Chalumeau, Violin, 2 Viole all'inglese, 2 Violins 'in tromba marina', 2 Harpsichords, RV 555*; *Concerto in D min. for 2 Oboes, Bassoon, 2 Violins, RV 566*; *Double Trumpet Concerto in D, RV 781*; *Concerto in F for Viola d'amore, 2 Horns, 2 Oboes &*

Bassoon, RV 97; Concerto in F for Violin, 2 Oboes, Bassoon, 2 Horns, RV 574; Concerto in D for Violin, 2 Oboes, 2 Horns, RV 562
Hyp. CDA 67073. Soloists, King's Cons., King

This is one of the most attractive of all the CD groupings of Vivaldi's often extraordinarily scored multiple concertos, in which the period-instrument playing is not only expert, but constantly tweaks the ear. The braying horns often dominate, especially in RV 562 and RV 574. The oboes are used to decorate the *Grave* of the latter, and elegantly open the finale of the former, before a bravura violin sends sparks flying. The *Concerto funèbre*, not surprisingly, opens with a *Largo* and combines the remarkable solo combination of muted oboe, tenor chalumeau, a trio of viole all'inglese, accompanied by muted strings. Then (in RV 555) comes the most remarkable array of all. Vivaldi even throws in a pair of harpsichords for good measure, and they are given some most attractive solo passages and are used to provide a gentle rocking background for a most engaging violin soliloquy in the central *Largo*. Throughout, the solo playing is wonderfully stylish and appealing, and Robert King maintains a fine vigour in *Allegros* and an often gentle espressivo in slow movements. The recording is first class. Very highly recommended.

'Concerti con molti istromenti': Concerto in G min. for Oboe solo, Violin solo, 2 Flutes & 2 Oboes, RV 576; Concerto in G min. for Oboe solo, Violin solo, 2 Flutes & 2 Oboes, RV 577; Concerto in F for Violin, 2 Oboes & 2 Horns, RV 574; Concerto in F for Violin, 2 Oboes & 2 Horns, RV 569; Sinfonia for Strings in C, RV 192.
Naïve OP 30283. Soloists, Freiburg Bar. O, Von der Goltz

We know of the excellence of Gottfried von der Goltz's period-instrument Freiburg Baroque Orchestra from their outstanding DVD of the Bach *Brandenburg Concertos*. They are no less stimulating in these Vivaldi concertos, written for Dresden, to which they bring a remarkable range of instrumental colour and dynamic, much vitality and expressive finesse. Slow movements, usually played gently, are always memorable, as in the *Grave* of RV 569 or the *Larghetto* of RV 576, and the excellence of their horn players is demonstrated vigorously in RV 574. A splendid collection, vividly recorded.

Double Cello Concerto in G min., RV 531; Concerto for Flute, Oboe, Bassoon & Violin in F (La tempesta di mare), RV 570; Concerto funèbre in B flat for Violin, Oboe, Salmoè & 3 Viole all'inglese, RV 579; Flute Concerto in G min. (La notte), RV 439; Violin Concertos in D (L'inquietudine), RV 234; in E (Il riposo – per il Natale), RV 270; in A (Per eco in lontano), RV 552.
Virgin 5 45424-2. Europa Galante, Biondi

This collection of some of Vivaldi's most imaginative concertos, played on period instruments, is just as attractive as its looks. All the special effects, from the ghost and sleep evocations in *La notte* to the echoing second violin in RV 552, are neatly managed, and the atmosphere of the *Concerto funèbre* is well sustained. This concerto features a theme taken from *Tito Manlio*, where it was used as part of a procession to execution, and the scoring is very telling. Fabio Biondi leads an excellent team of soloists and directs sparkling accompaniments, with a touch of vintage dryness to the bouquet of string-timbre. Excellent recording.

Double Concertos: for 2 Cellos in G min., RV 531; for Violin, Cello in F (Il Proteo ò sia il mondoa rovescio), RV 544; for 2 Violins in A (per eco in lontano), RV 552. Triple Concertos: for 3 Violins in F, RV 551; for Violin & 2 Cellos in C, RV 561. Quadruple Concertos: for 2 Violins & 2 Cellos in C, RV 561; in D, RV 564.
Teldec 4509 94552-2. Coin and soloists, Il Giardino Armonico, Antonini

An exceptionally rewarding collection of concertos for multiple, stringed instruments. Christophe Coin leads an excellent team of soloists and the imaginative continuo (organ, harpsichord and archlute) adds to the colour of performances which are full of life, yet which also reveal the music's more subtle touches and are remarkably free from the exaggerated stylistic devices often associated with period instruments. The recording is excellent.

Violin Concertos in D (L'inquietudine), RV 234; in E min., RV 273; in E flat (La tempesta di mare), Op. 8/5; Double Violin Concerto in D min., Op. 3/11; Double Violin Sonata in D min. (La Follia), RV 63. (i) Aria: ***Andromeda liberate: Sovvente il sole***.
DG 477 7463. Hope, COE, (i) with Von Otter

Some exhilarating playing here. This collection begins with a dynamic account of the *'L'inquietudine'*, where the brilliance of the virtuosic writing is tempered with a timbre of both warmth and beauty. The opening of the *E minor Concerto* sounds darkly imposing, while *La tempesta di mare* is as exciting as it gets. Anne Sofie von Otter sings her aria with great beauty (and what a meltingly haunting aria it is too!). The CD ends with a vibrantly stylish account of the *Double Concerto in D minor*, from *L'estro armonico*. Superb recording and top production standards from DG.

(i) **Gloria in D, RV 588; Gloria in D, RV 589**; (ii-iii) **Beatus vir in C, RV 597; Dixit Dominus in D, RV 594**; (iv; iii) **Magnificat in G min., RV 610**
Ⓑ Double Decca (DDD/ADD) 443 455-2 (2). (i) Russell, Kwella, Wilkens, Bowen, St John's College, Cambridge, Ch., Wren O, Guest; (ii) J. Smith, Buchanan, Watts, Partridge, Shirley-Quirk, ECO, Cleobury; (iii) King's College, Cambridge, Ch.; (iv) Castle, Cockerham, King, ASMF, Ledger

The two settings of the *Gloria* make an apt and illuminating pairing. Both in D major, they have many points in common, presenting fascinating comparisons, when RV 588 is as inspired as its better-known companion. Guest directs strong and well-paced readings, with RV 588 the more lively. Good, warm recording to match the performances. *Dixit Dominus* cannot fail to attract those who have enjoyed the better-known *Gloria*. What caps this outstanding Vivaldi compilation is the earlier King's account of the inspired *Magnificat in G minor*. Ledger uses the small-scale setting and opts for boys' voices in the solos such as the beautiful duet, *Esurientes*, which is most winning. The performance overall is very compelling and moving, and the singing has all the accustomed beauty of King's. The transfer of an outstanding (1976) analogue recording is admirable, even richer than its digital companions.

(i) *Stabat Mater, RV 621*; *Clarae stella scintillate (Motet), RV 625*; *Concerto funèbre in B flat for Violin, Oboe, Salmoè & 3 Viole all'inglese, RV 579*; *Concerto sacra in D for Violin & Cello, with Organ obbligato, RV 554a*; *Sonata 4 al Santo Sepolcro in E flat for Strings, RV 130*.

Naïve OP 30367. (i) Mingardo; Concerto Italiano, Alessandrini

The deep contralto timbre of Sara Mingardo is especially telling in Vivaldi's *Stabat Mater*, and she is very moving in the agonized closing section. This performance is appropriately framed by the *Concerto funèbre* and similarly solemn 'Santo Sepolcro' Sonata. The other concertos which frame the contrasting motet, 'O bright stars shine forth', match its very different mood, and Mingardo successfully lightens her voice and style. Fine performances throughout.

Orlando furioso (complete, CD version)

CPO 777 095- 2 (3). Desler, Kennedy, De Liso, Gregoire, Coro da Camera Italiano, Modo Antiquo, Sardelli

Orlando furioso has a complex plot tied up with *Alcina* and *Orlando* (which we know from Handel). Orlando is well named, of course, for he goes mad at the end of Act II but recovers at the end of the opera in time to bless the marriage of the real lovers, Angelica and Medoro. The opera takes a little while to get going, but soon produces some splendid music for Orlando (the brilliant mezzo, Anne Desler), the engaging soprano Angelica (Nicki Kennedy) and of course Alcina (Marina De Liso) while Medoro's Act I aria '*I break the chains*' is particularly dramatic. But all the solo singing is of quality and the Camera Italiano Chorus and Modo Antiquo complete a fine supporting group, directed with spirit by Federico Maria Sardelli. Excellent recording, too, makes this enjoyable listening.

Arias from: *L'Atenaide*; *Catone in Utica*; *L'incoronazione di Dario*; *Griselda* (with *Sinfonia*); *Ottone in villa* (with *Sinfonia*); *Tito Manlio*; *Tamerlano (Sinfonia)*

®® Hyp. Helios CDH 55279. Emma Kirkby, Brandenburg Cons., Goodman

This delightful collection was recorded in 1994 when Emma Kirkby was at the very peak of her form. Whether she is singing alone, or in duet with an oboe (as in *Tito Manlio*), or with herself in the echo aria, *L'ombre, l'aure, e ancora il rio* (from *Ottone in villa*) she continually delights the ear and the senses. And how gently touching she is in *Non mi lusinga vana speranza* from *L'incoronazione di Dario*, and how stirringly regal in the closing *Se in campo armato*, with trumpet, from *Catone in Utica*. Roy Goodman's accompaniments with the Brandenburg Consort are a model of taste and maintain a nicely intimate atmosphere.

'Heroes': Arias from: *Andromeda liberata*; *Demofoonte*; *Farnace*; *Giustino*; *L'Olimpiade*; *Orlando finto pazzo*; *Orlando furioso*; *Ottone in villa*; *Tieteburga*; *Il Tigrane*; *Tito Manlio*
Virgin 3 63414-2. Jaroussky, Ens. Matheus, Spinosi

The French counter-tenor Philippe Jaroussky here gives an astonishing virtuoso performance in 15 arias from Vivaldi operas, well chosen to represent the three main periods of his operatic output. Brilliant, florid arias alternate with warmly lyrical ones. His fast divisions are flawless, breathtaking in their daring, with no suspicion of any intrusive aspirate. Perhaps even more remarkable are the intense, expansive, lyrical arias, which offer a refreshing view of the composer in their warmth, notably a *Larghetto* aria from *L'Olimpiade*, a late work, and the even more extended *E minor aria* Vivaldi contributed to a *Serenata* jointly composed with others, *Andromeda liberata*. This is a thrilling disc of rarities, very well accompanied and clearly recorded.

Opera arias and scenas: *Il Bajazet (Il Tamerlano): Anch'il mar par che sommerga*; *Dorilla in Tempe: Dell'aura al sussurrar*; *Il Farnace: Gelido in ogni vena*; *La Fida Ninfa: Alma oppressa*; *Dite, oimè*; *Griselda: Dopo un'orrida procella*; *Il Giustino: Sventurata navicella*; *Sorte, che m'invitasti . . . Ho nel petto un cor sì forte*. *L'Olimpiade: Tra le follie . . . Siam navi all'onde algenti*; *L'Orlando finto pazzo: Qual favellar? . . . Anderò volerò griderò*; *Il Teuzzone: Di trombe guerriere*. Arias with unidentified sources: *Di due rai languir costante*; *Zeffiretti, che sussurrate*.
Decca 466 569-2. Bartoli, Il Giardino Armonico (with Arnold Schoenberg Ch.)

This remarkable collection is valuable as much for its exploration of rare Vivaldi operas as for coloratura singing of extraordinary bravura and technical security. It is a pity that the programme (understandably) opens with the excerpt from *Dorilla in Tempe*, with its echoes of *Spring* from *The Four Seasons*, as the chorus, although enthusiastic in praising those seasonal joys, is less than sharply focused. But the following aria from *Griselda*, with its stormy horns and fiendish leaps and runs, shows just how expertly Cecilia Bartoli can deliver the kind of thrilling virtuosity expected by Vivaldi's audiences of their famous castrato soloists. Farnace's tragic aria, *Gelido in ogni vena* (based on the

Winter concerto), shows the other side of the coin with some exquisite lyrical singing of lovely descending chromatics. In short, this is dazzling singing of remarkable music, most stylishly and vividly accompanied. Indeed, the Storm aria from *Il Bajazet* brings a delivery of such speed and sharpness of articulation that the rapid fire of a musical machine-gun springs instantly to mind. Moreover, Decca have done their star mezzo proud with fine documentation including full translations.

WAGNER, Richard (1813–83)

Götterdämmerung: Dawn and Siegfried's Rhine Journey; Siegfried's Death and Funeral Music. Lohengrin: Preludes to Acts I & III. Die Meistersinger von Nürnberg: Overture. Das Rheingold: Entry of the Gods into Valhalla. Rienzi: Overture. Siegfried: Forest Murmurs. Tannhäuser: Overture. Die Walküre: Ride of the Valkyries; Wotan's Farewell and Magic Fire Music.
ⓑⓑ EMI Gemini 586248-(2). BPO, Tennstedt

This bargain Gemini two-CD set comprises two early digital collections (1981 and '83) of Wagner's orchestral music which were quite a sonic revelation in the early days of compact disc. With steely metallic cymbal clashes in the *Ride of the Valkyries* and a splendid thwack at the opening of the *Entry of the Gods into Valhalla*, the sense of spectacle is in no doubt. The sound could ideally be more opulent in the middle and bass (the brass is also a bit dry), but the brilliance is demonstrable. There is plenty of weight – the climax of *Siegfried's Funeral March* has massive penetration – and fine detail too, especially in the atmospheric *Forest Murmurs*. Tennstedt amalgamates something from the combined Furtwängler and Klemperer traditions with his broad, spacious reading, and the playing throughout is of the finest quality, always maintaining a high level of tension. The opening and closing sections of the *Tannhäuser Overture* are given a restrained nobility of feeling without any loss of power or impact. Similarly, the richly contoured string melody at the opening of *Rienzi* is elegiacally moulded, and later, when the brass enter in the allegro, there is no suggestion of the bandstand. In the Act I *Lohengrin Prelude*, Tennstedt lingers in the *pianissimo* sections, creating radiant detail, then presses on just before the climax.

Der fliegende Holländer (complete, DVD version)
DG DVD 073 4433. Rundgren, Ligendza, McIntyre, Bav. State Op. Ch. & O, Sawallisch

Der fliegende Holländer (complete, CD version)
DG 437 778-2 (2). Weikl, Studer, Sotin, Domingo, Seiffert, Ch. & O of German Op., Berlin, Sinopoli

The Bavarian State Opera production has taken some time to reach us on DVD. It was recorded in May 1974 and the production filmed the following autumn.

The adaptation by the Czech director Václav Kâslík is the second to appear on film (there was a monochrome and highly individual version in 1964 by Joachim Herz) and it succeeds in gripping the viewer visually as successfully as does Wolfgang Sawallisch musically. Indeed Sawallisch is the reason to investigate this set, for he gets gloriously eloquent playing from his wonderful Bavarian forces. No complaints about the soloists either: Catarina Ligendza makes an excellent Senta and Donald McIntyre is an effective Dutchman. The colour is as good as can be expected for a performance now 35 years old.

Sinopoli's CD version is also an intensely involving performance, volatile in the choice of often extreme speeds. The choral singing is electrifying, and the line-up of principals is arguably finer than any other. Cheryl Studer is a deeply moving Senta, not just immaculate vocally but conveying the intense vulnerability of the character in finely detailed singing. Bernd Weikl is a dark-toned, firmly focused Dutchman, strong and incisive. Hans Sotin is similarly firm and dark, nicely contrasted as Daland, and the luxury casting may well be judged from the choice of Plácido Domingo as an impressive, forthright Erik and Peter Seiffert as a ringing Steersman. Full, vivid sound and a top choice in this opera.

Lohengrin (complete, CD version)
DG 437 808-2 (3). Jerusalem, Studer, Meier, Welker, Moll, Schmidt, V. State Op. Ch., VPO, Abbado

That Abbado's speeds are generally faster than Solti's rival Decca set (with the Act III *Prelude* a notable exception) means that the complete opera is squeezed on to three instead of four discs, giving it a clear advantage. As Elsa, matching her earlier Bayreuth performance on Philips, Cheryl Studer is at her sweetest and purest, bringing out the heroine's naïvety more touchingly than Jessye Norman (on Solti's Decca set), whose weighty, mezzo-ish tone is thrillingly rich but is more suited to portraying other Wagner heroines than this. Though there are signs that Siegfried Jerusalem's voice is not as fresh as it once was, he sings commandingly, conveying both beauty and a true Heldentenor quality. Where Plácido Domingo for Solti, producing an even more beautiful tone, tends to use full voice for such intimate solos as *In fernem Land* and *Mein lieber Schwann*, Jerusalem sings them with tender restraint and gentler tone. Among the others, Waltraud Meier as Ortrud and Kurt Moll as King Heinrich are both superb, as fine as any predecessors; and though in the role of Telramund, Hartmut Welker's baritone is not ideally steady, that tends to underline the weakness of the character next to the positive Ortrud.

Die Meistersinger von Nürnberg (complete, DVD version)
DG DVD 073 4160 (2). Jerusalem, Weikl, Prey, Haggender, Clark, Schiml, Schenk, Bayreuth Festival Ch & O, Stein (Director: Wolfgang Wagner; V/D: Brian Large)

It is extraordinary largesse that we are so spoilt for choice with DVDs of *Die Meistersinger*, and several alternative versions will give great satisfaction. Wolfgang Wagner's production in 1984 assembled an exceptionally starry cast, with not a single weak link and with many strengths. This DVD offers a recording, made live but without an audience. The exception is the great *Quintet* in Act III, which appears to have been recorded separately with the singers miming their roles, a small flaw in what is otherwise an immaculate and revelatory film, directed by Brian Large. Wolfgang Wagner's sets and costumes are grandly traditional, and add greatly to the impact of the piece. Siegfried Jerusalem as Walther is one of the most heady-timbred of Heldentenoren, and sings with heroic tone in the Prize Song, making a magnificent climax. Bernd Weikl is a characterful, strong-toned Sachs and Mari Anne Haggender is a vivacious Eva, singing very sweetly, shading her tone down beautifully for the *Quintet*. Hermann Prey as Beckmesser is both characterful and unusually mellifluous of tone, not guying the character too much, and Manfred Schenk as Pogner, Graham Clark as David and Marga Schiml are all first rate. An outstanding version, with Horst Stein pacing the massive work splendidly.

The Mastersingers of Nuremberg (CD version, sung in English)

Chan. (ADD) 3148 (4). Remedios, Curphey, Hammond-Stroud, Bailey, Dempsey, Mangin, Sadler's Wells Ch. & O, Goodall

This recording of *The Mastersingers* in English, made by the BBC at Sadler's Wells in February 1968, marks an iconic moment in the history of opera in England. That is so not just because Goodall here demonstrates how strong the team of Sadler's Wells singers was in Wagner, but the whole project pointed the way forward to the emergence in due course of English National Opera at the Coliseum, a genuine 'Volksoper' rival to the grand international company at Covent Garden.

Goodall had been hibernating for many years, having earlier made a name for himself conducting (among much else) the first performance of Benjamin Britten's *Peter Grimes*. It was then an inspired choice to have him conduct Wagner at Sadler's Wells, and he seized it eagerly, as this glowing performance amply demonstrates in every bar. Goodall himself patiently helped to train the singers of the 1960s Sadler's Wells company in singing Wagner as he wanted it. His speeds are almost always very slow, but the singers respond superbly, revelling in the expansiveness instead of finding it a trial.

Alberto Remedios was then at his peak as a Wagner tenor, pure and unstrained throughout, rising magnificently to the challenge of the Prize Song in Act III, an exhilarating moment which sends you away joyfully, as the audience here plainly felt. Norman Bailey too was an outstanding Sachs, firm and focused, the wise philosopher; Noel Mangin is a clear-toned Pogner, and Gregory Dempsey is a bright, lively David, well contrasted with Remedios, while Derek Hammond-Stroud is a delightfully characterful Beckmesser, pointing the humour infectiously, though maybe the voice is too firm and strong for this character.

The women in the cast are not quite on this level, but Margaret Curphey as Eva sings with winning firmness and purity, and Ann Robson is a lively

Magdalene. It is striking that not one of the singers has even the suspicion of a wobble, and the excellent casting equally involves the other Masters and the Nightwatchman sung by Stafford Dean. Consistently adding to the glow of the performance is the singing of the chorus and the playing of the orchestra. It is astonishing, remembering the variable quality of latter-day companies, that the team at Sadler's Wells in the 1960s was so fine, quite a revelation. The radio recording captures the atmosphere thrillingly, a credit to the 1968 engineers, as well as to those making this transfer.

Parsifal (complete, CD version)

DG 477 6006 (4). Domingo, Meier, Struckmann, Selig, Bankl, Anger, V. State Op. Ch. & O,
   Thielemann

Christian Thielemann conducts an incandescent account of *Parsifal*, recorded live at a sequence of performances at the Vienna State Opera in June 2005. The performance is crowned by the magnificent singing and acting of Plácido Domingo in the title-role. It is astonishing that in his sixties he can produce such glorious, cleanly focused tone, powerful and even youthful-sounding, in keeping with the character of the young hero. Even in a live account his voice remains fresh to the end of this long opera. Comparably fine is the Kundry of Waltraud Meier, in glorious voice, attacking even the most exposed top notes with freshness, clarity and precision. Though the others are rather less impressive, they all sing well, with Franz-Josef Selig darkly powerful if occasionally unsteady as Gurnemanz and Falk Struckmann as Amfortas initially gritty-toned, later focusing more cleanly in Act III. Wolfgang Bankl is an excellent Klingsor, attacking the role incisively, while Ain Anger as Titurel completes a well-balanced team. Thielemann remains the hero, alongside Domingo, bringing dedication to this quasi-religious score combined with passion and dramatic bite. He keeps speeds flowing well, while letting the music breathe spaciously, with the choral singing magnificent throughout, and with the recording – made in collaboration with Austrian Radio – vividly atmospheric. This now takes pride of place for this opera, even ahead of Karajan's deeply spiritual and equally dedicated account.

Der Ring des Nibelungen (DVD version) *Das Rheingold*

Warner DVD 2564 62318-2. Tomlinson, Clark, Finnie, Von Kannen, Hölle, Kang, Svendén,
   Bayreuth Festival O, Barenboim (Director: Harry Kupfer; V/D: Horant H. Hohlfeld)

Die Walküre

Warner DVD 2564 62319-2 (2). Elming, Secunde, Tomlinson, Finnie, Evans, Hölle,
   Bayreuth Festival O, Barenboim (Director: Harry Kupfer; V/D: Horant H. Hohlfeld)

Siegfried

Warner DVD 2564 62320-2 (2). Jerusalem, Clark, Tomlinson, Von Kannen, Evans, Kang,
   Svendén, Bayreuth Festival O, Barenboim (Director: Harry Kupfer; V/D: Horant H.
   Hohlfeld)

Götterdämmerung

Warner DVD 2564 62321-2 (2). Jerusalem, Evans, Brinkmann, Bundschuh, Kang, Von
  Kannen, Bayreuth Festival O, Barenboim (Director: Harry Kupfer; V/D: Horant H.
  Hohlfeld)

Harry Kupfer's Bayreuth production of the *Ring* cycle, recorded in 1991 and
1992, involves minimal stylized sets, evocatively lit. Generally conventional
costumes, with occasional modern touches as in male characters wearing trilbies (not everybody's choice), result in a cycle which tells the complex story of
each part of the tetralogy as clearly and graphically as possible. Under the direction of Wolfgang Wagner each section was filmed as a straight performance
in the Festspielhaus but without an audience, giving more air to the sound.

Rheingold opens in a shimmering green light with the Rhinemaidens dancing and the gold shining from a great cavity in the river bed. Alberich is
characterfully sung by Günter von Kannen with firm, clear tone, as he steals
the gold. The gods, waiting to enter the newly built Valhalla, are pictured in a
simple, bare setting, and are again controversially depicted, with many of them
wearing green fronds, and with John Tomlinson in dark glasses as Wotan,
their powerful leader. Linda Finnie sings with fresh, clear tone as Fricka and
Graham Clark makes a picturesque Loge, preening himself in a blond wig. The
giants, Fasolt and Fafner (Matthias Hölle and Philip Kang both excellent) are
then portrayed as genuinely gigantic figures with prosthetic arms and enormous bodies. Wotan's and Loge's coup in stealing the gold back from Alberich
in Nibelheim is then atmospherically portrayed, and so is the handing of the
gold to the giants in payment for their work, including the Tarnhelm and the
Ring. The Rainbow Bridge in the final scene is suggested by vertical strip lighting in the relevant colours, illuminating Daniel Barenboim's powerful
conducting, a thrilling conclusion.

Die Walküre benefits not just from an excellent cast with no weak links but
from the thrustful conducting of Daniel Barenboim, giving full weight to the
big moments like the opening of Wotan's Farewell in Act III. The Kupfer settings are similar to those in *Rheingold*, with space-age implications in the
minimal sets, evocative lighting and clever use of long perspectives. Poul Elming as Siegmund (wearing fatigues!) comes out with ringing top notes, yet
sings with the most tender emotion on greeting Sieglinde, beautifully sung by
Nadine Secunde. Linda Finnie as Fricka makes the role seem nobler than
usual, opposite the compelling Wotan of John Tomlinson. Anne Evans sings
magnificently as Brünnhilde, fresh and bright, with clear, firm tone.

In *Siegfried* the Harry Kupfer production ingeniously conveys such tricky
moments as the arrival of the bear in Act I and the flying of the Woodbird in
Act II very graphically without descending into unwanted comic effects. Here
the light soprano, Hilde Leidland, sings freshly and clearly. Graham Clark as
the shifty Mime is splendidly contrasted with the strong Siegfried of Siegfried
Jerusalem, the most mellifluous Heldentenor of his generation. As the Wanderer, John Tomlinson remains a tower of strength, poignantly struck down at

his defeat at the hands of the callous Siegfried. The climax of Act III with Anne Evans at her peak as Brüunnhilde is exhilarating, aided by Daniel Barenboim's powerful conducting.

Götterdämmerung opens with the Norns literally weaving their thread, and with Anne Evans in radiant voice singing superbly opposite the fine, clear Siegfried of Siegfried Jerusalem. The clarity of sound in the Rhine Journey is a delight, and in the Gibichung Hall scenes the Hagen of Philip Kang is genuinely sinister. Eva-Maria Bundschuh as Gutrune sings very sweetly, though Bodo Brinkmann as Gunther is too wobbly. The Alberich of Günter von Kannen is again excellent, and Barenboim brings out the darkness of the score most compellingly. In the calling of the Vassals in Act II the Bayreuth Chorus makes the most of its brief moment, all, like Siegfried himself, wearing boiler suits. The final Immolation scene is vividly done, with Anne Evans rising superbly to the challenge, though Kupfer's device, after the fall of Valhalla, to have members of a modern audience watching TV sets is an odd intrusion for the final curtain, and one not welcomed by I.M.

Der Ring des Nibelungen (complete, CD version)

Ⓜ Decca (ADD) 455 555-2 (14). Nilsson, Windgassen, Flagstad, Fischer-Dieskau, Hotter, London, Ludwig, Neidlinger, Frick, Svanholm, Stolze, Böhme, Hoffgen, Sutherland, Crespin, King, Watson, Ch. & VPO, Solti

Ⓜ Testament 141 412 9 (14). 1955 Bayreuth recording, cond. Keilberth (details below)

It would be to take the easy option to suggest that the top choice for Wagner's epic *Ring* cycle on CD is Solti's pioneering version for Decca, especially now it is so nicely packaged and relatively inexpensive. Indeed, it is hard to go wrong with that choice, the peak of achievement for the conductor and many of his cast, commanding and magnificent.

Also, readers might also be interested to hear Deryck Cooke's 'An introduction to the Ring', released in conjunction with the Solti *Ring*, a scholarly lecture, with its riveting discourse demonstrating just how many of the leading ideas in the *Ring* develop from one another, springing from an original germ (Decca 443 581-2 (2)).

Decca have also reissued Boehm's fine (1967) Bayreuth Festival set, which captures the unique atmosphere and acoustic of the Festspielhaus very vividly. Birgit Nilsson as Brünnhilde and Wolfgang Windgassen as Siegfried are both a degree more volatile and passionate than they were in the Solti cycle. Gustav Neidlinger as Alberich is also superb, as he was in the Solti set, and the only major reservation concerns the Wotan of Theo Adam in a performance searchingly intense and finely detailed, but often unsteady of tone even at that period. The sound, only occasionally restricted, has been vividly transferred (Decca 478 2367 (14)).

However, Testament have released Joseph Keilberth's recordings, taken live from the 1955 *Ring* cycle at Bayreuth, which was the very first recording in stereo, some years before the Decca set, which was recorded in the studio. This earlier set had been languishing in the archives, and it was thanks to the enterprise of Stewart Brown of Testament that finally, after much negotiation, the cycle appeared.

When Wieland Wagner invited Keilberth to conduct the *Ring* at Bayreuth, he was consciously aiming to present a reading manifestly contrasted with that of Hans Knappertsbusch's spacious and contemplative version. Keilberth, by contrast, is urgent and passionate, and the thrust of the performance makes the result intensely exciting, inspiring the great Wagnerian singers in the cast to give of their finest. Testament have released the complete cycle at mid-price, and the individual operas are discussed below. However, in the complete boxed set, the first version of *Götterdämmerung* with the original cast is included and, fine though that is, the cast of the second cycle of the *Ring* at Bayreuth is even finer – see below.

Das Rheingold (complete, CD version)
Testament (ADD) SBT2 1390 (2). Hotter, Neidlinger, Lustig, Weber, Bayreuth Festival O, Keilberth

Keilberth's complete recording of the *Ring* cycle emerges on disc for the first time, half a century late, as a constant revelation. The first astonishing thing is the clarity of the voices and the cleanness of the separation between them, scarcely rivalled by any more recent recordings. Vivid and immediate, the three Rhinemaidens are sharply defined in contrast with each other, with directional effects very clear. It means that the orchestra is relatively recessed, but the atmospheric beauty of the Bayreuth orchestra's playing is well caught, and the big climaxes come over vividly, as for example Donner's smiting of the anvil (even though no metallic clattering is conveyed). Another thrilling moment comes in Wotan's final monologue with the first emergence of the Sword Theme. Keilberth's conducting throughout is electrically intense, far more dynamic than that of his fellow Bayreuth conductor, Hans Knappertsbusch.

Die Walküre (complete, CD version)
Testament SBT4 1391 (4). Varnay, Hotter, Brouwenstijn, Vinay, Greindl, Bayreuth Festival O, Keilberth

Hans Hotter's interpretation of the role of Wotan is well known from a number of versions, but here he not only sings with urgency, his voice is in wonderfully fresh condition, perfectly focused. 'Wotan's Farewell' has never been more powerfully presented, with his agony over having to punish his favourite daughter most movingly conveyed. Astrid Varnay as Brünnhilde is similarly moving, and so are Gré Brouwenstijn as Sieglinde and the darkly baritonal Ramón Vinay (Toscanini's choice as Otello) singing Siegmund, with Josef Greindl massive of voice as Hunding. The end of Act I, when the twins fall into each other's arms, brings another great orgasmic moment, and the recording, originally made by Decca and now beautifully reprocessed, far outshines in quality the radio recordings of Bayreuth that have appeared on various labels.

Siegfried (complete, CD version)

Testament SBT4 1392 (4). Windgassen, Kuen, Hotter, Varnay, Neidlinger, Bayreuth
   Festival O, Keilberth

Fine as the recording of the 1955 *Walküre* is in the Testament processing, the
Siegfried of that year is even more impressive, with even greater weight in the
orchestral sound, with the brass and timpani astonishingly vivid. In this section of the *Ring* cycle that is particularly important, when Wagner more than
ever relies on darkened orchestration. The voices are vividly caught too, with a
wonderful sense of presence, and Wolfgang Windgassen as Siegfried (also the
Siegfried of the Solti cycle) is in gloriously fresh voice, superbly contrasted with
the mean-sounding but comparably well-focused tenor of Paul Kuen as Mime.
Gustav Neidlinger too is clear and incisive as Alberich, with Josef Greindl
darkly majestic as Fafner. The duetting of Varnay and Windgassen as Siegfried
and Brünnhilde then makes a thrillingly passionate conclusion in Keilberth's
thrustful reading.

Götterdämmerung (complete, CD version of 2nd cycle recording)

Testament (ADD) SBT4 1433 (4). Mödl, Windgassen, Hotter, Ilosvey, Neidlinger, Greindl,
   Brouwenstijn, Bayreuth Festival Ch. & O, Keilberth

Recorded in 1955 during the second cycle of the *Ring* at Bayreuth under Keilberth, this is an important supplement to the complete Keilberth cycle that
Testament issued earlier, with arguably two important cast-changes making it
even more attractive: Martha Mödl instead of Astrid Varnay, more powerful if
less girlish, and Hans Hotter as Gunther certainly finer than Hermann Uhde,
who was rested in order to sing in the Bayreuth *Fliegende Holländer*. Wolfgang
Windgassen as Siegfried is again remarkable, not just for his unstrained power
but for the moments of tenderness.

   Keilberth's conducting is incandescent, more urgent than Hans Knappertsbusch or Furtwängler, making the big dramatic moments totally thrilling,
surging with excitement, with the fulfilment of the final scene movingly caught.
The impact is all the greater thanks to the excellent stereo sound obtained by
the Decca engineers, even if the string focus can be a little fizzy. As before,
words are astonishingly clear.

Tannhäuser (complete (Dresden) DVD version, plus Paris *Bacchanale*)

DG DVD 073 4446 (2). Wenkoff, G. Jones, Weikl, Sotin, Bayreuth Festival Ch. & O, C. Davis
   (Stage Director: Götz Friedrich; V/D: Thomas Olofsson)

This 1978 *Tannhäuser* was the first time a production had been filmed complete
at Bayreuth; considering that, the visual balance and the sound are remarkably
impressive. Obviously the artists were aware that history was being made, and
the concentration and tension of the performance are unmistakable. The sets are
not opulent but are faithful to the composer's intentions, and Sir Colin Davis's
conducting is full of inspiration and vitality. The star performance is Dame

Gwyneth Jones's gloriously sung Elisabeth and Venus, but Spas Wenkoff is strong in the title-role and Bernd Weikl is a superb Wolfram. The production offers the original Dresden version, plus the Paris *Bacchanale*, handled with effective eroticism. All in all, a remarkable achievement.

Tannhäuser (complete (Paris) CD version)
DG 427 625-2 (3). Domingo, Studer, Baltsa, Salminen, Schmidt, Ch. & Philh. O, Sinopoli

Plácido Domingo as Tannhäuser for Sinopoli brings balm to the ears, producing sounds of much power as well as beauty. Sinopoli here makes one of his most passionately committed opera recordings, warmer and more flexible than Decca's Solti version, always individual, with fine detail brought out, always persuasive and never wilful. Agnes Baltsa is not ideally opulent of tone as Venus, but she is the complete seductress. Cheryl Studer – who sang the role of Elisabeth for Sinopoli at Bayreuth – gives a most sensitive performance, not always even of tone but creating a movingly intense portrait of the heroine, vulnerable and very feminine. Matti Salminen in one of his last recordings makes a superb Landgrave and Andreas Schmidt a noble Wolfram, even though his legato could be smoother in *O Star of Eve*.

Tristan und Isolde (complete, DVD version)
DG DVD 073 4439 (2). Jerusalem, Meier, Hölle, Struckmann, Bayreuth Festival Ch. & O, Barenboim

Tristan und Isolde (complete, CD version)
EMI 9 6686402(3) (3). Stemme, Domingo, Fujimura, Pape, Bär, ROHCG Ch. & O, Pappano

Barenboim's DVD is not a recording of a live performance but was made over a seven-day period, without an audience, in 1995. The result is very successful indeed, having the best of both worlds and offering an inherent spontaneity. The production is plain and the performance not voluptuous either, but with a splendid partnership of Siegfried Jerusalem at his finest and the rich-voiced Waltraud Meier also at her freshest, and the casting topped by Matthias Hölle's resonant bass as King Mark. Barenboim is in his element and the Bayreuth Festival Orchestra provide a richly intense backing

When Plácido Domingo suggested to EMI that as a culmination to his unique career he would like to record *Tristan und Isolde*, the record company boldly took up the challenge and with luxury casting produced what is instantly recognizable as a classic recording, worthy successor to the great Furtwängler version of 1952 with Flagstad as Isolde. The glory of this set is not only the radiant singing of Domingo, still in glorious, full-throated voice in his sixties, but the warmly understanding conducting of Antonio Pappano with the Covent Garden Orchestra, more volatile than that of Furtwängler but just as concentrated. Domingo, at once heroic and lyrical, not only offers the most beautiful assumption on disc since Windgassen for Boehm at Bayreuth in 1966, but he sings with a passion beyond that of most Heldentenoren, and he is matched by the tenderly girlish Isolde of Nina Stemme. Hers may not be a big, noble soprano like those of Flagstad or Birgit Nilsson, and in Act II she comes to sound a little stressed, but with fine projection and subtle shading her portrait is the more passionate and more feminine. Mihoko Fujimura as Brangäne is clear and tender too – her warnings in the love duet creep exquisitely on the ear – and René Pape as King Mark is unmatched by any contemporary. Olaf Bär with his lieder-like command of detail is a fine Kurwenal, with such stars as Ian Bostridge as the Shepherd and Rolando Villazón as the Young Sailor filling in smaller parts. The set includes a bonus CD-ROM with libretto and synopsis.

WALLACE, William (1860-1940)

Symphonic Poems 1 (The Passing of Beatrice); 3 (Sister Helen); 5 (Sir William Wallace); 6 (Villon)
Hyp. CDA 66848. BBC Scottish SO, Brabbins

Like Hamish MacCunn, William Wallace was born in Greenock, near Glasgow. *Sir William Wallace*'s Scottish character is immediately obvious at the brooding opening; the main theme, 'Scots wha' hae', emerges only slowly but is celebrated more openly towards the end. *Villon*, an irreverent medieval poet, was a hero of a different kind, and Wallace's programme draws on the thoughts of his philosophical ballads (which are named in the synopsis) in music that is both reflective and vividly colourful. The very romantic *Passing of Beatrice* is a sensuous vision of Paradise, lusciously Wagnerian with an unashamedly Tristanesque close, reflecting the heroine's final transformation. The scoring is sensuously rich, yet it retains the spiritually ethereal quality of the narrative, rather as Wagner does in *Parsifal*. The final piece here is based on Rossetti. What is so remarkable is not only the quality of the musical material throughout these works, but also the composer's skill and confidence in handling it: they are musically every bit as well crafted as the symphonic poems of Liszt. Clearly the BBC Scottish Symphony Orchestra enjoy playing them. The result is remarkably satisfying.

WALTON, William (1902-83)

(i) Capriccio burlesco; (ii) Music for Children; Portsmouth Point Overture; (i) The Quest (ballet suite); Scapino Overture; (ii) Siesta; (i; iii) Sinfonia concertante
Lyrita SRCD 224. Composer, with (i) LSO; (ii) LPO; (iii) Katin

When Walton made these recordings he was in his late sixties, and his speeds had grown a degree slower and safer. If *Portsmouth Point* loses some of its fizz at so moderate a speed, there is no doubting the commitment of the playing, brought out superbly by the vintage Lyrita sound. By contrast *Scapino* suffers hardly at all from the slower speed, rather the opposite, with the opening (if anything) even jauntier and the big cello melody drawn out more expressively. *Siesta* too brings out the piece's romantically lyrical side, rather than making it a relatively cool intermezzo. The *Capriccio burlesco* and the ten little pieces of the *Music for Children* are delightful too, with the subtleties of the instrumentation beautifully demonstrated. Much the biggest work here is the *Sinfonia concertante*, and in the outer movements the performance lacks the thrust that Walton himself gave it in his very first, wartime recording in which Phyllis Sellick was a scintillating soloist. Yet Peter Katin is a very responsive soloist too, and the central slow movement is much warmer and more passionate, with orchestral detail rather clearer. It is good too to have the first stereo recording of the suite from Walton's wartime ballet based on Spenser's 'Faerie Queene', *The Quest*, only a fraction of the whole, but a magical score, bright and colourful and unfailingly enjoyable.

(i) *Cello Concerto*; (ii) *Viola Concerto*; (iii) *Violin Concerto. Scapino*; *Coronation Marches: Crown Imperial*; *Orb and Sceptre*; *Façade Suites 1 & 2*; *Henry V: Suite. Symphonies 1 & 2*; *Variations on a Theme of Hindemith*; (iv) *Coronation Te Deum*; *Belshazzar's Feast*.
Decca 470 508-2 (4). (i) Cohen; (ii) Neubauer; (iii) Little; (iv) Terfel, L'inviti, Wayneflete
  Singers, Winchester Cathedral Ch.; Bournemouth Ch. & SO, Litton or Hill

Decca's four-disc Walton Edition offers consistently fine versions of all the composer's most important orchestral works, some of them unsurpassed by rival versions, with Andrew Litton an idiomatic Waltonian with a natural feeling for the jazzy syncopations. This set brings together the three Litton discs previously issued by Decca, but with important additions. The third of the four CDs, never originally issued with the others, contains outstanding versions of the *Viola Concerto* and *Hindemith Variations*, plus the two Walton *Façade Suites*.

Where most latter-day interpreters of the *Viola Concerto* have taken a very expansive view of the lyrical first movement, *Andante comodo*, Paul Neubauer comes nearer than anyone to following the example of the original interpreters on disc, Frederick Riddle and William Primrose, in adopting a flowing tempo, encouraged by the composer. It makes Neubauer's and Litton's far more persuasive than other modern versions, with no expressive self-indulgence and with the brisker passages in this movement also taken faster than has become usual. Neubauer's tone is taut and firm to match, clean rather than fruity, with the central Scherzo taken excitingly fast. He then relaxes beautifully for the hauntingly lovely epilogue, ending on a whispered *pianissimo*. Litton also encourages wide dynamic contrasts, with the big tuttis bringing an element of wildness in brassy syncopations. The *Hindemith Variations* also delivers a performance with contrasts heightened, not just of dynamic but of speed, extreme in both directions. This goes with an exceptional transparency in the orchestral textures, well caught in the recording and bringing out the refinement of Walton's orchestration. *Façade*, predictably, is a fun performance, although the warm acoustic runs the danger of taking some edge off these witty parodies.

Two of the other discs are the same as before, with Tasmin Little's heartfelt reading of the *Violin Concerto* very well coupled with Litton's outstanding account of the *Second Symphony* and *Scapino*, and Robert Cohen's thoughtful reading of the *Cello Concerto* in coupling with the *First Symphony*. Not since Previn's vintage recordings of Walton has a conductor so thrillingly conveyed the element of wildness in Walton's finest inspirations, notably in the *First Symphony*. Litton's success lies not just in his ability to screw up tension to breaking point but also in his treatment of the jazzy syncopations which are a vital element in this music. Like Previn – and, for that matter, Walton himself – Litton treats the jazz rhythms with a degree of idiomatic freedom, consistently making the music crackle with electric energy. In the *Symphony*, Litton more than anyone makes the finale into a fitting culmination, bold and brazen, resolving into the concluding climax triumphantly on a shattering outburst of timpani.

In the *Cello Concerto*, Litton is both mercurial and tender and his hushed, meditative approach is powerfully compelling. The way that Cohen makes the opening note of the slow finale seem to emerge from afar is magical. Tasmin Little as the soloist in the *Violin Concerto* gives the most tenderly beautiful performance, matching Litton in her control of Waltonian contrasts between tender lyricism and sparkling wit. Like Litton, she is able to hold full tension through pauses, often daringly extending them as in a live performance, so that the cadenzas in the first and last movements have rare intensity. This is a work which has generated many inspired performances, not least from woman violinists, and Little in spontaneity and tenderness is unsurpassed.

Litton's powerful account of *Belshazzar's Feast* brings a fresh, cleanly focused choral sound that, with the help of keenly atmospheric recording, points up more clearly than usual the terracing between the different groupings of voices. Recorded in Winchester Cathedral, the reverberation time is formidably long, yet, thanks to brilliant balancing, there is ample detail and fine focus in exceptionally incisive choral and orchestral sound. The great benefit is that this emerges as a performance on a bigger scale than its rivals, with the contrast between full chorus and semi-chorus the more sharply established. Bryn Terfel is a most dramatic baritone soloist, pointing the words as no one else has with deeply expressive and individual colourings, notably in the 'shopping list' – 'Babylon was a great city' – and in his spine-chilling narration describing the writing on the wall. This disc also includes the two coronation marches – *Crown Imperial* is particularly stirring – the *Coronation Te Deum* (sounding suitably imposing and very richly recorded) and the *Henry V*

Suite, with David Hill, chorus-master in *Belshazzar*, ably standing in for Litton in *Orb and Sceptre* and the *Te Deum*.

Sadly, the classic accounts of Previn's version of the *First Symphony* and Szell's account of the *Second* are currently unavailable on CD. However, the composer's own performance of the *First Symphony* is available, coupled with his version of *Belshazzar's Feast*, on EMI.

Viola Concerto; Violin Concerto

Ⓜ EMI 5 62813-2. Kennedy, RPO, Previn - **VAUGHAN WILLIAMS**: *The Lark Ascending*

(i–ii) Viola Concerto; (i; iii) Violin Concerto; (iv) Partita for Orchestra; Symphony 1 in B flat min.; (iv–v) Belshazzar's Feast

Ⓑ EMI stereo/mono 9 68944-2 (2) (i) Y. Menuhin; (ii) New Philh. O; (iii) LSO; (iv) Philh. O; (v) Bell, Philh. Ch.; cond. composer

Nigel Kennedy's achievement in giving equally rich and expressive performances of both *Concertos* makes for an ideal coupling, helped by the unique insight of André Previn as a Waltonian. Kennedy on the viola produces tone as rich and firm as on his usual violin. The Scherzo has never been recorded with more panache than here, and the finale brings a magic moment in the return of the main theme from the opening, hushed and intense. In the *Violin Concerto* Kennedy gives a warmly relaxed reading, in which he dashes off the bravura passages with great flair. He may miss some of the more searchingly introspective moments, but there are few Walton recordings as richly rewarding as this, helped by warm, atmospheric sound, and with the bonus of a highly sensitive account of Vaughan Williams's masterly evocation of *The Lark Ascending*.

However, the EMI collection has great historical interest as the composer, for many years his own finest interpreter, directs throughout. Fine performances (made in 1968/9) of both *Concertos* from Menuhin, who is in reasonably good form in the *Violin Concerto* and makes a very good showing in the masterly *Viola Concerto*. But many Waltonians will not approve of the extremely slow account of the *Viola Concerto* first movement, and undoubtedly Nigel Kennedy's performances of both works are superior. However, it is good to have such an important recording as that of the *First Symphony*, sharply illuminating and resurrected after some years of unavailability. *Belshazzar's Feast* obviously has authenticity too, but the singing of the Philharmonia Chorus, although good, is not ideally incisive; and some reservations could be expressed about Donald Bell's contribution, which might have been more imaginative. The recording is extremely clear, if a little on the dry side. The *Partita* is generally more successful. It was commissioned by the Cleveland Orchestra and first performed in 1958. The writing is typical of Walton's earlier style, having something of the hurly-burly of *Portsmouth Point*, and the finale, *Giga burlesca*, more than once reminds the listener of *Scapino*.

Violin Concerto
Onyx 4016. Ehnes, Vancouver SO, Tovey – **KORNGOLD**; **BARBER**: *Violin Concertos*

Ehnes gives perhaps the finest of all accounts of Walton's *Violin Concerto* on record. He sets his seal on his performance from the magical opening bars onwards, played exquisitely by soloist and orchestra alike, and all the way through the work brings out its full emotional thrust without vulgarity or exaggeration. Unlike most latter-day interpreters, Ehnes has taken note of the example of the work's commissioner and dedicatee, Jascha Heifetz. Where latterly the work has generally spread to well over half an hour, Ehnes takes exactly 30 minutes, and the result again is all the stronger. He is helped by the powerful playing of the Vancouver Symphony Orchestra under its music director, Bramwell Tovey. An outstanding disc in every way, with its equally outstanding couplings.

(i) *Façade* (complete); (ii) *Orb and Sceptre*; (iii) *Siesta*; *Overtures: Portsmouth Point*; *Scapino*
Ⓜ Australian Decca Eloquence mono/stereo 480 3783. (i) Sitwell, Pears, E. Op. Group Ens., Collins; (ii) LSO, Sargent; (iii) LPO, Boult (with **BAX**: *Coronation March* (LSO, Sargent). **BLISS**: *Welcome the Queen* (LSO, composer))

Anthony Collins's 1954 recording of *Façade* is a gramophone classic. With their cut-glass accents and beautifully manicured diphthongs, Pears and Sitwell, richly musical in their inflexion, are in complete sympathy with this wonderful work. Dame Edith Sitwell had one of the richest and most characteristic of speaking voices, and here she recites her early poems to the witty music of the youthful Walton with relish. Peter Pears is hardly less arresting in the fast poems, rattling off the lines like the Grande Dame herself, to demonstrate how near to nonsense pure poetry can be. Of course, there are flaws in Dame Edith's contribution over rhythm. She has no idea whatever of offbeat accentuation or jazz syncopation in *Old Sir Faulk*, but any such criticism fades in the richness of her characterization. The sound is sharply defined and vivid in a way few digital recordings can match. Boult's mono recordings of the Walton shorter works make an intelligent coupling: both *Scapino* and *Siesta* come off very well, and even if *Portsmouth Point* doesn't quite match the earlier, 78-r.p.m. recording in rhythmic bite, it is very good by any standards. Sargent's *Orb and Sceptre* and Bax's *Coronation March* offer both relaxed and effective readings of these royal favourites, while Bliss's lusty and lively version of his own *Welcome the Queen* (in stereo) is as enjoyable as ever. However, it is for *Façade* that this CD is an essential purchase.

Façade: Suites 1 & 2
ⒷⒷ Hyp. Helios CDH 55099. E. N. Philh. O, Lloyd-Jones – **BLISS**: *Checkmate* (ballet): *Suite*. **LAMBERT**: *Horoscope: Suite*

Brilliantly witty and humorous performances of the two orchestral suites that Walton himself fashioned from his 'Entertainment'. This is music which, with its outrageous quotations, can make one chuckle out loud. Moreover it offers, to quote Lambert, 'one good tune after another', all scored with wonderful felicity. The playing here could hardly be bettered, and the recording is in the demonstration bracket with its natural presence and bloom. A very real bargain.

Sinfonia concertante for Orchestra with Piano (original version)
Ⓜ Dutton CDLX 7223. Stott, RPO, Handley with **BRIDGE**: *Phantasm*. **IRELAND**: *Piano Concerto*

Kathryn Stott, warmly and strongly accompanied by Vernon Handley and the RPO, gives an outstanding reading of the *Sinfonia concertante*'s original version, and the result seems to strengthen what is a consistently memorable work, built from vintage Walton material. First-rate recorded sound (originally on Conifer) and couplings that are both generous and apt, particularly the splendid version of the Ireland *Piano Concerto*.

As You Like It; Hamlet
Chan. 10436X. Gielgud, Bott, ASMF, Marriner

Thanks to the diligence of Christopher Palmer, Walton's score for *Hamlet* offers some 40 minutes of music, a rich and colourful suite, superbly played and recorded, and much enhanced by the contribution of Sir John Gielgud in two of Shakespeare's soliloquies, 'O that this too, too solid flesh' and 'To be or not to be'. The selection of music from the pre-war film of *As You Like It* makes a valuable fill-up. It adds the splendid setting of *Under the greenwood tree* in a radiant performance by Catherine Bott. Marriner and the Academy draw out all the romantic warmth of both scores, and the sound is richly atmospheric to match.

The Battle of Britain: Suite. Escape Me Never: Suite. The First of the Few: Spitfire Prelude and Fugue. Three Sisters; A Wartime Sketchbook
Chan. 8870. ASMF, Marriner

The *Spitfire Prelude and Fugue*, from *The First of the Few*, was immediately turned into a highly successful concert-piece: from its imposing fanfare opening to the thrilling fugue, it is rightly one of the composer's most popular pieces. But we owe it to Christopher Palmer that there is the 'Wartime Sketchbook', drawing on material from three of the wartime films, plus scraps from the much later *Battle of Britain* film music, and not least the theme from the credits of the film *Went the Day Well*, which opens the *Suite*. It is undoubtedly one of the most stirring pieces ever written; by that we mean by any composer – not just Walton. The following *Bicycle-chase* is as exhilarating as the Scherzo (*Gay Berlin*) is vivaciously enjoyable. The brief suite from the music for Olivier's film of Chekhov's *The Three Sisters*, from much later, brings more than one setting of the *Tsar's Hymn* and a charming imitation of *Swan Lake*. Earliest on the disc is *Escape Me Never*, the first of Walton's film scores, written in 1935 in a more popular idiom; but the war-inspired music is what this delightful disc is really about. Marriner and the Academy give richly idiomatic performances, full of panache. Aptly opulent recording.

Henry V: A Shakespeare Scenario (arr. Palmer)
Chan. 10437X. Plummer (nar.), Westminster Cathedral Ch., ASMF, Marriner

Few film scores can match Walton's for the Olivier film of *Henry V* in its range and imagination. From the opening bars, the drama is vividly evoked, with Walton's rich musical imagination delivered with maximum impact. The set-piece numbers such as *Agincourt* are as spectacular as the *Interlude: At the French Court* is charming. The 'Scenario' recorded here, devised by Christopher Palmer, lasts just over an hour and, as a concert performance of a film score, it cannot be faulted. The most controversial change is to 'borrow' the first section of the march that Walton wrote much later for a projected television series on Churchill's *History of the English-speaking Peoples*; otherwise the Chorus's call to arms, *Now all the youth of England is on fire*, would have had no music to introduce it. As an appendix, three short pieces are included which Walton quoted in his score. Sir Neville Marriner caps even his previous recordings in this series, with the Academy and Westminster Choir producing heart-felt playing and singing in sumptuous sound. Christopher Plummer makes an excellent substitute for Olivier, unselfconsciously adopting a comparably grand style.

Macbeth: Fanfare & March; Major Barbara (suite); Richard III
(Shakespeare scenario)
Ⓜ Chan. 10435X. Gielgud (nar.), ASMF, Marriner

Walton's music to *Richard III* is hardly less impressive than that of his master-piece, *Henry V*. From the vibrant fanfares which open the score, via the imposing music for the Coronation scene, to the dramatic *Death of Richard*, there is much to relish in this colourful and atmospheric score. If Sir John Gielgud tends to underplay his part with his great 'Now is the winter of our discontent' speech, working to the underlying music – much of it eliminated in the film – may have cramped his style. But the performance has all the panache one could ask for, leading up to the return of the grand Henry Tudor theme at the end. The six-minute piece based on Walton's music for Gielgud's wartime production of *Macbeth* is much rarer and very valuable too, anticipating in its

Elizabethan dance-music the *Henry V* film score (along with yet another impressive fanfare). *Major Barbara* also brings vintage Walton material. Marriner and the Academy give performances just as ripely committed as in their other recordings in the series, helped by sonorous Chandos sound.

Troilus and Cressida (complete, CD version)

Chan. 9370/1 (2). A. Davies, Howarth, Howard, Robson, Opie, Bayley, Thornton, Owen-Lewis, Opera N. Ch., E. N. Philh., Hickox

Few operas since Puccini have such a rich store of memorable tunes as *Troilus and Cressida*. As Chandos's magnificent recording shows, based on Opera North's 1995 production – using Walton's tautened score of 1976 but with the original soprano register restored for Cressida – this red-bloodedly romantic opera on a big classical subject deserves to enter the regular repertoire. Judith Howarth portrays the heroine as girlishly vulnerable, rising superbly in the big challenges of the love duets and final death scene. Arthur Davies is an aptly Italianate Troilus, an ardent lover, and there is not a weak link in the cast, with Nigel Robson a finely pointed Pandarus, comic but not camp, avoiding any echoes of Peter Pears, the originator. As Evande, Cressida's maid, Yvonne Howard produces firm, rich mezzo tone, and the role of Calkas, Cressida's father, is magnificently sung by Clive Bayley. The role of Diomede, Cressida's Greek suitor, can seem one-dimensional, but Alan Opie, in one of his finest performances on record, sharpens the focus, making him a genuine threat, a noble enemy. Richard Hickox draws magnetic performances from chorus and orchestra alike, bringing out many parallels with the early Walton of *Belshazzar's Feast* and the *First Symphony*. As for the recorded sound, the bloom of the Leeds Town Hall acoustics allows the fullest detail from the orchestra, enhancing the Mediterranean warmth of the score, helped by a wide dynamic range. The many atmospheric effects, often off stage, are clearly and precisely focused, and the placing of the voices on the stereo stage is also unusually precise.

WARLOCK, Peter (1894–1930)

Capriol Suite (for strings)

ⓑⓑ Naxos 8.550823. Bournemouth Sinf., Richard Studt (with Concert: *English String Music*)

This is just about the finest available performance of Warlock's masterly *Capriol Suite*. There is a memorable account conducted by Vernon Handley on Chandos (CHAN 8808), but that uses the full orchestral score, whereas the Naxos version sounds just as the composer conceived it. The rest of the programme is a splendid collection of English string works which includes Britten's

Frank Bridge Variations, Holst's *St Paul's Suite* and Vaughan Williams's *Dives and Lazarus*. Demonstration sound.

WAXMAN, Franz (1906–67)

Rebecca (complete film score)
🅱️🅱️ Naxos 8.557549. Slovak RSO, Adriano

Rebecca (1940) is regarded as Waxman's finest score and it is easy to hear why. Waxman sweeps you immediately into the world of Daphne du Maurier's bestseller. The score is an integral part of Hitchcock's film, with the Rebecca theme used to portray the ghostly presence of Max de Winter's dead first wife. Throughout, the music brilliantly portrays the often haunting and creepy atmosphere of this gothic fantasy. It is not all gloomy though, with numbers such as the *Lobby Waltz* providing a haunting piece of nostalgia. Adriano (and others) have made a splendid job of assembling this score, some of which had to be reconstructed from the soundtrack, while other music, not used in the final film, is also restored here. Both the performance and recording are very good and, at super-bargain price, this is an obvious acquisition for all film-music aficionados.

WEBER, Carl Maria von (1786–1826)

Clarinet Concertos 1, Op. 73; 2, Op. 74; Clarinet Quintet, Op. 34
(version for clarinet and strings)
Sony SACD 88697 37632-2. Fabio di Càsola, Russian Chamber Philharmonic, St
   Petersburg, Juri Gilbo

It was a celebrated contemporary clarinettist, Heinrich Baermann, who attracted Weber to the instrument. He had a special clarinet made with ten keys to extend the instrument's range, and Weber wrote a total of ten pieces for him to play on it, all of them delightfully tuneful, and with roulades galore to test the virtuosity of the player, who here comes up trumps. Such enticing works, admirable show-pieces too, have received many recordings, notably scintillating accounts of the two *Concertos* from our own Emma Johnson (on ASV), but Martin Fröst on BIS (SACD) is hardly less seductive, and he, like the light-hearted Sabine Meyer (on HMV), also offers the arrangement of the *Quintet*. However, Fabio di Càsola's performances are dazzling and Juri Gilbo's persuasive partnership in slow movements is romantic in the best Weberian operatic style. The twirly-whirly *Menuetto capriccio* of the arranged *Quintet* is deliciously done, and the closing *giocoso* is also wonderfully infectious. Then the performances are capped by the bravura scales in the final jaunty *Allegro polacca* of No. 2. The SACD sound is splendidly atmospheric, so this can be strongly recommended.

Symphonies 1 in C; 2 in C. Die drei Pintos: Entr'acte. Silvana: Dance of the Young Nobles; Torch Dance. Turandot: Overture; Act II: March; Act V: Funeral March

ⓑⓑ Naxos 8.550928. Queensland PO, Georgiadis

Weber wrote his two *Symphonies* in the same year (1807) and, though both are in C major, each has its own individuality. The witty orchestration and operatic character of the writing are splendidly caught in these sparkling Queensland performances, while in the slow movements the orchestral soloists relish their solos, for all the world like vocal cantilenas. The recording is in the demonstration class, and the disc is made the more attractive for the inclusion of orchestral excerpts from two little-known operas and incidental music from *Turandot*. The *Entr'acte* from the incomplete *Die drei Pintos* was put together by Mahler from Weber's sketches.

Overtures: Abu Hassan; Der Beherrscher der Geister (Ruler of the Spirits); Euryanthe; Der Freischütz; Jubel; Oberon; Preciosa

EMI Encore (ADD) 5 75644-2. Philh. O, Sawallisch

Weber overtures represent some of the most attractive and memorable overtures in the classical repertoire, yet choosing just one collection is not easy. None is ideal. There is Karajan's DG collection which includes some of the most beautifully played examples of this repertoire – the masterful *Oberon* and *Der Freischütz* are peerless – yet it may be said that Karajan lacks some of the romantic excitement found in these vibrant works. Sawallisch's 1958 selection has the advantage of the Philharmonia at their peak. The orchestral playing is superb and the excitement of *Der Freischütz*, the Turkish colourings of *Abu Hassan* and the contrasts of *Euryanthe* (the timpanist notably) are presented with a strong sense of the individual character of each piece. There is real orchestral virtuosity in *The Ruler of the Spirits* and the spectacular appearance of *God Save the Queen* as the apotheosis of *Jubel* will cheer anyone up. The snag is the over-bright, sharply focused recording, with a very light bass. Another collection worth considering is Ansermet's, on a newly released Australian Decca Eloquence CD (480 0123). What the performances lack in polish they more than make up for in lusty spirit and are presented in vintage Decca sound. The CD also includes the delightful Weber *Bassoon Concerto in F*.

Clarinet Quintet (Grand Quintetto) in B flat, Op. 34

ⓜ Australian Decca Eloquence (ADD) 476 2447. De Peyer, Melos Ens. – **HUMMEL**: *Piano Quintet; Piano Septet*

Weber's *Clarinet Quintet* was written at a time when the clarinet was still fighting for acceptance as a solo instrument; even though Mozart, Beethoven and

Schubert had used its novel colours with the utmost felicity, there remained plenty of scope for more virtuosic treatment. This Weber undertook in his concertos and in the *Quintet*, which is delightful music as well as being a willing vehicle for the soloist's display of pyrotechnics. Gervase de Peyer is in his element, immaculate and brilliant, and given superb support from the Melos Ensemble. The 1959 recording is unbelievably warm and vivid.

Der Freischütz (complete, DVD version)

Arthaus mono DVD 01 271. Kozub, Frick, Saunders, Mathis, Grundheber, Blankenheim, Minetti, Sotin, Krause, Hamburg State Op. Ch. & PO, Ludwig (Director: Rolf Liebermann; V/D: Joachim Hess)

A fascinating early example of filmed opera in remarkably vivid colour, dating from 1968. The cast pre-recorded the music in mono within an attractive acoustic, then acted and sang the opera on stage, miming very successfully to the pre-recording. The production and sets are traditional, very much so. But the principals are excellent singers every one, with Gottlob Frick's melodramatic portrayal of Kaspar almost stealing the show. If, as Kilian, Franz Grundheber's Act I aria is a bit too self-satisfied, the main problem is that Max, the hero (Ernst Kozub), although he sings ardently, looks so morose throughout the opera that one wonders what Agathe can see in him. However, both she (the sweet-voiced Arlene Saunders) and the delightful Ännchen (a young Edith Mathis), are charmers in their central scenes, which contain the heroine's two most famous arias, very well sung. The Wolf's Glen scene, dominated by a sinister Samiel (Bernhard Minetti), is staged quite spectacularly, with an impressive storm, even if it is not as rivetingly scary as the famous Keilberth audio recording. However, the opera's closing scene, with Hans Sotin magnificently commanding as the Hermit who intervenes to provide the happy ending, is very successful. In all – allowances being made for the dated production – this is most enjoyable and a considerable achievement when one realizes it is over 40 years old! There is, for once, a good accompanying booklet, with synopsis and full documentation.

Der Freischütz (complete, CD version)

Teldec 4509 97758-2 (2). Orgonasova, Schäfer, Wottrich, Salminen, Berlin R. Ch., BPO, Harnoncourt

Harnoncourt's electrifying and refreshing version of this operatic warhorse was recorded live at concert performances in the Philharmonie in Berlin in 1995, and the engineers have worked wonders in conveying the atmosphere of a stage performance rather than a concert one, not least in the Wolf's Glen scene, helped by recording of a very wide dynamic range. Harnoncourt clarifies textures and paces the drama well, making it sound fresh and new. The cast is first rate, with Orgonasova singing radiantly as Agathe, not just pure but sensuous of tone, floating high *pianissimos* ravishingly. Christine Schäfer, sweet and expressive, makes Ännchen into far more than just a soubrette character, and Erich Wottrich as Max is aptly heroic and unstrained, if hardly beautiful.

The line-up of baritones and basses is impressive too, all firm and clear, contrasting sharply with one another, a team unlikely to be bettered today. A clear first choice among modern, digital recordings.

WEBERN, Anton (1883–1945)

Collected works: Disc 1: (i) *Im Sommerwind*; *5 Movements for String Quartet* (orchestral version), *Op. 5*; *Passacaglia, Op. 1*; *6 Pieces for Large Orchestra, Op. 6*. Arrangements of: Bach: *Musical Offering: Fugue*; Schubert: *6 German Dances, D.820*

Disc 2: (i) *5 Pieces for Orchestra* (1913); *Symphony, Op. 21*; *Variations for Orchestra, Op. 30*; (i; v) *Das Augenlicht, Op. 26*; *Cantatas* (i; iii; v) *1, Op. 29*; (i; iii–v) *2, Op. 31*; (i; iii) *3 Orchesterlieder* (1913–24)

Disc 3: (ii; vi) *Concerto for 9 Instruments, Op. 24*; (ii) *5 Pieces for Orchestra, Op. 10*; (ii; vi) *Piano Quintet*; Op. posth. *Quartet, Op. 22* (for piano, violin, clarinet & saxophone); (ii–iii; v; vii) *5 Canons on Latin Texts, Op. 15*; (ii; v) *Entflieht auf leichten Kähnen, Op. 2*; (ii; vii) *2 Lieder, Op. 8*; *4 Lieder, Op. 13*; *6 Lieder, Op. 14*; (ii–iii) *5 Geistliche Lieder, Op. 15*; *5 Canons, Op. 16*; *3 Lieder, Op. 18*; (ii; v) *2 Lieder, Op. 19*; (ii–iii) *3 Volkstexte, Op. 17*

Disc 4: (iii; viii) *3 Gedichte* (1899–1903); *8 frühe Lieder* (1901–4); *3 Avenarius Lieder* (1903–4); *5 Dehmel Lieder* (1906–8); *5 George Lieder, Op. 3*; *5 George Lieder, Op. 4*; *4 George Lieder* (1908–9); *4 Lieder, Op. 12*; *3 Jone Gesänge, Op. 23*; *3 Jone Lieder, Op. 25*

Disc 5: (ix) *6 Bagatelles for String Quartet, Op. 9*; *(Langsamer) Slow Movement for String Quartet* (1905); *5 Movements for String Quartet, Op. 5*; (ix–x) *3 Pieces for String Quartet* (1913); (ix) *Rondo for String Quartet* (1906); *String Quartet* (1905); *String Quartet, Op. 28*; *String Trio, Op. 20*; *Movement for String Trio, Op. posth.* (1925)

Disc 6: (xi–xii) *Cello Sonata* (1914); *2 Pieces for Cello & Piano* (1899); *3 Small Pieces for Cello & Piano, Op. 11*; (xiii–xii) *4 Pieces for Violin & Piano, Op. 7*; Piano: (xiv) *Kinderstück* (1924 & 1925); (xv) *Movement* (1906); (xiv) *Piece* (1925); (xv) *Sonata Movement (Rondo)* (1906); (xiv) *Variations, Op. 27*
DG 457 637-2 (6). (i) BPO; (ii) Ens. Intercontemporain; (i–ii) cond. Boulez; (iii) Oelze; (iv) Finley; (v) BBC Singers; (vi) Aimard; (vii) Pollet; (viii) Schneider; (ix) Emerson Qt; (x) McCormick; (xi) Hagen; (xii) Maisenberg; (xiii) Kremer; (xiv) Zimerman; (xv) Cascioli

This monumental DG set goes far further than the earlier Sony collection in its illumination of Webern as one of the great musical pioneers of the twentieth century. The first point is that where the earlier set limited itself to the numbered works, this one covers so much more (on six discs instead of three) with a far fuller portrait presented in the early works. Both sets include such offerings as the arrangements of Bach (the *Ricercar* from the *Musical Offering*) and Schubert (a collection of waltzes). Boulez's interpretations of the numbered works have developed too, with the Berlin Philharmonic exceptionally responsive, bringing out often unsuspected warmth and beauty. The point and purposefulness of these performances is particularly helpful in making such thorny late inspirations as the two *Cantatas* so much more readily approachable. The vocal soloists have been chosen ideally, with the fresh-toned Christiane Oelze taking on the majority of songs, but with Françoise Pollet and Gerald Finley equally assured. Nor could the starry list of instrumental contributors be bettered, including as it does such luminaries as the Emerson Quartet and Krystian Zimerman; and the recordings, made over a period of years, are uniformly excellent.

WEILL, Kurt (1900–1950)

Die Dreigroschenoper (The Threepenny Opera) (complete)
Decca 430 075-2. Kollo, Lemper, Milva, Adorf, Dernesch, Berlin RIAS Chamber Ch. & Sinf., Mauceri

On Decca there are obvious discrepancies between the opera-singers, René Kollo and Helga Dernesch, and those in the cabaret tradition, notably the vibrant and provocative Ute Lemper (Polly Peachum) and the gloriously dark-voiced and characterful Milva (Jenny). That entails downward modulation in various numbers, as it did with Lotte Lenya, but the changes from the original are far less extreme. Kollo is good, but Dernesch is even more compelling. The co-ordination of music and presentation makes for a vividly enjoyable experience, even if committed Weill enthusiasts will inevitably disagree with some of the controversial textual and interpretative decisions.

WIDOR, Charles-Marie (1844–1937)

Organ Symphonies: 1 in C min.: Méditation (only); *2 in D*; *3 in E min.: Prélude, Adagio & Finale*; *4 in F min., Op. 13/1–4*; *5 in F min.*; *6 in G min., Op. 42/1–2*; *9 in C min. (Gothique), Op. 70*
Warner Apex 2564 62297-2 (2). Marie-Claire Alain (Cavaillé-Coll organs, Saint-Étienne de Caen & Église de Saint-Germain-en-Laye)

For this Apex reissue Warner have combined two sets of recordings, from 1970 and 1977, which jointly offer an impressive overall coverage of this repertoire. Marie-Claire Alain contents herself with playing just the *Méditation* from the uneven *First Symphony*, and only three movements from the *Third*. Here the Saint-Germain organ sounds very orchestral and the colouring of the gentle

Adagio (a perpetual canon) is very effective. The later *Symphonies* are more impressive works than the earlier group of Op. 13. The *Fifth* is justly the most famous. These are classic, authoritative performances, given spacious ana-logue sound with just a touch of harshness to add a little edge in *fortissimos*.

WIENIAWSKI, Henryk (1835-80)

(i) *Violin Concertos 1–2*; (ii) *Caprice in A min*. (arr. Kreisler); *Obertass-Mazurka, Op. 19/1*; *Polonaise de concert 1 in D, Op. 4*; *Polonaise brillante 2, Op. 21*; *Scherzo-tarantelle, Op. 16*

Ⓜ EMI (ADD) 5 66059-2. Perlman, with (i) LPO, Ozawa; (ii) Sanders

Perlman gives scintillating performances, full of flair, and is excellently accompanied. The recording, from 1973, is warm, vivid and well balanced. It is preferable to Perlman's digital remake of the *Second Concerto*. The mid-priced reissue includes a mini-recital of shorter pieces, often dazzling, but losing some of their appeal from Perlman's insistence on a microphone spotlight. Samuel Sanders comes more into the picture in the introductions for the two *Polonaises*, although the violin still remains far too near the microphone. Even so, brilliant all the same.

WILLIAMS, Grace (1906-77)

(i) *Carillons for Oboe & Orchestra*; (ii) *Trumpet Concerto*. *Fantasia on Welsh Nursery Tunes*; (iii) *Penillion*; (iv) *Sea Sketches* (for string orchestra)

Lyrita (ADD) SRCD 323. (i) Camden; (ii) Snell; both with LSO; (iii) RPO; all cond. Groves; (iv) ECO, Atherton

It is good to have this attractive programme of works restored to the catalogue, all by a woman composer who (rarely among twentieth-century female musi-cians) glowingly shows that she believes in pleasing the listener's ear. No barbed wire here, and no lack of imaginative resource either, particularly in the memorably individual *Sea Sketches*, a masterly suite of five contrasted move-ments which catch the sea's unpredictability as well as its formidable energy. Grace Williams focuses her scene-painting more acutely than is common, while the two slow sections, the seductive *Channel sirens* and the *Calm sea in summer*, are balmily, sensuously impressionistic, the former taking a some-what unpromising idea and turning it into true poetry. The other works here range attractively from the simple – and at one time quite well-known – *Welsh Tunes Fantasia* (which is a good deal more than a colourfully orchestrated pot-pourri) through two crisply conceived concertante pieces, to *Penillion*, written for the National Youth Orchestra of Wales. 'Penillion' is the Welsh word for stanza, and this is a set of four colourful, resourceful pieces, easy on the ear but full of individual touches; although Williams does not use any folk material, she retains the idea of a central melodic line (on the trumpet in the first two pieces) in stanza form. The trumpet and oboe concertante pieces – superbly played by soloists from the LSO of the early 1970s – both show the affection and understanding of individual instrumental timbre which mark the composer's work. Excellent performances throughout (especially the vivid sea music) and very good analogue sound. This CD is surely an ideal representation of the composer at her most appealing.

WILLIAMSON, Malcolm (1931–2003)

Concerto grosso; *Our Man in Havana: Suite*. *Santiago de Espada Overture*; *Sinfonietta*
Chan. 10359. Iceland SO, Gamba

Our Man in Havana, based on Graham Greene's novel, is among the most colourful of post-war British operas, with its catchy Cuban rhythms and its tunes first cousin to those in Broadway musicals. Until this excellent disc, the first of a projected Williamson series, not a note of it had been recorded, and this suite of four substantial movements makes one long for a full-scale stage revival. The *Concerto grosso* and *Sinfonietta* are both exercises in Williamson's attractive brand of neoclassicism, and the *Overture, Santiago de Espada*, written in 1956, well before the rest, is even more approachable, one of Williamson's first essays in tonality after his early experiments with serialism. Rumon Gamba conducts fresh, crisp performances with the Iceland Symphony Orchestra, very well recorded.

(i) *Organ Concerto*; (ii) *Piano Concerto 3*; (iii) *Sonata for 2 Pianos*
Lyrita (ADD) SRCD 280. Composer (piano or organ), with (i–ii) LPO; (i) Boult; (ii) Dommett; (iii) Richard Rodney Bennett

There are few more immediately rewarding couplings of post-war keyboard concertos than this (and one could wish the *Piano Concerto* was better accompanied). Williamson composed them both in the early 1960s, and they represent two clearly contrasted sides of his creative character. The *Organ Concerto*, written in tribute to Sir Adrian Boult, uses the conductor's initials, ACB, as a dominating motive, and though some of the writing – for the orchestra as well as the organ – is spectacular, it is essentially a tough and ambitious piece, with the two powerful outer movements framing a beautiful and lyrical *Largo* for strings and organ alone. *Piano Concerto No. 3* in four movements has immediate attractions in the catchy melodies and snappy rhythms, which ought to make it a popular success in the line of the Rachmaninov *Concertos*. Unfortunately, the performance has an accompaniment that is less than punchy, and the red-bloodedness of the writing is not fully realized. The performance of the

Organ Concerto is quite different in every way. Excellent recording. The remarkable *Sonata for Two Pianos*, inspired by the composer's stay in Sweden, encapsulates in six continuous sections (and just seven and a half minutes of music) a Swedish winter and the arrival of spring 'with the serenity of a great release into a world of warmth and light'. The performance is definitive.

WIRÉN, Dag (1905–86)

(i–ii) *Miniature Suite* (for cello & piano), *Op. 8b*; (ii) (Piano) *Improvisations*; *Little Suite*; *Sonatina, Op. 25*; *Theme & Variations, Op. 5*; (iii) *3 Sea Poems*; (iv; ii) *2 Songs from Hösthorn, Op. 13*
BIS CD 797. (i) Thedéen; (ii) Bojsten; (iii) Jubilate Ch., Riska; (iv) Högman

Dag Wirén was a miniaturist par excellence and few of the individual movements recorded here detain the listener for more than two or three minutes. The early (and inventive) *Theme and Variations*, Op. 5, is the longest work. Although it is slight, the *Sonatina for Piano* often touches a deeper vein of feeling than one might expect to encounter. Good performances from all concerned, and the usual truthful BIS recording.

WOLF, Hugo (1860–1903)

Italian Serenade; *Penthesilea* (symphonic poem); *Scherzo and Finale*; *Der Corregidor* (opera): *Prelude and Intermezzo*
(BB) Warner Apex 0927 49582-2. O de Paris, Barenboim

For those who know only Wolf's *Italian Serenade* and enjoy the subtle word-painting of the Lieder, this orchestral collection will come as something of a shock. The early three-part symphonic poem, *Penthesilea* (1883–5), is turbulently and voluptuously romantic in a style of post-Lisztian hyperbole, while the *Prelude* to *Der Corregidor* is Wagnerian in its expansive opulence. Barenboim plays both with uninhibited exuberance and almost convinces the listener that *Penthesilea* is worthy of standing alongside the music of Strauss. The *Intermezzo*, however, is almost in the style of French ballet music, and the well-known *Serenade*, of course, is similarly lightweight and sunny. The *Scherzo and Finale* of 1876–7 shows the precocious skill of an 18-year-old: it is music of more than a little substance and is felicitously scored, although Wagner briefly raises his head again in the *Finale*. Barenboim makes the very most of all these pieces, and they are played with much conviction. The recording is rather resonant but otherwise acceptable.

Spanisches Liederbuch (complete)

Ⓜ DG (ADD) 457 726-2 (2). Schwarzkopf, Fischer-Dieskau, Moore

In this superb DG reissue, the sacred songs provide a dark, intense prelude, with Fischer-Dieskau at his very finest, sustaining slow tempi impeccably. Schwarzkopf's dedication comes out in the three songs suitable for a woman's voice; but it is in the secular songs, particularly those which contain laughter in the music, where she is at her most memorable. Gerald Moore is balanced rather too backwardly – something the transfer cannot correct – but gives superb support.

WOLFF, Albert, with the Paris Conservatoire Orchestra

Overtures: **SAINT-SAËNS**: *La Princesse Jaune*. **BERLIOZ**: *Benvenuto Cellini*; *Le Carnaval romain*; *Le Corsaire*; *Les Francs-juges*; *Le Roi Lear*. **ADAM**: *Si j'étais roi*. **HÉROLD**: *Zampa*. **REZNIČEK**: *Donna Diana*. **SUPPÉ**: *Pique Dame*. **NICOLAI**: *The Merry Wives of Windsor*.

Ⓜ Australian Decca Eloquence (ADD) 480 2385 (2) – **AUBER**: *Overtures*

These recordings from the 1950s readily demonstrate a Gallic style of orchestral playing which now has all but disappeared, with performances of much character and personality. Five of the overtures, those by Adam, Hérold, Rezniček, Suppé and Nicolai, were originally released in 1958 under the title 'Overtures in Hi-Fi', and they have never sounded better, with only a certain tubbiness betraying their age. Just listen to the way Wolff points the strings in *Si j'étais roi*, and the genial vitality which pervades the music-making throughout. Even the obvious fluff in the brass in *Zampa* (at 3 minutes 25 seconds) seems acceptable under the circumstances. The rest of the items are in (good) mono sound. Both *Le Roi Lear* and *Les Francs-juges Overtures* were (and remain) comparative rarities, yet both are excellent works, while the latter contains one of the best tunes Berlioz ever wrote. Even more rare is the delightful *La Princesse Jaune Overture* of Saint-Saëns, which certainly tickles the ear. They are coupled with Wolff's classic recordings of Auber overtures, making this collection very valuable.

WOLF-FERRARI, Ermanno (1876–1948)

La dama boba: Overture. I gioielli della Madonna: Suite. Overtures & Intermezzi from: *L'amore medico*; *Il campiello*; *I quattro rusteghi*; *Il segreto di Susanna*. (i) *Suite-Concertino in F, for Bassoon and Orchestra, Op. 16*.

Chan. 10511. BBC PO, Noseda, (i) with Geoghegan

A warm welcome to a superb collection of Wolf-Ferrari's sparkling orchestral music. Beginning with the dramatic *Festa popolare* from *The Jewels of the Madonna*, Wolf-Ferrari provides an endless succession of sweetly tuneful music with ear-tickling orchestrations, lively dances contrasting with beautiful intermezzi, such as the delicately delicious one from *I quattro rusteghi*. The *Suite-Concertino in F* is a great rarity – and what a charmer it is, with Chandos's recent find, the superb bassoonist Karen Geoghegan, bringing out all the colour of this score. The second movement, *Strimpellata*, is especially catchy, but this CD abounds with catchy melodies. The overture to *Il segreto di Susanna* sparkles brightly, and the scurrying string-writing in the overture to the opera, *L'amore medico*, is exhilarating. The Chandos recording is first class, with the deep, resonant bass-drum in *L'amore medico* marvellously captured.

WOOD, Haydn (1882–1959)

Apollo Overture; *A Brown Bird Singing* (paraphrase for orchestra); *London Cameos* (suite): *Miniature Overture: The City*; *St James's Park in the Spring*; *A State Ball at Buckingham Palace*. *Mannin Veen* (Manx tone-poem); *Moods* (suite): *Joyousness* (concert waltz). *Mylecharane* (rhapsody); *The Seafarer (A Nautical Rhapsody)*; *Serenade to Youth*; *Sketch of a Dandy*.
Marco Polo 8.223402. Czech-Slovak RSO (Bratislava), Leaper

Haydn Wood, an almost exact contemporary of Eric Coates and nearly as talented, spent his childhood on the Isle of Man, and much of his best music is permeated with Manx folk-themes (original or simulated). *Mannin Veen* ('Dear Isle of Man') is a splendid piece, based on four such folksongs. The companion rhapsody, *Mylecharane*, also uses folk material, if less memorably, and *The Seafarer* is a wittily scored selection of famous shanties, neatly stitched together. The only failure here is *Apollo*, which uses less interesting material and is overambitious and inflated. But the English waltzes are enchanting confections and *Sketch of a Dandy* is frothy and elegant. Adrian Leaper is clearly much in sympathy with this repertoire and knows just how to pace it; his Czech players obviously relish the easy tunefulness and the sheer craft of the writing. With excellent recording in what is surely an ideal acoustic, this is very highly recommendable.

WUNDERLICH, Fritz (tenor)

'The Magic of Wunderlich', arias from: **HANDEL**: *Serse* (with Bav. RSO, Kubelik). **MOZART**: *Don Giovanni* (with Munich PO, Rieger); *Die*

Entfürung aus dem Serail (with Bav. State Op. O, Jochum); *Die Zauberflöte* (with BPO, Boehm). **LORTZING**: *Zar und Zimmermann* (with Bamberg SO, Gierster). **BIZET**: *Les Pêcheurs de perles* (Munich RSO, Stein). **TCHAIKOVSKY**: *Eugene Onegin* (with Bav. State Op. O, Gerdes). **VERDI**: *Rigoletto*. **BELLINI**: *La sonnambula* (with Munich RSO, Eichhorn); *La traviata* (with Bav. RSO, Bartoletti). **PUCCINI**: *Tosca* (with Baden-Baden SW R.O, Smola). **KÁLMÁN**: *Gräfin Mariza*. **STOLZ**: *Frühjahrsparade* (with V. Volksoper, Stolz). **HAYDN**: *The Creation* (with BPO, Karajan). **GLUCK**: *Iphigénie en Tauride* (with Bav. RSO, Kubelik). **MAILLART**: *Les Dragons de Villars* (with Munich RSO, Moltkau). **R. STRAUSS**: *Der Rosenkavalier* (with Bav. State Op. O, Kempe). Songs: **SPOLIANSKY**: *Heute nacht oder nie*. **MAY**: *Ein Lied geht um die Welt*. **BRODSZKY**: *Be my love*. **LARA**: *Granada* (with Graunke SO, Carste). **KREUTZER**: *Das Nachtlager von Granada* (Munich RSO, Eichhorn). **R. STRAUSS**: *Heimliche Aufforderung*; *Ich trage meine Minne*; *Morgen*; *Ständchen*; *Zueignung* (with Bav. RSO, Koetsier). Bonus DVD: Arias from: **ROSSINI**: *Il barbiere di Siviglia*. **TCHAIKOVSKY**: *Eugene Onegin* (with Bav. State Op. O, Keilberth)

(M) DG mono/stereo 477 5575 (2) with bonus DVD

For those not wishing to buy the seven-CD set of Wunderlich in DG's Originals series, this carefully compiled two-CD set is the answer. Many of his most famous recordings are here, with stylish examples of his Tchaikovsky and Verdi, and very lively excerpts from *Serse* and, of course, some delicious Mozart. He is no less sophisticated in the lighter numbers, of which a good selection have been included (the Kálmán number is most winning) and the popular numbers like Lara's *Granada* sound fresh and un-hackneyed. There's the odd rarity too, such as the little-known aria from Maillart's *Les Dragons de Villars* which makes one long to hear the whole work. It is Wunderlich's consistent artistry and golden voice which permeate this set and he never lets you down in either beauty or style. The bonus DVD gives us a chance to see him working in the opera house, and again one laments his death at the incredibly early age of 36. There are no texts included, but the booklet notes are very good and there is a fair sprinkling of photographs. Excellent transfers.

XENAKIS, Iannis (1922–2001)

Antikhthon; *Aroura*; (i) *Synaphaï (Connexities for Piano & Orchestra)*
Explore (ADD) EXP 0047. New Philh. O, Howarth; (i) with Madge

Using higher mathematics as well as a computer (slide-rule and graph paper to hand), Xenakis managed to produce works which to some ears actually sound like music, but to others are incomprehensible. The composer's imagination, which defies any kind of technique, is in no doubt; however, for many the results are barren. The most ambitious of these three works, *Antikhthon*, is hypnotic in its range of colour, even if it fails to get you thinking of the infinite, as the composer intends. Excellent performances (so far as one can tell) and brilliant recording (from Decca, dating from 1975).

YOST, Michél (1754–86)

Clarinet Concertos 7 in B flat; 8 in E flat; 9 in B flat; 11 in B flat
MDG 301 0718-2. Klöcker, Prague CO

Not many collectors will have heard of Yost before discovering this CD. But here are four delightfully bubbly *Concertos*, brimming with excellent tunes and plenty of wit, with any moments of drama soon pushed away with sunny abandon. This is a delightful CD and it is hard to imagine better performances or recordings.

YSAŸE, Eugène (1858–1931)

6 Sonatas for Solo Violin, Op. 27
BB Naxos 8.555996. Kaler

As is well known, the six *Sonatas* Ysaÿe published in 1924 were written for the six greatest virtuosi of the day: Szigeti, Kreisler, Enescu, Jacques Thibaud and (less well remembered nowadays) Manuel Quiroga and Mathieu Crickboom. They are held in special regard by violinists who enjoy overcoming the technical challenges they pose. Ilya Kaler was a gold medallist in the Sibelius, Paganini and Tchaikovsky competitions and is a virtuoso of the first order. These are commanding accounts, which characterize the particular qualities of each *Sonata* to impressive effect.

ZANDONAI, Riccardo (1883–1944)

Francesca da Rimini
Arthaus DVD 101 363. Dessi, Armiliato, Marchigiana Ch. & PO, Barbacini (Director: Massimo Gasparon; V/D: Rossi)

Dubbed 'the Italian Tristan', Riccardo Zandonai's telling of the legendary love story of Paolo and Francesca is drawn from a play by Gabriele d'Annunzio to a libretto by Tito Ricordi. It is a thoroughly workmanlike piece, attractive in its idiom but with melodies that only rarely stick in the memory. Before the first performance in 1914, Ricordi was much more concerned over the success of this piece than for the latest opera of Puccini, the composer who brought profits to his publishing firm.

The performance on this DVD under Barbacini is a warm and purposeful one, recorded live in 2004 at the Sferisterio Opera Festival in Macerata. Singing is good if not outstanding, led by the Francesca of Daniela Dessi and the Paolo of Fabio Armiliato. Paolo is one of the three Malatesta brothers, but Francesca is betrothed to Giovanni the Lame, though she thinks she is going to marry the brother she loves, Paolo, dubbed 'the handsome'. The story echoes that of *Tristan and Isolde*, and in the opening scene a jester refers to that legend as well as to the legend of King Arthur and Guinevere. The climax comes when Paolo and Francesca are caught *in flagrante* and both are killed, a sequence that Zandonai passes over with surprising speed before the final curtain. A flawed work, but one well worth hearing in a warm and sympathetic performance like this, with traditional costumes and a stylized, single set.

ZELENKA, Jan (1679-1745)

Complete Orchestral Works: *Capriccios 1–5*; *Concerto à 8 concertanti*; *Hipocondrie à 7 concertanti*; *Melodrama de St Wenceslao: Symphonia*; *Ouverture à 7 concertanti*; *Simphonie à 8 concertanti*
CPO 999 897-2 (3). Neu-Eröffnete O, Sonnentheil

A contemporary of Bach and Handel, Jan Dismas Zelenka was among the most original composers of the period but is still something of a mystery figure when no portrait survives. Unlike his great contemporaries, he remained an underling in the world of his time. Happily, his music has survived, and this fine collection of his complete orchestral works is compiled from three separate discs issued earlier. All the works, including the five multi-movement *Capriccios* and the oddly named *Hipocondrie*, involve elaborate concertante writing and, although the soloists here are not as starry as those on the earlier set (which involved Heinz Holliger and Barry Tuckwell), the use of period instruments instead of modern adds to the freshness and bite, with the natural horns, above all, breathtakingly brilliant in music that ranges wide in its emotions.

ZEMLINSKY, Alexander von (1871-1942)

(i) *Cymbeline* (incidental music); (ii) *Lyrische Symphonie, Op. 18*
Chan. 10069. Czech PO, Beaumont, with (i) Březina, Bremen Shakespeare Company (members); (ii) Karlsen, Grundheber

Along with *Die Seejungfrau*, the *Lyric Symphony* is the most performed and recorded of Zemlinsky's works, but this Czech recording has a special claim to attention in that it is based on a new critical edition of the score by Antony Beaumont himself. This clears up the odd engravers' and copyists' errors and expunges a few cymbal crashes which Zemlinsky himself removed during rehearsals. Textual matters aside, this performance is very fine indeed and, in the Norwegian soprano Turid Karlsen and Franz Grundheber, it has dedicated soloists. The incidental music to *Cymbeline* makes an attractive coupling, also edited by the conductor. Scored for full-scale orchestra, including triple wind, harp, harmonium, celesta and a substantial array of off-stage instruments, it is full of resonance and inventive sonorities. It makes a good introduction to the composer and, like the *Symphonie*, is very well recorded.

Choral Music: (i) *Aurikelchen*; (ii–iii) *Frühlingsbegräbnis*; (i) *Frühlingsglaube*; *Geheimnis*; *Minnelied*; (i; iv) *Hochzeitgesang*; (ii) *Psalms 13, 23 & 83*. Orchestral Lieder: (v) *2 Gesänge* (for baritone & orchestra); (vi) *6 Maeterlinck Gesänge, Op. 13*; (vii) *Maiblumen blühten überall*; (viii) *Symphonische Gesänge, Op. 20*; (vii) *Waldgespräch*.
EMI Gemini 5 86079-2 (2). (i) Mülheimer Kantorei; (ii) Düsseldorf State Musikvereins Ch.; (iii) with Voigt, Albert; (iv) Blum; (v) Schmidt; (vi) Urmana; (vii) Isokoski; (viii) Volle; Gürzenich O & Cologne PO, Conlon

The major choral works here are Zemlinsky's passionate and intense settings of the three *Psalms*. In a manner recognizable from his operas, the first two bring sensuous writing more apt for the *Song of Solomon* than the *Psalms*; the third (LXXXIII) brings dramatic martial music. Those three items as well as the cantata, *The Burial of Spring*, in seven compact movments, were recorded live in Cologne and bring warm, committed performances under Conlon as a dedicated Zemlinsky interpreter. The other, lighter items were recorded later in the studio.

The two major solo works are both for soprano: *Waldgespräch* an Eichendorff/Loreley ballad, accompanied by a pair of horns, harp and strings, and *Maiblumen blühten überall*, inspired by Schoenberg's *Verklaerte Nacht* and supported no less alluringly by a string sextet. Soile Isokoski responds with passion to both works, and Andreas Schmidt is no less responsive in the *Zwei Gesänge*, orchestrated by Antony Beaumont, both very Wagnerian in feeling. Michael Volle proves boldly dramatic in the *Symphonische Gesänge*, and if Violeta Urmana is less than ideally seductive in the Maeterlinck cycle, as always with Zemlinsky the orchestral sounds are as luscious as ever, with Conlon a splendidly supportive accompanist; and translations are included.

Abbreviations

AAM Academy of Ancient Music
Ac. Academy, Academic
Amb. S. Ambrosian Singers
arr. arranged, arrangement
ASMF Academy of
St Martin-in-the-Fields
Ⓑ bargain-price CD
Ⓑ super-bargain-price CD
Bar. Baroque
Bav. Bavarian
BBC British Broadcasting
Corporation
BPO Berlin Philharmonic Orchestra
Cap. Capriccio
CBSO City of Birmingham
Symphony Orchestra
CfP Classics for Pleasure
Ch. Choir; Chorale; Chorus
Chan. Chandos
CO Chamber Orchestra
COE Chamber Orchestra of Europe
Col. Aur. Collegium Aureum
Col. Mus. 90 Collegium Musicum 90
Col. Mus. Ant. Musica Antiqua,
Cologne
Concg. O Royal Concertgebouw
Orchestra of Amsterdam
cond. conductor, conducted
Cons. Consort
DG Deutsche Grammophon
E. England, English
E. Bar. Sol. English Baroque Soloists
ECO English Chamber Orchestra
ENO English National Opera
Company
Ens. Ensemble
Fr. French
GO Gewandhaus Orchestra
HM Harmonia Mundi

Hyp. Hyperion
L. London
LA Los Angeles
LMP London Mozart Players
LOP Lamoureux Orchestra of Paris
LPO London Philharmonic
Orchestra
LSO London Symphony Orchestra
Ⓜ mid-price CD
Met. Metropolitan
min. minor
movt movement
N. North, Northern
nar. narrated
Nat. National
Nim. Nimbus
None. Nonesuch
NY New York
O Orchestra, Orchestre
OAE Orchestra of the Age of
Enlightenment
Op. Opera (in performance listings);
opus (in music titles)
orch. orchestrated
ORR Orchestre Révolutionnaire
et Romantique
ORTF L'Orchestre de la radio
et télévision française
Ph. Philips
Phd. Philadelphia
Philh. Philharmonia
PO Philharmonic Orchestra
Qt Quartet
R. Radio
RLPO Royal Liverpool Philharmonic
Orchestra
ROHCG Royal Opera House, Covent
Garden
RPO Royal Philharmonic Orchestra

RSNO Royal Scottish National Orchestra
RSO Radio Symphony Orchestra
RTE Radio Television Eireann
SCO Scottish Chamber Orchestra
Sinf. Sinfonietta
SO Symphony Orchestra
Soc. Society
Sol. Ven. I Solisti Veneti

SRO Suisse Romande Orchestra
Sup. Supraphon
V. Vienna
V/D Video Director
Van. Vanguard
VPO Vienna Philharmonic Orchestra
VSO Vienna Symphony Orchestra